GILBERT AND SULLIVAN

MICHAEL AINGER

GILBERT AND SULLIVAN

A Dual Biography

OXFORD

UNIVERSITY PRESS

2002

OXFORD
UNIVERSITY PRESS

Oxford   New York

Auckland   Bangkok   Buenos Aires   Cape Town   Chennai
Dar es Salaam   Delhi   Hong Kong   Istanbul   Karachi   Kolkata
Kuala Lumpur   Madrid   Melbourne   Mexico City   Mumbai   Nairobi
São Paulo   Shanghai   Singapore   Taipei   Tokyo   Toronto

Copyright © 2002 by Oxford University Press, Inc.

Published by Oxford University Press, Inc.
198 Madison Avenue, New York, New York 10016

www.oup.com

Oxford is a registered trademark of Oxford University Press

Library of Congress Cataloging-in-Publication Data
Ainger, Michael.
Gilbert and Sullivan : a dual biography / Michael Ainger.
p.   cm.
Includes bibliographical references.
ISBN 0-19-514769-3
1. Sullivan, Arthur, Sir, 1842–1900. Operas.   2. Sullivan, Arthur, Sir, 1842–1900—
Criticism and interpretation.   3. Gilbert, W. S. (William Schwenck),
1836–1911—Criticism and interpretation.   I. Title.
ML410.S95 A77 2002
782.1'2'0922—dc21
[B]   2001056046

2 4 6 8 9 7 5 3 1

Printed in the United States of America
on acid-free paper

FOR MARY

PREFACE

IT IS FIFTY YEARS SINCE the last joint biography of Gilbert and Sullivan based on original research was published. When Leslie Baily published *The Gilbert and Sullivan Book* in 1952, Dame Bridget D'Oyly Carte was still alive, and although Baily was given access to correspondence in her possession, the full D'Oyly Carte collection of letters and other documents did not then exist. Dame Bridget left her papers to the D'Oyly Carte Opera Trust and those papers now reside in the Theatre Museum, London. In writing *Gilbert and Sullivan: A Dual Biography,* I have made particular use of this collection as well as the other great repositories of Gilbert and Sullivan material to be found in the British Library, at the Pierpont Morgan Library in New York, and at the Beinecke Rare Book and Manuscript Library, Yale University.

I should like to record my thanks to the staff at all the libraries and archives at which I have worked in preparation of this book: the Beinecke Rare Book and Manuscript Library, Yale University; the British Library; the British Library Newspaper Library at Colindale; the Family Records Centre, Islington; the Genealogical Society, London; the Guildhall Library, London; the Hampshire County Record Office, Winchester; the London Metropolitan Archives; the New York Public Library; the Pierpont Morgan Library, New York; the Principal Registry of the Public Records Office, Somerset House (now in Holborn); the Public Record Office, Kew; the Surrey County Record Office, Kingston-upon-Thames; the Theatre Museum, Covent Garden; the Victoria and Albert Museum Archives; the Westminster City Archives; and the Wiltshire County Record Office, Trowbridge. I owe particular thanks to Adrian Blunt, deputy librarian of the Honourable Society of the Inner Temple; to Ian Martin, general manager, and Mary Gilhooly, archivist, of the D'Oyly Carte Opera Company; and especially Catherine Haill, curator of the D'Oyly Carte collection at the Theatre Museum for her unfailing patience and kindness. Grateful thanks are due to my editors at Oxford University Press: Maribeth Anderson Payne, Robert Milks, and Ellen Welch. My thanks also are due to those who have helped me at various stages: John Dodd, Peter Joslin, the late John McCauley, the late Joe McCauley, Jo McNamee, Bernadette O'Mahony, Jonathan Pyefinch; and to Elizabeth Menezes, Camilla Cutts, and David Menezes, whose encouragement and enthusiasm to promote the book, even before it was completed, are much appreciated.

Above all, I must thank my family: Bernard, Teresa, Paul, Catherine, and Maria for their encouragement and expertise—from the technicalities of rescuing chapters lost in the mysteries of my computer to the art of writing a book proposal. To my wife, Mary, are due the greatest thanks of all. Without her, this project would have been impossible.

Of great assistance in tracking Gilbert and Sullivan and their families around London was the series of maps of Victorian London published by Alan Godfrey; together with census records, the maps made it possible to find Portland Place in Hammersmith, where Gilbert lived as a young child, and Ponsonby Street in Pimlico, where the Sullivan family lived after Thomas Sullivan had left the army. The maps of "Gilbert and Sullivan's London" in this book bear no specific date. My intention was to produce maps that would be helpful for the reader in locating places mentioned. I suppose they represent London around the year 1900: after Shaftesbury Avenue and Charing Cross Road had been built, but before the development of Kingsway and the Aldwych. My original amateur sketches were turned into professional maps by Nick Bullmore and Latitude, who also produced the final version of the "Gilbert Family Tree." The "Sullivan Family Tree" appeared originally in *Arthur Sullivan: A Victorian Musician* by Arthur Jacobs. Every effort has been made to contact the Estate of the late Arthur Jacobs, and the tree has been reproduced by permission of his agent, David Bolt Associates.

Wherever possible, I have quoted from original documents, and I generally have left the quotations unedited, preferring the reader to see what was actually written rather than what the writer thinks should have been written. In order to represent the frequent underlining in letters, I have followed the convention of using *italics* to represent one underline, *italics and one underline* to represent a double underline, and ***bold italics and an underline*** to represent triple underlining. Quotations from the librettos are taken from Gilbert's *Original Plays*, published by Chatto and Windus, which he was revising for publication at the time of his death. Quotations from original documents have been made from the Gilbert Papers in the British Library; from Sullivan's diaries (1881–1900) held at the Beinecke Rare Book and Manuscript Library, Yale University; from correspondence and from Sullivan's 1879/80 diary, by permission of the Pierpont Morgan Library, New York, Gilbert & Sullivan Collection; and by permission of the D'Oyly Carte Opera Trust for material for which they hold the copyright in the D'Oyly Carte collection of the Theatre Museum. Grateful thanks are extended to the Royal Theatrical Fund, 11 Garrick Street, London WC2E 9AR, for permission granted to quote from previously unpublished letters and other material written by Sir W. S. Gilbert.

Two books stand out from all others on Gilbert and Sullivan: *Arthur Sullivan: A Victorian Musician* by Arthur Jacobs (1984), and *W. S. Gilbert: A Classic Victorian & His Theatre* by Jane Stedman (1996), both published by Oxford University Press. It is intended that *Gilbert and Sullivan: A Dual Biography* should complement these two books, appealing perhaps to the wider audience of those who are drawn to the names Gilbert and Sullivan in collaboration, the reason for their enduring fame. But they were individuals, each a master in his own field; and their individual lives are as interesting as their collaboration. In personality and in life experiences they were opposites, but they shared a sense of humor and the result has brought laughter and enjoyment to succeeding generations. The individual components each of them brought to the partnership are as mysterious as in any human life; their mixing together produced the magic that is "Gilbert and Sullivan."

CONTENTS

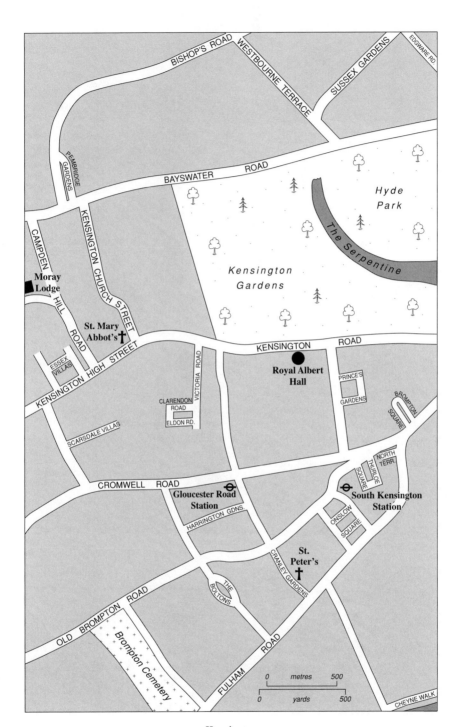

Kensington

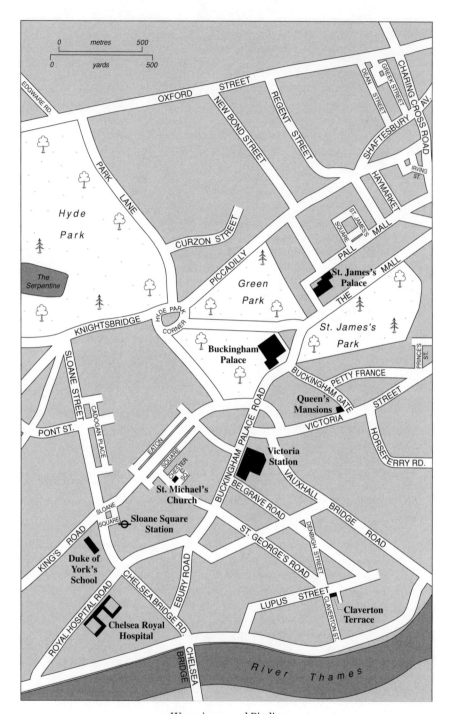

Westminster and Pimlico

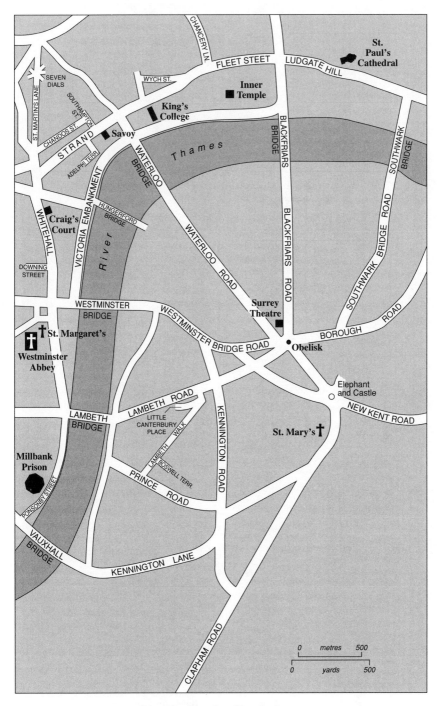

The Strand and Lambeth

Gilbert and Sullivan's theaterland

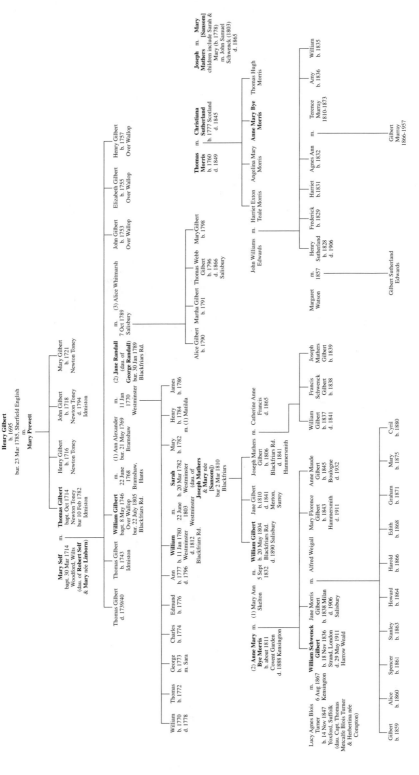

Gilbert's family tree.

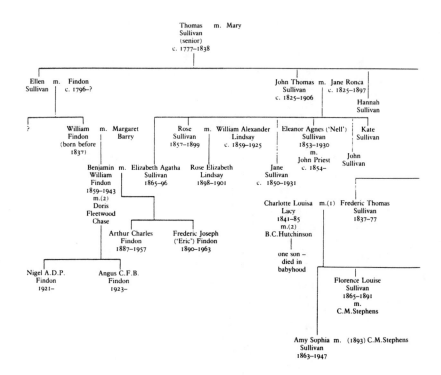

Sullivan's family tree (By permission of David Bolt Associates)

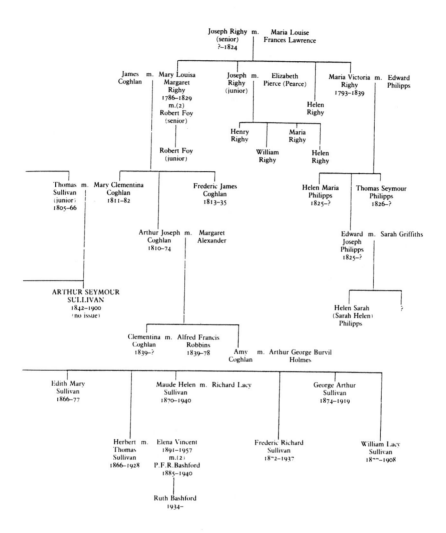

GILBERT AND SULLIVAN

CURTAIN-RAISER

The London Grocer and the Irish Soldier

On 18 July 1805, *The Times* announced the death of William Gilbert, Esq., of Lower Tooting. Five weeks earlier, unannounced by *The Times*, the first child of Thomas Sullivan had been born in Cork. Before the end of the century, the names "Gilbert and Sullivan" would be linked in the most famous theatrical partnership of the Victorian period. Who then were these two men, William Gilbert and Thomas Sullivan, one English and the other Irish, whose descendants were destined to make such a mark on the nineteenth century and beyond?

William Gilbert, great-grandfather of W. S. Gilbert, was born on 14 April 1746, the son of Thomas and Mary Gilbert of Over Wallop in Hampshire.[1] The family had owned a smallholding in Newton Toney, three or four miles away across the border in neighboring Wiltshire, but about 1739, the family property had been sold.[2] It was a period when the standard of living of many yeomen with small holdings was in decline and the future for Thomas Gilbert's sons looked bleak if they were to stay on the land. So, when he was fifteen years of age, William Gilbert left home to serve his apprenticeship to a shopkeeper.[3] His father had laid £300 aside for him on completion of his apprenticeship and the money was intended to set him up in life.[4] The opportunity carried with it a responsibility. In an age when property was wealth and status, the Gilbert family had seen the loss of their property and the lowering of their own status in the eyes of their neighbors. It would be for William to reverse the family fortune and, by the industry for which the yeoman class was renowned, improve his status and one day become a gentleman. A hundred years later, that same attitude toward property and ownership was to prove central in the character of W. S. Gilbert, who insisted that his written works should be respected as his personal property.

His years of apprenticeship over, William set out for London to make his fortune. He opened up his first business as a grocer in Westminster, in a street called Long

Ditch, which ran north from Westminster Abbey to the newly built George Street leading to Westminster Bridge.[5] The elegant houses of George Street and the open spaces of St James's Park nearby were in sharp contrast to other meaner, squalid parts of Westminster. At that time, before Victoria Street had been carved through it, the houses in the narrow streets and alleys heaved with an ever-growing population. Not far away from Long Ditch were Pye Street and its wretched rookery and Anne Street with its prostitutes, both within the shadow of Westminster Abbey. Near the ill-sounding Long Ditch were Pickpocket Alley and Thieving Lane, descriptive names of streets to be avoided.

Once established in London, William returned briefly to rural Hampshire and to Ann Alexander, the girl he intended to marry. The wedding took place in Bramshaw on 22 June 1768, and Ann accompanied her ambitious young husband to London and to the harsh realities of an overcrowded city.[6] Ann's life in Westminster was to be short-lived. The following spring she went back to Bramshaw, probably to have her first child. There she died and was buried on 21 May 1769.[7] They had been married for less than a year.

William married again the following year: this time a London girl, Jane Randall. They were married at the bride's parish church, St. George's, Hanover Square, on 11 January 1770, and their first son, William, was born on 2 November in the same year.[8] They were to have ten children in all, only five of whom survived into adulthood.[9] This was not an exceptional mortality rate; at the end of the eighteenth century, four of every ten children died before the age of five. Their firstborn, William, fell victim to the unhealthy Westminster environment and it was their seventh child, another William, born 11 January 1780, who was to survive to inherit his father's business.

By 1775, the name Long Ditch had been changed to the infinitely more acceptable Prince's Street, and at number 5 William Gilbert pursued his business. It was one of the many "corner shops" with which the district teemed. There were no set opening hours; William Gilbert would have opened up his shop before breakfast and stayed open until he went to bed. Around the corner from Prince's Street (now called Storey's Gate) was Tothill Street and along the same thoroughfare, separated by what is still called the Broadway, was Petty France. At number 15 lived a soap maker, Joseph Mathers, with his wife and family.[10] Joseph became a lifelong friend of William Gilbert, and the future of his two daughters, Mary and Sarah, was to be bound up intimately with the Gilbert family.

The completion of Blackfriars Bridge in 1769 and the development of the area of Southwark, south of the Thames, led to a migration from the slums of Westminster to what many hoped was a brighter future on the other side of the river. William Gilbert was alive to the business potential. While retaining his business premises in Prince's Street, and providing himself with a substantial mortgage of £1,500,[11] he moved his family in 1788 and set up a second shop just south of Blackfriars Bridge, at number 5 Great Surrey Street.[12] Their new house, built shortly after the opening of Blackfriars Bridge, was part of a terrace of tall four-story houses with the ground floor converted into a shop.[13] The move to Blackfriars coincided with the lowering of the import duty on tea, which put it within the reach of the poor; many grocers, William Gilbert among them, boosted their business by trading now as tea dealers. Scarcely a year after the move, in January 1789, when William the younger, W. S. Gilbert's grandfather, was only eight, Jane Gilbert died.[14] She was not yet forty; she had given birth to ten children in nineteen years and may have been pregnant again or a victim of the increasingly unhealthy environment of Commerce Row, at the upper end of Great Surrey Street. The unsanitary conditions, with consumption rife, were to claim several members of the family.

William the elder had never lost touch with his roots in Hampshire and Wiltshire and had stayed close to one family in particular, the Whitmarsh family, who were grocers. On 7 October 1789, only nine months after Jane's death, William married Alice Whitmarsh in Salisbury.[15]

With his third wife, William was to have five more children, although two were to die in infancy. The district may well have been unhealthy, but business flourished. By the end of the century, William Gilbert owned a whole block of premises, from number 22 to number 26 Commerce Row, as well as the family house at number 5 and another house and shop in Holland Street nearby.[16]

Three sons were to follow their father into the grocery business: George, the eldest and therefore expected to succeed to the ownership, who was born in 1773; William, born in 1780; and Henry, born four years later. But, in 1793, George did something unforgivable. Before he was twenty-one, he fathered a child. George and the mother-to-be, Sarah, married before the birth, so the child was actually born in wedlock, but the fact remained that little George William Henry Gilbert had been *conceived* outside wedlock and was not therefore "lawfully begotten." It was in William Gilbert's code of right-mindedness to disown this, his first grandson. As further punishment, George was no longer considered worthy of succeeding his father. Succession to the family business would now pass to the second son, William the younger.

William the younger was only thirteen and still had his apprenticeship to serve, which in time he completed with Thomas Slater, a grocer at Fenchurch Street. Over the years, the Gilberts had kept up their friendship with the Mathers family in Petty France, and on 7 June 1803, at St. Margaret's Westminster, William the younger married Sarah Mathers, whom he had known since childhood. A few months later, in October, Sarah's sister Mary, then aged twenty-five, married John Samuel Schwenck, a gentleman and a man of property.[17] The two sisters were close and the newly married Schwencks moved south of the River to Canterbury Villas, twenty minutes walk away from the Gilberts at the other end of Great Surrey Street, or to give it its later name, Blackfriars Road. The Schwencks chose to live away from the increasingly crowded area at the top of the road, and preferred what was still a more rural setting, beyond the Obelisk, which marked the entry into London.

Now that William the younger had reached his majority and was able to take over from his father, William Gilbert the elder considered he was in a position to prepare for retirement as a country gentleman. He had bought a country estate at Tooting in Surrey and had his portrait painted, and when he drew up his will in September 1803 he considered he was entitled to call himself a "gentleman." By then his third wife, Alice, had died, leaving him with three young children. Although a widower for the third time, he could look back on his life and feel satisfied that he had achieved the goal that had been set for him. From his beginnings in a family forced to sell off its property, from his early days as an apprentice to a shopkeeper, he had by his own energy, foresight, and abilities risen to become a successful and respected business-man and a man of property. William Gilbert had moved up the social scale. On 20 May 1804, a grandson was born whom he could this time recognize as "lawfully be-gotten": William Gilbert, who was to be the father of W. S. Gilbert.[18]

To judge from the flurry of codicils and additional notes to his will, William Gilbert knew his end was close and on Tuesday evening, 16 July 1805, he died at his house in Blackfriars Road. His burial service took place at Christ Church, Blackfri-ars Road, the following week, and his name was recorded in the parish register with the all-important "Esqr." added. It seems that the rector, Thomas Ackland, also rec-ognized that old Will Gilbert had status.

IN THE SULLIVAN FAMILY a story had grown up about the army career of Arthur's grandfather, Thomas Sullivan. It was a story that Arthur Sullivan himself had been happy to believe, or at least happy to offer to his first biographer as the official ver-sion. The true story of his grandfather is more interesting.

He was born about 1777 in Cathair Oisín, anglicized to Caherweeshen, County Kerry, a townland between Tralee and the Slieve Mish Mountains. He worked as a farm laborer and had moved to Cork, where his wife, Mary, gave birth to their first child, Thomas. If the future on the land had looked bleak to Thomas Gilbert, it looked even more bleak to the young Irishman. The Great Famine still lay in the fu-ture, but there had been famine in Ireland in 1800 and living conditions were des-perately poor. Whether or not he was drunk when he took "the King's shilling" as the family story went, or whether, like a number of his compatriots, he thought the army offered him a better and more exciting future, he enrolled in the Fifty-eighth Regiment of Foot on 25 June 1806.[19] A few weeks later he was transferred to the Fifty-seventh Foot (later to become the West Middlesex Regiment) and sailed to join the Second Battalion stationed on the island of Jersey. It was only then, after joining his regiment in Jersey, that on 28 July he received his king's shilling, or more pre-cisely 10 guineas, the equivalent of three months' pay and almost certainly more than he had ever had in his life. Thereafter, his pay was to be a shilling a day.[20]

While Thomas Sullivan and the Second Battalion of the Fifty-seventh Foot were guarding Jersey and providing a front line of defense against any possible invasion from Napoleon, the duke of Wellington and his army were engaging with the French on the Iberian Peninsula. Following the battle of Albuera, in May 1811, when the First Battalion of the Fifty-seventh sustained horrendous losses, the need for reinforcements was paramount. On 13 July, Thomas Sullivan was among the men transferred to the First Battalion who embarked for Portugal, landing in Lisbon on 3 August.[21]

The soldiers were met by intense heat, filthy living conditions, and widespread disease. Sickness now ranked as a major enemy facing Wellington's army, and Thomas Sullivan was not immune. By the middle of October, he was in the hospital, but after a month he was strong enough to rejoin his regiment and was in action before the end of the year. He saw active service again the following year in both Portugal and Spain until the end of August 1812, when sick or wounded, he spent a week in the hospital in Spain. He recovered in time to join Wellington's retreating army as they marched back toward Portugal. Supplies were dangerously low, the men were starving, and on 15 November the rain set in. In appalling conditions, they trudged their way until nightfall, when they came to a halt under the trees with the rain still pouring down relentlessly. The men were in a wretched condition and without rations, because their witless quartermaster general had sent the supplies down the wrong road. Their only food was the acorns lying about in the woods.[22]

In the early hours of 17 November 1812, the officers were awakened by the sound of musket fire. Hundreds of black pigs had run through the woods nearby, disturbing but at the same time tantalizing the starving soldiers. Many set off in pursuit of this promising breakfast, and among them was Thomas Sullivan. When the men finally straggled back, they found a far from understanding Wellington. Two of them were hanged for "the shameful and unmilitary practice of shooting pigs in the woods."[23] Thomas Sullivan kept his head well down and stayed in the woods. Where he went to is not known, but when his company next mustered at Plasencia at the end of November he was still missing. His friends covered for him. When his name was called, they said he had left the parade, sick because of the heat. The pay sergeant accepted the excuse. At the next muster at the end of December, Sullivan was still missing. His friends tried the same excuse, but the captain was not to be fooled. After making the necessary enquiries, he wrote against Sullivan's name: "this man appears to have been missing since 17 Nov[r]." [24]

Sullivan picked his time well to emerge, probably during the Christmas festivities. He must have had a very plausible story. Somehow, this fair-haired, blue-eyed little Irishman charmed his way back and no punishment was recorded against him.[25]

In the following year, on 21 June 1813, Sullivan took part in the battle of Vitoria, which proved to be the turning point of the Peninsular War. The army had marched four hundred miles in forty days to face the French army and on the day of the battle the Fifty-seventh had covered about twenty miles since three o'clock in the morning. The battle started in drizzling rain at 8:30 a.m. and was over by the end of the afternoon. Instead of ordering his men to set off immediately in pursuit of the enemy, Wellington allowed the exhausted infantry to rest. That evening, the looting began.

The soldiers plundered the French stores, where there was food in plenty and money galore.

When the pursuit did begin, the Fifty-seventh were in a division that pursued the French into the Pyrenees, where Sullivan was engaged in fierce fighting at Roncesvalles on 25 July 1813. They remained in the Pyrenees until the beginning of November. From the pass of Roncesvalles, now snowbound, they moved down to the Nivelle, and in the bloody encounter that followed, they overran the French troops. They met stiffer resistance at the River Nive, where Thomas Sullivan and his fellow soldiers were locked in a battle that could swing either way, with positions being decided at bayonet point.

After a winter billeted out in towns and villages in the southwest of France, the main body of the allied army moved off in February 1814, pushing the French further north, and on 24 May they entered Bordeaux. Sullivan and the men of the Fifty-seventh were to march no further north. They had been engaged on active duty for eighteen months, marching and fighting. They were hardened and experienced soldiers, Wellington's veterans. He had once called them "the scum of the earth" but was now prepared to admit that "there never was an army in the world, in better spirits, better order or better discipline."[26] They were now needed elsewhere. On 4 June 1814, Sullivan embarked at Bordeaux for America.[27]

The War of 1812, as it is called, between Britain and the United States, was in its last months when Sullivan disembarked with his regiment near Quebec. The Fifty-seventh moved further up the St. Lawrence River and quartered at Brockville, building a substantial stockade and barracks. Sullivan was in action in November and December, and then the war came to an end with the signing of the treaty of Ghent on 24 December 1814.

Back in Europe, following his escape from Elba, Napoleon was reported to have entered Paris on 20 March 1815. Although Wellington did not expect Napoleon to march north immediately, he wanted to be ready for him. His army was greatly depleted because of the use of so many of his veterans in America. Now that there was peace in America, it was time to move the troops back to Europe in readiness. The Fifty-seventh was among those who set sail. They arrived in England in May just as Wellington's army was mustering in Flanders for the decisive confrontation with Napoleon. From Portsmouth, the Fifty-seventh was due to sail on to Ghent. On 16 May 1815, a few weeks before the battle of Waterloo, Thomas Sullivan deserted.[28]

Again, it is not known where he went. It had been four years since he had left Jersey. He had been through four years of active soldiering in the most bloody encounters, had escaped with his life after intense fighting in Spain, in the Pyrenees, and in Canada; and all for a shilling a day. His little son Thomas, now nearly ten years old, had been admitted to the Royal Military Asylum for the children of soldiers of the Regular Army in 1814.[29] It would seem that Thomas Sullivan's priorities at that time did not coincide with the army's. How was he to know that it was the eve of an historic battle? As it happened, his regiment did not engage in the battle of Waterloo.

They arrived in Ghent on the day after the battle, and in the aftermath of Waterloo were sent down to Paris, where they camped in peace in the Bois de Boulogne.[30]

Sullivan would certainly not have considered himself a deserter. If he were, why did he turn up in Portsmouth on 25 July?[31] What story did he have to tell? A convincing one evidently, because he was enrolled in the army again, and the incident was not referred to in his final army records. He could not rejoin his old regiment, who were still in France, so he was enlisted in the Second Battalion of the Sixty-sixth Regiment of Foot (later to become the Berkshire Regiment). Two years later, he embarked for St. Helena, where the First Battalion formed part of the garrison on the island, and where his wife was able to join him. His pay was now 7 pence a day; the heady days of a shilling a day were over.[32]

The Sullivans returned to England in 1821. Thomas was sent to Chatham, where he was invalided out of the army and paid up to 11 October. In order to qualify for a pension, he was medically examined on 21 December. His age was recorded as forty-three, and his total service in the army reckoned as eighteen years three months. His "complaint," or reason, for being awarded a pension, was written down as "Worn out & undersize" [sic]. Thomas Sullivan was five feet three-fourths inch tall. On his discharge certificate, his commanding officer wrote against the word "Conduct": "Very good."[33] Only rarely did a soldier receive a better commendation than "very good." Despite Private Thomas Sullivan's occasional display of independence of spirit, he was considered a very good soldier.

In 1830, when he was fifty-two or so, Thomas Sullivan became an in-pensioner of the Royal Chelsea Hospital, where he was to spend the rest of his days.

PART 1

1836-1866

By Different Routes
to the Stage Door

CHAPTER ONE

1836-1853

Gilbert: A Dramatic Childhood;
Sullivan: A Musical Background

WILLIAM SCHWENCK GILBERT gave two short autobiographical accounts to magazines: one to *The Theatre* in 1883 and another to the *Strand* magazine in 1893. They often have been quoted in writing his biography, but they are to be approached with caution. They are pithy and amusing, and their similarity suggests an often told tale. The questions a biographer would really like to ask him are diverted by the author's moving rapidly on to the next selected episode. The early part, concerning his beginnings, is quickly passed over in what turns out to be a series of little smokescreens.

"Date of birth, 18 November, 1836. Birthplace, 17, Southampton Street, Strand," he says in one of these autobiographies, "in the house of my grandfather, who had known Dr Johnson, Garrick and Reynolds."[1] Who was this grandfather? Gilbert omits to tell his reader that this grandfather was not named Gilbert, and so deflects attention away from a mere grocer. It was not considered socially acceptable to have come from a family of tradespeople.

Before continuing with this story in the direction Gilbert would like to take us, let us return to the Gilbert family and the grandfather we have already met.

When William Gilbert took over the family business, he was twenty-five. With two associates who had worked for his father, he began trading as "Gilbert, Grumitt & Cock, grocers & tea dealers."[2] Two more children were born to William and Sarah in the next few years: Joseph Mathers, born in April 1806, and Jane, born three years later. By this time, Sarah was already beginning to show signs of the consumption that finally claimed her at the end of February 1810. Two years after his wife's death, struck down by the same dread disease, William Gilbert died, and on 26 April 1812 he was buried from the parish church of Christ Church. The following month his obituary appeared in *The Gentleman's Magazine*:

Aged 32, Mr. William Gilbert, Blackfriars-road, grocer; highly respected for his integrity in his dealings with the world, and much esteemed by his numerous friends and acquaintances. . . . He lost an amiable wife about two and a half years ago, through the same melancholy cause, only 27 years of age. They have left three young children to lament their loss; who, however, are well provided for; and their friends are happy in knowing that they are placed by his will under the protection of guardians, who will as far as possible supply the care, and mitigate the loss, of parental affection and tenderness.[3]

The guardians referred to were the Schwencks, their mother's sister Mary and her husband, John Samuel, who had no children of their own but who now found themselves with three little children to care for, with the eldest, William, still only seven years old. They probably took them to live at Canterbury Villas initially, but in need of a larger house and with London spreading beyond the Obelisk, they moved away from Lambeth to Nightingale Lane, Clapham, on the south side of the Common. The care and affection hoped for by friends were certainly provided by Aunt Mary and her husband; both William and his brother, Joseph, were to pass the name Schwenck on to their sons, William Schwenck and Francis Schwenck Gilbert. Mary Schwenck was to prove herself to be not only a kindly mother figure but also a woman of strong character, as later events will show.

Their father had left the financial future of the three children secure. He divided most of his property between the two boys, giving one house to Jane as well as the interest on £1,000 invested for all three of them. The rest of his property was to be invested in stocks and the interest to be equally divided among his children on their coming of age, the management of these legacies being left in the safe hands of John William Schwenck and his wife, Mary. Because the fortunes of the three children were linked in this way, William would have to wait until Jane was twenty-one before he attained financial independence, by which time he would be twenty-six.[4]

No information survives about their immediate future, except a few facts about the movements of William. At the age of fourteen, young William Gilbert went into the service of the East India Company as a midshipman. After three years, he left the service and spent the next four years in Italy. When he was twenty-one, he returned to England, matriculated at Guy's Hospital, spent some time as an assistant surgeon in the Navy and became a member of the Royal College of Surgeons in 1830. In the same year, he came into the inheritance that gave him the independence to live as a gentleman and to occupy himself as he chose. That year also, he had privately printed a volume of his own poems and two years later, on 5 September 1832, he married Mary Ann Skelton at St. James's Piccadilly.[5] It was about this time that he had another volume privately printed, a tragedy in blank verse on the same theme as that of Romini's libretto of *Norma*.[6] His own personal tragedy was the death of his young wife, Mary Ann. It is not known when she died, nor what William Gilbert did over the next few years. Writing would emerge again as a central feature of his life,

4 Portland Place, Hammersmith, where Gilbert spent his early childhood

but he published nothing until many years later. After that came a stream of books. Thanks to A. S. Byatt's 1998 edition of *English Short Stories*, William Gilbert is in print again, with a story entitled "The Sacristan of St Botolph."

A little more than three years after his first marriage, on 12 February 1836, William Gilbert, now aged thirty-one, married Anne Mary Bye Morris, the twenty-four-year-old daughter of Thomas and Christiana Morris. And so we come to the grandfather that W. S. Gilbert mentioned in his autobiography: Thomas Morris. He and his Scottish born wife, Christiana Sutherland, had married at the end of the eighteenth century, when Thomas was already forty. Their first child, named Thomas, died when he was seven weeks old, but they went on to have five other children. The last four children, including Anne Mary Bye, who was their fifth child, were all baptized together at St. Paul's, Covent Garden, on 31 July 1813.[7]

Thomas Morris was an apothecary who had run his chemist and druggist shop at 8 Chandos Street, Covent Garden, for about thirty years since the beginning of the century.[8] The status of apothecaries changed during the nineteenth century and they were leaving their shops to become "proper doctors." The Society of Apothecaries led the way in providing a formal medical education in advance of the physicians and surgeons; even so, Thomas Morris only received his diploma (L.S.A.) in 1839 when he was already seventy-nine, and had by that time been carrying on his medical practice for ten years or so from 17 Southampton Street.[9]

Southampton Street, originally part of the duke of Bedford's estate, runs down from the Piazza, Covent Garden, to the Strand, which it enters almost directly opposite what is now the Savoy. Number 17 was in the middle of five large houses, at the top end of Southampton Street, built at the beginning of the eighteenth century. The houses have long since been demolished, but two similar houses on the other side of the road still stand, number 26 and number 27, where David Garrick had lived before moving to Adelphi Terrace.[10] Garrick died in 1779, so if Thomas Morris had met him, the meeting must have taken place during Thomas's apprenticeship years in London.

Before the first year of their marriage was out, Anne Gilbert returned home to have her first baby, and on Friday, 18 November 1836, William Schwenck Gilbert was born. The Gilberts stayed at Southampton Street until at least 11 January 1837, when the little boy was baptized at St Paul's, Covent Garden, with John Samuel and Mary Schwenck as his godparents.[11] Gilbert's family called him Schwenck, and he was to be known as Uncle Schwenck to his nephews and nieces to the end of his days. The young family then left the smoke and fog of London and went westward to their home in Hammersmith, with its fresher air, surrounded as it still was by market gardens and nurseries.

Number 4 Portland Place stood at the border of the parish of Hammersmith, a border that is now marked by the Metropolitan and District Line of the London Underground. At the end of a short terrace, built on three floors with a basement, and with its porticoed main door at the side, away from the road, it was a comfortable size for the new family and their two servants. This was the house in which W. S. Gilbert spent his early childhood, where in the little walled garden at the rear he played and where he became conscious of the world about him. His was a privileged existence, but he soon became aware of the less privileged living nearby. The suffering of the poor was to be a major theme in the writings of William Gilbert senior, and W. S. Gilbert never forgot the poor of Hammersmith. The house in Portland Place still stands today. At some stage, the house was stuccoed over, and the road renamed Addison Bridge Place.

No doubt, one of the reasons for choosing to live in Hammersmith was that Anne Gilbert's elder sister Harriet had already moved there with her husband, John Edwards. They lived a short walk away, along the King's Street, now called the Hammersmith Road, in a large three-story, brick house called "Fairlawn" adjoining the Red Cow public house. The house belonged to Harriet's mother-in-law, Ann Edwards, and they lived there with John's sister and their six children. In the same house lived Catherine Weigall and her three young children.[12] This was most likely part of the Weigall family W. S. Gilbert would be connected with all his life. The Gilberts were probably frequent visitors and the children of the families became close cousins.

Sutherland Edwards, the eldest of the children and eight years older than Schwenck, later worked on the staff of *Punch*. He went out to Australia early in the 1840s, and after his return was a correspondent for *The Times* before becoming the first editor of the *Graphic*. His younger sister, Agnes, four years older than her cousin Schwenck, went out to Australia in 1860 as a governess. Her first position was of short duration, but soon after she was employed to look after the young children of the widowed Australian politician Terence Murray, whom she married in August of that year, when she was twenty-eight and her husband fifty.[13] Terence Murray was knighted in 1869, whereupon Agnes became Lady Murray, and, after his death in 1875, she returned to England with her son Gilbert Murray, named after W. S. Gilbert's "very interesting and handsome old father," as Murray himself related.[14] Gilbert Murray was to become one of the leading Greek scholars of his day and professor of Greek at Oxford.

In 1838, William Gilbert took Anne and Schwenck on an extended visit to Italy. His previous visit to Italy had resembled the Grand Tour of young gentlemen in the eighteenth century, spending the years from seventeen to twenty-one completing his education as an alternative to university. Now he was completing his young wife's education. But there was a complication. Anne was already pregnant when they left England accompanied by two female companions, one of whom was probably Anne's sister Angelina. Their movements at the beginning of their journey are unknown; they may have traveled through France down to Marseille, but they were certainly in Naples at the end of July, when William Gilbert was granted a passport to travel north.[15] This was in the days before the reunification of Italy, when Naples was part of the Kingdom of the Two Sicilies, and the passport was required to travel into the Kingdom of Sardinia in the north west. There, in Milan, on 5 October 1838, Jane Morris Gilbert was born.

To his first biographer, Edith Browne, W. S. Gilbert told a story about an event that occurred while they were in Naples, an event that left its mark on the young Schwenck. One day, his nurse had taken him out when she was accosted by two men who managed to persuade her that they had been sent by "the English gentleman" to pick up the child and take him home. Once the boy was in their possession, the kidnappers demanded a ransom of £25 for his return, a sum that his father was only too willing to hand over. Gilbert assured Edith Browne that, many years later when he visited Naples, he recognized part of the route he had been taken along "riding in front of a man on an animal."[16] Whatever he remembered of the incident itself, no doubt frequently referred to in family stories and creating an image in his young mind that then became the reality, it made a deep impression, and the idea of babies being stolen or switched at birth became a recurrent theme in his writing.

The Gilberts returned to life in Hammersmith. By 1841, William Gilbert's brother, Joseph, and his sister, Jane, were both suffering from consumption. In June that year, having let out the house in Nightingale Lane, Clapham, Joseph and his wife, Catherine, with their three sons went to stay with the Schwencks who had settled further away from the encroaching city, in Merton, Surrey.[17] As Joseph grew worse, he and Catherine went down to Brighton; they had contemplated a trip to Italy or the south of France but because he was too weak to travel, in the end they had to settle for

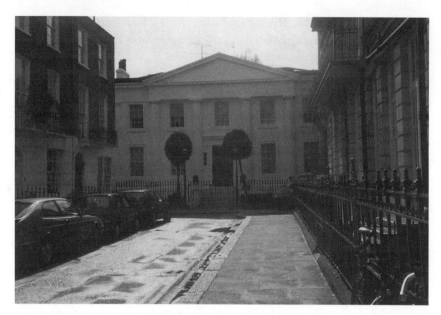

Western Grammar School, where Gilbert was a pupil for three years from 1846

Hammersmith, whose clean air, away from the noxious smoke of London, made it a popular area for people suffering from chest complaints.

After being bedridden for four months, Jane Gilbert, who still lived with the Schwencks, was the first of the two invalids to succumb to the disease. She died on 5 October 1841. Jane had proved very wise with her inheritance, either under John Samuel Schwenck's guidance or because of her own good business sense. She owned five cottages in Merton as well as houses in Blackfriars, Clapham, Paddington, the Edgware Road, and 5 Portland Place, the house next door to her brother in Hammersmith. Her brothers were the main beneficiaries of these properties.[18]

Before arriving at Hammersmith, Joseph had already made his will in October. Although Catherine was optimistic about the future and spoke of going to the continent in the spring, Joseph was now very weak and had little time left.[19] A codicil was added to his will. It was undated and witnessed not by a solicitor but by William Gilbert's two servants. William had evidently persuaded his brother that it was imperative to name him as the joint guardian of his children with Catherine. He realized that there was a strong possibility that Catherine, still only in her twenties, would marry again. If she were to marry or die, then he would share the guardianship with the Schwencks, and after their death he would be sole guardian.[20]

Joseph Mathers Gilbert died at Portland Place on 20 November 1841. Unlike his sister, Joseph had no property to dispose of; even the house in Nightingale Lane was still the property of the Schwencks. His estate, in life annuities, Assam Tea shares, and other securities was to be managed by John Samuel Schwenck as trustee to provide an income for his family. The will had been carefully drawn up by the lawyers and seemed to be beyond dispute. The codicil proved to be a different matter.

By 1843, William and Anne Gilbert had three children of their own, Mary Florence Gilbert having been born in Hammersmith, but William Gilbert continued to be a vigilant and zealous guardian of his brother's children. At Christmas 1844, Catherine and her two surviving sons, Francis Schwenck, now seven years of age, and Joseph, two years younger, came to stay with the Gilberts until the New Year. When the time came for Catherine to leave Portland Place, the little boys stayed on a little longer with their cousins. After a few days, she sent word asking the Gilberts to have the boys brought home to her. Her request was refused. She rushed around to Portland Place to recover her children. An emotional and chaotic scene ensued. Catherine Gilbert maintained that force was used to take the children away from her. William Gilbert was adamant that the children should remain in his care. What little Schwenck saw of all this or thought about it, cannot be known; for sure, the notion of kidnapping entered further into his consciousness.

To obtain custody of her children, Catherine now commenced a legal struggle. She claimed that William Gilbert had wanted to draw up a deed after his brother's death, which would give him an interest in the children's property in the event of their death. On 21 January, Catherine was granted habeas corpus, and the children were returned to her.[21] For his part, William Gilbert had become aware that Catherine Gilbert had begun a relationship with a lieutenant in the East India Company's Service, and he had begun to act, as he saw it, in the best interests of the children by removing them from an immoral environment.[22] The other guardians named in the will were the Schwencks, and it was against them that Catherine brought her action, causing great distress, as Mary Schwenck explained to Mrs West of Pangbourn, "If you have read any thing of Mrs. Cath Gilberts law proceedings, in the papers,—against us—I must inform you, it is *all incorrect*, & put in,—*as it is*,—I think to annoy us. . . . I do not think, the Gent[n.] will ever marry her—if he does he must be very much attached to her indeed."[23]

The adverse publicity sent both the Gilberts and the Schwencks scuttling. William Gilbert and his family left Portland Place for good and sailed off to Boulogne, where Anne Gilbert gave birth to her last child, Anne Maude. The Schwencks left London even further behind by moving down to Weybridge in Surrey. The Gilberts returned briefly in June, staying with the Schwencks until the court case. In the Court of Exchequer on 9 July 1845, judgment was granted in favor of Catherine Gilbert.[24]

When Ann Maude was weaned, the Gilberts went back to Boulogne, where they were to live for the next two years, among the middle-class English who found that life in this pleasant French watering place was cheaper than it was in England.

In the meantime, Schwenck's grandmother, Christiana Morris, had died at Southampton Street on 3 April, aged sixty-eight. At that date, the Gilberts were almost certainly already in France. It is probable that Anne Gilbert had not returned from France when her mother was ill. Perhaps she did not realize that her mother's condition was serious; on the death certificate the cause of death was given as "chronic catarrh."[25] Or perhaps it would have been too much for her to travel at that stage in her pregnancy. Whatever the case, a serious rupture occurred in the family, and Anne's father refused to have anything more to do with her. It may have been that he linked the publicity over the Catherine Gilbert affair with his wife's premature death. When Thomas Morris made out his will a few weeks before his own death on 14 January 1849, at the age of eighty-eight, it was as though his daughter Anne had never existed. He had no property to leave, but his estate was divided between his surviving children, with the exception of Anne. His will was not proved until nearly two years later, on 28 October 1850.[26] This can only mean that it had been disputed and it would be reasonable to assume that William Gilbert was the cause of the delay.

The eight-year-old William Schwenck had his first experience of school while the family were living in Boulogne, where he probably attended one of the many establishments set up by the English for the education of their children. During his two years in France, he learned to speak and read French fluently; it was a fluency he never lost. His education in the written language, however, was limited as he left France when he was only ten, and his subsequent education in England never made good the deficiency. Of life in Boulogne he always retained fond memories, frequently returning in later years, choosing it for part of his honeymoon, and making "delightful Boulogne" the subject of a "Bab Ballad."

The Gilberts returned to England in 1847 and moved into Brompton, an area that had become fashionable for the more affluent. They settled into 17 Brompton Square, and a little before his eleventh birthday, Schwenck became a pupil at Western Grammar School in North Terrace, no more than a five-minute walk from his new home. Western Grammar School was termed an "independent proprietary school," meaning that the parents were shareholders, or "proprietors." As well as "the doctrines of Christianity as taught by the Established Church," the curriculum included Latin, Greek, French, English, and mathematics, with "occasional lectures in science and art," but the school did not encourage the performing arts. John B. Buckstone, the actor-manager, had tried to place one of his sons in the school some years before, but his application had been rejected, as he explained in a letter to *The Times*, "on the ground that I am an actor, and that the son of such a parent in a public school would incite in the boys a desire to see plays, which would unsettle their minds."[27]

The front part of the Grammar School, pedimented and stucco-faced, still stands in North Terrace, but the building is now a private house.[28]

When Schwenck was nearly fourteen, it was time for him to leave home for his initiation into manhood; not as an apprentice like his grandfather, nor as a midshipman like his father, but more appropriately for the son of a gentleman, at a school that would prepare boys for the university. Gilbert said in his autobiography: "I went to school at Ealing, presided over by Dr. Nicholas—a pedagogue who appears more than once in Thackeray's pages as 'Dr. Tickle-us of Great Ealing School.'"[29] But the Dr. George Nicholas of Thackeray had died in harness in 1829. His son, Dr. Francis Nicholas, had taken over and was the schoolmaster when Gilbert was a pupil there.[30] Ealing was a small school in Gilbert's time, with only about forty boarders, aged between seven and sixteen, and only fifteen of these pupils were aged thirteen and over. Dr Nicholas was assisted by two nongraduate masters and several governesses for the younger pupils.[31] It was, however, a school that could boast some famous past pupils: Thackeray was at the school as a small boy before leaving in 1822 to go to Charterhouse; T. H. Huxley spent two unhappy years there; and the older Dr. Nicholas considered his star pupil to have been John Henry Newman, who went to Oxford in 1817.

Like many teenage boys, Gilbert tended to idleness at school, although he faithfully completed his weekly verse translations in Latin and Greek, winning several prizes for his efforts. Laying a few old ghosts in his "Bab Ballad" called "Haunted," years later, he recalled:

> First and worst in the grim array—
> Ghosts of ghosts that have gone their way,
> Which I wouldn't revive for a single day
>   For all the wealth of PLUTUS—
> Are the horrible ghosts that schooldays scared:
> If the classical ghost that BRUTUS dared
> Was the ghost of his "Caesar" unprepared,
>   I'm sure I pity BRUTUS.[32]

If he retained unhappy memories of Ealing, at least it had the advantage over Western Grammar of allowing him to explore his theatrical talents. Already he showed his preference for total control of a production: he would write the play, direct it himself, and also paint the scenery. Stories about his being violent at rehearsals in order to get his own way are without foundation; however, Gilbert did admit to a friend years later that he did not think he was a popular boy.[33] One of the plays he wrote and produced was a melodrama called *Guy Fawkes*, in which he played the principal part. "Blowing up" Parliament would emerge again in more humorous style in his mature writings. In February 1852, *The Corsican Brothers* by Dion Boucicault opened at the Princess's Theatre in Oxford Street. After Gilbert had seen it, he decided that the stage was preferable to school, packed his bag, went off to the Princess's Theatre and nervously asked to see Charles Kean, the actor-manager. Unfortunately for the boy, Kean knew William Gilbert senior, and, as soon as he realized the boy's identity, sent him straight home to his father.

Escape from school was to come about in a totally different way from the one planned by the unhappy pupil. At the end of 1852, Gilbert contracted typhoid. When the critical stage of the illness was past, his parents took him to France to convalesce. While they were in Paris, the Gilbert family witnessed a procession through the streets in which they caught sight of the emperor and empress passing by in their carriage. The Spanish princess, Eugénie, had not been readily welcomed by the French people, and fears for her safety kept her out of public view, so the most likely date for this procession is 30 January 1853, when Napoleon III and Eugénie were returning to the Tuileries from their wedding in Notre Dame.[34] The earliest surviving piece of Gilbertian verse dates from this occasion. It entered into the family repertoire of stories and was passed down to the next generation. One of Gilbert's nieces recited it many years later to Leslie Baily, who published it in *The Gilbert and Sullivan Book* (1952).

Completely recovered from his illness and back home in England, Gilbert enrolled as an occasional student at King's College, London, in March 1853.[35] It would appear that he never returned to Ealing where he had spent little more than two years. Gilbert's school days were over.

ARTHUR SEYMOUR SULLIVAN's father, Thomas, had entered the Royal Military Asylum (later to be called the Duke of York's School), Chelsea, on 24 June 1814, at the age of nine.[36] It was three years since he had seen his own father, who at that moment was sailing from Bordeaux to America to take part in a conflict of which, like many a soldier, he had scant knowledge. His mother, Mary Sullivan, had made the decision that the education the army offered was the best hope for her son's future. As we have seen, Thomas was able to enjoy an unofficial visit the following year, when his father probably took the opportunity to see his ten-year-old son before he had changed beyond recognition. But in 1817, when young Thomas was still only twelve, he had to say good-bye to his parents when they sailed off to Saint Helena. With both his parents still away, it was his own decision, therefore, on 4 September 1820, when at the age of fifteen he had come to the end of his time at military school, and he volunteered to go to the Royal Military College, Sandhurst.[37]

Thomas Sullivan had received his basic musical training in the band at the Royal Asylum, where he had shown genuine talent and now, as a bandsman in the army, was entering in a humble but very real way on his own musical career. Having no family of his own at Sandhurst, Thomas was befriended by the Coghlan family and came to know them well, especially the girl he was later to marry, Mary Clementina Coghlan, then only nine years old. She was born on 2 November 1811 at Great Marlow in Buckinghamshire, where the Royal Military College was then established before its move to Sandhurst in 1812. Clementina, or Clemmie as she was called by Thomas, was partly Italian: her grandfather Joseph Righi had come over to England from Nice, then part of the Kingdom of Sardinia, and lived with the Coghlans in Camberley until his death in 1824. Clementina was particularly close to one of her aunts, Maria Victoria Righi (or, with the anglicized spelling, Righy), who became Mrs. Edward Philipps, and Arthur Sullivan was to continue this connection with

Brompton Square, where the Gilbert family lived while Schwenck
was a pupil at Western Grammar

later generations of the Philipps family. It is from this line of the family that the name
Seymour was derived.[38] According to a family story, Clementina was educated at a
convent school in nearby Easthampstead, and then assisted her parents in running a
"ladies' seminary" at Blackwater, Camberley.[39]

When he was twenty-nine, after fourteen years in the army, Thomas Sullivan left
on 31 December 1834 to begin life as a civilian.[40] He probably moved to London, to
the district he was already familiar with at Chelsea, and close to his parents at the
Royal Military Hospital, where his mother is said to have worked as a nurse after her
husband's admission. Nothing is known of Thomas's movements during the next
two years, but later events would suggest that he frequently visited Sandhurst to see
Clementina Coghlan, that they were planning to get married, and that he wanted to
establish himself as securely as possible as a music teacher beforehand. They married on Clementina's twenty-fifth birthday, 2 November 1836, and rented rooms at
number 10 Sloane Square, a stone's throw from the Chelsea Hospital. There, at 9:15
on Christmas morning 1837, their first son, Frederick Thomas Sullivan, was born.[41]
The old soldier Thomas Sullivan lived long enough to see his first grandchild, but
shortly after, on 6 February 1838, he died at the Royal Military Hospital.[42] He was
about sixty years of age.

It is not known when Thomas Sullivan's mother died, but soon after the death of
his father, Thomas with Clementina and the baby Frederick moved south of the river.

Lambeth was being developed with simple but respectable housing and Thomas Sullivan became the first tenant of a new house in Bolwell Terrace at a rent of £20 a year.[43] The young music teacher found it impossible in this modest area of London to make a living simply by teaching. He could not even afford the rent. By 1841, he was sharing the house with another music teacher and his wife and child.[44] Thomas had already taken on a second job that would give him a reliable income of a guinea a week playing the clarinet at the Surrey Theatre at the lower end of Blackfriars Road.

Into the already crowded house at 8 Bolwell Terrace on 13 May 1842, Arthur Sullivan was born. His parents had him baptized on 31 July at St. Mary at Lambeth with the names Arthur Seymour.[45] Clementina Sullivan was the center and heart of the family, true to both Irish and Italian tradition, remaining a powerful presence for Arthur Sullivan throughout her life. The boys called her "mum," in contrast to the more formal "mama" in the Gilbert household. She doted on her younger son—preserving all his letters and even keeping his first baby garment. Thomas Sullivan worked diligently as the provider of the family, playing the clarinet in the evening, teaching and copying orchestral parts during the day. Despite all his efforts, he could not make the kind of progress he had hoped for in civilian life, and on 28 April 1845 he reenlisted at the Royal Military College, this time as sergeant bandmaster.[46] The college band was small: counting the bandmaster, it numbered only a dozen.[47] His pay was only three shillings a day but accommodation would be paid for. The opportunity to return to the college relieved him from the monotonous grind he had led for the last six years. "It was like the coming of a new day," he wrote to a friend.[48]

By the time he was three, Arthur Sullivan had left Lambeth and it is unlikely that he retained any clear memory of the little terraced house.[49] His early, happy memories were of Sandhurst and of York Town, where they moved after a few years, and nearby Frimley, where his brother went to school. It was a part of the country he would frequently return to in later life.

In reminiscences given to Arthur Lawrence, his first biographer, Sullivan spoke about making "discoveries" on the piano when he was about four or five and of acquiring a good knowledge of the instruments in his father's band, managing to achieve a degree of proficiency on many. Musical theory may have been taught by his father and it seems that Arthur was very young when he started composing; by the age of eight, he had produced his first composition: an anthem, "By the waters of Babylon."[50] Church music and military music were his foundation, a combination that would be immortalized in "Onward Christian Soldiers."

Arthur started his formal education at the local National School but, when he was nine (the age Thomas Sullivan was when he left home to go to the military school), his father decided that a private education was preferable and sent him to a school run by William Gordon Plees at 20 Albert Terrace, Bishop's Road, Bayswater.[51] Hundreds of these little schools in private houses were dotted around the more affluent areas, often consisting of no more than three or four pupils. Mr. Plees opened his school in 1851 and Arthur was one of its first pupils. Music, or at least singing, would have formed part of his curriculum, and fortunately Mr. Plees had a lodger in the house who allowed Arthur to practice on her piano.

For the next two years, young Arthur Sullivan attended the little school in Bayswater, but he was becoming impatient to develop his musical talent and had set his heart on going to a choir school. First he had to persuade his father.

CHAPTER TWO

1853-1858

The Chapel Royal and King's College

THOMAS SULLIVAN WANTED his son to receive a good general education before devoting himself to music. Arthur Sullivan, on the other hand, was eager to receive a good musical education as soon as possible. He thought he could best achieve this in one of the leading choir schools, and decided on the Chapel Royal, where Purcell, he had learned, had once been a chorister. Only when Arthur was already nearly twelve did his father at last agree; and he began by enlisting the help of his local clergyman, the Rev. Percy Smith, who on 23 March 1854 wrote to the Rev. Thomas Helmore, master of Her Majesty's Chapels Royal.

As there was still no reply to that letter a fortnight later, the impatient pupil took the affair into his own hands and decided to try the personal approach. Armed with a letter from his father, Sullivan — accompanied by his schoolmaster, Mr. Plees — set off on Saturday, 8 April, to see Sir George Smart, who had been the organist at the Chapel Royal since 1822. When Sullivan first saw him, he thought Smart was a funny old gentleman; but that old gentleman, then nearly eighty, was to be of great help to Sullivan's future education. Sullivan had chosen wisely. George Smart read the letter, patted Sullivan on the head, and told him he must go and see Thomas Helmore, who lived in Onslow Square, Brompton. But Helmore had moved two weeks before to Cheyne Walk, Chelsea — a twenty-minute walk away.

Eventually, Thomas Helmore heard Sullivan as he accompanied himself and sang a piece called "With Verdure Clad." Helmore then questioned him on the catechism. He had other candidates for the vacancy at the Chapel Royal, but he liked Sullivan's voice and was also impressed by his appearance and his manner — Sullivan's good looks and his famous charm were already working in his favor. Two difficulties stood in the way: first, his age — Sullivan was nearly twelve, which was older than the usual starting age; and second, his home was too far away to allow him to reach the Chapel Royal during the vacation periods, when the boys still had to perform their duties. Plees suggested that it would be possible for Sullivan to stay with him during the vacations and so overcome the second difficulty. Helmore was sufficiently impressed by the boy to write that evening to the Rev. Percy Smith with the news that he would ask the subdean the next day to admit him.

On 10 April, Sullivan learned that he had been accepted and two days later, on Wednesday 12 April 1854, he became a chorister of the Chapel Royal.

The boys of the Chapel Royal, ten in number, boarded with the master in a house in Cheyne Walk that was large enough to accommodate the choristers as well as Helmore's own family. Chelsea embankment had not been built and Cheyne Walk ran along the shore of the Thames, a broad road with taverns and coffee shops. The boys had to walk from Cheyne Walk to St. James's Palace and back, a round trip of about five miles, twice every Sunday and major Feast Day, including Christmas Day: a journey made all the more difficult because of the heavy gold coats the boys had to wear. Sullivan found the walk exhausting and had to lie down and rest in between morning and evening services. At times, the walk was hazardous and on at least one occasion the choir boys, unescorted and glaringly obvious in their gold, attracted the unwelcome attention of a gang of young hooligans and were forced to forgo their dignity, hitch up their coats, and run for it.

Sullivan quickly gained experience as a chorister. On Maundy Thursday, the day after his admission to the Chapel Royal, he sang in a duet from "Blessed is he that considereth the poor and needy" by James Nares, a former organist at the Chapel Royal, and on 25 April, he was called on to sing "Rejoice Greatly" from the *Messiah* as part of a concert at St. Mark's College on the patron's feast day.

Apart from regular duties at the Chapel Royal, the choristers formed part of larger choirs at special occasions. On 10 May, they took part, as one of eighteen choirs, in the "Sons of the Clergy" Festival at St. Paul's Cathedral; and when the Crystal Palace opened on 10 June, having been rebuilt on its new site at Sydenham, the choristers formed part of a choir of 1,500 who sang Handel's "Hallelujah Chorus" in the presence of Queen Victoria and Prince Albert—an early experience for Sullivan of performing before a large audience for the grand occasion.

Helmore, composer of hymn tunes as well as teacher, had been vice principal and director of music at St. Mark's College Chelsea, the first national training school for teachers, before his appointment at the Chapel Royal. Not only was it his responsibility to give the boys a sound musical training but he also was charged with supervising their general education, including Scripture and Latin. In contrast to the young Gilbert, Sullivan was happy at school. For Sullivan, an authority figure was not someone to be resented but someone to be befriended and won over by his natural charm. Sullivan's respect for Thomas Helmore developed into a friendship that was to last until Helmore's death in 1890.

One schoolroom incident at Cheyne Walk stood out in Sullivan's memory years later. It happened in September 1854 in the early days of the Crimean War, before criticism of the British army's performance at Sebastopol had been voiced. Sullivan recalled that Helmore had one day come into class and told them to put away their books while he gave them the best English history lesson possible. He then read them W. H. Russell's *Times* report of the battle of the Alma. The boys, and Helmore, were moved to tears at the tales of bravery of the British soldiers.[1] Gilbert also read that report along with other reports on the Crimean War, and he, too, was affected by them, as we shall see.

Musical composition, rather than soldiering, was what occupied Arthur Sullivan's mind. He would even compose while others were asleep—something he was to make a habit of in later life. One of his early efforts, a madrigal entitled "O lady dear," written in a yellow manuscript book, contains the inscription: "Written while lying outside the bed one night, undressed, and in deadly fear lest Mr. Helmore should come in."[2]

One of his compositions was an anthem, "Sing unto the Lord and bless His name." He showed it to Sir George Smart, who arranged for it to be sung one evening in the Chapel in front of the bishop of London. The bishop sent for Sullivan to congratulate him on his clever composition, and, not omitting to remind him that there was "something higher to attend to," shook his hand and gave him half a sovereign.[3]

The quality of his voice, together with his attractive looks and personality, meant that Sullivan was frequently called on to sing solo parts, and there are several stories of his being patted on the head afterward by some dignitary or other and given half a sovereign. One such story tells of the duke of Wellington singling him out at the end of a service. It is true that the duke went regularly to the Chapel Royal on Sundays, but he had been dead for two years by the time Sullivan became a chorister.

Fred Sullivan was by now working in an architect's office in London, training to be an architect himself. He was not far from Cheyne Walk and would call in to see his younger brother, at the same time keeping the other choristers amused with his comic songs. At first Helmore was not too happy when he discovered him in the schoolroom but, when he came to know Fred better, he grew to like his friendly, cheerful manner. Fred was a natural comedian. The writer and librettist Francis Burnand described him as "one of the most naturally comic little men I ever came across."[4]

At the end of June 1855, Sullivan was given an unexpected break from the Chapel Royal when he was sent home to recuperate following an illness, and shortly afterward he went on holiday to Devon with the family of Cunningham Bridgeman, a fellow chorister. In greater leisure than he enjoyed at the Chapel Royal, he used part of the time to compose, and produced a sacred song, "O Israel," which he dedicated to Bridgeman's mother. It became his first published work and he was still only thirteen.[5]

His own mother felt the separation from her son keenly and never more so than at Christmastime when, she said, she would miss his "little happy face and black eyes" at the dinner table.[6] Although most of his time was spent separated from them, Sullivan was secure in the love of both his parents, and in the knowledge that the sacrifices they made were for his benefit.

In the spring of 1856, Sullivan heard that there was to be a competitive examination at the Royal Academy of Music for a scholarship founded in memory of Felix Mendelssohn. The idea of instituting a Mendelssohn Scholarship had been around since at least 1848, when Jenny Lind, the famous Swedish soprano, had given her services in a London concert to help endow the scholarship. At the outset, the intention was to combine with the Leipzig Conservatory in raising funds. Later, as funding or enthusiasm were not forthcoming in Leipzig, Sir George Smart, the chairman, and the rest of the committee decided to go ahead on their own to provide the scholarship for a boy to benefit from studying at both the Royal Academy and at Leipzig.

Sullivan was the youngest of the seventeen candidates on the first day of the examination, Saturday, 28 June 1856, but at the end of the first round, the number of competitors was reduced to two: Sullivan and the oldest of the candidates, seventeen-year-old Joseph Barnby, who had been a chorister at York Minster. The deciding examination took place on Friday, 4 July. After subjecting the two finalists to a more searching examination, the judges needed more time to confer and Sullivan had to go back to Cheyne Walk to begin the agonizing wait for the result. The letter arrived that evening. Sullivan tore open the envelope to find he had won the coveted scholarship. It was an unforgettable moment: a moment he preserved by framing the letter and keeping it for the rest of his life. Sullivan's joy was shared by his proud parents, who were immediately notified by Helmore, who also offered to accommodate the young scholar while he attended the academy. The scholarship was initially for one year, entitling him to free tuition at the academy commencing on 21 September 1856.

Sullivan's piano tutor at the academy was William Sterndale Bennett, a composer as well as pianist and conductor of the Philharmonic Society. Apart from his weekly lesson with Bennett, Sullivan received another lesson from Arthur O'Leary, a young pianist who had studied at Leipzig, and whose role was to coach selected pupils at the Royal Academy. Sullivan was taught harmony and composition by John Goss, a former Chapel Royal chorister, organist at St. Paul's Cathedral, composer, and also a neighbor in Cheyne Walk. Required by the academy to take a second instrumental study, Sullivan chose the violin.

In his last year at the Chapel Royal, where he continued while studying at the academy, there were signs that Sullivan was not always as seriously devoted to his work as Helmore would have liked. Writing to Mrs. Sullivan on 29 November 1856, Helmore suggested that Sullivan should work harder, and was spending too much time at play. Helmore's suggestion was that he should compose a song or an anthem every week as concrete proof that he was working. It was a criticism that would be leveled at Sullivan throughout his life, but in his defense in those early days it could be argued that one of his difficulties was that he was having to combine two worlds: the world of student at a music college and that of chorister.

After more than eleven years as bandmaster at Sandhurst, Thomas Sullivan was discharged from the army on the last day of December 1856. That was not to be the end of his connection with the military. In 1857, the Royal Military School of Music was founded and at the beginning of May, Thomas Sullivan took up his post as professor of clarinet as a civilian. His salary was to be £115 a year, a considerable improvement on his pay as a bandmaster. Before Thomas had received his first salary payment, Arthur made an early demand on him, asking him for two guineas to allow him to subscribe to the season's Philharmonic concerts, something his master for composition, John Goss, had strongly recommended.

The six Philharmonic concerts, conducted by Sterndale Bennett, were held fortnightly on Mondays from 20 April until 29 June. It was an ideal opportunity for the young student to hear a substantial program of music, although limited in the sense that new vogue composers such as Robert Schumann and Richard Wagner were not acceptable. There were usually two symphonies and two overtures played at each concert. In the course of the season, five Beethoven symphonies and also Mendelssohn's *Scotch* Symphony were played. On 18 May, Sullivan heard Anton Rubinstein play his Concerto for Pianoforte in G as well as two more of his own compositions. At the first concert he had the opportunity to hear the famous cellist Alfredo Piatti and in the last concert Clara Schumann played "17 Variations Sérieuses" of Mendelssohn.[7]

Before the end of the Philharmonic season, Sullivan's voice had broken and his days as a choirboy were over. His final performance as a Chapel Royal chorister was at the first Handel Festival at the Crystal Palace, and on 22 June 1857 his membership of the Chapel Royal ended.

He was also nearing the end of his year at the Royal Academy of Music, and a few weeks later the principal, Cipriani Potter, reported to George Smart and the members of the Mendelssohn Committee on Sullivan's progress:

> Sullivan (A.S.) played a most excellent examination today, he is greatly improved on the Piano, in Harmony has been most industrious, considerably advanced in Counterpoint, canons &c—. A Duette & chorus of his composition was performed at our last concert (July 14th) which was much admired; therefore as the Mendelssohn Committee have allowed him the advantage of another year, I feel that he is fully deserving of his election.[8]

The duet and chorus referred to had been composed by Sullivan to Shakespeare's "It was a lover and his lass."[9]

By the autumn, Thomas and Clementina Sullivan had moved to 3 Ponsonby Street in Pimlico. Arthur and Frederick joined them and the family were all together again. Pimlico, which came to be popularly known as stucco land, had recently been developed by Thomas Cubitt after his completion of Belgravia. The houses were more modest than those in the wealthier district of Belgravia, although still intended as middle-class housing. The tall stuccoed houses of Ponsonby Street, built on four

The houses of Ponsonby Street, now incorporated into Millbank

floors with the top floor, a garret, intended as servant accommodation, were not well situated. On the other side of the road stood a row of wharves and a saw mill; and the houses themselves lay in the shadow of the walls of the Millbank Prison. As in the old days in Lambeth, the rent of the whole house was too much for Thomas Sullivan, and they shared with another family, the Sullivans occupying the lower floors.[10] There was no question of employing a servant. The house was however ideally situated for Thomas Sullivan to travel to and from Kneller Hall. After his day's work and a short train ride to Vauxhall Station, it was just a few minutes walk across Vauxhall Bridge to reach home.

The situation of Ponsonby Street brought two other benefits to the Sullivan family. Along the same thoroughfare was Crescent Terrace and at number 1, above a grocer's shop, lived Alfred J. Hipkins with his wife and two children. Hipkins worked for Broadwood's, the piano manufacturers in Horseferry Road. As well as being a clerk for the firm, Hipkins was also a music teacher, proficient on both harpsichord and clavichord. He proved to be an invaluable contact for Thomas Sullivan, who soon began to teach at Broadwood's to the benefit of his son. Further along the road, at number 10 Crescent Terrace, lived the Lacy family.[11] The eldest daughter, Charlotte, was seventeen when the Sullivans moved in, and she became the focal point of Frederick Sullivan's interest.

The whole of that road was renamed Grosvenor Road and is now Millbank. Millbank Prison was swept away long ago to become the site of the Tate Gallery. The wharves are no more, and in their place neat public gardens run along the side of the Thames. The houses of Ponsonby Street are still there, restored, with their white stucco standing out more clearly than it did in smoke-filled Victorian London. Because of redevelopment and renumbering, it has not been possible to pinpoint which house was number 3 Ponsonby Street.

Apart from Charlotte Lacy, Frederick Sullivan found another interest in Pimlico with the formation of the Pimlico Dramatic Society, who gave their performances in Ebury Street. Arthur joined his brother for at least one performance, providing an ensemble made up of students from the Royal Academy, which he conducted. The society came to an early end when the duke of Westminster banned dramatic activities on his land. The theater was still considered by many in the 1850s to be less than respectable.

Toward the end of his second year at the Royal Academy, in May 1858, Sullivan was invited to a meeting with George Smart to discuss his future prospects, and shortly afterwards he received official notification of his reelection as Mendelssohn Scholar for another year to allow him to go to Leipzig. To help him overcome the language barrier, Mrs. Klingemann, the wife of the honorary secretary of the Mendelssohn Committee, offered to give free German lessons twice a week and so ease his transition into studies at the conservatory.

Sullivan had the confidence, support, and encouragement of a number of people who believed in his exceptional musical abilities. Winning the Mendelssohn Scholarship was a vital part of his musical formation, but equally important was the continued support of the committee, not simply as a body, but as individuals who were anxious to see their chosen candidate succeed, and in whom they placed great hope for the future of English music. The exact makeup of the original committee is not certain, but it is unlikely to have changed much before 1864 when Sir George Smart resigned as chairman and his place was taken by Cipriani Potter. Other members of the committee at that time were Otto Goldschmidt, the pianist and composer, also the husband of Jenny Lind, and, at twenty-nine, the youngest member of the committee; Julius Benedict, conductor and composer (in 1862) of *The Lily of Killarney*; J. W. Davison, the musical critic of *The Times*; Henry Chorley, a critic on the staff of the *Athenaeum*; Charles Lucas, composer and a future principal of the Royal Academy of Music; and Sterndale Bennett.[12] But Sullivan's greatest supporter and inspiration was his father, who after his work at Kneller Hall would then go on to Broadwood's to teach on a few evenings a week in order to earn enough money to support his son in his musical studies. Henry Broadwood himself also contributed to the young musician's studies, giving £30 to help toward Sullivan's expenses at Leipzig.[13]

Sullivan's studies at the Royal Academy ended with his final concert on 13 July 1858, when his Overture in D Minor, dedicated to John Goss, was played, and in September 1858 Sullivan set out for Leipzig and the next stage of his musical education.

IN THE AUTUMN OF 1853, Gilbert became a full-time student at King's College, London. He joined the department of general literature and science, which meant that his studies were to be in classics and mathematics. The education of the department was regarded as "that type of culture best fitted to produce the ideal Christian gentleman in which [the] college specialized." In a report of the department in 1855, the belief was firmly expressed "that careful training in the classics and mathematics was the basis of an education which was universally secure and lasting."[14] Soon the numbers doing classics were to fall dramatically and the professors were lamenting that they were having to accept students who were totally unfit to follow the course. In other words, the "secure and lasting" was giving way to a period of change.

The success of the Great Exhibition of 1851 in Hyde Park had heralded a period of peace and prosperity. For some, now that the threat of revolution had subsided with the collapse of the Chartist Movement, it was an opportunity to return to the old, stable society led by its aristocracy. For others, it was an age of change and inventiveness; instead of the ubiquitous "change and decay" seen by H. F. Lyte, the writer of "Abide with me," they saw the possibility of change leading to a better future. The old world had been modernized with the coming of the railways and the telegraph. Gilbert had been born into the modern world. As a modern young man, he cut his hair short, grew side-whiskers, and wore trousers. The old world had died with his grandfather, Thomas Morris, "the last man in London, I believe," said Gilbert, "who wore Hessian boots and a pig-tail."[15]

For the present, Gilbert had come to King's College, back to the Strand and a short distance from where he had been born. Fleet Street and the Strand, a single thoroughfare stretching from the City to the borders of Westminster—the hub of London, alive with print shops and lawyers' chambers at the Fleet Street end, and every kind of shop in the Strand: hatters and hosiers, wigmakers and jewelers, fishmongers and bakers, and with the roadway itself choked with horse-drawn vehicles leaving behind the all-pervading smell of dung. Much of Gilbert's working life was to be centered around the Strand and Fleet Street: his university days at King's College, his legal studies at the Inner Temple, his days as a journalist, his early work as a dramatist at the Gaiety, and eventually his greatest triumphs at the Opera Comique and the Savoy.

As a student at King's, Gilbert became active in a society called the Scientific Society, formerly the Engineering Society. At an "extraordinary meeting" on 31 October 1854, a student named Geary proposed that the "Society be dissolved and that its funds and property be devoted to the founding of a Shakespearean Reading Society." This motion was seconded, but Gilbert moved an amendment, "that the Society be also called a Dramatic as well as a Shakespearean Reading Society." The amendment was carried. The matter was then referred to the Principal of King's College, Dr. Jelf, who gave his signed approval in the Minute Book. The officers of the old society resigned and new officers were elected and amongst them was Gilbert, as one of the secretaries. Three years later the Engineering Society was reestablished, on 18 November 1857—after Gilbert had left King's College.[16]

How much of this was Gilbert's doing, as sometimes suggested? He played his part, certainly, but as a seventeen-year-old student he was hardly in a position to influence the college principal. That it was not Gilbert's intention to take over the society and to change its character can be seen from later minutes. The day following the extraordinary meeting, on 1 November, a paper was read on "The Scientific Education of the Working Man," followed by a discussion in which Gilbert was one of five speakers, and the following week, on 8 November 1854, Gilbert read a paper on "The Theory of Apparitions." He was in no hurry to change to purely dramatic questions. In the minutes, his name occurs frequently as a contributor to discussions; but of course, as one of the secretaries, he was in a privileged position to mention his own contributions.

What particularly captured Gilbert's attention in 1854 was the fighting in the Crimean War. The battle of the Alma in September, followed by the battles of Balaclava in October and Inkerman in November, were all reported by W. H. Russell in his graphic accounts in *The Times*. Gilbert's imagination was fired by the exploits of the British soldiers and he pictured himself as an artillery officer. Although the war effectively ended when the Russians abandoned Sebastopol in October 1855, peace was not signed until the treaty of Paris on 30 March 1856. Gilbert's own recollections of his attempt to gain a commission have to be read against this timetable, because there is a discrepancy in the dates. He said, in his autobiographical account, that he prepared for the army examinations in December 1856. The Crimean War, however, was already over by that date.

During the long vacation of 1855, no doubt after discussions with his father, Gilbert had come to a decision about his future, and when he returned at the beginning of the Michaelmas Term, he was admitted to membership of the Inner Temple. Law studies did not follow immediately, but his membership did entitle him to commence dining at the Inner Temple and so begin to "keep terms," a necessary requirement before being called to the bar. Legal studies would come later. However, he was at the same time attracted by the prospect of a career in the army.

After the initial wave of enthusiasm for the war by the British public, the mood had changed when an army that they considered invincible failed to take Sebastopol. Voices of criticism were raised against the generals, and against the aristocrats who administered the war from their offices in Whitehall. To raise the quality of leadership in the army, the idea of a competitive examination for commissions was put into operation.

Examinations were held in August 1855 for commissions in the Royal Artillery and the Engineers. Gilbert, then only eighteen, was too young to enter, but would qualify when he was nineteen in November. However, in October 1855 the minimum age was raised to twenty, and so Gilbert would still be too young. Therefore, when he said in his autobiographical account that he applied to Lord Panmure, the secretary of state for war, for a dispensation, it was because he was *below* the age limit and not, as he recalled years later, because he was *above* the limit. The next examinations were to be held after Christmas, in January 1856, and were to be more rigorous than the first examinations held. There was to be a preliminary examination in mathematics, at which a third of the candidates would be eliminated, to be followed by optional subjects including classics. The examination was not canceled as Gilbert recalled, but took place in January as planned, and further examination sessions were held later in the year and in the following year.[17] Perhaps with the Crimean War coming to an end, Gilbert had lost interest.

What did interest Gilbert was writing plays. He said he used to write plays for home performance, and certainly his mother and his two younger sisters were all interested in amateur dramatics.[18] Home for the Gilberts was no longer in Brompton Square, but in a larger and grander house, at 21 Thurloe Square, on the other side of Brompton Road. By the time he was eighteen, Gilbert had become more ambitious and had written a burlesque, which he sent to every manager in London. The total rejection of his work baffled him, but did not put him off.

Not that writing plays for a living was a practical proposition. It was still necessary for him to follow a profession and earn his livelihood. He had changed his mind about a military career, and for some unexplained reason he did not pursue his law studies at this stage. Neither did he proceed to Oxford after obtaining his B.A. at King's College, as he originally intended. His father must have agreed to his change of mind from law to the army in 1855 and perhaps he was not now prepared to countenance another change of mind; or perhaps Gilbert was quite simply tired of being a student. Sullivan, secure in his precocious talent, had been clear from an early age that his future lay with music; Gilbert was not at all clear where his future lay and would only find a home for his talents, in his own words: "after a touch at two or three professions."[19]

The second reform resulting from criticism over official handling of the Crimean War was aimed at the mediocrity of the administration, and competitive examinations to the civil service were introduced. In 1857, the year he received his degree, Gilbert was successful in obtaining an assistant clerkship in the newly formed Education Department. He was one of thirty-four clerks in the department and as a third-class assistant clerk he received a salary of £100 a year, which would increase each year by annual increments of £5. After ten years service, he could look forward to £150 a year.[20] The dream of being a heroic artillery officer fighting for his country had been replaced by the reality of being a third-class clerk fighting to stave off boredom.

Mr. and Mrs. Gilbert saw their eldest two children leave home in 1857: Schwenck, who found lodgings in a boarding house in Pimlico, and Jane, who on 7 September, a month before her twentieth birthday, married Alfred Weigall, a miniature portrait painter. The family were not to be far away from each other: Jane and Alfred moved to Kensington, where they lived at number 8 Clarendon Road, a turning off Victoria Road, to which the rest of the family moved shortly after.[21] The lodging house that Schwenck lived in has never been located but is likely to have been in the old district of Pimlico, near Sloane Square, and therefore, in those days before the Metropolitan and District Railway, within reasonable walking distance of his office in Downing Street.

The same year, 1857, saw the first published work of William Gilbert senior, with the appearance of *On the Present System of Rating for the Relief of the Poor in the Metropolis*. The following year he published *Dives and Lazarus, the Adventures of an Obscure Medical Man in a Low Neighbourhood*: titles that reveal his strong social conscience. His radical political leanings found a natural home among like-minded men when he became a member of the Reform Club. His son's only work in print by this time was a translation of the laughing-song from Auber's *Manon Lescaut*, which he wrote for the soprano Euphrosyne Parepa, whom he had known since childhood and who was later to marry Carl Rosa. The piece was printed in the playbill of one of Alfred Mellon's promenade concerts. Gilbert was not sure of the year of its appearance. He suggested 1858, but what he did remember clearly was the immense pride he felt when he went to those promenade concerts—nightly, he tells us—just to stand next to someone in the audience reading his words. It was to be a few more years before W. S. Gilbert was to catch up with his father and to appear more regularly before the public in print.

CHAPTER THREE

1858-1862

Sullivan at Leipzig; Gilbert at Law

THE CONSERVATORY AT LEIPZIG had been founded by Mendelssohn only fifteen years before Sullivan's arrival in September 1858. Its director was Konrad Schlemitz, although Ignaz Moscheles, who had originally been invited by Mendelssohn to take charge of piano tuition, effectively ran the institute. George Smart wrote to Moscheles to recommend Sullivan and to point out that composition was his strongest subject. For his part, Moscheles was glad to welcome the promising young musician, assuring Smart that Sullivan's program of studies would be drawn up bearing his particular talent in mind.

Moscheles himself and Louis Plaidy taught Sullivan piano; Moritz Hauptmann, the eminent violinist who had taught Joachim, taught him counterpoint, as did Ernst Friederich Richter; and Julius Rietz was his master for composition. Orchestral training was in the hands of Ferdinand David, who had been concertmaster of the Gewandhaus Orchestra under Mendelssohn. Sullivan also received three violin lessons a week. All in all, he found this to be too many lessons at first, far different from the practice at the Royal Academy. In addition, there were the Gewandhaus concerts to attend every Thursday, and on Friday evenings an *Abend Unterhaltung*, or evening entertainment, which gave the students an opportunity to perform in front of their fellow students and teachers, as soloists, in ensembles, or even to perform their own compositions.

Sullivan's charm endeared him to Moscheles and his teachers. It also allowed Sullivan to live a little more cheaply as he received weekly invitations to supper with the Moscheles and the Davids. He was just as popular with his fellow students. One of them, Walter Bache, liked him immediately, and writing home mentioned Sullivan's "great talent" in composition.[1] Three other friends of the Leipzig days were Franklin Taylor, who lodged at one time in the same house as Sullivan, Carl Rose (later to be known as Carl Rosa), and John Francis Barnett, who recalled Sullivan's popularity and his "charming boyish ways."[2] Sullivan, Franklin Taylor, Walter Bache, and Carl Rosa frequently met at the house of Barnett's aunt, Mrs. John Barnett (the wife of the composer), and every Sunday she kept open house for them, feeding them as well as providing an opportunity for an enjoyable musical evening.

Mrs. Barnett had gone to Leipzig to be with her three children—Domenico, Rosamund, and Clara—while they studied at the conservatory. Sullivan was sufficiently taken with Rosamund to dedicate to her a song he had written: "Ich möchte hinaus es jauchzen."[3] Rosamund's younger sister, Clara, was infatuated by the "smiling youth with an oval, olive-tinted face, dark eyes, a large generous mouth and a crop of dark curly hair."[4] She was only fourteen, and it is not surprising that Sullivan was more interested in her older sister. Sullivan made a deep impression on Clara, which she recalled more than fifty years later when she came to write her reminiscences. She remembered his youthful flirting with other girls, which she took so seriously at the time; but she also remembered his generosity when, to surprise her, he had secretly copied out the parts of a string quartet she had composed, and had a few of their friends rehearse it in order to play it to her at a party.

Toward the end of his first year at Leipzig, in May 1859, Sullivan's String Quartet in D Minor was played at an *Abend Unterhaltung,* and that summer the Mendelssohn Committee renewed his scholarship for a further year. In September, Moscheles was able to report to Sir George Smart that he was very pleased with Sullivan's progress in playing, as well as in composition, mentioning that he was just finishing a new overture. Sullivan had already given his father his own progress report for his first year: he felt that progress was only really noticeable in about May, language difficulties having held him back in the early months.

Summer activities included a concert in June, which gave Sullivan the opportunity of meeting Franz Liszt who conducted and performed at the piano, impressing Sullivan by the power but also by the delicacy of his playing. The previous day, Sullivan had been invited to the house of Ferdinand David, who was entertaining Liszt, and the day ended with a game of whist in which Sullivan joined, walking home with Liszt afterward.

In his second year, encouraged by Ferdinand David, Sullivan gave more attention to developing his skills as a conductor and found himself called on more and more in this role. In October, his quartet was performed again at an *Abend Unterhaltung,* and later in the year, he not only had to conduct an operetta by Reinecke but had to adapt the orchestration to suit an orchestra consisting mainly of strings. That year, Sullivan's professor of composition, Julius Rietz, left the conservatory to take up a post in Dresden, and at celebrations in his honor, Sullivan was called on to conduct a concert of Rietz's works.

At the end-of-year examinations, the *Prüfungskonzert,* on 25 May 1860, Sullivan conducted his own overture, *Der Rosenfest,* based on Thomas Moore's poem, "Lalla Rookh." He enjoyed the experience immensely, was not in the least nervous, and thrilled to the enthusiastic applause at the end. He had wondered how the press would receive the Mendelssohnian style of his overture, but the notices proved to be favorable and encouraging.

The period of Sullivan's studies at Leipzig was due to end that year, but Moscheles and Plaidy were both in favor of his staying until the following Easter to improve his playing and to give him a chance to play in the Grand Public Examination. Earlier in the year, Sullivan had written an anthem, "We Have Heard With Our Ears," which he dedicated to Sir George Smart, sending him an additional copy to be passed on to Thomas Helmore; and now George Smart wrote to Sullivan offering £5 to help toward the expenses for his extended period of study. Only then did Sullivan write to his father with the news, forwarding George Smart's letter. He realized that the demands on his father would probably be too much to allow him to stay on at Leipzig. His devoted father, however, was quite prepared to work even harder for the sake of his son's future. He increased his teaching at Broadwood's to four evenings a week, but confessed that, with his duties at Kneller Hall, he had taken on almost too much. Arthur could scarcely find the words to thank him. He promised not only to work hard but also to do what he could to repay his father's sacrifices and try to make the rest of his days happy and comfortable. News that Schlemitz, the director of the conservatory, had exempted Sullivan in his last two terms from his £6 tuition fees came as a bonus.

By the beginning of his final year, Sullivan was only too conscious of the benefits he had derived from Leipzig, and the opportunity it had given him to hear more music than was ever played in England. He saw it as one of his tasks to raise the standard of orchestral playing in England, and to produce something of the light and shade that he said was characteristic of the German orchestras. That was his youthful ambition; it would be some years before he would be in a position to act on it.

He started work on a symphony, but by the end of November he abandoned it, explaining to his father, after finishing the first movement, that he could not shake off the influence of Schumann in the second subject. In a postscript to the same letter he mentioned that he was writing music to the *Tempest*. In August that year, Leipzig suffered the biggest storm in living memory. Sullivan never mentioned a connection between the storm and his music; perhaps no connection existed. It was more likely to have been Mendelssohn's *A Midsummer Night's Dream* that influenced his choice of Shakespearean subject.

Early in 1861, Sullivan humorously assured Clara Barnett that his *Tempest* music was "going to take the world by 'storm.'"[5] His early confidence gave way to doubts, and by February Sullivan was complaining to his father about his slow progress. With his father's encouragement, Sullivan pushed on and managed to complete the work in time. In the Prüfung on Saturday 7 April 1861, a selection from the *Tempest* was heard for the first time and was warmly received. Sullivan had the great satisfaction of being called forward three times afterward in response to the applause. To add to his satisfaction, he learned that Mendelssohn's brother was in the audience to hear his work and felt honored afterward to receive an invitation from him to dinner.

Moscheles was delighted with it; he thought it "sounded fresh and clear," and that it heralded the beginning of Sullivan's career as a genuine artist.[6] On 10 April, Sullivan was awarded his diploma from the conservatory, and a few days later he left Leipzig.

Shortly after his return to London and to his family at 3 Ponsonby Street, Sullivan wrote to George Smart in his capacity as chairman of the "Mendelssohn Scholarship Committee," to express his "heartfelt thanks" for the opportunities his scholarship had opened up for him, providing him with "a first rate education, and one that does not fall to the lot of everyone." He was honored to have had such distinguished teachers. "I trust my future career will prove how entirely I have appreciated and endeavoured to benefit by them."[7]

His musical education completed, Sullivan had three aims: to earn his living, to repay his parents for all the sacrifices they had made for him, and to develop his own career as a musician. He advertised for pupils; on four afternoons a week he went over to Helmore's house in Cheyne Walk to teach the choristers basic subjects; and he began studying the organ under George Cooper, the assistant organist at St. Paul's Cathedral and now organist at the Chapel Royal. After only a few months tuition, he heard of a vacancy through an old friend of Thomas Helmore, was introduced to the Rev. Joseph Hariman Hamilton, vicar of St. Michael's Church, Chester Square, and given a trial. Hamilton's daughter remembered how she was "quite enthralled by the performance of the E minor Fugue of Bach, one of the pieces played by the slim, curly-headed, black-eyed youth."[8] She became one of Sullivan's first pupils in organ and harmony, and then acted as his assistant for many years.

He was to hold the post for eight years and, for the dual role of organist and choirmaster, Sullivan is said to have received a yearly salary of £80.[9] At least it gave him a regular income, even though the regularity of its hours did not suit Sullivan's temperament. The tenors and basses for his choir were recruited from the local police station. It was a good training ground, teaching music to singers of limited musical knowledge — hard work, but all carried out in good humor. He had the respect of his "gallant constables," as he called them, and he said years later that he sometimes thought of them when composing the music for *The Pirates of Penzance*.[10]

Earning his basic living as a church organist was not enough; Sullivan needed to make progress as a composer in a world in which the help of influential friends was vital. One such friend was Henry Chorley. Now in his fifties, Chorley had been a critic for the *Athenaeum* since 1830 and with J. W. Davison was one of the most influential critics of the day. Largely self-educated, Chorley had tried his hand at novels and plays but without success. His "strange voice" and "foppish manners" were commented on by Charlotte Brontë when she met him,[11] and yet Charles Dickens was frequently in his company and treated him as a close friend. Shortly after Sullivan's return from Leipzig, Chorley arranged for Sullivan to play some of his *Tempest* music at a gathering at his house in West Eaton Place. Chorley had also invited

George Grove and, in view of Grove's position as secretary to the Crystal Palace, it is likely that he hoped to impress him.[12]

Grove had started out as a civil engineer, superintending the construction of lighthouses in the West Indies but had changed direction and, after a period as secretary to the Society of Arts, had taken over as secretary to the Crystal Palace, where he was concerned particularly with developing its music concerts. Although Grove was more than twenty years older than Sullivan, an immediate rapport was struck between the two men and an enduring friendship developed. Sullivan set about revising his *Tempest* and Grove arranged for its first performance at the Crystal Palace the following spring. But shortly before the scheduled performance, Grove suffered the personal tragedy of losing his eight-year-old daughter Lucy to scarlet fever. In his deep sorrow, he found solace by throwing himself into his work, and admitted that Sullivan's affection and support had comforted him in his grief.[13]

The *Tempest*, with a narration by Henry Chorley, was given its first public performance on Saturday afternoon, 5 April 1862, conducted by August Manns. Sullivan said he woke up next morning and found himself famous. The report in *The Times* was enthusiastic, praising "a decided vein of melody, a strong feeling of dramatic expression, and a happy fancy in the treatment of the orchestra." A little background was supplied about the new composer.

> Mr. Arthur Sullivan, originally a pupil of Mr. Goss, in the Royal Academy of Music, was selected by the Committee of the Mendelssohn Testimonial Fund to be sent to Leipsic as "Mendelssohn Scholar." . . . The concert-room was crowded to the doors, and a success was obtained by the young musician of which he, and those who first discerned the germs of talent in him, may well feel proud.[14]

Stung by the omission of his own role in the details of Sullivan's education, Thomas Helmore immediately wrote to *The Times* to point out that the "young English composer, Arthur Seymour Sullivan" had entered the Chapel Royal in April 1854, and left in June 1857; "and it seems just to the oldest school of English composers that this fact should not be wholly ignored in any notice of his educational career."[15] Sullivan responded at once and in an attempt to heal his old master's wounded feelings assured Helmore that he was conscious he owed more to him than to perhaps anyone else.

The following Saturday, 12 April 1862, the *Tempest* was repeated at the Crystal Palace. Chorley had taken along Charles Dickens, who afterward met Sullivan and, in his usual energetic manner, gripped Sullivan's hand in hearty congratulation.

Sullivan became a frequent visitor to the Crystal Palace. After the Saturday afternoon concerts, Grove used to invite a group of young men back to his house in Sydenham. Among the group were Franklin Taylor, Sullivan's friend from Leipzig, and Lionel Lewin, a young poet whose words were to inspire Sullivan in composing some of his songs.

St. James's Hall was to be the setting for Sullivan's next appearance in public, this time as a performer. On 9 May, he took part in the same concert as his father. Thomas Sullivan directed the military bands of "Messrs John Broadwood and Sons' Manufactory," and Arthur Sullivan appeared as accompanist, and as part of a piano quartet in a piece by Walter Macfarren.[16] St. James's Hall, just off Piccadilly, had been built by Thomas Chappell in 1858 and was the home of Chappell's "Saturday and Monday Popular Concerts" to be immortalized later by Gilbert in *The Mikado*.

Shortly after the *Tempest*, Sullivan began a new work. Chorley provided him with the libretto for an opera called *The Sapphire Necklace*, and Sullivan worked at it over the next year. It proved to be a blind alley. Chorley was no better as a librettist than he was as a novelist or dramatist. Sullivan found it impossible to produce a decent score, and only parts of the work were ever performed. It is certain that he was working on this opera in August 1862 when he received an invitation from Lady Smart to go down to Blackheath to spend the day with her and Sir George, as she specifically referred to the opera in her letter. After the visit to Blackheath, Sullivan had a copy of the *Tempest* made especially for Sir George Smart, and in October he dedicated the music to him.

Sullivan's friendship with George Grove led to his spending more and more time at Sydenham, often staying at Grove's house, and through Grove he was appointed professor of pianoforte and ballad singing at the Crystal Palace School of Art.[17] He was back in London on 17 September 1862, when he was best man at the wedding of his brother Frederic (the spelling now changed from Frederick) to Charlotte Louisa Lacy at St. Margaret's Westminster, where the officiating priest was Sullivan's master from the Chapel Royal and now a firm family friend, the Rev. Thomas Helmore.[18] Having returned to Sydenham and George Grove, Sullivan invited Helmore to dinner a week later, bringing together those two great influences in his life.

The *Tempest* was heard again at the Crystal Palace, when a selection was played on 22 November. Sullivan attended the performance and went on to dine at George Grove's with Joseph Joachim, the great violinist, and his new friend Fred Clay, three years older than Sullivan and a promising musician. Afterward, they entertained their host with an impromptu concert including Bach's sonatas for violin and piano, and a few pieces of Spohr, interspersed with "no end of pleasant nonsensical small-talk," Sullivan related to a friend, Nina Lehmann. The three of them then returned home together "smoking gorgeous cigars, running down Meyerbeer and praising Auber."[19]

Friendship with Chorley had drawn Sullivan into a wider circle of friends that included the Lehmanns. Frederick Lehmann, a wealthy German-born merchant, and his wife, Nina, eldest of eight daughters of the Edinburgh publisher Robert Chambers, were friends of Charles Dickens as well as of Chorley. Nina Lehmann, eleven years older than Sullivan, was an excellent pianist; she became friend and confidante, and Sullivan's correspondence with her was to continue over the years.

In December, the Lehmanns invited Sullivan and Chorley to join them on a trip to Paris with Charles Dickens, who was commuting frequently between England and France at that time, visiting the young actress, Ellen Ternan. On one occasion, Sullivan went with Dickens and Chorley to hear the celebrated mezzo-soprano Madame Viardot (Pauline Garcia) in Gluck's *Orpheus*. It was such an emotional performance, said Sullivan, that they were all moved to tears, though Dickens was more likely moved by the story of doomed love in the opera. Through Madame Viardot, Sullivan gained an introduction to Rossini and visited him several times over the next few days, once finding there his fellow student from Leipzig, Carl Rosa, playing a violin sonata. Rossini showed genuine interest in the *Tempest* music, and together they played a pianoforte arrangement of part of it. On the final visit, on 12 December 1862, Rossini presented him with his photograph, inscribed: "Offert a mon jeune Collègue Arthur S. Sullivan."[20] Before they left Paris, the Lehmanns and their party all went to the Opera Comique to see David's *Lalla Rookh,* which Sullivan found "very pretty, but rather monotonous."[21]

He had scarcely arrived home from Paris when he received his next social invitation. Otto Goldschmidt and Jenny Lind, in particular, were impressed with the *Tempest*, playing the music frequently, and they invited Sullivan to go down to St. Leonard's-on-Sea to spend Christmas Eve with them. He would still have time to return for his organ duties on Christmas Day.

Sullivan had been back in England for little more than eighteen months. He was still only twenty years old but was already considered a rising star in the musical world. With the continuing support of influential members of the Mendelssohn Committee—the critics Chorley and Davison; Otto Goldschmidt and Jenny Lind—and now with a newly formed friendship with another influential person, George Grove, his musical future looked promising. He was mixing socially with rich people like the Lehmanns, and had made the acquaintance of famous artists of the day such as Charles Dickens and Rossini. For a boy from modest beginnings, his progress had been rapid. He was engaged on his next important piece, the opera with Chorley, and through his association with Rossini felt inspired "with a love for the stage and things operatic."[22] His opera with Chorley was to prove a false start, but at this point, on the threshold of his career, he would never have imagined that "the stage and things operatic" were to prove the main source of his enduring fame.

W. S. GILBERT STARTED the year 1859 in the obscurity of the education offices in Downing Street. The work of the department was expanding rapidly and the number of assistant clerks grew in the next year from thirty-four to fifty-two.[23] The increasing importance of the department meant little to Gilbert, who did not see his talents best suited to the civil service. The original head of the education department, James Kay-Shuttleworth, was succeeded in the course of the year by Robert Lowe. As an albino, with chronic near-sightedness, Lowe was an easy target for the political cartoonist. Although Gilbert was a gifted caricaturist, no cartoon of his boss has survived; but later, in one of his plays, Gilbert was to attract considerable attention to himself by caricaturing several politicians, one of them Robert Lowe. The details can wait until later.

Perhaps in answer to his country's need; perhaps because his mind was turning again to the military; or perhaps simply out of boredom in "the detestable thraldom of this baleful office," as he described it,[24] Gilbert decided to join the militia. He enrolled with the Fifth West Yorkshire Militia and on 10 March 1859 he was gazetted Ensign.[25] His career with the Fifth West Yorkshire was brief. This was the year when the government, nervous about Napoleon III after his victory over Austria, and reckoning that he was not a man to be trusted, decided on the need for riflemen; in answer to the call "Riflemen form," regiments of Rifle Volunteers began to spring up. One such regiment was the Civil Service Rifle Volunteers, and F and G Company (Whitehall), as it came to be called, first met on 16 December 1859, presided over by Tom Taylor, who apart from being secretary to the Board of Health was a prolific and successful dramatist. This company was recruited from the government offices in Whitehall and the War Office. More volunteers joined over the months and with a complement of two hundred men, it became necessary to form another company and increase the establishment of officers. They had the democratic notion that officers should be elected from the ranks, and on 5 April 1860, Color Sergeant W. S. Gilbert was elected by his fellow militiamen to become Lieutenant of the Second Company. On 11 April, the first "march out" was held at Wimbledon, where Lieutenant Gilbert received his baptism as an officer in the pouring rain.[26]

On completion of two years as an assistant clerk, Gilbert's salary had risen to £110 a year. But the cost of the outfit for a lieutenant was about £30, more than a quarter of his salary. It was possible to recoup some, if not most, of the cost of the uniform by claiming expenses for attendance at a training course for officers. It was obligatory for every officer to attend the school of instruction at Wellington Barracks and obtain his certificate of proficiency within two years of his appointment.[27] When he first put that expensive uniform on and looked at himself in the glass, Lieutenant Gilbert was no doubt suitably impressed. At six feet four, with an upright military bearing, the handsome twenty-three-year-old officer cut a fine figure. At least one visit to his parents and his teenage sisters while in military dress must have been made. His parents were now living at 21 Victoria Road, near Jane and Alfred Weigall, in the new town of Kensington. An even better place to be seen would have been at the so-called church parade in nearby Hyde Park on a Sunday morning. Not that Gilbert went to church, but he was not averse to the social gathering after church in the park. If he did stroll along Victoria Road while in uniform, did a curtain twitch on the other side of the road, at the house of Mrs. Turner and her two daughters? Grace Turner was then nineteen; but little Lucy was only twelve, perhaps a little too young to be interested in the man who was to be her husband before her teenage years were over.

Not all Gilbert's visits home were made in uniform, although it might have helped him one night as he was making his way back to his lodgings. On 1 October 1860 he related the incident in a letter to *The Times*. As he was walking along Knightsbridge Road, he met "three Guardsman walking arm in arm with as many women. I gave them a wide berth, but one of the fellows deliberately came up to me and struck me violently on the chest with his elbow. The blow sent me staggering into the road in a most undignified manner." Gilbert grabbed the man, threatening to hold him until the police came. There was a struggle, the man broke away, "and one of the other two soldiers exclaimed, 'Let's give him a bit of belt.'" As they were about to lay into Gilbert, he grabbed one of the men. Fortunately, a passerby joined in on Gilbert's side. "After a short struggle the fellows broke from us, and finding that the odds were as much as two to three against them, the cowardly ruffians took to flight like so many startled sheep."[28] Gilbert goes on to suggest a way of avoiding this kind of attack by stitching the belts on to the soldiers' uniforms. But that avowed purpose of the letter is not as interesting as the actual account of what took place, revealing Gilbert's physical courage in being quite prepared to take on three men at the same time rather than to cower under their attack.

The Civil Service Rifle Volunteers (C.S.R.V.) gave Gilbert not only the military interest he required but also a dramatic opportunity. On 18 July 1860, the C.S.R.V. presented Tom Taylor's *A Lesson for Life* at the Lyric. The part of Crouch, one of the undergraduates of St. Barnabas College, Cambridge, was played by Lieutenant W. S. Gilbert, and that of Vivian, another undergraduate, by Captain Tom Hood. Also in the cast were Captain Tom Taylor, Ensign Edmund Yates, and two young ladies who appeared by special permission: Ellen Terry (aged fourteen) and Kate Terry (aged sixteen).[29] It was a minor galaxy of stars. Edmund Yates worked at the General Post Office but also was making his way in journalism and was acting editor of *Temple Bar*. Tom Hood, son of the poet Thomas Hood, and the Terry family were to be important players in Gilbert's future.

The company's performance of *A Lesson for Life* was successful enough to be repeated "By Special Demand" the following year, on 22 May, at the Lyceum. In between his two appearances as an actor, Gilbert was still writing unsuccessfully for the theater. A letter survives, dated 17 October 1860, written to W. H. Swanborough of the Strand Theatre, proposing a farce that Gilbert had written with the Strand company in mind.[30] The manager was not impressed.

On 3 January 1861, John Samuel Schwenck died in Brixton, where he and his wife had moved from Weybridge toward the end of their life. He left virtually all his wealth to his wife. In his short autobiography, W. S. Gilbert says: "Coming unexpectedly into a capital sum of £300," without saying where it came from.[31] This legacy almost certainly came from his great-aunt and godmother, Mary Schwenck, now a wealthy woman in her own right. The situation of her two godsons was not promising: Francis Schwenck, with no profession, was languishing at 3 Michael's Grove (now Egerton Terrace) in the house of his maternal grandmother, and William Schwenck was languishing in his assistant clerkship at the education department.[32] It is very likely that she offered to set them both up in life but with conditions. The sum of money William received, and therefore probably Francis, was coincidentally the same as their great-grandfather had received to start him out, and on which he had built so successfully. If they had inherited any of their great-grandfather's industry and flair, they would be successful. The sum was probably tied to a particular purpose: to take up a profession. Francis chose to be a civil engineer; William chose to be a barrister.

Gilbert tells us: "On the happiest day of my life I sent in my resignation. With £100 I paid my call to the Bar (I had previously entered myself as a student at the Inner Temple), with another £100 I obtained access to a conveyancer's chambers, and with the third £100 I furnished a set of chambers of my own, and began life afresh as a barrister-at-law."[33] His pupilage was undertaken at Pump Court in the Inner Temple, under Watkins Wilkins (later a judge), and he took chambers in Clement's Inn.

The law, or rather the "capital sum," had enabled Gilbert to escape from the civil service and embark on a profession, but he still felt the need to write. Clement Scott recalled that Gilbert told him that "when he broke away from 10 to 4 drudgery of the Education Office, he purchased a quire or so of blue foolscap paper, a packet of quill pens, and a few wood blocks, and commenced to fire away with pen and pencil, mainly for the comic papers."[34] In the autumn of 1861, he submitted a poem, called "Satisfied Isaiah Jones," to *Good Words*. It was rejected, because the editor thought that, although it was clever and amusing, it was too long. On 21 September 1861, a new weekly journal appeared called *Fun*. The editor was H. J. Byron, only two years older than Gilbert but already successful in writing for the stage, and who was to write the longest running play of the century, *Our Boys*, to be produced in 1875. The *Fun* office was in a room over the shop at number 80 Fleet Street owned by Charles Maclean, a carver and gilder who was manager of the "Commercial Plate Glass Co." and the first proprietor of the paper. *Fun* was situated a few doors away from *Punch*, at number 85. Payment at *Fun* was £1 a column, whether prose or verse, and fractions of columns were paid in proportion, and similarly illustrations were paid according to size. Gilbert took great pains over producing an article three-quarters of a column long, did a half-page drawing on wood and sent them to the paper.

A day or two later, Gilbert received a request from H. J. Byron to contribute a weekly column and a half-page drawing every week for *Fun*. Gilbert was staggered. "I hardly knew how to treat the offer, for it seemed to me that into that short article I had poured all I knew. I was empty. I had exhausted myself; I didn't know any more."[35] But he said he would try.

The writers for *Fun* were, in the main, a group of young writers in their twenties beginning to make their way in journalism. They included: Clement Scott, at twenty years of age the youngest, a clerk in the War Office who was later to earn his reputation as dramatic critic for the *Daily Telegraph*; Henry Leigh, who went on to translate and adapt French comic operas; Jeff Prowse, who had a talent for writing humorous verse and invented a character called "Nicholas"; Francis Burnand, educated at Eton and Trinity College, Cambridge, where he had founded the Cambridge Amateur Dramatic Club, who was with *Fun* for a short time before moving up the road to *Punch* in 1862, and eventually becoming its editor. Two older men, in their forties, were part of the team: E. L. Blanchard, already established as a journalist and editor, who produced a yearly pantomime at Drury Lane; and Arthur Sketchley, who in former days was a clergyman called George Rose and now wrote "Mrs. Brown's monologues" for *Fun*. And there was Tom Robertson, seven years older than Gilbert, and who was to become famous as a dramatist and stage manager. In that role he was to be a major influence on Gilbert's life.

Many weekly contributions were to follow from Gilbert, including one drawing signed "Bab," before there appeared in the edition of 1 February 1862 his first humorous poem, called "The Advent of Spring." Gilbert's career as a writer was coming to life.

CHAPTER FOUR

1863-1866

Gilbert and Sullivan:
The Ballad Writers

WHEN GILBERT GAVE UP the monotony of life in the civil service, at the same time he gave up a secure salary. Weekly contributions to *Fun* provided a regular income, but at £1 a column, it was hardly a princely one. Family connections helped him when he took over as London correspondent for *Invalide Russe* from his cousin Sutherland Edwards; something that, according to Clement Scott, caused either envy or awe in the other writers of *Fun*, but lean times lay ahead.[1]

Uncertainty surrounds what has been suggested as Gilbert's first play to actually reach the stage. In 1863, the German-born actor Charles Fechter, who had taken over as lessee at the Lyceum, produced a play called *Bel Demonio*, in which he and Kate Terry took the leading roles. The play opened on 31 October with a curtain-raiser called *Uncle Baby* by one W. Gilbert—not W. S. Gilbert. It was a play he never admitted as his own. The manuscript deposited with the lord chamberlain's office bears the date 1858, and lines concerning "temperance" have led to the speculation that the play was by Gilbert's father, who had strict views on the subject.[2] *Uncle Baby* was panned a few weeks later by *Punch*, in a review written in the form of a parody of the play, but it survived the criticism and ran until Christmas. Certainly Gilbert collaborated with his father that year when he provided the illustrations for William Gilbert's first novel, *Shirley Hall Asylum, or, The Memoirs of a Monomaniac*.

Writing, whether for journals or for the stage, consumed more of Gilbert's energy and enthusiasm than did his study of law. All that was required of him, before he was considered eligible to be called to the bar, was to attend for a whole year the lectures of two readers of the Inns of Court. A public examination was still only optional. He also was required to have kept twelve terms, that is, to have dined three days in each term in the hall of the Inner Temple.[3] He had already "kept terms" for a period from

1855 following his admission to membership of the Inner Temple, allowing him to be called only two years after leaving the education department.

And so, on 17 November 1863, the day before his twenty-seventh birthday, Gilbert was called to the bar. His first brief was to interpret for a Frenchman in a case at Westminster. The Frenchman won his case and put it all down to his interpreter. "He met me in the hall," Gilbert related, "and, rushing up to me, threw his arms round my neck and kissed me on both cheeks. That was my first fee."[4]

His second brief produced his second fee: a boot thrown by an old lady accused of picking pockets. "My Maiden Brief," the short story he wrote arising from his experience, proved more lucrative than his appearance in court. *Cornhill* magazine published the story and paid him eight guineas.

Over the next few months, the occasional poem from Gilbert was published in *Fun,* and, on 19 March 1864, Gilbert's first poem to contain comic characters, "The Baron Klopfzetterheim; or, The Beautiful Bertha and the Big Bad Brothers of Bonn," appeared. The poem, in five parts, ran for five consecutive weeks, accompanied by Gilbert's grotesque little drawings of the baron and his sons.

Gilbert wrote only two more poems in 1864 and was having little success as a barrister. He reckoned that in his first two years at the bar he earned no more than £75. This was probably his lowest point financially. The next year was to bring an upturn in his fortunes.

Ownership of *Fun* changed hands and was now the property of Edward Wylam, and Tom Hood took over as editor on 20 May 1865. H. J. Byron had decided to go into theater management with Marie Bancroft, still then Marie Wilton, and in April they had opened the reconditioned Prince of Wales's Theatre in Charlotte Street, St. Pancras. Previously, the theater had been known as the Queen's Theatre, or to give it its more popular name, "The Dust Hole." At the same time, Tom Robertson, following his success in 1864 with *David Garrick* at the Haymarket, joined the Prince of Wales's to produce *Society*. He invited Gilbert to attend rehearsals, an experience that altered Gilbert's perception of stage direction. Until then, Gilbert had been writing plays for others to produce, but now he saw in action a dramatist who was stage managing, or directing, his own work and producing something new. Many years later he was to say of Tom Robertson, that he "invented stage-management." What impressed him was the "life and variety and nature" that Robertson brought to a scene.[5] The Prince of Wales's company with Marie Bancroft was similarly innovative, creating a new style in acting and moving away from the highly charged, emotional displays of the old style.

His change of career to the law, and now his closer involvement with the theater, had not lessened Gilbert's interest in the militia. No longer in the civil service, he had to look elsewhere for a regiment, and settled on the Royal Aberdeenshire Highlanders for which he qualified, having had a Scottish grandmother, and on 15 June 1865 he took up his appointment as lieutenant.[6] Every year for the next thirteen years he would be called on to attend "militia training" with the regiment.

A month beforehand, on 16 May 1865, Gilbert's godmother Mary Schwenck had died at Brixton; now, on 3 July, her will was proved, and this formidable woman had her final say. Mary Schwenck had known the Gilberts better than anyone. She had known them all: from the first William Gilbert, the great-grandfather, down to her godson William Schwenck. She knew in particular the strength of personality of William Schwenck and his father and was a match for the pair of them. Her last will and testament is wonderfully revealing. Through the lawyer's jargon her own strong voice comes out clearly. She would have no nonsense from William senior in the matter of her will. Having stated her bequests to him (several oil paintings, including a portrait of himself, two houses, and some shares), she then requires that he execute a release of all claims and demands on her will and on the will of her late husband, and if he did not satisfactorily comply with that request within two calendar months, then she revoked his bequests and directed that his share go back into the residuary estate.

How many times, one wonders, did she have to say when he was a little boy: "You have been given a fair share with the other children. If you argue any more you will get nothing." The speed with which this will was proved showed that William Gilbert did not argue. He had been firmly put in his place. To her godson she gave £500, two houses in the Edgware Road, and shares in Assam Tea and Norwich Union. She made similar gifts to Francis Schwenck Gilbert, although his property was a little better, the old family house in Nightingale Lane, Clapham, and her present house in Brixton. She said pointedly that she would have made Francis Schwenck one of the executors of her will, but his profession necessitated frequent absence from London. She did not even contemplate appointing William Schwenck as an executor, clearly thinking that to do so would have led to a dispute. She then made it crystal clear that she would have no dispute over her will. If any dispute or litigation were to arise in reference to her estate, then the share of the person causing the dispute would be forfeited and go to her godson and great-nephew Francis Schwenck Gilbert. Having dealt earlier with Gilbert senior, her last remarks were evidently intended for the attention of Gilbert junior. She then rubs salt into the already smarting wounds of William Schwenck, the lawyer, by adding that if her executors need any legal advice, they should consult her solicitors.[7] William Schwenck Gilbert was too sensitive to what he probably considered an insult ever to mention his godmother as his fairy godmother. He never referred to the benefits he had received from her. It is true he always kept the name Schwenck; but it is well known that he disliked the name intensely.

In 1865, Gilbert moved from Clement's Inn to chambers at 3 South Square, Gray's Inn, off the north side of High Holborn. It was here he wrote his first ballad to be signed "Bab." It was entitled "To my Absent Husband," and appeared in *Punch* on 14 October 1865. It was in these same rooms that Gilbert founded a club called "The Serious Family." The subscription for each member was 2 guineas, although Gilbert was exempted as he undertook to supply a rump steak, a Stilton

cheese, whisky and soda, and bottled ale every Saturday night for the term of his natural life. Tom Hood was appointed "Head of the Family," and Gilbert was known as
"l'enfant terrible."[8] The first meeting was held on 23 December 1865 and each member signed the attendance book: Tom Hood, W. Prowse, W. S. Gilbert, Henry S.
Leigh, Clement Scott, Paul Gray, and George Rose.[9] The members varied a little
over the months, "nearly all of them more or less known at the time" as Gilbert said
of them years later, "& all of them careless, light-hearted free-lances of about my own
age, with but few memories of the past & fewer forebodings of the future—literary
gad-flies who basked in the sunlight of their own small successes, & who bore
mishaps lightly as matters which were quite in the normal order of things."[10]

"Bab" and "l'enfant terrible" as nicknames bear some similarity. Which came
first? The usually accepted story is that "Bab" was Gilbert's nickname as a child.
Perhaps. But it is a strange nickname for the eldest child of a family: Gilbert's sister
Jane was born before he was two years old. The Gilberts were a very formal family:
the parents were Mama and Papa, and Gilbert was called Schwenck by them and by
the rest of the family. Even at the end of his days, his father, who by this time knew
how much his son disliked the name Schwenck, could not bring himself to refer to
him by his Christian name. A letter survives in which he addresses his son as "My
dear Gilbert."[11] "Bab" was most likely an invention of W. S. Gilbert.

Saturday nights were spent at Gilbert's chambers, and Friday nights were spent
with Tom Hood by more or less the same group of young men. Out of these pleasant evenings among friends came a set of short stories, *A Bunch of Keys, Where They
Were Found and What They Might Have Unlocked*, edited by Tom Hood for publication at Christmas 1865. Gilbert contributed the short story "Key to the Strong
Room." Other contributions came from Tom Hood, Tom Robertson, Clement
Scott, Jeff Prowse, and Thomas Archer. The book was described by Tom Hood as a
labor of love in which the editor had a sinecure as that role could have been filled by
any of the contributors.[12] Further socializing on other nights of the week, perhaps
after the theater or the music hall, took place at the Arundel Club in Salisbury Street,
off the Strand, a club of which most of the *Fun* gang were members.

Having been successful in placing one ballad with *Punch*, Gilbert tried another,
"The Yarn of the Nancy Bell," a parody of Coleridge's "The Rime of the Ancient
Mariner." Mark Lemon, the editor, rejected it as being too cannibalistic for his readers, but it was published in *Fun* on 3 March 1866. Despite its gruesome subject, it
proved to be one of the most popular of the Bab ballads.

Now that Gilbert's financial position had been transformed by his legacy from
Mary Schwenck, he considered that he was in a position to get married. The young
lady he had been courting for some months was Annie Thomas, who lived in Eldon
Road off Victoria Road, and who was, therefore, a neighbor of his parents. She was
a keen horsewoman and Victoria Road was ideally situated. Behind the Gilberts'
house, the Blackmans ran a large riding school, and at the top of the road lay the
open spaces of Kensington Gardens and Hyde Park with its famous Rotten Row.

Annie Thomas was a novelist and used the young W. S. Gilbert as the model for her character Roydon Fleming in *Played Out*, which she published in 1866.[13] Gilbert may have been suitable as the model for a character in a novel, but he was not the model of the husband Mrs. Thomas had in mind for her daughter, and his proposal of marriage was refused.

Financially, the situation had improved for Gilbert; but he had reached a low point in his life. Turned down in marriage, unsuccessful at the bar, and still unaccepted as a writer of burlesques, he was depressed. In that frame of mind, seeing things out of proportion and feeling a thorough failure, he wrote a serious ballad called "Haunted" for 24 March 1866 with the byline "By our Depressed Contributor." He was feeling antisociety generally:

> Ghosts of fraudulent joint-stock banks,
> Ghosts of "copy, declined with thanks,"
> Of novels returned in endless ranks,
>   And thousands more I suffer.
> The only line to fitly grace
> My humble tomb, when I've run my race,
> Is, "Reader, this is the resting-place
>   Of an unsuccessful duffer."[14]

Gilbert was never to reach such a low point again.

His depression soon passed and in a more hopeful mood on 9 June 1866 in "To My Bride (Whoever she may be)" he advertised himself as an eligible bachelor:

> . . . of *circa* two-and-thirty,
> Tall, gentlemanly, but extremely plain,
>   And, when you're intimate, you call him "BERTIE."
>   Neat—dresses well; his temper has been classified
>   As hasty; but he's very quickly pacified.[15]

On 23 June 1866, another ballad appeared, entitled "To My Steed," suggesting his mind was back on horse riding. He was a keen horseman and even without Annie Thomas he still went riding in the park. But then he noticed someone else. Someone who shared his love of riding. Someone who had been there all the time. The little girl who lived over the road from his parents; except that she was no longer a little girl. Lucy Turner was now eighteen; fair-haired, blue-eyed, and very pretty.

Lucy's mother and father had married in India. Her mother, Herbertina Compton, was the daughter of Sir Herbert Compton, lord chief justice of Bombay; her father, Thomas Metcalfe Blois Turner, was a captain in the Bombay Engineers in the East India Company Service. They had two other children, Grace and Samuel Compton, and were expecting their third child when, on 7 July 1847, Captain Thomas Turner died suddenly, at the age of thirty-seven. At that point the Turner family took over. Herbertina's brother-in-law, Captain Henry Blois Turner, was granted extended leave to take his brother's family home to England.[16] Home was, in the first place, the house of his father, Dr. Thomas Turner, at 31 Curzon Street, in Mayfair. Thomas Turner, doctor of medicine from Trinity College, Cambridge, was the *paterfamilias* of the numerous Turner family and, now a widower, lived with his unmarried sister, Grace, his three unmarried daughters, Lucretia, Mary, and Emma, and seven servants to attend to their needs.[17] Herbertina soon left Curzon Street to be taken down to a house the family owned in Suffolk, and in which they retained three servants ready to receive them when required. In that house, called "The Grove" in the village of Yoxford, Lucy Agnes Blois Turner was born on 14 November 1847.[18]

By 1852, before Lucy was five, Mrs Turner had moved back to London, taking with her two servants from Suffolk, and they settled into 4 Marlborough Villas, in Victoria Road, Kensington. At its northern end, opposite Kensington Gardens, Victoria Road was still open and semirural, before the area had been developed and before the tall, elegant houses with their porticoes had been built. Into one of those new houses, number 21, the Gilberts were to move many years later. With little recollection of her early Suffolk days, Lucy grew up as a true Kensington girl.

Gilbert would not have known when he first started to court Lucy exactly what kind of family he was getting himself into. At first, there was only the widowed mother with her three children. But gradually he was introduced to the rest of the family. There was the family at Curzon Street, now including Lucy's cousin Richard, home from India for his education; and then there was the family at Upper Wimpole Street, four more unmarried sisters of Lucy's grandfather, in their grand house with the butler, the cook, two lady's maids, the housemaid, the footman, and the kitchen maid.[19] There were Turners in Suffolk and Turners in Norfolk. Gilbert found the number of female relatives overwhelming and one day would make a family joke out of it, which in its public form would go round the world.

On 15 March 1866, Gilbert had been elected to the Northern Circuit.[20] His first brief did not come along until a few months later, after military training and after the summer vacation. It was the case of an Irish woman accused of stealing a coat and it came to court at St. George's Hall in Liverpool. Marie Bancroft, Squire Butterfield (to become Mr. Bancroft the following year), and the rest of the Prince of Wales's Company who were in Liverpool to open Tom Robertson's *Ours* on 23 August, went along at Gilbert's invitation, to witness his performance in court. Years later, Gilbert related what happened next:

> No sooner had I got up than the old dame, who seemed to realise that I was against her, began shouting, 'Ah, ye divil, sit down. Don't listen to him yer honour! He's known in all the slums of Liverpool. Sit down, ye spalpeen. He's as drunk as a lord, yer honner—begging your lordship's pardon.' Whenever I attempted to resume my speech, I was flooded by the torrent of the old lady's eloquence, and I had at last to throw myself on the protection of the Recorder, who was too convulsed with laughter to interfere.[21]

Arthur Sullivan in 1864, at the time of *Kenilworth* (From the collection of Peter Joslin)

Gilbert collaborated with his father again in 1866, providing illustrations for *The Magic Mirror*, "a round of tales for the young and old," and following on from the success of *A Bunch of Keys* in 1865, Tom Hood edited another collection of stories for publication at Christmas 1866 called *Rates and Taxes*. Gilbert's share was a short story entitled "Maxwell and I." Hood also edited *Warne's Christmas Annual*, to which Gilbert contributed "The Lawyer's Story," as well as an illustrated story called "The History of the Gentleman Who Was Born at an Advanced Age," an example of topsy-turvydom at its most ludicrous extreme; and *Ruy Blas*, described as "A preposterous piece of nonsense for private representation" and in which the lyrics were written to such tunes as "Oh, Dear, What Can the Matter Be?" the "Laughing Song" from *Manon Lescaut*, and "A Hunting We Will Go."[22]

The agreeable reversal of his personal fortune was matched by a sudden change in Gilbert's dramatic fortunes. Gilbert thought of Tom Robertson as one of the best and staunchest friends it had been his good fortune to know. He had learned much about stagecraft by watching him at rehearsal and Robertson had also encouraged Gilbert in his own writing for the stage. Robertson had been engaged by Miss Herbert, lessee of the St. James's Theatre, to write a piece for her. Robertson's play would not be ready for several months and she needed someone to write a play to be ready for Christmas, only a few weeks away. Robertson suggested Gilbert, and on his recommendation Miss Herbert agreed. Gilbert chose to do a burlesque of Donizetti's opera *L'Elisir d'Amore* and called it *Dulcamara, or The Little Duck and the Great Quack*. He said it was written in ten days and rehearsed in a week.[23] The stage manager at the St. James's at that time was a relatively unknown actor, Henry Irving, and the part of the great quack was played by Frank Mathews, who had a double encore with Gilbert's parody of "Champagne Charley."

After the first night, Gilbert took a dozen friends, including Henry Irving, to supper at the Arundel Club, something that in later years he would be totally incapable of doing, saying, "I would as soon invite friends to supper after a forthcoming amputation at the hip-joint."[24] The piece was moderately successful, holding its own until Tom Robertson's play, *A Rapid Thaw,* opened on 2 March 1867. *Dulcamara* was favorably compared by one critic to the work of Planché. Years later, Lucy Turner, as Lady Gilbert, recalled how pleased they both were to hear that. From her remark, it is clear that by Christmas, Gilbert and Lucy Turner were already settled in their relationship. She must have been the only person who saw every single first night of Gilbert's works in London, from *Dulcamara* to his last play in 1911.

Once *Dulcamara* was into production, Gilbert was approached by the manager concerning payment. What happened then was often told by Gilbert. He modestly asked for £30. The surprised manager wrote him out a check for the amount, and then said, "Now take a bit of advice from an old stager who knows what he is talking about: never sell so good a piece as this for £30 again." "And I never have," Gilbert liked to relate.[25]

The old system of selling a play outright was beginning to break down, but was still being used by managers if they thought they could get away with it. As recently as 1861, Tom Taylor had sold his record-breaking *Our American Cousin* to the Haymarket for £150. Frank Burnand, far more experienced in the theater than Gilbert at this stage, had taken a share of the profits, making £2,000 from his play *Ixion* and then in 1866, the same year as *Dulcamara*, making £2,000 from *Black-eyed Susan*.[26] Gilbert's account is amusing, and he told it partly to raise a laugh. But he was deadly serious. He never trusted another theater manager again, and this was to lead to the most bitter disputes. Now that Gilbert had at last had one of his burlesques put on stage, his dramatic career was launched. In his own words, he was "afloat on the dramatic stream."[27]

EARLY IN THE NEW YEAR, 1863, Sullivan was invited to stay over at the Lehmanns and shortly after was in Manchester as a guest at Charles Hallé's house The occasion was a performance by Hallé's orchestra of the *Tempest*. From Manchester, Sullivan wrote to Mrs. Lehmann in humorous vein about his experience. On the evening before the concert, he was taken to a ball where he was "shown about like a stuffed gorilla" while he "stood about in easy and graceful postures conscious of being gazed upon." The next evening, Thursday 22 January, the concert was a genuine success. The performance was warmly applauded and when Sullivan appeared on the platform, in response to Hallé's repeated signals, his breath was "literally taken away by the noise."[28] Sullivan was still only twenty-one but was already a celebrity.

He was sufficiently established to be elected, in February 1863, to the "Musical Society" of London; and also to be commissioned to write music for royal occasions. To celebrate the wedding of the prince of Wales, Sullivan wrote two pieces: a Procession March, performed by military bands at the Crystal Palace on the day of the wedding of the prince to Princess Alexandra of Denmark; and the Princess of Wales's March, also for military bands, performed at a concert on 14 March at the Crystal Palace in the presence of the prince and the new princess of Wales. In addition, to celebrate Alexandra's arrival in the country, he had written a song called "Bride from the North," with words once again by Chorley.

In later years, Sullivan said that the first guineas that he gave up, in order to devote himself to what he wanted to do, were those that came from teaching, which he hated. He was happy to free himself from private tuition and from the lessons he gave at the Chapel Royal. His parents were the beneficiaries of his first earnings from composition. He moved them from Ponsonby Street to 47 Claverton Terrace, a short row of houses in Lupus Street. The exact situation of these houses was opposite the junction of St. George's Road with Lupus Street. They no longer exist, and the site is now occupied by Pimlico School. For the first time in London his parents were able to occupy a house to themselves, and were at last able to afford a servant and so release Clementina Sullivan from domestic chores.[29]

Chorley's libretto for *The Sapphire Necklace* remained unfinished. Sullivan must have wondered how much was due to his own inexperience as much as to the quality of the libretto, and he approached Michael Costa, director of music at Covent Garden. At any rate, it was worthwhile cultivating the friendship of such an influential musician; Costa had been conductor of the Philharmonic concerts from 1847 to 1854 and of the Birmingham Festival since 1849. Sullivan's intention for the moment was to learn as much as possible about grand opera. He began by asking to watch rehearsals and ended up by accepting the post of organist at the theater.

Saturday afternoon concerts at the Crystal Palace continued to be an integral part of musical and social life for Sullivan. John Millais, at thirty-four already established as one of England's greatest artists, was now part of the group who met together with George Grove afterward, as were Francis Burnand and Fred Clay, who was probably Sullivan's closest friend at this time. Clay's background was totally different from that of Sullivan. His father, James Clay, was M.P. for Hull and Fred Clay worked as private secretary to the parliamentary secretary to the Treasury, before eventually giving up the civil service for music.

Sometimes, the group would go on to one of two wealthy families living in Sydenham: the von Glehns and the Scott Russells. Robert von Glehn was a successful merchant, born in Russia, but a naturalized British subject. He lived with his English wife and their ten children and eight servants in a large house called "Peak Hill Lodge." The other family would have appeared just as prosperous to Sullivan, although in reality their position was not as secure as that of the von Glehns. The Scott Russells lived in a house called Westwood Lodge, which stood on Sydenham Hill. John Scott Russell, a Scot, was a graduate from Glasgow University and had temporarily held, at the age of twenty-six, the chair of natural philosophy at Edinburgh University. Mrs. Scott Russell was the daughter of Sir Daniel Toler Osborne, twelfth baronet of Tipperary.[30] John Scott Russell had worked as a marine engineer and naval architect in Edinburgh before moving to London where he became secretary of the Royal Society of Arts. In 1847, he became joint secretary preparing for the Great Exhibition and at the same time he went into a shipbuilding venture on the Isle of Dogs, becoming involved in building "The Great Eastern" for Isambard Kingdom Brunel.[31] The Scott Russells had a son and three daughters: Louise, Rachel, and Alice. When Sullivan first knew them in 1863, when he was twenty-one, Louise Scott Russell (known by her nickname Lady) was twenty-two, Rachel (known as Chenny) was eighteen, and Alice (known as Dickie) was sixteen.

The three Scott Russell girls were described by Ernest von Glehn as "beautiful and accomplished."[32] Sullivan was just as much at ease with them as he had been with the Barnett girls in Leipzig. He had an attractive personality and an ease of manner that made him popular with everyone he met. He enjoyed their company and they delighted in his. He became a frequent visitor to both the von Glehns and the Scott Russells and was an entertaining companion. When Sullivan introduced Fred Clay to both houses, and he and Clay proceeded to play duets on the piano, their listeners were dazzled by their skill. The two young musicians were always welcome guests.

Sullivan's social life was flourishing; but in the latter half of 1863, his musical production was looking a little thin. He had been back from Leipzig for over two years; the *Tempest*, although revised in England, had been composed in Leipzig; and the two commissioned pieces for the wedding of the prince of Wales had not been followed by further commissions. He had published three songs in 1863, but had devoted time to an opera that was not going to succeed. Michael Costa provided help by asking him to write a ballet for Covent Garden, and although Sullivan accepted the commission, it was time for him to take the initiative and produce an important work of his own.

Using as his inspiration Walter Scott's novel *Kenilworth* he started work on a cantata, with Henry Chorley once more providing the words. His intention was to offer it to the Birmingham Festival for performance in September 1864; but he needed influence to get the work accepted. He approached Michael Costa again, asking him on 15 February to put in a word on his behalf to the Birmingham Festival committee. Costa obliged and on 3 March the committee accepted the cantata. Sullivan showed his gratitude by paying Costa the compliment of asking him to look over the finished score and offer his advice before it was printed for performance.

Sullivan completed his ballet, *L'île enchantée*, which was performed on 14 May 1864 at Covent Garden as an afterpiece to Bellini's opera *La Sonnambula*. He was not immediately happy with it; he had found himself too restricted by the demands made on him, saying he felt like a musical carpenter, and was reluctant to undertake any more ballet music. Later he recognized that he had written music that was good enough to be recycled for use in other works. He turned his mind to *Kenilworth* and as time drew on, his work became more concentrated as he slaved on in the way he was to continue all his life, sometimes working through the night and neglecting to eat properly. "Last evening I even forgot my supper," he told his mother, "and was painfully reminded of the oversight when my watch conveyed the intelligence that it was 4 a.m."[33]

At the beginning of September, Sullivan traveled up to Birmingham for the first rehearsal of his cantata, which he was to conduct himself. He felt that the rehearsal went extremely well, giving him every confidence for the performance on Thursday, 8 September. He wrote to his father the day before the performance asking him to travel up to Birmingham with Fred so as not to miss the opportunity of hearing the work performed. Why the invitation failed to include his mother is not known; no mention is made in any of his letters of his mother attending any performance of his music. For whatever reason, Thomas Sullivan was unable to go to Birmingham and, reporting back to his father after the performance, Sullivan told him that he was "dreadfully nervous" when he went on the platform, but by the end of the performance, with the applause ringing in his ears, he was convinced of its success.[34]

After the festival, Sullivan stayed on with friends in Edgbaston. He had no plans for another serious work, and only published two songs that year, one of them, "Sweet Day, So Cool" to the words of George Herbert, which he dedicated to Jenny Lind Goldschmidt. He could not work steadily, dividing his time between work and a social life. When he worked, he did so intensively, giving the task his total concentration until it was finished. Afterward he felt so exhausted, he needed a long time to recover, and so there would be a period of idling, of doing what he wanted. That is the way he was now working; it suited him, and he was not to change throughout his life.

The early part of 1865 was a period of prolonged relaxation for Sullivan. In July he spent some time in Farnham, Hampshire, at the home of a friend from the old Sandhurst days, Colonel Patrick Paget, to whom he dedicated "An Idyll for the Violoncello," written especially for him. Afterward, he went off to Belfast where he stayed at Richmond Lodge, Holywood, as a guest of the Dunvilles. He also came to know the Tennent family, already known to his mother, and in particular Annie Tennent, who wanted any letters she had written to him destroyed in case anybody should one day write his biography. She had her way. Nothing is known about that relationship. But another relationship did develop around this time. Sullivan had been a frequent visitor to the Scott Russells for two years and now he and Rachel Scott Russell were in love. He was only twenty-three; he had no money; he could not offer her the sort of life she was used to, in a house as grand as the one she lived in. He knew that her mother would not tolerate the idea of her daughter marrying anyone unable to provide richly for her, so they kept quiet about their love; at least, they kept it hidden from Rachel's parents.

In a letter from Belfast, Sullivan had confessed to his mother that his life there had been lazy, but he had insisted he would be able to work "like a horse" when he got back. Already he had ideas for the first movement of a symphony "with a real *Irish* flavour about it."[35] That symphony was ready by the next spring, and on 10 March 1866 at the Crystal Place, Sullivan conducted his Symphony in E Flat, *In Ireland*. He was reluctant to call it the *Irish* Symphony because of Mendelssohn's *Scotch* Symphony but regretted that decision years later when Stanford named his work an *Irish* Symphony. A second performance of Sullivan's symphony followed shortly after, on 11 April 1866, given by the Musical Society of London at St James's Hall.

The symphony did not make Sullivan rich. He was not yet in a position to go to Rachel's parents and ask for their daughter's hand, even though he had increased his output of songs. He published six Shakespearean songs in 1866, including some of his most enduring—"Orpheus with his Lute," "The Willow Song," and "O Mistress Mine," which he sold to Metzler's for 5 guineas each; he had also written three songs for Chappell's, including "If Doughty Deeds," which he dedicated to Mrs. Scott Russell, and for each of which he received 10 guineas. Then, persuaded by George Grove that it was unwise to sell the songs outright, he wrote "Will He Come?" which he offered to Boosey's on a royalty basis. "And oh the difference to me!" he said later.[36] By now he had established a wider reputation for himself: as well as being the promising young composer of serious music, he was becoming known to a larger audience as the writer of popular ballads.

Meanwhile, the opportunity for a little piece of theatrical fun came his way—something apparently trivial that would not overtax him. Sullivan used to go along to Saturday evening entertainments at Moray Lodge, Campden Hill. They were referred to as "Moray Minstrel" gatherings. Moray Lodge was the home of Arthur Lewis, partner in the firm of Lewis and Allenby, of Regent Street. Arthur Lewis, later to marry Kate Terry, used to hold his entertainments on the last Saturday of the month from January to April each year. After one of these entertainments in which Offenbach's *Les deux aveugles* was performed, Frank Burnand suggested to Sullivan that they should write something together that would just be for performance among friends. Sullivan agreed and Burnand began to work on Maddison Morton's farce *Box and Cox*, turning the title round and changing the character of Mrs. Bouncer into Sergeant Bouncer. Burnand was living in Belgrave Road at the time, not far from Claverton Terrace, and would take each number around to Sullivan as he had finished it. Rehearsals were held in Burnand's house, and on Wednesday, 23 May 1866, at 11:30, *Cox and Box* was performed for the first time. Cox was played by Harold Power; Box by George Du Maurier, the *Punch* cartoonist; and Bouncer by John Forster. The late hour allowed Burnand's guests, including the actor Edward Sothern and the manager John Buckstone, to come from the theater.[37]

That is Burnand's story, but it has been disputed. Arthur Lewis claimed that the first performance took place at Moray Lodge, three days later, on 26 May 1866. Normally, as noted, the Moray Lodge performances took place from January to April and Arthur Lewis would have asked them to perform their work at an extra Saturday gathering. Possibly Lewis considered the performance at Burnand's house as the final rehearsal; Burnand, however, had invited guests, and considered it a performance. It has also been disputed that it took place in 1866 at all, and that the first performance was really in 1867. The only person to put that forward was John Forster, who played Bouncer, and who kept a diary and also a collection of all the Moray Minstrel programs. But if the *Cox and Box* performance was an *extra*, and not part of the Moray Minstrel schedule, then Lewis would not necessarily have provided programs.

Sullivan recalled that he only wrote out the vocal parts because, as he was the accompanist, no accompaniment needed to be written. He also recalled that the orchestration was written much later. The evidence points to 1866 as the year of the first performance—*private* performance—of *Cox and Box*. What is surprising is that, having first heard it, nobody set about ensuring a public performance soon afterward. To have sat on such a work for another year is difficult to understand now, but Sullivan would not have considered this as a major work of the kind he was intending to write.

A concert more in keeping with his mind at the time was arranged by Sullivan himself, with the influential assistance of Jenny Lind Goldschmidt, and took place on Wednesday 11 July 1866 at St James's Hall. The program, devoted to Sullivan's music, included his symphony, a selection from *Kenilworth*, and the overture to his opera with Chorley, *The Sapphire Necklace*. Jenny Lind Goldschmidt sang Sullivan's "Sweet Day, So Cool," which he had dedicated to her, and also "Orpheus with his Lute," which became a Victorian favorite, and Charles Santley, probably the finest baritone of the time, sang "O Mistress Mine," dedicated to him by the composer.[38] They both performed without fee as an act of generosity and encouragement to the young composer. The audience included George Grove and John Goss, his old master of composition, who was fulsome in his praise for Sullivan's symphony, urging him to go on and become one of the greatest of composers of symphonies. Davison in *The Times* thought it was his best musical work, but was frightened of the influence of Schumann and Mendelssohn, advising him to use Haydn and Mozart as his models.

By this time, Sullivan had already been commissioned by the Norwich Festival, where the conductor was Julius Benedict, another member of the Mendelssohn Committee, to write an orchestral work for performance in October, but in August, Sullivan had still made no progress with it. Rachel Scott Russell urged him on and accused him of not getting down to work. Having received an invitation from Rachel to spend a week with the family, Sullivan replied that he was fearful of spending the time with her because she had an enervating influence on him. She reacted smartly suggesting that perhaps if they saw less of each other, he would produce more work: if he were serious about wanting to marry her, he would be ready to get down to some good, hard, honest work. Sullivan was not likely to respond to such hectoring.

In the middle of September, Sullivan received two further offers of work. The first he willingly accepted as it could lead to "greater things": he had been asked to conduct a concert at the Crystal Palace in place of August Manns. The second he accepted as it was an honor he could not refuse: Sterndale Bennett offered him the professorship of composition at the Royal Academy of Music.[39] With less than a month to go to the festival, Sullivan had still produced nothing for Norwich and was becoming despondent. He wrote to his father suggesting that he should abandon the idea. Thomas Sullivan, in a tone quite different from Rachel's, urged him not to give up. "Something will probably occur which will put new vigour and fresh thoughts into you."[40]

Sullivan was staying down at Sydenham, and a few days after that encouraging letter from his father, in the early hours of Sunday, 23 September 1866, he was woken up by his brother, who broke down as he tried to tell him that their beloved father had died. Thomas Sullivan had gone to bed shortly before midnight when he was suddenly seized with chest pains. He called Clementina as she came up to bed. She tried rubbing his chest to relieve the pain, but he suddenly cried out and his eyes began to roll. Clementina screamed for Eliza, the maid, to come down out of bed and to hold him while she ran for a doctor. They were back in a few minutes, but it was too late. Thomas Sullivan had died. He was sixty-one.

That close, loving family had been torn apart. "My dear, dear Father," Sullivan wrote to Nina Lehmann, ". . . Oh, it is so hard, it is so terribly hard to think that I shall never see his dear face again, or hear his cheery voice saying 'God bless you, my boy.'"[41] His mother was distraught; Clementina and Thomas had known each other since they were children and had been married for thirty years. It was such a sudden and bitter blow to them all. The admirable Thomas Sullivan had gone.

The funeral took place on Friday, 28 September, and Thomas Sullivan's body was laid to rest in Brompton Cemetery. George Grove was not present but wrote that day to comfort his friend and assure him that he had been thinking of him all day. Sullivan received the letter that same evening, and on the last page he sketched his first idea of *In Memoriam*. His father's words had come true: he had found the inspiration he needed to finish his composition for the Norwich Festival. A week later *In Memoriam* was completed.

No doubt remembering what a help work had been to him at the time of his own daughter's death, George Grove arranged to go down to the Isle of Wight with Sullivan to visit Alfred Tennyson. Some time before, Grove had proposed the idea of a song-cycle for Sullivan to set to music and for Millais to illustrate.[42] Sullivan and Grove traveled down together on 17 October. They spent a pleasant evening with Mr. and Mrs. Tennyson, with Sullivan providing music on an out-of-tune piano, followed by Tennyson reading a selection of his poems to them. The song-cycle, however, was going to prove a long, drawn-out project as Tennyson was later to have second thoughts about the poems he had written.

Sullivan's diary for the rest of the year included several engagements. On 30 October, he was at the festival in Norwich for the performance of *In Memoriam*: his tribute to his father—the grief and sadness of its opening giving way to a cheery melody for woodwind and finishing on a note of triumphant celebration. A few weeks later, on 24 November, at the Crystal Palace, his Concerto for Cello and Orchestra was played by Piatti with August Manns conducting; and on 6 December, having stayed up all night talking to a friend, Sullivan caught an early train from Euston to arrive at Manchester in time for a two and one-half hour rehearsal. That evening, with the Hallé Orchestra, Sullivan gave the fourth performance of his symphony.

To some extent, work had helped Sullivan through the months following his father's death. Now he was to be the sole provider for his mother. Fred and Charlotte Sullivan had a young family and, living in Clapham, were not near enough to provide much emotional comfort.

The year 1866 had been a mixed one for Sullivan, with the death of his father dominating what had been a productive period in his life: a symphony, a cello concerto, ten songs, and for the theater a short ballet and a little gem, *Cox and Box*, which, although it had been performed privately, had yet to burst onto the London stage.

Part II

1867-1877

Establishing Reputations:
From *Cox and Box* to *The Sorcerer*

CHAPTER FIVE

1867-1868

Gilbert and Sullivan in the Theater

THE BEGINNING OF 1867 heralded another year of promise for Arthur Sullivan. He was self-confident and was still exploring the range of his talents in music. His latest ballad, "If Doughty Deeds," dedicated to Mrs. Scott Russell, was first heard in public on 31 January, when it was sung at a ballad concert by Charles Santley. Sullivan was still close to Chorley, playing at a party at Chorley's house for Valentine's Day, and arrangements were in hand for a performance of what survived of his attempted opera with Chorley, the overture and two songs, to be performed on 13 April at the Crystal Place and conducted by August Manns. In February, Sullivan paid his second visit to Tennyson on the Isle of Wight, hoping to receive his poems and embark on the composition of the music. Tennyson read him all twelve of the songs, which Sullivan thought were "absolutely lovely."[1] However, Tennyson was reluctant to part with them, considering them too light and fearing they would harm his reputation. Despite his attempts at persuasion, Sullivan had to sail on the ferry to Portsmouth without the poems, but at least the poet had undertaken to revise what he had written and continue with the project.

In March, Sullivan was asked to supervise the music in a benefit performance to be put on at the Adelphi in May for one of the *Punch* artists, Charles Bennett, who was seriously ill and whose wife was expecting their ninth child. Bennett died on 2 May, before the performance, and the benefit was redesignated to his widow and orphans. One of the items chosen for the program was *Cox and Box*. George Du Maurier was to repeat his success as Box, Quintin Twiss was asked to play Cox, and Arthur Blunt (later to be known as Arthur Cecil) to play Bouncer. Before the performance at the Adelphi, the whole program was rehearsed at Moray Lodge, and then put on at one of the regular gatherings on Saturday 27 April. For the Moray Lodge performance, Sullivan supplied the accompaniment himself as before, but for the Adelphi he would have to provide orchestration.

He put off any attempt at scoring and only began work on Monday 6 May, with the performance at the Adelphi just five days away; he managed—just, completing the task with a marathon session on Friday night. Understandably, he had no time left to compose an overture.

At the Adelphi, in the afternoon of Saturday 11 May 1867, the first public performance of *Cox and Box*, with orchestration, took place. It was followed by a packed program, including Offenbach's *Les deux aveugles* and Tom Taylor's *A Sheep in Wolf's Clothing* with the staff of *Punch* in the cast, assisted by the Terry sisters, Kate, Ellen, and Florence (aged twelve).[2] In the audience sat Gilbert, as critic for *Fun*, who considered that "Mr. Sullivan's music is, in many places, of too high a class for the grotesquely absurd plot to which it is wedded."[3]

Another member of the audience on that Saturday afternoon was Thomas German Reed, who arranged with Sullivan and Burnand to give a further performance of *Cox and Box*, another benefit performance, at the Gallery of Illustration in Lower Regent Street. German Reed, formerly musical director at the Haymarket, had toured with his wife, Priscilla Horton, since the 1840s as entertainers. German Reed played the piano and Priscilla sang. In the mid-1850s, they had started their "Illustrative Gatherings," so called in an attempt to overcome the reluctance of many early Victorians to be seen at a "play" in a conventional theater. Later the German Reeds were to become interested in nurturing the talents of Gilbert as well as Sullivan's friend Fred Clay.

Little time now remained before Sullivan's next work was due, and as usual Sullivan had left it to the last moment. He had agreed to write an overture for the Philharmonic Society to be performed on 3 June, less than three weeks away, and the work was still to be scored. After his customary intense period of work, he delivered the manuscript score of his overture *Marmion* to the copyist on Tuesday 28 May.

Sullivan's relationship with Rachel Scott Russell was still unknown to her parents. In the week following *Cox and Box* at Moray Lodge, the relationship had become more intense. After a day together in London, they traveled back to Sydenham. "Do you remember that night you took me down in the train to Sydenham," she asked him a year later. "You literally conquered & subdued me there."[4]

Shortly afterward, Rachel went to Paris with her parents; the possibility had arisen that the family would move to Paris, where interest was being shown in John Scott Russell's plan for a Channel train ferry. Arrangements had already been made for the sale of Westwood Lodge by auction. Rachel fully expected that Sullivan would come over to Paris to visit her. When he failed to arrive and she learned that he had spent Sunday 19 May at Sydenham she was angry, and the news that he had spent the previous Sunday with Nina Lehmann at Westbourne Terrace made her intensely jealous. In that mood she wrote to him, rejecting his pressing need to finish his overture as his reason for not visiting her in Paris. As for *Marmion*, she told him it "is the only piece you ever wrote, that I don't care a straw about—they may hiss it for all I care."[5]

That letter drew an equally angry response from Sullivan; her dismissal of his music had touched the nerve she intended. Rachel asked to be forgiven for what she called her "wicked letter," insisting that she loved his music and pleading with him to take her away, saying that she longed for his kisses.[6] She was still too jealous to let him go and see Mrs. Lehmann and instead wanted him to work at his overture at the Scott Russells' house. She reminded him that he had told her there were times when he could not trust himself.

Two days after that letter, on 26 May, Sullivan and Rachel met at Sydenham and had the chance to make up and sort out their differences. But within a few days Rachel was again saying she was concerned about his "purity" and wondered whether his heart could be steadfast and true. Then for a while affairs were back on an even keel. The Paris project had fallen through and the family house, Westwood Lodge, was not to be sold for the present.

On 3 June, Sullivan's overture *Marmion*, inspired by Walter Scott's poem of that name, was performed by the Philharmonic Society at St. James's Hall. It had been especially written for the Philharmonic and formed part of one of their regular lengthy concerts, which included Mozart's *Jupiter* symphony, Beethoven's eighth, and a concerto for piano in E-flat by Benedict. Sullivan was not satisfied with his overture and was to revise it later in the year for performance at the Crystal Palace.

If only he had something settled, like a conductorship, suggested Rachel, the day after the *Marmion* concert. She was beginning to worry about the wisdom of marrying soon; and she was still jealous of other women and the physical influence they had on Sullivan. She hated his flirting and hoped he would not "go back to the candle that burnt all the purity" out of his young life.[7] She complained that his letters were now short. It seemed to her that, unless he was with her, he did not think about her. Now that they had "tried the utmost," he seemed to be different.[8]

It was a turbulent relationship. Rachel had a bright, effervescent personality. She was intelligent, artistic, romantic, and frustrated as a young woman in the society of the time. She envied men their freedom. Sullivan had his career, and that she was more than willing to further; but she was frustrated by him, by his not driving on in the way she herself would have liked. She oscillated between yearning to go away with him and being fearful of losing what independence she possessed.

While his relationship with Rachel blew hot and cold, Sullivan received an offer that provided a much needed source of regular income: the post of organist at St. Peter's, Cranley Gardens. He had originally only agreed to play the organ at the consecration of the church and, because of his other commitments, shared the duties with his assistant, François Cellier, brother of Alfred Cellier, both of whom were old Chapel Royal choristers. Sullivan was to hold the post until 1872.

That summer it was the turn of France to stage another Great Exhibition, and in July Sullivan and Grove traveled to Paris. Each succeeding exhibition in London and Paris, after the Great Exhibition of 1851, was bigger and grander than its predecessor, and the Paris Exhibition of 1867 was intended to be the biggest and grandest of them all. Sullivan had been appointed as a "commissioner" to supervise the British musical contributions.

He had reached a stage in his life when his position was ambiguous. Called on by his country to represent it at an international exhibition, and acclaimed in the concert halls at home as the bright hope of the future in English music, he still had to earn his regular income as a church organist. In his private life, he was too poor to be an acceptable suitor for Rachel Scott Russell, and at the same time his popularity in society was pulling him away from any consistent work. He was at a crossroads. He was spending more and more time in the company of the fashionable people of the day and loved it. He liked the company, he liked to entertain others, and he enjoyed the lifestyle of the rich, in the houses of the rich. He also had begun to gamble at cards with people who were better cushioned financially to play for high stakes than he was, and he was running up debts.

Rachel was growing impatient. She had given herself to Sullivan and marriage should automatically follow. She quickened the pace. On 28 July, she told her parents of their wish to marry. To Mrs. Scott Russell the news came as a bombshell. The next day, she wrote to Sullivan expressing her shock and grieving that her trust in him had been misplaced. She would not consider his relationship with Rachel as anything other than that of a friend; she banned him from their house and assured him that there was no circumstance that could possibly alter her decision.

Sullivan drafted a reply the next day saying that he was just as determined as Mrs. Scott Russell and as long as Rachel held to their engagement, he would feel honor-bound to consider her as his future wife.

The shock that Mrs. Scott Russell felt at the news of Rachel and Sullivan's desire to marry must have been matched by the setback that Sullivan himself felt. For the first time in his life, his charm was of no avail. Mrs. Scott Russell had given no reason in her letter for his unsuitability. We must assume, as no doubt Sullivan did, that he was unsuitable because he was not sufficiently wealthy to provide Rachel with the sort of life her mother expected for her, and that he did not have the background to marry into the family. Fred Clay, who had been accepted as a suitable husband for their youngest daughter, Alice, was also a musician, but his father was an M.P., and he also was wealthy.

Banning Sullivan from the house was Mrs. Scott Russell's first prong of attack; the second was to send Rachel away. Rachel was to join her father in Switzerland where he was going to work as a consultant to the St. Gothard Railway Company. Despite Sullivan's protestations of resolve, Rachel had her doubts and questioned whether her love and honor were safe in his hands, mentioning a comment from Grove that he thought Sullivan did not know what devotion meant. The relationship was already on shaky ground. Before going away in August, Rachel asked Sullivan to send her some token that she could wear always, and send back to him when he had broken faith. She said her mother was adamant: "she will _**never**_ let us marry."[9] Rachel asked him to burn her letters and tell her whether he had shown any part of them to anyone.

St. Peter's, Cranley Gardens, where Sullivan was the organist for a few years from 1867

Sullivan insisted that his love was true and firm and that they only had to wait. Reassured, Rachel urged him to write an opera for the next year, and also urged him to secrecy in their letters, which were passed through George Grove.

In her final letters before leaving for Switzerland, her mood changes from letter to letter. At one moment she is buoyed up with the hope of a life together, a week later she is questioning Sullivan's sincerity, quoting a comment from Fred Clay that Sullivan was not given to matrimony. On 24 August, she refers to a little gold ring as the visible sign of their great inward love, and she asks him to be true to her, and by the memory of his father to be noble and good.

Four days later, having promised her mother only to write "friendly" letters to Sullivan, Rachel left to join her father in Zurich.[10]

GILBERT, TOO, WAS IN LOVE. He had taken over the tenancy of 28 Eldon Road from Mrs. Thomas, the mother of his former girlfriend Annie Thomas, and had moved in well in advance of his wedding day. Whatever preparations had to be made for the new household would undoubtedly have been made under the supervision of Lucy. She was ideally placed, living just around the corner in Victoria Road. Now that Jane and Alfred Weigall and the grandchildren had moved and would soon be settling in Salisbury, Mr. and Mrs. Gilbert had themselves made their final move, together with their remaining daughters, to the north of Kensington High Street, to 14 Pembridge Gardens in Notting Hill Gate, only a few minutes' walk from the open country.

In July, Gilbert received a letter from Annie Thomas to tell him about her coming marriage to the Rev. Pender Cudlip. Gilbert replied humorously, feigning jealousy but hoping she would be happy, provided her husband shared her love of horses. He was genuinely pleased for her and in a postscript, with a skull and crossbones drawn across it, joked about his own impending marriage in the first week of August.

On 6 August 1867, William Schwenck Gilbert, aged thirty, married Lucy Agnes Blois Turner, aged nineteen, at St. Mary Abbots, Kensington. Lucy's cousin, the Rev. Herbert Turner, officiated.[11] Afterward, the young couple went to France for their honeymoon, and from there Willie and Lucy wrote a joint letter, emphasising their oneness, and probably addressed to one of Lucy's numerous aunts. Only a fragment of the letter has survived:

> [LUCY:] Willie says he would be delighted to spend a few days at Heydon [in Norfolk]. But cannot promise at present as he does not know what work he may have to do, if the Burlesques come out he must be present at the rehearsals, but nothing is as yet decided—We return to Hotel Christol [in Boulogne] when we leave this & are to have the same room—which will be jolly.
>
> [WILLIE:] She desires me to remember her to you very kindly & to say that she has cut her hair in an absurd fashion, to come in a sort of fringe over the forehead, which makes people stare. She looks like this. [He provided a sketch of Lucy's new hairstyle][12]

Gilbert found in marriage a security that he had never known. Years later he told a friend that Lucy was "his centre of every bit of happiness he had, his only peace, his only safety, his guardian angel, the only person he trusted unchangingly."[13] After his marriage to Lucy there followed a creative outburst. Only four Bab Ballads had appeared in the first half of the year; twenty more would appear before the end. They poured out almost every week in *Fun* and the flow was unabated throughout 1868. Most of the Bab Ballads, and nearly all the famous ones, were written after Gilbert's marriage, at 28 Eldon Road, and not in his lawyer's chambers at Clement's Inn.

Gilbert's stagework at the time was no less prolific. Already in July he had collaborated with the *Fun* team (H. J. Byron, Tom Hood, H. S. Leigh, Arthur Sketchley, and Jeff Prowse) to produce *Robinson Crusoe or the Injun Bride & the Injured Wife* at the Haymarket. Tom Hood, James Molloy, Arthur Sketchley, and Clement Scott were all in the cast, along with Gilbert who played the part of "An Invisible Black." The libretto had gone on sale on 26 July at the *Fun* office, with the proceeds going to the widowed mother of Paul Gray, one of the *Fun* writers, who had recently died. In the same month, in Liverpool, Gilbert's burlesque of Donizetti's opera *La Figlia del Reggimento*, which he called *La Vivandière; or True to the Corps* had opened with Maria

Simpson's company. In London, on 4 November, Gilbert's farce, *Allow me to Explain*, was produced at the Prince of Wales's Theatre with Squire Bancroft and George Honey in the leading roles; and on 5 December his *Highly Improbable* was produced at the Royalty Theatre with Nellie Bromley in the cast. Also in December came the Christmas pantomime at the Lyceum, Gilbert's *Harlequin Cock-Robin and Jenny Wren*, which earned him £60. Preparations also were in hand to bring *La Vivandière* to London, but in fact that would take place after Christmas. On 22 January 1868, it shared the bill with H. J. Byron's *Dearer than Life* at the Queen's Theatre with Henrietta Hodson, J. L. Toole, Maria Simpson, and Harriette Everard in the cast.[14]

It is little wonder that Lucy had said in her honeymoon letter that "Willie" was reluctant to commit himself to any visit to the country in case the burlesques came out. After *La Vivandière*, Gilbert was described by *The Times* as "long celebrated as one of the cleverest artists of *Fun*, and more recently known as a smart writer of burlesques. . . . It has been his evident ambition to produce an extravaganza more elegant in its tone than the generality of burlesques."[15]

Gilbert still found time to contribute to Tom Hood's third Christmas Book *On the Cards* with a story called "The Converted Clown" with his own illustrations; and also to write "The Triumph of Vice," as well as providing illustrations to stories by Arthur Sketchley and Edward Draper for *The Savage Club Papers*. The *Fun* gang had now evidently changed their allegiance from the Arundel to the Savage Club.

JUST AS GEORGE GROVE had intervened to help Sullivan at a time of crisis when his father had died, so now, during the absence of Rachel, he approached Sullivan to accompany him on a proposed trip to Vienna in search of Schubert's "lost music" of *Rosamunde*. The directors of the Crystal Palace gave their financial support, but Sullivan added to this by selling three songs ("In the Summer Long Ago," "The Moon in Silent Brightness," and "We Gathered the Roses") to Metzler for 35 guineas, probably to help finance himself.[16] Before leaving with Grove, he had received news that Tennyson's revised poems were now ready for him. They would have to await his return.

Sullivan and Grove set off on the first leg of their journey on 26 September with Fred Sullivan, who accompanied them as far as Paris. From there they traveled on to Baden Baden, where Sullivan saw Madame Viardot Garcia again and where he met Clara Schumann for the first time. According to Grove, writing to Mrs. Sullivan, Arthur was extremely nervous at the prospect of meeting her. In the same letter, Grove assured Mrs. Sullivan that her son was in good company and that they were being economical, no doubt allaying any suspicion she may have about Arthur's love of a gamble. Then, via Munich and Salzburg, they made their way to Vienna, where they arrived on Saturday 5 October.

In Vienna, their search for Schubert's music began. Their point of contact was a music publisher by the name of Spina. From him, they received a letter of introduction to Dr. Eduard Schneider, a lawyer and son of Schubert's sister Therese. From Schneider they obtained manuscripts of the Symphony in C Major, the Symphony in C Minor, and an Overture in D. Sullivan went through the manuscripts copying themes and making notes. They had found some of the *Rosamunde* music at Spina's shop, but it was incomplete. Grove was disappointed and on Thursday, 10 October, they had called on Schneider again to say good-bye, when Grove decided to have a final search in the cupboard, where he had located the earlier manuscripts. There, at the back of the cupboard, at the bottom of a pile of music two feet high, he found what he had come for: the part-books of the whole of the music of *Rosamunde*, which had lain in the cupboard for almost fifty years. In haste and excitement, they began to copy the music with Ferdinand Poull, a music librarian, who had been called in to help them. They worked continuously until two in the morning of Friday and then went out to celebrate in the deserted streets of Vienna—with a game of leap-frog.[17]

While Grove stayed on in Vienna, on 12 October Sullivan left for Prague and then traveled on to Leipzig, where Grove joined him on the following Thursday. Together they went to the Gewandhaus concert that evening and listened to *In Memoriam*. Sullivan was thrilled by its reception and the applause that he was called on to acknowledge. Afterward, they dined with Ferdinand David and Anton Rubinstein, who had played his own D Minor Pianoforte Concerto at the concert.

Their last destination on their travels was Dresden, where they heard Wagner's *Rienzi*—a great disappointment, according to Sullivan. Then they returned to England—almost a month after they had set out on their momentous search—and were rewarded for all their efforts when August Manns conducted the first complete performance of *Rosamunde* on 10 November 1867 at the Crystal Palace.

Over the next few months, Sullivan was kept busy. He had already provided an overture for *Cox and Box* for another benefit for Charles Bennett, when the whole program was repeated in July at the Theatre Royal, Manchester, raising £1,000,[18] and now he completed the music for *The Contrabandista*, a comic opera that German Reed had commissioned Sullivan and Burnand to write after seeing *Cox and Box* in May. German Reed had taken a lease on the new St. George's Hall in Langham Place, renaming it St. George's Opera House. *The Contrabandista* opened on 18 December but only lasted a few weeks. German Reed had engaged a large orchestra and chorus but could not cover his expenses, and before long the Reeds would have to return to the Gallery in Regent Street, and to a piano and harmonium accompaniment.

Letters were still passing between Sullivan and Rachel, although letters from Rachel were more frequent than Sullivan's to her. She did not like what he told her about all the late night parties he was going to, and his smoking. She urged him to write an opera and even suggested a subject: Francesca da Rimini. She felt miserable separated from him and wanted to marry the following year, hoping that Sullivan would by then be free of debt. By the end of the year, she was feeling wretched, as

Sullivan had failed to send her a letter or even a card for Christmas or the New Year.

Rachel returned to England in January 1868, still hoping they would marry in May, but sad to think that Sullivan could not stand the test of her being away; if the physical passion was absent, she said, then for Sullivan there was nothing. She begged him to go to her mother and ask for her hand. Sullivan had made no attempt to see Mrs. Scott Russell, so Rachel threatened to tell her herself of their intention to marry. The recriminations ceased when a few days later they met at the Crystal Palace and there was a reconciliation. Rachel was happy to have him back in her life and was reluctant to let him go again, even though she felt his love had changed.

It was Rachel who eventually broke the news to her mother that she and Sullivan still planned to marry. Mrs. Scott Russell sobbed all night and the next day the whole Scott Russell family went into deliberations over the couple's future. The general opinion was that Sullivan must have money laid by before they married. Rachel urged him to deny himself for her sake and to give up his way of life that, she said, was moral and physical ruin. Her father had his own opinion: they should marry straight away or break it off. But Rachel was contrary: she did not want to marry straight away—she wanted a period of peace, to know her own mind truly and clearly. She told Sullivan she loved him but feared rushing into marriage.

In late March, Sullivan was invited to Worcester by Sir Frederick Gore Ouseley, and during his stay he was asked by the Three Choirs Festival Committee to provide a work for the following year. At the same time, Rachel had been in raptures listening to his *In Memoriam* at the Crystal Palace concert on 28 March, afterward urging him to work on something big, another symphony or a concerto. Reconciled once more, they met a few days later in Grove's office at the Crystal Palace.

Less than a week after that meeting, Sullivan made an agreement with Boosey's, by which the firm would pay him £400 a year for three years, in return for publishing rights in his works, without prejudice to his royalties. This would have given a sufficient income over the first years of marriage. But that was not what Sullivan had in mind. There is no mention of this new income in letters from Rachel, and it is just as likely that Sullivan needed the money to pay his debts and fuel his lifestyle.

Since February, Sullivan had begun to seek consolation in Louise Scott Russell. She called him "Dearest Arthur," but did not want him to refer to her as his "little woman."[19] The situation was becoming complicated. She talked about Rachel's passionate outbursts and the unevenness of her love, and said she imagined that would have suited Sullivan. Despite her earlier reluctance, Louise began signing herself as "Little Woman."[20] Meanwhile, Rachel was warning that she would not marry him until he had "a nice balance at [his] bankers."[21] She accused Sullivan of being self-indulgent, of frittering his life away, going to parties and not getting down to any work. He could remove the obstacles to their marriage simply by working.

On 16 July Sullivan sold an opera, *The False Heiress* (possibly an alternative title to *The Sapphire Necklace*), to Metzler for £275. Years later he was to buy the opera back.[22] It is most unlikely that he was trying to build up his bank balance for

Gilbert and Kitty at the time of their marriage in 1867 (From Leslie Baily's
The Gilbert and Sullivan Book, published by Cassell & Co. All attempts at tracing
the copyright holder have been unsuccessful)

Rachel's sake; much more likely that his gambling was getting him more into debt.
Marriage to Rachel looked increasingly unrealistic. By August, Rachel felt that Sullivan's once changeless love had drifted away from her. She felt heartbroken. After
a farewell in Grove's office at Crystal Palace, she returned to Switzerland with her
father.

While Sullivan was going through the turmoil of his personal life, unsure of his future with Rachel and unable to balance his financial accounts, a young musician introduced himself who was to provide direction in Sullivan's life as well as the means of his solving all his financial difficulties. All that lay in the future. For the present, the young musician was an unknown. His name was Richard D'Oyly Carte.

Richard D'Oyly Carte was born on 3 May 1844 at 61 Greek Street, Soho. His father, Richard Carte, had been a professional flautist before joining the flute-making business of Rudall & Rose in 1850. Six years later, the firm of Rudall, Rose, Carte, & Co. expanded into the military musical instrument business when they bought up Key & Co. with premises at 20 Charing Cross. Richard D'Oyly Carte owed the name D'Oyly to his mother's side of the family. His mother, Eliza Jones, daughter of Rev. Thomas Jones, was a woman of decisive character, totally dedicated to the welfare of her family.[23]

The Carte family lived in Dartmouth Park Road, near Hampstead. D'Oyly was the eldest of six children, two boys and four girls. Music predominated in the Carte household, where the children were taught at least one musical instrument, as well as singing and the "theory of music." D'Oyly was reputed to be able to read a complete musical score "as the ordinary person reads a book."[24] He was educated at University College School until he was sixteen, and then went to University College, London, for a year where he matriculated in 1861, but instead of continuing his studies for a degree, he joined his father in his firm at Charing Cross.

D'Oyly Carte wrote to Sullivan to interest him in an operetta he had written called *Dr. Ambrosias, His Secret*, an "Opera di camera" in two acts. It was to be performed privately on 8 August 1868 at St. George's Hall. Sullivan did not reply to Carte's letter until after the performance:

> Dear Sir,
> I must regret that I could not avail myself of your kind invitation for Saturday last. I was out of town, during the week & only returned on Saturday evening, when I had to fulfil a dinner engagement. Hoping that your performance was successful
> I am, very truly yours
> Arthur S. Sullivan [25]

Until then, D'Oyly Carte had already been actively involved in amateur theatricals. Among his papers, a program has survived of a theatrical evening he organized at Stroud Green, Hornsey, for 1 February 1866. It was a full evening of entertainment, including a short selection of vocal and instrumental music, followed by a comedy-drama with a cast that seems to have been made up of relations and close friends, as well as a performance of the successful farce *Ici on parle français*, in which D'Oyly Carte played Mr. Spriggins, Miss B. J. Prowse appeared as Anna Maria, the servant, and her elder sister played Mrs. Spriggins. Miss Blanche Julia Prowse, then only thirteen, was later to become Mrs D'Oyly Carte. Her father, like D'Oyly's father, owned a musical instrument business, later to combine with another firm to become Keith, Prowse, & Co., a famous booking agency.

With no inkling of the importance of D'Oyly Carte in his future life, Sullivan was still in a state of uncertainty with Rachel. He arranged to visit her while she was in Switzerland, and she was thrilled when he told her that he intended to write an opera. She had long before suggested the theme of "Francesca da Rimini," but Sullivan, preferring an English setting, had chosen the Lancelot and Guinevere story rather than that of Paolo and Francesca. In mid-August, Rachel asked Sullivan to take the *Guinevere* book with him when he went to Switzerland, which suggests the libretto was already completed, although it may have existed only as a scenario. It is not certain who had provided the book or scenario, but Sullivan began writing with Lionel Lewin about this time and later, in April 1872, published the ballad "Guinevere!" to Lewin's words.

A few days later, Rachel wrote to Sullivan aghast at the news that Fred Clay had broken off his engagement to her sister Alice. This would not have been news to Sullivan. Such good friends as he and Fred Clay had no doubt discussed their possible futures together. Clay had made a decision about his. Sullivan was not so decisive, but it was becoming more and more obvious that he and Rachel would never marry. On Saturday 12 September, Sullivan and Rachel met in Zurich, and Sullivan dined with Rachel and her father. It was in fact a farewell but nothing seems to have been clear-cut. Rachel had agreed that it would be best for him not to write. Two months later, on 17 November, Rachel wrote to him saying that she found the silence terrible. Life was empty without him. If his love should change he was to send her a token. She begged him to send her a line.

In the meantime, Sullivan was seeing Louise. Louise was unhappy when Sullivan told her that he was tempted by other women; he must be faithful to his future wife and his little woman, she told him. She hoped he was kissing nobody but his little woman; and then, after a particularly painful letter from Sullivan, she complained, "Why did you say you loved me?" She suggested he should throw himself into his work. If he were not "good," she could not see him.[26] On Saturday 28 November, they met at the Crystal Palace concert. She reminded him of the letter that he had promised to write to Rachel, telling her that he was convinced that she would never be his wife.

Following that reminder, Sullivan chose not to see Louise for a week, but soon they were discussing their next assignation. "I hope it wont rain because the little bench near the gate is safest & best," she wrote.[27] She was delighted to be loved and to be told that she was loved. The relationship was as painful as that between Sullivan and Rachel. On 7 December Louise wrote: "If you can do a thing which gives me pain, & do it knowingly & with intent to hurt me is it love?"[28] She said she had kissed his letters and then burned them. They met again on 12 December, when *The Tempest* was performed at the Crystal Palace, then on 18 December, Louise wrote Sullivan a letter of good-bye. He had revealed something about himself in a letter to her, and when she replied she referred to "that terrible thing" that he had mentioned. She refused to be a passing fancy.[29]

Inevitably, the emotional turmoil coupled with his heavy social life affected Sullivan's musical output at this time. He was still writing and having pieces published, and he was also working at "The Window," the song-cycle with Tennyson; but he was not working on any large work. By his own standards, he was not making best use of his talents.

AFTER *LA VIVANDIÈRE* HAD been successfully launched on its 120-night run, Gilbert went to Paris in February 1868 as the drama critic for the *Illustrated Times* writing under the byline "The Theatrical Lounger." In terms that provide a vivid contrast to the emotional turmoil of Sullivan at the time, Gilbert wrote to Lucy from the Hotel de Lille et d'Albion in Paris:

> Dearest Kits
> I was very glad to get your letter as I have been thinking of you ever since I left. I am pretty comfortable here—very high up (5th floor) but a pleasant room when one gets to it. The weather is lovely I have been writing all day in my room with the window open & without a fire. . . . I have sent P. Oliver the rest of the burlesque—I have had two hard days' work at it. . . . Paris seems to be very full of French people & more English are here than I expected to find. . . . I don't much like being a bachelor—& I find a difficulty in getting up in the morning. I have, however, bought some chocolate to console myself with. I wish you were here, old girl.
> Good bye my darling. God bless you—I think of you very often—& long to be with you again. My hand is quite cramped with writing. . . .
> Ever your devoted
> Old husband
>   A BOY [30]

(The burlesque sent to P. Oliver refers to *The Merry Zingara*, due to open at the Royalty in March.)

The letter betrays a tension in Gilbert between the formal and the familiar. He had been brought up to be very formal. He always referred to men by their surname, and familiarity did not come easily to him. He had invented the name "Bab" for himself and "Kitten" for Lucy, which became "Kits," as in this letter, and then settled down as "Kitty," the name by which Lucy became known to a large number of her friends. In this letter, he signed himself not "Willie," as Kitty called him, but "A BOY."

"Bab," "Kitten," and "Boy" suggest a world of children and animals in which Gilbert was comfortable, and he became well known later for his love of children and animals. It is not that Gilbert was frightened of life, as sometimes suggested; Gilbert played his full part in the adult world of the army, the law, and the stage, but he was bothered by the problem of flawed human nature in the adult world about him. The "wicked world" lay at the center of his thinking, and he was able to offer an escape for his audiences, creating alternative worlds of his own fancy; worlds full of his own characters who, although bearing all the appearances of normality (such as judges, soldiers, policemen, or generals' daughters), behaved and spoke in a way that was often absurd but conveyed with the utmost seriousness.

The burlesque Gilbert had mentioned in his letter to Kitty was produced on 21 March 1868 at the Royalty. It was called *The Merry Zingara; or the Tipsy Gipsy and the Pipsy Wipsy*, a parody on *The Bohemian Girl*, replacing Francis Burnand's highly successful *Black-eyed Susan*. Gilbert thought that it suffered by comparison with Burnand's burlesque; nevertheless, *The Merry Zingara* managed to run for 120 nights. Pattie Oliver was evidently pleased enough with Gilbert's work to include *The Merrie Zingara* in her benefit program on 24 June, along with Burnand's *Black-eyed Susan* and concluded her program with Gilbert's *Highly Improbable*. All three pieces were repeated the next day.

Bab Ballads were still appearing almost every week in *Fun* and on 11 April 1868, a ballad appeared for which Gilbert received £1.5.6 and £1.5.0 for the five drawings. It was called "Trial by Jury." It was subtitled "An Operetta" and the scene was set in "A Court of Law at Westminster." In this ballad, "Edwin, sued by Angelina" make their first appearance, the Counsel for the Plaintiff approaches his case "With a sense of deep emotion," and the Judge settles the matter by declaring "Place your briefs upon the shelf / I will marry her myself!" at which point they are all invited to the wedding breakfast at "Five hundred and eleven, Eaton Square!"[31]

After attending the annual militia training session at Aberdeen, with the new rank from 7 July 1868 of Captain,[32] Gilbert set about publishing a collection of "Bab Ballads," using his original drawings. He worked initially through the owner of *Fun*, Edward Wylam, who was willing to accept the terms proposed by Gilbert: £90 for a first edition of two thousand copies of the "Bab Ballads." If a second edition were needed, then Gilbert would receive £50 for a run of one thousand copies. Publication day was set for 15 November 1868.

That settled, Gilbert and Kitty went off to Boulogne to spend a fortnight at the Hotel Christol. Gilbert made good use of both his militia training and his holiday as sources of inspiration for several pieces in the autumn. He wrote "A Military Training" for *London Society* that appeared in September, another article for the same paper called "Britons in Boulogne" for November, and a ballad called "Boulogne," which appeared in *Fun* on 12 September. He later provided three ballads for *Tom Hood's Comic Annual for 1868*, including "A Boulogne Table d'Hote." In addition, he undertook to provide the illustrations for a serial by his father, *King George's Middy*, a boys' adventure story, which ran for a year in *Good Words for the Young*, and proved to be extremely popular.

The publication day in November set for the "Bab Ballads" was not met, and a few weeks later Gilbert found out that the publisher Hotten, with whom the agreement had been drawn up, had printed more than the two thousand copies originally agreed. Gilbert demanded full payment for a second edition of the book. Hotten of-

28 Eldon Road — where Gilbert and Kitty started married life

fered to meet Gilbert to sort out the difficulty. Gilbert would not hear of it. He had found out from the printers that 263 extra copies had been printed, considered that Hotten had broken his contract, and unless he received the payment he had stipulated he threatened to put the matter in the hands of his solicitor and instruct him to apply for an injunction. Hotten felt that Gilbert was being unjust and wanted to hand the book over to another publisher. Meanwhile the printer, Judd, contacted Gilbert to inform him that they had only made up two thousand complete copies, and that he was holding the remaining copies. He was clearly distressed by the argument that had arisen, and in a tone that would find an echo in later disputes involving Gilbert, he pleaded, "Cannot this disagreeable matter be settled amicably?"[33] Gilbert was not content until the extra sheets were destroyed, then asked for a *pro rata* payment of the copies that had been printed but now no longer existed, namely £13.3.0, and threatened legal proceedings if the book were not published within two days of receipt of his letter.

Gilbert's next piece for the theater was by then nearing production. It had been commissioned by John Hollingshead, who had left journalism and his post as drama critic for the *Daily News* to go into theatrical management. Hollingshead was undertaking a major new venture in the Strand: the building of the Gaiety Theatre, for which he had engaged C. J. Phipps, the most experienced of theatrical architects. To his brand new theater Hollingshead brought a reform that would not be lost on D'Oyly Carte when he came to build his own theater in the Strand a decade later:

tipping was prohibited; there was to be no booking fee, no charge for taking care of coats, cloaks, or hats. The one payment at the door covered everything.[34]

When the Gaiety opened its doors in the evening of 21 December 1868, the builders' hammers had only just fallen silent. The carpenters had not ceded the stage to the actors until late afternoon, barely leaving time for a final rehearsal. A large flashing light, powered by the biggest battery available, had been fixed to the top of the Gaiety, advertising a new age in theaters, but it was to be removed soon after the opening in case it frightened the horses below in the Strand. As the audience made its way into this most modern and advanced theater, the ladies were treated to scented fans, inscribed with the evening's program: a curtain-raiser—*The Two Harlequins*, adapted from French by Gilbert à Beckett; the main piece—a comedy, *On the Cards* (another adaption, this time by Alfred Thompson), with Madge Robertson and Nellie Farren in the cast; and the afterpiece—an operatic extravaganza, *Robert the Devil; or The Nun, the Dun, and the Son of a Gun*, a parody of Meyerbeer's opera *Robert le Diable*, by W. S. Gilbert.

The cast for *Robert the Devil* included Richard Barker as Bertram, Nellie Farren as Robert the Devil, Miss Tremaine as Albert (Prince of Granada), and Constance Loseby as Rainbault: that is, three male roles were taken by women, something that Gilbert would later outlaw in his operas with Sullivan. The program also announced that Gilbert's burlesque would include two ballets with two comic dancers (Two Mysterious Fiddlers) who were played by Messrs. Dauban and Warde. John Dauban (or D'Auban) was later to be the choreographer of nearly all the Gilbert and Sullivan operas. Of that first night *The Times* reported: "Like the other extravaganzas from the same pen, *Robert the Devil* shows an endeavour to avoid the ordinary vulgarities of grotesque drama, and bring its most elegant contingencies into the foreground. . . . The burlesque has been received with a storm of approbation."[35]

In the audience on that first night of *Robert the Devil* at the Gaiety, sat Arthur Sullivan as one of the many first-night guests of John Hollingshead.[36] After his entry into theatrical circles, Sullivan's own circle of friends and associates was now beginning to overlap with Gilbert's. Gilbert and Sullivan each knew of the other's existence and of his work. So far their paths had not crossed; but they were getting closer.

1869-1871

The Meeting of Gilbert and Sullivan—*Thespis*

GILBERT HAD NOW ACHIEVED a reputation for the cleverness of his burlesques and the refinement that he had brought to an old genre. Six months after the opening of the Gaiety, another theater opened at the other end of the Strand, in King William Street. Gilbert had produced a successful burlesque for the Gaiety and it was hoped he could do the same for the Charing Cross. The theater opened on 19 June 1869 with Gilbert's *The Pretty Druidess; or The Mother, The Maid and The Mistletoe Bough*, a parody of Bellini's opera *Norma*, the same opera his father had used as a basis for his blank verse tragedy more than thirty years earlier.

The quality of his burlesques brought Gilbert to the attention of the German Reeds, who asked him to write a piece for them. It was a new challenge for Gilbert and proved an excellent training ground for the operas to come. He had to write for a small, stock company consisting of little more than soprano (Rosa D'Erina—real name Rose O'Toole), tenor (Arthur Cecil), bass (Thomas German Reed), and contralto (Priscilla Horton Reed), giving Gilbert the opportunity to develop the contralto part in a comic role to match the versatility of Mrs. German Reed. Gilbert wrote them a "musical comedietta" called *No Cards* and was paid £150, the fee he would receive for each piece he wrote for the German Reeds. The difference between these pieces and a burlesque was that the music was written to his lyrics instead of his fitting words to existing tunes, allowing Gilbert to exercise his talents as a lyricist. In *No Cards*, Gilbert made use of part of one of his "Bab Ballads," "The Precocious Baby," sung to the air of the "Whistling Oyster." Apart from the long lost tune of that number, German Reed supplied the music.

The German Reeds had returned to the Gallery of Illustration in Regent Street and *No Cards* formed part of a double bill with *Cox and Box*, now back to its piano and harmonium accompaniment, opening on Easter Monday, 29 March 1869. German Reed played the part of Cox, Arthur Cecil was Box, and J. Seymour played

Bouncer. *Cox and Box* and *No Cards* ran for 139 performances and then in mid-August went to the provinces.[1] Although a piece by Gilbert and a piece by Sullivan had been playing together at the Gallery of Illustration, by no means does it follow that Gilbert ran into Sullivan there. Sullivan had completed his work long before, and as with the operas he was to write with Gilbert, he would have made no further appearance.

It was about March 1869 that Gilbert and Kitty moved into 8 Essex Villas, a mid-Victorian semidetached villa on the Phillimore estate, north of Kensington High Street. It was, and still is today, an elegant and peaceful district, near to but sheltered from the bustle of the main road. It was from Essex Villas that Gilbert wrote on 16 April 1869 to John Hollingshead about a new departure in his work in the theater. Hollingshead recalled the play and his relationship with Gilbert in his *Gaiety Chronicles*, remembering Gilbert as "somewhat of a martinet in his stage management, but . . . more right than wrong, and . . . consequently an able director of his own pieces." He remembered that the manuscript of *An Old Score* was printed—"a great advantage to a busy manager, I read it, and was so struck with its clever dialogue, that I put it in rehearsal at once."[2]

The speed with which he put the play into rehearsal was not quite as fast as he remembered, and it was on that point that Gilbert wrote to him, reminding Hollingshead of its existence. *An Old Score* opened at the Gaiety on 26 July 1869 with a cast that included Rosina Ranoe, later to become Mrs. Frank Burnand. According to Hollingshead, when he considered later why it had not been a great success with the public, the play had "one great fault—it was 'too clever by half.' Too true to nature—disagreeable nature. Not enough make-believe sauce."[3]

Gilbert's first comedy and his latest burlesque, *The Pretty Druidess*, had not exactly set the town alight, but his first piece for the Gallery of Illustration was an outstanding success and he was at work on a second piece, this time teaming up with Fred Clay, who was to write the music. The new piece, *Ages Ago*, opened at the Gallery of Illustration on 22 November 1869, with the music dedicated by Clay to Arthur Sullivan. A new soprano, Fanny Holland, appeared in the cast together with Arthur Cecil and the German Reeds. It was in this play that Gilbert first used the idea of ancestral portraits coming to life. *Ages Ago* was an even greater success than Gilbert's first piece for the Gallery, running for 350 performances and so outdoing *Cox and Box*.[4]

Apart from the four pieces that he actually put on the stage in 1869, Gilbert wrote a farce called *A Medical Man*, his contribution to a collection by Clement Scott called *Drawing-Room Plays and Parlour Pantomimes*, which was brought out in time for Christmas.[5] Individual "Bab Ballads" had continued to appear, with gaps around the time of the move to Essex Villas and rehearsals for *An Old Score*, but the rate of production of the ballads was beginning to slacken off by the end of the year.

Gilbert's father was in the news in 1869. Apart from having two books published, *Lucrezia Borgia, Duchess of Ferrara* and *Sir Thomas Branston*, a novel, he was the unwitting cause of a dispute over a play by Tom Taylor called *Mary Warner*, which opened at the Haymarket on 21 June 1869. Several critics, including the critic of *The Times*, said that the play was an adaptation of William Gilbert's novel *Margaret Meadows*. Tom Taylor hastened to assure the editor and readers of *The Times* that this was not the case. It was true that Mr. Gilbert suggested the subject, he said, but "a misunderstanding . . . led me to believe that Mr. Gilbert had relinquished all notion of making dramatic use of the subject."[6] Misunderstanding or not, William Gilbert was awarded £200 after arbitration but he refused the right to be named as coauthor. The play was taken off after only four weeks.

W. S. Gilbert had taken his father's side in the dispute, adding his own contribution by writing a parody of *Mary Warner* for *Fun*. Gilbert and his father saw eye to eye on many subjects, but their choice of clubs placed them in opposing camps politically. While his father, as a liberal, was a member of the Reform Club, W. S. Gilbert became in 1869 a member of the Junior Carlton Club, which was definitely for conservatives. The younger Gilbert may well have been fond of tilting at British institutions from time to time, but politically he was conservative.

"I had for some time determined to try the experiment of a blank verse burlesque in which a picturesque story should be told in a strain of mock-heroic seriousness."[7] That is how Gilbert spoke of the origin of his next piece, *The Princess*, for which he took Tennyson's poem "The Princess," using both the story and the subject matter of womens' rights. He decided to cast three women to play the roles of the three young men (Hilarion, Cyril, and Florian) who disguise themselves as women, and presumably to keep the balance in the battle scene, cast three women to play the parts of Gama's sons (Arac, Guron, and Scynthius). He called it "A Whimsical Allegory Being a Respectful Perversion of Mr. Tennyson's Poem." The music was taken from Auber and Offenbach with one song, "Like a teetotum, with a guitar" sung to Rossini's "Largo al factotum della città."[8] *The Princess* opened on 8 January 1870 at the Olympic Theatre, the first of four pieces Gilbert was to produce in 1870. It ran until mid-April and then went on tour in the provinces.

The Charing Cross Theatre produced Gilbert's second piece for 1870, another musical entertainment, with Fred Clay providing the score, called *The Gentleman in Black*. The gentleman in black of the title is the king of the gnomes, who has the power to transfer souls. The souls of the wicked baron and a simple peasant are transferred into each other's body for a month. It is learned later that the baron and the peasant had been exchanged at the age of three weeks: the peasant was really the baron and the baron, the peasant. The fact that the baron appears to be twenty years older than the peasant is explained by the baron saying that he has lived a fast life. (A similar discrepancy between Captain Corcoran and Ralph Rackstraw in *HMS Pinafore* is later left unexplained—Captain Corcoran had led a sober life.)

The Gentleman in Black opened on 26 May and then a few weeks later, on 20 June 1870, came Gilbert's next piece for the Gallery of Illustration, *Our Island Home*, replacing *Ages Ago*, which had come to the end of its run in its initial form two days before. The company at the Gallery had now been joined by Corney Grain, and it may have been for this opera that German Reed had written to Sullivan asking him to set the music, describing it as a "comic one-act entertainment" for soprano, contralto, tenor, baritone, and bass. Sullivan declined this first opportunity of working with Gilbert, and German Reed had to set the music himself. *Our Island Home* introduces the Pirate King who is "never sick at sea" and who was apprenticed by his "stupid" nurse to a "pirate" instead of a "pilot."[9] A tricky situation concerning the completion of his indentures is solved when it is realized that he was born on the Greenwich meridian and the island he is on is 50° east, so he had reached twenty-one, twenty minutes beforehand.

With *Our Island Home* appearing on 20 June, it is difficult to see how much training with the Royal Aberdeenshire Highlanders Gilbert was able to attend. The training period that year started in June, but Gilbert did not always attend the complete session. A letter survives, written about this time to Kitty from Fort George, on the Moray Firth, in which Gilbert addresses her as "My darling old Girl," and tells her about a march to Inverness, when he carried "the knapsack of a man who had fallen out fainting, on the road. . . . We had a jolly dance yesterday," he goes on to say, "You should see me dance a reel!"[10]

ALL THROUGH THE MONTHS of silence, with no letter from Sullivan, Rachel suffered and hoped. A young man by the name of Frank Rausch whom she met in Switzerland was showing an intense interest in her. He was the son of a wealthy industrialist from Schaffhausen and an ideal partner for Rachel, from her mother's point of view. Rachel was not interested in him; she was still in love with Sullivan. Frank Rausch gave up and turned his attention to her sister Alice who, since the end of her engagement to Fred Clay, had become engaged to a Mr. Baxter. Poor Mr. Baxter was ditched and, before the end of the year, Alice was to become Mrs. Frank Rausch.

Rachel found the silence from Sullivan unbearable. Why did he not write to her, she asked. Her loneliness was extreme. Her mind went back over the moments of happiness in the six years of her love for him; and now it had all come to an end. Bowing to the inevitable, she sent him back the ring. It was good-bye. "I hear you are changed & ill—God help you—& give you strength & courage to bear it all—You have others to work for & your beautiful genius to work for—& I—nor any other woman on Gods earth—is worth wasting one's life for."[11]

Shortly after this letter, Sullivan received written confirmation of the request from the Worcester Festival Committee that they would like him to write an oratorio for their next festival. No doubt he remembered the times Rachel had upbraided him for frittering his talents away. He had produced no serious work since *Marmion* in June 1867. It was time for the prodigal son to return. For the present, it was still his *Cox and Box* that claimed his attention, while he negotiated terms with German Reed for its appearance at the Gallery of Illustration.

Rachel Scott Russell returned home from Switzerland in March. Despite the note of finality and acceptance in her last letter from Switzerland, she began writing to Sullivan again. In May she went to see *Cox and Box*. "The new things are too delightful," she told him, "— only it made me sad — because I remembered when every note of it was written — and our discussions as to the pro and con of certain changes over the little white piano which then stood in the dining-room."[12]

She sent Sullivan flowers for his birthday on 13 May. She had heard from George Grove that he was going to work on *The Prodigal Son* for the Worcester Festival and wanted him to put in an unaccompanied quartet for her. (To the aptly chosen words "They went astray . . ." there is a canon, first for soprano and bass, then for alto and tenor — unaccompanied.)[13] She begged him to write. Sullivan did not write to Rachel, but he wrote to George Grove, leaving it to Grove to pass on his feelings to Rachel. He said he could not write directly to Rachel because of the pain that it would give *him*, a notion that Rachel understandably found difficult to comprehend. On 4 June she wrote him a long, sad letter. The tears fell freely over her words as she wrote, blurring the letters on the page and leaving an indelible mark of her sorrow. She could not believe that the love of six years should die like this. "Oh! *why* did you take all my strength & the best years of my bright young life only to throw them away at the end. The tears come welling up from the agony even as I write."[14] She wanted to see him once more. They did meet again: Sullivan accompanied by Arthur Cecil went with Rachel to an Ella's concert on 15 June, and they met again, alone this time, at the end of the month. When she told him about the financial difficulties her family were now in, Sullivan only laughed. He could not believe her; the Scott Russells had always seemed to him to be the picture of wealth in their luxurious home.

When Sullivan asked Rachel to copy *The Prodigal Son*, she was overjoyed and asked him to conduct from her copy. "I should *so* like it, & I will try & do it beautifully & will make as few mistakes as possible."[15]

On Friday 10 September, Sullivan conducted the first performance of *The Prodigal Son* at the Three Choirs Festival in Worcester Cathedral. Rachel was there, and afterward Sullivan saw her off on the train. The next day she wrote to him, "*I glory* to think that you *could* not have written [thus] before I knew you."[16]

After his prolonged exertions with *The Prodigal Son*, Sullivan felt the need to go right away. With a few friends, including Arthur Cecil, he spent several days in Brussels, and then moved on to Paris intending to stay about a month in the hope also of improving his French. Rachel wrote to him in Paris on 26 October. She wondered whether he was going to do any work there on projects she knew he had in mind: a symphony in D, the Guinevere opera. She reminded him of past times together. "The beginning of winter is always sad, & it brings back to me those bright days when you came in the afternoons & we sat round the fire & we had tea & chatted such nonsense — such *sweet* nonsense — & then you played on the piano in the red firelight & it was so delicious within & without. Oh! it was delightful."[17]

8 Essex Villas — the first house Gilbert bought for his own occupation

On his return to London, Sullivan prepared for a performance of *The Prodigal Son* at the Crystal Palace scheduled for the 11 December in a program that included *In Memoriam*. Unfortunately, two of the soloists (Tietjens and Sims Reeves) cried off and the substitute tenor playing the part of the Prodigal was so weak, Sullivan confessed later "it was *Hamlet* with the part of Hamlet omitted."[18] John Goss was there, and wrote to congratulate Sullivan. "All you have done is most masterly." He praised his conducting, thought his orchestration superb, and hoped Sullivan would try another oratorio, but he sounded a note of warning: "putting out all your strength—but not the strength of a few weeks or months, whatever your immediate friends may say."[19] Sullivan would never be capable of that long, sustained work. He preferred short, intensive bursts, followed by long periods of inactivity.

Sullivan and Rachel met again on Christmas Day when Sullivan gave her a camellia. In January she was going to leave for Russia to stay with her brother Norman who was working for Baird and Co., a shipbuilding and engineering firm. She wrote to him a few days later to tell him that she would see him on Friday, 31 December, when she would burn all her letters. Whether the meeting actually took place or not, no letters were burned. She expected to see him on New Year's Day, but Sullivan failed to appear. On 5 January, Rachel left for St. Petersburg, without a word of farewell from Sullivan. Louise now stepped in again to offer Sullivan comfort as his "Little Woman," although she assured him his love was past.

The last letter from Rachel to Sullivan was written on 9 May. She could not let his birthday pass without a word. Her final words to him were, "God bless you—&

send everything that is bright & golden & blessed to you—& watch over you & keep all care & pain & trouble from your dear head."[20] Louise wrote again, on 24 May 1870, telling Sullivan that her sister Alice had had a baby: "Another destiny come to weave itself into ours."[21]

And so the long relationship with Rachel Scott Russell was over. Sullivan kept the letters from both girls all his life. The love of Rachel Scott Russell was known in his family as the "one serious love-affair" of his life and the blame for their failing to marry was laid firmly at the door of Mrs. Scott Russell, "the vain mother who thought the young composer not good enough for her daughter to take in marriage."[22] Sullivan never really recovered from being refused and considered not good enough, and the relationship was doomed from that moment; but as time went on he possibly came to realize that the relationship would always be a stormy one and that his freedom was being eroded. He had never approached the Scott Russells to ask for their daughter's hand, as would have been expected of a serious suitor, and appeared reluctant to alter his own lifestyle in order to be able to offer Rachel financial security. The whole picture is impossible to recreate in complete fairness to Sullivan without his side of the correspondence, but Rachel's letters reveal how slow he was to come to a decision, and how he preferred to let the relationship die out rather than put an end to it.

AT THE BEGINNING OF July 1870, Gilbert and Fred Clay were back at the Gallery of Illustration for rehearsals of a shortened form of *Ages Ago*, which would open on 11 July. Clay invited Sullivan along to one of the rehearsals to meet Gilbert and performed the formal introduction. Gilbert immediately challenged Sullivan with a prepared question. "I am pleased to meet you Mr. Sullivan, because you will be able to settle a question which has arisen between Mr. Clay and myself." He then adapted a few lines of the play he was writing at the time, *The Palace of Truth*, asking if:

> . . . the result would be the same,
> Whether [your lordship] chose to play upon
> The simple tetrachord of Mercury
> That knew no diatonic interval,
> Or the elaborate dis-diapason
> (Four tetrachords, and one redundant note),
> Embracing in its perfect consonance
> All simple, double and inverted chords![23]

Gilbert once said of Sullivan that he always understood a joke immediately and never needed an explanation. Presumably this occasion was no exception. Gilbert's account of the meeting says, "Sullivan reflected for a moment, and asked me to oblige him by repeating my question. I did so, and he replied that it was a very nice point, and he would like to think it over before giving a definite reply."[24] Sullivan's noncommittal answer was the perfect reply and Gilbert's jokey comment that he thought that, twenty years later Sullivan was "still hammering it out," was the opposite of the case. Sullivan had understood the joke and never gave it another moment's thought. It is an often quoted piece of nonsense, but it is in character for Gilbert that his first words to Sullivan were a challenge. Over the years there would be many other challenges that he would set Sullivan; Sullivan would answer them all, and then in his turn start to challenge Gilbert and get the best out of him.

After the meeting, Gilbert and Sullivan went their different ways. Neither of them thought of following up this first encounter. Gilbert went back to rehearsing *Ages Ago*, which opened on 11 July, introducing Leonora Braham, the Gallery's new soprano, to the public. Sullivan went off to continue work on an overture he was writing for the Birmingham Festival.

AS THE WAR BETWEEN Prussia and France in 1870 intensified, and as the Prussian Army moved closer to the French capital, Gilbert was asked by the *Observer* to go over to Paris to cover events in the unfolding conflict. He had recently entered into an agreement with Routledge and Sons to publish his second collection of *Bab Ballads* (on less favorable terms than those with Hotten for the first collection); and had just undertaken to provide illustrations for *Good Words for the Young*. He sent off the illustrations he had completed to Dalziels, who were cutting his blocks, and on 6 September he left for France.

Years later, Gilbert wrote a story of what happened to him as he had crossed the channel on his journey over to France, when he encountered an attractive stranger in a plaid shawl. She was desperate to visit her sick husband in France but was without a passport. Gilbert agreed to pass her off as his wife and then gave her 20 gold sovereigns in exchange for two £10 notes. The notes turned out to be forgeries and the lady and her husband, whom Gilbert met later by chance at the theater, proved to be two notorious swindlers. The story, entitled "The Lady in the Plaid Shawl," and subtitled "A Scrap of Autobiography," was originally published in the *Daily Mail* in 1908 to raise money for the Union Jack Fund. Perhaps it is just one of Gilbert's jokes. But Gilbert's stories, like Gilbert's plays, usually contain a fantastic element, the supernatural or the highly improbable. "The Lady in the Plaid Shawl," like Gilbert's story "My Maiden Brief," may be embellished, but it is plausible.[25]

His stay in Paris was short. With the danger of the Prussian invasion of the capital increasing, Gilbert was quickly recalled by telegram. He left on the last train out of Paris. After it had passed over the bridge at Creil, French engineers blew the bridge.

From the dangers of a besieged Paris, Gilbert returned to the comparative peace of life as a dramatist in London. The success of *The Princess* had brought his work to the attention of John Baldwin Buckstone, manager of the Haymarket since 1853, and now nearly seventy years of age. Buckstone had written numerous farces and other dramatic pieces, playing in them himself as the "low comedian," and his comic talents and reputation guaranteed a laugh as soon as he appeared on stage. Buckstone had asked Gilbert to write a piece for the Haymarket, and Gilbert decided to write what he called "a blank verse fairy comedy," based on the French story "Le Palais de la Vérité," in which a magic spell prevents lying and deceitfulness. Gilbert's *The Palace of Truth* opened on 19 November with a cast that included Buckstone, W. H. Kendal, and Kendal's wife, Madge Robertson. It was an immediate success. As far as Francis Burnand was concerned, it "had taken the town by storm."[26]

By the time *The Palace of Truth* opened, Gilbert was already at work on three other ideas. His favorite author, Charles Dickens, had died in 1870 and now Gilbert contacted Charles Dickens junior asking for permission to dramatize *Great Expectations*. He received that permission, but two other commissions were more pressing. The Court Theatre in Sloane Square had recently opened, and the manager, Marie Litton, asked Gilbert for a play for January; meanwhile, the German Reeds wanted him to write a new piece to replace *Our Island Home* at the Gallery of Illustration.

Gilbert rehearsed the two plays simultaneously and they opened within days of each other. The first, at the Court on Wednesday 25 January 1871, was *Randall's Thumb*, a play in which Gilbert introduces several characters who pretend to be what they are not—a married couple of thirty-five years pretend to be on their honeymoon, and a young honeymoon couple pretend to have been married for five years—but the main storyline is concerned with unmasking a villain. Good triumphs over evil, and gentlemanly conduct wins out through the love of a virtuous woman. What is interesting now is not the storyline but the portrayal of characters who are themselves playing a role, pretending to be different from what they are in reality. This question of appearance and reality, the playing of roles, mistaken identity, and the similar subject of characters being forced, by a spell or potion, to play out roles that differ from their role in daily life, occurs again and again in Gilbert's works, including the operas with Sullivan. It is not so much a question of "topsy-turvy" as inside-out—is the person that you see the real person?

The Monday after the appearance of *Randall's Thumb*, *A Sensation Novel*, with music by Florian Pascal, opened at the Gallery of Illustration. A few days later, the man who had been so influential in introducing Gilbert to the stage, Tom Robertson, died. Years later, Gilbert related how at the funeral, he had the frightening experience of thinking he saw Robertson standing on the other side of the grave. It is impossible to discover now, but intriguing to ponder: what was the content of Gilbert's paper as a student when he wrote "The theory of apparitions"?

Paul Gray, Jeff Prowse, and now Tom Robertson: three of Gilbert's "Serious Family" had died within the space of five years. Three of Gilbert's old friends, three of that "thoughtless devil-may care crew of irresponsible young free-lances" as Gilbert referred to them, were dead.[27]

The extraordinary output of 1871 continued with two more pieces for the Court. On 15 April appeared a comedy drama called *Creatures of Impulse*, accompanied by the music of Alberto Randegger, which appeared in the same month as a short story by the same title in *Tinsley's Magazine*. *Creatures of Impulse* was another of Gilbert's plays in which the characters are transformed: this time, due to a fairy's spell, the bully becomes a coward, the coward becomes courageous, and the shy girl becomes expansive in her behavior. On 28 May, *Great Expectations* was presented at the Court. In later years, Gilbert ridiculed the censorship of those days, giving as an example Magwitch's words to Pip "Here you are, in chambers fit for a Lord." Gilbert recalled how the "MS. was returned to the theatre with the word 'Lord' struck out, and 'Heaven' substituted in pencil."[28]

By now, Gilbert's work was being introduced to American audiences, and Gilbert used a theatrical agent, Edward English, to further his American business. *Randall's Thumb* opened at Wallack's Theater, New York, on 9 May 1871, and the following month *Great Expectations* made its appearance.[29] This was only the beginning of a stream of Gilbert's work in America, long before the first appearance of a Gilbert and Sullivan opera.

SUMMER 1870—AND the music Sullivan had written for the song-cycle with Tennyson had still not been published. The process had taken so long, and Millais was so impatient with Tennyson's delay, that the drawings he had done for the proposed volume "had all been dispersed," as he told Sullivan, and he found it impossible to start again. Only one drawing was being engraved and that would be the sum of Millais's contribution.[30] It was another three months before Tennyson finally, and reluctantly, agreed to the publication of the songs. Writing to Sullivan on 6 November 1870, Tennyson agreed to their being published by Christmas, provided that it was mentioned in the preface that they had been written four years earlier. *The Window, or The Song of the Wrens* made its appearance at the end of the year. The idea of bringing together the leading men of the day in poetry, music, and painting had not been a success and none of the three was satisfied.

Greater success came to Sullivan when he conducted his overture *Di Ballo* at the Birmingham Festival on 31 August. Immediately afterward, he felt the need to relax after his usual intensive effort. Instead of taking off for the continent, he went home for his mother's birthday, tired, but satisfied with the enthusiastic reception given to his overture. He had shown his ability to charm an audience with his melodies and his graceful instrumentation, appealing not only to the educated ear but also to the less sophisticated. Music from Sullivan of a more earnest character was heard again before the year was out when he conducted a performance of *The Prodigal Son* in Edinburgh.

By 1871, Sullivan had moved with his mother to Albert Mansions in Victoria Street, where he now employed a cook as well as four other servants. Fred and Charlotte had moved back to Pimlico with their five children, after a short spell in the country at Hendon, and were now living at 40 Denbigh Street, nearer to Fred's office in Buckingham Palace Road, and nearer to the world of the theater, which was becoming a second career for him.[31]

Yet another International Exhibition was held in 1871. Partly with the profits from the first great exhibition, South Kensington was the site of further development, including the Albert Hall, which was opened on 29 March. Henry Cole, a leading member of the committee responsible for all the exhibitions in London since 1851, had commissioned Sullivan to write a cantata for performance at the Albert Hall, and on 1 May Sullivan conducted *On Shore and Sea*, which he had composed to a libretto by Tom Taylor. Sullivan's choice of subject met with adverse criticism in the press. Unlike Sterndale Bennett and Macfarren who had been "intensely national," Sullivan had accepted a libretto, said the *Graphic*, "which laid the action in an Italian port, on the Mediterranean Sea, and among the barbarians of Northern Africa."[32]

Ironically, the next month Sullivan was asked to turn his eyes across the sea to France, when he was appointed to the committee organizing the Mansion House Relief Fund for people suffering hardship in Paris, following the fall of the Paris Commune at the end of May, when up to 30,000 had lost their lives. Sullivan made a short trip to Paris with George Grove, William von Glehn, and William Simpson, an artist and war correspondent for the *Illustrated London News*. Writing to his mother from Paris on 5 June 1871, Sullivan assured her that he was safe, and told her of the ruins in the city, "the result of the uncontrolled, devilish spite of these ruffians of the Commune."[33]

The Paris that Sullivan had known had already been destroyed with the fall of the empire. The emperor, Napoleon III, and his empress Eugénie had gone into exile, and all the royal followers at the Tuileries court had dispersed. Eugénie had made her escape from Paris at the same time as Gilbert was making his. She had landed in England and within a few days had leased a large house in Chislehurst, called Camden Place (now the clubhouse of the Chislehurst Golf Club). There she was joined by her sons (and later by Napoleon III), as well as secretaries, ladies, and gentlemen of the court, and more than twenty servants. One of the ladies-in-waiting to Eugénie was Madame Conneau, wife of Napoleon III's senior physician, and an accomplished singer. Sullivan had often accompanied her on the piano in Paris and later he visited both Madame Conneau and Eugénie at Chislehurst.

He had rented a cottage a mile or two from Chislehurst, at Widmore Farm, Bromley, where he worked on the incidental music to *The Merchant of Venice*, due to open at the Prince's Theatre, Manchester, on 9 September. In the meantime, Sullivan had been asked by Henry Hersee, one of the directors of the Royal National Opera, to conduct during a season being organized to promote English opera. The scheme proved to be a failure, but the idea was to exercise the mind of another composer, who at this time, August 1871, was still trying to make his own way as a composer of light opera.

Richard D'Oyly Carte wrote two operettas for the Opera Comique, a theater that had only been open since the previous October. The first, *Marie*, had a short run and was soon followed by *The Doctor in Spite of Himself*, adapted from Molière's *Le médecin malgré lui*, which ran until November. Its place was taken by German opéra bouffe, but D'Oyly Carte was convinced that what the French or the Germans could do the English could do better. As a composer, he was not the person to put English comic opera on the map, but he had begun to use his entrepreneurial skills to harness and encourage the talents of others. In 1869 he had set up an agency, with the clumsy title of "Messrs. Rudall, Rose, Carte, & Co's London Opera, Concert and Choir Agency," which was established in Craig's Court, just south of Trafalgar Square. He was still a long way from being able to develop his idea for English comic opera: running an agency was a beginning, but he had no theater at his disposal, nor did he have the necessary financial backing to go further. However, a leading manager had already spotted the potential success of bringing together the talents of Gilbert and Sullivan.

John Hollingshead invited Gilbert to repeat his success of 1868 and produce another Christmas extravaganza for the Gaiety, this time to music by Sullivan. Gilbert was already engaged on two other pieces at the time which were both to be ready before Christmas. A piece for the Gaiety would be a very rushed affair, but he agreed. Sullivan had just finished his music for *The Merchant of Venice* and after a performance of the music at Crystal Palace on 28 October, was going off to Scotland for the grouse season; but he also agreed. In late September or early October, notices were appearing in the Gaiety programs to announce that "The Christmas Operatic Extravaganza will be written by W. S. Gilbert, with original music by Arthur Sullivan."[34]

After the opening of *The Merchant of Venice*, Sullivan remained in Manchester, staying at the house of J. H. Agnew, to whom he had dedicated the music. From Manchester he wrote to J. W. Davison, telling him about the projected performance of the music at the Crystal Palace and explaining that he would not be able to return to London for the funeral of Cipriani Potter, chairman of the Mendelssohn Scholarship Committee, of which Sullivan was now a member. From Manchester, he traveled up to Scotland with Agnew for the grouse shooting. The hardship this entailed for him he portrayed in a letter to "Dearest Mum." He seemed none too pleased with his first day "& have got to do two days more," he complained, ". . . walking up & down these awful, endless hills they call moors."[35] The only compensation he found was in the thought that all his expenses were paid, including the rail fare.

Gilbert's first piece before Christmas, *On Guard*, was written for the Court Theatre and opened on 28 October 1871. It ran for only a month, by which time it had already opened in America.[36] Before the end of that month, Gilbert had roughed out a sketch plot for the piece with Sullivan. At the same time he was working on a much more substantial piece, *Pygmalion and Galatea*. With his mind still on classical themes, he had come up with the idea of *Thespis; or the Gods Grown Old* for the Gaiety. On 30 October Gilbert's agent, Edward English, wrote to R. M. Field of the

Boston Museum Theatre telling him that W. S. Gilbert and Arthur Sullivan were doing an opéra bouffe in English for the Gaiety at Christmas. "It is expected to be a big thing," he wrote. He enclosed a rough sketch of the piece and said he believed that Gilbert and Sullivan were hard at work on the piece.[37] Not yet — Gilbert's mind was still mainly concentrated on *Pygmalion and Galatea*. As for the "rough sketch," an outline scenario has survived and is in the British Library, but Gilbert would not have allowed such a rough sketch to be sent to America. This scenario therefore represents a stage in the construction of the piece before Edward English's letter of 30 October.[38]

Pygmalion and Galatea opened at the Haymarket on 9 December 1871 and Gilbert would have been busy with rehearsals for about three weeks before that. Nevertheless, he must have started writing the lyrics for *Thespis* during this period. Years later, he recalled that *Thespis* was put together in less than three weeks followed by a week's rehearsal, and gave a similar period of time, that is, five weeks in all, to a correspondent in 1902. To that same correspondent, a Mr. de Strzelecki, he said he was unable to read the proofs for *Thespis* because he was in America at the time.[39] His memory was probably faulty about this. He remembered being in America before the opening there of *Pygmalion and Galatea*, but it was his play *The Palace of Truth* that opened in America in December.[40] He was only at the stage of agreeing the assignment of the American rights to *Pygmalion and Galatea* in December. It would have been impossible for Gilbert to travel to America and back in time for rehearsals of *Thespis*. If we take the longer of the two periods that Gilbert gave for the production of *Thespis*, then he started writing the lyrics and sending them to Sullivan shortly after 20 November, while he was still rehearsing *Pygmalion and Galatea*. (The American production of *Pygmalion and Galatea* did not appear at Wallack's Theatre, New York, until 1 October 1872, after Gilbert's visit to America in June.)[41]

Pygmalion and Galatea was to prove Gilbert's greatest financial success outside the operas and was to be revived many times.

It is often mentioned that in *Thespis* Gilbert was writing for an existing team of actors at the Gaiety, and not for a specially selected company as with the later operas; but up to that point Gilbert's experience had been precisely that of writing for the company of the theater that had commissioned the work. The actors were not new to him; he had written *Robert the Devil* for the Gaiety and the cast for that piece included many of those to appear in *Thespis*. A newcomer to the Gaiety was Fred Sullivan, who was to play the part of Apollo, and his engagement by Hollingshead may have had some influence on Arthur Sullivan's agreement to set the music to such an intentionally ephemeral piece as a Christmas extravaganza.

The part of Thespis was to be played by Johnny Toole, a leading comedian of the day and one of the stars of the Gaiety. Toole was still on his customary tour until 18 December, when he returned to the Gaiety and went straight into rehearsals for *Thespis*, with just a week to go before the opening.[42] Speaking of the rehearsals to his first biographer, Sullivan recalled:

Until Gilbert took the matter in hand choruses were dummy concerns, and were practically nothing more than a part of the stage setting. It was in "Thespis" that Gilbert began to carry out his expressed determination to get the chorus to play its proper part in the performance.

Sullivan also recalled how limited he felt in having to write music for "people without voices!"[43] He was not writing music for posterity, and it is not surprising that the score was not preserved but was later "recycled" by Sullivan.

Gilbert was trying yet another variation of his combination of the improbable (or the impossible—a group of gods on Mount Olympus) and the day-to-day reality (a theatrical company). The plot reveals people pretending to be other than what they are (the actors take over the roles of the gods), and the confusion that results from this state of affairs is only resolved by everyone reverting to their original positions, although finishing up a little wiser.

The most famous piece of music from *Thespis*, which was used again in *The Pirates of Penzance,* was the chorus sung by the troupe of actors climbing Mount Olympus, "Climbing over Rocky Mountain," with the solos sung by Daphne (Annie Tremaine) and Nicemis (Constance Loseby). Another number that survived and became a famous "ballad" was "Cousin Robin" (later known as "Little Maid of Arcadee") sung by Sparkeion (Mlle Clary). Careful detective work has reproduced what is thought to be the ballet music from act 2 of *Thespis*, taken from *L'Ile enchantée*, and part of which was used again in a later ballet by Sullivan.[44]

Thespis; or, The Gods Grown Old, "an entirely original Grotesque Opera in Two Acts," had its first night on Tuesday, 26 December 1871. The theater was packed; the audience was looking forward to seeing Johnnie Toole and Nellie Farren as much as being entertained by the joint work of Messrs. Gilbert and Sullivan. The production may have been rushed in composition and scamped in rehearsal, but Gilbert did not fail to ensure an important detail: the libretto was on sale in every part of the theater for a shilling (6d in the pit and the gallery) and, having assigned the American rights to R. M. Field of Boston, Gilbert included a "Caution to American Pirates."[45] Sullivan conducted, and the ballet was provided by the Payne brothers, assisted by a troupe of five female dancers.

The program for the evening opened at 7 p.m. with Henry J. Byron's *Dearer Than Life*, starring Johnnie Toole, and the curtain went up on the first Gilbert and Sullivan production, *Thespis*, at 9:30 p.m. "I have rarely seen anything so beautiful put upon the stage," wrote Sullivan to his mother.[46] According to the *Morning Advertiser*, the scenery was "rich in artistic effect" and the costumes were "brilliant with colours and spangles. . . . Miss E. Farren [was] in a suit of something that looks as like the real quicksilver as anything can well do."[47] Nellie Farren, as Mercury, was a major attraction in herself; she had a dynamic and agreeable stage presence and was described by Hollingshead as cheeky in tone but "without the slightest tinge of offensive vulgarity."[48] Clement Scott in the *Daily Telegraph* was full of praise:

Some of the numbers will certainly live, and the impression caused by the music as a whole is that it will have more than a passing interest.... A ludicrous ballad for Mr. Toole, commencing, "I once knew a chap who discharged a function on the North-South-Eastern-Diddlesex Junction" [*sic*], is quite in the spirit of the well-known compositions of "Bab," and, as it has been fitted with a lively tune and a rattling chorus, a hearty encore was inevitable.[49]

Unfortunately, that lively tune and rattling chorus have not been discovered. Clement Scott was disappointed that the audience on that first night was not as appreciative as they might have been. "*Thespis* is too good to be put on one side and cold-shouldered in this fashion; and we anticipate that judicious curtailment and constant rehearsal will enable us to tell a very different tale."[50] Curtailment was certainly needed: *Thespis*, due to finish at 11 p.m., was still running after midnight, and the audience was becoming restless.

The *Daily News* thought that on the whole the burlesque was a success "and will doubtless amuse the public for some time to come."[51] *Thespis* was still playing to full houses in the middle of February and ran for sixty-four performances until 8 March 1872, everything that could be expected of a Christmas extravaganza. There had been encores on that first night for Toole, for Nellie Farren and for Mlle Clary, but no encore for Gilbert and Sullivan — yet.

CHAPTER SEVEN

1872-1873

Different Worlds:
Gilbert's *The Wicked World*;
Sullivan's *The Light of the World*

SUCCESSFUL THOUGH *THESPIS* WAS, it belonged in Gilbert's mind to the world of burlesque and pantomime and not to the world of drama in which he was now making his mark. *The Princess, The Palace of Truth,* and now *Pygmalion and Galatea* were surely the prelude to more important works. At the beginning of 1872, he was negotiating terms with Buckstone for a third play for the Haymarket, and suggesting 5 guineas a night for a guaranteed one hundred nights, the fee then reducing to 3 guineas. Buckstone, good-humoredly, hoped that if the next play was another success, Gilbert would not ask for an even higher fee. Buckstone was pleased to keep Gilbert at the Haymarket, and offered him a piece of advice that was not devoid of self-interest: not to write himself out by "supplying all sorts of houses" with his work.[1] As for Gilbert, the next piece was to receive considerable time and attention.

The American public was already familiar with Gilbert's work. Following *Randall's Thumb* at Wallack's, the *New York Times*, on 31 December 1871, had carried a long review of *Pygmalion and Galatea* that had first appeared in the *Daily News*.[2] The ground was being prepared for its successful launch in America in 1872. Gilbert's reputation in England was confirmed by an article that appeared in *Era*, on 28 January 1872, saying that "he possesses in a more striking degree than his fellow labourers the rare gift of originality ... His *Princess* was the first conspicuous sign of talent which borders on genius."[3]

Not everyone saw Gilbert's work as a benefit to society. He was beginning to attract criticism for the view of life he portrayed in his plays. To some, his view that total honesty would lead to an impossible situation for the normal functioning of society, as he put forward in *The Palace of Truth*, was a cynical view of humanity and something to be resisted. The masters of Harrow School were not in favor of Gilbert's views and declared that *The Palace of Truth* was not an appropriate play for their pupils.[4] Inevitably, the more it created controversy, the more interesting Gilbert's work became to the public.

In June, Gilbert made a visit to the United States to make arrangements for the appearance of *Pygmalion and Galatea*. It was a short stay, three days in New York and two in Boston;[5] productions were planned for Wallack's in New York on 1 October, and then on 23 October for the Globe in Boston.

He was back in England in time for militia training. Instead of the usual training period in June, the Royal Aberdeenshire Highlanders held what they called autumn maneuvers, starting on 5 August. The highlight of the month that they spent at Aldershot was a visit and inspection from General Sherman. This was followed by two weeks' maneuvers on Salisbury Plain before the regiment returned to Aberdeen on 13 September.[6]

Gilbert returned to work on his new play for the Haymarket after the vacation period, but he also was working on other pieces that autumn. *A Medical Man*, which he had originally written for Clement Scott's Christmas book of 1869, was produced at St George's Hall on 24 October, and four days later, *Happy Arcadia* opened—a new piece for the Gallery of Illustration, for which he had collaborated once more with Fred Clay.

On 4 January 1873, Gilbert's long-awaited play, *The Wicked World,* opened at the Haymarket. The structure of *The Wicked World* is similar to that of *Thespis*: instead of a theatrical group arriving on Olympus and changing places with the gods, three mortal men are exchanged with their fairy counterparts (in Gilbert's fairyland every fairy has a counterpart in the real world, "the wicked world"). The men's arrival in fairyland plays havoc among the fairy sisters who compete for their love and resort to hypocrisy and lying to win the love of the mortals. The resulting confusion is only undone when the men return to earth and the fairies return to their former state of happiness—without mortal love—but wiser than before.

What raised eyebrows over *The Wicked World* was Gilbert's treatment of love—"mortal love," as he called it—the cause of most of the problems in the world. When it was allowed to enter fairyland it caused jealousy and enmity among the blameless fairies. Gilbert's view of the world was by many regarded as cynical.

The Times reviewed it favorably on 6 January: "The expected throng which filled on Saturday night every part of the Haymarket Theatre proved beyond a doubt the strong hold which Mr. W. S. Gilbert, striking into a new path, has upon the public mind." It praised his originality since *The Palace of Truth* which "gave dramatic form and colour to a well-known tale by Madame de Genlis," making it possible to portray fairyland in poetic language in a theatrical play, instead of leaving fairyland to the burlesque and the pantomime. He had invented "a new species of drama," and made it popular. "The audience on Saturday night perfectly knew what sort of play they were about to see, and they were not only curious, but prepared to be highly gratified."[7]

The *Pall Mall Gazette* took a contrary point of view of *The Wicked World*, saying on 6 January that "Mr. Gilbert's fancy is agile enough, but his imagination seems cold and inert," the characters were mere shadows, "inanimate creatures" who could not attract the sympathy of the audience.[8] Two weeks later, on 23 January, the *Pall Mall Gazette* published a letter signed "AMUETOS," which said that the play "fails as an imaginative conception," that it betrayed "coarseness of workmanship," occasionally hardening into "actual offensiveness." The letter went on to call parts of the play "vulgar and coarse" and one scene "indecent."[9] This was too much for Gilbert and he sued for libel.

The notoriety attached to *The Wicked World* and its condemnation as "indecent" were enough to contribute to its success at the box office. Certainly Buckstone, as the manager, was more than happy and on 12 January he wrote to Gilbert, saying, "Let me congratulate you on the success of 'The Wicked World' as I know you were anxious and nervous, about your third venture at the Haymarket, and indeed so was I."[10] *The Wicked World* ran for 175 performances and Gilbert sold the autumn touring rights to Buckstone for £200.

Never one for passively letting events run their course, while he was waiting for his case against the *Pall Mall Gazette* to come to court, Gilbert hit on the idea of a burlesque of his own play under the title *The Happy Land*. It was written in double-quick time, the manuscript was submitted for licence to William Bodham Donne, the Reader of Plays, on 3 February, and approval was given five days later. The play was to cause even more excitement than *The Wicked World*. It opened on 3 March 1873 at the Court Theatre, advertised as written by F. Tomline and Gilbert à Beckett.

Three characters in the play—Mr. G. (played by David Fisher), Mr. A. (played by Edward Righton), and Mr. L. (played by W. J. Hill)—were made up and dressed like Gladstone, Ayrton (president of the Board of Works), and Lowe (the chancellor of the Exchequer) who was Gilbert's former boss at the Education Office. Two days later, the lord chamberlain's attention was drawn to the fact that three members of the government were being impersonated on stage at the Court. That evening he himself went to the theater and, finding that the "personalities" of the three gentlemen were not in the manuscript submitted to him, ordered that the play be suspended. Comparison with the prompt copy revealed eighteen quarto pages of additions, interpolations, and deviations from the original licensed text, and the original manuscript gave no indication of the intention to "point the allusions to individuals."[11] Marie Litton begged to be allowed to perform the play as originally licensed, promising to stick closely to the text and not to make any allusions to individual personalities. With those guarantees, the lord chamberlain relicensed the play.

On 8 March, *The Happy Land* appeared again. Despite the lack of makeup, everybody understood the allusions perfectly and every seat in the house had been booked in advance.

The notoriety of the play was increasing public desire to see it, as well as giving rise to much speculation as to the true identity of the author calling himself F. Tomline.

Gilbert confessed to Fred Clay that the "general scheme of the piece" was his, but because he wanted to avoid being seen writing a burlesque of his own work, à Beckett had assumed authorship. Correspondence with Marie Litton later in the year, concerning payment for *The Happy Land*, would suggest that Gilbert's part in the production of the play was a little more than just suggesting the "general scheme."[12]

He had already negotiated terms for his next play at the Court, asking for £3 a night with a guarantee of eighty nights. The play was an adaptation of the French farce *Le chapeau de paille d'Italie* by Labiche and Marc-Michel, and initially Gilbert called it "Hunting a Hat." It was expected that the play would be brought on in July, but *The Happy Land* ran successfully until 14 November and the new play, now called *The Wedding March*, opened on 15 November. Gilbert later said it had only taken him a day and a half to write and it brought him £2,500.[13]

The Royalty, Dean Street, was the scene of Gilbert's next play. It was another adaptation from French, this time from Meilhac and Halévy's *Le Roi Candaule*, which Gilbert initially had named *The Realm of Joy*, using the name Tomline again. The Reader of Plays was against granting it a licence, but the lord chamberlain, having learned from experience, thought that banning the play would only give it more publicity and the licence was approved.[14] *The Realm of Joy* opened on 18 October, changing its name during the course of its run to *Realms of Joy*.

Gilbert v. Enoch, Gilbert's libel action against the publisher of the *Pall Mall Gazette*, came before Mr. Justice Brett and a special jury in the Court of Common Pleas on 27 November 1873. Parts of the first act and the whole of the second and third acts of *The Wicked World* were read out in court. Also read were relevant parts of the *Pall Mall Gazette*'s criticism, including the line spoken by the character Ethais, who says he is returning to earth, "where women are not devils — till they're dead," a line, claimed the paper, which was "unfit to be spoken in a theatre at all." Gilbert had asked Buckstone and other members of the profession to testify on his behalf as experts. Cross-examination of Buckstone, hard of hearing but sure of his timing, turned into a performance that was enjoyed by everybody present, including the judge. Guided by the judge, the jury found that both the play and the article in the *Pall Mall Gazette* were innocent, and judgment was in favor of the defendant, with Gilbert having to pay costs.[15]

Judgment had been pronounced in a court of law, but Gilbert wanted to have the last word. As far as he was concerned, as he explained in a letter to *The Times* on 2 December, it had been decided in court that his work did not deserve "the strictures with which that journal [the *Pall Mall Gazette*] has visited it."[16]

The year had been dominated by controversy surrounding two of Gilbert's plays, *The Wicked World* and *The Happy Land*, but in May 1873, *More "Bab" Ballads*, published by Routledge, had made a peaceful appearance to the delight of the readers of *Fun*. The collection of 35 ballads with illustrations included the last of his ballads, "Old Paul and Old Tim," which had first appeared on 28 January 1871. Separately, Gilbert had expanded "Trial by Jury" to provide a libretto that Carl

Rosa had asked for, intending to produce a one-act operetta for which Rosa would write the music.

Meanwhile, Gilbert was hard at work on his next play for the Haymarket to appear early in 1874, another play that was to land him in controversy. It had already caused controversy between Gilbert and Buckstone before it appeared. As it was not ready when Buckstone returned in the autumn from his provincial tour with the Haymarket company, he planned to put on a replacement. Gilbert was furious; he accused Buckstone of breaking his agreement and threatened legal action. Buckstone ignored the threat, and calmed Gilbert down by saying, "I presumed I was suiting your convenience by giving you more time—I do not want to argue."[17]

IN CONTRAST TO GILBERT, Sullivan enjoyed a public persona that was above controversy. His friendship with the rich and the aristocratic had even reached the height of friendship with royalty. Alfred, duke of Edinburgh, the second son of Queen Victoria, was an amateur violinist and had befriended Sullivan, who was only two years older than him. The friendship developed about the beginning of 1872. On 9 January, the duke of Edinburgh had attended a performance of *Thespis* at the Gaiety and in April was in correspondence with Sullivan, addressing him in the familiar form "My dear Sullivan." The prince of Wales had recently recovered from typhoid, and Sullivan was commissioned to write a *Te Deum* in gratitude for the prince's recovery. Sullivan wanted to dedicate the music to the queen, and the duke of Edinburgh ensured that he received the appropriate royal permission to do so.

The *Te Deum* was performed at a concert at the Crystal Palace, with choir and orchestra totaling 2,000 performers, and to an audience of 26,000. "In this new work by our young countryman," wrote *The Times*, "we are glad to be able to speak in terms of unqualified praise. It is not only, in our opinion, the most finished composition for which we are indebted to his pen but an honour to English art."[18] The concert was well attended by royalty, including the duke of Edinburgh and Princess Louise, the twenty-three-year-old daughter of Queen Victoria, but the queen herself was not present.

The private life of Sullivan was not proceeding as smoothly. *Thespis* had provided a much needed boost to his finances, but at the beginning of 1872 he was again financially embarrassed. He had hoped to sell the rights of some of his works to Boosey, but they had put him off until June. The situation was bad enough to reduce him to writing a begging letter to Frederick Lehmann, the husband of Nina, asking for a loan of £300. Lehmann recognized that he would not be helping Sullivan by lending him money, probably to pay off gambling debts. His reply was short and to the point: "I must say no to your request, and I have not the heart to add another word to so disagreeable a communication."[19]

Sullivan was in "a state of great anxiety."[20] He now occupied larger premises in Albert Mansions, was still supporting his mother, from whom he was careful to hide

W. S. Gilbert—the young dramatist (V&A Picture Library)

the extent of his gambling habit, and he had a certain social standing to maintain. It is also around this time that he began to suffer from the kidney ailment that was to plague him for the rest of his life. Somehow he managed to arrange his finances until June, when Boosey paid £500 for the rights to *Cox and Box and The Prodigal Son*, as well as "Birds in the Night" and other songs.[21]

In September, Sullivan conducted part of his *Te Deum* at the Norwich Festival. "Mr. Sullivan's charmingly melodious and impressive music was, if we may judge by the frequent applause bestowed upon it, not only understood, but thoroughly enjoyed," said *The Times*.[22] Sullivan related in a letter to his mother that the president of the festival, Lord Stafford, had invited him to stay at Cossey Hall, five miles outside Norwich. "I can't describe the place because I only got a glimpse of the exterior as I drove up, but it looks magnificent. . . . There is a fine chapel which Lord Stafford took me to see in the moonlight, & a little dim lamp was burning in front of the altar."[23] The Staffords were an old Catholic family and the lamp kept burning in front of the altar was a symbol of the presence of Christ, the light of the world. It is quite possible that there, or later reflecting on that scene, Sullivan had the idea for the theme of his next oratorio, *The Light of the World*. In a letter the following May, he referred to his working on his oratorio since Michaelmas, so the idea originated from about this time.[24]

After Cossey Hall, Sullivan returned to Norwich to rehearse "Guinevere," the song that he had written to Lionel Lewin's words. With Lionel Lewin, Sullivan had written three other songs in 1872, "Golden Days," "None but I Can Say," and "Once Again." In all, he published eight songs in that year, including one called "Oh! ma charmante" to words by Victor Hugo and dedicated to Mme Conneau. His output of hymns also had increased, following the popular "Onward Christian Soldiers" of the previous year. Much of his music at this period was religious, including his oratorio for the Birmingham Festival of 1873. Not that Sullivan was becoming pious in his outlook; he was still the bright, humorous character he had always been, joining the von Glehns at Sydenham on Christmas Eve for the performance of a farce called "Christmas Eve in a Lighthouse," in which he was one of the performers, along with Lionel Lewin and Ernest von Glehn. According to von Glehn, Sullivan never got round to learning his lines and ad-libbed madly throughout, his spontaneity only adding to everyone's enjoyment.[25]

As for the other family at Sydenham that Sullivan had visited so frequently in the past, the Scott Russells saw their second daughter leave the family home, when Rachel married William Henn Holmes, a cousin of the composer Villiers Stanford, and whose family were old friends of the Scott Russells. Holmes and Rachel went off to live in India, where Holmes worked as a civil servant. The eldest of the girls, Louise, never married. She was to die from tuberculosis in 1878, aged thirty-seven.

The Light of the World absorbed Sullivan for much of 1873. Writing to J. W. Davison in May, he told him, "I never get out in the world as my Oratorio takes all my time and thought." Sullivan was not quite the recluse his letter to Davison suggests.

In January, he had been a guest at a house party given by Baron Meyer Rothschild at Mentmore in Buckinghamshire, and in early May he went up to Oxford to visit his friend Lionel Lewin, who was a student at Pembroke College. Their friendship was to come to an abrupt end in 1874 with the premature death of Lewin. Older friends, from the days of the Mendelssohn Scholarship and from his early years after Leipzig, had already died: George Smart and, more recently, Henry Chorley who had died in February 1872.

While he was at Oxford, Sullivan paid a Sunday afternoon call on the dean of Christ Church, Dr. Henry Liddell, whose daughter, Alice, had been the "model" for Lewis Carroll's *Alice's Adventures in Wonderland*, which had appeared in 1865. Sullivan returned to the Liddells after dinner to join in the social and musical gathering, when the eldest daughter of the family, Lorna Charlotte, sang Sullivan's "Orpheus with his Lute." Next day he lunched with them, and after attending a lecture by John Ruskin, at that time Slade Professor of Fine Art, Sullivan returned to the Liddells for tea with Prince Leopold, the twenty-year-old youngest son of Queen Victoria, who was then a student at Christ Church.

At the time of all the controversy provoked by Gilbert's *The Wicked World*, Sullivan's *The Light of the World* received its first performance on 27 August 1873 at the Birmingham Festival. The duke of Edinburgh made a point of attending, particularly as the music was dedicated to the Grand Duchess Marie Alexandrovna of Russia, who was to become his wife in 1874. Sullivan met "a hearty and unanimous greeting" when he appeared on the platform to conduct his new oratorio. "The last outgrowth of his genius . . . leaves far behind all that had preceded it," wrote *The Times*.[26] The duke of Edinburgh rushed to congratulate Sullivan at the end of the performance and, when the cheering had subsided, they drove off together afterward.

Sullivan's social position, no less than his musical reputation, was firmly established. He was thirty years of age; still young, still promising great things for serious music in England, and on 18 October an "All Sullivan" promenade concert was performed at Covent Garden.

And then, about this time, John Hollingshead commissioned Sullivan again for the Gaiety, to write incidental music for *The Merry Wives of Windsor*. This was to prove no simple excursion into the theater. It would in fact be many more years before Sullivan wrote for the concert hall again.

CHAPTER EIGHT

1874-1875

Trial by Jury

CHARITY, GILBERT'S NEW PLAY for the Haymarket, opened on 3 January 1874. His serious intention was to portray the different standards shown by society toward men and women: a woman who has fallen only once is harshly condemned; whereas a man, no matter how wayward his behavior, escapes all condemnation. Buckstone was uneasy at the thought of putting on a straightforward serious play and wanted to lighten it with comedy. The comedy sat uneasily with the theme and the play suffered from it. Some found the play offensive because a fallen woman is shown kindness by a bishop, and is given hope with the possibility of a new start in Australia. The play was unsuccessful in London, losing £200 a week by late February, but fared better in the provinces.

A fortnight later, on 17 January 1874, Gilbert's second play of the year, an adaptation from a popular novel (*Ought We to Visit Her?*) opened at the Royalty Theatre under the management of Henrietta Hodson, who played one of the leading parts with Charles Wyndham. During the last rehearsal, a heated argument took place between Gilbert and Miss Hodson. Gilbert lost his temper; she called him a "floody bool" and told him to go home to bed. Gilbert stormed out of the theater, bumped into Marie Litton, and treated her to his version of events.

Nearly three weeks after the opening of the play, Gilbert received a letter from Miss Hodson's solicitors. They had been informed by their client that Gilbert had been slandering her to Miss Litton and others, saying that she used "disgusting and obscene language." Unless Gilbert was willing to sign an apology, which they would write on her behalf, Miss Hodson was prepared to take him to court.[1]

It was not until a month later that Gilbert signed the apology prepared by the solicitors, and he begged Henrietta Hodson not to publish it. She agreed, but instead circulated it to all the leading members of the dramatic profession in London, and the apology found its way into the pages of the *Hornet*. As far as Gilbert was concerned, this placed friendly relations between them out of the question.

Henrietta Hodson was a colorful character, a strong personality with an equally strong temper. She had acted with Henry Irving in Manchester in the days before Irving was famous, and in 1863 had left the stage to marry. She returned three years later, when she first appeared on the stage in London, and in 1868 she left her husband for the journalist Henry Labouchère, later a well-known radical politician, whom she was to marry on the death of her husband in 1887. Labouchère had bought the Queen's Theatre, Long Acre, when Hodson was a member of the company there, and then in 1870 she took over as manager of the reopened Royalty Theatre in Dean Street. Gilbert's skirmish with Henrietta Hodson in 1874 was not the end of their disagreement; a full-scale battle was not far away.

Shortly after the opening of *Ought We to Visit Her?* Carl Rosa's wife, Euphrosyne, died on 21 January, aged thirty-seven. Gilbert, who was the same age and had known her since childhood, attended her funeral at Highgate Cemetery, along with Michael Costa, Charles Santley, Alberto Randegger, and members of the Carl Rosa company. Carl Rosa no longer had the heart to continue with his work. His opera company had to finish its season without him and was then disbanded temporarily.[2] The idea of setting Gilbert's libretto, *Trial by Jury*, was out of the question.

A further setback for Gilbert soon followed. *Charity* was running at a loss Buckstone could not sustain, and he was forced to withdraw the play in March. But before the end of the month Gilbert had another play ready for production at the Criterion. Once again, Gilbert was to be disappointed. Due to open on 21 March as a curtain-raiser, with music by Alfred Cellier, *Topsyturvydom* had to be postponed because the theater was still upside down due to redecoration. When the piece finally made its appearance, it was a failure. The *Athenaeum* described it as "clever, but rather remote . . . an exercise rather than an amusement."[3]

Gilbert soon bounced back, this time with an idea for Henry Irving, telling Irving he had thought of a really powerful part for him. Irving was interested, and Gilbert sent him a sketch of the play, which Irving liked. Gilbert carried on with the play, but when he approached Irving again, Irving had lost interest. Gilbert turned to William Montague at the Globe and sold the play to him, so he thought, but Montague left suddenly for San Francisco and Gilbert was left with the play on his hands. He tried Irving again in August, telling him that he had now improved on the original sketch, and had completed about an act and a half. Irving showed no interest and the matter was dropped.[4]

In contrast to the series of setbacks Gilbert had experienced, the comedietta, "White Willow," written the previous year and now renamed *Sweethearts*, made its appearance and was a success. It opened on 7 November 1874 at the Prince of Wales's with Marie Wilton (Mrs. Bancroft) in the cast. It was with her husband, Squire Bancroft, playing opposite her that Mrs. Bancroft was to take this play all round the country, keeping it as a favorite in their repertoire.

On 20 November 1874, another member of the "Serious Family" died: Tom Hood, the editor of *Fun*. Hood's choice to succeed him as editor was Henry Sampson, who had previously worked for the *Hornet*, the paper that had published Gilbert's apology to Henrietta Hodson. Writing to the Dalziels, the owners of *Fun*, on 30 November, Gilbert declared that he was unable to preserve his self-respect and work under someone who had been associated with the *Hornet*. He would write no more for them, but would send two columns for the next three weeks that he had already written. This three-week contribution, Gilbert's last for *Fun*, began to appear on 12 December and was called *Rosencrantz and Guildenstern*, a parody of *Hamlet*. Gilbert's Hamlet is totally self-absorbed and given to soliloquizing in melodramatic fashion. At one point in Gilbert's stage directions, Hamlet "stalks to chair, throws himself into it" before uttering the line, "To be—or not to be." The play within a play in Gilbert's parody is accompanied by trumpets and drums. "Cannot he woo without an orchestra at his elbow?" says one of the players.[4] It is surely no coincidence that Henry Irving, who loved incidental music in his Shakespearean productions, had scored a notable success as Hamlet earlier in the year.

In the three years since *Thespis*, Gilbert had produced eleven pieces with mixed success. On his hands was a twelfth piece, for which he had been looking for a home since Carl Rosa had returned the libretto to him. The opportunity to use it was not far away.

HAVING BEEN INVITED by the Society for Propagating Christian Knowledge to edit *Church Hymns, with Tunes*, Sullivan devoted most of 1874 to the task. He published thirty-six new hymns in the course of the year and the hymnal contained forty-five hymn tunes either composed by Sullivan or arranged by him. It was a formidable achievement and some of those tunes have remained popular to the present time, such as "Hushed Was the Evening Hymn," and "It Came upon the Midnight Clear," which Sullivan developed from a tune known as "Noel." They appeared alongside the most popular of all his hymn tunes, "Onward, Christian Soldiers," to which he gave the name "St. Gertrude."

He also published twelve new songs, including two to words by Burnand and one, "The Distant Shore," to words by Gilbert. The following year was to see the publication of two more Gilbert and Sullivan songs: "Sweethearts," inspired by Gilbert's successful play, and "The Love That Loves Me Not," which Sullivan dedicated to Mrs. Beach Grant. Toward the end of the year, Sullivan wrote "Thou'rt Passing Hence, My Brother" in memory of his father. In a letter to his mother, on 21 September, Sullivan mentioned the song, saying that he had dated it 22 September, the anniversary of his father's death. "It is . . . curious that I should have done it just now," he wrote. "Time passes very quickly—It doesn't seem eight years since dear Father died—bless him."[5]

Before leaving for the continent that summer, Sullivan was called on to provide music to celebrate the visit of Russian royalty. First he provided the orchestration for an arrangement by Joseph Barnby of the Russian national anthem, and second he arranged two unaccompanied vocal pieces of Russian church music, which he conducted himself at a concert on 18 May at the Albert Hall in honor of the czar.

In contrast to the music required for official occasions, the popular taste of the time was the bright and tuneful music of the Parisian operas written by Offenbach. The young D'Oyly Carte thought it was time for English comic opera to show that what the French could do the English could surpass. He had tried as a composer, but realized he did not have the talent. Next, on 5 June 1874, he took over the management of the Opera Comique, hoping to establish a home for the kind of opera he had in mind; but he was short of money and the scheme fell through by November. Carte did not give up easily. He would try again later.

While Carte was dreaming and scheming about comic opera, Sullivan took his summer vacation on the continent, leaving on 21 July. The first leg of his journey took him to Coburg, where he met up with his friends, including the soprano Christine Nilsson and her French husband, Auguste Rouzeaud. With the Rouzeauds, Sullivan traveled on to Franzensbad, in Bohemia, where they were met at the station by Mrs. Beach Grant, who was to become a close friend of Sullivan over the years. Writing to his mother, Sullivan described Mrs. Grant as "a perfect specimen of a high bred, charming American lady . . . very intelligent, well educated, pretty manners, & as cheery as a bird."[6]

The party moved on to Dresden, where they were joined by the Lindsays: Sir Coutts Lindsay, a Scottish baronet, aged fifty, and his wife, Caroline, a little younger than Sullivan, the granddaughter of Nathan Rothschild. So congenial did they find each other's company in Dresden that the Lindsays invited them all to spend more time together at their home in Balcarres, Fifeshire, the following month.

Sullivan arrived back in London on 23 August, only to leave a week later for Liverpool in preparation for a performance of *The Light of the World*. From Liverpool, he went to Wigan to join the night train for Edinburgh, which Mrs. Grant had boarded in London. After breakfast in Edinburgh, they continued their journey to the station at Kilconquhar, two miles from the Firth of Forth, where they were met by the Lindsays and the Rouzeauds and then driven to Balcarres. "The place is very beautiful & we can see the sea spread out before us," he wrote to his mother. "We walk & potter about, the usual country house life, but I am hard at work in my room today as I only lark about after lunch — & work every morning."[7]

For most of September, Sullivan enjoyed the country house life at Balcarres, returning to Liverpool in time for a rehearsal on the day before his oratorio on 29 September. While Liverpool listened to Sullivan's serious music, London enjoyed his lighter side when *Cox and Box* made another appearance in September, this time at the Gaiety, with Fred Sullivan in the cast.

It was with his lighter music in mind that, early in November, Sullivan made a trip to Paris, possibly in search of a librettist. He visited his friend Mrs. Grant, and also contacted Albert Millaud, who had worked as a librettist with Offenbach. If Sullivan was thinking of writing an opera at this time, this suggests that he was not contemplating a grand opera, but something more suited to the light opera that was in Carte's mind; the operas Sullivan saw while in Paris were Offenbach's *Orfée aux enfers*, *La Périchole*, and *Madame l'Archiduc*. However, for the moment, he took the matter no further, and when he returned to England it was to start work on the incidental music for *The Merry Wives of Windsor*, which John Hollingshead had asked him to write for the Gaiety.

His work was interrupted at the end of November by an invitation to stay at Eastwell Park, near Ashford in Kent, the home of the newly married duke and duchess of Edinburgh. A royal invitation was not to be refused, but he was dangerously short of time. After the visit, he had less than three weeks to complete *The Merry Wives of Windsor*, and writing to the critic, Joseph Bennett, he confessed that shortness of time had obliged him to make use of part of the music from his ballet *L'Ile enchantée*.[8]

The sequence of events over the next few weeks is not certain, but the leading players were circling around the idea of something new in comic opera. Richard D'Oyly Carte had given up as manager of the Opera Comique in November, but then in January 1875 became acting manager for Selina Dolaro and her company in a season of light opera at the Royalty. John Hollingshead, having put on Offenbach's *Les deux aveugles* and *La Princesse de Trébizonde* as well as *Cox and Box* at the Gaiety, then took over as manager of the Opera Comique on 19 January 1875. Fred Sullivan, having played in *Cox and Box* at the Gaiety, where Arthur Sullivan had agreed to write *The Merry Wives of Windsor* for John Hollingshead, had now joined Selina Dolaro at the Royalty, where Arthur Sullivan agreed to write a short piece for Richard D'Oyly Carte. The Sullivan brothers were seeing more of each other now since Fred had taken 7 Albert Mansions for his office premises, and Arthur was showing an interest in writing for the theater again. But as yet there was no librettist for Sullivan.

On 23 January 1875 a notice for the Royalty Theatre appeared in *The Times*; "In Preparation, a New Comic Opera composed expressly for this theatre by Mr. Arthur Sullivan, in which Madame Dolaro and Nellie Bromley will appear." The notice appeared four more times over the next week.[9] Gilbert would doubtless have heard of the intended comic opera in theatrical circles and would have seen the notice in *The Times*, but did not immediately rush round to see Carte at the Royalty. What was holding him back? He had a libretto on his hands and it was not Gilbert's practice to let his work lie idle. One of the drawbacks may have been that Henrietta Hodson was the lessee of the Royalty, and Gilbert would not have wanted to be associated with her in any way after their notorious dispute. It is therefore possible that Carte, knowing of the libretto, had some persuading to do with Gilbert.

In the meantime, Selina Dolaro opened on 30 January 1875 with Offenbach's *La Périchole*, preceded by a curtain-raiser called *Awaking*. It was another three weeks before Carte persuaded Gilbert to take his libretto around to Sullivan. On Saturday morning, 20 February 1875, a still somewhat reluctant Gilbert called at Albert Mansions in Victoria Street.[10] It had been snowing and when Gilbert appeared at Sullivan's door with the libretto, his fur coat was still covered in snow after his walk. Sullivan recalled what happened next:

> [Gilbert] read it through, and it seemed to me, in a perturbed sort of way, with a gradual crescendo of indignation, in the manner of a man considerably disappointed with what he had written. As soon as he had come to the last word he closed up the manuscript violently, apparently unconscious of the fact that he had achieved his purpose so far as I was concerned, inasmuch as I was screaming with laughter the whole time.[11]

Less than five weeks after Sullivan had received the libretto from Gilbert, the music was completed, the cast was rehearsed, and their little masterpiece was ready for performance.

On Maundy Thursday, 25 March 1875, at the Royalty Theatre, Dean Street, the evening's entertainment opened at 7:15 with a farce going by the extraordinary name of *Cryptoconchoidsyphonostomata or While It's To Be Had.* It was followed at 8:15 by the main item on the program, *La Périchole*, with Selina Dolaro as La Périchole and Fred Sullivan as Don Andres.[12] Then at 10:15 came the first performance of *Trial by Jury*, "A novel and entirely original Dramatic Cantata, music by Arthur Sullivan, book by W. S. Gilbert." Sullivan conducted the first performance.

How would Gilbert and Sullivan fare, coming immediately after a piece by the popular Offenbach? "To judge by the unceasing and almost boisterous hilarity which formed a sort of running commentary on the part of the audience," said *The Times*, "*Trial by Jury* suffered nothing whatever from so dangerous a juxtaposition. On the contrary, it may fairly be said to have borne away the palm."[13] The sheer enjoyment the audience experienced came not from the words or the music alone but from the unusually happy combination of the two, a point that was seized on by the critics as exceptional: "so completely is each imbued with the same spirit," commented the *Daily News*, "that it would be as difficult to conceive the existence of Mr. Gilbert's verses without Mr. Sullivan's music, as of Mr. Sullivan's music without Mr. Gilbert's verses. Each gives each a double charm."[14]

Gone was the mythological setting, as on Mount Olympus in *Thespis*. The setting was the meticulously accurate depiction of a court of law. Nothing could be more serious than a court of law; no one could be more sober than a learned judge; never was there a more solid institution than British justice—and now the world had been turned upside down. The court of law had become the scene of humor and frivolity; the learned judge had shown himself to be as fickle as the defendant, and the justice system turned out to be flawed by human frailty. And Sullivan had grasped the joke at one reading of the libretto. From the first chords, before ever a line is sung, Sullivan's music sets the scene of mock-seriousness and proceeds to dance its way through the whole piece. His parodies of Handel at the entrance of the Judge, and of Italian operatic style in general in "A Nice Dilemma," have often been quoted; his humorous use of the orchestra runs throughout, and can be heard, for example, in the reeling effect produced by the strings to the words "That she is reeling / Is plain to see!" and in Sullivan's use of the bassoon to point up one of Gilbert's dubious puns or spurious rhymes, as in "To marry two at once is Burglaree!" The bassoon accompaniment is used to similar effect earlier in the Usher's plea: "From bias free of every kind, / This trial must be tried," as though Sullivan is saying, "Don't you believe it!"

As with *Thespis*, the cast was not specially selected, but was simply the existing company of the theater, and as such was to see a number of changes over the months. Special praise was reserved for Fred Sullivan, "whose blending of official dignity, condescension and, at the right moment, extravagant humour," said the *Daily Telegraph*, "made the character of the Judge stand out with all requisite prominence, and added much to the interest of the piece."[15] His success in the main part overshadowed that of Nellie Bromley, whose name had been used as a draw for the piece in its initial advertisement.

There was no performance on 26 March, Good Friday, and then on the Saturday a new curtain-raiser was put on, *A Good Night's Rest*, but *La Périchole* and its highly successful afterpiece *Trial by Jury* continued to run until Saturday 12 June, when the Royalty closed for the summer.

After the successful launch of *Trial by Jury*, Sullivan entered into another partnership, this time with Bolton Rowe, who became more famous later when he reverted to his real name of B. C. Stephenson. Stephenson and Sullivan produced a short opera called *The Zoo*, which opened on 5 June 1875 at St. James's Theatre, where it ran for eighteen performances, and then transferred to the Haymarket until 9 July. After that it moved to the Philharmonic, Islington, as a curtain-raiser to Offenbach's *Les Géorgiennes*.

Gilbert, too, produced another musical entertainment after *Trial by Jury*, once more for the German Reeds. *Eyes and No Eyes*, with music by Florian Pascal, for six performers including Leonora Braham as the soprano, opened on 5 July at St. George's Hall. The piece is particularly remembered for its opening scene: the character Clochette is discovered alone on stage at her spinning wheel, an opening that Gilbert would make use of again many years later.

Both Gilbert and Sullivan had continued their own individual careers, which had not suddenly come to an end because of the success of their latest collaboration. The implications of that fateful day, 20 February, when Sullivan agreed to set Gilbert's libretto, had not yet been fully realized. Yet, it would change the lives of both men, and also that of Richard D'Oyly Carte.

CHAPTER NINE

1875-1876

In Search of a Manager

ON 6 JUNE 1875, the *Era* announced that Madame Selina Dolaro was to start a tour with her company on 21 June "to perform *La Périchole, La Fille de Madame Angot* and Arthur Sullivan and W. S. Gilbert's Dramatic Cantata 'TRIAL BY JURY.'" All communications were to be addressed to Mr. R. D'Oyly Carte. And so the first tour of a Gilbert and Sullivan opera, organized by D'Oyly Carte, was set on its way. The tour went to Manchester, Nottingham, Sheffield, Liverpool, Newcastle-on-Tyne, then back to Manchester and Sheffield again: a total period of ten weeks in England before crossing the Irish Sea to Dublin, where the company opened on 5 September at the Gaiety Theatre.[1]

The owners of the Gaiety, Dublin, were John and Michael Gunn. John Gunn managed the Gaiety and Michael Gunn the Theatre Royal. Carte interested Michael Gunn in his work and also interested Helen Lenoir, a young actress in the Theatre Royal company who had previously played at the Gaiety Theatre, Glasgow, in *The Great Divorce Case*. They both listened eagerly to Carte as he told them about his dreams for comic opera in England. Helen Lenoir was sufficiently intrigued to accept Carte's offer to work for him and to join Frank Desprez, his assistant, in the agency in Craig's Court. Michael Gunn and his cousin, George Edwardes, were to follow later when Carte became more established. Gunn did not confine his interest to Carte and his plans for the future; he was also attracted by one of the members of the touring company called Bessie Sudlow, who was shortly to become Mrs. Gunn.

Helen Lenoir was the stage name of Helen Couper-Black, twenty-three years of age and daughter of the procurator fiscal of Wigtown in Dumfries and Galloway.[2] She had been on the stage for less than a year when she met Carte, having completed three years as a student at University College London, in 1874. She proved to be invaluable to Carte. Whereas Carte was the man of ideas and grand schemes, a risk taker, energetic, persuasive, and a rapid talker, Helen Lenoir had an unerring eye for detail, was patient, calm, tactful, and conciliatory. Both of them were, in today's term, "workaholics." They proved a formidable team, and it is important to recognize that Miss Lenoir was there from the beginning of the venture, and her role in the success of Gilbert and Sullivan (and D'Oyly Carte) is inestimable.

In the summer, Gilbert undertook his usual militia training, which took place in 1875 at Redhill, a piece of moorland about ten miles from Aberdeen. The highlight of the year for the Royal Aberdeenshire Highlanders was a change in regimental dress: from that year Gilbert donned the kilt as part of his uniform.[3] Now he could dance a reel with his kilt twirling about his legs. After the rigors of military training, Gilbert returned to Kitty and a quiet summer vacation taken that year at Trouville and Boulogne.

Sullivan's continental trips took him further afield. In July, he escorted Mrs. Grant and her children, now including a new baby, together with a nurse and maid, for part of her journey to the German spa at Kissingen. Sullivan's intention was to accompany them as far as Cologne, but Mrs. Grant fell ill on the journey, and he felt obliged to stay with them all the way to Kissingen to make sure they arrived safely before leaving them and heading for his own destination, Paris. After a short stay he returned to London, but within a fortnight was off to the continent again, traveling with the Lindsays to Cadenabbia on Lake Como. They made the long, uncomfortable, and exhausting crossing of the Alps by carriage and then drove down into Italy, where Sullivan luxuriated in the warm climate. "This morning Lindsay & I got up & bathed in the Lake at *six o'clock*," he wrote to his mother. "Then we returned to bed for two or three hours & dozed. Breakfast at 9.30. Since then we have been largely writing letters. Our rooms are en suite overlooking the Lake, with a wide stone covered in balcony which makes a beautiful room, & where we sit & take our meals. It is all very beautiful and very sweetly lazy."[4]

At the end of his Italian vacation Sullivan returned to Paris, staying there three weeks and meeting up with Mrs. Grant and her family again. Once more he came to the assistance of Mrs. Grant, offering to escort her son Douglas to England, where the boy was to spend a year at school.

In the autumn, Gilbert was hard at work on his next two plays. Carl Rosa had recovered sufficiently after the loss of his wife, to return to his company and had asked Gilbert and Sullivan to write a two-act comic opera for him. Gilbert replied on 4 October telling him that he was already working on two plays: one for his friend John Hare at the Court, which would keep him busy until 1 December, and the other for the actor Edward Sothern, which would take him to 1 January 1876. After that, Gilbert would be prepared not to take on any new work until March so that he could work on the libretto for Carl Rosa. He estimated that the principal numbers would be ready for Sullivan by 1 February.

The Royalty reopened on 11 October. *Trial by Jury* still appeared as the afterpiece to *La Périchole*; and Fred Sullivan was still playing the Learned Judge, but from September he had been feeling weak and unwell, the first ominous signs of his tuberculosis. Gilbert and Sullivan's one-act piece was more than holding its own alongside the immensely popular Offenbach. Whereas Offenbach's opera was a foreign import set in Lima, in distant Peru, *Trial by Jury* was set in London and was homegrown. It was outdoing the French at opéra bouffe; a follow-up was essential. But was the next piece of English comic opera to come from Sullivan and Gilbert, or was it to be Gilbert and Benedict? Although he had two pieces in hand, and had put off Carl Rosa until the following spring, Gilbert was tempted by the possibility of working on an opera with Sir Julius Benedict.

In October, Gilbert was in correspondence with Benedict, but by December it was clear that taking on anything extra at that time was out of the question. Reluctantly, he wrote to Benedict again, expressing his regret but hoping they would be able to collaborate in the future.

Carte's hopes of bringing Gilbert and Sullivan together again were facing stiff opposition. He may have brought them together once, but that was no guarantee of being able to do so again. Gilbert and Sullivan were two decidedly independent spirits, each at the top of his profession; Carte was a theatrical agent, with some management experience, but with no permanent theater at his disposal, and without the financial resources to set up the kind of company he had in mind. Nevertheless Carte, more aware than anyone of the Gilbert and Sullivan potential, entered into the lists competing for their work. With George Dolby, another theatrical agent, he looked for financial backing to put on a revival of *Thespis* at the Criterion before Christmas. Gilbert contacted Sullivan:

> They seem very anxious to have it and wanted me to name definite terms. Of course I couldn't answer for *you*, but they pressed me so much to give them an idea of what our terms would be likely to be that I suggested that possibly we might be disposed to accept two guineas a night *each* with a guarantee of 100 nights minimum. Does this meet your views, & if so, could you get it done in time. I am going to re-write a considerable portion of the dialogue.[5]

D'Oyly Carte and Selina Dolaro had given up management of the Royalty; their place had been taken by Charles Morton, the old music-hall impresario. Gilbert reminded Morton that for every copy of the libretto sold in the theater he received 2 pence under an agreement with Madame Dolaro, and assumed the agreement would continue. The weekly check for 18 guineas continued to reach Gilbert during the run of *Trial by Jury*; and he regularly passed on 9 guineas to Sullivan. Short business letters were a commonplace between the two men at this period; on 9 November, Gilbert added to his letter the comment, "No news of Thespis."[6] Again on 11 November, he added "No news about Thespis,"[7] and then on 23 November wrote, "I have heard no more about Thespis. It is astonishing how quickly these capitalists dry up under the magic influence of the words 'cash down.' "[8] This was not a reference to Carte but to the financial backers Carte had been trying to persuade to put their money into the revival of *Thespis*.

A new "star" appeared in the cast of *Trial by Jury* in November, when W. S. Penley, aged twenty-three, took over as the Foreman of the Jury. He was a natural comedian and captivated the audience with his facial expressions and vocal inflection in the few solo lines the Foreman has in the piece. In the same month, a pirate version of *Trial by Jury* opened in New York at the Eagle Theatre and, to Gilbert's particular annoyance, a pirate version of the libretto went on sale.

In the early hours of the same day, Gilbert noted at the end of the manuscript that he had been writing for a year for the Court Theatre, "Finished Monday 15th November, 1875, at 12.40 a.m. Thank God."[9] The play was *Broken Hearts*, in which Gilbert said he had invested a great part of himself as well as a great part of his time. Gilbert was particularly sensitive about the play and it was to lead to some battered, even broken friendships. He sent an advance copy of the play to his old friend Clement Scott, now editor of the *Theatre*, who was initially pleased with it. Gilbert told Scott that he was determined to show he was not devoid of "a mysterious quality called 'sympathy' . . . with what success, remains to be seen."[10]

Gilbert's *Broken Hearts*, "An entirely original fairy play," is set in "a tropical landscape," on an island where a group of women have fled the old world after their hearts had been broken through the loss of their lovers. The only male presence allowed is that of their servant, "a deformed ill-favoured dwarf, hump-backed and one-eyed" and therefore no threat to their maidenhood. Peace is shattered by the arrival of Prince Florian, who through his own thoughtlessness and selfish behavior brings unhappiness to the community and hastens the death of one of the women. It has been said that in conversation with the American actress Mary Anderson, Gilbert claimed he had put more of his real self into *Broken Hearts* than any other play,[11] but it is in the realm of ideas rather than in the development of character that Gilbert reveals anything of himself in the play. It is the "wicked world" again, in which, into a tranquil world of women, a man enters, bringing "mortal love" to disturb the tranquillity.

As Gilbert's most serious play and the one he had the highest opinion of, *Broken Hearts* cannot be said to explore the depths of human emotion. It reveals little of romantic love, and what he described to Clement Scott as "the mysterious quality called sympathy" only appears now as sentimentality. *Broken Hearts* shows the essential seriousness of Gilbert: he saw the world about him as seriously flawed. He tried creating alternative worlds. At the serious level his success was partial and temporary; but in creating crazy worlds to which his audience could escape for a few hours of laughter, he was to be preeminently successful.

Gilbert had written *Broken Hearts* for his great friend John Hare. Hare liked to direct the plays at his theater and Gilbert always insisted on "stage managing" his own plays; consequently they clashed at rehearsals. They were both quick-tempered men, although they could calm down just as quickly. Their friendship survived—on

Richard D'Oyly Carte (V&A Picture Library)

this occasion. *Broken Hearts* opened on 9 December 1875; Gilbert managed at the last moment to get two returned stalls for Sullivan who had dashed down from Glasgow in order to be at the opening night.[12] The play was generally well reviewed but Clement Scott in a later article mentioned Burnand's joke about going to see "Broken Parts," which stung Gilbert into calling his comments "most offensive, and likely to cause a great deal of injury to my play." He described "Burnand's attempt at wit is silly and coarse. . . . I am not by any means a thin-skinned man, but in this case I feel bound to take exception to your treatment of me and my serious work."[13]

Sullivan's hasty trip to London had taken him away from Glasgow, where he had been appointed conductor of the Glasgow Choral and Orchestral Union for a series of concerts in the city hall, over a period of six weeks beginning on Tuesday 16 November 1875. Other venues had been arranged: in one week alone he conducted in Greenock, Dundee, and Perth, as well as the concert in Glasgow.

While he was away, he was having his apartment in Albert Mansions decorated throughout and insisted that his mother move out, suggesting that she stay at the Grosvenor Hotel in nearby Buckingham Palace Road. No doubt she spent Christmas that year with Fred and Charlotte and the grandchildren, while Sullivan preferred to stay in Scotland and spend the time with the Lindsays at Balcarres. "Christmas day was beautiful and we had a tree in the afternoon for the servants," he told his mother. "Yesterday, Lindsay & I went for a long walk along the seashore. The view of the Firth of Forth at this moment is divine from my window."[14]

The end of Gilbert's year was punctuated with a lively correspondence with the "Royal Aquarium & Summer & Winter Garden Society, Limited," which was being established on a site opposite Westminster Abbey. Sullivan had accepted the post of director of music and was appointed to the committee; Gilbert had been approached by the secretary, Wybrow Robertson, husband of Marie Litton, asking him to lend his name to the society by becoming a Fellow on payment of 5 guineas. Now, in December, he was asked to pay "seven guineas entrance fee & subscription of two guineas." Gilbert considered that this request differed from the original request, and he objected.[15]

A bitter exchange of letters followed between Gilbert and Wybrow Robertson. At one stage, Robertson offered to pay Gilbert's 2 guineas for him. "I am not in the habit of asking any one . . . to pay my debts for me," replied Gilbert. "If I owe the money I will pay it myself—if I don't owe it, I will not rest until I have obtained the privileges I claim without it."[16] If it was a matter of justice, then Gilbert would pursue it to the end.

The executive committee meanwhile revised the question of fees and announced that the Council of Fellows would be exempted from paying any entrance fee. Nevertheless, the dispute between Gilbert and Robertson rolled on; Gilbert would not let it rest, even writing two letters on Christmas Day. The board of directors disclaimed any responsibility for what Wybrow Robertson may have said to Gilbert, and in the end Gilbert had to accept their position. He paid his 2 guineas subscription and sent a long letter to the chairman of the directors recapitulating the correspondence, but it was not until his final letter on 30 January 1876 that he felt he had had his say. This long-running argument had started on 2 December, while Gilbert was in the middle of rehearsing *Broken Hearts*. This was not an example of the hot-blooded Gilbert, angrily responding on the spur of the moment. It was a sustained attack, over a period of nearly two months, returning to the argument again and again. He was not driven by raw anger but by a sense of justice mingled with a liberal portion of wanting to prove himself right by winning the argument.

Two episodes that occurred around this time serve to illustrate Gilbert's sense of justice. The first concerned an Italian organ-grinder, by the name of Paolo Frati, who refused to go away from Essex Villas when Gilbert unmistakably signaled to him to do so. Gilbert had the man arrested. Frati was later charged, and the next day at the Hammersmith Police Court was fined 10 shillings, which included 5 shillings for an interpreter. Gilbert then paid both the fine and the costs.[17] To have given the man a penny would have been much easier, but then Gilbert would not have won the argument.

In the second episode, Gilbert's footman, James Saunders, who was moving on to a new situation, was suspected of trying to leave with his uniform inside his portmanteau. As Saunders was about to leave the house, Kitty stopped him and asked him to empty his bag. Inside was the uniform. To make matters worse, Gilbert found that the man had been wearing his shirts and socks and had, on the day of his departure, helped himself from Gilbert's cigars out of the box in his study. Gilbert felt honor-bound "from a strict sense of justice" to point this out to the man's new employer, but finished his letter to him by saying, "I may add that I shall be glad to learn that you do not consider my charges against Saunders to be so grave as to render your employing him out of the question."[18] Gilbert had already written to Saunders telling him what he proposed doing, saying that he was happy to give him "an excellent general character." But it was his duty, he told him, to relate the circumstances to the new employer for him to evaluate.[19]

Gilbert was struggling with contrary emotions: to do the right thing out of a sense of duty, and at the same time to avoid causing permanent damage to the offending person. Time and time again, we find Gilbert fighting hard to win the argument, and if he wins he enjoys being magnanimous in victory. If he loses, and he often loses, he accepts the decision, but not with bowed head and certainly not in silence.

After *Broken Hearts*, the second piece that Gilbert had contracted to write was a play for Edward Sothern, who had made his reputation by his comic portrayal of Lord Dundreary in Tom Taylor's highly successful *Our American Cousin*. Sothern had written to Gilbert in April, saying that he was taking over the management of the Haymarket and wanted a piece for December. "As I shall not be in it we cannot get at Loggerheads," he pointed out.[20] It was agreed that the play "Abel Druce" would be ready by the end of December. That deadline was not met, and even in January, Gilbert was asking for an extension until the end of February. "It is simply from anxiety to do it thoroughly well," he told Sothern.[21]

Trial by Jury was now coming toward the end of its run at the Royalty. At the end of November, *La Périchole* had been replaced by Lecocq's *La Fille de Madame Angot*, which would see out the rest of the season. On 2 December, Charles Morton called on Gilbert to tell him that he was taking over as manager of the Opera Comique after Christmas, "& he wants to know our terms for 'Trial by Jury' for 50 or 60 nights there," Gilbert said in a letter to Sullivan. "I told him I would consult you & let him know. I should think £2 a night, if he guarantees 60 nights, would be enough[.] Dont you think so?"[22] Sullivan agreed to 2 *guineas* per performance, for not less than fifty performances.

Selina Dolaro's season at the Royalty ended on 18 December, by which time *Trial by Jury* had completed 131 performances, and Gilbert and Sullivan had settled with Morton to put the piece on at the Opera Comique in January 1876. Carte had missed out again: his plans for a revival of *Thespis* had fallen through because of a lack of funding and now his mind turned to commissioning a new piece from Gilbert and Sullivan. In the middle of December, he approached Gilbert, who set out terms. "I have no doubt," Gilbert assured him, "that the piece could be put into your hands, completed in every respect, in the course of March."[23]

During Gilbert's negotiations with Morton and then Carte, Sullivan had been in Scotland; after his Christmas stay with the Lindsays he had returned to Glasgow for an extra concert on New Year's Day when his *Di Ballo* overture was included in the program. He then returned to London; not to Albert Mansions, as the decorators were still there, but to temporary accommodation at 2 Albert Street, Victoria Square, just behind the Royal Mews. Neither Gilbert nor Carte lost any time in contacting him. Gilbert wrote on Tuesday 4 January 1876, "I'll be with you by 11 on Wednesday—so that we can discuss the matter, before Carte arrives."[24]

Trial by Jury made its appearance at the Opera Comique on 13 January, following Offenbach's *Madame L'Archiduc*. Fred Sullivan and W. S. Penley were in their old parts and the musical director for this run was Hamilton Clarke, who, with the stage manager Richard Barker, was to work with Gilbert and Sullivan in later pieces.

For the present, Sullivan's mind was occupied with other concerns. Royal pressure had been brought to bear on him to accept the position of "Professional Director" of the new National Training School for Music. Sullivan did not want the post: he was not a natural administrator, he hated teaching, and his own inclination and judgment pointed him in the opposite direction. He was also aware that he did not have the unanimous support of the committee, which had been established to direct the institution. He was officially offered the post on Saturday 8 January, and initially turned down the offer. On 12 January, he went to see Sir Henry Cole, the prime mover in establishing the school of music, and talked through his anxieties. Cole satisfied him on his concerns about the support of the committee and on 13 January, the day *Trial by Jury* opened at the Opera Comique, Sullivan replied to the duke of Edinburgh. He wrote two letters, an unofficial letter in which he told the duke of Edinburgh about his doubts and his difficulty in accepting the post; and an official letter accepting the post of professor of composition and principal "acting in concert with the Board of principal Professors." He assured the duke that he would devote his "best energies to the School in the hope that it may become recognized by the State." The fee for his services during the first year was to be £400.[25]

At the same time, Gilbert was having problems with Charles Morton. Morton had been selling Gilbert's libretto at the Opera Comique for 1½d instead of 2d as at the Royalty. "I shall be obliged by a cheque for the balance at your convenience," wrote

Gilbert on 26 January 1876, adding, "I will see Sullivan at once about the two act piece."[26] So Carte had another competitor for the work of Gilbert and Sullivan.

After consultation and dinner at Gilbert's house in Essex Villas on Sunday 6 February, Gilbert and Sullivan wrote a joint letter to Morton, dated 7 February 1876, saying they were prepared to write a piece for the Opera Comique and stipulating 4 guineas a night, with a guaranteed minimum of "120 performances in town & country, within eight months of first production."[27] The dinner at Essex Villas had not been all business. A complaint from Gilbert's elderly next-door neighbor that Gilbert was in the habit of holding parties every Sunday evening suggests that on 6 February a good deal of laughter traveled through the walls of Essex Villas.

Meanwhile, Carte had been in touch with both Gilbert and Sullivan. Gilbert wrote to Sullivan on 15 February. "I have heard from Carte. He is going to Charing X & wants the one act piece as soon as possible. Have you told him about 'money down'"?[28]

Further progress had been made with the proposal of an opera for Charles Morton: a draft agreement had been sent to Gilbert, which he in turn sent off to Sullivan for his approval on 28 February. Shortly after, Sullivan left for Paris. The trip was partly business, in the hope of arranging a performance of his symphony, a hope that was unrealized; and partly for pleasure, including a visit to the newly finished Opéra to see a performance of Gounod's *Jeanne d'Arc*—a disappointment to Sullivan.

Gilbert told Carte on 1 March that he and Sullivan were ready to begin work on their one act "Bouffe." There was no reply from Carte for a week; he was unable to raise the "money down" that Gilbert and Sullivan had demanded, but he was still hoping to keep them to their agreement to write a piece for him. "Now this won't do," wrote Gilbert on 11 March, "either for Sullivan or myself: if we're to be businesslike, you must be businesslike too. . . . [w]e can't hold ourselves at your disposal whenever you want us."[29]

After all Gilbert's efforts to write a play for Edward Sothern at the Haymarket, Sothern had suddenly changed his mind and gone to America. From New York on 10 February he had written to Gilbert asking him to write another play to be ready in October. This time Sothern wanted to act in it himself and wanted Gilbert to write him a serious part, different from anything else he had done. "I hope you will see your way to this—," he told Gilbert, "for I know no one else who can write me the class of piece I so much want—."[30] By this time Gilbert was well into act 3 of "Abel Druce," yet without complaint he agreed to write another play for Sothern—but at a price.

For Pygmalion I have already received, from all sources, about £5000. The Wicked World has brought me £2000, nearly—The Palace of Truth about £2200. From "Broken Hearts"—a financial failure here, I am already assured £1000. I mention this to prepare your mind for my asking a larger sum for the sole & entire right of my new piece. For that right, for ten years, I want 2000 guineas — to be paid as follows 1000 guineas on delivery of MS. the balance within one year of such delivery.[31]

Confident in Gilbert's ability, Sothern agreed. "My faith in you is great — or I wd. not so unreservedly agree to all you stipulate."[32]

By the end of March, problems had arisen over arriving at an agreement with Charles Morton. Gilbert had received a draft agreement from Morton's solicitor but found it unsatisfactory. Although Sullivan was still in Paris, Gilbert was confident he was acting for both of them when he wrote to Morton declining "any further fruitless correspondence on the subject." If Morton could not agree to the terms set out by Gilbert and Sullivan, then they would have no difficulty in finding a manager who would.[33] Morton did not pursue the matter any further, and shortly afterward gave up the management of the Opera Comique.

Trial by Jury ended its run on 5 May 1876, after ninety-six performances at the Opera Comique. There were two more performances on 13 and 23 May at Alexandra Palace, Wood Green, where it was advertised as "with the original cast," probably meaning the cast from the Opera Comique. Fred Sullivan, in poor health, had left the cast in March, and his place as the Judge had been taken over by W. S. Penley. With the backing of Tom Chappell, Fred Sullivan now entered the competition for the opportunity to manage a Gilbert and Sullivan piece. Arrangements were well advanced by 14 May, when Gilbert wrote to Fred, "I have arranged with your brother to do The Wedding March as a burlesque opera & to set about it at once. I'll get the first act ready by the end of next week — say the third June, & the piece will be finished, as far as I can see, by the fifteenth June."[34]

Why this particular project fell through is not known. Perhaps the state of Fred Sullivan's health made it impossible for him to continue with his plan. It was the latest in a lengthening line of failed attempts to produce a follow-up to *Trial by Jury*. Only one man had not given up despite two failed attempts: Richard D'Oyly Carte — and he was determined to succeed.

CHAPTER TEN

1876

· ◆⋟⟵⟶◯ ◯⟵⟶⟨◆ ·

Sullivan Is Honored; Gilbert Is Ridiculed

SULLIVAN CAME BACK FROM France to the affairs of the National Training School for Music. The school was formally opened by Queen Victoria on 16 April and on 13 May the queen made an official visit with her eldest daughter Princess Victoria. To Sullivan's relief, he was to be called principal of the school, rather than given the clumsy title of professional director, which had first been suggested.

For much of the year, Sullivan divided his time between the School of Music and the Royal Aquarium, supervising the musical arrangements and conducting concerts there every Thursday. The Aquarium was not a success and Sullivan was glad to resign and free himself from the regular commitment. More important to him was the autumn series of concerts he was soon to conduct in Glasgow. The season started on 21 November when he conducted extracts from *The Light of the World*, and lasted for five weeks when he included in the final program part of *The Tempest*.

He was now Dr. Sullivan. To give him an appropriate title to match his academic position, Sullivan had been awarded the honorary degree of doctor of music by Cambridge University in June. He shared his pride with his mother, writing to her from Trinity College, Cambridge: "Dearest Mum . . .The deed is done and I am Mus. Doc.," and signing off, "God Bless you, y[ours] affectly. AS. Mus. Doc."[1]

Gilbert's relations with his mother could not be more different at this time. Part of the correspondence between them has survived, despite Gilbert's practice of not keeping personal correspondence. That some letters survive at all suggests either that Gilbert considered them as business correspondence, or possibly, as they survived his mother's death, that he wanted to preserve something of hers.

Mr. and Mrs. Gilbert had been married for forty years and had come to the conclusion that it would be better if they lived apart. Gilbert was of the opinion that a quarrel was the cause of his parents' rift; his mother said that this was not the case. Certainly, Gilbert senior was, in the words of one of his granddaughters who lived with him, "a tempestuous old gentleman, but," she added, "very kind to us children."[2] Mrs. Gilbert insisted to her son that the separation "was the result of weeks of calm deliberation and entirely against the wishes as he and you well know of your sisters and myself—He left home of his own accord and without the slightest reason and is of course at liberty to return if he chooses."[3] Her son took this at its face value and assumed that she would take him back. Not so; now that he had left, she did not want him back.

At the time of the separation, Gilbert senior had legally assigned the house in Pembridge Gardens to his wife. In addition, he allowed her £400 a year for household expenses and made a separate allowance of £400 a year to his two daughters, Florence and Maude. At that time, he hoped to earn enough for himself from his writing, but fell seriously ill and was close to death. When he recovered, his doctors told him he should not return to writing, and so his income was reduced to about £150 or £160 a year. Gilbert junior asked his mother to reconsider the situation, as his father's income was now insufficient for him to live "like a gentleman." He suggested that she either allow him the use of two rooms in her house, or give up some of her allowance for him. Other members of the family, Gilbert's aunt (presumably Harriet Edwards, his mother's sister), and his own sister Jane and her husband, who were looking after Gilbert senior in Salisbury, also appealed to her on her husband's behalf. Her reaction to these appeals, her son termed "cold and formal."[4] Gilbert made one last appeal to his mother: ". . . it is impossible to disregard the fact that he has been *most dangerously* ill—that he is still in a very delicate state of health—that he is in his 73rd. year—that he has no settled home." Within the last fortnight, Gilbert claimed, his father had "given practical proof of his great interest" in the welfare of his wife and daughters. "I mention this to show you that he, at all events, is not entirely lost to those feelings of regard which forty years of intimate association must have aroused in the mind of any person not absolutely lost to all feeling of humanity."[5]

When it was finally clear to Gilbert that his mother was not to be moved, he wrote his final letter to her, on Tuesday 6 June 1876, addressing her simply as "Madam,

> . . . I shall proceed to Salisbury on Wednesday, & lay the whole correspondence before him. I may add that I have hitherto, in your interests, induced him to believe that when he was in danger of his life, you hurried home from Paris, & were unremitting in your personal enquiries after him, until he was pronounced out of danger. It will now be my duty to tell him the bare facts of the case—that you delayed two days in Paris after receiving a copy of Dr Coates' letter describing the perilous state of his health, & that on his return you exhibited no interest whatever in his critical condition.[6]

That is the last recorded contact between Gilbert and his mother. His father continued to live in Salisbury with Jane and her family and he visited his son regularly. He did write again, publishing another half-dozen books by 1882, including his

Memoirs of a Cynic. He had been a difficult husband, and his own son had spoken "seriously to him on the error he committed in endeavouring to impose unnecessary restrictions" on his wife and daughters;[7] but it is also clear that the difficulties were not all one-sided. Anne Gilbert had been abandoned by the three men who were closest to her: her husband, her son, and, most significantly of all, by her own father thirty years earlier.

At the same time as these family matters were being discussed, Gilbert was preparing for a move from Essex Villas. In mid-May he sold one of his houses, 297 Edgware Road, for £850 and a week later he offered £4,075 for the ground lease of 24 The Boltons, a large semidetached villa with a garden big enough for a tennis court. The Boltons was the centerpiece of an estate built south of the Old Brompton Road, and consisted of two crescents of imposing stuccoed villas, with the Church of St. Mary in the middle.

Gilbert set out his requirements for the builder before he took up residence: a marble chimney piece to be installed in the main bedroom and double-glazing for the study window to deaden the sound of St. Mary's church bell. While the alterations were being carried out, Gilbert went off to join the Royal Aberdeenshire Highlanders for a fortnight, having been given leave for the first fortnight of the training session that took place that year at Redhill.

Gilbert and Kitty had moved into The Boltons by 23 July, and two days later Gilbert wrote from his new address questioning the mess bill he had received from the regiment. It seemed to him that he was being charged for a whole month instead of the fortnight he spent with them. He wanted to know if all officers who were on leave "were placed on the same footing," otherwise, he said, "I must decline to pay for more messing than I actually enjoyed—if that term can be reasonably applied to the food that was placed before me by the messman. There is an item of £1.3.9 for beer. I never touch beer. Possibly this may include spirits. I certainly did not drink 50 glasses of brandy during the twelve days I was with the regiment."[8]

The argument dragged on without Gilbert receiving satisfaction and on 17 October he offered to resign his commission. His commanding officer, Colonel Innes, endeavored to pacify him. Gilbert, however, thought that in resigning his commission he was taking the only step, he told Colonel Innes, that was "consistent with the preservation of my self-respect."[9] In the end Gilbert was prevailed on to withdraw his resignation and he continued to serve in the regiment for a little longer.

On 11 September 1876, Gilbert's play, which he had originally written for Edward Sothern under the title "Abel Druce," and that he now called *Dan'l Druce*, opened at the Haymarket. The cast included Hermann Vezin, Forbes Robertson, and Marion Terry—now nineteen years old—as Dorothy. Gilbert acknowledged that the plot was in part inspired by George Eliot's *Silas Marner*, but his development of the idea is original. One of his characters, Reuben Haines, "a sergeant of horse," is of particular interest as a forerunner of Jack Point. His patter trips merrily off his tongue as he courts Dorothy: "If thou wilt be my wife I will so coll thee, coax thee, cosset thee, court thee, cajole thee, with deftly turned compliment, pleasant whimsy, delicate jest and tuneful madrigal." Reuben also knows the pain of rejection: he is given a line that is gratuitous in the context of the play, but significant given Gilbert's recent correspondence with his mother—"My mother always disliked me and kept me at a distance; but *she* was a Scotchwoman and not liable to be imposed on."[10]

Three weeks later, on 2 October, *Princess Toto*, a comic opera by Gilbert and Fred Clay, opened at the Strand Theatre. It had already had a trial run in the provinces, opening at the Theatre Royal, Nottingham, on 1 July. Clay had bought a ten-year lease on the acting and publishing rights from Gilbert for £525.[11] Gilbert was not involved in the stage management, nor in the casting, and disagreed with the casting of Kate Santley as Princess Toto. To avoid any criticism being leveled at him, he made it publicly known that the play was Clay's property, and that it had been Clay's decision to stage the piece.

Gilbert's major preoccupation at that time was his play for Edward Sothern, *The Ne'er-do-Weel*. Even before he had sent him the manuscript, Gilbert received Sothern's check for £1,000. He was reluctant to let his name appear as the author of the play, preferring to see whether it would succeed on its own merits. Sothern thought differently: he wanted the pull that Gilbert's name would bring. The play was not yet finished; Gilbert was still having difficulty with the last act, and was about to rewrite it: "in justice to us both I won't hurry it," he assured Sothern.[12] Sothern had every confidence but tried again to impress on Gilbert how important it was that his name should appear as the author.

Gilbert was not convinced, "With the enormous value of your name in the cast, there will be no need of mine," he told him.[13] But Sothern persisted. He suggested that the work should be in both their names, and as Sothern was now a naturalized American he could copyright the play. When Sothern eventually received the play, he changed his mind. He saw weaknesses in it, and wrote to Gilbert offering to return the play and pay a forfeit of £500. He made several suggestions for improving the play and pleaded, "I hope you won't swear at me in your heart, but I have been building up such hopes on this play."[14]

Sothern's letter came as a bitter disappointment, not least because of the money involved, "& counting on the dead certainty of receiving it," Gilbert told him, "I have made arrangements which I should have the greatest difficulty in cancelling."[15] Gilbert's expensive move to The Boltons had depended on Sothern's money. He suggested that instead of returning £500 to him (the £1,000 received from Sothern less the forfeit of £500), he would play the piece and give one-half of the fees to Sothern until he had paid back the £500 he owed. On the same day, Sothern sent a slightly revised letter to Gilbert, confusing the situation. "The more I read yr. comedy the more I like it—but the part of Roll makes me nervous—however I shall play it in N.Y. & we'll see the result."[16] For the time being at least, *The Ne'er-do-Weel* was back in Edward Sothern's court.

Throughout all this correspondence, no sign appears of Gilbert's famous anger.

Toward Sothern, an extremely nervous man who changed his mind from one letter to the next, who was eager to succeed in a new role but terrified of failing, Gilbert was patient and understanding, anxious to write a play that would please him. His attitude to Henrietta Hodson was of a different order and now this particular problem had resurfaced.

Buckstone had taken over the management of the Haymarket again after a short spell by John S. Clarke. He planned to put on *Pygmalion and Galatea* and wrote to Gilbert suggesting a cast that included Henrietta Hodson in the part of Cynisca. Gilbert objected because, he said, "it is impossible to stage manage a piece satisfactorily when the stage manager (in this case myself) & a leading actress are not on speaking terms."[17] Threatened with legal action by Miss Hodson's solicitors, Gilbert waived his objection. He claimed that he had not known that Miss Hodson already had an engagement as a member of the Haymarket company. He wrote to Miss Hodson on 29 November, explaining what had happened and concluded, "I have only to add that I have no desire to injure you, either in your profession or out of it, & that if you are willing to meet me, for the purposes of this rehearsal, on friendly terms, the ground of my solitary objection is at once removed."[18]

Three days before the first rehearsal, called for 6 December, Gilbert wrote to Buckstone. He presumed that Marion Terry, whom he had coached at home, was to play the part of Galatea. "I suppose Miss Hodson plays 'Cynisca'—but I have not heard from her."[19]

Gilbert had supposed incorrectly: Henrietta Hodson claimed that as she was the leading lady of the Haymarket company, the part of Galatea was hers by right. After an explanation from Gilbert, Marion Terry surrendered her claim to the part, and Gilbert notified Henrietta Hodson that he withdrew his objection to her playing Galatea. Having won her point, Miss Hodson reverted to the role of Cynisca.

When it came to rehearsals, Gilbert asked the stage manager, Henry Howe, to observe his conduct and to check him if there were "any act or word which may smack of discourtesy towards that lady."[20] In practice, partly to avoid conflict and at the same time to show his coolness toward her without being literally discourteous, Gilbert gave Henrietta Hodson little or no direction in rehearsal. Eventually, *Pygmalion and Galatea* took the stage and all appeared to be at peace.

Buckstone's next revival at the Haymarket was to be *The Palace of Truth*. After discussion with Gilbert, Buckstone offered Henrietta Hodson the part of Mirza. Miss Hodson insisted that she was entitled to play the part of Zeolide, the part originally played by Madge Robertson. Gilbert told Buckstone that he had no objection to Miss Hodson as Zeolide, provided Buckstone could find "an efficient Mirza . . . Mirza is a part that requires a [strong] actress with a thorough command of the stage—whereas Zeolide is a part that an intelligent young lady with Miss Terry's personal advantages could be trained to play."[21]

On the same day, Gilbert wrote to Miss Hodson expressing the same views. To protect himself from future criticism, Gilbert asked Buckstone to put it in writing that his decision had not been influenced by him. Buckstone obliged by writing that he did not require Miss Hodson's services for the next season, and added, "she is too expensive."[22]

Henrietta Hodson was furious and wrote to Buckstone convinced that Gilbert was behind his decision, claiming that Gilbert had been persecuting her and intended to drive her out of the theater. Gilbert rejected her allegations, sending her a copy of his correspondence with Buckstone, saying he left it to her solicitor to explain that she had no case against him. If she did decide to go to court, Gilbert told her, "I have only to express my most earnest desire that the question between us may be finally settled by a jury."[23] The following day Gilbert passed on copies of his carefully compiled correspondence to George Lewis, Miss Hodson's solicitor.

Advised by Lewis that she had no case against Gilbert, Henrietta Hodson decided on an alternative way to attack him. In April she published a pamphlet: *A Letter from Miss Henrietta Hodson, An Actress to The members of the Dramatic Profession, being a relation of the Persecution which she has suffered from Mr. William Schwenck Gilbert, A Dramatic Author*. Her tactic was to go outside the documentary evidence of letters written by the people involved in the dispute, which on their own did not give her a case for Gilbert to answer, and to build her case on reported conversations, which could not be substantiated, but that would be damaging to Gilbert, whether they were accurate or not. She referred to conversations with Gilbert as early as 1874, when, she said, he had told her "he had invariably quarrelled with every one with whom he had been professionally connected." She claimed he had told her stories of how he had humiliated actresses, including Madge Robertson, and that "before he forgave her, he had forced her to cry and humbly sue for pardon." At the final rehearsal of *Ought We to Visit Her?* she claimed that Gilbert "jumped up, and commenced pulling his hair and dancing like a maniac." When Gilbert had been obliged by her solicitors to sign an apology, she claimed, Gilbert "appeared in a position approaching madness." As to rehearsals for *Pygmalion and Galatea*, she described his behavior toward her as a studied insult. "He neither spoke to nor looked at me, but only recognised my presence by a distant bow." She said that Kate Terry and Gilbert would sit on the stage while she was rehearsing, and laugh and talk together.

A few weeks later, Gilbert responded by publishing his own pamphlet: *W. S. Gilbert, A Letter addressed to the Members of the Dramatic Profession in reply to Miss Henrietta Hodson's Pamphlet. 18 May 1877*. Gilbert's case kept closely to the evidence that he had carefully collected since the first time that Henrietta Hodson had threatened him with legal action. He ignored the reported conversations with her, but mentioned that Henry Howe was willing to testify that Gilbert's conduct toward her at rehearsals of *Pygmalion and Galatea* had been most courteous. He did not mention the incident about making Madge Robertson (Mrs. Kendal) cry. However, he had already written to Mrs. Kendal to say, "I should be extremely sorry if you believed, for the moment, that I, at any time, made any such statement. . . . I have placed the matter in the hands of my solicitors—in the mean time I must content myself with assuring you that Miss Hodson's statement is entirely false."[24] In his pamphlet, Gilbert quoted from a letter Henrietta Hodson had written him on 3 March, after Buckstone's letter saying that he was not renewing her contract. She had written, "You are fully capable of either having dictated it to him or of having forged it to suit your own purposes." In view of this, said Gilbert, he would never meet her again, and that was the reason she was not in the cast of *The Palace of Truth*.

The long and acrimonious battle was at an end. It had begun when the volatile Gilbert had reacted angrily to Henrietta Hodson at rehearsal; and the equally volatile Miss Hodson had humiliated him. Both were stubborn; neither would take steps toward a reconciliation, and in the end the reputation of each of them was damaged by a private quarrel made public among their fellow professionals.

CHAPTER ELEVEN

The Comedy Opera Company
and *The Sorcerer*

FOR THE SAKE OF HIS HEALTH, Fred Sullivan had moved away from Pimlico to the open spaces of Fulham, to the opposite end of the King's Road from Sloane Square, where he had been born. He rented Northumberland House, a large Georgian house in a short terrace standing on the King's Road itself. He now had seven children: the eldest was thirteen, the youngest two, and Charlotte was expecting her eighth child. By January 1877, Fred had become seriously ill, and as his death drew near, Arthur spent more and more time at Northumberland House. During one of his watches by his brother's bedside, he began to sketch out, to the words of Adelaide Procter, "The Lost Chord," which was to be the best-selling song in the country for many years to come.

Fred Sullivan died on 18 January 1877, aged thirty-nine. His body was laid in the same grave as his father's at Brompton Cemetery and both Gilbert and Fred Clay were among the mourners at his funeral. Mrs. Sullivan moved to Fulham to live with Charlotte and the grandchildren, and no doubt the financial responsibility of supporting the family now fell entirely on Arthur Sullivan. Standards were maintained, however; they continued to live in Northumberland House and kept two servants — a cook and a nurse. Arthur was a regular Sunday visitor, his cousin B. W. Findon recalled, often taking with him Fred Clay or Alfred Cellier, and providing the children with some musical fun.[1] When Fred's last child was born, he was named after Charlotte's brother, William Lacy Sullivan.

In the same year that Arthur Sullivan lost his brother he gained a lifelong friend, Fanny Ronalds. She was an accomplished amateur contralto and her name became closely associated with "The Lost Chord," which she sang frequently at social gatherings. By her own instructions, a manuscript copy of the song was buried with her.

It was obviously of romantic significance to both Sullivan and Fanny Ronalds and marks the time when their friendship began.

Fanny Ronalds, born Mary Frances Carter on 23 August 1839, was a beautiful American from Boston who had married Pierre Lorillard Ronalds in 1859. Later, her name was linked with that of Leonard Jerome, Winston Churchill's grandfather, and she was certainly a frequent visitor to the Jeromes' summer villa in Newport. Jerome's daughter Jennie, who later married Randolph Churchill, remembered Fanny Ronalds singing to them as children at bedtime. When Leonard Jerome's wife, Clarissa, exasperated by her husband's philandering, decided to move to Paris with her daughters, Fanny Ronalds did likewise, taking her two children, Fanny and Regie. It was in Paris that Sullivan first met her in 1867 and recalled years later to his nephew Herbert how, at that time "all Paris . . . from the Emperor downwards was at her feet."[2] Allowing for the inflated language, that meant that a number of extremely wealthy, and probably married, Frenchmen (among them Napoleon III) were vying at the very least for her attention, if not for her favors. When the empire fell and the empress Eugénie fled to England, Fanny Ronalds followed her current lover to Algiers, where she became part of the court of the Bey, before moving to England and settling finally in London.[3] At 7 Cadogan Place, in the heartland of red-and-white Victorian architecture, she became well known for her Sunday soirees, where Fanny sang and Sullivan played, and where her beauty is said to have attracted the attention of the prince of Wales.

The relationship of Sullivan and Fanny Ronalds was to last, despite stormy passages, until Sullivan's death twenty-three years later. Fanny was in no position to seek a divorce; the ensuing scandal would make it out of the question. In public, Mr. Sullivan and Mrs. Ronalds were friends; privately, everybody was aware that they were lovers. That arrangement may well have suited Sullivan who did not want the ties of married life. Whether it suited Fanny Ronalds we shall never know; there was no alternative, given the social thinking of the time.

FIFTY BAB BALLADS, with the original drawings, was officially published by Routledge in 1877 but had already made its appearance before Christmas. Gilbert had also rewritten his comedy *Committed for Trial*, which was produced as *On Bail* by Charles Wyndham at the Criterion Theatre on 3 February 1877, with limited success, lasting only five weeks. Gilbert gave a small boost to his income, however, by selling, in what had become a lean period for him, the country rights of three of his plays: *Pygmalion and Galatea*, *The Wicked World*, and *The Wedding March*, for a grand total of £78.[4]

Two years had passed since the opening of *Trial by Jury*, and no follow-up had materialized despite the early attempts to capitalize on their success. Gilbert and Sullivan next came together when, on 1 March 1877, *Trial by Jury* made another appearance, as part of a benefit performance in aid of Henry Compton, a famous comic actor of the day and grandfather of the writer Compton Mackenzie. Guest performers added to the interest, with Gilbert in the nonspeaking role of the Associate, W. S. Penley and a young musical entertainer called George Grossmith in the Jury, and Emily Cross, Florence Terry, and Marion Terry among the Bridesmaids. Sullivan conducted and was musical director for the whole program. Two days later, with W. S. Penley back as the Foreman of the Jury, *Trial by Jury* was revived as an afterpiece to Tom Taylor's *Babes and Beetles*, at the Strand Theatre, where it ran for seventy-three performances until 26 May 1877.

The next attempt to make use of Sullivan's talents came from Lewis Carroll, who was considering a dramatization of his *Alice's Adventures in Wonderland*. Sullivan put him off, but Carroll persisted. If the book were dramatized first, then Sullivan admitted he would possibly write the music, but that suggestion was not acceptable to Carroll; he wanted the music written first. Sullivan was not persuaded by Carroll's arguments and must have cringed at Carroll's writing, "what I know of your music is so delicious (they tell me I have not a musical ear—so my criticism is valueless, I fear)."[5]

Of greater value to Sullivan, and Gilbert, was the attempt by Richard D'Oyly Carte to establish an opera company specifically for English comic opera. Carte had by now built up a highly successful agency, and a glance at his prospectus issued in March 1877 reveals an impressive list of clients: singers (including Adelina Patti and Antoinette Sterling), instrumentalists (such as Clara Schumann and Franklin Taylor), composers (including Benedict, Gounod, and Offenbach), and a considerable number of "Opéra Bouffe" performers and "Entertainers," such as Mr. and Mrs. German Reed, Mr. and Mrs. Howard Paul, and George Grossmith.

Carte was as ambitious as his list of clients was impressive. He estimated that at that stage of his career he was earning about as much as Gilbert and Sullivan, but he lacked the financial resources necessary to move on to the next stage. For that he needed men with capital, and he succeeded in interesting four men who would become the directors of his Comedy Opera Company. Two of them were music publishers, George Metzler and his associate Frank Chappell, and the other two were Augustus Collard Drake, chairman of the new company, and Edward Hodgson Bayley, a businessman with a fleet of water carts and a contract for damping down the dusty streets of the capital. Carte was now in a position to approach Gilbert and Sullivan with a greater degree of confidence.

Sullivan had changed his apartment in Albert Mansions after his mother had moved down to Fulham, and from number 9, on 5 June 1877, he wrote to Carte laying out the terms he and Gilbert wanted for a two-act piece: a 200-guineas (£210) advance on delivery of the manuscript—words and music; 6 guineas (£6.6.) a performance for the entire run; and the country right to be reserved to themselves. Sullivan estimated that they would have the piece ready for performance by the end of September.

At last, the collaboration of Gilbert and Sullivan in a new two-act opera looked imminent. Where others had tried and failed, Richard D'Oyly Carte was on the threshold of succeeding. For Gilbert, the projected work with Sullivan was coming at a critical moment in his career, when his reputation had received a setback following his dispute with Henrietta Hodson.

Closer to home, Gilbert's friendship with John Hare had run into trouble. Back in February, Hare had written saying that he thought it better if they were not "associated in business relations. . . . I cannot forget that we have never met on a business ground without some serious unpleasantness resulting from it." He complained of Gilbert's treatment of him after the production of *Broken Hearts*, when Gilbert had blamed him for its comparative failure: "you rarely let an opportunity pass, without reminding me that you think the piece will be a great success, when revived & 'properly done.' " For the sake of their friendship, he thought, it would be better not to work with Gilbert in the future: "highly as I value your work, I value your friendship more."6

In reply, Gilbert expressed his deep disappointment at being banned from Hare's theater, as he expressed it, but in the end had to bow to Hare's decision: "I accept this position at the hand of my oldest & most valued friend, with a sense of humiliation which I trust it may never be his lot to experience."7

A complication arose in June when Hare's wife, Mary, dropped Kitty as a friend, claiming that Gilbert had been cold toward her husband. Gilbert was unaware of such behavior on his part. "When I make (or believe that I have made) a friend, I do my best to retain him. Perhaps you may have remarked this. My wife has this in common with me that she also values her friends most highly, & feels it very bitterly when she loses them."8

In his professional life, and now in his personal life, Gilbert was turning people away from him. He was able to accept that relationships with Henrietta Hodson and Labouchère were permanently estranged, but he could not accept without pain the possibility of losing a personal friend he had known since the old days at the Prince of Wales's. His friendship with Hare had started in 1865 when they had been introduced by Tom Robertson, when Hare was a twenty-one-year-old beginner on the stage, and when Gilbert had not yet produced anything in the theater. They were to have another misunderstanding the following year when Hare was hurt by remarks Gilbert made in a conversation about professional matters that Hare had taken personally. "You should know me well enough," wrote Gilbert, "to be aware that, when I have anything to say, I talk *to* people — not *of* them. . . . I can only regret that the experience of the past twelve years has not proved to you that I am capable of stalwart, if not demonstrative friendship."9

At a time of broken relationships for Gilbert came the moment of sealing a new collaboration with Sullivan. Sullivan had gone away to Paris in June, but was back in London in time to sign the contract with the directors of the Comedy Opera Company on 4 July for the production of the two-act opera scheduled for 29 October. Unlike Gilbert, Sullivan was enjoying good social relationships, and the immediate

Northumberland House — Fred Sullivan's home in Fulham,
where Arthur Sullivan composed "The Lost Chord"

future looked bright indeed. On Friday 6 July, he was giving a dinner party at his apartment in Albert Mansions and Princess Louise had agreed to come. He could hardly contain his joy. He wrote to his mother telling her to fill the apartment with roses: "masses of them, and one in every single thing I have. Hooray! Blow the expense."[10] Among his guests for this royal occasion were Lady Lindsay, Mrs. Clay Ker Seymer (Fred Clay's sister-in-law), Charles Santley, and Mrs. Ronalds.

Although the contract settling terms between Gilbert and Sullivan and the directors of the Comedy Opera Company had now been signed, Carte's own terms with the directors had still to be decided. Carte claimed that he should be entitled to a share in the profits along with the directors. That was only fair, he argued, as it had been his idea and it was he who had negotiated the whole business. As for his role as manager, it was worth at least £15 a week. "— *less* would not pay me."[11] He received no immediate response and business relations were always to be strained between Carte and the directors.

As soon as the contract had been signed for the opera, Gilbert set to work. He chose as the basis for his plot the short story he had written the previous Christmas for the *Graphic*: *An Elixir of Love*, in which a love philter supplied to the Rev. Stanley Gay, curate of Ploverleigh in Dorsetshire, by Messrs. Baylis and Culpepper, magicians, of St. Martin's Lane, London, results in the villagers of Ploverleigh falling in love with the first person they set eyes on. It is a variation on Gilbert's favorite theme of people being forced to change their normal pattern of behavior as the result of a spell or charm.

1877

To his first biographer, Edith Browne, Gilbert outlined the method that he and Sullivan used for the production of their operas, and that procedure varied little over the years. His plot books, large bound copy books, also give an indication of his method of working. In a new plot book, Gilbert would write out a first draft. Then he would start again, modifying the first draft, and elaborating as he went along. He wrote on the right-hand page of the book and, on the opposite page, he would make additional points as they occurred to him, or make a sketch of a character, or a costume, or even draw the odd caricature of himself scowling at what he had just written. After many drafts, when he was reasonably satisfied, he would write up a neat version of the plot or scenario on quarto sheets to read to Sullivan. The two of them would then decide on the musical situations and the number of ballads for the soloists, the ensembles, choruses, and so on. Then Gilbert would set about writing the lyrics for the musical numbers in act 1, sending them singly or in batches to Sullivan, who would start writing the music. Only when Gilbert had finished all the lyrics would he start work on the dialogue, during which time Sullivan was finishing the music. Sullivan left the scoring of the whole opera until the end, partly to avoid having to make changes to a full score late in the day. Sullivan knew he could score rapidly but this method of working put him under intense pressure as the date of the opening night approached, forcing him to spend long hours at scoring while rehearsals were going on. Gilbert's libretto, as a completed book of words of the opera, did not materialize until rehearsals had already started on act 1, and only a short time before the score was completed.

Before the end of July 1877, Gilbert and Sullivan were clear about the number of characters and the types of voices required for casting. Gilbert had modified the plot of his short story, making Alexis (of the Grenadier Guards and son of the elderly baronet Sir Marmaduke Pointdextre) the person who procures the love philter from the magician (John Wellington Wells of number 70 St. Mary Axe); the curate (Dr. Daly) is as much a victim of the love potion as the villagers, and Aline (daughter of a Lady of Ancient Lineage, Lady Sangazure) is persuaded by her betrothed, Alexis, also to take the potion.

Building on his experience of writing for the German Reeds, and no doubt for financial reasons spelled out by Carte, Gilbert kept the number of characters to soprano (Aline), contralto (Lady Sangazure), tenor (Alexis), and bass (Sir Marmaduke), plus two "comedy roles" (John Wellington Wells and Dr. Daly), two other small female roles (Mrs. Partlet and her daughter, Constance), and an even smaller part for a Notary. As for casting, it has sometimes been suggested that Gilbert chose a number of unknown actors so that he could more easily mold them, or browbeat them, into his way of doing things, treating them like marionettes. That was not the case. All three—Gilbert, Sullivan, and Carte—were involved in the casting. Carte was only too aware of the need to keep expenses down, and the sort of work that Gilbert and Sullivan had in mind did not call for the great singers of the day. Gilbert in particular wanted actors, or singers who would be able to act adequately with help from him. Sullivan was able to write music for virtually any kind of voice, although he had not been happy with some of the voices in *Thespis*.

One of the first to be engaged was Mrs. Howard Paul. She was on Carte's books and known to both Gilbert and Sullivan, who had given her permission to use numbers from *Trial by Jury* in her entertainments.[12] Mrs. Howard Paul, born Isabella Featherstone, was a contralto and versatile actress who had played Lady Macbeth at Drury Lane, and Her Highness of Gerolstein at Covent Garden. She toured with her American husband and a small group of actors giving musical entertainments and comic monologues. She was in her mid-forties, was not in good health and, as Gilbert and Sullivan were soon to discover, her voice was deteriorating. Mrs. Howard Paul wanted them to look at a young performer in her company called Rutland Barrington, and they all went along one evening to see him, including Helen Lenoir, already acting as Carte's assistant rather than his secretary.[13]

Barrington impressed them sufficiently to be offered a contract at £6 a week to play the part of the vicar, Dr. Daly. He was twenty-four and had been on the stage for three years, most of that time with Mr. and Mrs. Howard Paul.[14] They also engaged Harriette Everard, who had worked with Gilbert before and was an actress who could sing, rather than a singer. Turning to the singers: Alice May, Giulia Warwick (sopranos), and Richard Temple (bass) were already on Carte's books, and, for the tenor role, Carte engaged George Bentham from Her Majesty's Opera Company. Apart from the very small part of the Notary, for which Fred Clifton was engaged, there was still one very important gap in the casting: the major comedy role, the part of John Wellington Wells.

The Sorcerer was not the only piece Gilbert was working on at this time. He was also completing a "farcical comedy" called *Engaged*, which opened on Wednesday 3 October at the Haymarket under the management of John S. Clarke, with a cast including Marion Terry, George Honey, and Lucy Buckstone. Gilbert insisted that the piece "should be played with the most perfect earnestness and gravity throughout. . . . [t]he characters, one and all, should appear to believe, throughout, in the perfect sincerity of their words and actions. Directly the actors show that they are conscious of the absurdity of their utterances the piece begins to drag."[15] This was a point of view that could be said to apply fairly well to the operas he would write with Sullivan.

To complicate matters for Gilbert as he worked on *The Sorcerer*, Sothern was having grave doubts about the *Ne'er-do-Weel*. He was sure it would fail, and that he would fail along with the play. Gilbert was "surprised & disappointed"; he had altered and realtered the piece to suit Sothern and from the financial point of view was not in a position to return Sothern's £1,050, which was tied up with the mortgage on his house. But he offered to take the piece back, work at it, produce it in London and in the country and, if it were successful, have it produced in both America and Australia. Then he would pay Sothern two-thirds of everything he earned on it until he had paid him £2,100.[16]

When Gilbert then sent his new play, *Engaged*, over to Sothern in Boston, Sothern was excited about it and became more enthusiastic about *The Ne'er-do-Weel*, wanting to play it at Wallack's in New York, and hoping that Gilbert would be able to go over for some of the rehearsals.

While Gilbert struggled to repay his debt to Sothern and at the same time maintain the standard of living appropriate to a successful professional man living in The Boltons, Kitty and her sister came into an inheritance from their aunt, Mary Turner, who had died in Brighton in September leaving each of them £1,000.[17] Unfortunately the inheritance was not immediately forthcoming, as future events will show.

For some months, Gilbert had been conducting all his own business because his agent, Edward English, had died suddenly from a heart attack in the autumn of 1875. Initially, Gilbert had been happy to work through English's associate, Blackmore, until Blackmore demanded 10 percent on all fees that came through him. Such a rate Gilbert found unacceptable. Without an agent acting for him, business letters were a constant part of Gilbert's life as he pursued his interests and kept an eye on the production of his pieces, protecting his property and ensuring that he received what was due to him. His play, *Sweethearts*, was the cause of further acrimony between Gilbert and the Kendals. Gilbert had fallen out with the Kendals for some unknown reason at the time of *Broken Hearts* and refused to let them perform any of his plays. When he discovered that they were playing *Sweethearts* in the provinces, he wrote to object. Kendal, who would not answer Gilbert's letters personally, informed Gilbert, through a secretary, that he did not want to hear from him. "So long as you refrain from trespassing on my property, so long will you be spared the humiliation of being taken to task for so doing," was Gilbert's response.[18]

Sullivan, too, was busy with other work, writing incidental music to act 5 of *Henry VIII*, scheduled to open on 28 August 1877 at the Theatre Royal, Manchester. On Saturday 18 August, he was still hard at work and wrote to his mother in Fulham: "Don't expect me to-morrow, as I must have a quiet day's work. I shall then be able to get it finished by Tuesday or Wednesday."[19] Only then would he be able to start work on Gilbert's lyrics for *The Sorcerer*.

The prospect of a good income from an opera with Gilbert must have been particularly encouraging. His family responsibilities and expenses were greater since his brother's death, and when his eldest nephew, Herbert, was nine years old, the age Sullivan was when he left home, he placed the boy in a school. "I will take Bertie down to Brighton tomorrow (Sunday) by the 5.50 train from Victoria," he wrote to his mother on Saturday 8 September, adding, "I have to see my doctor again at 2."[20] His kidney problems were becoming worse and he was heading for a serious attack. At the end of September, he traveled up to Scotland with Fanny Ronalds for a house party given by the Lindsays at Balcarres. On Friday 5 October, they put together a little concert for the villagers. Sullivan played a duet with Charles Wortley, Lady Lindsay played the violin, and Mrs. Ronalds sang several pieces including "The Lost Chord."[21] The following Sunday, Sullivan was leaving Balcarres when he was suddenly taken ill on the way to the station, was rushed back to the house, and had to spend several more days with the Lindsays before he was fit enough to travel.

Once he was back in London, Sullivan returned to work on act 1 of *The Sorcerer*. It was not only Sullivan who was behind schedule. Gilbert only started writing the lyrics of act 2 in the middle of October: in his pressed-copy book, between 15 and 18 October 1877, there is an original lyric for the beginning of act 2, which is a variation on the opening given by Ian Bradley in *The Complete Annotated Gilbert & Sullivan*. As the copy is from Gilbert's letter book, it can be assumed that it is the version that he first sent to Sullivan.[22]

By 23 October 1877, Sullivan had finished composing the music for act 1 and promptly wrote to Mrs. Howard Paul. She had expected to receive the music in advance of rehearsals, but Sullivan preferred her to "read it all through" with him first, sensitive to the fact that her singing role was not as prominent in the first act as she had anticipated. "The second of course will be far more important now you are going to take the part of the Spirit Fiend."[23]

Mrs. Howard Paul would find that later changes in act 2 meant that she was not to play the Spirit Fiend after all, that her solo was to be cut, and, even more significantly, that Gilbert was to give her not a single line of dialogue.

The first music rehearsal for principals took place on Saturday morning, 27 October. The original intention had been to open on 1 November but the opening was now rescheduled for Saturday 17 November, only three weeks away—and there was still no one for the part of the sorcerer. It was probably on Tuesday 30 October, when Sullivan was at the Beefsteak Club with Arthur Cecil, that he told Cecil that they still needed a comedy lead for the opera. Cecil tentatively suggested Grossmith. "The very man!" replied Sullivan.[24]

Sullivan had met Grossmith when he played a juror in Henry Compton's benefit in March, and he had also met him at a dinner party after which Grossmith, with Arthur Cecil and Alfred Cellier and a few other friends, went around to Sullivan's rooms in Albert Mansions, where they all "sang, played, and chatted till an early hour in the morning."[25] Grossmith, twenty-nine years old at the time of *The Sorcerer*, had made his first professional appearance as an entertainer in about 1870. His father, also named George Grossmith, was a well-known entertainer and, together, father and son used to do an autumn tour of the provinces. He had not, however, given up his main occupation as a Bow Street reporter. In the summer of 1871 he had toured with Mr. and Mrs. Howard Paul, and had once appeared at the Gallery of Illustration, playing in Tom Robertson's *Society*, when Gilbert as the "Theatrical Lounger" for the *Illustrated Times* had written that "Mr. Grossmith has comic powers of no mean order."[26]

After his conversation with Arthur Cecil, Sullivan wrote to Grossmith, from the Beefsteak Club. "Are you inclined to go on the stage for a time? There is a part in the new piece I am doing with Gilbert which I think you would play admirably. I can't find a good man for it."[27]

Mary Frances Ronalds (By permission of Peter Joslin)

Grossmith was flattered by the compliment but unsure what to do. He had a provincial tour arranged with his father and the income from that was assured. His father advised him against accepting the engagement, thinking that his voice was not good enough. Still unsure, Grossmith went to see Sullivan. What happened then is told by Grossmith.

[Sullivan] struck the D (fourth line in treble clef, if you please), and said, "Sing it out as loud as you can." I did. Sullivan looked up, with a most humorous expression on his face—even his eye-glass seemed to smile—and he simply said, "Beautiful!" Sullivan then sang, "My name is John Wellington Wells," and said, "You can do that?"

I replied, "Yes; I can do that."

"Very well," said Sir Arthur, "if you can do that, you can do the rest."[28]

It is interesting that Sullivan struck a D for Grossmith to sing, when the note he has to sustain in the song is an F. By the way Grossmith sang that D, Sullivan knew he would have no difficulty in taking him up to an F in the context of the song. He also had heard enough of Grossmith before to know that he could sing the part.

After his interview with Sullivan, Grossmith went off to The Boltons to see Gilbert. It was not their first meeting; Grossmith had played the Judge in a production of *Trial by Jury* in Bayswater, where Gilbert had supervised the rehearsals and coached him. Gilbert read him the opening speech of J. W. Wells and told him that the part had assumed a greater importance than he had first planned. "I saw that the part would suit me excellently," Grossmith related, "but I said to Mr. Gilbert, 'For the part of a Magician I should have thought you require a fine man with a fine voice.' I can still see Mr. Gilbert's humorous expression as he replied. 'No, that is just what we don't want.'"[29]

Grossmith still had to agree terms with Carte. He wanted 18 guineas a week; Carte offered him 15. They went to lunch and when Grossmith was feeling more mellow after "a lunch of oysters and most excellent Steinberg Cabinet," Carte again offered him 15 fifteen guineas a week.[30] This time, Grossmith accepted. Grossmith learned later that the directors of the Comedy Opera Company were opposed to his engagement, but their opinion carried little weight with Carte. Mrs. Howard Paul, who had written to Grossmith encouraging him to accept the part, was overjoyed when he accepted, and invited him to celebrate with Barrington and a few other friends with a firework display on 5 November in the garden of her house in Bedford Park.

Sullivan was now into scoring the opera. He wrote to "Dearest Mum" on 1 November, the eve of her sixty-sixth birthday, wishing her "many years to come" and telling her that he had been "*slaving*" at the new work. "The book is brilliant, & the music I think very pretty and good. All the company are good & like it very much. The scoring will be a tremendous labour, but I don't mind that, as I can do it quickly, & there is no more composition to be done."[31]

The early music rehearsals had taken place with Sullivan sitting on the stage at the piano, and with the company, principals, and chorus, sitting in a semicircle. Only the vocal parts were written at this stage; Sullivan supplied the accompaniment himself as he went through the music. Gilbert also attended the music rehearsals, noting whatever he needed to help him arrange the "business" of the numbers in prepara-

George Grossmith (V&A Picture Library)

tion for the stage rehearsals. "Of course, I planned out the whole stage-management beforehand," he explained to the critic William Archer, "on my model stage, with blocks three inches high to represent men, and two and a half inches to represent women." It was all clear in his mind before he started rehearsals. The actors believed in him, he said, and lent themselves "heartily to all I required of them."[32]

"My goodness, how we all stood in awe of them at the early rehearsals of the *Sorcerer*!" Rutland Barrington recalled.[33] Grossmith remembered how exact Sullivan was in musical rehearsals and how strict Gilbert was when it came to his turn. "The music rehearsals are child's play in comparison with the stage rehearsals. Mr. Gilbert is a perfect autocrat, insisting that his words should be delivered even to an inflection of the voice, as he dictates."[34]

As the rehearsals progressed Barrington became uneasy at the thought of portraying a clergyman on the stage. He took his problem to Gilbert, saying that he thought the public would "take either very kindly" to him "or absolutely hoot" him off the stage for ever. Gilbert "was very sympathetic," Barrington recalled, "but his reply, 'I quite agree with you,' left me in a state of uncertainty."[35]

The final rehearsal on Friday 16 November, started at 7:30, and was a long affair in the course of which Gilbert and Sullivan decided on last-minute revisions and cuts, giving Sullivan further work on the day of the performance. He had had no time to write an overture and adapted the "Graceful Dance" from his music to *Henry VIII*. Sullivan never did get around to writing an overture for *The Sorcerer*; the task was completed by Hamilton Clarke.

At last they were ready for the first performance of a two-act Gilbert and Sullivan opera at the Opera Comique. The Opera Comique had opened in October 1870 and the advertised address of "299 Strand" indicated not the site of the theater but the entrance next door to "The Spotted Dog" public house. It led down a flight of steps into a well-lit passage, which ran under Holywell Street (a road running parallel to the Strand), and then did a sharp right turn as it bordered the Globe Theatre, to finish with steps leading up into the Opera Comique. A separate orchestra section entrance stood in Wych Street, also parallel to the Strand, and the dressing-rooms were up a flight of about thirty stone stairs into houses in Holywell Street. Conditions were cramped: George Grossmith, Rutland Barrington, Richard Temple, and Fred Clifton all shared the same dressing room. The two theaters, the Globe and the Opera Comique, were back to back, with adjoining stages; they had not been built to last, situated as they were in an overcrowded, run-down district destined for redevelopment. The "rickety twins," as they were called, stood in fact until the end of the century, when they were closed; shortly after, the area was redeveloped and Wych Street gave way to the Aldwych.

At 8:00 p.m. on 17 November 1877, the program opened with *Dora's Dream*, a curtain-raiser by Arthur Cecil and Alfred Cellier, with Richard Temple and Giulia Warwick in the cast. Then, at 8:45 p.m., the curtain went up on *The Sorcerer*. It was a nervous moment for both Gilbert and Sullivan; and each man dealt with it in his own way. Once the baton was in his hand, Sullivan was soon enjoying being out front; while Gilbert, having left Kitty and his guests in a box, walked the Embankment, or went to another theater, or called in at the Beefsteak—and this was to be his habit on every first night.

"Happy Young Heart" sung by Alice May (Aline) was encored, and so was the duet "Welcome Joy," by Richard Temple (Sir Marmaduke) and Mrs. Howard Paul (Lady Sangazure), who still possessed the ability to put over a song even if her voice was showing signs of wear. A glance at her vocal line shows that her voice had very little top left: at her verse in the duet she comes in a third lower than the first verse sung by the bass-baritone. She also was to have had a solo following her recitative after Aline's ballad. It appears in a copy of the libretto, written in Helen Lenoir's hand, but may have been one of the cuts following the dress rehearsal. George Grossmith's patter song received an encore, as did the quintet in act 2, "I rejoice that it's decided."

While Gilbert walked and fretted, the audience laughed and applauded. They had come to be entertained, to forget their worries, to laugh at Gilbert's words, and to be enchanted by Sullivan's melodies. But the comedy of *The Sorcerer* does not arise solely from the words, the characters, or the situations; it abounds in the music. No character could be more of a pompous prig than Alexis, and whereas his recitative before the act 2 finale sounds serious enough, the orchestration is comic in its portrayal of mock surprise and suspense. As in *Trial by Jury*, Sullivan uses the bassoon to comic effect, both in Wells's patter song and again when Constance addresses her "plain old man" in the act 2 ensemble. And in the joyful chorus "Now to the banquet we press," Sullivan plays with Gilbert's word order in the reversal of "jam, buns / buns, jam," adding to the infectious jollity of the number.

Sullivan told his mother that he had written music that he thought was "pretty and good," a description that matches the eighteenth-century style gavotte for Sir Marmaduke and Lady Sangazure that delighted the audience with its old-world charm, and also the simple ballad for Dr. Daly, in which the music subtly adds to the humor. "Messrs W. S. Gilbert and Arthur Sullivan have once again combined their efforts with the happiest result," said *The Times*. ". . . A more careful performance of a new work of its kind has rarely been witnessed."[36]

By the end of the performance, Gilbert had returned in time to hear the verdict of the audience. Gilbert and Sullivan were called, reported *The Times*, "amid applause, the genuine nature of which could never once have been mistaken. In short, the audience had been diverted from the rise of the curtain to the fall, and the laughter was incessant."[37]

In reviews that followed, individual performers came in for praise, particularly Rutland Barrington as Dr. Daly, and also George Grossmith who, with Harriette Everard, communicated Gilbert's humor with the right degree of seriousness. Not so fortunate in the reviews was George Bentham, who could be excused on the first night because he was suffering from a sore throat, but who eventually had to be replaced.

After the opening, Sullivan's immediate concern was to work at the piano score so as to have it ready as soon as possible for Metzler's to publish. The management of the Strand Theatre were now expressing an interest in revising *The Zoo*, and in a letter to his friend Alan Cole, Sullivan wondered whether he would be interested in rewriting it with him. Nothing came of the suggestion of reviving *The Zoo*, but Gilbert was already talking about doing another piece together.

For the present, it was time for Sullivan to take off for a rest and a change, traveling over to France with his French valet, Silva, and spending Christmas in Paris. At this time of the year, the memory of his brother was particularly close. On Christmas Day, he came out of mourning for the day. "I don't see why I should wear black on dear old Fred's birthday," he told his mother. "So I brighten up, & shall drink a glass of wine to his memory, bless him. . . . He would have done the same for me I know." It was no use "grieving and repining" he told her. They had responsibilities, he said encouragingly, which they had to face courageously. "I hope I shall come back strong and well, for I have much to do this forthcoming year."[38]

Before the end of the year, Gilbert was ready with a sketch plot for a new piece with Sullivan.

Part III

1877-1884

The G&S Phenomenon:
From *HMS Pinafore* to *Princess Ida*

1877-1878

HMS Pinafore

A FORTNIGHT INTO THE RUN of *The Sorcerer*, Mrs. Howard Paul became ill and her young understudy, Rosina Brandram, made her first appearance in a Gilbert and Sullivan opera on Monday, 3 December 1877.[1] Together with George Grossmith, Rutland Barrington, and Richard Temple, Rosina Brandram would become one of the much-loved "stars" of the developing stock company. For the moment, though, she had to be content with the role of understudy to the ailing Mrs. Howard Paul.

At the beginning of December 1877, Gilbert, Sullivan, and Carte had agreed terms with the directors of the Comedy Opera Company for a new opera, insisting on a guaranteed minimum run. By Christmas, Gilbert had completed his sketch plot and, not knowing Sullivan had gone over to Paris, called at Albert Mansions on Christmas Day to talk it over with him. On 27 December, he wrote to Sullivan enclosing a copy of the plot, eager to know what he thought of it: "there is a good deal of fun in it which I haven't set down on paper. Among other things a song (kind of 'Judge's song'[)] for the First Lord—tracing his career as office boy in cotton brokers office[,] clerk, traveller, junior partner & First Lord of Britain's Navy."

He insisted disingenuously that there would be no *"personality"* in this, as the First Lord would be a radical, in contrast to the actual First Lord, W. H. Smith, in the conservative government. He made suggestions as to casting and then turned to costumes, ambitiously proposing that they might have the sailors' uniforms made in Portsmouth.[2]

What did the sketch plot consist of at this stage? Gilbert would have written several versions in his plot book before arriving at the version he thought ready to present to Sullivan, and then would have copied it out on quarto sheets. Among Gilbert's papers in the British Library is an incomplete copy of an early sketch plot written on separate sheets. As Gilbert would have moved on to writing the lyrics of act 1 afterward, and would not have returned to the stage of rewriting the plot in this form, it is fair to assume that the version in his papers was the same as the one he sent Sullivan. It already included the name of the ship and suggested casting.

> The Pinafore is a line-of-battle ship, commanded by Capt. Corcoran (*Barrington?*[)] an excellent officer, beloved by his crew, whom he treats with fatherly consideration. All the crew are devoted to him—but no one so much as Ralph Rackstraw—(*Tenor*) the Captain's coxswain, who also secretly loves Josephine, the Captain's daughter.
> The act opens with a chorus of men-o-war's men, who are buying buns & peppermint drops of Mrs. Cripps (*Miss Everard*) a Portsmouth bum-boat woman.[3]

The Bumboat Woman had made her first appearance in Gilbert's "Bab Ballad" of 1870 entitled "The Bumboat Woman's Story," in which she was called Poll Pineapple, and also called Little Buttercup by the commander of the *Hot Cross Bun*, Lieutenant Belaye, whom she loved. The crew on the *Hot Cross Bun* never used "a big, big D—," but then they all turned out to be "simple girls" all in love with the "kind Lieutenant Belaye."[4]

As he unfolds his plot, the other major characters are introduced: "a malignant, blackbrowed, white-faced scoundrel called Dick Deadeye"; and the First Lord: "In his eyes all ranks (but one) are merged in one common equality.... He has only recently been appointed First Lord—is wholly ignorant of naval affairs ... & is invariably accompanied by an admiring crowd of female relatives who, headed by his elderly cousin Hebe (*Mrs. H. Paul?*) [later crossed out] attend him on all ceremonial occasions."[5]

The female relatives had previously appeared in a "Bab Ballad": "Captain Reece" written in 1868, in which the commander of *The Mantelpiece*, "adored by all his men," bears striking similarities to Captain Corcoran.

> You have a daughter, CAPTAIN REECE,
> Ten female cousins and a niece,
> A ma, if what I'm told is true,
> Six sisters, and an aunt or two.[6]

Gilbert would take the ladies away from the captain and transfer them to Sir Joseph, at the same time making the joke much more pointedly a family joke. When he wrote that ballad in 1868, he was still reeling from the plethora of Lucy's female relatives who surrounded him. He decided to give a middle-aged lady character, originally to be played by Mrs. Howard Paul, the name of his mother-in-law Hebe (short for Herbertina, and the name used by Lucy's relatives), a character who would be the leading (bossy) relative of a chorus of sisters and cousins and aunts. As it turned out, the character of Hebe was played by an attractive young woman in her twenties, and Gilbert's "mother-in-law" joke was consequently softened.

The major difference between the sketch plot and the finished libretto appears in the section that becomes the finale of act 1. When Ralph explains to the members of

1877–1878

the crew that his love has been rejected by Josephine, the Captain's daughter, the First Lord is on stage.

Ralph explains, in a ballad, that he loves a maiden of high rank (without naming her)—that his love is despised because he is a common sailor. The First Lord is indignant, and advises the crew, if they are men, not to stand this insult to their order, but to carry the girl off, whoever she may be, & compel her to marry their noble-hearted comrade. The crew are excited to enthusiasm by the First Lord's sympathy and in a spirited chorus declare their intention to carry the girl off that night, in accordance with his advice.[7]

According to Gilbert's diary, he worked at the lyrics of the act 1 finale on 28 March and then on 31 March, unhappy with the original version, returned to the scheme of act 1. Remnants of the original act 1 finale remain. The original sketch plot has Ralph explaining to the First Lord, in a ballad, that his love has been rejected. When the First Lord was removed from this scene, Gilbert switched to the character of the First Lord's cousin, Hebe, who has no other function in the scene. Ralph sings to Hebe:

> The maiden treats my love with scorn,
>   Rejects my humble gift, my lady;
> She says I am ignobly born,
>   And cuts my hopes adrift, my lady.[8]

It is just possible that those lines were originally addressed to Sir Joseph with the words "your honour," where now they are "my lady." Gilbert had already written the dialogue of act 1 at the end of April, and Ralph's lines addressed to Sir Joseph in that act always end with "your honour."

The other remnant from the original finale is in the "spirited chorus" in which they "declare their intention to carry the girl off." In the ensemble of the finished version, Josephine who has now been brought on, joins in the singing of these words:

> With wooing words and loving song,
> We'll chase the lagging hours along,
> And if $\begin{cases} \text{I find} \\ \text{we find} \end{cases}$ the maiden coy,
> $\begin{cases} \text{I'll} \\ \text{we'll} \end{cases}$ murmur forth decorous joy
>   In dreamy roundelays![9]

These lines have little sense when sung by Josephine.

BUSINESS AT THE OPERA Comique was down over the Christmas period due to the preference of the public for pantomimes at that time of year, although only in Christmas week itself did takings fail to cover expenses. The directors of the Comedy Opera Company, inexperienced in the theater, took fright and were anxious to reduce the guaranteed number of nights that Gilbert and Sullivan had stipulated for the new opera. On 2 January 1878, on his way home along the Strand after a visit to the Gaiety, Gilbert happened to bump into Carte, who told him what the directors wanted to do. Gilbert absolutely refused to change the terms assuming that, as he had not heard from the directors, they had accepted them.

The next day, Gilbert had woken with a bad headache, and had breakfasted in bed. He received a delivery of eight hundred cigars, walked to Westerton's, the bookseller's at Hyde Park Corner, to buy a diary, and then walked back, taking the long route home through Hyde Park to help him clear his head. From then on, having written up the first two days of 1878, Gilbert kept the diary consistently until the last day of the year.

What sort of a document is it? At the beginning of the year Gilbert records mostly business matters, meetings he had and points discussed. On 1 January, for example, he wrote: "Lunched Neville [manager of the Olympic Theatre] & Ld. Londesborough [lessee]. Neerdoweel to be put in rehearsal at once. M.T. [Marion Terry] to be offered engagement. Suggested Faust & Marguerite subject."[10] He included financial matters, which were coded, presumably to keep such details from any prying eyes, for example—"I am to have £UX for Wedding March."[11] He began the year by recording letters received and letters sent, but abandoned that idea before the end of January. He recorded what he was working on: *6 January*—"Wrote at amateur pantomime";[12] and also commented on his state of health: "Bad headache," "Rather seedy." As his social life and business life overlapped, visits to the theatre are briefly recorded as are visits to his clubs: *12 January*—"Home at 6.15 to dress for P. of W. 'Diplomacy' at P of W. Success—*distinct*. Bfst. [Beefsteak Club] afterwards."[13]

Gilbert and Kitty's social life included entertaining guests to dinner most weeks and dining out with friends once or twice a week. Among their closest friends at this time were John Hare and his wife, Mary, and the painter Marcus Stone and his wife. Gilbert's father often called, sometimes staying overnight, and his sister Jane and her husband, Alfred, stayed for a few days. Kitty's mother and her sister, Grace, also were regular visitors, as were Gilbert's Aunt Harriet and his cousin Agnes (Lady Murray).

It was at the time of one of Gilbert senior's visits that a problem arose concerning Kitty's legacies from the Turner family. In a will proved on 9 September 1875, Kitty had been left by her godmother, Lucretia Anne Turner, the sum of £150.[14] As already mentioned, another aunt, Mary Turner, had died in September 1877, leaving £1,000 each to Kitty, her sister, and Kitty's brother Samuel Compton Turner.[15] Kitty had received neither legacy by the end of 1877. On 4 January 1878, she received a letter from her father's brother, who had taken charge of Herbertina when her husband died. Henry had reached the rank of lieutenant-general in the India army before retiring, and was now the senior member of the numerous Turner family, executor to both wills, and clearly intent on looking after the family interests. In his letter to Kitty, General Turner insisted on seeing her marriage settlement before agreeing to pay the first of the legacies, the £150 from Aunt Lucretia.

Gilbert immediately sought advice from his solicitor, who told him that General Turner had no right to see the settlement.[16] Replying to Kitty's uncle, and addressing him, "Dear Sir," Gilbert ended: "Acting upon their advice I altogether decline to comply with your request."[17] It is tempting to see this letter as an example of Gilbert's no-nonsense approach to requests he objected to, but subsequent events suggest that Gilbert was acting too hastily.

The motive behind General Turner's request cannot now be known, but the considerable sum of £1,000 had yet to be settled. Neither will had stated explicitly that the legacy to Kitty was for her sole use, and General Turner may have been reluctant simply to hand over these legacies to Gilbert. It happened that Gilbert senior was staying over with Gilbert and Kitty, and father and son sat up late one night discussing the situation. Following that discussion, Gilbert junior wrote to General Turner's solicitor asking for his authority to demand to see the settlement, and Gilbert senior placed his own affairs concerning a "settlement" in the hands of his son's solicitors.[18] It would appear that Gilbert was not able to dismiss General Turner as simply as he had first thought. When the checks finally arrived, Gilbert and Kitty went to the bank together to pay them in and to instruct the manager to credit them against the loan for the purchase of their house in The Boltons.[19]

Much of Gilbert's time at the beginning of 1878 was taken up with completing *The Ne'er-do-Weel* and arranging for its production at the Olympic Theatre. He also had agreed to join with Robert Reece, Frank Burnand, and Henry J. Byron in writing a pantomime for John Hollingshead at the Gaiety. Gilbert's share was to write the second of the four scenes of *The Forty Thieves*. He went further: he also was to perform in the harlequinade and approached his task with the utmost seriousness, being coached regularly by John D'Auban. At the same time, he was anxious to start work on the opera. Because Sullivan was in France, no discussion about the new opera had been possible, and the sketch plot had still not been read to Carte nor to the directors of the Comedy Opera Company.

On 8 January, Gilbert wrote what appeared to be an innocuous letter to "Mr. Carte": "Will you kindly reserve two stalls for me tomorrow (Wednesday) Evening? ... P.S. Will you let me have a note agreeing to terms for new piece? Sullivan is delighted with the plot. Ill send it to you whenever you like —"[20]

The request for tickets was genuine enough: they were for Marcus Stone and his wife, who went to see *The Sorcerer* as arranged.[21] But Gilbert noted in his diary that he had written to Carte "asking for note agreeing to terms for a new piece."[22] The letter was formally addressed to "Mr. Carte" and was clearly meant to be preserved as a record that the terms agreed verbally with the directors were assumed by Gilbert to be still in existence. He wrote to Sullivan the same day to keep him informed. The letter was kept carefully by Carte and, when matters came to a head with the directors, it appeared later as an exhibit in court and was referred to in affidavits sworn by Carte, Gilbert, and Sullivan. It appears that Carte was already looking ahead to the time when he would be able to work independently of the directors.

Gilbert started work on the lyrics for *HMS Pinafore* on 10 January, beginning with the opening chorus, but then spent two days writing his scene of the pantomime. Time had to be given to rehearsals at the Gaiety, and he also was coaching Marion Terry for her part in *The Ne'er-do-Weel*. In the meantime, he had read the plot to Carte, who was "much pleased," and a week later to the directors, also "much pleased." By then Gilbert had written the Captain's song, "I am the Captain of the *Pinafore*" and by the end of the month also had written the First Lord's song, "When I Was a Lad."

While Gilbert was making progress, Carte was still having difficulties with the directors, with the "Company" as he called them in a letter to Sullivan. The directors were uneasy about the box office returns and were regretting the terms agreed with Gilbert and Sullivan for the new opera. Just as serious, from Carte's point of view, was their reluctance to settle terms with him in his role as manager. In his reply, written on 5 February, Sullivan tried to reassure Carte by telling him that he would only deal with the directors through him. "And I shan't deal with them at all, unless they make up their minds to settle your business quickly. They ought to have done it long ago."[23]

The cautious attitude shown by the directors was not Carte's approach. He was prepared to take risks and had already begun to make preparations for a company to take *The Sorcerer* on tour, asking Sullivan for advice to help him settle a cast. Carte thought that George Bentham was not good enough for a London theater and had engaged another tenor, George Power, although he was quite willing to try Bentham in the touring company. Sullivan agreed, but was less happy with Carte's choice of Furneaux Cook for Dr. Daly.

> I wish you could find someone else among your Barytone list. . . . There will be no part for Mrs. Paul I believe in the new piece. When does the "Sorcerer" tour begin[?] Good bye my dear Doyly. Keep good and virtuous. I shall be home at the end of the month, & have received nothing yet from Gilbert. I have lost all my money gambling — a regular facer.[24]

Sullivan's openness with Carte about his gambling contrasts with his letter from Nice to his mother, in which he tells her: "I went to Monaco the other day, to have a look at the gaming tables. I staked a few five franc pieces, & came away the winner of 100 francs! I confess the gaming table — that is sheer chance — has no attraction for me. Tomorrow I shall make a colossal effort and go to Church to counter balance the wickedness of gambling."[25]

It was not until 24 February that Gilbert copied out the five numbers he had already written and posted them off. He had been preoccupied with rehearsals of *The Ne'er-do-Weel* and with rehearsals for the Gaiety pantomime, including his own rehearsals for the harlequinade. On the day of the pantomime, Wednesday, 13 February, he attended rehearsals of *The Ne'er-do-Weel* in the morning, lunched with Marion and Florence Terry at Simpson's in the Strand, and then took them to the Gaiety for the pantomime. Hollingshead was left with an abiding memory: "the gem of the performance was the grimly earnest and determined harlequin of W. S. Gilbert. It gave me an idea of what Oliver Cromwell would have made of the character." Hollingshead was, however, generous in his praise of Gilbert's "kindness and liberality" in the time and energy he had given to the whole venture, which produced a total of £700 to be "distributed between the general theatrical fund and other charities including the 'Home for Lost and Starving Dogs.' "[26]

Two days later, Gilbert took a break from his hectic routine by going for a long weekend to Brighton with Kitty and Marion Terry. After rehearsals in the morning, they all three lunched at Victoria Station and then took the train down to the coast, staying in a lodging house, which Gilbert described as small "but clean and comfortable." It was not a total break: Gilbert worked at his play over the weekend and still coached Marion Terry, but otherwise they were able to relax, walking on the pier, going to the theater and a pantomime, and also going to see Herr Frikell, "the world-famed conjuror," as he styled himself.[27] Gilbert was not impressed: "—atrocious entertainment—left when half over—atmosphere putrid—"; but the evening was warm enough for them to go and sit for a while on the Esplanade.[28] They were back in London in time for rehearsals on Tuesday.

On Monday 25 February, *The Ne'er-do-Weel* opened at the Olympic. The first two acts went well, but the third act—the act that Sothern had thought weak—was a failure. The next morning Gilbert tried to work, but the attempt was fruitless. He knew that the third act needed rewriting but was temporarily out of fresh ideas. Instead, he cheered himself up after lunch by going with Kitty to hire fancy dress for a ball they had been invited to for Wednesday evening. Tuesday evening he went to Francis Burnand's house in Russell Square with Tom Taylor, James Albery, Robert Reece, and Charles Merritt to draw up the rules for the new Dramatic Authors' Society. He finished up at the Beefsteak afterward, and only got home at 3:30 a.m. The following morning his diary reads: "Rather seedy"[29]—probably a slight hangover, but Gilbert never admitted to such things. At the fancy ball that evening, he met Neville and suggested that, in view of the poor third act, he should reconstruct *The Ne'er-do-Weel*. The Gilberts did not arrive home from the Ball until 3 a.m., and the next morning Gilbert was feeling unwell again, recording "Headache" in his diary.[30]

The Ne'er-do-Weel was withdrawn and Gilbert immediately began to rewrite the third act, staying up late one night until 4 a.m. On 6 March, Ash Wednesday, he woke in pain—a pain he recognized immediately. It was gout. He wasted no time but went straight around to his doctor, Oscar Clayton, in Harley Street, and then took his prescription to be made up by Squires the chemists, in Oxford Street. Then he was off to rehearsals for a revival of *Tom Cobb*; and home again to work at act 3 of *The Ne'er-do-Weel*, all the time with his gout getting worse: "went to bed at 3 a.m. Gout much

worse—couldn't sleep—got up at 4.30—lighted fire in study—read until 6.45—
Then went to bed & slept till 9.30."[31] The next day he was only able to walk through
his rehearsal for another performance of the Gaiety pantomime, and after a dinner
engagement he slept on the sofa until 1:30 a.m. before going to bed.

However, the gout in his foot began to improve. He kept up his pace, working at
The Ne'er-do-Weel the next evening until 2 a.m., and the following morning, 8 March,
rehearsing the touring company of *The Sorcerer* at the Opera Comique. On Saturday 9 March, he traveled down to Brighton with the rest of the company for a performance of *Forty Thieves*, followed by supper at the "Ship" and bed at 3:45 a.m.
The next morning, unsurprisingly, he woke with a slight headache—and went
swimming before breakfast.

Gilbert drove himself on: rehearsing, working at *The Ne'er-do-Weel*, which he had
now renamed *The Vagabond*, and all the time keeping up a busy social life. At the
end of the evening when his dinner guests had left for home, Gilbert returned to his
work. "*11 March*: . . . Burnands to dinner—They left at 11—Very seedy—tried to
work—couldn't—to bed, at 1.30."[32] "*12 March*: . . . went to Stones . . . afterwards
home—worked."[33] "*13 March*: . . . Reception . . . home by 11. 30—Worked."[34]

Following Gilbert's rehearsal of *The Sorcerer* on Friday 8 March, the touring company gave a matinee performance at the Opera Comique the next day and then,
under their musical director Hamilton Clarke, opened their tour on Monday 11
March at the Prince of Wales's Theatre, Liverpool. Despite Sullivan's advice, Carte
had not been able to find a baritone better than Furneaux Cook who played Dr. Daly,
and, as arranged, George Bentham was taken as Alexis. In addition, Rosina Brandram was cast as Lady Sangazure and two newcomers were engaged: Arthur Rousbey to play Sir Marmaduke and J. H. Ryley, from the Kate Santley Opera Company,
to play J. W. Wells. At the Opera Comique, meanwhile, Giulia Warwick had taken
over from Alice May as Aline and would remain in the part until the end of the run.

The day the touring company opened in Liverpool, Sullivan returned home from
Nice. He had been away for nearly three months enjoying the winter sunshine of the
Mediterranean and keeping well away from the pressures of work, including those of
the National Training School for Music. He had not been able to escape altogether:
in mid-January, he had received a telegram from the secretary of the British Commission charged with preparations for another international exhibition in Paris. Reluctantly, he had been obliged to leave the "beautiful sunshine and lovely flowers" for
the cold of Paris and two meetings on Saturday, 19, and Monday, 21 January.[35]

Having done his duty, Sullivan had returned to his friends in Nice, one of whom,
Madame Conneau, organized a concert for him on Monday, 18 February, when he
conducted his music for *The Merchant of Venice*, his overture *Di Ballo*, and the
"Graceful Dance" from *Henry VIII*. On Friday, 22 February, he left Nice by carriage
for Genoa taking the coast road, lunching at the border town of Mentone and spending the night at Bordighera, so he told his mother in a letter; but, writing to his
housekeeper, he said he spent a night on the road. The next day they drove on

"through the quaintest, dirtiest, most picturesque old towns & villages as far as Albenga" where they caught a train for the last leg of the journey. Having arrived in Genoa, and knowing how much it would please his mother, he gave a vivid description in his letter of the church of San Lorenzo with "the interior magnificently prepared for the funeral mass for the Pope the day after tomorrow."[36] At the end of the week he started out on his return journey to London via Paris.

Sullivan's first task on his return to London was to respond to an invitation from the Leeds Festival Committee to compose an oratorio for them for the 1880 festival. Frederick Spark, secretary to the Festival Committee, had first written to Sullivan as early as 2 January. As there was no reply from Sullivan, Spark wrote again on 29 January. After another fortnight, Spark sent a third letter. The day after his return from France, Sullivan sent a telegram to Spark and the same day sat down to write his reply. He told Spark that at first he had been reluctant to accept because of his health and had been waiting to see if he improved. Now in better health, he felt ready to undertake a composition for Leeds. "I could not, however, undertake the composition of an oratorio which should occupy the whole of a concert. For that I should have no time."[37] He suggested a shorter work, about the length of *The Prodigal Son*. The state of his health and the commitment to write another opera with Gilbert, together with his responsibilities at the National Training School, combined to make Sullivan reluctant to take on a lengthy serious work; it would have put on him a pressure he wanted to avoid. His reluctance to take on such work, however, with more than two years notice, does raise a question about Sullivan's desire to dedicate himself to serious composition. He was still only thirty-five, but most of his serious work already lay behind him.

The Leeds Committee agreed to Sullivan's proposal of a shorter work and offered to pay him 100 guineas. Out of this Sullivan had to pay his own expenses, including the cost of providing copies for orchestra and chorus. His choice of subject was initially "David and Jonathan" and he intended to provide the libretto himself. He was earning almost 100 guineas a month from *The Sorcerer*, and it is not difficult to understand Sullivan's reluctance to give so much time and energy to Leeds when he could earn much more by doing what came naturally to him. This pull in two directions was to trouble him for most of his life.

Sullivan could now turn his attention to the new opera and the lyrics that Gilbert had already sent him at the end of February. Because of his preoccupation with *The Vagabond*, Gilbert had not progressed any further with the lyrics. On 22 March he went straight from rehearsing *The Vagabond* at the Olympic to the Opera Comique for a rehearsal of *Trial by Jury*, with George Grossmith as the Judge and Rutland Barrington as the Counsel. The next day *Trial by Jury* joined the program with *The Sorcerer* and continued until the end of *The Sorcerer*'s run, another fifty-six performances.

A heavy fall of snow on 24 March kept Sullivan from driving down to Fulham to make his Sunday visit to his mother. The enforced absence, though, gave him the opportunity to finish a trio, "Morn, Happy Morn," which he was writing for John Hare, for a new play, *Olivia*, due to open at the Court the following week. The same day, Gilbert returned to work on the opera, rewriting the First Lord's song and finishing it before going to bed. He took it around to Albert Mansions the next day and met Charles Santley, who sang him Sullivan's new song. Gilbert reciprocated by reading the First Lord's song, sent for a box for Sullivan at the Olympic, and then drove with him to the National Training School. That evening was the first night of the reconstructed play, *The Vagabond*, at the Olympic: "house crammed—. . . Piece went magnificently," Gilbert commented in his diary.[38]

Sunday's snow soon melted. The tennis season had arrived. Gilbert had already marked out a court in his garden and, on Thursday morning, out came the rackets, and he and Kitty played their first game of the year before he settled down to work on the opera. Gilbert was working on the opera every day now, but it was far from finished. He had barely made a start on act 2, writing the "Proverb Song" on 5 April; Neville was already asking for another play for the Olympic; and his obligations to Sothern were never far from his mind. Something had to give in his heavy schedule, and he decided he would relieve the pressure on himself by resigning from the Royal Aberdeenshire Highlanders whose summer training session was approaching fast. On 6 April, he wrote out his resignation and sent it to Colonel Innes. This time it was accepted and with the official resignation date given as 24 April, and with his previous service as an officer in the militia taken into consideration, he was entitled to retire with the honorary rank of major.

Gilbert now turned his mind to the set for *HMS Pinafore*. He had originally intended to make his preliminary sketches at Greenwich, but Sullivan, through his friendship with Lord Beresford, at that time a young captain in the navy, arranged a visit to Portsmouth. On Saturday morning, 13 April, the two men caught the 10:30 from Victoria arriving in the naval town at 1:00 p.m. They lunched with Lord Beresford on board the *Thunderer*, were given a tour of the ship, and then went on board the *Invincible*, followed by the *Victory* and the *St. Vincent*, on both of which Gilbert was busy making his sketches. By 4:40 p.m., they were back on the train to Victoria.

The next day Gilbert set to work, building a model from the sketches he had made at Portsmouth. By 7:30 p.m. on the second day, the model was finished and after dinner Gilbert took it over to Carte at the Opera Comique. When he arrived home he made an attempt to pick up his work on the opera: "could not—read instead—bed at 3."[39] On Tuesday evening, he was back at the Opera Comique to settle details about the construction of the set from his model, and while he was there decided to go on in *Trial by Jury*. Whether that was appreciated, enjoyed, or dreaded by the rest of the cast is not recorded in his diary. He was in holiday mood: he and Kitty were planning a trip to Paris for Easter and had invited Marion Terry to join them. Gilbert ordered new clothes from White's in Regent Street, bought the life of Goethe and *Faust*, in preparation for his new play at the Olympic, and on

Good Friday, 19 April, wrote the "Bumboat Woman's Confession," afterward driving over to Hampstead with Kitty to play tennis in a drill shed.

On the Saturday morning, although he was leaving on holiday that evening, Gilbert made a start on the dialogue of act 1 of the opera, and after lunch took his latest lyrics over to Sullivan. Then it was off with Kitty and Marion Terry to catch the 8:35 p.m. from Victoria.

They were in Paris by 6:15 in the morning. Kitty and Marion went to bed for a few hours, while Gilbert went for a walk, rejoining the ladies for breakfast. It was Easter Sunday; they were in Paris, but they still kept up the custom of Sunday afternoon visiting, calling on their friends, the Hares, and Marcus Stone and his wife, just as they did when they were in Kensington. Over the next three days they visited the sights: the Louvre, Notre Dame, the Palais de Luxembourg, Versailles; they went shopping on the rue de Rivoli; went to the theater in the evening; and walked along the boulevards, stopping for a drink at a pavement café.

They moved on to Brussels, catching the night train and arriving at six o'clock in the morning. This time Gilbert went to bed for a few hours' sleep on arrival at the hotel. A visit to the battle site of Waterloo in the afternoon left him with a "furious headache," forcing him to lie down when they returned to the hotel and miss dinner. Later he felt well enough to go for a walk with the ladies—"bought frogs & duck," but the headache got worse and he was in bed by 10:30.[40] The next few days were spent sight-seeing: first, in Brussels, including watching the lace-makers; and then it was on to Antwerp for another rapid tour. They attended High Mass in the Cathedral on Sunday, and in the evening caught the train back to Brussels on the first leg of their journey home—a journey that gave Gilbert the opportunity to make use of his fluent French. "Row with old woman as to coupé—she complained to guard—lied—nothing came of it—changed to another train—another row with another old woman, as to people crowding in carriage—arrived at Brussels just in time to catch train to Calais—."[41]

They were back at The Boltons by 7:00 a.m. Monday morning. After breakfast, a bath, and a few hours in bed, Gilbert took Kitty and Marion to the Haymarket Theatre, and then walked to Regent Street, where he proceeded to have an argument with White about the clothes he had bought from him before the holiday.

While Gilbert had been away, Sullivan had been struggling to compose the music for the opera in between bouts of excruciating pain from a kidney stone. He felt isolated in London: "Everyone is out of town for Easter except myself," he told his mother. "I haven't been out this week except to dine, as I am in the full swing of my new work. It will be bright & probably more popular than the Sorcerer, but it is not so clever."[42]

While Sullivan struggled to work, Carte battled with the directors who were trying to keep down costs by cutting the size of the chorus. Carte appealed to Sullivan for help. On Tuesday 23 April, the eve of the first music rehearsal for *HMS Pinafore*, Sullivan wrote Carte an official letter addressed "Dear Sir" instead of his usual

"Dear D'Oyly" and clearly intended for the directors. "The men chorus play such an important part in the new piece, that the present chorus must be strengthened. I shall therefore advise your making up the number to 6 tenors and 8 basses. Please see that everyone is present tomorrow to begin at 11.30 and that the Stage is ready with seats and Piano."[43]

On the same day, he wrote a hasty note to Carte to express a different concern:

I am very much distressed about Mrs. Howard Paul. I am most anxious to have her in the cast, but there is *absolutely nothing* for her to do, I want a lady for concerted pieces only—The "1re. Relation" has not a single line to herself.[44]

Carte had already started to renew contracts for the new opera. George Grossmith signed for 18 guineas a week, the rate he had originally asked for when he joined the company; and the day before Sullivan's note to Carte, Mrs. Howard Paul had signed for 10 guineas a week "to sing and act as principal contralto & character during the period of the run."[45] At that stage, Carte still had no clear idea of the size of the part that Gilbert was writing for her.

Gilbert caught up with the music rehearsals on Tuesday 30 April, after his return from Paris and Brussels. The opening of *HMS Pinafore* was less than a month away and both men were under pressure. No neat cutoff point existed when the libretto was completed and handed over to Sullivan for him to compose the music. The lyrics were not yet finished; on 1 May, Gilbert and Sullivan met at the Beefsteak, and returned to Albert Mansions for a conference on the words and music for act 1. Two days later, after a game of tennis with Kitty before breakfast, Gilbert worked at the dialogue and at alterations in the lyrics, which he then sent off to Sullivan. After music rehearsal the next day, Saturday, he read act 1 to the company and then it was home for more tennis with friends.

Even before Gilbert had written the dialogue of act 2, he was already thinking of his next piece of work, and on Sunday, 5 May, he started writing the plot of a play for Neville at the Olympic, giving it the working title of "Faust." In the evening, it was back to work on *Pinafore*, when Sullivan called at the Boltons after dinner for a long discussion on act 2 until after two in the morning. Stage rehearsals started the next day. Gilbert's original idea of having the sailors' uniforms made in Portsmouth had proved too expensive, and he and Carte went straight from rehearsal to the Army & Navy stores in Victoria Street and then to Mathews, the costumiers, who agreed to send them an estimate for sale or hire.

While rehearsals of act 1 continued, Sullivan was writing the music and Gilbert the dialogue of act 2. By 13 May, Gilbert was ready to read act 2 to the company, but he was still not satisfied. He noted in his diary, "determined to cut Mrs. Paul's part out—."[46] He wrote to her on 17 May. No copy of that letter has survived; nor any reply, if indeed there was one; but the upshot was that Mrs. Howard Paul left the cast. The tiny singing part of Hebe, all that remained of the original character, now had to be filled and it was left to Carte to find someone with only a week to go to the performance. Carte remembered a twenty-four-year-old contralto, Jessie Bond, whom he had heard sing at St. George's Hall and had approached after the performance offering to act as her agent. She was on holiday in Liverpool, where her family lived, and Carte sent her a telegram: "Would you like comic opera call eleven oclock my office D'Oyly Carte."

"It was like a trumpet call!" she recalled.[47] Jessie Bond readily accepted a contract for £3 a week. And so began the stage career of one of the best-known singers in the Gilbert and Sullivan operas. Only three years earlier, she had started at the Royal Academy of Music studying under Manuel Garcia; she had no stage experience but had sung at concerts in Manchester, at the Crystal Palace, Langham Hall, and the Queen's Theatre. She was to join one other newcomer to the cast for *HMS Pinafore;* for the part of Josephine, Carte had engaged an Australian soprano, Emma Howson, unknown in England, but who had previously performed in America.

Sullivan's score was now complete except for the overture. He sketched out the general lines and asked Alfred Cellier, who had become musical director the previous December, to complete the detail.[48] It was Cellier's role to take over the conducting after the first night, and the stage management, carried out to Gilbert's instructions, would then be supervised by Charles Harris. The management team at the Opera Comique was completed by Richard Barker, later to be joined by Michael Gunn, as business manager.

Kitty accompanied Gilbert to the Opera Comique during the final week of rehearsals. Sometimes she was joined by other guests: Beatrice Lake (a young relative), John Hare, and friends from the Beefsteak Club. On the Friday, Gilbert and Sullivan rehearsed the company in the morning, and Gilbert stayed at the theater until 5:30 p.m. checking on every detail. That evening, the 178th and final performance of *The Sorcerer*, was followed by a night rehearsal—"Everything smooth," wrote Gilbert in his diary. He left the theater at 3:35 a.m. and went to the Beefsteak for supper, finally arriving home at 4:30 a.m.[49]

On Saturday 25 May, the day of the opening of *HMS Pinafore*, Gilbert was at the theater in the afternoon making sure that everything on the set was in order; then it was off to the Beefsteak for dinner and to dress for the evening. He was back at the theater again by eight o'clock to "put finishing touches &c." as he wrote in his diary, but he was probably fussing about nervously, making others feel as agitated as himself. "Rowdy gallery," he noted, "singing songs &c. Piece went extremely well— I went in & out three or four times during evening. Enthusiastic call for self & Sullivan."[50]

Enthusiastic calls had been the order of the evening: Captain Corcoran's song, the First Lord's song, the ensemble at the end of act 1, "Never Mind the Why and Wherefore," and "He Is an Englishman" were all encored.

Sullivan had told his mother that the music would be "bright & probably more popular" than *The Sorcerer* and it was the tunefulness and breezy quality of the music that endeared it to so many. The most famous songs from the opera were all written for people with limited voices: the First Lord's song, where Sullivan allows the words to dominate, but provides additional humor even through a tum-tum accompaniment; the Captains' song in which "What never?—Hardly ever!" are commented on by the bassoon; and Little Buttercup's simple but catchy waltz tune, not rising above a D, written for a singer with a low voice rather than a true contralto. Once again, Gilbert and Sullivan had delighted their audience. "The curtain fell amidst enthusiastic applause," said the *Era*, "and Messrs. Gilbert and Sullivan and the principal performers were called to the footlights, and greeted most heartily . . . the success of the comic opera and the genuine enjoyment the audience had derived from it was unquestionable."[51]

Gilbert chose to relax afterward with the gentlemen of the Beefsteak Club, where he enjoyed the hearty congratulations of the members including his cousin Sutherland Edwards; it was even sweeter to be praised in the presence of some who may not have felt so inclined to participate, although they were present that evening, such as Labouchère and W. H. Kendal.

The next day Gilbert's father called: he was a frequent Sunday visitor, but on that Sunday especially proud of his son's success of the previous evening. "Good reviews in Observer & Era," noted Gilbert. He went over to Albert Mansions to see Sullivan, to compare notes and to arrange for cuts on Monday. Mrs. Sullivan was there: another proud parent come to congratulate her son. They had to wait until Monday for the reviews in the daily papers. *The Times* gave prominence to the performances of Grossmith, Barrington, and Harriette Everard. "The vocal achievements of these artists are not of the highest order, but their *parlato* style does full justice to the humorous sallies of Mr. Gilbert." The reviewer admitted Sullivan's "decided success" and then qualified his praise: "we cannot suppress a word of regret that the composer on whom before all others the chances of a national school of music depend should confine himself, or be confined by circumstances, to a class of production which, however attractive, is hardly worthy of the efforts of an accomplished and serious artist."[52]

On Monday, Gilbert and Sullivan cut a hornpipe in act 1 and Captain Corcoran's "Fair Moon" serenade at the beginning of act 2 (which was later reinstated), and Gilbert decided to turn some of the dialogue into recitative. After all the anxiety and the exertion, and finally the triumph, both Gilbert and Sullivan deserved a rest. Sullivan had been ill, off and on, for months and had struggled through the composition and rehearsals. Even Gilbert, who usually moved straight on to the next piece in hand, took a complete break from writing by playing tennis, enjoying a picnic lunch one day in Richmond Park with Kitty and Marion Terry, spending quiet evenings at home with Kitty (frequently joined by Marion Terry), and on one occasion reading *David Copperfield* to them both.

Sullivan had little time to relax: his talents were in demand for the latest international exhibition in Paris. As he crossed the Channel, he witnessed a shipping disaster when two German warships, the *König Wilhelm* and the *Grosser Kurfürst*, collided off the English coast, with the loss of more than half the crew of nearly five hundred men on the *Grosser Kurfürst*.[53] Like the rest of the passengers on his ship, Sullivan was a helpless spectator as the stricken ship sank beneath the water "in clear bright sunshine, & the water like a calm lake," he told his mother. "It was too horrible, & then we saw all the boats rowing about, picking up the survivors — some so exhausted that they had to be lifted on to the ships."[54]

That trip to Paris was the first of several that Sullivan had to make during the next two months organizing the British musical contribution to the exhibition. When the last concert was over, Sullivan breathed a sigh of relief: "musically we were very successful, & everyone speaks very highly of us," he wrote to a friend. "On Wednesday I go back to England, & shall not move again for some time."[55] He had no thought of a follow-up to *HMS Pinafore*.

CHAPTER THIRTEEN

1878-1879

Troubled Waters

A MONTH AFTER THE OPENING of *HMS Pinafore*, following a wet and cool early June, London was hit by a mini-heatwave. A hot and sticky evening in the theater was not an attraction, especially when sweltering in heavy serge, or constricted by a tight corset, in an atmosphere made unbearable by the heat issuing from the gaslight. Even the bright and breezy *Pinafore* at the Opera Comique would find it difficult to survive in such conditions. In the event, the very hot weather lasted only five days, ending on 30 June with a thunderstorm, but a week later it was warm again. One of the directors of the company, Edward Bayley, was becoming nervous about profits and wrote to Carte on 6 July: "I hope you will get Gilbert & Sullivan's *agreement in writing* to a break at once. I do not care to go on as a Company without it. The hot weather is returning & I object to putting my head in a noose."[1]

With the firm backing of Gilbert and Sullivan, Carte kept the Opera Comique open despite the temporary setback caused by the warm weather. In accounts explaining the slow start of *HMS Pinafore*, the hot weather has usually been put forward as a reason, but it has been exaggerated. The weather in July was mixed, with only three hot days in the middle of the month, soon followed by a thunderstorm, heavy rain, and cooler conditions.[2] In a letter to his mother of 16 August, Sullivan refers to the changeable weather that summer when he says, "What extraordinary weather we are having. It has been beautiful sunshine all the morning, & now suddenly there comes on heavy rain & thunder. The coolness however is good for the [promenade] Concerts & the 'Pinafore.'"[3]

Soon after the start of *Pinafore*, Gilbert began to feel unwell; he mentioned nothing specific in his diary, but simply wrote "seedy," "too ill to work," "still seedy." He felt in need of a vacation and suggested a "world tour" to Kitty, who was excited at the idea. The next day, 1 July, Gilbert went along to Cook's to make enquiries about the tour, and then arranged with his friend Frank Locker at the *Graphic* to write a series of articles for the paper during the trip, sending a weekly page and three wood-cuts. No sooner was that settled when the possibility of going to America on a project with John Hare sidetracked the world tour. In the middle of these exciting speculations, Gilbert was brought down to earth when a letter from Neville arrived telling him that he wanted his "Faust" play to be ready by November, forcing Gilbert to conclude that neither the world tour nor the American project was practicable. To compensate Kitty in her disappointment at not seeing the world, or even America, Gilbert drove into town with her and "bought diamonds & chain." For himself, and for the sake of his health, Gilbert settled for a few days in Margate.[4]

His health cannot have been improved when he had a serious clash at the Opera Comique with the stage manager, Charles Harris. A few days earlier, Gilbert had already clashed with Harris when he heard that Harris, without Gilbert's or Sullivan's permission, had arranged for a performance of *The Sorcerer* at the Crystal Palace for Saturday, 29 June. It was too late to refuse permission, Gilbert informed Harris, and they had no wish to embarrass the Crystal Palace company, but their agreement to the performance going ahead was dependent on one condition, he told him: "your entire share of the profits must be handed over intact, to the Victoria Hospital for Children, Gough House, Chelsea, in the joint names of Mr. Sullivan & myself."[5]

After dining at the Beefsteak on 4 July, Gilbert called at the Opera Comique. What he saw infuriated him. Harris had altered some of the stage business without consulting him. Gilbert would not tolerate such interference and a row followed. The next day Gilbert saw the directors: "Harris not to be allowed to enter theatre again," was the outcome recorded in his diary.[6] Harris was not in fact to work on a Gilbert and Sullivan opera in England again until *Utopia, Limited* in 1893.

On Tuesday 9 July, Gilbert left on his own for Margate. On his way to the station, he called in at Watherston's, the jeweler in Pall Mall, to order diamond earrings for Kitty and then left Charing Cross by the one o'clock train. His original intention was to book in at a hotel, but he was met at Westgate by Marion and Florence Terry, who had rented a house there with their mother. He accepted an invitation to stay with them and wrote to Kitty asking her to join them. The next day he booked rooms in a hotel and went to meet Kitty at the station. "I was rather late—caught it," he noted ruefully in his diary.[7]

Every morning over the next five days Gilbert walked the two miles or so to Margate to take a swim before breakfast. "After breakfast, loafed about—walked with Mrs. on Esplanade." All mention of feeling ill, a feature for eleven consecutive days before the holiday, had disappeared from the diary. The following Tuesday, they returned to London but only to collect their luggage. That same evening they caught the nine o'clock train to Southampton to cross over to France and continue their vacation there with John and Mary Hare.[8]

At Trouville, Kitty joined Gilbert for the daily swim before breakfast, and John and Mary Hare joined them both for cribbage after dinner. The stakes were modest: in three days Gilbert ended up 4 shillings ahead. They broke from their mainly seaside vacation to take a short sight-seeing trip to Rouen, staying at the Hotel d'Angleterre, which Gilbert noted in his diary as "beastly & extortionate." Then it was back to the coast, this time Dieppe, where the Hares left for London, while Gilbert and Kitty went on to Le Tréport. On the first morning they both went swimming, despite the rough sea, but on the second day Gilbert had failed to check the times of high tide: "Got up & went to bathe—," he noted, "but found no water—."[9]

For the last part of their holiday in Boulogne, they had invited Kitty's niece, Beatrice Lake, to join them and booked in at the Hotel Christol, where they had spent part of their honeymoon. They stayed ten days, swimming every morning, but mixed bathing was not allowed: Kitty swam with Beatrice at one part of the beach, while Gilbert was obliged to swim alone. They walked, they listened to the band, they drove over to Wimereux, and one evening Gilbert managed to sit through two acts of *Carmen* at the theater: "wretched performance," he noted. And every evening after a stroll, he bought cakes or ice cream as an end-of-day treat. After an early swim on Monday, 5 August, they sailed for Folkestone and home arriving at Charing Cross at seven o'clock: "home—dined—bed early—."[10]

Sullivan was meanwhile hard at work. He had been appointed as principal conductor for an eight-week season of promenade concerts at Covent Garden with Alfred Cellier as assistant conductor. The season opened on Saturday, 3 August, when Sullivan was given "the cordial greeting due to the position he enjoys among our native artists," said *The Times*. "[He] is no common labourer in the field of art, and merits all the distinction that may be conferred on him."[11]

The opening concert included a selection from *The Sorcerer*, but it was a selection from *HMS Pinafore*, compiled by Hamilton Clarke, which later in the month captured the public imagination. On Saturday, 24 August, "the chief attraction," said *The Times*, was "a highly effective 'selection' from Mr. Sullivan's comic opera *H.M.S. Pinafore* . . . comprising some of the most striking melodies—such as the opening chorus, Josephine's first song, the songs of Sir J. Porter and Captain Corcoran, that of 'Little Buttercup,' and a large portion of the finale to Act 1." It was Sullivan's belief that the *Pinafore* selection at the promenade concerts contributed to the increased interest at the Opera Comique; certainly the concerts were a huge success. Sullivan conducted Hamilton Clarke's selection several more times before the end of the season, by which time the success of *Pinafore* at the Opera Comique was assured.[12]

Having devoted so much time and energy to his stagebound *Pinafore*, Gilbert decided to buy a seagoing craft for himself. He advertised in *The Times* and saw several yachts before finding the *Druidess* on the Isle of Wight. Gilbert and Kitty joined the yacht on Thursday 12 September at Southsea and after "shopping to buy stores &c.," Gilbert recorded, they were "under weigh at 12.30" with their hired crew. Their first cruise tested their resolve to become sailors. Before long they were struck by a squall and all night they had to struggle through rough seas, arriving at Dungeness only at daybreak. In calmer waters, they sailed on to Dover, where they managed to find a tug to tow them into port. The next two days were spent in the harbor, living on board, but on Sunday, when they had intended to sail on to Ramsgate, the weather was too treacherous. Gilbert and Kitty set out for home on dry land, leaving instructions for the crew to sail the yacht to Greenhithe when the weather improved, and to dock her there.[13]

When he returned to London, Gilbert called on Sullivan at Covent Garden on 20 September in the hope of persuading him to write another opera. It was not Sullivan's intention to continue writing comic operas; he had taken to heart the comments about his real place being in serious music. Others expected greater things from him. However, in June, when he had run into difficulty preparing a libretto for the "David and Jonathan" that he had agreed to write for Leeds, Gilbert had offered to help, and it had been agreed that Gilbert would provide a book based on Henry Hart Milman's *The Martyr of Antioch*. Now, in September, Sullivan "half-consented" to write another piece for the Opera Comique.[14]

Three days later Gilbert and Carte met Sullivan at Covent Garden, and all three walked down to the Strand to take a look at the site at Beaufort Buildings on which Carte proposed to build a new theater and realize his dream. Afterward, Gilbert walked all the way back to Victoria Street with Sullivan. Both Gilbert and Carte were exerting pressure in their different ways and Sullivan was caught in a pincer movement. Gilbert was more than willing to write another opera; *HMS Pinafore* was now playing to full houses and looked set for a long run, providing him with a steady income. Carte had his eyes on the future, to the days when he was no longer bound by the directors of the Comedy Opera Company but was the proprietor of his own theater, built for English comic opera. The time would come when he would say he had built the theater for the Gilbert and Sullivan operas, but at this stage he was not even sure of another opera from Sullivan. It was not that Sullivan had any definite plans; even his next serious project was to be written in conjunction with Gilbert, and he had not written any serious piece outside the theater for five years. Although flanked by two such decisive characters as Gilbert and Carte, Sullivan still wavered; he had to be wooed, as he would have to be wooed, even more ardently and more persuasively, over the years for almost every other opera.

The three men were brought closer together because they had a common enemy: the directors of the Comedy Opera Company. The directors were businessmen, looking after their own interests; when profits were down, they wanted to cut and run; now that profits were up, they were content to hold on to what they considered to be their property. With the backing of Gilbert and Sullivan, Carte had had to fight to keep *HMS Pinafore* afloat, and now all three could see most of the profits going into the directors' pockets. Sullivan obliged Carte with another letter in September, addressed "My dear Carte" instead of his usual "My dear D'Oyly" and clearly intended for official purposes. He complained that the orchestra was down in number and indifferent in quality. "I beg to give you notice that if the deficiencies are not supplied by Saturday and the efficiency of the Orchestra increased by engaging better players both of the wind and stringed instruments I shall withdraw my music from the theatre on Monday Night."[15] It was another letter for Carte to use initially to force the directors to increase their expenses, but also another letter to keep carefully for later use.

Since Gilbert had returned from his sailing trip on the *Druidess*, he had gone back to work on "Faust" and at the same time was helping Marion Terry prepare for her part in *Two Orphans*, which opened at the Olympic on 23 September. She had been staying at The Boltons since 17 September, and each night Gilbert waited up until she returned from the theater. This went on until Sunday 6 October, when Gilbert noted in his diary, "At home all afternoon & evening. Row." There is no mention of the cause or subject of the "row," or indeed who was involved, but the next day Marion Terry, who had been staying with them for the past three weeks, left.[16]

It is an appropriate moment to look at the "Xs" that appear from time to time in Gilbert's diary and to consider whether he was using a secret code to denote experiences, possibly sexual, which he wanted to keep hidden. In Gilbert's diary, the entries that have an "X" against them can be divided into two. The first category consists of those entries against which the "cross" appears in the body of the text, for example, to mark the point for an insertion; or against a scrap of dialogue intended for *Pinafore*; or against a simple entry, such as "Went to Club x—Thence home—very seedy." There are few entries in this category. The second category, a much larger one, consists of "Xs" in the margin, and they almost always occur against an entry referring to MT, Marion Terry. It was Gilbert's practice while Marion Terry was rehearsing or acting in one of his plays at the Olympic to escort her from the theater, by cab or on foot, to one of the stations on the various railway lines of the time (Metropolitan Railway, Metropolitan & District Railway, West London Railway, Hammersmith & City Railway), all now incorporated into the London Underground system. What at first sight may appear to be various addresses in London are instead the names of stations that Gilbert mentions: Temple, St. James's Park, Gloucester Road, High Street [Kensington], Queen's Road Bayswater (he called it Bayswater Road), Earls Court, Uxbridge Road (which closed in 1941), Latimer Road, Notting Hill (now called Ladbroke Grove), and Westbourne Park.

It is possible that Kitty thought that he was being overprotective of Marion Terry, escorting her from the theater, and now staying up every night like an anxious father waiting for her to come home safely. They had known Marion Terry since she was a child, but she was now twenty-five. On one occasion, Gilbert and Marion had walked down the Strand together and he had bought her buns and ginger beer at Marshalls, the baker's, opposite Charing Cross Station. Not exactly the behavior of a man trying to impress a young lady; more like the behavior of a man treating a young lady like the little girl he had known for years. Perhaps rumors had reached Kitty's ears: her husband had been frequently seen out with Marion Terry. It is impossible to say when the "Xs" were made—before the row, during it, or afterward. But it seems as though Gilbert was looking out for railway stations as his eye scanned the entries. He missed a few, whereas he put a cross against this innocent looking entry on 9 April: "Went to Gloucester Rd—then to A. Sullivan he was out—"[17] (from Gilbert's Gloucester Road to Sullivan's Victoria, or vice versa, the quickest route was via "Sloane Square and South Kensington stations").

Whatever the details of that heated discussion, perhaps Kitty thought it was time he stopped his overprotective behavior toward Marion Terry. Kitty and Gilbert remained friends with the Terry girls who still came to lunch occasionally, but Gilbert's escorting days were over and Marion never stayed with them again.

There are three further crosses: two against visits to the Carlton Club, which was not his regular club—then they disappear. The crosses in Gilbert's diary seem to draw attention to an entry rather than denote a hidden meaning.

In the autumn of 1878, Gilbert was busy but led a less hectic life than in the first half of the year, which had ended with his being unwell. He was already preparing for next season's sailing by taking navigation lessons from a tutor who called at his house; he was still working at "Faust," and rehearsing the cast for a revival of *The Wedding March* at the Charing Cross Theatre, now renamed the Folly.

Sullivan called on Gilbert on 4 November, arriving at 10:30 and remaining until three o'clock in the morning. He was treated to a reading of *Gretchen*, as Gilbert now called his "Faust" play, then they played cribbage and Gilbert won 13 shillings from his vastly more experienced card-playing colleague. Gilbert does not say in his diary why Sullivan called; perhaps it was simply a social call, but it is more likely that Sullivan wanted to discuss affairs at the Opera Comique. The theater was going to be closed in December by order of the Ministry of Works while improvements were made to the drainage, sewage, and water supply in accordance with the Public Health Act of 1875. After the closure, Carte would have to negotiate a new lease with the owner, Lord Kilmorey, through his agent the earl of Dunraven. Carte's intention was to take a personal lease on the Opera Comique for six months after the reopening of the theater. The directors, suspecting Carte's motive, were not happy at such a proposal. Sullivan agreed to support Carte and wrote to the directors on 13 November.

As "amicus curiae," he said, he strongly recommended that they accept Carte's proposal.[18] His own relations with the directors and with Carte were equally friendly, he claimed, and he sought an amiable settlement to the dispute. However, knowing of Carte's plans to build a new theater, Sullivan was well aware that Carte had no intention of continuing his connection with the company a moment longer than was absolutely necessary.

For Gilbert, the pace of work was beginning to quicken again. He had read the first three acts of *Gretchen* to the principals at the Olympic Theatre, Neville was pleased with it, but suggested changes to act 3, which Gilbert worked at before moving on to act 4. Rehearsals for the revival of *The Wedding March* at the Folly had begun on 9 November, and immediately after the play opened on 23 November, Gilbert offered to write an adaptation of *La Cagnotte* for Selina Dolaro. He had already agreed in October to write another play for Edward Sothern for the £1,050 he owed, but in December offered to release Sothern from the contract, offering to send him the American fees on *Engaged* instead. Sothern preferred to have the new play.

In the middle of all this activity, Gilbert began work on the next opera. By Sunday morning, 8 December, he had sketched out a plot and then went over to see Sullivan. In the evening, after a reception that they both attended, Gilbert returned to Albert Mansions and he and Sullivan talked over the opera until three in the morning. Three days later Gilbert worked again at the plot, and that evening Sullivan dined with the Gilberts at The Boltons. On 14 December, Gilbert finished *Gretchen* and gave himself a week's rest from all work.

By Christmas, Gilbert was back into his routine of working in the mornings, but had not returned to working late at night. On 23 December, Marion Terry arrived at The Boltons with a Christmas present, but would not go in, and on Christmas Eve, Kitty's mother and Grace arrived to stay over. Gilbert called in at the Opera Comique, where there was a preholiday atmosphere before the theater closed for a month, and then he went on to the Olympic Theatre and its Christmas festivities, finally arriving home at 4:30 a.m. On Christmas morning he woke with a hangover. "Headache from bad champagne last night," he wrote in his diary. On Christmas Day, Gilbert, Kitty, and the Turners were joined by Gilbert's father, and after dinner they went round to the Hares, who were entertaining Marcus Stone and his wife. The day ended up with cribbage and with Gilbert losing £3.[19]

A few days after Christmas, Sullivan had an all-male celebration, inviting Gilbert and a few friends to dinner at the Garrick, followed by cards in his rooms at Albert Mansions, where the stakes were a little different from those at cribbage with John Hare. Gilbert arrived home at 3:30 in the morning—£17 better off.

Now that the Opera Comique was closed and the touring company had completed its tour of *HMS Pinafore* and *The Sorcerer*, London and the provinces were both without a Gilbert and Sullivan opera. The focus of attention had now shifted to America, where a pirate version of *Pinafore* had opened at the Boston Museum on 25 November, to instant success. Sullivan's tunes were hummed and whistled everywhere, turned out on barrel organs and blasted out by brass bands. Gilbert's words became catchphrases: "What never?—Well, hardly ever" was so overused that one harassed newspaper editor warned his reporters that he never wanted to see that phrase again. "What never?" one of his staff asked bravely.

Companies sprang up in theaters all over New York, and in no time *Pinafore* was a craze in America. One American manager, John Ford, offered Sullivan £1,000 to go over and conduct *Pinafore* for a few nights in Philadelphia. Sullivan preferred to involve his two colleagues and Carte devised a scheme to take the authentic *Pinafore* to America, but it would be a whole year before any plans could be put into action.

The year 1879 promised a considerable increase in fortune. Sullivan shared some of his good fortune with Fanny Ronalds. He wrote to his father's old friend, Alfred Hipkins, with a request that Broadwoods take Mrs. Ronalds's piano from 84 Sloane

Street, tune it, and return it to her new address, 104 Sloane Street. A few weeks later, he wrote again, offering to pay for the hire of Fanny's piano. "She is a *very* old friend of mine, not well off, the best amateur singer in London, & has sung my songs in London, Paris & New York as if she had a royalty upon them! . . . I can easily afford it, for I have had a very good year with the 'Pinafore' & 'Lost Chord.'"[20]

CARTE SUCCEEDED IN OBTAINING the lease of the Opera Comique for six months beginning 1 February 1879. He was determined that, at the end of that period, 31 July 1879, he would be rid of the directors of the Comedy Opera Company and free to make his own arrangements for the future, to his benefit and to the benefit of Gilbert and Sullivan and their operas. Carte, aged thirty-four, abounding in energy and with the ambition to match, was about to embark on the most decisive year of his career. For the moment he had his schemes and his dreams; but it could all still end in disaster.

Gilbert and Sullivan were starting the year with a successful money-spinner set to endure for some time to come. Sullivan was content with that, and apart from the worry of having to compose *The Martyr of Antioch* as soon as Gilbert had provided him with the book, had no personal projects in mind. Gilbert, however, did have other projects before continuing his work with Sullivan, the first of which was to see *Gretchen* into production. And that was Gilbert's first difficulty of the year; he did not see eye to eye with Neville, the manager of the Olympic.

"Let us distinctly understand one another," he wrote in a letter to Neville on 3 February, ". . . unless I am accorded the full privileges which are conceded to me in every other theatre with which I am connected, *I will not put my foot within the walls of the Olympic.*" He was insisting on the "unquestioned right to make all engagements" and "an absolute control over the stage management of the piece from first to last."[21] Without these privileges, as he called them, he would not stage manage the play. The problem was eventually ironed out sufficiently to allow Gilbert to feel that his honor was intact, and that he could go ahead with the stage management of *Gretchen*.

A more serious problem arose when W. H. Kendal was overheard to remark in the Beefsteak that Gilbert had acted dishonorably toward Sothern. According to John Hollingshead, who had been in the club at the time of the remark, Kendal did not believe that Gilbert had ever returned any of the money he had received for *The Vagabond*. Gilbert was indignant. His integrity as a man of honor had been questioned. Gilbert was only too aware of his debt, and according to their latest agreement, he was to write another play for Sothern for the £1,050 he still owed him. Gilbert demanded an apology from Kendal, who denied accusing Gilbert of acting dishonorably; and Gilbert, armed with a letter of confirmation from Sothern concerning their agreement, insisted that there was not "one particle of foundation for the statement to Hollingshead &c."[22] This unhappy affair, added to the earlier disputes with Kendal, was to result in an estrangement lasting thirty years.

A repercussion from the Kendal affair was that John Hare, now sharing the management of the Court with Kendal, distanced himself from Gilbert. His excuse for not responding to an invitation from the Gilberts to dinner was that Gilbert's behavior toward his wife Mary had been unfriendly. Gilbert rejected the accusation. Hare's action, he suggested, was caused either because his mind had been prejudiced against Gilbert "by the malicious utterances of persons who are interested in dividing us" or because he felt that it was difficult to remain "on intimate terms" with the Gilberts and their "declared enemies." What particularly hurt Gilbert, he told Hare, was Hare's inability "to appreciate the value of an old and often-tried friendship."[23]

Kitty was at one with her husband. She, too, was losing a friend for what seemed to her no good reason. She wrote to Mary Hare sharing her husband's indignation at what she saw as the wrong done to them, and showed the same attention to detail as her husband in putting forward the documentary evidence to support her case. "You are of course at liberty to give your version of our quarrel," she wrote to Mary Hare, "as we shall most certainly give ours."[24]

At the time of his personal battles and setbacks, Gilbert could at least take comfort in the financial success he was having in America. In February, *Engaged* had done well at the Park Theatre, New York; in the first four weeks, Gilbert's share of the takings was $3,144.68 (£641.15.0). *Engaged* also played at the Chestnut Street Theatre in Philadelphia in March, and at the Opera House Baltimore where his share for the week ending 22 March was $1,083.60 (£221.3.0). But in London, where *Gretchen* opened on 24 March at the Olympic, Gilbert was faced with failure. When he found out that Lord Londesborough, determined not to lose any money over the venture, had posted a fortnight's notice in the Green Room at the end of the first night, he was exasperated.

He took to the sea, this time trying out a new yacht, the *Pleione*, which was moored at Dartmouth. Gilbert and Kitty, accompanied by their friend Mrs. Playfair, spent the whole of Easter week on board, enjoying a restful time in the picturesque harbor, taking only one short cruise before returning to London by train the following Monday, 21 April.

On 24 April, Sullivan, Gilbert, and Carte all met at Albert Mansions to make arrangements for America. The plan was to start on 7 October; they would each share one-third of the profits, with traveling and hotel expenses being paid out of the gross receipts. *Pinafore* was doing good business again at the Opera Comique after the enforced break, and a touring company had undertaken a short tour, in April and May, to Liverpool and Birmingham. Carte wanted to extend the touring side of the business but also needed to go to America to settle a good theatre in New York. At the present he had only been offered the Lyceum, on Fourth Avenue, which he described as "an inferior house."[25]

Gilbert could now afford to take life at a more leisurely pace. With the success of *Pinafore* continuing in London, the prospect of making money out of *Pinafore* in

America, and with another opera in the making, the need to take on whatever work was offered had receded. He abandoned his translation of *La Cagnotte* for Selina Dolaro, offering to give her what he had already done of acts 1 and 2. He often called on Sullivan, inviting him to lunch on several occasions and Sullivan invited Gilbert to join a group of friends, including the duke of Edinburgh, to celebrate his thirty-seventh birthday at the Garrick. Afterward, they went on to Sullivan's rooms, where the musical entertainment included songs from Fanny Ronalds. After the departure of the duke of Edinburgh, the cards were brought out and they finished the evening with cribbage.

Gilbert and Sullivan met Carte again on 12 June when they drew up a "Memorandum of Agreement" for the American tour.[26] Carte then sailed for New York. Michael Gunn took over Carte's business in England, sending out two companies to take *Pinafore* around the country: the "B" Company, with Richard Mansfield as Sir Joseph Porter, which would finish up at the end of the year in Torquay; and the "A" Company, with W. S. Penley as Sir Joseph, and which would include a new contralto, Alice Barnett, as Little Buttercup.

Carte arrived in New York on 24 June. He had his eye on two theaters: the Fifth Avenue and the Standard. He met up with Fred Clay, already in New York on his own business, and discussed terms first with Henderson, the lessee and manager of the Standard. Then it was on to see Ford in Philadelphia to discuss terms over the management of the Fifth Avenue Theatre. The newness of the Fifth Avenue probably appealed to Carte. It had been open only two years, having been rebuilt following a fire in 1873, but the old marble front of the first theater had been retained. It was well situated, on the south side of West Twenty-Fourth Street, between Fifth and Sixth Avenues. Nothing had been decided by 11 July when Carte received a telegram from Michael Gunn. The directors of the Comedy Opera Company in London had received a letter on 8 July from George Lewis, the solicitor acting on behalf of Sullivan, giving them notice to withdraw *Pinafore* on 31 July. The next day, 12 July, the directors claimed the right to play *Pinafore* and stated their intention to take another theater to do so, and at the same time swore that Carte had agreed to renew with them. Carte cabled back to Gunn denying such an agreement.

A week later, Carte was still without an agreement on the Fifth Avenue Theatre, and was finding it difficult to settle on the terms he had agreed with Gilbert and Sullivan before leaving for New York. He cabled Sullivan, "negotiations difficult . . . you must take half profits between you or share risk."[27]

While waiting to settle terms in New York, Carte had arranged a concert for Sullivan with the Handel and Haydn Society of Boston and, after advertising in the New York *Herald*, had been auditioning chorus singers at the Steinway Hall, on East Fourteenth Street. When he finally settled with Ford for the Fifth Avenue, the terms were not what he had originally wanted, but at least he was guaranteed a good theater. It was Ford who was to manage the theater for a twelve-week tenancy starting on 1 December, an arrangement that would greatly disappoint Gilbert and Sullivan.

Carte stayed a week longer in America to finalize arrangements for tours outside New York, and on Wednesday, 30 July set sail for England and the continuing battle with the directors of the Comedy Opera Company.

By this time, Sullivan was in Paris. Two days before, he had undergone an operation to crush a kidney stone. Now out of pain he was planning to leave on 31 July for Pontresina in Switzerland. In London, the final day of the agreement between Carte and the directors of the Comedy Opera Company had arrived. The directors were not prepared to let their profitable enterprise be taken from them without a fight. Immediately after Carte's telegram of 12 July to Michael Gunn, the directors had applied for an injunction against Gunn, to prevent him handling receipts from the opera, and at the same time they applied for a receiver. An interim injunction was granted to them, but when the case was heard in the Chancery Division of the High Court on 21 July, the motion failed and Gunn was allowed to continue to act for Carte in his absence.

The directors wasted no time in putting into operation their plan to set up in competition to the Opera Comique, making an offer to the chorus members that most of them found too good to refuse. According to Richard Barker only "ten ladies and two gentlemen" from the old chorus stayed at the Opera Comique.[28] The directors also managed to induce three principals from the touring company—Michael Dwyer (Captain Corcoran), Arthur Rousbey (Dick Deadeye), and Percy Blandford (Ralph)—to join them, and they engaged J. G. Taylor to play Sir Joseph and act as stage manager. Their musical director was Auguste van Biene, who had been musical director of the touring company until May.

Michael Gunn wrote to Sullivan asking him for confirmation that the band parts were Sullivan's personal property, and that the Comedy Opera Company had no claim on them. Sullivan was only too ready to assert that the band parts were his "and they should not go out of the Opera Comique Theatre *without my permission.*"[29] Then Sullivan hurriedly contacted John Hollingshead asking him to return the band parts of *The Merry Wives of Windsor*, and also the parts for *Thespis* that Hollingshead still held on loan. He knew that Hollingshead's opinion was that the band parts belonged to him and were only loaned for the performances, and he wanted to use Hollingshead's practice as a precedent. "I shall be much obliged," he wrote to Hollingshead, "if you will do this, my Dear John, as your name is weighty in a court of law."[30]

The directors had succeeded in setting up a company that they considered to be a viable rival to that of the Opera Comique. They had leased the Imperial (Royal Aquarium) Theatre from 1 August and were ready to open—apart from one thing: they had no scenery.

On 31 July, during the performance of *Pinafore* at the Opera Comique, a boarding party from the rival *Pinafore* swooped in an attempt to carry off the set. Gilbert described what happened next in a letter to Sullivan: "Barker resisted their approach & was knocked down stairs & seriously hurt—There was an alarm among the audience who raised a cry of fire—appeased however by Grossmith who made them a speech from the stage. Barker has applied for summonses against Drake & Bayley, & the case comes on next Monday. . . . Let us know how you are by return, & that you approve of what I've done."[31]

Gilbert was asking for Sullivan's approval of his sending out a notice to be carried by sandwich-board men announcing that the author and composer of HMS Pinafore "in face of the fact that the piece is being played at another theatre," felt it necessary to state that the piece played at the Opera Comique was by the original company, under their supervision, and had their full approval and consent.[32] Gilbert also had applied for an injunction to prevent the directors from putting on their alternative Pinafore, and the petition was heard by the Master of the Rolls on 1 August. The injunction was granted, but at appeal in the afternoon the injunction was dissolved, on the grounds that Lewis's letter of 8 July on Sullivan's behalf and the directors' reply of 9 July had not been submitted as evidence. The directors were, therefore, allowed to go ahead with their scheduled performance that evening at the Imperial.

From Monday, 4 August, Michael Gunn renamed the two touring companies, so as to leave no doubt whose companies they were: the "A" Company became Mr. D'Oyly Carte's "1st 'Pinafore' Company" and the "B" Company became Mr. D'Oyly Carte's "2nd 'Pinafore' Company." With business safely settled in Gunn's hands and nothing more likely to happen until the case with the directors came up in November, Gilbert told Sullivan he was going on a short cruise on his yacht, but would be back to see Carte as soon as he arrived home from America. After that, Gilbert had planned a vacation in Trouville. Meanwhile, he kept Sullivan up to date with progress on the new opera. "I've broken the neck of act 2 & see my way clearly to the end. I think it comes out very well." Gilbert explained the "Tarantara" business—a talisman to help the policemen work up their courage. "When concealed in act 2, and the robbers approach, their courage begins to fail them, but recourse to Tarantara (pianissimo) has the desired effect." Gilbert wanted it to be an important feature, but only offered it as a suggestion. "If you don't like it," he said, "it shan't be done."[33]

Sullivan received the letter in Pontresina, while convalescing at the Roseg Hotel in the company of a large English contingent including the Bancrofts, Joseph Barnby and his wife, Otto Goldschmidt, Rudolph Lehmann, and Arthur Cecil. When the opportunity arose to help raise funds for the English church at Pontresina, a performance of Cox and Box was put on at the hotel on 26 August with an illustrious cast: Sullivan played Cox, Arthur Cecil was Box, Joseph Barnby was Bouncer, and Otto Goldschmidt at the piano supplied the accompaniment.

On the same day Carte, whose life since his return from America had been all "rush and turmoil," wrote a long letter to Sullivan to bring him up to date with developments and to share his anxieties over the directors of the Comedy Opera Company. More happily, he was able to report to Sullivan that he had arranged for the Handel and Haydn Society in Boston to play The Prodigal Son, and was hoping to arrange further concerts in New York and Philadelphia. And with his newly acquired experience of American audiences, he was keen to discuss the prospective tour of *The Sorcerer, Pinafore,* and the new opera:

> Now as regards cast—our people must all be *strong singers.* The people there are nearly all splendid singers. . . . They like "emotional" singing and acting. The placid English style wont do and I assure you that if we took out such a Company as the Opera Comique we should make a big failure as likely as not.

He was negotiating with both Ryley and Penley for the parts of John Wellington Wells and Sir Joseph, and suggested Alice Barnett for Mrs. Partlet and Buttercup, and for the part of Ruth in the new opera. "I think [she] wd. be first rate she has *much* improved in her acting . . . and Everard positively declines going." As for the soprano, Carte had already engaged for the Opera Comique an American soprano, Blanche Roosevelt, who went by the name of Rosavella. "I am inclined to think," he told Sullivan, "that Rosavella's voice may be too thin for America. . . . They are accustomed to hear big voices and fine singers." Carte had in mind another singer, Helene Crosmond. "The only question is terms. . . . She asked me £100 a week—I offered her £20—there we are." So there was to be no Helene Crosmond, but she recommended a tenor, Hugh Talbot, who sang under the name of Talbo. "He wants to go and would be cheap. I know of no one. Power or anyone like that wd. not be listened to in New York. Helene Crosmond says that Talbo is the best Faust she has ever played with."[34]

It is evident that Carte was making the running as regards casting, then referring to Sullivan for his approval, and only later would he consult with Gilbert. With the inclusion of Alice Barnett in the cast of the new opera, Sullivan would be able to write for Ruth a real contralto's part for the first time. Blanche Roosevelt was eventually chosen as the soprano and Talbo went as the tenor but proved to be a disaster.

Before the case against the Comedy Opera Company came to court, Carte wanted to make sure that Sullivan was well protected legally and advised him that he should have "the *best* legal advice possible. The man you want is Frederic Stanley who is a chancery lawyer—the cleverest man in the profession—the man who understands thoroughly all theatrical business, who never makes a mistake, and never loses a suit."[35]

Sullivan was to follow Carte's advice in engaging Stanley, not only in this case, but also eleven years later against Gilbert, when the involvement would be one of the causes of a continuing dispute between the two men. "Take my tip," repeated Carte, *"Stanley is our man"* (Carte's emphasis). For Sullivan's more immediate satisfaction, Carte told him that he had paid the money due to him from the tours to Gilbert, half of which was for Sullivan, together with a bonus: "I have taken the liberty of sending an additional 100 guineas which Gunn and I hope you will let us do as we have done better than we expected."[36]

Carte was on the verge of achieving the ambition he had worked for over the past ten years: the total control of a theater dedicated to the performance of English comic opera, and more specifically the operas of Gilbert and Sullivan. That was not the extent of his ambition; he still intended to build his own theater and to be free from having to ask other people for leases. For the present, he had the worry of the court case against the Comedy Opera Company, the outcome of which was impossible to foretell, no matter how clever the solicitor he had engaged. If that affair were successfully completed, then he would be able to set sail for the New World and a bright future.

CHAPTER FOURTEEN

1879-1880

America and *The Pirates of Penzance*

OPPOSITION TO THE "ORIGINAL" *Pinafore* came closer to home when, on 8 September 1879, the Comedy Opera Company transferred their production to the Olympic Theatre, in Wych Street, only a hundred yards away from the Opera Comique. The "alternative" *Pinafore* was now in its second month and the directors meanwhile kept up the pressure on Carte, threatening that they would make a claim for damages against him, and against any other manager who played the piece without their permission. They extended their range of targets by threatening that "every actor taking part in the performance without their permission" would incur a penalty of £2 a performance.[1]

Before he could start out for America, Carte had other concerns to settle, the principal of which was agreeing terms with Gilbert and Sullivan. When Gilbert had learned that he and Sullivan would have to be content with a half share of the net profits in New York, he met with Sullivan on 14 September to discuss the issue. The following day he wrote to Carte, reminding him of their agreement in June. "It seems that on your visiting America, you ascertained that you could have the 5th. Avenue Theatre on certain terms —*or* Ford would take the theatre & pay orchestra & advertisements, on condition that he received, not a stated sum per night, *but 40 per cent of the gross receipts.*" This was not in the spirit of the agreement Gilbert and Sullivan had made with Carte. As far as they were concerned, Carte had made a managerial decision that was in his own interests and not in the interests of all three. Under their agreement, said Gilbert, Carte was bound to take the theater himself. "Under no circumstances could we agree to pay Ford 40 per cent of gross receipts, in return for his sharing the money responsibility with you."[2]

The letter is tough but not as strident in tone as many of Gilbert's letters to managers. As it was a joint letter, its tone was perhaps tempered by Sullivan. The purpose of going to America was to pocket as many dollars as possible instead of letting everything go to the pirates, and neither Gilbert nor Sullivan was prepared to go to all the trouble involved, only to see another American, Ford, take 40 percent of their profits. Gilbert followed up the letter by calling that evening on Carte at the Opera Comique, but he was no more successful in person than he had been in correspondence. Carte could not now move from the position he had agreed with Ford. Dissatisfied, they conferred again and on 4 October Sullivan wrote to Carte. Again the letter was on behalf of both Gilbert and Sullivan, and Sullivan's more forthright tone than usual suggests Gilbert's influence. "We agree to your proposition subject to your giving us in addition one sixth of your net profits—your net profit to be calculated over the whole tour. I think you had better close with this & save all further bother and negotiation. . . . Pray say that you agree to our amendment & the thing is off our mind."[3]

The agreement was not signed until 23 October, after the court case against the Comedy Opera Company. Gilbert and Sullivan agreed to complete the new opera by 1 December 1879, an aim that was not realized, and all three agreed to stay in America for twelve weeks from 1 December, and not to leave without the consent of the other two.

Two actions had come to court on 15 October 1879. The first was brought by the Comedy Opera Company against Michael Gunn, in which the motion was made that the receiver should pay over to the company the net receipts up to 31 July, when their tenancy of the Opera Comique came to an end. This motion was refused on the grounds that the receiver had not yet passed his accounts, and no case of urgent need for the money had been made out by the company. The second action was brought by Gilbert and Sullivan against the Comedy Opera Company to prevent them from playing *HMS Pinafore* without their permission and infringing their copyright. That motion also was refused, and the Comedy Opera Company were free to continue their performance of *Pinafore*. The opera had been written for the Comedy Opera Company to produce, and it had not been sufficiently established that their right to produce the opera had ceased on 31 July 1879, with their loss of the lease of the Opera Comique and their removal to another theater. The fight over the ownership of the copyright and performing rights would have to be continued, and would not come to court again for almost eighteen months.[4]

The Comedy Opera Company managed to limp along with their rival *Pinafore* at the Olympic until 25 October, when their production was withdrawn, after a total run of ninety-one performances. On the same day, Sullivan left London for Liverpool, ready to embark with Gilbert for America on the *Bothnia*. The day before, he had been occupied by an endless stream of visitors and well-wishers, he had dined with the Lindsays, and then returned home to write "Edward Grey," to words by Tennyson.

Carte was due to follow Gilbert and Sullivan a week later, sailing on the *Gallia* on 1 November. The directors of the Comedy Opera Company were out to stop him. They obtained a court order, dated 30 October, to the effect that Carte who, they claimed, owed them £150, should pay a security of £250 and not leave the country until his debt was cleared. Carte left London at midnight on 31 October, and it was only when he had reached Liverpool that the directors acted on the order. Carte had little time to spare. He cabled Helen Lenoir to pay the £250 into court. The directors were still not satisfied. They insisted on being paid the £150, which, they claimed, he still owed. If he was to catch the boat Carte had no alternative. He paid the £150, but he did so under protest.[5]

For the American tour Carte had done his best to put together a strong singing cast. As he had proposed to Sullivan in August, he had engaged J. H. Ryley and Blanche Roosevelt, who by this time had already appeared as Josephine at the Opera Comique during September. Furneaux Cook had been engaged to sing Captain Corcoran and also the part of Dr. Daly in *The Sorcerer*; Fred Clifton, the original Notary in *The Sorcerer*, was to sing that role and also to play Bill Bobstay in *Pinafore*. Again with the New York audience in mind, Carte had engaged an American baritone, John Clarke, who sang under the name of Signor Brocolini and had played Dick Deadeye in the "1st *Pinafore* Company" during October. As well as Alice Barnett, Carte took two other contraltos from the Opera Comique: Rosina Brandram (for Mrs. Partlet in *The Sorcerer*) and Jessie Bond, who would add the role of Constance in *The Sorcerer* to her usual role of Hebe in *Pinafore*. The decision to take Jessie Bond was a risk. Before leaving England she had missed a number of performances at the Opera Comique through ill health, her place being taken by her understudy from the chorus, Marion Johnson.

Accompanied by Alfred Cellier, Gilbert and Sullivan arrived in New York on Wednesday, 5 November, and were met by their old friend Fred Clay, still there since Carte's visit in June and preparing for the production of *Princess Toto*. They were feted at "a splendid reception," Sullivan told his mother, at the Lotus Club on Saturday, 8 November, by "the most prominent men in New York," and Carte arrived with the rest of the company on Tuesday, 11 November.[6] Rehearsals started the next day. Sullivan thought it was "a first rate chorus and the Principals are the best who have ever been put together for the immortal Pinafore."[7] Sullivan had begun his stay in New York with his friend Mrs. Grant and her husband, David Beach Grant, at 361 West Twenty-third Street. He found Beach Grant "the kindest host possible" and thought his younger brother Suydam, "the dearest fellow in the world, so thoughtful & so unselfish. Mrs. Grant is just as sweet and dear as she always was," he assured his mother. "She sends her love to you & says that she does her best to make me feel I have a mother here!"[8] In an earlier letter to his mother Sullivan had given his first impression of Americans: "I must do the Americans the justice to say that they are most wonderfully kind & hospitable — the moment a man sees you, he wants to know what he can do for you, & means it too."[9]

As well as rehearsals and social functions, and what seemed to Sullivan like endless interviews, he had to travel to Boston to conduct *The Prodigal Son* on 23 November, performed by the Handel and Haydn Society. But he still had so much work to do on the new opera that, on 4 December, he left the Grants' house to move to an apartment at 45 East Twentieth Street, only a few blocks away from the Fifth Avenue Theatre.

Pinafore had opened at the Fifth Avenue on Monday, 1 December, and according to Sullivan, in a letter to his mother, it was "magnificent."[10] Not all that magnificent, however, from the point of view of Gilbert and Sullivan's share of the takings: in the first week, their share was $441.80 each (£110); in the second week, $85.33 (£21); in the third week, nothing. They were not going to get rich in America out of *Pinafore*; everything depended on the success of *The Pirates of Penzance*. Sullivan had composed most of the music in England but he still had to score the whole opera in New York and rewrite act 1, as he had left all his sketches for that act in London. There was little more than a fortnight to go before opening night. "It is a great nuisance," he told his mother, "as I have to rewrite it all now, & can't recollect every number I did. We hope to get it out in a fortnight from next Saturday—27th. I think it will be a great success, for it is exquisitely funny, & the music is strikingly tuneful & catching."[11]

As he worked on the opera Sullivan began to keep a diary, something he was going to do for the next twenty years, although there are often gaps, especially toward the end of his life. He recorded work done, people seen, and engagements, and in that sense it is similar to Gilbert's diary; but, unlike Gilbert, Sullivan was expansive when writing about his journeys abroad, describing new places and new experiences. At no time did he choose to use the diary for self-analysis or to question his own motives. From the beginning he uses L.W. (Little Woman) when referring to Fanny Ronalds in her intimate role in his life, whereas he would refer to her as Mrs. Ronalds or Mrs. R. when she appeared in a public role. The intimate details that Sullivan kept hidden under lock and key were only revealed after his death, when the locks on his diaries were broken open. He recorded in simple code his sexual experiences, using (1) or (2) or a tick, or an expression in German, such as "Himm[e]lische Nacht (2)." The code appears against the initials L.W. for Fanny Ronalds, but also against different initials representing other women in his life.

He was working now into the early hours of the morning, sometimes until 4:30 or five o'clock. Alfred Cellier lent his assistance by writing an accompaniment (not a full orchestral score), for act 2 to be sent over for the first performance in England, and later helped Sullivan out by completing the overture for the American production.

By 12 December, when Sullivan found himself imprisoned in his hotel room and cut off from his social life because of pressure of work, he had revised his opinion of America and Americans: "I wish I were in England," he wrote to his mother. "If anyone wants thoroughly to appreciate England let him come to America—that will shew him what England is worth. I will not put on paper my feelings with reference to many things in this land of liberty & freedom, but I will give them to you freely when I return."[12]

To complete the music for act 1, Sullivan resorted to reusing a piece from *Thespis*.

Rutland Barrington as the Sergeant of Police in *The Pirates of Penzance*
(V&A Picture Library)

It is well known that the chorus in act 1 of *The Pirates of Penzance*, "Climbing over Rocky Mountain," originally appeared in *Thespis*, and although Gilbert made a few changes to the words to adapt them to a different scene, a phrase like "Scaling rough and rugged passes," more appropriate to climbing a mountain as in *Thespis* than clambering over rocks on the Cornish coastland, remains to reveal its origin. In a letter to a correspondent in 1902, Gilbert explained the "history of the transfer," how Sullivan had left "nearly all the score of Act I" in London, that "his marvellous memory enabled him to reproduce a considerable part of it—almost note for note, as he subsequently discovered on comparing the new with the old score."[13] But Sullivan could not recall, said Gilbert, the girls' chorus in act 1, and Gilbert suggested using the chorus from *Thespis*.

This account by Gilbert was given twenty-two years after the event and could be subject to the faults of memory over a long period of time, although remaining substantially true. It could also be the version that Gilbert was prepared to admit. Certainly there was no "score" in England for Sullivan to compare with his finished score in America, and there are one or two other questions left unanswered. What happened to the original chorus written by Gilbert? Unused lyrics in one piece are sometimes "recycled" and appear elsewhere, or at least they were preserved amongst Gilbert's papers; but this chorus has disappeared. Did Sullivan have difficulty in setting the original, and rather than rewrite it, did Gilbert (or Sullivan) then suggest substituting the chorus from *Thespis*? Why did Sullivan have the music (and words) of *Thespis* with him in America? He had recently received the "parts" back from John Hollingshead, as he requested in his letter to Hollingshead of 30 July 1879, but if he also had the words with him, he must have been carrying the orchestral score of *Thespis*, or at least the piano score. Why did he pack *Thespis* on his last busy day in England and yet leave behind his sketches for act 1?

The decision to make the substitution was probably made quite early by Sullivan, perhaps in England where he saw the possibility of using the chorus before packing *Thespis* to take with him. He had, after all, sketched out most of the opera by then. There is no mention of the chorus in Sullivan's diary, which probably means that the transfer had been made before the first entry on 8 December and before he had finished all the numbers in act 1; Ruth's song, for example, in act 1 was not written until 15 December, the same day as the first music rehearsal.

Sullivan took a short break from work, skipping dinner in the process, when he went with Gilbert to a concert of the Mendelssohn Glee Club on 16 December, and noted in his diary that he heard his part-song, "The Long Day Closes." "Admirably sung & encored."[14] Gilbert went on to a reception afterward, and was altogether more free than Sullivan at this stage to attend social functions, going to a ball given on 8 December at the fashionable restaurant Delmonico's. Both men however went to a ball on 11 December at Astor House, opposite City Hall, and to another on 18 December at Delmonico's. If Gilbert followed his normal pattern for first nights, however, he kept clear of the Standard Theatre on 13 December, where Fred Clay was producing their joint work, *Princess Toto*.

After one of Sullivan's typically grueling days, Friday, 19 December, which he spent scoring then conducting *Pinafore* in the evening—before continuing to score all through the night until six o'clock in the morning—he wrote to his mother so that she would have the letter in time for the New Year. He was particularly disenchanted with New York:

> I am sick of the place and the people. It is like a provincial English town—only ill bred, rough and swaggering—I am bitterly disappointed in everything around me. The people in the shops are insolent and ill mannered and with the exception of half a dozen people in your circle like the Grants, Barlows &c, there is no real lady or gentleman to be found.[15]

Sullivan much preferred the deferential society that still existed in England, where people knew their place. The greater self-confidence of the average American he interpreted as insolence, but reserved his severest criticism for the press. "The pressmen are an unscrupulous, lying, inquisitive, and mischievous set who will do anything & print anything. . . . Republicanism is the curse of the country, everyone is not only equal to, but better than his neighbour, and the consequence is insolence and churlishness in all the lower orders."[16] Having unburdened himself to his mother on the ills of American society, Sullivan went back to scoring an opera in which a mirror is held up to English society, where an incompetent army officer lies to save his own skin, and allows his daughters to marry a bunch of scoundrels when he finds out they are really "noblemen gone wrong."

Sullivan worked on, through Christmas, stopping to have Christmas dinner with the Grants, until he had finished the whole score at seven o'clock in the morning of Sunday, 28 December, three days before the opening performance. On 29 December, Sullivan was "in despair" after a dress rehearsal of act 2 had gone badly; but the final dress rehearsal on 30 December was a success, and afterward Sullivan, Cellier, Gilbert, and Clay all worked at the overture with Cellier completing the orchestration and the others copying the parts.

At 2:00 p.m. (in England), on Friday, 30 December, when Sullivan was about to start a full band rehearsal of act 2 in New York, a performance of *The Pirates of Penzance* opened at the Bijou Theatre, Paignton, in order to secure the copyright in England. The "2nd *Pinafore* Company," who were appearing in Torquay, had one rehearsal after their performance on Monday, 29 December, and traveled to Paignton on the morning of the performance. Richard Mansfield played the Major-General, Fanny Harrison was Ruth, Emilie Petrelli—who had sung in the rival *Pinafore* with the Comedy Opera Company—was Josephine, and the Sergeant of Police was played by Fred Billington. Billington had joined the "2nd London Company" in September appearing first as Bill Bobstay and then as Dick Deadeye before becoming part of the "2nd *Pinafore* Company" in December. He was to have a long and successful career with the D'Oyly Carte company, a career that only ended with his death in 1917. The cast also included John Le Hay, who played the part of James, one of the pirates, a part that did not appear in the New York production.

Even among the small audience at the Royal Bijou Theatre on that afternoon, social distinctions were maintained in the seating: the best seats, the "sofa stalls," were 3 shillings, the "second seats" cost 2 shillings, and there was also room in the theater for an "area" at 1 shilling and even a "gallery" at 6 pence.[17] The small audience, probably outnumbered by the company, witnessed a performance without an overture (it had not been finished), without scenery, with makeshift costumes and with a cast who, although underrehearsed and having to read their lines and music, were able performers.

The next evening in New York, at eight o'clock, the first "genuine" performance of *The Pirates of Penzance; or, The Slave of Duty* opened at the Fifth Avenue Theatre. Not only Gilbert but Sullivan, too, was in a nervous state as well as being exhausted following his long hours of composing and scoring. In the morning he had held a band rehearsal for the overture; in the afternoon he tried to rest, but was unable to sleep. Gilbert arrived at 5:30. Sullivan got up, "miserably ill." Slowly he dressed for the theater and then went off to the New-York Club on West Twenty-fifth Street:

> got to New York Club at 7:30. Had 12 oysters & a glass of champagne. Went to the Theatre. House crammed with the élite of New York. Went into the Orchestra, more dead than alive, but got better when I took the stick in my hand—fine reception. Piece went marvellously well—Grand success.[18]

"The laughter & applause continued through the whole piece until the very end," Sullivan told his mother, "and then there were thunder calls for Gilbert & myself after every Act.... The libretto is ingenious, clever, wonderfully funny in parts, & sometimes brilliant in dialogue—beautifully written for music, as is all Gilbert does, and all the action & business perfect." As for the music, Sullivan thought it, "infinitely superior in every way to the Pinafore—*tunier* and more developed—of a higher class altogether. I think that in time it will be more popular."[19]

The theater programs for the evening highlighted the costumes: "Elaborate Costumes imported from Europe, made by Mme. Latreille, of Paris, Mme. Alias and Mr. Nathan of London, from designs, made by 'Faustin.' The Ladies' Dresses by Messrs. Bloom, of New York." "The New York ladies are raving about them," Sullivan wrote to his mother. He was full of praise for the performers, with the exception of Hugh Talbot, the tenor, who had not learned his lines and forgot his music. "We shall, I think, have to get rid of him."[20]

The Pirates was well received both by the audience—nine encores—and by the press: "a palpable hit," said the New York *Herald*.[21] J. H. Ryley was considered a great success, with his acting ability making up for what he lacked in vocal talent. The character of the Major-General had proved a worthy successor to that of Sir Joseph

Porter. It has been suggested that Gilbert's model for the Major-General was Sir Garnet Wolseley, partly because of Grossmith's makeup, in the later English production, which included the large moustache of Wolseley; but Major-General Stanley was no more modeled on Wolseley than Sir Joseph Porter could be said to have been modeled on Nelson simply because George Grossmith made himself up to resemble him. For the idea of the Major-General it is only necessary to look at the examination requirements for entry into the Royal Artillery, which Gilbert was subjected to twenty years or so earlier, in which mathematics had figured so large, to say nothing of the importance of classical history. Closer to home, at the time Gilbert was drawing up his sketch plot for *The Pirates*, at the end of 1878, his acrimonious tussle with Kitty's uncle, General Turner, was still fresh in his mind. General Turner was one of the "old school" of officers, having been commissioned in 1825, and whose "military knowledge" did not extend much beyond "the beginning of the century."

An unusual element in the composition of *The Pirates of Penzance* was the distance in time between Gilbert's conception of the plot and creation of his characters, and Sullivan's composition of the music. When Gilbert created the four main comedy characters—the Major-General, the Pirate King, the Sergeant of Police, and Ruth—he had in mind Grossmith, Temple, Barrington, and Everard. By the time Sullivan came to write the music and the American tour had been planned with a different cast in mind, Sullivan was writing for Ryley, Brocolini, Fred Clifton, and Alice Barnett. The difference was particularly noticeable in the singing part written for Alice Barnett, which has a good sprinkling of low Gs in her act 1 solo; and in the part for Fred Clifton, in which the Sergeant of Police is more of a bass-baritone than the lighter baritone normally associated with the parts played by Rutland Barrington.

Sullivan's wit matches Gilbert's throughout the opera. He indulges in parody of grand opera in the recitatives and in such melodramatic situations as the policemen's reluctance to go in pursuit of the pirates: "Away, Away!" "Yes, yes, we go," and so on in act 2; he provides descriptive accompaniments, as in the "plodding" introduction to "When the foeman bares his steel"; and matches music to words perfectly in the "Chattering chorus" of the girls in act 1, "How Beautifully Blue the Sky." Sullivan responded to Gilbert's even more developed use of the chorus (pirates, policemen, and the General's daughters) and their involvement in the action, by providing music in distinctive styles for the three groups.

By Saturday, 3 January 1880, the end of the first (short) week of *The Pirates*, Gilbert and Sullivan's share of the net profits was $691.21 (£172) each, and at the end of the first full week they each received $1,148.31 (£287). In the third and fourth week each share rose to over $1,200 (£300) and then began to fall back, but even at the end of February, their last full week, they each received $931.60 (£232).[22]

Apart from the company in New York, Carte launched three other companies. The first opened in Philadelphia on 9 February, at which Sullivan conducted; then the company toured New England. The second opened at Newark, New Jersey, on 16 February going on to a wide-ranging tour through Pennsylvania, Ohio, Indiana,

Michigan, Missouri, as far west as Nebraska, and then to Iowa, Minnesota, and Wisconsin. The third company opened at Buffalo, where Sullivan again conducted the opening performances, and then moved over to Chicago before heading south to St. Louis, right down to New Orleans, and then back through Memphis, Nashville, and Louisville.[23]

On 12 February, Gilbert wrote to Marion Johnson, Jessie Bond's understudy as Hebe in England, giving her some idea of the work involved in preparing the companies.

My dear Johnny,
I am just ashamed of myself for having left your kind letter so long unanswered, but if you had any idea how bothered and badgered I have been with rehearsals you would not be very angry with me. We have to rehearse four country companies at once, and no Barker to help us, so you may believe that our hands are pretty full. . . . Chorus ladies get £3 a week out here—dont you wish you might get it.
    Everything is dear out here, so that £3 a week is not so much as it seems.
. . . Jessie Bond has been very ill with pneumonia, but she is alright again now.
I shall be very glad to get back to the old faces at the Opera Comique.
Give my love to all the ladies—and with same to yourself.[24]

Jessie Bond's illnesses are something of a mystery. In her memoirs she referred to an abscess on her ankle, which left the joint permanently stiff; Gilbert referred to her pneumonia; and Sullivan noted in his diary, on 1 January 1880, that he had to call a doctor for "Jessie Bond with one of her fits."[25] Both Gilbert and Sullivan had generously helped Jessie Bond out by paying medical fees for her in America, and the letter to Marion Johnson shows that Gilbert had a more friendly attitude to the members of the cast than his reputation as a martinet usually allows. At least, he was popular with the ladies. While he was in America he received a letter from a chorus member, in one of the companies he had rehearsed, who simply signed herself "Cynisca." "How it started, God only knows, I flattered myself I was fascinated by your ability. . . . If you for a moment think I have a sinful thought connected with you, you have sadly mistaken me, my feeling for you is of the *head alone.* . . . Think of me with respect for I deserve it, there is no shame in the feeling I bear you—."[26] Whatever Gilbert may have made of all that, the letter managed to survive among his papers over the years, despite his normal practice of destroying personal, as opposed to business, correspondence.

Early in the new year Sullivan was offered the conductorship of the Leeds Festival for October 1880, at a fee of 200 guineas in addition to his existing fee of 100 guineas for composing *The Martyr of Antioch.* He replied immediately giving his conditional acceptance, and then in a longer letter on 28 January expressed his appreciation of the honor while asking for some control over the selection of the programs. The festival committee was nervous. They had hoped to avoid the battle for control they had experienced with Michael Costa when he was the conductor. Frederick Spark replied on 14 February, making clear their reluctance to hand over control; Sullivan's advice would be welcome, but they felt "responsible to the public for the programme."[27] This reply was not exactly what Sullivan had wanted, but it was sufficiently open to allow him to accept the post.

With the hectic rehearsal period behind them, and the last of the touring companies under way in Buffalo on 21 February, Gilbert, Sullivan, and Carte relaxed with a trip to Niagara.

From Niagara, Sullivan traveled up to Ottawa as the guest of Princess Louise and her husband, the marquess of Lorne, governor-general of Canada. "After lunch played lawn tennis in the court," he wrote in his diary, "and toboggined [sic] for the first time. Great parliamentary dinner at night."[28] Meanwhile, Gilbert and Carte returned to New York in time for an "Irish Famine Matinee" of The Pirates on 25 February, which raised $394.75 (£98).[29]

Gilbert, Sullivan, and Carte were approaching the end of their own tour. While The Pirates of Penzance flourished in America, back in London HMS Pinafore had come to the end of its run at the Opera Comique on 20 February 1880, after 571 performances. A children's HMS Pinafore, produced by Richard Barker and François Cellier in December 1879, would continue giving matinee performances until 20 March. After that, the theater would be empty until the first London performance of The Pirates of Penzance. Helen Lenoir had already left London and the Opera Comique, and was on her way to New York, while Michael Gunn was looking after the two touring companies. But for the moment the major focus of attention for Gilbert, Sullivan, and Carte was still America.

During their last week in New York, while Sullivan was in Canada, Gilbert and Carte discussed future plans. The American venture had proved a great success financially. The three men had worked together closely and effectively to ensure that success. They were now working for themselves; they had seen off the Comedy Opera Company and were their own bosses. So successful had they been that they were planning to repeat the project in the autumn with their next opera; this time at Booth's Theatre, and with a different manager, Henry E. Abbey.[30] But even at this early stage, there were cracks beginning to appear in what seemed a solid foundation. Sullivan confided to Fred Clay that he had been hurt by the jokes that Gilbert made at his expense,[31] and an even more serious problem arose in Gilbert's conversation with Carte.

Ever since his first encounter with a manager over payment for his work, in which he came off the worse, Gilbert had driven as hard a bargain as possible. Now that he was receiving a share of the profits, instead of a fee, he was pushing for an increased share. In his forthright, even overbearing manner, Gilbert asked Carte what he thought he himself brought to the concern. As Gilbert saw it, he told Carte provocatively, all the manager had to do in London was to look after the advertisements and sign the contracts when performers were engaged. Gilbert estimated Carte's services at £1,000 a year. He even suggested to Carte that he and Sullivan might take a theater themselves and employ a manager; not that he and Sullivan had any intention of doing this, he hastened to add.[32] The mere suggestion, however, was threatening to Carte, and was clearly intended to put Carte in his place. The role of the manager was a blind spot for Gilbert; he would never be able to accept Carte as an equal member in the partnership.

Gilbert and Sullivan sailed for England on Wednesday, 3 March, on board the *Gallia*, the ship that had brought Helen Lenoir to New York. She was to work with D'Oyly Carte initially before taking over all the American business, and would continue to represent Carte's interests in America during the winter months over the next six years. The *Gallia* docked in Liverpool on 13 March, exactly three weeks before the opening of *The Pirates of Penzance* at the Opera Comique. Gilbert and Sullivan went straight into rehearsal. The old favorites were there: Grossmith (Major-General Stanley), Barrington (Sergeant of Police), Temple, who had refused to go to America for less than £20 a week (Pirate King), and Harriette Everard (Ruth). With Jessie Bond and Rosina Brandram still in America, Julia Gwynne and Lilian La Rue, who had both been understudies and appeared in curtain-raisers, played Edith and Kate. George Power had been retained to play Frederic and opposite him was an attractive newcomer, Marion Hood, presumably engaged by Helen Lenoir, to take over as leading soprano in the role of Mabel.

Disaster struck at one of the last rehearsals before opening night, when a piece of scenery fell forward, catching Harriette Everard on the side of the head, partly scalping her and leaving her badly injured. Her understudy, Emily Cross, had to take over at twenty-four hours' notice.

By now a London audience knew what to expect from a Gilbert and Sullivan opera and they were not disappointed. "The anticipation of the treat to be derived from Mr. Gilbert's rich vein of satirical humour," said the *Daily News*, "and Mr. Sullivan's genial and tuneful music were fully realized . . . before an audience that crowded every portion of the building, and by whom the piece was received throughout with enthusiastic applause."[33] Almost every number was encored, and Barrington's song, "When a Felon's Not Engaged in His Employment," received a double encore. Barrington himself was described by *The Times* as "absolutely sublime."[34]

Because of the success that always greeted Barrington when he sang "The Enterprising Burglar" song, it occurred to him "that an encore verse would be very nice, and in a rash moment," he recalled, "I one day presumed to ask Gilbert to give me one. He informed me that 'encore' meant 'sing it again.'"[35]

Davison in *The Times* had particularly praised Sullivan's contribution, remarking on his "skill and ingenuity" in overcoming the "disadvantageous circumstances" of writing music for Gilbert's parodies, and then he bemoaned "what might have been, or, perhaps might still be if Mr. Sullivan would attempt a genuine dramatic effort."[36] Despite all the praise in other directions, despite all his success in writing with Gilbert, Sullivan was always stung by the criticism of the "serious" critic, and the words of the criticism stayed with him. At least in *The Martyr of Antioch* he would have an opportunity to satisfy the critics.

CHAPTER FIFTEEN

1880-1881

Patience

FOLLOWING THE LOSS OF Harriette Everard, *The Pirates* received another setback a few weeks after the opening at the Opera Comique. George Grossmith was called away in the middle of a performance to go to his father who had collapsed while dining at the Savage Club, and who subsequently died on 24 April. Frank Thornton took over as General Stanley for the rest of the performance and until Grossmith's return. "Three understudies in the course of the first three weeks!" wrote Gilbert to the critic Alfred Watson. "It's hard lines. The question now arises, 'Quis understudiet, understudiodes?'"[1] It is not clear who the third understudy was, unless Gilbert was counting Julia Gwynne, whose role would be taken over by Jessie Bond when she returned from America.

Despite these setbacks, *The Pirates* looked set for a long run, and now it was time for Gilbert, Sullivan, and Carte to settle on terms for the future, especially in the light of Gilbert and Carte's discussion in New York. Rather than wait until the end of the run, when the net profits could then be worked out and apportioned in three ways, Gilbert and Sullivan asked Carte for a three-monthly calculation. Carte objected. He sent a long letter addressed to them both on 8 April. What he did, he told them, was "fully worth one third of the *net* profits of the entire enterprise."[2] There would inevitably be a loss at some time during the run and that loss, borne by him, would eat into his profit. In Carte's opinion, a three-monthly division was against their spirit of understanding. "I understood that we were to stand or fall together." Carte was being optimistic, if not naive; the common enemy had disappeared and now infighting would always be a danger. Gilbert had already demonstrated that in New York. Carte wanted to keep to the spirit of the original agreement drawn up by Gilbert in June 1879, and signed by all three in October of that year, but in view of the success of *The Pirates* in America, he agreed to hand over to them two-thirds of the net profits on the opera, both in London and in America. But he would only make interim payments to them on the understanding that the final calculation of profits would be made at the end of the run of *The Pirates*.

Wounded by Gilbert's remarks in New York about his contribution, Carte spelled out at great length how the enterprise would not have existed at all, if it had not been for his willingness to take risks and persist in his attempts:

> If there is any copyright in a man's ideas and in his working them out then the manipulation of the English Comedy Opera scheme is my copyright. I made a pretty good thing out of it, but so did you. . . . It is easy to think that someone else might have done it, but as a matter of fact no one did, from 1870 to 1877, until I did, and if I had not done it it might not have been done at all.[3]

Carte was rightly proud of his part in bringing Gilbert and Sullivan together for a series of operas. But at that stage only three two-act operas by Gilbert and Sullivan had been written under Carte's management. His struggle was only just beginning; he now had to keep them together, but he expected to be recognized as an equal partner. At that moment, he told them, he had a legal action pending against him that could result in bankruptcy

> or crushing, lifelong debt. . . . I have thus staked all I have in the world, my name and position included, on the Opera Comique affair, and for what? Not certainly to secure the fag end of the run of the Pinafore, I never expected to get anything to speak of out of that. Not certainly to simply substitute you for the Comedy Opera Company and place myself in a position in which it can be discussed what my services are worth and what you could get a manager for if I do not see my way to hand over to you more than ⅔rds of the net profits of the theatre.[4]

Carte was fighting hard to put his case and convince both Gilbert and Sullivan of the worth of his contribution. It is more than likely that Sullivan was already convinced, but convincing Gilbert was a different matter. Carte had been stung by Gilbert's remarks in New York about the little he had to do as manager.

> If [Gilbert] were to spend a few days with me at my office and the theatre he would find out the mistake of this. My work never finishes. . . . I have been able to dine at home only on Sundays, can take no holidays for any time, and it is simply a slavery, which I have cheerfully gone through for a chance of making a good lot of money, but which I do not think you would get a man at a salary to do. . . . I have worked loyally with you from the first day and have worked hard, and I don't think you ought to put the screw on me now or want to play heads you win and tails I lose.[5]

Having made his case forcefully, and at times excitedly, Carte looked forward to a more settled and certain future with Gilbert and Sullivan. "As I told Gunn—'Gilbert and Sullivan are pretty hard to make a bargain with but when once it is settled they are simply perfect to deal with'."[6] The rumblings from Gilbert fell silent—but it was to be only a lull.

A memo dated 11 May 1880 among the D'Oyly Carte papers shows that Carte had entered into an agreement with Henry E. Abbey of Booth's Theatre, commencing on 29 November 1880, that "W. S. Gilbert and Arthur Sullivan . . . agree to write a new Opera in time for production in New York on such 29th Nov. 1880."[7] The timing is intriguing: in May, Sullivan had not yet started to compose *The Martyr of Antioch*, and Gilbert had not started on a sketch plot for a new opera. Sullivan would have had September and part of October to write the music for the opera, perhaps leaving the scoring for New York. He was setting himself a tight schedule, confident that he could work quickly under pressure. But at what cost to himself? Carte left Liverpool for New York on 12 June, and stayed until 31 July when he returned with Helen Lenoir. There was no further mention of the agreement with Henry E. Abbey. That was the end of any plan to repeat the success of *The Pirates* in America.

Soon after the memo dated 11 May, Gilbert had turned his mind to a sketch plot of the new opera that at that time was planned for America. His first thought, which he discussed with Sullivan, was a plot based on the "aesthetic school of poets," but he quickly abandoned the idea, because he thought, as he explained to Sullivan, there would be "great difficulty in getting the chorus to dress & make up aesthetically."[8] He was thinking of an American chorus and possibly of the difficulty in putting across successfully in America the parody he had in mind; the audience would have been unclear about who was being parodied. Oscar Wilde, still only in his twenties and unknown in America, was already well known in London, and many of his poems had appeared in magazines. Gilbert turned to one of his "Bab Ballads," "The Rival Curates," in which appears Mr. Clayton Hooper, curate at Spiffton-extra-Sooper, as mild mannered as he possibly could be, until the day he found out that there was another curate, Hopley Porter at Assesmilk-cum-Worter, who was even milder.

So Gilbert set to work on this new idea, interspersed with cruises on his new sixty-eight-foot yacht, the *Pleione*, until the pressure was taken off by the breakdown of the agreement to produce the opera by November in America. Gilbert could then proceed at a more leisurely pace, and Sullivan could, no doubt, breathe a deep sigh of relief.

Harriette Everard had sufficiently recovered from her injuries to return to the cast of *The Pirates* for the second half of June, but then in July a fresh problem arose when the company, which had been in America, returned to England. It was anticipated that Jessie Bond would play Edith and that Julia Gwynne would move from Edith to Kate; but it also was anticipated that Alice Barnett would take over as Ruth. Harriette Everard had not been informed of the change, and neither had Gilbert. After being refused "admission to the stage" by Richard Barker, a distraught Miss Everard appealed to Gilbert, who replied to her on 9 July 1880:

There seems to be some question as to whether the music of Ruth is well within the compass of your voice. This is a matter upon which I can give no opinion, but however this may be, Mr. Barker has no reason to treat you otherwise than with proper courtesy, & I will take care that he does.

He tells me that he received instructions from Mr. Gunn, to withdraw you from the part. This I take the liberty to disbelieve, but I will write to Mr. Gunn & find out exactly how the matter stands.[9]

Gilbert would not have mildly accepted Gunn's decision; he must have been convinced by Sullivan that Harriette Everard would not have done justice to the music, and that the opera would have suffered. That was to be the end of Harriette Everard's career with Gilbert and Sullivan. She was to die two years later from tuberculosis.

Sullivan started work on *The Martyr of Antioch* in July, and by 31 August he was rehearsing it with the Leeds Festival choir. It was seven years since *The Light of the World*, and his return to the concert hall must have given him some anxiety. To add to his anxiety, rumors of dissatisfaction from the committee of the National Training School, following an adverse report from examiners, brought him to the point of resignation. He was convinced that Hallé, annoyed at being passed over for the Leeds conductorship, had influenced his fellow examiners in drawing up the report. It is probable that Sullivan was only too pleased at the prospect of giving up the responsibilities connected with the school, but the duke of Edinburgh persuaded him to put off such a move.

At the same time, Carte was agitating for Sullivan's closer involvement in the ongoing legal battle with the Comedy Opera Company. Carte had meanwhile retained Stanley as Sullivan's solicitor and had paid him 20 guineas. Stanley was now reading up on the affair and obtaining affidavits on Sullivan's behalf, but Carte was not willing to bear all the expenses himself. He was prepared to work as hard as necessary "to thrash" the directors of the Comedy Opera Company, he told Sullivan, but

> I cannot put my hand into my pocket and pay the lawyers fees to prosecute a claim of yours for damages when I get no share if you obtain them. I was at work at your business yesterday continuously with 3 hours interval from 11.30 in the morning, all the way in the train [from Liverpool] till 2.0 this morning at Richmond Villas [Carte's home, in Holloway, North London]. I don't know whether I can get down to you today. . . . If I can I will and show you the papers, but please *reply definitely to this*.[10]

Carte's letter pleading for a reply lay unopened on Sullivan's desk at Albert Mansions. Sullivan had already left for the continent — for a brief stay at Spa, a health resort in Belgium, before going on to Paris. He was suffering again from kidney stones and taking drugs to relieve the pain. "Thank God for morphia, and chloral and all these other blessed things which enable us to bear our ills!" said George Grove, writing to Mrs. Sullivan. In the same letter he said of his old friend, "I see very little of Arthur, but I am bound up in him. He is to me always the same dear genial sympathetic boy that he was when I first knew him in 62.... I hear other people say he has changed—but to *me* never, and he *never will.*"[11]

After two full days of rehearsal the Leeds Festival opened on Wednesday, 13 October, and over the next four days the program was to include seven "grand performances" ending with a "People's Festival Concert" on the Saturday evening. On Friday morning, 15 October, Sullivan conducted the first performance of *The Martyr of Antioch*, which he had dedicated to the princess of Wales. Joseph Bennett, writing for the *Daily Telegraph*, could not hide his disappointment with the work, even while praising Sullivan: "Mr. Sullivan is most charming when represented by the incense, flowers and songs of Apollo's maidens," whereas for "the poor Christians," said Bennett, Sullivan had written music whose "lugubrious strains appear as uninteresting as they are sombre."[12]

Later in the year, *The Martyr of Antioch* was repeated by the Sacred Harmonic Society, by Joseph Barnby's Choir, and on Saturday 11 December, at the Crystal Palace. *The Times* was qualified in its praise: a composer with Sullivan's "vein of melody" and "singular skill of writing for the voice" was capable of something higher than the *Martyr of Antioch,* "and it is for that reason that we have thought it necessary to point out its imperfections."[13]

His old friend Joseph Barnby and his wife were more encouraging and sent their "sincere and hearty congratulations on the achievement of a great work. No matter what the Public may say of it you have created a work which is an honour to England."[14]

Out of his fee of 300 guineas for the Festival, Sullivan sent a cheque for £25 to the City of Leeds hospital funds, the designated charity of the festival committee. Gilbert had not traveled up to Leeds and had refused a fee from Sullivan for his contribution; but Sullivan, in recognition of Gilbert's work, presented him with a silver cup on which he had inscribed "Martyr of Antioch, W. S. Gilbert from his friend Arthur Sullivan."[15] In acknowledgment, Gilbert assured him that he expected no other reward than the honor of being associated with Sullivan "in a success which, I suppose, will endure until music itself shall die."[16]

It was their next work together that was preoccupying Gilbert at the time. He had become uneasy with his plot for the new opera. With two clerics as the main characters, he felt that he was leaving himself open to a charge of irreverence. He went back to his original plan, making the two rivals "a couple of yearning 'aesthetics' and the young ladies their ardent admirers," rearranging his plot accordingly. Having satisfied himself that he had solved his problem, he set about satisfying Sullivan.

> Although it is about two thirds finished, I don't feel comfortable about it. I mistrust the clerical element. . . . I can get much more fun out of the subject as I propose to alter it, & the general scheme of the piece will remain as at present.

The Hussars will become æsthetic young men (abandoning their profession for the purpose)—in this latter capacity they will carry lilies in their hands, wear long hair, & stand in stained glass attitudes.[17]

Aestheticism can be understood partly as a reaction to the new industrial age, when mechanical inventions dominated a world in which the usefulness of an object signified its value. Art and poetry would celebrate that which had no practical use. Art had no need to instruct; a work of art simply existed, as something beautiful in itself. It was Ruskin, not himself an advocate of aestheticism, who said that a lily was beautiful but useless; and it was Oscar Wilde who used the lily as a symbol of his own brand of aestheticism. Wilde owed more to Pater, however, who advocated the love of art for its own sake.

The aesthetic movement grew out of the second phase of Pre-Raphaelitism in the 1860s and 1870s, represented by Dante Gabriel Rossetti, William Morris, and Edward Burne-Jones. Rossetti's sensual paintings, together with his sensual poetry, were attacked as obscene by Robert Buchanan in an article called "The Fleshly School of Poetry," which appeared in 1871. Burne-Jones had been launched into fame when he exhibited eight paintings at the opening of the Grosvenor Gallery in 1877; and Morris became more famous for design than for painting, his company helping revolutionize Victorian taste with its designs for tapestries, wallpaper, pottery, tiles, and stained glass in which Burne-Jones specialized. James McNeill Whistler had already initiated the craze for collecting blue-and-white porcelain after his discovery of Japanese art in the 1860s, and Gilbert made fun in Bunthorne's lines:

> Such a judge of blue-and-white and other kinds of pottery—
> From early Oriental down to modern terra-cotta-ry [18]

As a cult, aestheticism achieved notoriety through Oscar Wilde at Oxford in the late 1870s. In 1878, Wilde had attended a fancy dress ball wearing plum-red breeches and silk stockings, and at one time had filled his rooms at Oxford with lilies. He was the subject of a series of cartoons by du Maurier in *Punch*, and was the most notorious example of the new fad of aestheticism that carried its own vocabulary, using such epithets as "precious," "utter," "intense," and "consummate."

It was clear to Gilbert that he could give his audience more to laugh at by satirizing Wilde and the aesthetes than ever he could from ridiculing two clergymen. The Rev. Lawn Tennison of his clerical version became Reginald Bunthorne, a fleshly poet, and the other cleric became Algernon Grosvenor, named after the Gallery. Later, when Gilbert learned that an Algernon Grosvenor really existed, he changed Grosvenor's name to Archibald. Bunthorne is not modeled solely on Oscar Wilde but appears to be an amalgam of several personalities: Wilde, Rossetti, and Algernon Charles Swinburne, whose poetry is parodied in Bunthorne's aptly named poem, "Oh, Hollow, Hollow, Hollow," reflecting some of Swinburne's poetry—dependent on sound and empty of sense. Grossmith made himself up partly to resemble Whistler, with the white streak in his hair, and the monocle, and his use of Whistler's famous "Ha! Ha!" as a vocal mannerism.

Adapting the plot and the lyrics he had already written, changing the character of Patience from the village schoolmistress to the village milkmaid, Gilbert then embarked on the rest of the lyrics for his aesthetic theme, extending the aesthetic passion for flowers to the vegetable kingdom in general:

> Then a sentimental passion of a vegetable fashion must excite your languid spleen.
> An attachment *à la Plato* for a bashful young potato, or a not-too-French French bean!

Everything went into Gilbert's melting pot and out of it came some of his cleverest lyrics, aimed at ridiculing the populist idea of aestheticism, if not the movement itself, and summing up his attitude to aestheticism in the line:

> The meaning doesn't matter if it's only idle chatter of a transcendental kind.[19]

Gilbert was not the only playwright to satirize the aesthetics. On 20 November, James Albery's play *Where's the Cat?* opened at the Criterion. Gilbert wrote to Albery immediately to tell him that he was two-thirds of the way through his piece, and did not want it suggested that this new piece was inspired by Albery's play. Francis Burnand was also at work on a satire of the aesthetics. His play, *The Colonel*, was to appear on 2 February 1881 at the Prince of Wales's, but was eventually eclipsed by *Patience*.

As yet, Sullivan had scarcely set any of the music for *Patience*. Carte was still pursuing him over legal business concerning the Comedy Opera Company, making sure that their affidavits left no loose ends that could be exploited in court, and with Gilbert, calling on Sullivan on 21 November for a three-hour discussion on legal matters.

Before the end of the year, Sullivan took off for the Riviera, demonstrating to himself that he had good intentions by packing Gilbert's lyrics in his luggage. He stopped in Paris on Christmas Eve and visited his niece, Amy, who was at school there, before heading south to Nice with Edward Hall, his stockbroker friend. In the New Year they were joined by Sullivan's close friend Edward Dicey, editor of *The Observer* and expert on foreign affairs. Sullivan took out Gilbert's lyrics and looked them over.

> The year 1881 opens when I am still at Nice with Edward Hall. Having brought with me some numbers of the new Opera (Patience) Gilbert & I intend doing, I occasionally try to find a few ideas—amongst them, I sketch Bunthorne's song "The particularly good young man." But my natural indolence aided by the sunshine, prevent my doing any real work. I enjoy myself in the "dolce far niente," occasionally go over to Monte Carlo where I frequently see (Laura) Countess of Wilton who lives in Sir Fred: Johnstone's Villa, Le Nid.[20]

Over the next ten days the pages in his diary were left blank. The new opera could wait. On 11 January he set out on a slow journey home: Turin, Paris, and then back to London. Back to a new club, the Marlborough, for which he had been proposed by the duke of Edinburgh. Back to domestic duties, taking his mother, Mrs. Ronalds's daughter, Fanny, and his own nephew to see *Mother Goose* at Drury Lane.

Just before Sullivan had left for France, Carte had made up the accounts ready for inspection by Sullivan, and by Gilbert, too, who had just returned from a week in Paris. It is likely that Sullivan was content with the accounts; Gilbert was not. "I am sorry that you are dissatisfied with the manner in which the accounts are kept," said Carte in a letter to Gilbert on 21 December 1880. "I don't think that an error of £50 or so on transactions extending over about nine months and involving the turning over of about £30,000 is very out of the way."[21] He suggested that it might be better if Gilbert and Sullivan appointed their own auditor to go through the books and report back to them on the way the books were kept.

Gilbert was watching Carte like a hawk. He wanted every penny accounted for and was suspicious of any discrepancy. It was unreasonable behavior on Gilbert's part, and potentially dangerous to their business arrangement. Gilbert must have been aware that Carte was not in a position to finance the building of a new theater out of his own resources, the question that was now occupying Carte. Carte had kept his eye on the site in the Strand that he had shown Gilbert and Sullivan in 1879, before they went to America. In order to secure the site, a syndicate had to be formed for the "Savoy Land scheme," as Carte called it. It was Carte's scheme and Carte's planning, but Michael Gunn joined him in interesting businessmen to form the syndicate, with Carte and Gunn each taking a share. Gunn also was responsible for negotiating additional loans for building the theater itself. D'Oyly Carte and Michael Gunn were close friends as well as business associates, and Carte said of him later, "I have a greater respect and regard for him than I think for any man living except my father."[22]

The site for the new theater was on a piece of ground that sloped down steeply toward the Thames embankment and was reached from Beaufort Buildings off the Strand, where Carte had moved his office a few years earlier. Carte's first notion was to call the theater the Beaufort Theatre, but later he changed the name to the Savoy, as the site of the ancient Savoy Palace was close by. The architect commissioned by Carte was C. J. Phipps, the leading theatrical architect of the day, who had designed John Hollingshead's Gaiety.

IN JANUARY 1881, Edward Sothern died. Gilbert had written another play for him, *Foggerty's Fairy*, which Sothern had hoped to open at the Park Theatre, New York, in September 1880. He had arrived in England in June 1880 for a six-week break, but during that period had fallen seriously ill. Shortly after Sothern's death, Gilbert contacted his sister, Mrs. Cowan, offering to help her in whatever way he could, and suggesting she might like to "underlet" *Foggerty's Fairy*. J. L. Toole was approached, after Gilbert had agreed to pay Mrs. Cowan £525 for the play, and to give her half of what he received for the piece until she had received in all 1,500 guineas. The deal with Toole fell through, and the piece finally went to Charles Wyndham at the Criterion. When all the financial dealings with Gilbert had at last been settled, Mrs. Cowan wrote to thank him: "Allow me to say that of all the people with whom I have had any dealings in reference to money since my Brother's death, you have treated me with the greatest kindness & fairness & I feel grateful to you for sparing me any trouble or anxiety."[23]

By now, Marion Hood and George Power had left the cast at the Opera Comique, replaced by Emilie Petrelli and Durward Lely, a Scottish tenor who had taken over as Frederic in November 1880. *The Pirates of Penzance* was still running well as the time approached for the final stage in the fight against the Comedy Opera Company. It was only eighteen months since Carte had broken with the Comedy Opera Company, and with Gilbert and Sullivan he could boast an unrivaled success: a long-running opera at the Opera Comique, four other companies performing Gilbert and Sullivan pieces; the completion of a successful tour in America, not only in New York but with three other companies touring most of the eastern half of the United States. They were giants in the theatrical world and were now going to court against the defunct Comedy Opera Company Limited to decide who held the ownership of the copyright at the time of the breakup, and who would be obliged to pay damages.

The trial took place in the Chancery Division of the High Court of Justice before Mr. Justice Fry, on 2 and 3 March 1881. Gilbert and Sullivan had claimed that the right to perform their work had expired on 31 July 1879, and had demanded an account of profits, and damages. The issue turned on the construction of the original agreement Gilbert and Sullivan had entered into, and the meaning of the word "run." The judge ruled that as the word "run" was being used in a technical sense in the agreement, then interpretation would be made in the light of evidence from members of the theatrical profession. The Comedy Opera Company declared that *Pinafore* had been discontinued in December 1879 because of essential repairs to the drainage system. Counsel for Gilbert and Sullivan argued differently: they now claimed that the piece had been discontinued because of the pantomime season, which made other theatrical performances fall flat, and that the "run" had come to an end. They also claimed that the "run" would have come to an end when the Comedy Opera Company changed the theater and the cast. Gilbert, Sullivan, and Carte had obtained the affidavits of fifty-one members of the profession in order to establish the accepted meaning of the word "run," and among those to be cross-examined in court were George Grossmith, Squire Bancroft, and Henry Irving.

Mr. Justice Fry's judgment was that the five-week interruption at Christmas 1878 had put an end to the "run," and that the change of theater and cast later would have ended the "run" if it had still counted. As Gilbert and Sullivan had not asked for substantial damages, the judge awarded 1 shilling.[24] A few months later the Comedy Opera Company was compulsorily wound up.[25]

So, it had been decided in a court of law that the initial run of *HMS Pinafore* had come to an end on 24 December 1878, after seven months and about 250 performances. Ever since, whenever the initial run of *HMS Pinafore* is mentioned, it has always been calculated at 571 performances. It would appear therefore, that by common opinion, the judgment was erroneous.

Sullivan was now into his usual period of intense work in order to complete the score of *Patience* in time, while also appearing on two occasions in his other capacity, as the foremost composer of serious music in the land, when he conducted *The Martyr of Antioch* at St. James's Hall on 18 March, and then on 7 April before the prince of Wales at the Albert Hall. Meanwhile, the rehearsals were under way. The last performance of *The Pirates of Penzance* had taken place on Saturday, 2 April, leaving three full weeks before the opening night.

After a dress rehearsal on 20 April, Sullivan worked through the night, completing the opera and sketching out the overture. He finished at 5:30 in the morning and by eleven o'clock he was at a full rehearsal with the orchestra. Then he went straight into a rehearsal for orchestra and singers. He was exhausted. He thought everyone was singing flat and had a "heated discussion . . . about things generally" with Gilbert, who was himself tense and anxious.[26]

That evening Sullivan gave his sketch of the overture to Eugene D'Albert to score. D'Albert was a seventeen-year-old student at the National Training School and winner of the Mendelssohn Scholarship that year. For Sullivan to have given him the overture to score indicates not only his belief in D'Albert's abilities but also that he did not consider it worth spending time himself on writing a specially composed overture that would be largely ignored by an audience still finding seats and chatting. Instead, at the end of his exhausting day, he went round to the Argus club and lost £450 at cards.

The final dress rehearsal went off very smoothly, Sullivan thought, and afterward he joined Gilbert and Kitty, Fanny Ronalds, with her daughter and father, and Tom Chappell for an oyster supper.

Among the audience packed into the Opera Comique on Saturday, 23 April, sat Oscar Wilde, "looking forward to being greatly amused," as he told George Grossmith.[27] Wilde did not have to wait long to be amused as the curtain rose revealing the "twenty love-sick maidens" in dresses and groupings reminiscent of a Burne-Jones painting, and the whole audience no doubt immediately recognized Patience as she made her entrance dressed in the milkmaid's costume made famous in Luke Fildes's picture, *Where Are You Going to, My Pretty Maid?* It had been Gilbert's original intention to have the dresses designed by du Maurier, but in the end had designed them himself. Gilbert, artist as well as writer, was presenting a visual parody as well as a literary satire. The contrast between the dull greens of the maidens' dresses and the bright reds of the dragoon guards was striking; and just as striking a contrast was provided by Sullivan's music for the two groups, when the languorous strains of the maidens give way to the energetic tones of the dragoons as they burst on the scene with "The Soldiers of Our Queen." Each group is played off against the other in the ensemble when the dragoons sing indignantly, "Now Is Not This Ridiculous," while the maidens continue "In a Doleful Train," oblivious to their military charms.

Wilde would certainly have recognized himself in Bunthorne, but also in Grosvenor, especially when Grosvenor says, "These gifts—irksome as they are—were given to me for the enjoyment and delectation of my fellow-creatures. I am a trustee for Beauty, and it is my duty to see that the conditions of my trust are faithfully discharged."[28] If Wilde had not already said something similar, he soon would. *Patience* reveals Gilbert at his cleverest as a lyricist of the patter song: "If You're Anxious for to Shine," "If You Want a Receipt for That Popular Mystery," "When I First Put This Uniform On," and "So Go to Him and Say to Him," and each one provided by Sullivan with the music to make them memorable.

There is less in the way of parody from Sullivan in *Patience* than in the earlier operas, but many humorous touches, as in the melodramatic accompaniment of crashing chords in Bunthorne's "Am I Alone and Unobserved." Even in the otherwise plainest of accompaniments, the humor is there, as in the duet between Patience and Angela, "Long Years Ago—Fourteen Maybe," where the possibility of Patience having loved as a child is pointed up with the pizzicato of "Cupid's bow-string."

One of Sullivan's brightest pieces is the quintet in act 2, "If Saphir I Choose to Marry," which also reappears at the end of the opera. It is not the vocal line that is particularly outstanding, but the syncopated accompaniment provided by the clarinet, and the scintillating dance tune to which the cast dance off to "everyday normality" while the brideless Bunthorne is left to his self-admiration. Not an amusing note to finish on for Oscar Wilde!

There had been "widespread public interest in the new effort of so distinguished a musician and so eminent a literary humorist; and accordingly, the pretty theatre in the Strand was crowded in every part," said the *Daily News*.[29] Sullivan took eight encores on that first night. The cast included a new soprano in the part of Patience, the twenty-eight-year-old Leonora Braham, who, after her time with the German Reeds had since played Princess Toto in New York. According to the *Daily News* she "sang with brightness of voice and refinement of style, and acted with unaffected naïveté and grace."[30] Durward Lely, the Scottish tenor, played the English aristocratic army officer, Lieutenant the Duke of Dunstable, and the former understudies Frank Thornton and Julia Gwynne were given the minor parts of Major Murgatroyd and the Lady Saphir. The part of the Lady Ella went to a beautiful young actress called May Fortescue, who, with Jessie Bond and Julia Gwynne, "contributed much to the attractiveness of the principal group of 'rapturous maidens.'"[31] "Perhaps the most remarkable piece of acting" in *Patience*, thought the reviewer in *The Times* "was Miss Alice Barnett's, Lady Jane. A masterpiece of humorous impersonation."[32]

After the first night of *Patience*, Sullivan relaxed in the Fielding Club with a lemon and soda and a few friends—Albert Randegger, John Hare, and others—before going on to the Argus, where he managed to recoup some of his losses from two nights before and finished ahead by £300. The next day, he informed Carte that he would write only one more opera with Gilbert, and then he would turn his mind to a grand opera for Covent Garden.

CHAPTER SIXTEEN

The Savoy Theatre

INSTEAD OF LOOKING immediately for a plot for the next opera, Gilbert turned his attention to his new eighty-five-foot yacht built for him by John Harvey at Wivenhoe, on the River Colne in Essex. The *Chloris* was launched from Wivenhoe on 30 April 1881, witnessed by a few friends, including Lady Katherine Coke and her daughter Sybil, who was to be a close and lifelong friend of both Gilbert and Kitty.

Since the previous November Gilbert had been in correspondence with Harvey, and on his visits to the shipyard at Wivenhoe had been introduced to Harvey's son, John Martin Harvey, who was more keen on acting than working for his father at shipbuilding. Gilbert allowed the young man to make use of his library of books on board the *Pleione*, recommended an acting tutor, and after a period gave him an audition. Later in the year, Gilbert introduced him to Charles Wyndham during rehearsals for *Foggerty's Fairy*. It led to an engagement at the Court, where Marion Terry was in the cast. Gilbert asked her to "speak a word or two to him now and then." Marion Terry failed to do so. If she had, said Harvey, he would have fainted on the spot.[1] John Martin Harvey never forgot Gilbert's readiness to guide his first steps in the theater and, when he had achieved fame himself, he still referred to Gilbert as his old mentor.

A few weeks after the opening of *Patience*, a complication arose in the relationship between Sullivan and Fanny Ronalds. During one of her visits to Albert Mansions, she caught sight of a telegram from another woman—"painful scene in consequence," Sullivan recorded in his diary. Only the day before this "painful scene" he had given Fanny £300 as a share of his earnings. Fanny, however, did not see herself as a kept woman; for her, their relationship was one of love, which excluded the possibility of others. In consequence, on the afternoon of 17 May, Sullivan went around to Gloucester Place to see the other woman, confirming the end of their affair—"another painful interview," he wrote. The following day, he recorded that L.W. called and stayed from 12:30 until two o'clock. "Storm over," says the diary.[2] The events are recorded dispassionately, as inevitable inconveniences, and no more. For Sullivan, his relationship with Fanny was not exclusive of others. He was not married to her; there would be other women in his life in the future.

For the time being, he found the society of men less complicated. On 12 May, he gave his annual birthday dinner at the Garrick for fourteen guests, including the duke of Edinburgh, Fred Clay, Edward Hall (his stockbroker), John Millais, Gilbert, and Tom Chappell. The next day, he formally resigned as principal of the National Training School and in the evening dined at the Marlborough Club with the duke of Edinburgh. On 17 May, there was another men-only session, when Sullivan dined at Millais's house, where the guests included Anthony Trollope, Fred Clay, and Thomas Hardy. Two days later, he left with Clay for a week in Paris.

While Gilbert was cruising with Kitty on his new yacht and Sullivan was enjoying his social round, Carte was hard at work planning for the future. At the end of 1880, Carte had renewed his tenancy of the Opera Comique for a further twenty-six weeks while he was waiting for his new theater to be built. Richard Barker would then take over the Opera Comique, but he wanted Carte to continue to work with him in putting on a series of light operas. Carte declined; he had hoped to be able to concentrate on his own work with Gilbert and Sullivan at the Savoy, but with Sullivan now saying that he would write only one more opera with Gilbert, Carte's own future plans were in doubt. Michael Gunn also was keen on acquiring a London theater, and wanted Carte to be involved with casting and to bring to the concern his expertise and experience.

Carte was uncertain. He wanted to consult Gilbert and Sullivan and invited them both to go and see him. Sullivan's social calendar did not allow it, but Gilbert went along. As Sullivan had not yet informed Gilbert of his intention to write only one more opera with him, Carte was at the disadvantage of not being able to give him the complete picture. Gilbert's view was clear. "He thought that if I were engaging artists for another English Opera Company, 'grit' might get into the machinery, however fairly we might intend to act," said Carte, reporting on the meeting later to Sullivan. "I therefore gave up the idea as I am bound to say that his objections seemed perfectly reasonable, and I thought that they would probably be entertained by you also."

Keeping Sullivan abreast of events was not Carte's sole reason for writing. He had another motive. "I look upon the operas by you and Gilbert as my mainstay. And I want to remind you that I rely on your promise to let me have under any circumstances another piece to follow Patience—if necessary for the opening of the new Theatre."[3] Now was the time, Carte suggested, to tell Gilbert that after the next piece he would probably not write another work with him for a long time.

Of the three men, Gilbert was the only one at that time who had a clear idea of the future. They would continue to produce operas at the new theater and go on to even greater financial success. Carte would have endorsed Gilbert's idea—it was his own idea after all, but he was not sure about being able to hold Sullivan, and was subtly putting pressure on him; if he could hold Sullivan for one more opera—then perhaps future events would produce another opportunity.

By the time Sullivan returned from Paris, Fanny Ronalds was ready to let their relationship continue as before. Sullivan went round to see her at 7 Cadogan Place. After making love to Fanny on that Friday, 27 May, Sullivan dined at Edward Hall's in Bloomsbury Road, but had to excuse himself in the course of the evening to rush away to St. James's Hall to accompany Fanny as she sang "The Lost Chord." He returned to Hall's house after the concert, and then finished his crowded day by going to a party given by Lady Molesworth for Princess Louise. This was Sullivan at his happiest: entertaining others and being entertained himself; appearing in public one moment, and enjoying the company of royalty the next. And then on 2 June, "John Millais gave a splendid ball at his new house in Palace Gate," Sullivan recorded in his diary, "and there I ran up against Chenny! (R.S.R.) whom I had not met since her marriage and departure for India. We sat on the stairs talking for 3 hours! She was as handsome as ever."[4]

A cruise that Sullivan undertook at the end of June 1881, overshadowed anything that Gilbert might do in his new yacht. With Fred Clay, he had been invited by the duke of Edinburgh to join him, as admiral of the Reserve Fleet, on the fleet's annual maneuvers in the Baltic. Sullivan was accommodated on the *HMS Hercules*. "I have a lovely cabin in the Admiral's quarters at the stern of the ship," Sullivan told his mother, "and am very luxuriously lodged altogether. . . . The officers seem pleasant fellows, the ship is splendid, the sea like glass, & the weather heavenly, and I have nothing to do."[5] But it was not the cruise so much as the royal personages Sullivan met that made this trip so memorable for him.

At Copenhagen they were the dinner guests of King Christian IX and the queen; and at St. Petersburg they were driven to a villa kept for royal guests, close to Czar Alexander III's villa, heavily guarded following the assassination of his father in March. At the end of their visit, they were seen off by the czar and czarina, accompanied by guns firing royal salutes; and when they docked at Kiel they were met by the twenty-two-year-old Prince William of Prussia, eldest son of Queen Victoria's daughter Victoria, and the future kaiser of Germany during World War I. The young prince greeted Sullivan by singing, "He Polished Up the Handle of the Big Front Door" from *Pinafore*. "I burst out laughing," Sullivan recorded, "and so did everyone. It was too funny."[6]

It was a sweet moment for Sullivan to savor. He had been a welcome guest in royal households, acceptable to those at the very pinnacle of his society; fourteen years before he had been considered an unacceptable suitor in the haughty eyes of Mrs. Scott Russell.

On his arrival back in London, Sullivan took Fanny Ronalds to see the new apartment block in which he had leased rooms for himself and his secretary, Walter

Smythe. Sullivan was acquiring a royal-sounding address: No 1, Queen's Mansions, Victoria Street.

He was the guest of royalty again at the beginning of August, staying one night at Osborne in the Isle of Wight, by invitation of the prince of Wales, during the yachting week at Cowes. But it was not long before he was off to the continent, catching the night boat over to Calais. He was accompanied by Fanny Ronalds and her mother, Mrs. Carter, and for part of the way by his friend Edward Dicey. Fanny and Mrs. Carter were heading for Bad Ems near Koblenz, to take the "cure" at the spa there, while Sullivan went on to the spa at Homburg, about forty-five miles away. With the city of Frankfurt close by, Sullivan grasped the opportunity to escape from the monotony of the spa by visiting the opera, seeing *Fidelio* and *Rigoletto,* and on 23 August he drove over to Ems to wish Fanny Ronalds a happy birthday. On 5 September they met up at Kassel, near the Belgian border, staying in the Hotel König von Preussen. They visited the castle at Wilhelmshöhe, of great interest to Sullivan as it was there that Napoleon III was held prisoner, in some luxury, at the end of the Franco-Prussian War.

From Kassel they crossed into France, staying at the chateau of the marquis d'Aoust near Douai. On a visit to the town, Sullivan tried out the new organ in the church of Saint Jacques and accompanied Fanny Ronalds as she sang "The Lost Chord" and "Oh, for the Wings of a Dove." It had been a romantic reunion for Sullivan and Fanny since 5 September at Kassel, and in these few weeks they had been able to spend all day in each other's company, rather than the few hours that was normally the case back in London. Fanny had Sullivan to herself again after his earlier wandering away in May. They traveled back to England separately, Sullivan making his way via Paris before arriving on 25 September in London.

Gilbert and Kitty had also spent most of July and August away, sailing on their yacht, the *Chloris.* Gilbert's mind was never far away from work, and even on his yacht he was in correspondence with Henry Irving, offering to write him a play on the same subject as *Rigoletto.* He was in contact as well with Carte, arranging for the scenery they would need for *Patience* when it was transferred to the new theater. Emden, the scenic designer, had to modify some of Gilbert's original ideas: "In place of the pool," Carte wrote on 1 September, "we propose to have a little stream of real water trickling down some rocks on the prompt side into a little pool."[7]

In August, Carte had formed a new company to take *Patience* round the country, with a new leading comedian as Bunthorne. This was George Thorne at the start of his long career with Gilbert and Sullivan operas; for many audiences around the country, it was his name that they would associate with all the "Grossmith" parts. Plans were already in hand to take *Patience* to America and Helen Lenoir left Liverpool on 25 August to supervise the preparations. On 22 September 1881, at the Standard Theatre, New York, *Patience* opened with J. H. Ryley as Bunthorne.

Carte gave himself no time to rest. Mrs. Carte had taken their two boys down to

Broadstairs for a vacation, but Carte carried on working and worrying, trying to ensure that all the money promised to him from lenders came in on time. Throughout September, preparations were being made for opening the Savoy and for winding up at the Opera Comique. Richard Barker, disappointed that Carte would not go in with him in developing another opera company, still wanted Carte to stay on at the Opera Comique until 3 October, when John Hollingshead had agreed to join him. The first piece Barker had lined up was Gilbert and Clay's *Princess Toto*. When Gilbert heard, he wrote to Clay objecting that he had not been consulted, saying that it was "an act of marked discourtesy."[8] But Clay had bought the performing rights and Gilbert was obliged to concede that Clay was only acting within his rights. They came to an amicable agreement, however, over Richard Temple, who was asked to stay behind at the Opera Comique and play in *Princess Toto*, instead of joining the cast of *Patience* at the Savoy.

A few days before the new theater was due to open, Sullivan made a belated inspection of the orchestra pit, was not satisfied with it, and asked Carte to have it raised by eight inches. The work involved did not cause any additional delay. The opening of the theater was already delayed because of the complication of installing the electric light. It was to be the first time it had been attempted to light a theater or any public building entirely by electricity. In a prospectus issued to the public, Carte explained that the theater was to be lit by 1,200 "incandescent lamps" made by J. W. Swan of Newcastle-on-Tyne, and that the current was to be generated by large steam engines of 120 hp standing on open ground near the theater. Technical difficulties led to the curtailment of the original plan of lighting both stage and auditorium by electricity for the opening night, and a decision was taken to continue a little longer with gas lighting for the stage. Carte stressed in his prospectus how the new electricity would improve not only the lighting but also the atmosphere in the theater. A gaslight consumed as much oxygen as several people, making the air foul as well as hot, whereas an electric lamp, he argued, consumed no oxygen and gave off no perceptible heat.

On Saturday 8 October, *Patience* was played for the last time at its old home in the Opera Comique. A full-day rehearsal ran from 11:00 a.m. until 4:30 p.m. on Monday, 10 October, and then at last everything was ready for the first performance of *Patience* at the Savoy.

The new theater had a seating capacity for 1,292 people, with eighteen private boxes and a gallery that could seat over four hundred. "A perfect view of the stage can be had from every seat in the house," reported *The Times*.[9] The main colors used in decorating the theater were white, pale yellow, and gold; the gold was only used "for backgrounds, or in large masses, and not following what may be called, for want of a worse name, the gingerbread school of decorative art for gilding relief-work or mouldings."[10] Venetian red was used for the walls of the boxes, the dress circle, and the gallery; the stall seats were covered in dark blue plush and the same color was used for the seats in the gallery; the box curtains were of cinnamon silk, richly brocaded, and in place of a painted act-drop was a stage curtain "of gold-coloured satin, quilted, having a fringe at the bottom and a valance of embroidery of the character of Spanish work."[11]

When the curtain opened at that first performance at the Savoy Theatre, it was to reveal the whole cast of *Patience* in their costumes to lead the audience as they stood to sing the national anthem. Then, before Sullivan raised his baton for the start of the overture, D'Oyly Carte stepped on to the stage to make a brief announcement. Only the auditorium would be lit by electricity on this first night. It was only an experiment and the experiment might fail. As a precaution, one gaslight would be kept burning, and if the electricity should fail, then the whole theater could be immediately lit by gas. The excited but apprehensive audience applauded the manager as he left the stage, and as the gaslight was lowered in the theater a hushed expectancy fell on the audience. "As if by the wave of a fairy's wand," reported the *Daily Chronicle*, "the theatre immediately became filled with a soft, soothing light, clearer and far more grateful [*sic*] than gas."[12] Spontaneously, a cheer went up from the excited and relieved auditorium.

At the end of the performance, Sullivan returned for supper to The Boltons with Gilbert and Kitty. He did not leave them until three in the morning, when he went back to Albert Mansions to change, and then drive to Liverpool Street station to catch the 5:10 train for Norwich for a rehearsal of *The Martyr of Antioch*. At the performance the following evening, 12 October, Sullivan devoted his mind to a combined work of Gilbert and Sullivan totally different in character from their combined work in *Patience*. Meanwhile, Gilbert turned his own mind to their next combined work at the Savoy.

CHAPTER SEVENTEEN

1881-1882

Iolanthe

WHILE PATIENCE RAN SUCCESSFULLY at the new Savoy Theatre in London, *The Sorcerer, Pinafore,* and *The Pirates* were all still alive and being performed, along with *Patience*, by four separate companies around the country. In America, *Patience* had been running for a month at the Standard Theatre New York, and had also been played in Boston. In Australia, J. C. Williamson had bought the rights to perform the Gilbert and Sullivan operas and operated several companies to tour Australia and New Zealand. And it was only two years since Gilbert, Sullivan, and Carte had broken away from the Comedy Opera Company. How much longer could this phenomenal success continue? Carte had other ideas to extend his business empire; Sullivan was hoping for fresh ideas to pursue his career in serious music; and Gilbert had an idea for the next opera at the Savoy.

"Gilbert came, & sketched out idea of new piece," Sullivan wrote in his diary on 19 October 1881. "Ld Chancellor, Com: in Chief, Peers, fairies, &c—funny, but at present vague."[1] Vague maybe; but it was an idea, and Gilbert would work at it and worry it until it took shape in the form of a plot.

Sullivan had in mind a long trip abroad, further abroad than usual, this time to Egypt in the company of Edward Dicey, who had published accounts of his travels in Egypt ten years earlier. Sullivan had other engagements to fulfill before his departure. On 24 October, he went to hear Eugene D'Albert, his former student at the National School, to whom he had entrusted the scoring of the overture to *Patience*, and who was playing his own piano concerto at St. James's Hall: "immense enthusiasm," Sullivan recorded; "reminded me of my first appearance at the C. P. with the 'tempest' in 1862.'"[2] At the end of November he had a royal engagement when he was invited to Eastwell Park by the duke of Edinburgh, and on 15 December he was at the Criterion for the first night of Gilbert's play, *Foggerty's Fairy*. He admired its cleverness but found it on the whole unsatisfactory, dreamlike. On the day before his departure for Egypt, Gilbert called at Albert Mansions and showed him the lyrics he had already written for their new opera.

Now that Carte had successfully completed the Savoy Theatre, he could give his attention to the further development of the "Ground Scheme," financed by the syndicate he had formed with Michael Gunn. It was a scheme that would culminate in the building of the Savoy Hotel. He had two other projects that autumn, both in America: first, the American production of *Claude Duval*, by H. P. Stephens and Edward Solomon, an opera that he had first produced with Michael Gunn at the Olympic on 24 August; and, second, a lecture tour for Oscar Wilde.

Carte had originally approached Wilde on 30 September and received a positive response, provided the terms were acceptable. Carte wrote to a number of American managers, explaining his thinking behind the suggested tour, telling them that Wilde's name had often been quoted as "the originator of the aesthetic idea," and that Wilde was the author of a volume of poems that had been highly successful in English society."[3] For Carte, the tour might prove useful to the success of *Patience* in America; but in the event it would turn out to be wonderful publicity for Wilde himself.

Before his own departure for America, Carte supervised the first occasion electricity was to be used to light the stage at the Savoy, at the matinee performance on Wednesday, 28 December. Carte reassured the apprehensive audience and proceeded to demonstrate the safety of the new lighting by dramatically taking a hammer and breaking a lamp wrapped in a piece of muslin. To the relief and astonishment of the audience, reported *The Times*, "the flame was immediately extinguished without even singeing the muslin."[4] The applause for his dramatic demonstration was so enthusiastic that he had to return to the stage and take two curtain calls before the audience were satisfied. The following day, 29 December, was the occasion for the 250th performance of *Patience* in London and the 100th at the Standard Theatre, New York, and two days later, on 31 December 1881, Carte set sail from Liverpool on the Cunard Liner, the *Servia*, bound for New York.

Gilbert and Kitty had been booked to sail with Carte on the *Servia*, but for some unknown reason decided to cancel.[5] Perhaps Gilbert was reluctant to give up time while he was struggling with the new opera; even by mid-February he told Sullivan he was having immense difficulty with act 2. Now that he was earning a considerable salary from *Patience*, the days of writing four plays a year were well behind him. Four London theaters, however, were performing works by Gilbert in the autumn of 1881. Apart from *Patience* at the Savoy, *Princess Toto* ran at the Opera Comique until December, *Foggerty's Fairy* had a short run at the Criterion, and, at the Court in Sloane Square, John Clayton produced a revival of *Engaged* with Marion Terry, W. H. Denny, and H. J. Byron in the cast. Byron, who was already suffering from tuberculosis and would die the following April, was having difficulty learning his lines: "[he] not only does not know a word of the third Act—but he has only a glimmering of the other two," complained Gilbert to Clayton, with less than a week to go before the scheduled opening night.[6]

New Year's Day 1882, a Sunday, saw Carte on a steamer bound for New York, Sullivan on a steamer passing through the Suez Canal on his way to Cairo, and Gilbert keeping a close eye on affairs at the Savoy. Michael Gunn continued to supervise the touring companies and in Carte's absence had taken over affairs at the Savoy as well, only to find Gilbert a close presence. Gilbert was becoming increasingly anxious about the accounts. His quarterly check that he received from Gunn was less than he had expected, and he calculated that the expenses at the Savoy were excessive. "Of course I know that the Savoy is a most expensive theatre," he wrote to Gunn, "—but there cant be a difference of £40 per night in the expenses! But this we'll settle with Carte when he returns."7 But Gilbert could not sit still and wait for Carte to return. A few days later, after examining the detailed expenditure, Gilbert wrote to Carte to share his anxieties. He calculated that if they took on average £120 a night at the Savoy, they would be losing at the rate of £3,000 a year. "Of course you will see at once that this is simple ruination, & must be stopped forthwith." Gilbert then complained about particular items of expenditure in a way that he would repeat eight years later, but then with devastating consequences for the partnership.

"I find among other items of expenditure," he complained, "that we are paying no less than £210 per week for advertising." Gilbert's understanding was that any increase in expenditure on advertising would be covered by the increase in rent at the Savoy, charged to the "firm" of Gilbert, Sullivan, and Carte. "In any case there is no need, now, to advertise to anything like this extent. No theatre stands less in need of advertisement than the Savoy." He questioned additional costs for the chorus, and complained that the gas bill was £10 a week more than at the Opera Comique, "& this with electric light! What the cost of lighting will be when we have to pay for electric lighting as well as gas, God only knows."8

In February, Gilbert had a telephone installed at The Boltons at a cost of £20 a year, and had another installed at the Savoy, at the prompt entrance so that he would be able to hear the performance from his study, he told Sullivan. Gilbert had this in common with Carte: he embraced the modern world of the 1880s with its inventions of the incandescent lamp and the telephone, which could improve domestic life and could be harnessed to drive forward their business. But his relationship with Carte showed little else in common. Carte was a business associate, and as a manager had to be watched carefully in case he was benefiting unduly from Gilbert's property. Gilbert appeared to be totally unaware that the tone he adopted toward Carte was belittling and demoralizing.

In a conciliatory letter to Gilbert, Carte suggested that matters be left until they all met in London; but in a long letter to the more affable Sullivan, he was more expansive, complaining about Gilbert and his attitude.

I have suppressed my feelings as I want to avoid a storm being raised in my absence, but I feel "boiling over" when I think of it. . . . I have worked like a slave for four or five years, the last year and a half having been chiefly devoted to building a theatre expressly for your operas. The theatre is opened and turns out a success. The overwork and worry have tired me out physically and mentally, and I want to get away for a semi-holiday, something I have not had for five years and which I have certainly earned.

At the time they had discussed their agreement for the new theater, Gilbert had raised no objection, said Carte, "but when I am 3000 miles away he sees Gunn and raises up all this trouble and to a great extent spoils my holiday." He reminded Sullivan that the £500 increase in rent for the Savoy had been agreed by all three of them, and was to cover any substantial repair or redecoration. Gilbert's late reaction came as a surprise.

We often hear people say and I have heard you say that it is difficult to get on with Gilbert and <really sometimes it seems to me almost impossible> [crossed out] it really is. He takes views of things so totally unlike what any one else would. . . . If a discussion arises he will look at matters solely from his point of view, he will not see them from any other, will be very disagreeable about it. And will crush any difference of opinion with marvellously ingenious arguments which one knows all the time to be fallacious but which one cannot refute for the[,] moment. And at other times you know how nice and agreeable he can be. Well—I suppose his exceptional ways are part of his exceptional genius and that he could not write as he does if he were different. After all there is only one Gilbert, and I suppose it is of no use to talk about it.[9]

Carte detailed the reasons for the increased rent at the Savoy as opposed to the Opera Comique, a rent that he considered to be "one fifth less than the market value." He could not understand Gilbert's inconsistency in going back on an agreed price and accusing him of raising the rental. "It was my idea to build the theatre," he stressed. "*I did it.*" At the Savoy they would be able to make "£1000 to £1200 a week instead of £600 or £700. . . . All I get for this is that at this result Gilbert is aggrieved and angry (!!) . . . Money is not everything to me and I feel more about this tone he has taken than I care to say."[10]

In conclusion, Carte outlined his plans for the future. "When I get back to London I have got the great chambers and restaurant scheme which Gunn and I are going to float and must talk to you about it. . . . After that is disposed of (by next autumn I hope) the next thing ought to be the 'National Opera'!"[11]

These were Carte's three great schemes: the Savoy Theatre (already built); the Savoy Hotel (to be an outstanding success); and his opera house—which would prove to be a scheme too far.

In Egypt, Sullivan was far away from the discord, and not only physically; mentally he was able to shut himself off from those distant problems. "This is the most enervating place in the world I think," he wrote to his mother, "—if you once begin to be lazy, you can never stop, but are carried on with a mad impetus until from sheer exhaustion you write a letter or read one. I cant do any proper work here—but it doesn't matter."[12] It was a dangerous time to be in Egypt: a strong nationalist party was gathering force, only to be suppressed in July that year when the British fleet bombarded Alexandria and in September when British troops under Sir Garnet Wolseley occupied Cairo. In a humorous letter during the precarious times at the beginning of the year, Sullivan reassured his mother: "I am still alive—so are all my friends here—noone has been massacred! And I only hope they mean to leave us in safety."[13]

Taking the opportunity while in Egypt to hear an example of Arab music, Sullivan had arranged an invitation to listen to a group of musicians reputed to be "the best in Cairo."[14] He listened for three and a half hours, commenting afterward that the music was "impossible to describe, & impossible to note down."[15] He left exhausted. He was on more familiar ground when he went to the opera house in Cairo to see *Carmen*, and again to see Flotow's *Martha*. He was even more at home when given the chance to conduct in Alexandria, where he rehearsed orchestra and choir before giving a concert including Mozart's "12th Mass" and a selection from the *Messiah*.

Edward Dicey, however, was not simply an observer of the social scene but was in close contact with the leading players in political events. In a letter to his mother, Sullivan casually mentioned a few of the people Dicey was in correspondence with at the time: Lord Granville, the foreign secretary; Gambetta, the former French prime minister; and the khedive, Tewfik Pasha. Another major player was Sir Edward Malet, one of the two British consuls keeping Gladstone informed on affairs in Egypt. Sullivan went along to Malet's house one evening to meet the young sons of the prince of Wales: Albert, the future duke of Clarence, aged seventeen, and the future King George V, aged sixteen. "We had riotous games and separated at midnight," Sullivan wrote in his diary. "The Princes enjoyed themselves very much—were in riotously high spirits & knocked me about a good deal—I was in good spirits myself."[16] While Sullivan played with the princes, no doubt Dicey was engaged in more earnest conversation with Malet.

Sullivan's particular concern at the time was that his servant had proved to be a disaster, being "lazy, light headed, and worst of all [had] a tendency to drink," he wrote to his mother. He would have to dismiss him when they returned to England. "Oh, the bother of servants—and I shall have to get a cook also, besides a man. It is enough to make one marry—but the cure would be more awful than the disease. I can get rid of servants, but not a wife—especially if she is *my* wife."[17] On 19 March, he told his mother that the Shepheards Hotel was becoming crowded with Cook's tourists, "including of course a lot of parsons, who all sit together at the table d'hôte. . . . I wish they wouldn't wear black coats—they look so dirty & disreputable."[18] To avoid the lowly tourists, Dicey suggested they take an alternative route home.

They left Alexandria on 28 March bound for Naples. After a visit to Pompeii and Vesuvius, they traveled on to Rome and then to Turin, before making for Paris via the Mont Cenis tunnel. They reached Paris early in the morning on Monday, 10 April, and booked in at the Grand Hotel, meeting up with Mrs. Ronalds and Fanny, who were already there. On several evenings Sullivan dined with Mrs. Ronalds and her daughter, and with D.H. (presumably Mrs. Ronalds) when her daughter was not present. He also visited No 4, rue M.T., probably a brothel, every day he was in Paris, entering in his diary the symbols (1) or (2) as appropriate on four of the days. On one busy day, after visiting number 4, calling on the duke of Edinburgh for a chat, and dining with Mrs. Ronalds and her daughter, he went on to the New Club to indulge another passion, and lost £720 playing chemin-de-fer.

After four months abroad, Sullivan arrived back in London on 18 April and moved straight into his new apartment at 1 Queen's Mansions—his London home for the rest of his life. He had returned in time to conduct the anniversary performance of *Patience* on Monday, 24 April. "The theatre was crowded to the last seat, and the piece was listened to from beginning to end with unflagging attention and delight," reported *The Times*. "Mr. Sullivan, who has recently returned from his journey to Egypt, conducted, and was greeted with enthusiastic applause on his appearance in the orchestra."[19] Sullivan completed his evening at the Argus Club, where he lost £500.

No special celebrations marked Sullivan's fortieth birthday. His family called on him in the morning: his mother, Charlotte, and the children. Mrs. Sullivan still lived at Northumberland House in Fulham, even though Charlotte had married again in December 1881. Her husband, Ben Hutchinson, was a former army captain and thirteen years younger than Charlotte. In the afternoon, Sullivan attended a concert in aid of the Royal College of Music, newly founded from the old National Training School, and whose first principal was George Grove. The duke of Edinburgh played the violin, and Sullivan accompanied Madame Albani on the harmonium as she sang the Bach-Gounod "Ave Maria."

A few days later, Clementina Sullivan was taken ill. She had gone to Queen's Mansions, where Sullivan was listening to Courtice Pounds, a nineteen-year-old tenor who had joined the chorus of *Patience* the previous autumn. At lunch, she felt unwell and was taken home to Fulham. For a while she seemed to improve, but by 25 May her condition was causing concern. Sullivan visited her that evening: "Stayed an hour and found Mother still restless but a little more patient. Left her at 7.15 to return home to dinner."[20] At the same time, another crisis had arisen: Fanny Ronalds thought she was pregnant. "Important business with Mrs. R. Drove after dinner with D.H. to M., who advised delay in taking action until 20 June. Submitted to this advice (fee £1.1s.), returned home (2)."[21]

The following morning, 26 May, Sullivan wrote out a check for £1,000 for his stockbroker friend, Edward Hall, who had asked for a loan, promising to repay on 14 June: an ominous sign that Sullivan was unable to read with his mind already absorbed by his other worries. In the afternoon he drove over to Fulham. His mother had been given morphine to help her through the night and she was now very weak.

Sullivan asked the family doctor, Dr. Woodhouse, to call in a second doctor, Sir Henry Thompson. "They returned at midnight, & after a long exam: Thompson told me there was but little hope as her strength was failing her." Sullivan left at 3:30 in the morning, Saturday, 27 May, in order to get a few hours' sleep "— and regretted it afterwards," he recorded. At a quarter past eight, his niece Amy arrived at Queen's Mansions to fetch him. "I knew the worst was at hand—if not already over. I put on my clothes rapidly & was at Fulham before 9—the blinds were all down—Charlotte opened the door—I rushed upstairs, and was alone in the room—alone, that is with dear Mother's lifeless body—her soul had gone to God."[22]

Clementina Sullivan's body was laid to rest on Thursday, 1 June, in Brompton Cemetery, in the same grave as her husband and her son Frederic. The funeral service was conducted by the old family friend, Thomas Helmore. At the end of the day, Sullivan wrote in his diary, "home feeling dreadfully lonely."[23]

Sullivan was alone with his thoughts. His devoted mother had gone, the person whose love had always been there for him and to whom he had always remained a dutiful son. He had visited her regularly when he was in London, and when away kept in constant touch by letter. It was the one sure and unchanging relationship in his life. His relationship with Fanny Ronalds could not offer him the emotional stability he needed. Fanny was true to him and, as far as is known, Arthur Sullivan was the love of her life, following her earlier unsuccessful relationships. But Sullivan was not true to her. For him, their relationship was not satisfactory. He chose to spend long periods of time away from her; there were other women in his life, and even when with her in Paris he had spent most days visiting a brothel. It is ironic that, in the years ahead, and with their relationship changing in the course of time, Sullivan would find in Fanny's family, her parents, and children, a substitute for the family he had lost.

On 2 June, Sullivan's diary reads, "L.W. came—had seen A.C. symptoms beginning."[24] Fanny had not waited as the first doctor advised, but had consulted another doctor who had induced an abortion. "Things going well," Sullivan wrote in his diary on 5 June,[25] and on 7 June, "Letter from L.W. Last of 'cause' came away."[26] But then another woman appeared on the scene, someone who was possibly in Egypt with Sullivan. "Settled all 'off,'" noted Sullivan on 9 June,[27] and a few days later reassured Fanny that it was all over about Miss C. The next comment on the matter in his diary is intriguing:

Awful letter back—completely staggered & upset me. Couldn't do any work all day—walked out at 6, but returned as it rained so. L.W. just at door—came in for a few minutes, left in a "state" almost immediately. I dont know what to do.[28]

Whatever the contents of that "awful letter," Fanny Ronalds must have remonstrated with Sullivan over his conduct toward her. Did she upbraid him for his infidelity? It was that particular aspect of his character that Rachel Scott Russell had feared all those years ago. When Sullivan had seen Rachel in 1881, he had found that she was very little changed. In one respect, Sullivan had not changed either. Rachel had been spared a great deal of sorrow.

It was only a few weeks later, on 22 July 1882, that Rachel Scott Russell died from cholera at Varanasi (Benares) in India. Her husband, William Holmes, later returned to England with their two daughters. Rachel had left unfinished her translation, *Memoirs of Hector Berlioz*, which was completed by her sister-in-law Eleanor Holmes, and published in London in 1884. The news of her death reached England in the middle of August and when Sullivan heard, he wrote in his diary for 1881: "Chenny came to see me on 5th Oct: to say goodbye before returning to India—the last time I saw her poor girl."29

Before setting sail on his yacht for the summer, Gilbert produced a performance of *Broken Hearts* at the Savoy on 21 June to mark the farewell to the stage of Florence Terry. Then it was off to Devon, to sail the *Chloris* in waters where his romantically—and mistakenly—supposed ancestor Sir Humphrey Gilbert once sailed. On 27 July, Sullivan departed for Cornwall, as the guest of Lady Molesworth at Pencarrow, to work on the new opera. He worked on act 1, "framing" the finale and writing the "Invocation" and "the 'Peers' March" before leaving on 7 August to meet Gilbert at the Half Moon Hotel, Exeter. Between lunch and dinner together, they thrashed out any difficulties that Sullivan had encountered in the long finale to act 1 and then, armed with Gilbert's latest lyrics for act 2, Sullivan caught the train for London.

He continued to work on the opera, but only until 19 August, when he left for Bertich, a spa in Germany, with Fanny Ronalds and Mrs. Carter, and accompanied by his two servants, Louis and Adèle. Louis Jaegar, a twenty-year-old German from Hamburg whom Sullivan had employed after returning from Egypt, was to prove the best of all his valets, remaining in his service for the rest of Sullivan's life. For the moment, Louis was not used to his employer's requirements and they had left without Sullivan's diaries, his morphia injector, and his toothpaste. Sullivan had to write to his secretary to send them on to him. It was not that they had left in a hurry; the trip had been planned in advance. Sullivan had informed Carte about going abroad, but he had not felt inclined to tell Gilbert, even though he had seen him as recently as 7 August.

Anxious to go through their agreement for the opera before Sullivan left for Germany, Carte wrote asking Gilbert to meet them. "I am very sorry that Sullivan is going abroad," Gilbert replied on 10 August from the *Chloris*, "—he has no right to break his promise to begin rehearsals on the 6th. I cant possibly come up to town now—the agreement can wait until we meet."30

Carte's letter had another purpose: to discuss the possibility of releasing Frank Thornton from his contract. Frank Thornton had been with them since the days of *The Sorcerer* in which he had understudied George Grossmith and had a walk-on part as the "Oldest Inhabitant"; but Gilbert had no part for him in the new piece. Currently Thornton was playing the Major in *Patience* and had appeared in curtain-raisers, but Carte thought he deserved something more because of his devotion to the company since the very beginning, and because *Patience* was coming to an end. Gilbert disagreed: "[Thornton] is a most wholesome check on Grossmith & the best possible understudy—it would be madness, as it seems to me, to release him. . . .—The piece *may* run another year—of course it's not likely, but it *may*."[31]

While he was at Bertich, Sullivan did a little work on the opera, but was back in London on Monday, 12 September, the day rescheduled for the first music rehearsal at the Savoy. He arrived at Victoria Station at 6:30 a.m. and managed a few hours' sleep at home in Queen's Mansions before the arrival of Carte and François Cellier at eleven. They were probably relieved to find Sullivan there; as usual, he had cut things very fine. Any differences with Gilbert were ironed out, and Sullivan invited Gilbert and Kitty to dinner that Thursday, when his other guests were Fanny Ronalds and her daughter, as well Mr. and Mrs. Beach Grant and their daughter.

Much work remained to be done on the opera, and Sullivan was now into his phase of working until the early hours. It was his preferred time of working, free from all interruptions, and at a time when the clatter of hooves and the grinding of carriage wheels in Victoria Street had fallen silent. He was not an early riser, so he was not necessarily deprived of sleep. Nevertheless, he was working under pressure, as rehearsals had already started. He finished act 1 at 4:45 a.m. on 3 October, having made changes to the finale, and then began work the following evening on act 2, writing: "Fold Your Flapping Wings" (a song for Strephon that was eventually cut after severe criticism of the lyrics in the press); "Heigh-ho, Love Is a Thorn" (a song for Iolanthe, which also was cut); Iolanthe's ballad, "He Loves"; and "When Britain Really Ruled the Waves." After that long and productive session, Sullivan went to bed at 5 a.m. Then followed three days' rest from writing.

With the opening of the opera scheduled for late November, Gilbert and Sullivan appeared to be working well ahead of themselves; but the plan was to open in New York simultaneously in order to forestall the American pirates. Such a plan would entail rehearsing two companies and having the music ready to sail with the New York Company. Helen Lenoir was already in America, having sailed from Liverpool on 22 August. Despite all their careful attempts to keep plot, music, and even the title secret, word was leaked and a fairly detailed plot of the opera appeared in the columns of the *World* in early October. Gilbert suspected that the disenchanted Frank Thornton was the source of the leak. Writing to Carte on 13 October, he explained his reasons, saying that Thornton had been present when he read the piece to the cast, when act 1 was set in St. James's Park, but had not been at subsequent rehearsals when Gilbert had changed his mind about the setting. "I feel absolutely certain that he is the culprit."[32]

In the same letter, Gilbert stressed the need to settle the title of the opera. Until then they had been using the working title of "Perola." He asked Carte to write to Henry Irving for permission to call the opera *Iolanthe*, a title that Irving had already used for a piece in 1880. "I would write to him," said Gilbert, "but I fancy he is not particularly friends to me, as I have never disguised my opinion of his acting, & it has probably reached him—at least, so I guess from his constrained manner."[33]

Secrecy over the new opera was paramount; Carte was insistent that no details about the costumes should be leaked in America and find their way back to England. He warned Helen Lenoir: "They [Gilbert and Sullivan] are afraid that if it *gets once* to the Ld. Chamberlain's Office here that the sacred orders *The Garter*, Thistle, Patrick and Bath (above all the garter [)] are going on the Stage, the office may come down bang and forbid it being done."[34]

The question of the stage manager for New York still had to be decided when Gilbert, Sullivan, and Carte met on 19 October. Helen Lenoir was happy for Charles Harris to fill the role, but Harris was the man that Gilbert had had dismissed in 1878 for altering his stage business without consulting him. Gilbert had no objection, provided he was not brought into personal communication with him. An additional stage manager was required for a second company in America. Helen Lenoir was offered Thornton or W. H. Seymour. She chose Seymour. "Thornton is somewhat disappointed," wrote Carte, "but will get over it. . . . I am most desirous that you should have things done in America *as you wish* them, and as you think best."[35]

By 20 October, Sullivan had finished the composition of act 2 and two days later began scoring. The act 2 score was finished in less than a week, leaving him with just the overture to compose. Gilbert was still making changes but any amendments to the orchestral score had to leave with W. H. Seymour, who was shortly to embark for America. On 29 October, in a letter which shows signs of end-of-term levity, Sullivan sent Alfred Cellier in New York detailed notes on the numbers in the opera.

My dear Alfred,

Perola.

Its Rise, Fall, Use & Abuse: with a few remarks as to its ultimate influence on the current of thought of the nineteenth century.

————

Act I

Overture. Write one yourself.

No 1. Chorus. As originally written, the intro: was too short; a few additional bars are sent by Seymour with bandparts.

The curtain now rises on the 9th. bar.

. . .

No. 3. Invocation—The name Perola was originally "Iolanthe" which had 4 liquid syllables. Some name had to [be] put in an "O" and "Ah" or a "Come" before Perola.

. . .

5. Sprightly & lightly.

6. [Entrance and March of Peers] 4 bars side drums on stage before the trumpets, so that the cornets begin in sight of conductor. Then 4 bars I shall entrust

to you to compose—If you have any difficulty about this, Solomon is in New York & will probably help you.

Strings at letter E. heavy bows.

Keep all the instruments *pp* at G. except flutes & clarinets.

. . .

No 12. Ld. Chanc: Song

Strict time until 4th. Verse—let Riley [*sic*] take a little ad: lib I have taught Grossmith to sing it thus

[Sullivan included a musical quotation with the words "think that the rule might apply to the bar" [*sic*] shown as spoken through the accompaniment]

. . .

[As might be expected Sullivan wrote many notes on the long finale to act 1, ending with:]

Coda 2/4. I hope this will please you, as I took your advice & waited until I got what I think is a good phrase. It will remind you of "happy days" at Covent Garden, when all the audience had cleared out.

End of 1st. Act.

Act: 2.

No 1 Sentry's Song—1st. eight bars of song to be sung ad lib: like a gentleman at a public dinner without accompt.

. . .

No 4. Etude de Pizzicato! [Duet: "In vain to us you plead"]

The *chorus of men* (which is not in score) merely consists of the two "ha has" with Mount A. & Toll: & the "we go" at the end, all pp. When I first wrote the number, the peers were not on the stage—I have kept them on since then.

. . .

No 8. Patter song [the Nightmare song]—not too fast, & accompt. to be kept *down* [p.] so as to have a more mysterious & dreamy effect.

. . .

No 11A. [Iolanthe's "He loves"] 1st Verse—Simple pathos.

2nd Verse—*more* passionate.

12. ["It may not be"] you will find a difference in this number. *Full Score* is right. Perola to end pathetically instead of melodramatically [bar added] The wailing of the fairies to be *andante* & sustained, & the willaloo to die away. The Finale is a repeat of No 9.

I have thus dear <Edward> [crossed out] Alfred, (Edward Hall is in the room) tried to trace the history of Perola from its earliest development as handed down to us by tradition through the quaint old historian Gilbertus, commonly called the "Neverwrong." Should this attempt be successful in reviving an interest in the works of the too much neglected old composer, Sullivan I shall feel that my labour has not been thrown away.

Sullivan did not post that letter on the Sunday, when it was written; a full dress rehearsal of act 2 took place for the American company on Monday; and then on Tuesday, 31 October, returning to his letter, he added a few modifications.

The original duet between Phyllis and Strephon, which in Sullivan's notes had been described as being performed "Sprightly & lightly," was to be replaced by a new one that he had not yet written. "This will be sent to you on Saturday next," he told Alfred Cellier.[37] He tackled it on Sunday 5 November, but failed. He went for a walk, came back and finally started composing the duet at 1 a.m. By 4:10 a.m., he had scored it. The new duet was "None Shall Part Us," in which occurs, as described by Arthur Jacobs, "one of the most exquisite of Sullivan's chromatic modulations (at 'I to thee, and thou to me.')"[38] The "sprightly & lightly" duet of Phyllis and Strephon, "If We're Weak Enough to Tarry," had been moved to act 2, to replace a song by Phyllis. "This brightens up the 2nd. Act immensely," said Sullivan.[39]

He now had the unusual experience of being able to devote himself to rehearsals of the Savoy company without having to go home to finish composing and then scoring the opera in a race against time. Apart from conducting *The Martyr of Antioch* at Brighton on 7 November, Sullivan had ample time to write the overture entirely himself for the first time. He was working with an orchestra of twenty-nine at the Savoy: six first violins, four second violins, two violas, two cellos, two basses, two trombones, two flutes, two clarinets, two cornets, one oboe, one bassoon, two horns, and drums.[40] He made several attempts before pressure of time concentrated his efforts and he completed it at 7:00 a.m. on the morning of 24 November. That evening the final dress rehearsal lasted until 1:30 a.m., after which Sullivan went for supper with Tom Chappell to Rule's in Maiden Lane.

The first night audience for *Iolanthe; or, The Peer and the Peri* on Saturday, 25 November 1882, included a number of old friends and colleagues: Mrs. Ronalds, George Grove, Fred Clay, John Hollingshead, Lady Molesworth (in whose house a small part of the music was written), Captain Eyre Massey Shaw (Chief of the Metropolitan Fire Brigade), Gilbert's old friend Sir Bruce Seton, and, of course, Mrs. Gilbert. "The Savoy Theatre, lighted like no other theatre in Europe, and looking exceptionally brilliant on this occasion, was crammed to its utmost capacity," reported the *Era*.[41]

Gilbert's idea for *Iolanthe* had started with "The Fairy Curate," one of the "Bab Ballads":

> Once a fairy
> Light and airy
> Married with a mortal;[42]

It had gone through many changes and developments of plot before ending up as an opera. As the idea developed in Gilbert's mind, the fairy, Iolanthe, marries the most senior legal figure in the land, the Lord Chancellor; and in the Gilbertian topsy-turvy world, the common sense of the dainty fairies stands in contrast to the airy nonsense of the ponderous lords. Gilbert had not set out to write a satire on the House of Lords and on parliamentary procedures, but as the plot developed from its original idea Gilbert saw the opportunity to poke fun at them and provide a source of enjoyment for his audience with his absurd characters and clever lyrics.

For the critics, Gilbert became too serious when Strephon sang of the less fortunate in society turning to petty crime because of circumstances: Strephon himself might have been a criminal if he had had Fagin as a father. This was not the sort of thing that people expected from Gilbert and Sullivan, and as a result of criticism Gilbert decided to cut the number. The essentially serious Gilbert was no doubt disappointed to cut his lines; but the realistic Gilbert was also sensitive to what was good for business. The audiences wanted to be entertained, not instructed by Gilbert and Sullivan operas.

For the first time in the series of operas, the overture was Sullivan's and was superior in construction and orchestration to anything that had been done before. The music of the opera is wider in range than the previous operas: from the pathetic and sentimental tones for Iolanthe, through the bright and jaunty melody of "If We're Weak Enough to Tarry" and the joyful frolic in "Faint Heart Never Won Fair Lady," to the military brassiness of the Peer's march. Sullivan uses motifs for two of the characters, Iolanthe and the Lord Chancellor; the first, a plaintive melody on the oboe; the second, on the cellos, a solemn motif with just a suggestion of playfulness.

And then, of course, there are those numbers in which Sullivan provides music for Gilbert's most characteristically humorous lines: music that, at the very least, matches the lyrics. His music for the opening chorus, in which a chorus of fairies are not sure of the reasons why they dance the way they do, is accompanied by a pizzicato lightness together with a common-time ploddiness. In the Lord Chancellor's "Nightmare Song," in which Sullivan, perhaps more than anywhere else, has to subordinate his music to the author's words, the clever and varied accompaniment enhances the effectiveness of a very long patter song.

But one of Sullivan's finest achievements was the finale to act 1, which required much thought and discussion with Gilbert in its construction before arriving at its finished form. From the point of view of the dramatist, it consists of a series of dramatic situations that resolve the first act; the music demonstrates Sullivan's total comprehension of the absurd humor of it all, and, rather than resulting in unevenness, it results in a series of musical pieces that has never failed to delight successive generations of audiences.

One number that caused much excitement on the first night, and that Sullivan made great use of in his overture, was the Fairy Queen's song, "Oh, Foolish Fay." It is well known, and always quoted, that on the first night of *Iolanthe*, to the great amusement of those of the audience who knew him, Captain Eyre Massey Shaw, the Chief of the Metropolitan Fire Brigade, was in the audience to hear sung by the Fairy Queen, in all seriousness, the lines:

Oh, Captain Shaw!
  Type of true love kept under!
  Could thy Brigade
  With cold cascade
Quench my great love, I wonder![43]

Jessie Bond, in her "Reminiscences" says that "It was just a happy chance that set Captain Shaw . . . right in the middle of the stalls on that night of all others."[44] But it is more likely that it was not a complete surprise to the Fire Chief. On 25 July, Sullivan had invited Shaw to dinner at Queen's Mansions and could have warned him of what was coming; some, if not most, of the act 2 lyrics were ready by this time.

Sullivan's good nature and resilience were severely put to the test that day, when he was hit by a major financial tragedy, the culmination of a sorrowful year. His entry in his diary for the 25 November is stark; he is too numbed to elaborate.

At home all day—L.W. to tea. Received letter from E. A. Hall saying he was ruined & my money (about £7,000) lost, just before starting for the theatre— Dined with Smythe at home. 1st Performance of "Iolanthe" at the Savoy Theatre. House crammed, awfully nervous, more so than usual on going into the Orchestra—tremendous reception—1st. Act went splendidly—the 2nd. dragged & I was afraid it must be compressed—however it finished well & Gilbert & myself were called & heartily cheered. Very low afterwards—came home.[45]

A sad Sullivan but a delighted audience. It was another success for the author and composer and another triumph for the cast. "Of the principal artists," said *The Times*, "Mr. Grossmith deserves to be mentioned first. His mock gravity as the Lord Chancellor was inspired by genuine humour, and, without the ghost of a voice, he gave excellent effect to the three amusing songs allowed to him."[46] Second place was given to the excellence of Alice Barnett as the Fairy Queen. Doubt was thrown on the casting of Richard Temple in the part of Strephon by both *The Times* and the *Era*, but the rest of the cast were generally praised. "Miss Jessie Bond, as Iolanthe," said the *Era* "may be credited with all the grace, delicacy, and fascination we should expect from a fairy mother, and her singing of the really exquisite melody in the last scene was one of the most successful items in the entire opera."[47] The part of Private Willis, in Gilbert's mind originally intended for Rutland Barrington, was played by Charles Manners, who had been performing since August in one of the touring companies as Dick Deadeye and Samuel. Barrington was given a more important part as the Earl of Mountararat, one of the two main representatives of the House of Lords, alongside Durward Lely as Earl Tolloller.

Having given his audience an evening of intense enjoyment, Sullivan went home to face an uncertain future. He had hoped, after all, that this was to be his last opera with Gilbert, at least for some time. He would have to think again.

CHAPTER EIGHTEEN

1883-1884

Princess Ida

WHILE THE FIRST PROVINCIAL TOUR of *Iolanthe* set out from Bath at the end of 1882, in London Carte was feeling hard pressed because his team of loyal workers had been temporarily thinned out. Michael Gunn was producing a Christmas pantomime, Frank Desprez had taken the week's holiday promised him, George Edwardes (the younger — who had recently joined his older cousin at the Savoy) was ill with erysipolas, and Carte's major player, Helen Lenoir, was in America.

"The situation is that I am worried out of my life with detail," said Carte in a letter of 31 December 1882 to Helen Lenoir.[1] Carte's province was the grand scheme, adapting ideas to further his business, contacting the right people to convince them of the benefits of his latest plan. Detail was Helen Lenoir's forte. Carte wanted her back in London. He sounded desperate in his letter. "I *very* much wish you could [return] as your presence here would be most desirable in fact the word 'desirable' is altogether ludicrously inadequate to express the situation. Your presence would be *invaluable*."[2]

Helen Lenoir's work was unfinished in New York. *Iolanthe* had only been running a month, while two companies had opened at Boston and Philadelphia as recently as 4 December. She could not conscientiously close up her side of the business and return to England but would have to remain for several more months. It was imperative that Carte's interests in America should be protected. Just before the opening of *Iolanthe* in New York, the *Era*'s American correspondent had written, "Mr. Carte is not here although he was expected; and his affairs in America sadly need his personal attention, if he does not want to lose his prestige here."[3]

At some point in January 1883, perhaps during his trip to Paris that month, Sullivan realized that the only sure way of restoring his financial security was to collaborate with Gilbert on future operas — not on one opera only but a series. The previous summer, he had been looking forward to working with Bret Harte on an opera with an American theme and Harte had supplied him with a sketch plot in July. Harte had later turned the plot into a narrative published under the title, "At the Mission of San Carmel," and he sent a copy to Sullivan. The idea still tempted Sullivan, but he was conscious that it was his work with Gilbert that had brought him the financial success he needed, whatever the difficulties of working with Gilbert.

Unaware that Sullivan had not intended to write with him for a long time, Gilbert had meanwhile begun work on a new opera. This time, instead of taking as his starting point an idea from one of his "Bab Ballads," he went back to one of his plays, *The Princess*, written in 1870. This gave him a ready-made plot; he would need to make adaptations with Sullivan and write the lyrics, but much of his work was already done. The lyrics he had written for *The Princess* would not be suitable: they had been written to existing music, such as "Les trois cousines" from Offenbach's *La Périchole*, the Laughing Song from Auber's *Manon Lescaut*, and Rossini's "Largo al Factotum" from *Il Barbiere di Seviglia*. A departure from previous practice would be the use of a larger cast, entailing higher preliminary costs and necessarily eating into their profits in the early stages. Gilbert was taking a gamble, but Carte and Sullivan could have outvoted him if they disagreed, and there would be no point continuing if Sullivan were not happy with the plot.

By 8 February, Gilbert was ready with the adapted prologue from *The Princess*, which would become act 1 of *Princess Ida*. That same day all three—Gilbert, Sullivan, and Carte—went along to the office of Frank Stanley, who had drawn up a five-year agreement for them. Carte agreed to pay them each one-third of the net profits "after deducting all expenses and charges of producing the said operas." Included in the expenses was a rental of £4,000 a year for the Savoy Theatre, all rates, lighting expenses, and "repairs incidental to the performances and rendered necessary from time to time by ordinary wear and tear."[4] It was formal, legal language, intended to ensure as far as possible that there was no room for misinterpretation. The phrase beginning "repairs incidental to the performance" would prove to be at the center of the legal argument, although not the underlying cause, which in 1890 was to lead to so much controversy.

After signing the five-year agreement, Sullivan and Gilbert drove to the Savoy, having what Sullivan called "a slight breeze & explanation en route," and there Gilbert read him act 1 of what was to be *Princess Ida*.[5] Sullivan was sufficiently satisfied for Gilbert to be able to carry on with the adaptation of his own work and to supply Sullivan with the lyrics.

The following week at the Savoy, two special matinees took place. The first on Wednesday, 14 February was a benefit for Frank Thornton: a performance of *Broken Hearts* in which Thornton played Mousta; one of George Grossmith's musical sketches, "The Drinking Fountain"; and two numbers from Act 2 of *Patience*, with Thornton as Major Murgatroyd.[6] A fortnight later, Thornton left the Savoy company to play the Lord Chancellor and to be stage manager in a new touring company.

The second special matinee took place the very next day, Thursday, 15 February: a performance of *Iolanthe* for members of the theatrical profession. The company was presented with potentially their most critical audience, but "the humour and odd conceits with which the dialogue abounds," said *The Times*, "evoked, from what may be supposed to be a *blasé* audience the same laughter and applause as they nightly do for the public." The reviewer considered that Grossmith's Lord Chancellor had become "an exquisitely refined satire." Sullivan conducted the first act, and for that performance at least, the number of fairies adorned with electric stars in their hair had been increased to thirty.[7]

The Savoy now had orderly queuing outside its doors. At the end of December, Carte had carried out another revolution. In order to avoid the usual "struggling and pushing" outside the theater by those trying to buy unreserved tickets, he succeeded, with the assistance of the police, in persuading those waiting "to form *à la queue*, as they do in France and America, and quietly wait their turn."[8] Inside the theater, programs and cloakrooms were free of charge. The programs carried a warning that, "Any attendant detected in accepting money from visitors will be instantly dismissed; the public is therefore not to tempt the attendants by offering them gratuities."[9]

With affairs running smoothly at the Savoy, and Carte's full team back in place, Carte himself was able to cross the Atlantic to show his commitment to his affairs in America. He was more than confident that his business interests were in good hands and had implicit trust in Helen Lenoir, but personal contact was essential to keep the American managers happy. His stay was not a long one and, on 10 April, both Carte and Helen Lenoir left New York for Liverpool.

In the forefront of Sullivan's mind at this time were the preparations being made for the formal opening of the Royal College of Music. He noted in his diary on 29 April that the prince of Wales had said on shaking hands, " 'I congratulate you on the great honour we have in store for you'— I suppose he means he is going to place me on the Council of the R. C. of Music! what an honour!," thought Sullivan.[10] The following week, on Monday 3 May, Sullivan received a letter from the prime minister offering him a knighthood, "in recognition" wrote Gladstone, "of your distinguished talents as a composer and of the services which you have rendered to the promotion of the art of music generally in this country."[11] Sullivan humbly accepted. At the opening of the Royal College of Music on 7 May, the prince of Wales publicly announced Sullivan's knighthood, and that evening Sullivan attended a supper at the Lyceum Theatre with the prince of Wales and a "select party."[12]

Having signed an agreement under financial pressure with Gilbert and Carte for the next five years, Sullivan now found himself under a different kind of pressure from the musical world. The *Musical Review* remarked, "some things that Mr. Arthur Sullivan may do, Sir Arthur Sullivan ought not to do." It would look "rather more than odd," they cautioned, if the name of Sir Arthur Sullivan were to be linked with Mr. W. S. Gilbert in writing another comic opera. They wanted him to raise his mind to higher things: "it is to him that we look to wield the knightly sword—to do battle for the honour of English art."[13]

To mark the new stage in his life, Sullivan gave a dinner that would celebrate his forty-first birthday and at the same time celebrate his knighthood. It was an all-male gathering at Queen's Mansions on Sunday 14 May and the guests included the prince of Wales, the duke of Edinburgh, Millais, Gilbert, and Burnand. Musical entertainment for the guests was provided in part by Paolo Tosti and Madame Albani, and in part by a selection from *Iolanthe* relayed by telephone from the Savoy, where the cast had been specially assembled for a late-night performance starting at 11:15.

On 22 May, Sullivan went down "by special train" to Windsor Castle to be knighted along with George Grove, then aged sixty-three, and George Macfarren, aged seventy. He recorded the event in his diary in formal terms, leaving aside the emotion of the occasion. "I bowed low—then knelt down—the Queen took the Equerry's sword & laid it first on right then on left shoulder—said softly 'Sir Arthur' & gave me her hand to kiss—then I rose—bowed low again & backed out."[14]

Elated as he must have been by the honor, especially after the downturn in his fortunes in the previous year, Sullivan was not in good health. At the end of May, he traveled to Carlsbad (now called Karlovy Vary), a spa in Bohemia, in the hope that its waters would bring him some benefit. Fred Clay, also conscious of health problems, and Clay's sister-in-law were already there. Sullivan "began the cure at 7.15 a.m." on Monday, 4 June, and subjected himself to the tight regime, even going to bed at the unearthly hour for Sullivan of 10 p.m.[15] Fortified, he was back in London by early July.

In the summer of 1883, Gilbert had turned from the sea to the countryside, and rented a house for the summer at Eastbury, near Pinner. He had also decided to move from The Boltons to an even larger house that was being built in Harrington Gardens, a stone's throw away, on the other side of the Old Brompton Road. A plot of land, sufficient for two large houses, was acquired by the Hon. Henry Coke, husband of Lady Katherine, and he offered Gilbert a share. The two houses, numbers 39 and 41, later renumbered 19 and 21, were constructed at the same time. Atop Gilbert's house, fifty feet up, stands a model sailing ship, emblem of Gilbert's supposed ancestry. The ornate, even fussy façade imposes itself on its surroundings, in true Gilbertian style. Inside the house, Gilbert had ensured comfort: a large library with tall windows to ensure maximum light, central heating throughout, four bathrooms, a telephone, and electricity. The estimate to install the electric lighting came to £606.13.6, and included a dynamo capable of powering seventy lights.

In July, Gilbert sent one of his peremptory letters to the builders, informing them that he intended moving into his new house on 1 October, laying down strict orders as to what minimum accommodation should be ready by that date. Not even Gilbert could ensure that builders finished when they said they would. He moved in on 13 October, but the construction still resembled a building site to an outside observer. One such observer, out for a Sunday afternoon stroll with her friends, thought that the building must be unoccupied and decided to take a look around, only to find herself confronted by the towering figure of Gilbert. He was the model of courtesy, however, and insisted on giving his unexpected guests a tour of the premises.

Gilbert's correctness and sense of propriety were evident in his role of moral guardian of the female members of the Savoy company. Earlier in the year, May Fortescue, much admired by male members of the audience, had been the subject of a rumor spread by an officer of the Hussars, who claimed he was having an affair with her. When Gilbert learned what was going on, he found out the identity of the officer and hauled him in front of a solicitor to make a signed apology for the false rumor and to agree to pay all costs relating to an action that Miss Fortescue had initiated. And now Miss Fortescue was the object of a real peer's attentions after he had seen her in *Iolanthe*. The young nobleman, Lord Garmoyle, went so far as to propose marriage, and Miss Fortescue accepted. She informed Gilbert, who mentioned the matter in a letter to Carte, in the hope of furthering the career of another promising young member of the company. "By the way, Miss Fortescue is going to be married & leave the stage, at the end of Iolanthe. But she wants it kept a profound secret, & I wasn't to tell you anything about it. I hope Sybil Grey will be able to sing the music."[16] May Fortescue left the cast at the end of August but Sybil Grey was not chosen to replace her. Carte and Sullivan must have thought differently, and Gilbert was outvoted.

In the new opera, the part of Princess Ida was to be a more dramatic role than Leonora Braham had ever played with the company, and it was decided that they look elsewhere. Sullivan, Gilbert, Carte, and François Cellier all went to see Lillian Russell, an American soprano, who was appearing in Stephens and Solomon's work, *Virginia and Paul*. She was engaged for the part, but this particular engagement had repercussions that would make themselves felt for a long time to come.

At the end of July, Sullivan went to stay with the Gilberts at Eastbury in order to go through the whole of the new opera, which still bore the working title of *The Princess*. They made "alterations & modifications" together and Sullivan noted in his diary: "2nd. Act in good order—only wants a song for the Princess. 3rd. Act very nearly complete—left 1st. Act with [Gilbert] to make some alterations. Like the piece as now shaped out, very much."[17] An interesting comment from Sullivan, in view of what he had to say after the opera was produced. Sullivan also played tennis with Gilbert while he was at Eastbury; a fascinating contest to visualize, especially as it has been said that Gilbert arbitrarily extended the regulation measurements of a tennis court to allow him to get his service in.

Early in August, Sullivan moved away from London for a few weeks to a house he had rented to find the peace and quiet needed to continue with his composition of the new opera. He had made a start at Carlsbad and was now ready to start work on what was to be act 2. He was visited for a few days by Fanny Ronalds and her parents. There was little room in the house for privacy or intimacy between Sullivan and Fanny. His diary indicates that they had to make love in the shrubbery.

Sullivan had made steady progress on the opera writing four numbers on one day: the first two choruses of act 2, "Towards the Empyrean Heights" and "Mighty Maiden with a Mission"; the trio "I Am a Maiden" and "The Ape and the Lady." He had already written the other trio in act 2, "Gently, Gently" and he had finished most of the act 2 finale. In the middle of September, he returned to London to prepare for the Leeds Festival in October.

It was the first time Sullivan had conducted at Leeds since he had become Sir Arthur. He was conscious that his knighthood helped advance the status of English music, but the best-known names in conducting were still those of foreign-born musicians: Benedict, Costa, Hallé, Manns, and the rising star Hans Richter. *"Stupendous performance!"* Sullivan wrote in his diary after he had conducted Beethoven's *Grand Mass in D*. "Great cheering for me afterwards."[18]

And the approval of the audience was as vital to him as it is to any performer. He was certainly not the conductor of the Leeds Festival because of the money: 300 guineas for all the preparatory work, rehearsals, and performances was not going to restore his wealth. But it was even more important to him now, as Sir Arthur Sullivan, still to be engaged in serious music. More than one critic thought that he was in his rightful place, and Sullivan was beginning to agree.

After Leeds, Sullivan returned to the music of *Princess Ida*. Gilbert had made alterations to the first few numbers in act 1 at the end of September, and had suggested that the first act should finish with "O Dainty Triolet." Sullivan had other ideas and wanted the act to finish with the greater musical flourish provided by "For the rum-tum-tum / Of the military drum, / And the guns that go boom! boom!" Act 3 was to finish on the more serene music of "O Dainty Triolet." At the end of October, two more members of the Savoy company left: Charles Manners, whose part as Private Willis was taken over by Warwick Gray; and Alice Barnett, who had to give up because of poor health, her place being taken by Rose Carlingford. On Saturday, 10 November, with *Iolanthe* having passed its 350th performance, a new drawing-room entertainment was put on at the Savoy, as an addition to the program. It was called *The Drama on Crutches*, and in it George Grossmith did impersonations of famous members of the theatrical profession: Henry Irving, Ellen Terry, Corney Grain, and, to the joy of the Savoy audience, Gilbert and Sullivan.[19]

In November, music rehearsals began for *Princess Ida* and in the second half of the month Gilbert began rehearsals for his first play since *Foggerty's Fairy* in 1881. His new play was *Comedy and Tragedy*, which would open on 26 January 1884 at the Lyceum, with a beautiful young American actress, Mary Anderson, in the part of Clarice, and George Alexander, a young protégé of Henry Irving, playing the part of her husband. Mary Anderson had already appeared as Galatea in Gilbert's *Pygmalion and Galatea* in New York, and again in London in October 1883 at the Lyceum, and Gilbert had written *Comedy and Tragedy* expressly for her.

When stage rehearsals began for *Princess Ida* in December, Gilbert and Lillian Russell clashed. Russell failed to turn up for a rehearsal and Gilbert wanted her dismissed. Attempts by Carte to ensure her attendance at rehearsal by adding a new clause to her contract were to no avail, and Russell left the company, threatening to sue Carte for breach of contract. A late change in casting was necessary. Leonora Braham, who was to have played Lady Psyche, was called on to play Princess Ida, and Kate Chard came into the cast to replace her as Lady Psyche. In the absence of Alice Barnett, Rosina Brandram was given the part of Lady Blanche. It was Rosina Brandram's big opportunity; she had made a great impression with her singing of Iolanthe's ballad when she had substituted for Jessie Bond in September, and now she would never be dislodged from the role of principal contralto.

The small part of Chloe was given to a chorister, Miss Heathcote, who ran into a little difficulty with Gilbert. Gilbert wrote to Carte:

> Miss Heathcote was away from the theatre on Tuesday night—_ill_.
>
> Miss Heathcote was dancing at a fancy ball at the Albert Hall on Tuesday _night, well_.
>
> I met her there. . . .
>
> I think we must get rid of Miss Heathcote. . . . Miss H. does not seem to depend upon her salary as a means of livelihood. Her dress must have cost £15 if it cost a penny.[20]

Gilbert did not get his way, or perhaps he relented. Miss Heathcote played Chloe throughout the run of _Princess Ida_.

In early December, Sullivan was saddened by news of Fred Clay. On 4 December, after the second night at the Alhambra of Clay's new piece with George Sims, called the _Golden Ring_, Clay and Sims left the theater together. Shortly after chatting to Carte in the Strand and then turning into Bow Street, Fred Clay suffered a stroke and was carried into Bow Street Police Station. That night he had a second stroke, which left him unable to speak. Clay was only forty-four—a sobering thought for Sullivan, only three years younger, to see his closest friend of the old days suddenly struck down.

Another link with the past was weakened when Sullivan had to say good-bye to his brother's young family. His sister-in-law, Charlotte, had decided to make a new life for herself and her family and, with her husband and the children, left London on 14 December on the first stage of the journey to join her brother, William Lacy, who had settled in California. Her eldest son, Herbert, was now fourteen, and it was agreed that he would stay in England in the care of his uncle. That was the last time young Herbert was to see his mother. The next day he was sent to stay with a private tutor in Kilburn, while Sullivan threw himself into scoring _Princess Ida_—"heavy work," he noted in his diary.[21]

The usual rush had started. Not that Gilbert had yet finished. On Christmas Eve, Gilbert arrived at Queen's Mansions with a new lyric: a quintet for act 2, "The Woman of the Wisest Wit." Sullivan ended his Christmas Day by spending from midnight until five in the morning composing the new quintet, and then writing it out in full score. On 29 December, he took time out to take Herbert to the Surrey Theatre to see the pantomime *Jack and Jill*, but then it was home to carry on scoring the opera. The last two days of the year were days of intensive work: rewriting, scoring, and then turning to the overture, preferring to write it himself, leaving only a few copying details from the later parts of the opera. New Year's Eve was going to be no different from other nights as he worked away, rapidly and silently, smoking cigarette after cigarette and sipping a well-watered gin, unconscious of the passing time. At midnight, the door of his study opened and the servants came in to wish him "happy new year."[22]

The New Year 1884 started for Sullivan with an orchestral rehearsal in the morning. When it was over he walked out of the theater and into a snowstorm, and not a cab to be seen. To walk from the Savoy, along the Strand to Trafalgar Square, then down Whitehall and into Victoria Street is a pleasant though lengthy walk on a fine spring day. But Sullivan had to trudge home in the driving snow. Not a robust man at the best of times, and short of sleep, Sullivan arrived home exhausted. That day he composed "Nothing to Grumble At" and "I Built upon a Rock," the last of the songs to be rewritten.

Iolanthe ended its run, after 398 performances, on Tuesday, 1 January 1884, leaving three clear days before the opening of *Princess Ida; or, Castle Adamant*. On Wednesday there was a full musical rehearsal with cast and orchestra, followed in the evening by a dress rehearsal, which lasted from 7 p.m. until 2:00 in the morning. On Friday, 4 January, the full dress rehearsal was even longer, starting at 6:30 and not finishing until 2:30 in the morning. "I had a slight stiff neck," wrote Sullivan, "a dreadful pain—acute muscular rheumatism of the head & neck (left side)—had morphine injected—no good."[23] The following day, the idea of conducting the first night looked out of the question. Carte had a new print of the programs run off with François Cellier's name as conductor.

Sullivan was determined to conduct. At seven in the evening, he had another strong injection of morphine followed by a cup of strong black coffee to keep him awake. He crawled out of bed, dressed and "drove to the Theatre more dead than alive."[24] He was only ten minutes late going into the orchestra and then Sullivan the performer took over, buoyed up by the adrenaline, the reaction of the audience and the thought of the confidence he would give the performers, reassured to see his face on the other side of the footlights. The audience were then treated to one Sullivan gem after the other, transforming Gilbert's old piece *The Princess* into an opera. "The score of the new opera at the Savoy," wrote Hermann Klein in the *Sunday Times*, "may be summed up in a sentence—it is the best in every way that Sir Arthur Sullivan has produced, apart from his serious works. . . . Humour is almost as strong a point with Sir Arthur Sullivan as with his clever collaborator, and when attained by such legitimate means it is simply irresistible."[25]

Just as Sullivan had borrowed the idea of leitmotifs from Wagner when he wrote the music of *Iolanthe*, so with *Princess Ida* it might be said that he experimented with chromaticism, the succession of semitones in a melody, and used by Sullivan in short phrases, for example in "Oh, Dainty Triolet," producing a charming effect to match the lyrics. Sometimes the lyrics failed to inspire Sullivan, not surprisingly, for example, in "Come Mighty Must!" but also in the better written "I Built upon a Rock." Sullivan responded to jaunty rhythms and provided catchy tunes for "Oh Don't the Days Seem Lank and Long" as well as "And I'm a Peppery Kind of King." For Ida's world-weary lines, "The World Is But a Broken Toy," Sullivan produced one of his most beautiful, plaintive melodies.

It was their concerted work that captivated and held their audience. "Whatever may be thought of the abstract value of Gilbert and Sullivan's work," commented *The Times*, "it has the great merit of putting everyone in a good temper."[26]

At the end of *Princess Ida* came the usual call for the author and the composer. Sullivan took his bow with Gilbert, left the stage and collapsed. Frank Cellier and D'Oyly Carte rushed to his assistance and then, with his secretary, Walter Smythe, took him home and put him to bed. The state of his health was of national concern, and regular bulletins appeared in *The Times*. No details of his illness were issued beyond "muscular pains at the back of his neck, accompanied by a stiff neck."[27] Sullivan was clearly suffering from more than a stiff neck. He was exhausted, physically and mentally, and not a little worried about himself, after suffering a collapse so soon after Fred Clay's sudden illness.

By Saturday, 12 January, he was well enough, said an official bulletin, "to take a carriage drive, which appeared to have had a beneficial effect."[28] On Sunday, 20 January, he went to see Fred Clay, "our precious old Freddy," as he called him in a letter to Nina Lehmann. "He is bright, cheery, full of appreciation & sympathy but alas speechless still. How awful it is."[29]

It would not have been surprising for Sullivan, while recovering from his own illness, to look back on what had immediately preceded it and then to hold the nervous energy expended on *Princess Ida* as partly responsible. The "awful" condition of Fred Clay would have sharpened his thinking about the time he had left to achieve more in the world of serious music — a pressure made all the more acute by the expectations others had of him. On 29 January, when Carte came to call on him, Sullivan told him that he had made up his mind "not to write any more 'Savoy' pieces."[30]

Part IV

1884-1891

The Golden Years:
From *The Mikado* to the Carpet Quarrel

CHAPTER NINETEEN

1884-1885

The Mikado

THERE WAS NO MISTAKING Sullivan's resolve: he would write no more Savoy operas. But as his health improved, and as he grew stronger, so his resolve grew weaker. As early as 2 February 1884, in a letter to Bret Harte turning down the opportunity to work with him, appeared the hint that he might change his mind: "I have come to the decision of not writing any more operas for some time to come, for I have resolved to devote myself now, if not entirely, at least in a great measure, to more earnest work. . . . if I did yield to persuasion and write another, I should feel bound not to sever myself from my collaborateur Gilbert."[1]

Two days later, Sullivan left for Monte Carlo, to recuperate in the winter sunshine. That evening, the first provincial performance of *Princess Ida* took place in Glasgow at the start of a tour to all the major cities, including Dublin and Belfast. The company included David Fisher as King Gama, Fred Billington as King Hildebrand, Courtice Pounds as Hilarion, and Louie Henri playing the small part of Ada. In the chorus, and understudying David Fisher, was Louie Henri's seventeen-year-old husband, posing as her brother, and going by the name of H. A. Henri. Years later, he was to become famous as Henry A. Lytton. A week later, on 11 February in New York, with J. H. Ryley as King Gama, *Princess Ida* opened at the Fifth Avenue Theatre.

As well as the Savoy company and the New York company, six other companies toured the British Isles. In July, the "C" company was to become the "Repertory Company," with George Thorne as the leading comedian and with Alice Barnett, restored to health but not to the Savoy, in the main contralto roles. It was a formidable enterprise, taking Gilbert and Sullivan operas far and wide.

Before Gilbert had heard anything of Sullivan's wish to break their collaboration, he received a renewed offer of friendship from John Hare, who asked him to destroy an old letter of his "written in bitterness & temper," as he had destroyed a similar one from Gilbert, "& keep in its place this record of our unchanged feelings towards you."[2] Happy to have his old friend back, Gilbert replied, "Let our quarrel die & be buried, & let us agree that it shall never be referred to again by either of us."[3] Gilbert continued to work in peace on the next opera, having no idea of the bombshell that was about to burst on him. It came not directly from Sullivan, who found it quite easy to go away and put off any unpleasant business, but by courtesy of D'Oyly Carte.

On 22 March, Carte sent a formal letter to both Gilbert and Sullivan telling them that *Princess Ida* showed "signs of dropping" and therefore, by their agreement he was giving them six months' notice of a new opera being required.[4] Sullivan's reply from Brussels on 28 March showed a slight change in his position from January. He did not reject the idea outright, but said that he found it impossible "to do another piece of the character of those already written" with Gilbert. "The reason for this decision I can give you verbally when we meet. When I return to town, I must of course, talk the matter over with Gilbert and hear what his views on the subject are."[5]

That may have been satisfactory for Sullivan, but it left Carte, acting formally according to the contract, with the task of informing Gilbert immediately of the situation. "I scarcely know how to deal with such an announcement, coming as it does, through a third person," wrote Gilbert on 30 March and wasting no time in contacting Sullivan. Gilbert expressed his "unbounded surprise" and said that he was "absolutely at a loss to account for the decision" that Sullivan had made, hoping that he would reconsider. While Sullivan had been away, Gilbert had even written some of the lyrics of the next piece, reporting on progress to Sullivan in two letters to him, to which he had received no reply nor any indication from Sullivan that he was wasting his time.[6]

From Paris, on 2 April, two months after he had told Carte of his decision, Sullivan replied to Gilbert's letter. "I will be quite frank," he said. "With 'Princess Ida' I have come to the end of my tether—the end of my capability in that class of piece." Whatever meaning Sullivan intended to convey by "that class of piece," a possible interpretation is an inferior class of piece, and that is how Gilbert understood the words. Sullivan's further explanation made Gilbert feel even more uncomfortable. "It has hitherto been word setting. I might almost say syllable setting, for I have looked upon the words everywhere of such importance that I have been continually keeping down the music in order that not one should be lost." So far his letter had been clear, but when Sullivan came to express himself about what he wanted, he was merely echoing the critics and was vague. "I should like to set a story of human interest & probability," he said, "where the humourous words would come in a humourous (not serious) situation, & where, if the situation were a tender or dramatic one the words would be of a similar character." Gilbert would jump on such language, which unfortunately held his attention more than did Sullivan's statement at the end of the letter that he hoped that their different views would cause no break in their "chain of joint workmanship."[7] Sullivan had moved from the position of not writing any more for the Savoy, to a position in which he would write with Gilbert again provided that the next piece gave him greater musical freedom.

Sullivan's letter caused Gilbert "considerable pain." To be told that the libretti he had supplied had forced Sullivan to produce work that he considered to be inferior for a composer of his abilities could hardly be expected to do otherwise. "I cannot suppose that you intended to gall & wound me when you wrote of them as you did," said Gilbert in his next letter on 4 April. "I must assume that your letter was written hurriedly." Picking up on Sullivan's vague explanation of what he wanted, Gilbert told him that his desire that he should write "a libretto in which the humorous will come in a humorous situation, in & which [sic] a tender or dramatic situation will be treated tenderly & dramatically, you teach me the ABC of my profession. It is inconceivable that any sane author should ever write otherwise than as you propose I should write in future."[8]

The effect of Gilbert's letter on Sullivan was electric. He had to stop being vague and make his arguments specific. First of all, Sullivan did not want to offend Gilbert and was at pains to put himself right on that score. "It is I," he wrote on 7 April, "who feel hurt that you should put such a construction upon my words as to make them even seem to cast a reflection upon your works. I yield to no one in admiration of their matchless skill & genius and as I am not compelled to set anything I don't like, it is not very likely that I should have worked so long with you if I hadn't done so with real pleasure."[9] He rejected Gilbert's interpretation of his words and suggested that they should write something in which there was no burlesque, reminding Gilbert that he had himself more than once expressed his willingness to produce such a work. Sullivan then proceeded to discuss the new libretto that Gilbert had in mind. And so, the question had now become a specific question of the suitability of Gilbert's new libretto.

Having been galvanized into some hard thinking by Gilbert, Sullivan now came up with specific reasons as to why Gilbert's new ideas were not acceptable to him. Sullivan was beginning to take control. Gilbert's idea had been to develop a plot on the idea of people falling in love with each other against their wills as the result of a charm, in this case a magic lozenge. It was too much like *The Sorcerer*, and Sullivan could not see his way to setting it. Apart from anything else, people would say that they were repeating themselves. "Now pray do not say again or think, that I cast reflection on the pieces you have already written — I have enjoyed doing them with you and know of noone with whom I can write so sympathetically but I don't want my interest in our joint work to flag, and that is why I sincerely trust you will see your way to do something which will give me fresh vigour and energy."[10]

In a few days, and through a few letters exchanged between Gilbert and Sullivan, the problem that had lain dormant for two months had been grasped and taken apart but not yet solved. We can catch a glimpse of the extraordinary effect each of these two men was able to have on the other. Each of them had a high regard and respect for the professional ability, even genius, of the other and despite their differences, or rather because of them, they interacted to an unusual degree. At this stage, it was Sullivan who was challenging Gilbert to come up with an entirely new idea; it was Gilbert who was initially resisting that challenge and preferring to carry on along, what seemed to him, tried and tested lines. Each of them was capable of sparking off the other, either into an emotional reaction, or more positively, into a fresh burst of creative activity.

For the moment, the current difference was unsettled. Sullivan arrived back in London on 9 April and phoned Gilbert to arrange a meeting. The following afternoon, from two until four they discussed the new libretto. "Long argument on his part," wrote Sullivan in his diary, "—no concessions on either side. Complete deadlock, though quite friendly throughout."[11] Gilbert was at a standstill; he could not give up his plot and could not imagine himself producing the sort of plot that would satisfy Sullivan's demands. Despondently, he wrote to Sullivan the same day suggesting that, if Carte agreed, the next libretto should be written by someone else. "I am absolutely at a loss to know what it is that you want from me," he wrote. "You will understand how faintly I grasp your meaning when I tell you that your objections to my libretto really seem arbitrary & capricious. That they are nothing of the kind I am well persuaded—but, for all that, I can't fathom them."[12] For Gilbert to admit defeat, he must have been brought to an extemely low point.

It was not in Sullivan's temperament to leave Gilbert in that low state. He tried to reassure him. In an attempt to find a way forward, Sullivan met Carte and Helen Lenoir and, as a result, met Gilbert again on 15 April, this time willing to listen to any plan Gilbert had for modifying the original idea. It was agreed that Gilbert would send Sullivan a sketch of act 2, and then if Sullivan, after due consideration, found the subject uncongenial, Gilbert would look for a fresh idea.

Gilbert returned on 26 April with the revised sketch plot. Some of what he read Sullivan liked, but he needed more time to study it carefully. Within a week, he let Gilbert know that he was rejecting the new plot. Gilbert's understanding of the situation was different; as he had not heard from Sullivan and because Sullivan had earlier seemed satisfied with the sketch plot, then Gilbert had carried on working on it. "Anxious as I am, & have always been, to give all due weight to your suggestions, the time has arrived when I must state—& I do so with great reluctance—that I cannot consent to construct another plot for the next opera."[13]

Sullivan made no attempt to persuade Gilbert to reconsider. He felt he had done all he could. His reply was short: "The tone of your letter convinces me that your decision is final and therefore further discussion is useless. I regret it very much."[14] This short letter brought a much longer response from Gilbert. "And so ends a musical & literary association of seven years' standing—an association of exceptional reputation—an association unequalled in its monetary results, and hitherto undisturbed by a single jarring or discordant element." But Gilbert did not really want to end their association. He went on to talk about their distinctive roles as author and composer and how closely they worked together. What Gilbert did not want to do was to supply Sullivan with a series of pieces "on approval," although he recognized that he had to respect Sullivan's wishes when constructing a plot. Rather than abandon their collaboration altogether, he suggested that, if Carte approved, Sullivan should have a year in which to write a grand opera and, while pointing out that such an opera would not be suitable for the Savoy company, said he would be willing to write the libretto.[15]

Sullivan replied immediately: "I should be humiliated and grieved if anything in my words or manner had ever indicated that I claimed to see your librettos 'on approval.'" He agreed wholeheartedly with Gilbert's description of their "respective positions of author & composer," but admitted that he had felt uneasy about the subject Gilbert had proposed: "if, as you say, our collaboration is to end, I am bound in self-defence to put on record my own view of the cause of the disaster."[16] Whatever the result, Sullivan was happy to think that they could disagree without their friendship being broken.

Now in a strong position, Sullivan was challenging Gilbert to respond. Gilbert was hanging back. He was not used to being challenged in this way. It was he who had always thrown out the challenges to Sullivan, who in his turn had risen to every one of them. On 8 May, Gilbert asked, "am I to understand that if I construct another plot in which no supernatural element occurs, you will undertake to set it? Of course I mean a consistent plot, free from anachronisms, constructed in perfect good faith & to the best of my ability."[17]

Gilbert had finally risen to the challenge and Sullivan was delighted and relieved. Having gone to the edge, both men realized that they did not want to end, in Sullivan's words, "the collaboration which has been such a pleasure & advantage to us." If Gilbert would set a plot without the supernatural or the improbable, Sullivan would "gladly undertake to set it, without further discussing the matter, or asking what the subject is to be."[18] Gilbert asked for a month to get the old plot out of his system, when he would be ready to work on a new one. "All unpleasantness at an end," wrote Sullivan in his diary.[19]

As it happened, a month was more than Gilbert needed. One day in his study at Harrington Gardens he happened to glance at a Japanese executioner's sword hanging on the wall. It started a train of thought that he began to turn into a plot.[20] On 20 May, he sent Sullivan his sketch plot of *The Mikado*. "I think the subject excellent—funny," wrote Sullivan.[21] By the end of the month, Gilbert was able to sail away for the summer, in good heart. "I am just off yachting for four months or so —, off & on," he said to Frank Burnand, turning down the offer to write an article for *Punch*.[22]

WHILE THE LETTERS HAD been passing to and fro between Gilbert and Sullivan, a small but significant event took place on Wednesday, 30 April. Sullivan wrote in his

Richard Temple as the Mikado (V&A Picture Library)

diary, "Mrs. Scott Russell came to tea."[23] There is no comment, no mention of who instigated this contact, but it is significant that Sullivan had dined with Madame Rausch (Alice Scott Russell) at the Lehmanns' two days before, and had brought her home afterward.[24] It was twenty years since Sullivan used to frequent the home of the Scott Russells, when Mrs. Scott Russell was the mistress of a luxurious mid-Victorian household, with a company of servants at her beck and call, when she had a successful husband and three beautiful and talented daughters for whom she had such high ambitions. It was fifteen years since she had rejected Arthur Sullivan as a possible suitor for her daughter, because he was a poor, struggling musician. And now, an older and wiser Mrs. Scott Russell sat talking to the celebrated and rich Sir Arthur Sullivan in his luxurious apartment in Victoria Street. Two of her daughters were dead and her husband, having lost his business and having been forced to live in reduced circumstances in a small apartment on the Isle of Wight, also had died. The previous June, Mrs. Scott Russell had been granted a civil service pension of £90. Now she was alone. Four years later, on 9 October 1888, she was found dead in her apartment at Ventnor. Her clothes were alight and her left arm was burned to the bone in the fire. The inquest found that she had suffered a stroke while lying in front of the fire.[25]

THE ILLNESS AND DEPRESSION Sullivan had suffered following *Princess Ida* were now well behind him; he had settled with Gilbert over the next opera to be composed, and in the meantime his fortunes were being restored by the income brought in by *Princess Ida*. He could afford to entertain lavishly, and on Sunday, 8 June, he gave a dinner for a few of his aristocratic friends, with Lord and Lady Castlereagh as the principal guests. His after-dinner guests included Gilbert and Kitty, who were between yachting trips, as well as old friends like Mrs. Grant, Lady Katherine Coke and her daughter Sybil, and a Mrs. Ritchie. Fanny Ronalds's daughter was to be married shortly to Thomas Ritchie, an event that took place on 19 June at Holy Trinity Church in Sloane Square, with Sullivan at the organ playing Mendelssohn's Wedding March.

Princess Ida looked as though it was not going to run as well as hoped and, with no replacement ready, a decision had already been taken to bring on a revival of *The Sorcerer*. In early July, the takings for *Princess Ida* were down but picked up again later in the month. "Under these circumstances," Carte said to Gilbert in a letter of 5 August, "I thought it better not to commence the chorus rehearsals for The Sorcerer." Carte was afraid that if once word got out that *The Sorcerer* was to be revived, the news would kill what life was left in *Princess Ida*. Preparations went ahead. Hawes Craven was not available, and so Carte asked for a rough drawing from Gilbert to give Henry Emden, the new stage designer. Carte wanted Gilbert's advice not only on scenery but also on costumes and who was to make them, as well as advice on the set and costumes required for *Trial by Jury*. Sullivan promised to have the music ready for the alterations planned for act 2 by the middle of August, and Carte and Cellier would rehearse the music, leaving Sullivan to "put on any finishing touches."[26] Accompanied by Fanny Ronalds, her son and parents, Sullivan had moved out to Stagenhoe Park, in Hertfordshire, but was within reach of London if needed.

On Monday 18 August, Carte wrote again to Gilbert. "Since I wrote last things have changed about a good deal. The weather is scorching hot, the receipts are awful, the houses look shocking all our people are fagged out . . . some putting in medical certificates."[27] In the circumstances, Sullivan and Carte both thought it would be best to close the theater for a month, reopen with *Princess Ida* and at the same time start rehearsals for *The Sorcerer*. Gilbert agreed to the closure, but wanted to reopen with *The Sorcerer*.

Opposition from Gilbert was too much for Carte on his own. He went back to Sullivan. "I cannot deal with Gilbert in these matters alone, and annoying as it may be to have a business meeting in the middle of our closure, I think we must brace up and do it. Having had a discussion and settled all about everything we can then jog on as peacefully as may be until the 15th."[28]

Of course, to open with *The Sorcerer* on 15 September would have meant going into rehearsal straight away. Gilbert was prepared for that, but would Sullivan have been? Carte may have been reluctant to take part in a discussion with Gilbert alone, but he was confident of Sullivan's support for his own point of view and therefore confident of Sullivan's casting vote. The problem was to get Sullivan to a meeting. Carte tried another ploy. "If it is inconvenient for you to come up would you care about Gilbert and me coming down if I can get him, or would you rather not?"[29]

Wherever they met, Gilbert was outvoted again, and on Monday, 15 September *Princess Ida* reopened. Only a few days earlier, Sullivan had written the changes to act 2 of *The Sorcerer*, which he had promised Carte for the beginning of August, and the revival was ready to go into rehearsal.

On Saturday, 11 October, two days after the 246th and last performance of *Princess Ida*, Sullivan conducted the revivals of *The Sorcerer* and *Trial by Jury*. In his diary he recorded, "magnificent house — most brilliant & enthusiastic reception of the Opera — Excellently performed."[30] Far from being disappointed at being treated to a revival instead of a new opera, both audience and press were delighted to see the old favorites performed. The reviewer in *The Times* considered that *The Sorcerer* had not been sufficiently appreciated at its original production and went on to make a comment that has been echoed down the years: "Neither should Sir Arthur Sullivan's contribution to the common effort be underrated, Mr. Gilbert would be as impossible in this class of work without him as he would be without Mr. Gilbert. . . . It was only by working together that author and composer realized their full strength and struck the right vein. It was one of pure gold."[31] At that point, the reviewer assumed that the vein was exhausted. The rumor had been put about that the next opera was to be more serious.

The more serious work that Sullivan was indeed to be engaged on was for the Leeds Festival. On 30 September, Sullivan had been invited by the festival committee to write an orchestral piece for the next festival in 1886. Sullivan preferred to write "a short choral work . . . not necessarily sacred, but of an earnest character, about the length of (or shorter than) 'The Martyr of Antioch.'"[32] By the end of the year, the committee had agreed to his request.

It had been a year in which both Gilbert and Sullivan were actively involved in their roles as guardians. Sullivan took his fifteen-year-old nephew to Zurich to enroll him in the Polytechnic for training as an engineer, but, as Herbert did not speak German, he left him in the charge of a tutor in Freiburg to learn the language. Gilbert, as self-appointed moral guardian of his actresses, had taken up the case of May Fortescue, when in January Lord Garmoyle had broken off their engagement and fled the country. First Gilbert had ensured that she was not without employment or an income, by arranging that she play the part of Dorothy in a revival of *Dan'l Druce* at the Court Theatre in March; and second, he put her in touch with his solicitors so that she could sue Lord Garmoyle. The case came up in November 1884 and was uncontested by Lord Garmoyle, who was still abroad. May Fortescue was awarded £10,000 and with her capital she founded a theater company, regularly including in her repertoire plays by Gilbert.

After dinner at Harrington Gardens on Thursday, 20 November, Gilbert and Sullivan went through act 1 until 2 a.m. "Act still in an incomplete & somewhat crude condition," commented Sullivan afterwards in his diary, "but will shape out well."[33] By this stage, Gilbert had already made a start on the lyrics and a week later he sent seven numbers to Sullivan. On Monday, 8 December, Sullivan wrote Pish-Tush's song "For He Is Right," and the same day Gilbert called with a new finale for act 1 and the girls' chorus "Comes a Train of Little Ladies"—"both excellent" noted Sullivan.[34] The following day, Gilbert sent Sullivan the trio for Ko-Ko, Pooh-Bah, and Pish-Tush. Gilbert had set out the three verses: "I am so proud," "I heard one day," and "My brain it teems" side by side, while at the same time admitting that the different meters would probably not allow the verses to be sung together.

The fact that the verses were written alongside each other presented Sullivan with a challenge. He composed three separate melodies, as Gilbert had suggested, and then responded expertly, to the idea of a trio. The different melodies, at first sung separately and with distinctive accompaniments for each character, are cleverly interwoven with the music reflecting the state of mind of the characters as they proffer their individual excuses while ignoring the other two. The orchestral accompaniments complete the effect, with the brassy self-confidence of Pish-Tush, the quivering strings betraying the nervous state of Pooh-Bah and Ko-Ko, and the final staccato chords sounding the forbidding prospect of the executioner's sword.

Sullivan's diary, stating on 11 December "uncertainty changed to conviction," appears to refer to the possible pregnancy of Fanny Ronalds. "Things very bad—took

D.H. to M. usual course advised," he writes on 13 December. Then, on 19 December, he notes, "Signals of safety began." The next day, "Things going well." Finally, on 21 December, "Out of the wood."[35] As on the previous occasion, the comments suggest an induced abortion.

That same day, Sunday, 21 December, Sullivan wrote one of his most famous numbers, "Three Little Maids." Gilbert had sent Sullivan the "Three Little Maids" in the first batch on 27 November. The only change Gilbert made later to the original lyric occurs in the line sung by Pitti-Sing: "Won't have to wait very long, they say," which he originally wrote as "Wont have to wait very long, dare say!"[36]

"Three Little Maids" is one of the best examples of the individual genius of author and composer coming together to create a little masterpiece. Sullivan would take Gilbert's words and examine the meter carefully, finding his way into the song through the rhythm of the words, considering various rhythmic possibilities and also the mood of the number. Next came the creative leap when he would think of an appropriate melody and sketch it out on paper. At this stage he had a bright, little melody imitating the rhythm of Gilbert's words and capturing the mood of schoolgirl fun. Later he would frame the number, indicating the bars, rests, and perhaps an outline of the orchestration. When he came to the scoring in the final stages of his work, he was able to proceed rapidly, completing the creative process as he filled out the orchestration, producing the full effect he had held in his mind.

In this number, the light, tripping introduction on the strings and flutes sets the mood for the melody that follows, with the piccolo after "Everything is a source of fun" adding to the mood. The whole effect is charming to listen to, but that is only a part of the total effect produced on stage. Gilbert, too, had a performance in mind when he wrote the words for the three girls, and once the music had been played at rehearsal, he could work on the "business" with John D'Auban, the choreographer, assisted by the expertise of the Japanese from the Exhibition at Knightsbridge. The finished performance is what brought the house down on the first night. And underneath the words, the movements, the coquettishness of the girls, and the delightful music, was the absurdity of it all. Despite the black wigs, the Japanese dresses and makeup, the fans and the shuffling gait, everyone could recognize the trio as English girls straight out of a Kensington ladies' seminary.

The Japanese exhibition had opened on 10 January at Albert Gate, Knightsbridge, an event that could not have provided a better advertisement for *The Mikado*. The exhibition was laid out as a Japanese village comprising shops and houses, teahouses, and even a temple. It also included an entertainment provided by Japanese wrestlers and fencers, and a dance, or rather as *The Times* described it, "the [fantastic] posturing of three girls in slow measured time to a thrumming accompaniment kept up by some of the women on small stringed instruments."[37] For those in the audience at the Savoy who had witnessed the three girls' performance at Knightsbridge, the comparison to the "Three Little Maids" must have been exquisite in its contrast.

Durward Lely as Nanki-Poo in *The Mikado* (V&A Picture Library)

Although the "Three Little Maids" is perhaps one of the happiest examples of Gilbert finding the right words first time, not every first attempt at the lyrics was successful. Before he wrote "Behold the Lord High Executioner," for which Sullivan humorously composed a tune reminiscent of "A Fine Old English Gentleman," Gilbert had written the following entrance for Koko:

No one who in time gone by
 Ruled the roost in Titipu
Ever was, in public eye,
 Insignificant as you.
You were placed on civic throne
For a reason of our own
Though you rule in Titipu
You are but a parvenu!

 (*During this Koko has been bowing right & left, as if to high compliments.*)

Chorus (*coming down, in a confidential whisper to audience*)
That is the beauty of a chorus—
 When many people loudly sing,
We can express in tones sonorous
 That which we daren't in solo sing.
We can amuse ourselves in framing
Choice epithets of abusive blaming,
Which he imagines we're exclaiming
(*Falling back right & left*) "Here is a Health to our Civic King!
           "Here is a Health to our Civic King!
           "Here is a Health to our Civic King!
Koko (who has only heard the last lines,[)] bows with profound gratitude, right and left.[38]

Then followed Ko-Ko's song, "Taken from the County Jail," in a slightly different, longer version from the finished libretto, and that was perhaps shortened at Sullivan's suggestion.

These lyrics are among the papers that Gilbert sent to Sullivan and that survive in the D'Oyly Carte Collection. The manuscripts predate the licence copy of the libretto sent to the Lord Chamberlain. In Ian Bradley's *The Complete Annotated Gilbert & Sullivan*, he includes the licence copy version of "Were You Not to Ko-Ko Plighted," a much longer version than the song that became established later. There is an earlier manuscript by Gilbert, presumably the first version that he sent to Sullivan, which varies slightly from the licence copy. In it, Nanki-Poo's verse begins:

> Were you not to Koko plighted,
> And so soon to take his name,
> I, of course, should be delighted
> To reciprocate your flame—[39]

These lines were rewritten for the first-night performance, and then changed again to settle as:

> Were you not to Ko-Ko plighted,
> I would say in tender tone,
> "Loved one, let us be united—
> Let us be each other's own!"[40]

Sullivan continued to compose his music to Gilbert's lyrics, arising from a plot that, at Sullivan's insistence, was to have nothing of the supernatural nor of the improbable. It is true that the plot had nothing of the supernatural, but it was as improbable as ever. Instead of setting his story in fairyland or in a magical corner of England, Gilbert had set it at the other end of the world, as far away as possible from England, in an exotic land—but in which all his characters would behave like English men and women. After the not entirely successful experiment with *Princess Ida*, Gilbert had reverted to the tighter plotting for a limited cast of stock characters that had been so successful in the past: he wrote for two comedians, Ko-Ko (Grossmith) and Pooh-Bah (Barrington); a soprano, Yum-Yum (Leonora Braham); a contralto, Katisha (Rosina Brandram); a tenor, Nanki-Poo (Durward Lely); and a bass, the Mikado (Richard Temple). For the first time, Lely would be cast in the role of romantic hero, and a few minor characters were required: Pish-Tush (Frederick Bovill) and the other two little maids with Yum-Yum, Pitti-Sing (Jessie Bond) and Peep-Bo (Sybil Grey).

In an interview with the *New York Tribune* in August 1885, Gilbert discussed the casting for *The Mikado*: "The accident that Miss Braham, Miss Jessie Bond, and Miss Sybil Grey, are short in stature and all of a height, suggested the advisability of grouping them as three Japanese schoolgirls who should work together throughout the piece."[41] That particular combination of "schoolgirls" very nearly came unstuck. Leonora Braham's drinking was beginning to affect her performance and Carte remonstrated with her at the end of October 1884. He met Gilbert and Sullivan a few days later to consider whether to renew her contract for *The Mikado*, but "after protracted consideration" it was agreed to reengage her.[42]

Four companies were touring in 1885, keeping the Gilbert and Sullivan repertoire alive and taking the operas all over the British Isles. A fifth company, the "Children's Company," after a Christmas season of matinees at the Savoy, toured with *The Pirates of Penzance*. Gilbert organized his own private little company to give two performances, on 14 and 15 January 1885, of act 2 of *Patience* to a party of friends in his drawing room at Harrington Gardens. The select company invited to perform included George Grossmith, Richard Temple, Durward Lely, and May Fortescue; and in the role of Patience was Gilbert's young next-door neighbor, Sybil Coke. The harmonium and piano accompaniment was provided by no less than François Cellier and Sir Arthur Sullivan.[43] An elaborate way to encourage a young actress, but great fun for everybody involved.

A week after the joy and laughter of these domestic performances, Sullivan received a telegram from William Lacy in Los Angeles, bringing him the sad news that

Charlotte was dying, and was not expected to survive much longer. She died on 29 January, aged forty-three. She had had eight children with Fred Sullivan, and her ninth with her second husband, Ben Hutchinson. Writing later, William Lacy told Sullivan that Hutchinson had decided to return to England with his baby. "I think it is as well that he should separate from them now," said Lacy, "if he wishes to do so — he has been good and kind and a most attentive and patient nurse, is honest & good, but I suppose you know him well enough to understand that he is not capable of taking charge of this family and utterly unfit to lead & advise them." Lacy wanted to bring all the children over to England but had promised Charlotte that he would not do anything without Arthur Sullivan's approval. Of Fred's eight children, six were in America. The eldest, Amy, was twenty-one, and the youngest, William, was only six. One of the eight children, Edith, had died soon after her father in 1877. At the end of his letter to Sullivan, Lacy added, "if you can spare the time to come over here, I should like it very much."[44] And that is precisely what Sullivan decided to do.

Sensitive to the needs of his relatives, Sullivan needed no reminder of his family responsibilities. He had given Charlotte £2,000 when she went to America and was sending a yearly allowance of £300. To cover the costs of her final illness, he sent an additional £200.[45] He was contributing to his uncle John's rent with £50 a year and at some stage bought a house for his relatives, the Phillips, in Barbados.[46] He was already caring for Herbert and his education, and was now prepared to assume responsibility for the rest of Fred's children. For the time being at least, the children were to stay in their house in Los Angeles, under the care of the eldest girls, Amy, twenty-one, and Florence, aged eighteen. Just then Sullivan's mind was fully occupied. He had not yet finished composing the music for *The Mikado*; at the end of February, he was taking on the conductorship of the Philharmonic Concerts; and he still had a cantata to compose for Leeds in 1886. The cantata would have to wait.

Music rehearsals for *The Mikado* had begun on Tuesday, 27 January, while both Gilbert and Sullivan were still finishing writing the opera: it was only on 9 February that Sullivan composed the Mikado's song, "My object all sublime." Gilbert's reading of the opera to the company was scheduled for Monday, 16 February, and the day before he called on Sullivan with his last-minute alterations. Stage rehearsals started on 17 February; Sullivan preferred to give the first rehearsal a miss and use the time writing. He was now at his intense period of work and social occasions had to be limited. While he carried on with his scoring, he was happy to let Gilbert represent both of them at the anniversary dinner of the Dramatic and Musical Sick Fund, which took place at Willis's Rooms on 18 February, at which Gilbert replied to the toast to "Music and the Drama" proposed by Comyns Carr.[47]

On Friday 20 February, Sullivan rehearsed Brahms's Symphony in F (No. 3) for the Philharmonic Society in the morning, and in the afternoon rehearsed the finale to act 1 of *The Mikado* at the Savoy. He returned home at 4:30 exhausted, but after a short rest he was bright and lively enough to accompany Mrs. Chappell and Fanny Ronalds to a social evening at Whistler's. Sunday, 22 February, was a day of work,

The Three Little Maids in *The Mikado*—Sybil Grey, Leonora Braham, and Jessie Bond (V&A Picture Library)

making alterations to the finale of act 1 and writing "The flowers that bloom in the spring"; and the evening was a time of rest, going around to the Portland Club for a game of cards at ten and finding himself £20 richer by the end. The following Thursday, he made his first appearance as conductor at a Philharmonic concert, when he conducted Brahms's Symphony No. 3, in the first of a series of six concerts he was to conduct that season.

With his social life curtailed, Sullivan was feeling sorry for himself: he had not been to a party for over a week. "Feb 21—Mar 2," he wrote in his diary, "all these days ... writing & rehearsing & no drives, parties or recreation of any kind."[48] The following night he worked right through until 5 a.m. finishing the finale of act 1: "63 pages of score at one sitting!" he recorded.[49] Three days later he had the scoring finished, after a similar all-night session lasting until 5:45 Saturday morning.

By the time the first orchestral rehearsal was held, on Monday morning, 9 March, all the music had been completed apart from the finale of act 2 and Katisha's song, "Hearts Do Not Break!," which Sullivan went home to work on when the rehearsal finished at 5:00 p.m. The next day he had to rehearse the Philharmonic orchestra in the morning and then take a full music rehearsal, orchestra and voices, for *The Mikado* in the afternoon, having to rehearse at the Langham Hall while the set was being prepared at the Savoy. On Wednesday, the procedure was similar: Philharmonic rehearsal in the morning from 10:00 a.m. until 12:30 and then off for a stage rehearsal at the Lyceum in the afternoon. Tiredness was beginning to tell, and both men were in an anxious state. "Row with Gilbert about 'business'—all right afterwards."[50] Sullivan returned home to the last of his writing, which he completed at 10:00 p.m., and then took the manuscript to the theater for the copyist.

The first full dress rehearsal of the whole opera started at 11:30 on Thursday morning, 12 March, and lasted until 5:30 in the evening. Afterward, the Savoy company had to perform *The Sorcerer* and *Trial by Jury* for the last time, while Sullivan had to conduct Beethoven's Symphony in B flat (No. 4) at a Philharmonic concert. At the final dress rehearsal on Friday, 13 March, everything went smoothly except for George Grossmith, who was sick with nerves. Gilbert, too, was in his usual state of nerves, checking and rechecking everything, making whatever last-minute changes he thought would improve the performance. One such change was his decision to cut the Mikado's song, "My Object All Sublime." The chorus were astounded at the decision, and at their insistence the number was reinstated.

Friends and theatrical colleagues were among the audience that assembled for the first night of *The Mikado* on Saturday, 14 March 1885: Whistler; Kate Terry and her husband, Arthur Lewis; Comyns Carr; Kate Dickens and her husband, the artist Carlo Perugini; Corney Grain; Frank Burnand; and Mary Hare. Royalty was represented by the duke and duchess of Edinburgh. Queues for the unreserved seats had started early and many people were turned away disappointed. Before the curtain was raised, Gilbert had left the theater, too nervous to remain, preferring to walk and worry the time away elsewhere. For Sullivan, there was a "tremendous reception," he recorded later. "All went very well except Grossmith whose nervousness nearly upset the piece."[51]

Sullivan's opinion was not shared by the audience, who were prepared to overlook Grossmith's nervousness in their overall enjoyment of the opera. "From the moment the curtain rose on the Court swells in Japanese willow-plate attitudes to its final fall it is one long succession of uproarious laughter at the libretto and overwhelming applause for the music," said Rutland Barrington.[52]

Encores abounded, with a treble encore for "The Flowers That Bloom in the Spring" and a treble encore for "Three Little Maids," which was greeted with ecstatic applause.

Gilbert had taken his usual care over detail to ensure that, to all appearances, everything Japanese was genuine: the dresses, the set, and the use of the fans. Both Gilbert and Sullivan had received help from Algernon Mitford, a former attaché in Japan, and Gilbert was flattered to be complimented afterward on "the fidelity with which the local characteristics are reproduced."[53]

The Mikado sparkles with numbers that became immediately popular. Gilbert had given Durward Lely, a tenor who could act, an opportunity to prove himself with "A Wand'ring Minstrel," instead of the more usual tenor's ballad, and Lely showed that he was equal to the part. All the cast were praised by the press, including George Grossmith, whose "Little List" song, according to the *Daily News*, brought "a sudden hush of expectancy when Mr. Grossmith . . . appeared to be about to name the distinguished statesmen who, without any irreparable damage to their country, might be offered up as victims. . . . The outburst of merriment which followed on the conclusion of the lyric showed that the audience greatly enjoyed the joke of this evasion."[54] Leonora Braham justified her inclusion in the cast; the *Theatre* thought she "was more fascinating than ever, and more than once saved the action from dragging by her unaffected vivacity and winsome playfulness."[55]

The following day, Sullivan was able to resume his normal life: calling on the duke of Edinburgh in the afternoon, and in the evening dining at the home of Edward Sartoris, the widower of Adelaide Kemble, daughter of the actor Charles Kemble. After dinner he played two concertos with Joachim, and finished off the evening with cards at the Portland Club. On Monday, Gilbert and Sullivan met to discuss changes. They decided to move Ko-Ko's "Little List" to its present position instead of after the duet "Were You Not to Ko-Ko Plighted," and moved Yum-Yum's "The Sun, Whose Rays" to the beginning of act 2 instead of following the quartet "So Please You, Sir, We much Regret."

Shortly after the opening of *The Mikado*, a change was made in the casting. The baritone voice of Frederick Bovill, who played Pish-Tush, was not deep enough to bring out the bass line in the madrigal "Brightly Dawns Our Wedding Day," and so a new character was invented, Go-To, sung by Rudolph Lewis.

And with that change, *The Mikado* was off on its long run that would last until February 1887, the beginning of its phenomenal success that would take it all around the world.

CHAPTER TWENTY

1885-1887

Ruddigore

THREE WEEKS AFTER the opening of *The Mikado*, Marion Sambourne, a near neighbor and friend of the Gilberts in their Essex Villa days, tried to get a seat for the opera. "Went to Savoy," she wrote in her diary, "v. full, had to sit on dress circle steps."[1] *The Mikado* was playing not merely to full houses but to packed houses. But so far it was only London audiences who could see the opera; it still had to be taken to the rest of the country and to America.

Two companies had to be prepared. The first was prepared for purely home audiences and opened on 22 May 1885 at Northampton to give the first performance of *The Mikado* outside London. The second company was prepared with an American tour in mind, but that particular purpose was kept a closely guarded secret. The "D" company, of which Fred Billington, Frederick Frederici, and Courtice Pounds were members, was strengthened by the inclusion of George Thorne and Josephine Findlay, and opened with *The Mikado* at Brighton on 27 July, with Alfred Cellier as musical director. Courtice Pounds and Josephine Findlay had already gained valuable experience appearing as Nanki-Poo and Yum-Yum at the Savoy in June, and along with Kate Forster and Elsie Cameron, plucked from other touring companies, they were to form the company that in great secrecy would embark for America in August.

As his season of Philharmonic concerts at St. James's Hall was drawing to a close, Sullivan was able to get into the social swing, giving a dinner party at Queen's Mansions on 7 May, at which his guests included Princess Louise and her husband, the marquess of Lorne; and a month later, 7 June, he gave a dinner for the prince of Wales. On both occasions, the numerous after-dinner guests were treated to top-class entertainment: famous singers like Edward Lloyd, Antoinette Sterling, and Madame Albani; and entertainers such as George and Weedon Grossmith.

Social engagements were soon set aside as Sullivan prepared to leave for America, with the primary intention of visiting his nephews and nieces in Los Angeles. Accompanied by his valet, Louis Jaeger, he set sail from Liverpool on 20 June on board the Cunard steamer *Etruria*. Carte had traveled with him as far as Rugby and then returned to London, acting as messenger with a letter for L.W. Before Sullivan had left London, he had agreed with Gilbert and Carte to a scheme intended to circumvent the American copyright laws by assigning the copyright of his music for *The Mikado* to an American, George Lowell Tracy, with the necessary arrangements made by Helen Lenoir through A. P. Browne, a Boston lawyer.[2] Carte was planning to open with his American company in New York in the autumn and had negotiated with two American managers, John Stetson and James C. Duff, who were competing for *The Mikado*. Carte had decided to settle with Stetson, telling him in a letter on 13 June that Duff had gone to England "to get the Mikado and then haggled and haggled till he lost it, after which he wanted to agree all the terms."[3]

Carte set out to outwit Duff and prevent him putting on his own version of *The Mikado* ahead of him. Because of Carte's influence, London firms including Liberty's had refused to serve Duff; Carte bought up all the Japanese costumes in London, while his agent had been buying up all the Japanese costumes on the Parisian market. Similarly, Duff found himself cold-shouldered when he approached scenic artists in London. Carte spelled out his plan to Stetson: "If you can clear the date at the 5th Avenue I will get my company ready, you get your scenery in hand on the quiet at Boston, and the moment we hear of Duff's rehearsing and that we know when he proposes to open I will swoop quickly across with my company and be beforehand if only a week beforehand."

Carte's original intention had been to take over only the principals, but he revised his plan to include the chorus. If he announced in advance that he was going to engage the chorus in New York when he arrived, then he would "throw them off the scent." The extra cost would be worth it, he said, "I will spend anything to smash Mr. Duff."[4]

Adding to Carte's anxiety at this time, Gilbert had raised the issue of their respective positions in the management of the theater. Gilbert's interpretation of their contract was that they had equal shares in the management of the Savoy. Carte's reading was different. As far as he was concerned, the agreement gave him "the sole right of performance in London of all the operas." Gilbert and Sullivan each had a veto on the engagement of artists and also entire control of the stage and orchestra during rehearsals. To consult them on all management details would be impossible, he said, involving daily meetings and both of them devoting as much time to management as him.[5]

In reply, Gilbert pointed out that it was he and Sullivan who had "raised the theatre to its present position of exceptional prosperity and distinction." He did not contest Carte's interpretation of the contract, but accused Carte of treating him like "a hack author" employed simply to provide Carte with "pieces on certain terms." He would keep to the contract, "bound by its absolute and literal terms," but warned

Carte that the contract only had a few months to run.[6] Carte was surprised by Gilbert's reaction.

> Your note received grieved me very much — more than I can say. Must a dramatic author be considered a "hack" author if he does not arrange the number of stalls in a theatre where his opera is played? Must a novelist or a poet be considered a "hack" author if he does not superintend the working of the bookstalls at which his books are sold?

Carte envied Gilbert his position. "If I could be an author like you I would certainly not be a manager. I am simply the tradesman who sells your works of art."[7] Gilbert passed on his views to Sullivan and Sullivan confided in Carte. "From what I hear from Sullivan," said Carte in his next letter to Gilbert, ". . . I gather that your argument in favour of your and his having a share in the management of the theatre is that I might — if left alone . . . perhaps ruin the business. Of course you run this risk. But my reply is that I stand the whole risk of pecuniary loss."[8] He insisted on the practicalities of management, running not only a London theatre but also the provincial tours and the American and Australian business. That was his "raison d'être" in the triumvirate.

His answer failed to satisfy Gilbert. He did not, or would not, try to understand Carte's point of view. As Sullivan sailed for America, Gilbert was still expressing his dissatisfaction to him, making the comment that was to anger Carte in future years, that Carte "shows a disposition to kick away the ladder by which he has risen."[9]

On 21 June, acting on information received from Stetson, Helen Lenoir cabled Carte that Duff was starting rehearsals the next day.[10] The race was on. Against the clock, Carte rushed to engage his chorus for America. He wrote to Sullivan on 23 June, hoping Sullivan would receive the letter soon after his arrival in New York. "I have got a dose of it here. . . . I heard 90 (ninety) odd sing today. . . . It is now 7.0 and I am giddy."[11]

Sullivan arrived in New York on Monday 29 June. He was met by Suydam Grant and that evening dined with the Beach Grants. Under instructions from Carte, he had to contact A. P. Browne, the Boston lawyer, in case an affidavit was required concerning the assignment of the rights of *The Mikado* to Tracy. Another commission from Carte was to audition a new soprano, Geraldine Ulmar. Sullivan listened to her on 11 July, found her "a pretty and very intelligent girl,"[12] cabled his satisfaction to Carte, and Geraldine Ulmar was engaged.

The next day, Sunday, Sullivan started out at 9:00 a.m. on his long journey west: first to Chicago, then across Iowa, where there was a prohibition on serving alcohol. He decided against dining in Iowa. Then on to Denver, Colorado, stopping overnight, and next day playing the organ in the cathedral; then further west to Salt Lake City, arriving Saturday, 18 July. He visited "all the 'Brigham Young' family houses," bought several Mormon books and played the organ at the Tabernacle, "a really very

Blanche Prowse, about 1880 — the first Mrs. D'Oyly Carte
(From the collection of Peter Joslin)

good instrument (3 man^ls. etc.) made by a local Mormon a Swede."[13] After service at the Tabernacle on Sunday, he journeyed on to San Francisco, arriving there on Monday morning, 20 July—eight days after he had set out from the east coast. Rather than travel straight down to Los Angeles, still a small town in 1885, he chose to spend a few days in San Francisco, to see all he could, including Chinatown; but by Thursday, tired of being pestered by reporters, he left on the overnight train for Los Angeles, on the last leg of his journey. In the morning his three nieces, Amy, Florence, and the youngest of the girls, Maude, who was fifteen, were waiting at the station to meet him.

He spent six weeks with the children, enough time for him to weigh up the situation and to consider what was best for their future. Amy and Florence were old enough, and capable and responsible enough, to look after the smaller children; their uncle William Lacy, although not able to look after them himself, lived close by; and Sullivan began to make arrangements to buy the house for them and to employ a housekeeper.

A fortnight into his stay in California, Amy and Florence, together with William Lacy and his daughter Sophy, took their uncle on an expedition to the Yosemite Valley. They traveled all night by train to Madera, and then all day by stagecoach into the rugged beauty of what is now the Yosemite National Park. "30 hours travelling from Los Angeles without sleep or rest, in broiling heat and smothering dust," commented Sullivan in his diary.[14] The next day was more restful: on a pleasant morning, with the sunlight playing on the running stream of cool, clear water at their feet, Sullivan pulled off his socks and shoes and with his nieces paddled in the stream. After lunch they drove out to Mariposa "to see the *Big Trees*" he recorded. "They are wonderful."[15]

Far away from inquisitive newspaper reporters and a continent away from the proprieties expected of a knight of the realm, Sullivan relaxed with his brothers' children. For all his health problems, Sullivan was an excellent traveler, exhilarated by new sights and new experiences. He was free of illness on that grueling journey, and in the evening they went to a "barn-dance," with just a fiddler to provide the music and a caller to guide them through the dances. "All very primitive & enjoyable," Sullivan noted.[16]

Seen off at the station by the three girls and the Lacys, Sullivan left Los Angeles on 3 September. Without overnight stops on the return journey, he was back in Chicago by 8 September, and at the Grand Pacific Hotel took a much-needed bath. The next morning he was in New York, where Carte was waiting to meet him. He put up at the Brunswick Hotel and in the evening, with Carte, went to the Fifth Avenue Theatre to catch some of *The Mikado* before having supper with Suydam Grant at Delmonico's. After the lapse of a discreet interval, Sullivan met up with Fanny Ronalds, who had arrived in New York on 22 August, shortly after the opening of *The Mikado*.

D'OYLY CARTE HAD SAILED over from Liverpool on 8 August in great secrecy. He was registered as Mr. Henry Chapman, and the rest of the company had also registered under assumed names on board the Cunard liner, the *Aurania*. George Thorne went under the name of Mr. Fred Hurley, Fred Billington was Mr. E. Clarke, and Courtice Pounds was Felix Donn. All very plausible, but a few members of the company took the opportunity to use more far-fetched aliases: Kate Forster was Miss T. Caddy, and a glance down the passenger list reveals a Mr. P. P. Bitter, which looks suspicious, and a Mr. Touangue.[17] As they approached New York, secrecy was abandoned and on 14 August the company gave a concert consisting mostly of Gilbert and Sullivan numbers, but George Thorne added a song by George Grossmith, entitled "An Awful Little Scrub."[18]

They arrived in New York on Tuesday, 18 August, and the next day D'Oyly Carte's production of *The Mikado* opened at the Fifth Avenue Theatre, a week ahead of the rival Duff version at the Standard Theatre. That was not the end of the battle. Carte applied for an interim injunction to prevent Duff from playing *The Mikado* anywhere in America. His argument was that G. L. Tracy had the entire U.S. copyright of Sullivan's music, having made a piano arrangement from the orchestral score, and if anybody attempted to play *The Mikado*, Carte would proceed to prevent them under the statute laws of the United States.

Despite his best efforts, Carte was unsuccessful. On 29 September, in the United States Circuit court, Judge Wallace found in favor of Duff and Duff obtained "an injunction restraining D'Oyly Carte, Sir Arthur Sullivan, William S. Gilbert and others from commencing or pursuing any action or from procuring an injunction against him" anywhere in the United States. He was free to produce *The Mikado* anywhere he chose.[19]

On 21 August, two days after *The Mikado* opened in New York, D'Oyly Carte's wife, Blanche, died at their home at St. Alban's Bank, in Hampton, Middlesex. She was only thirty-two and her death certificate recorded that she had been suffering from pneumonia for a week. For some time, Blanche Carte had been in poor health, and that may have been the reason for Carte's move out of London and down to the riverside at Hampton. While Carte remained on business in America, presumably his two sons—Lucas, aged thirteen, and Rupert, aged eight—were in the care of relatives.

A gala performance of *The Mikado* was given on 24 September at the Fifth Avenue Theatre, with Sullivan conducting. "House crammed with a fashionable audience," he recorded. "Bouquets given to all the ladies. Very bright & spirited performance— great enthusiasm, & I had to make a speech."[20]

The first part of his speech was well received. He mentioned the kind reception "given to my friend Mr. Gilbert's work and my work" and spoke of "the extraordinary energy of our good friend and colleague, Mr. D'Oyly Carte," but when he went on to complain about the copyright laws in the country, it "wrought a rather un-

Helen Lenoir in the 1880s — the second Mrs. D'Oyly Carte
(Photograph courtesy of the D'Oyly Carte Opera Company Archive)

pleasant impression," according to the *New York Times*. It was not that they objected to his expressing his opinion, but that he had chosen his moment badly. "Mr. W. S. Gilbert no doubt harbours the same opinion as his co-labourer, but his literary judgement would have counselled him to defer their publication until a more suitable opportunity.... Perhaps, however," continued the *New York Times*, trying to finish on a kinder note, "if Mr. Gilbert were let loose in the orchestra he would play greater havoc than Sir Arthur on the rostrum."[21]

George Thorne had happier memories of Sullivan, recalling that he chartered "a special steamer and took the whole company up the river Hudson to West Point ... and a very charming outing it proved, the river scenery being beautiful."[22]

Carte's production of *The Mikado* opened in Philadelphia on 5 October at McCaull's Opera House. Additional luster was given to the evening by the presence of Sullivan, in the audience on this occasion and not in the conductor's chair, and at the end of the evening he went on to a celebratory supper given by McCaull at the Bellevue. Sullivan's three-month stay in America was at an end, and with Carte on 14 October he embarked on the *Eros*, a German liner, accompanied by Louis Jaeger and by Josephine Findlay, who was no longer needed in America after the engagement of Geraldine Ulmar. Miss Findlay would return to the Savoy to understudy Leonora Braham, and as they journeyed home Carte was not sure whether she would actually have to replace Miss Braham. Before going to America, Carte had written to Leonora Braham in July, warning her about her drinking. "It seems to me a thousand pities," he had said on 18 July, "that so admirable an artist as you are should wilfully prejudice her chances and injure her fortune in the way that you if you continue to do this sort of thing, will do."[23] In the event, Leonora Braham continued to play Yum-Yum for the rest of the run.

Waiting for Sullivan when he returned from America was a letter from Gilbert, written on 7 October, before he left for Egypt. He had a plot ready for the new opera, and enclosed four numbers with his letter. Unsure of *The Mikado*'s success in the early days of its run, Carte had given both Gilbert and Sullivan official notice in June that he required a new opera from them in six months' time, but Gilbert suggested to Sullivan the possibility of reviving *HMS Pinafore* after *The Mikado*; he was keen on doing a revival while they still had the original cast in the company. If they left it for another year, they might well lose Grossmith, Barrington, Jessie Bond, and Richard Temple.

Gilbert and Kitty left Cairo on 8 November and, via Venice reached Paris on the 18th. On the same day, Carte wrote to Gilbert at the Grand Hotel. Business had dropped a little at the Savoy, he said. "I think it would be well to get on now with the new piece, don't you?" He chatted on merrily, giving Gilbert little items of news: the idea of doing a "Children's *Patience*" had been abandoned, as both Gilbert and Sullivan were against the idea; and he wanted to put on *The Carp* as a curtain-raiser to *The Mikado*:

The Mikado now plays much closer than it did, we are obliged to spin out the interval rather to avoid finishing too early (as it is we finish generally before 11.0) and we really begin the Mikado a little too early. Sullivan quite agrees with me in this policy so I have a pretty little piece by Desprez with music by Alfred Cellier and have got it in hand.

They could start the evening performance at 7:45, begin *The Mikado* at 8:30 and finish at 11.00—"the proper time. Don't you think that will be much better?"[24]

Still smarting from his difference with Carte earlier in the year and now reading that Sullivan and Carte had made a decision without consulting him, Gilbert reacted. Ignoring Carte's friendly tone and leaving aside any niceties, Gilbert sent a curt reply objecting to the decision. If the piece were not abandoned, he insisted, "all friendly relations between us are at a definite end, & no consideration whatever will induce me to set foot in the Savoy again."[25]

Carte did not buckle under the onslaught; he replied firmly but reasonably to Gilbert on that Saturday, 21 November. He explained that it was common practice for them to put on a curtain-raiser "after the first rush of an opera." Gilbert had never before objected that he had not been consulted. If Gilbert had been in England, no doubt Carte would have spoken to him about the proposal. "But you were in Egypt and I did not wish to lose time. I spoke about the matter to Sullivan who *was* here." Carte pointed out that his view and Sullivan's view "should have equal consideration and weight" with Gilbert's. His point was valid, but what he failed to consider was that, in decision making among three people, a decision arrived at by two and then presented to the third begins to make that third person feel decidedly *de trop*. Gilbert was sensitive to the position; Carte was not. Carte agreed, however, to do nothing more about the curtain-raiser until they had discussed it further.

He put off their meeting until early the following week, telling Gilbert that he wanted to go down to Brighton. "My children are there and Sunday is my only chance of seeing them, added to which I am not well myself."[26] Before leaving for Brighton, Carte wrote to Sullivan, who had gone to Paris, sending him Gilbert's letter and enclosing a copy of his own reply.

> Gilbert returns this week today in fact and his readvent is being celebrated with a "row" as usual. Of course I know you will stick to me in this business. I don't mean to put up with this bullying tone any longer. And it is most ungrateful considering what I have done for his piece in America. . . . *I* don't mean to stand it.[27]

Eventually *The Carp* was put on as a curtain-raiser to *The Mikado*—but not until 11 February 1886, several months later.[28]

DOMESTIC AFFAIRS OCCUPIED Sullivan at the end of 1885 and the beginning of the new year. While he was in Paris, he had engaged two new servants: a chef, who did not remain long in his service, and a Belgian girl, aged twenty-two, called Clotilde Raquet, who entered his service as a kitchen maid on 15 December, and who was to remain with him for the rest of his life. Early in 1886 he had decided it was time for him to move into the age of electricity. He engaged the Swan & Edison Co. to provide electric light for his apartment at Queen's Mansions, and in early March, he had his own dynamo driven by a steam engine—"no noise or vibration," he commented in his diary.[29]

Of greater concern at the beginning of the year was the cantata he had promised the Leeds Festival committee for October. He had chosen Longfellow's poem, "The Golden Legend," and after attempting to produce a libretto himself soon found himself in difficulty. Help came from his old friend Joseph Bennett, whom he invited to dinner on 28 January. They talked the problem over and Sullivan confessed that the task of producing a libretto was beyond him. He had marked passages in the poem that he thought would make suitable incidents or scenes for a musical setting, but there was no relationship between the incidents. Bennett took the poem home to see what he could do.

The Leeds committee were already getting fidgety, anxious to know how Sullivan's work was proceeding, especially as they had heard in the press that he was working on *The Golden Legend* but had not informed them. Sullivan replied to Frederick Spark on 3 February, "very much annoyed at the 'enterprise' of the newspapers."[30] He assured Spark that Joseph Bennett was writing the libretto, and if it proved satisfactory he would start work at once.

Sullivan was certainly under considerable pressure of work. On 4 March he conducted the first Philharmonic concert of the season and on 8 March was in Bath to conduct *The Martyr of Antioch*, performed by the Bath Philharmonic Society, of which he was president. But what was pressing on Sullivan's mind was the thought of two works to be written: the new opera for the Savoy and his cantata for Leeds. He arranged for a substitute to replace him for the next Philharmonic Concert, scheduled for 18 March, while he began work on the new piece with Gilbert, tackling the finale of act 1; but pressure from Leeds was uppermost in his mind.

In advance of a meeting on Savoy business, arranged for 23 March, Carte wrote to Sullivan and Gilbert, setting out his own views of the current position and explaining that he could express his views better in writing than in conversation. He thought it *"most* desirable" for Sullivan to finish the new opera before beginning work for Leeds. He was clear in his opposition to bringing on a revival, especially after their experience with *The Sorcerer* revival, which he thought "practically thrown away" as the new opera was not ready. The same could happen to *Pinafore*. "We cannot as I believe calculate on more than two months good business possibly three out of Pinafore. Then the new opera will not be ready, down will go the receipts, and the Pinafore revival will be wasted."

Carte's proposal was to defer any revivals until after the next opera, or even until after the last opera they intended to write together. Then they could bring on a series of revivals, instead of producing revivals in between new operas. That way they would probably get a year's good business out of the revivals alone. He reminded Sullivan that the new opera should have been ready the previous December and sounded a note of warning: "we all three stand in equally [*sic*] in profit and *or loss* at the Savoy."[31]

In his diary, Sullivan summed up the eventual meeting: "Gilbert & Carte—long pow wow—adjourned for a week to see the result of a week's more performances of 'Mikado.'"[32]

Two days later, Sullivan was in Nottingham to conduct a performance of *The Martyr of Antioch*. He had still not made a start on the cantata and neither was he making any progress on the new opera. On 1 April came a request from the prince of Wales that he write the music to an ode by Tennyson for the opening of the Colonial and Indian Exhibition on 4 May. Reluctantly, Sullivan agreed. "How am I to get through this year's work?," he complained in his diary.[33]

But the accumulation of work was of his own making, because of his habit of putting work off until the last moment. Nevertheless, he was feeling the pressure. When Sullivan and Gilbert met Carte again on 3 April to review the situation, Sullivan was tense and responded angrily to Gilbert, who accused him of being late with the new opera. There was no alternative but to put off production until September or October. That evening Sullivan went to a reception for Liszt, who had just arrived from Paris and was about to be feted in London, in what turned out to be the last year of his life.

Once again Sullivan put off working on the cantata or the opera. He went to the races for the opening of the spring season at Epsom on 6 April; two days later he was at the Grosvenor Gallery for a reception for Liszt organized by Walter Bache, and the next day, 9 April, Sullivan escorted Liszt to a smoking concert at St. James's Hall.

The new opera had effectively been shelved. Now Sullivan had to get away from the distractions of London if he was to make any headway at all with *The Golden Legend*. He rented a cottage in York Town, and by chance it was next door to the house he had lived in for a time when his father was bandmaster at the Military College, and that was now let out by one of his father's old bandsmen. He moved in on 23 April and started work on *The Golden Legend* the very next day.

But the hoped-for period of calm composition eluded him. First of all he had musical engagements to fulfill: conducting his *Ode* for the Colonial and Indian Exhibition in Hyde Park, opened by Queen Victoria on 4 May; conducting his symphony at St. James's Hall on his birthday; and rehearsals and two more concerts for the Philharmonic Society on 19 May and 2 June. And second, there were the races: Derby Day at Epsom on 26 May, and the first week of June was Ascot week. Progress on *The Golden Legend* was slow. On 18 June, he left York Town and returned to London, still with a mountain to climb.

In the middle of May the New York company returned after completing its nine-month run of *The Mikado* at the Fifth Avenue Theatre. After two weeks at Liverpool and Manchester, they left for Germany where Carte had booked the Wallner Theatre in Berlin for 30 nights, opening on 2 June. "Some of the airs were rapturously encored," reported *The Times*, ". . . 'The flowers that bloom in the spring' . . . had to be repeated four times; while at the end the whole company was enthusiastically cheered and recalled thrice."[34]

Not at all sure that *The Mikado* would be a success in Germany, Sullivan had done his best to drum up powerful support. He had written to Sir Edward Malet, then the British ambassador in Berlin, and even to William, prince of Prussia, who was ill and unable to attend the first performance. In his reply, William told him how much he and his family were looking forward to seeing *The Mikado*, which he had heard so much about. He could not resist showing how well he still remembered *Pinafore*, hoping that they would have "polished up the handle of the big front door" for him, and reminded Sullivan of the time they had met in 1881, and "the charming musik on the yacht."[35]

After a month in London, Sullivan moved to the country again, out to Stagenhoe Park, to give all his attention to *The Golden Legend*. "I am quiet here," he reported to Fred Spark on 30 July. "The work is getting on satisfactorily."[36] Throughout August he toiled away, reporting regularly on his progress to Spark. "I am in the last throes of agony with 'The Golden Legend,' " he wrote on 16 August and then eight days later, "You will be glad to hear that the work is finished, and all in the copyist's and engraver's hands."[37] Sullivan had not been strictly accurate. His diary for 25 August records that it was the last day of scoring, finishing at 7:45 p.m. And on the following day he gave the last of the music to the copyist.[38]

Any hope of producing the next Savoy opera for October was abandoned. That was not a problem; *The Mikado* was still running well. Meeting at the Savoy on 6 September, Gilbert, Sullivan, and Carte decided to postpone the new opera until the end of November; but that still left Sullivan little time after the festival to complete the music. Choral rehearsals started in Leeds on 10 September, after which Sullivan returned to Stagenhoe Park until the end of the month. Three days of orchestral rehearsals were held in London and then on Friday, 8 October, with four servants, Sullivan left for Leeds. The Judge's Lodgings, lent to him by the mayor, were to be his home during the festival, and his house guests arrived the following Tuesday, among them Tosti and Mrs. Ronalds, with George Grove arriving the next day.

A heavy schedule of rehearsals and then the festival itself culminated on Saturday 16 October, with the first performance of *The Golden Legend*. Most of the press were ecstatic in their praise: "cheer after cheer rang through the hall," said the *Liverpool Mercury*; "the audience were excited and the choristers simply crazy. The girls pelted the composer with flowers. . . . such a frenzy of congratulations has surely never before rung in the ears of any living man as that amid which Sir Arthur left the platform."[39] *The Times* was more restrained: "The Leeds Festival may boast of having given life to a work which, if not of genius in the strict sense of the word, is at least likely to survive till our long expected English Beethoven appears on the stage."[40]

Gilbert added his congratulations to the flood that submerged Sullivan, not omitting to mention business at the same time: "I congratulate you heartily on the success of the Cantata which appears, from all accounts, to be the biggest thing you've done. I have quite finished the libretto (subject to any alterations you may suggest). . . . I can come up any day and go through the Ms with you."[41] Bowing to the obvious, but at the same time confident of *The Mikado*'s continued success, they had finally decided to produce the new opera at the end of January. After only a few weeks' rest Sullivan was ready to face the prospect, and on 5 November he went to dine with the Gilberts. After dinner, Gilbert read him the completed libretto of *Ruddygore* (to use the original spelling of the title).

Sullivan had already read the sketch plot and had even begun work on the finale to act 1 over six months earlier, but now Gilbert had completed all the lyrics. *Ruddygore*, as a parody of Victorian melodramas, was to be just as improbable as the other operas, with reversals of fortune as "a pure and blameless peasant" becomes a "bad baronet," and a once-bad baronet reforms and gives up "all his wild proceedings." The heroine changes the object of her love with dizzying rapidity, but always strictly in accordance with etiquette. And ghosts walk and talk with the living, and come back to life. But Sullivan did not appear to mind.

Not that Sullivan could concentrate purely on the music of *Ruddygore*. Three performances of *The Golden Legend* had been arranged for London. The first took place at the Albert Hall on 15 November with the Royal Albert Hall Choral Society; the second, with the Novello Oratorio Choir, on 23 November at St. James's Hall; and the third, again with the Novello Oratorio Choir, on 4 December at the Crystal Palace. Sullivan, at the age of forty-four, was at the height of his powers and his reputation had been enhanced by his latest work. If no longer the undisputed leading musician of his age, he was still the most popular and the best known.

Gilbert, too, was at the peak of his career, not as the leading dramatist any longer but as a librettist of unique talent and as a stage director of originality. Kitty urged her husband to have his portrait painted. Gilbert commissioned Frank Holl, who had been one of the early artists for the *Graphic*, the news magazine set up in 1869, and who had developed a reputation as a social realist. He had taken up the more lucrative work of portraiture later in his career and was greatly in demand. His portrait of Gilbert shows the mature dramatist, then aged forty-nine, in riding costume. No doubt this, too, was the suggestion of Kitty, not only capturing the more private persona of her husband, but also reminding her of the days, twenty years earlier, when they first rode together in Hyde Park and had fallen in love.

While Gilbert and Sullivan savoured the financial success derived from *The Mikado*, for Carte it was a period of readjustment following the death of his wife, a period in which he was attempting to build a new future for himself. It was also a time of major changes in personnel at the Savoy. Michael Gunn had given up supervising the touring companies in Britain and George Edwardes also was leaving. Edwardes had married Julia Gwynne in July, and after finding a financial backer, had agreed to go into management with John Hollingshead at the Gaiety. Not for the first time Carte offered Helen Lenoir a salary of £1,000 plus 10 percent on the net profit of all his business including London; once more she resisted the offer, and Carte was reluctant to put any pressure on her. He had referred the matter to Fladgate, his solicitor, in order to arrive at a fair and proper payment, and reminded Helen Lenoir, "I could not have done the business at all, at any rate on nothing like the same scale without you."[42]

Bathing in the glorious success of *The Golden Legend*, Sullivan was ready to overlook the fact that the new opera was not only improbable but also contained a strong element of the supernatural. He finished the choruses for act 1 of *Ruddygore* by the end of November and a start was made on the music rehearsals. Gilbert held his first stage rehearsal for act 1 on 15 December, and on 20 December Sullivan recorded that he had finished writing all the music except for two songs for Grossmith.

Gilbert spent Christmas in the country, at Breakspears, about nine or ten miles north of Uxbridge, in a house he rented for several years at this period of his life. Sullivan spent Christmas Day at Queen's Mansions with his nephew Herbert (now eighteen and working for an engineering firm in Leeds), with Fanny Ronalds and her family, and with Tom Chappell and his. All his employees received presents: to his secretary, Smythe, Sullivan gave £30, a silver pencil and notebook, and a turkey; to Louis he gave a desk and £2; and to Clotilde, now a year in his service, he gave £2 and a gold brooch.

Throughout the first half of January, rehearsals continued and Sullivan started scoring the opera. On 11 January, Gilbert called to suggest a new number in act 2 ("He Yields"); at 9:30 in the evening Gilbert called again, this time with the new words that Sullivan set and then scored that night, finishing at 6:10 in the morning. Two more all-night sessions followed before Sullivan finished the whole score at 4 a.m. on Friday 14 January. The next Wednesday, 19 January, *The Mikado* ended its run, after 672 performances. Two clear days were left before the opening of *Ruddygore; or, The Witch's Curse*. The final dress rehearsal, by now a semipublic affair attended by friends and critics, lasted for seven hours.

Following the success of *The Mikado*, the new opera was looked forward to with more excitement and a higher level of expectation than any other opera. The first night had certainly attracted a large number of celebrities, including Lord and Lady Randolph Churchill; the art world was represented by Millais, Whistler, Frank Holl, Marcus Stone, Carlo Perugini, and his wife, Kate Dickens; and the theatrical and musical worlds by Arthur Pinero, Francis Burnand, Kate Terry, and Madame Albani. The audience were all armed with their copy of the libretto, religiously following every word and causing a rustle of paper as they turned the page. It was an audience accustomed to the success of Gilbert and Sullivan operas. But this night was to be different from other first nights.

"The production of Gilbert and Sullivan's new operetta," reported *The Times*, ". . . was on Saturday evening accompanied by a phenomenon never before experienced at the Savoy Theatre. With the rapturous applause of a more than sympathetic first night audience . . . a small but very determined minority mingled hisses."[43] "There is no getting away from the fact," recalled Rutland Barrington, "that it was, for the Savoy, a very stormy first night, some of the malcontents in the gallery shouting 'Take it away—give us back *The Mikado*.'"[44]

The first act had gone well, it was bright and cheerful, with several numbers well received by the audience, such as Lely's song, "I Shipped, D'Ye See," and the hornpipe that followed. Grossmith's "My Boy You May Take It from me," and Jessie Bond's "To a Garden Full of Posies" were both successful. But during the second act, despite the popularity of the patter trio and the duet by Barrington and Jessie Bond, some of the audience grew restless. The plot came in for severe criticism, *The Times* having "no hesitation in attributing them [the hisses from the audience] to the feebleness of the second act and the downright stupidity of its *dénouement*."[45]

The set, too, was at fault. Two of the blinds or shutters that opened to reveal the ancestors in the ghost scene failed to function properly on the first night, and one of them came crashing onto the stage. "At the Savoy Theatre, where appliances are perfect, and where money is or should be no object, one expects something more realistic," said *The Times*.[46]

Opinion on the music was divided. "The whole of the music," said the *Daily News*, "is far removed above the ordinary level of comic opera, and is among the best things of this sort that Sir Arthur Sullivan has ever written."[47] For *The Times*, however, the "musical treatment of this scene [the Ghost scene] appears to be pitched in the wrong key. . . . [Sullivan] treats Mr. Gilbert's grotesque spectres as if they were a dreadful reality coming straight from the charnel house."[48]

Even the title did not escape criticism, *Ruddygore* being considered by the *Graphic* too coarse for a lady "on whose lips such a title would scarcely sound pretty."[49] Gilbert wrote to Sullivan on Sunday morning, sending the letter by hand, suggesting that Grossmith's song in the second act should be reset "to an air that would admit of his singing it *desperately*—almost in a passion—the torrent of which would take him off the stage at the end."[50] The song referred to was a patter song, "For Thirty-five Years I've Been Sober and Wary," but the change proposed by Gilbert would take time to put into operation. Gilbert and Carte called on Sullivan at Queen's Mansions on Sunday afternoon to discuss the opera and what they could do to improve it. They had no need to wait for Monday's papers to tell them that immediate cuts and changes were essential. But it was Monday before they decided not to bring the ghosts back to life. Other changes included reducing the act 2 finale to the short chorus "For Happy the Lily." On Tuesday, without the orchestra, a rehearsal was held to take the company through the alterations and the following Sunday, 30 January, Sullivan wrote the music to a new second act song for Grossmith, "Henceforth all the Crimes That I Find in The Times." The next day he scored the new, shorter finale.

Gilbert shared the opinion of the reviewer in *The Times*, and considered that Sullivan's music in the ghost scene had been too grand. In a letter to Alfred Watson, he suggested that the ghost music was "out of place in a comic opera. It is as though one inserted fifty lines of *Paradise Lost* into a farcical comedy."[51]

Reacting to criticism, Gilbert changed the spelling of the title to *Ruddigore*, a spelling that first made its appearance in newspapers on 2 February. The impression of failure with *Ruddigore* dogged Gilbert, even though in his heart he did not believe it. Its comparison with *The Mikado*, the onslaught of adverse criticism, his discomfiture with some of Sullivan's music, and his recognition that the second act as originally performed had serious weaknesses all contributed to the feeling of failure. It was nothing of the sort, despite the difficulties, but it was hard to lay that particular ghost.

In later years, Gilbert made several attempts to have *Ruddigore* revived, but was unsuccessful. It was left for later generations to enjoy. They would make no comparison with *The Mikado* but would treat *Ruddigore* as another Gilbert and Sullivan opera, with clever lyrics, amusing characters, and music that makes the opera distinctive; and they would be able to appreciate one of Gilbert and Sullivan's finest songs, "The Ghost's High Noon," without criticism of Sullivan's music being out of place. That particular song was, until then, the nearest Sullivan had come to grand opera in any of the previous works. It presaged the serious approach that he would adopt in his next opera with Gilbert.

CHAPTER TWENTY-ONE

1887-1888

"A Fresh Start"

A WEEK INTO RUDDIGORE, George Grossmith was taken ill. His understudy, H. A. Henri (Henry Lytton), twenty years of age, was called on to take over the role on Monday 31 January. Lytton was terrified as he stepped on to the stage in front of a silent audience, not knowing what to expect, appearing as replacement for the great George Grossmith.[1] Unlike the other leading comedy roles, the part of Robin Oakapple has a romantic element before its melodramatic development later; Lytton was handsome, had a pleasant light baritone voice, and could act. He was a success, and in time was to make his name in all the Grossmith parts. For the present, his glory in 1887 only lasted until 16 February, when Grossmith returned after his illness.[2] Gilbert was delighted with Lytton's performance, and sent him a gold-mounted walking stick in appreciation of his excellent performance. Lytton went on tour in April as Robin and before the end of the year was playing Sir Joseph in *Pinafore*. Gilbert remained a firm supporter over the years, and when H. A. Henri was considering changing his name, Gilbert suggested that he name himself after Marie Litton, in memory of the one-time manager of the Court Theatre, who had died a few years earlier.

More or less the same company that had taken *The Mikado* to America was now assembled for *Ruddigore*. They gave two matinee performances at the Savoy on 9 and 10 February and two days later sailed for New York, where they opened on 21 February at the Fifth Avenue Theatre. They were not, however, to achieve the same level of success with *Ruddigore* that they had enjoyed with *The Mikado*.

In early February, Sullivan left for Monte Carlo for a few weeks rest and quiet. At six o'clock in the morning of 23 February, his peace was shattered when an earthquake rocked the hotel in which he was staying. The inevitable panic followed, and although Sullivan maintained his usual calm at the time, afterward he described himself as feeling "quite sick."[3] More damage had been caused along the coast at the border town of Mentone, which Sullivan drove out to see the next day, and even more serious damage, including loss of life, sixty miles away at Savona. He left Monte Carlo a week later to travel down to Rome, where he received an invitation to conduct *The Golden Legend* on 26 March in Berlin, in honor of the kaiser's ninetieth birthday. If he were to be acclaimed for his serious music in Germany, that would indeed be the crowning moment of his career.

A few days later, Sullivan traveled further south to Naples, and there his old kidney ailment flared up, nailing him to his bed for two days. As he lay sick, he received an urgent letter from Carte, written on 5 March. Carte's prime concern was to bring Sullivan up to date on a question that required an immediate answer: whether the two of them were to involve themselves in the sale of the Carl Rosa Company, which Rosa wanted to turn into a limited company. If Sullivan were willing to join Carte in the purchase, all well and good; otherwise Carte would refuse the opportunity. For Carte the matter was urgent, and he pleaded, "like a dear boy wire me *at once*."[4]

After a lapse of three days, and with no reply from Sullivan, Carte wrote again with additional information: Carl Rosa was hoping to sell his whole company for about £88,000, but wanted to remain as managing director for five years for a salary of £1,500 a year.[5] Sullivan responded promptly with a telegram: "Must decline Rosa affair." Considering his relationship with Sullivan, Carte told Rosa, "I don't feel . . . that I can well go on without him."[6]

In his original letter, Carte had brought up a new problem concerning Leonora Braham. Unknown to Carte, she had been married in the previous June to Duncan Young, a former principal tenor in one of the touring companies, and she was now pregnant. "I have had to take her off," Carte reported, "on account of her increasing figure." The part of Rose Maybud had been taken over by Josephine Findlay, but Carte did not consider her strong enough to be the "Prima Donna" at the Savoy. "Are we to take Braham back after the accouchement?" he asked. "If not who are we to engage[?]"[7] Carte's own preference was to engage Marie Tempest—if he could get her. Marie Tempest was the twenty-three-year-old star of the new comic opera *Dorothy* by B. C. Stephenson (Sullivan's librettist for *The Zoo*) and Alfred Cellier. At Carte's request, Gilbert went to see her at the Gaiety, but found her too strident in tone and could not see her playing Rose Maybud.

The debate was finally settled by giving the role to Geraldine Ulmar, who had already played Rose Maybud in the New York production of *Ruddigore*, and who opened in the part at the Savoy on 7 May. She was well received, considering that she was taking over from a Savoy favorite, Leonora Braham, who had been the leading soprano since creating the part of Patience in 1881. "Compared with that of her charming predecessor, Miss Ulmar's style must be called a little *prononcé*," said *The Times*. ". . . At the same time she eschews vulgarity."[8]

The performance of *The Golden Legend* in Berlin turned out to be a disappointment. At rehearsal on 25 March, Sullivan thought that Pattini was "very uncertain as to time & phrasing," and the whole performance he considered to be third class.[9]

He spent two hours the next day rehearsing Pattini in the hope of redeeming the oratorio, but without success. "The performance itself is now a matter of history, alas!" was Sullivan's comment afterwards, "it was the most agonizing evening I have ever spent."[10] Although humiliated, he was not despondent; in his judgment, it was the performance and not the music itself that had failed. "The last chorus created a great effect," he wrote in his diary, "and I was recalled enthusiastically 3 times."[11]

In an attempt to make up for the comparative failure of 26 March, a further performance was scheduled for the following week. But this time Sullivan had managed to obtain the services of Albani. "Albani superb," Sullivan noted in his diary. After supper with the soprano and her husband, Ernest Gye, Sullivan presented her with a bracelet to show his gratitude.[12] For much of the remaining time in Berlin, Sullivan was the guest of royalty. He accompanied Princess Victoria as she sang "The Moon and I" from *The Mikado*, played duets with Princess Christian, and joined the royal family as they listened to a selection from *The Mikado* played by a regimental band, which was followed by another military band playing the same selection. Sullivan had indeed conquered Germany by his music: not by the earnest strains of *The Golden Legend*, but by the joyous melodies he had written to Gilbert's lyrics.

From Berlin to Leipzig is only about eighty miles — close enough for Sullivan to take the opportunity of going back for a brief visit to the place where his music had first been heard in Germany. It was his first visit in twenty-six years. The town had changed almost beyond recognition; "all the dear old fashioned houses are gone," he commented in a mood of nostalgia.[13] He returned to Berlin the next day and met up with Carte and Helen Lenoir, who were shortly to be followed by one of Carte's companies ready to open in Berlin with *The Mikado* and *Patience*. Sullivan rehearsed the orchestra on the day of the opening, and in the evening watched the performance from the royal box.

Sullivan had already missed the first two Philharmonic concerts of the season, but was back in time to conduct the third, on 21 April, and the fourth concert on 5 May. Two days later, he was at the Crystal Palace to hear a performance of *The Golden Legend* conducted by Manns, with an orchestra and choir which numbered 3,500, and with Albani, Patey, Lloyd, and Foli as the soloists. At the end, Sullivan was called to the platform, reported *The Times*, "to unanimous and prolonged applause."[14] The following week, Sullivan himself conducted another performance of *The Golden Legend*, this time given by the Leeds Philharmonic Society. By now the cantata had already crossed the Atlantic, having been heard first in Chicago in March, and then in May in a performance by the Boston Oratorio Society.

The sweetness of success that Sullivan tasted following *The Golden Legend* was to some extent tainted by the increased workload that he faced at the beginning of May. He still had to complete the season of concerts for the Philharmonic Society; another Savoy opera would soon be needed because of the uncertainty over *Ruddigore*; he had been asked to write a "Magnificat" for the Sons of the Clergy Festival; and he was invited by the prince of Wales to compose the music to an ode by Lewis Morris for the diamond jubilee of the queen. Sullivan found it difficult to cope with that number of demands. It worried him. In early May, he had to admit to John Stainer that he was unable to set the "Magnificat" for the Sons of the Clergy Festival at St. Paul's on 11 May. "I have been working at it since I returned from Berlin but all my efforts are weak and unworthy of the object. . . . You cannot be so vexed as I am myself."[15] In its place Stainer chose to conduct Sullivan's *In Memoriam.*

It was time to look at a new opera for the Savoy, and on 9 May, Gilbert and Carte called on Sullivan. Having served Sullivan up with a plot in *Ruddigore* that possessed both the improbable and the supernatural, Gilbert now tried again to persuade Sullivan to accept his old magic-lozenge plot—with modifications. Sullivan was unhappy with the idea, but they came to a compromise. Gilbert would write part of the plot and if it was unappealing to Sullivan, or if he foresaw difficulties with the musical settings, then the idea would be abandoned. They decided that, in the meantime, they would produce revivals for the next year or so. At least this decision had the advantage for Sullivan that he could put a new opera to the back of his mind.

What he could not put off was the ode for Queen Victoria's jubilee; if not exactly a royal command, it was a royal request, and impossible to refuse. He settled to his task, but not before seeing Lewis Morris on 12 June to discuss changes to his words that Sullivan thought necessary before setting the music. The "Jubilee Ode" was played on 4 July, when the queen laid the foundation stone at the Imperial Institute in South Kensington, a building that eventually became Imperial College.

The Philharmonic season had ended on Saturday, 25 June; and the next Savoy opera was still on the distant horizon. Sullivan was now able to relax. In the hot summer of 1887, to be on the water or beside the sea was an attractive proposition. With Fanny Ronalds, Sullivan joined a boating party on the Thames one Sunday in July; he went over to Trouville, on the Normandy coast, at the end of the month; he was on the Thames again a week later, in the company of Fanny Ronalds, Whistler, Carte, and Helen Lenoir, heading on a steamer from Hampton Court to the island that Carte had bought at Weybridge; and a few days later, he was down at Portsmouth and Cowes for the yachting season.

Gilbert spent the summer at Breakspears, partly working at his sketch plot for the next opera. Business was never far away from his mind, and it is probably at the end of August that he wrote to Carte, dating his letter simply "28th," "Im coming up to town on Thursday next—Can I see you then. . . . Try to get Sullivan to meet us. He ought to attend to business a little."[16]

Gilbert was not pleased with Sullivan at the time. In June, Jessie Bond had asked for the use of the theater to appear in a performance of Gilbert's *Broken Hearts* and Sullivan had refused. Gilbert did not disguise his own disappointment and told Sullivan that he thought he was being unreasonable, as the theater was lent freely to outsiders, the Royal College of Music, for example, while Jessie Bond was a member of their own company. Sullivan stuck to his initial decision.

Gilbert and Sullivan, such contrasting personalities, were different in the rela-

Jessie Bond (V&A Picture Library)

tionships that they had with members of the company. Gilbert, despite his reputation as a martinet, was closer to the company, getting to know them as individuals and supporting them whenever possible. When Marion Johnson left the Savoy to get married, Gilbert wrote to her. "My dear Johnny. I am exceedingly sorry to hear that we are going to lose you, but of course I knew that it must come sooner or later. . . . I hope you will look me up at rehearsals now and then, just to make it look like old times. Wishing you every possible happiness."[17]

Sullivan's note to her was friendly but less personal: "My dear child, I told you, if you wrote for my photograph, I would send you one. I have sent you the best I can find — it was taken in Canada."[18]

Admittedly, Gilbert's more familiar style was reserved for the ladies. To gentlemen, he was always formal. Unlike Sullivan, who was on first-name terms with a wide circle of friends, Gilbert always maintained the formal, "Dear Sullivan," "Dear Carte" in his letters. At the Beefsteak Club, he was equally formal. Whereas the members were mostly on first-name terms, Gilbert kept to the formal line of address. His friend the critic Alfred Watson said of him, "Gilbert was always Gilbert, never William. Willie would have been unthinkable."[19]

Whether Sullivan attended the meeting that Gilbert had arranged with Carte for Thursday, 1 September, is not known; but on Sunday, 4 September, Sullivan dined with the Gilberts and afterward Gilbert read him his new plot. Sullivan found it unsatisfactory. The plot seemed to lead nowhere, and the characters he thought were like puppets. "It is impossible to feel any sympathy with a single person. I don't see my way to setting it in its present form."[20] Gilbert was thwarted once again in his attempt to persuade Sullivan that his beloved lozenge plot would make a good opera. Once more Sullivan had challenged Gilbert to think again.

While Gilbert tried to come up with an idea for a new plot, Sullivan gave his attention to the Norwich Festival, where *The Golden Legend* was scheduled to be performed in October. He moved up to Norfolk on 8 September, leasing Brome Hall at Scole, and was joined by Fanny Ronalds and her parents two days later. After only a few days at Brome Hall, Sullivan was taken ill, and by 21 September he was too ill to get out of bed. His legs became swollen, and standing or walking caused intense pain. As the festival approached, he was showing signs of improving but was still far from well. Determined to appear, he struggled to the rehearsal on Monday, 10 October, and "hobbled on the platform."[21] At the performance the following Thursday, he still felt "very seedy, but managed to get through all right."[22]

Brought down low physically, Sullivan also was low in spirits. He notified the Philharmonic Society of his intention to resign from the conductorship, giving as his official reason failing health and increasing responsibilities. He gave a slightly different version to George Grove when he wrote to him on 12 October. He described the Philharmonic as the one great musical interest left to him, but said "it tied me down too much — to be compelled to be in London for four or five consecutive months in the year doesn't at all suit my restless nature. 2ndly. Although I look tough enough *I am not strong*, and I used to worry and fret about [the] things —."[23] In a letter to Joseph Bennett a few days later, he described his illness as bad urinary problems, and told Bennett that he was worried about the invitation he had received to present prizes as president of the Birmingham and Midland Institute at the Town Hall and to deliver an address. The thought terrified him and anyway he wanted to be free from all engagements and responsibilities for a time, so that he could be free to wander around the world. If he had the thought of the Town Hall address hanging over him, his peace of mind would be destroyed.

Ruddigore was into its last few weeks, and the first opera scheduled for revival, *HMS Pinafore*, was set to open on 12 November. Gilbert had learned of Sullivan's illness from Carte and on 26 October wrote to offer his commiserations, while at the same time attending to business matters, ironing out technical details for the revival. The next day Gilbert started rehearsals, and on 31 October Sullivan was happy to note in his diary that Gilbert had given up his original subject and "had found another about the 'Tower of London,' an entirely new departure, *much relieved!*"[24] By 3 November, Sullivan was dancing with joy: "I danced with every maid in the house."[25] The dancing was not because of Gilbert's letter, although it would have undoubtedly contributed to Sullivan's improved state of mind, but because of a party he threw at Brome Hall.

The last performance of *Ruddigore* took place on Saturday, 5 November 1887. Despite the talk of failure in its early days, it had run for 288 performances, longer than *Princess Ida*. That evening also was the last performance in the Savoy Company of Durward Lely, seven years after he had first appeared as principal tenor in *The Pirates of Penzance*. This was not Lely's decision; the triumvirate had decided that it was time for a change. The decision had been made in early October, even though they were doubtful about finding a suitable tenor. Carte expressed his concern to Gilbert: "Lely will certainly come and ask if he is not to be cast and this will be rather awkward as we may ultimately have to fall back on him.... If we are to make a change of course I must find some one that you will be satisfied with as to the acting."[26]

Their decision was to engage J. G. Robertson, brother of Gilbert's old friend Tom Robertson, and for that reason no doubt acceptable to Gilbert, although his acting ability was limited. The reason Carte gave Lely for not renewing his contract was that, as they were reviving *HMS Pinafore*, he would again be cast in the role of a sailor, straight after his role as Richard Dauntless in *Ruddigore*, and that might not go down well with the audience.

The rest of the company was reengaged, including Jessie Bond, now with the small part of Hebe, after playing the major part of Mad Margaret in *Ruddigore*. Carte wondered whether she would reengage for the part and suggested the possibility to Gilbert of "getting in a song for her."[27] That was not the only change Carte wanted. He was doubtful about Geraldine Ulmar being able to sing "Sorry Her Lot" effectively and suggested an alternative song. Gilbert resisted all changes. When Geraldine Ulmar tried the song at rehearsal she was applauded by the rest of the company and, overcome at the compliment, burst into tears. "I must confess," said Gilbert in a letter to Sullivan, "to a sneaking [kindness] for the only bit of literature in the piece!"[28]

Carte had not given up tinkering with *Pinafore*. Gilbert's reaction to Carte's next suggestion is not known but can easily be guessed. In a letter to Sullivan on 5 November, a week before the opening, Carte asked:

Have you considered the "Fair Moon" question?

I feel certain that it is a very serious and regrettable mistake if Barrington is allowed to sing it.

2. That it will be an equally serious and regrettable mistake if that very popular song is omitted[.]

Why cannot Brandram have it? We have a man on our chorus Medcalf who sings like a thorough artist and has a superb baritone voice . . .

P.S. I told Barrington that I thought that if I were he I would not attempt to sing the song. He expressed his perfect willingness to leave it out but his conviction that he would be successful in it.[29]

Perhaps Sullivan was discreet enough not to let the question reach Gilbert's ears. Certainly Carte was beginning to enter into an area of the production that Gilbert would have been quick to remind him was outside his province, if not his competence. That same letter from Carte carried a further piece of information for Sullivan's ears only. "I have some *interesting & important News*[;] should *like a quarter of an hour* quietly with you *on Wednesday*."[30] As Miss Lenoir had recently become "Helen" in Carte's letters to Sullivan, the news can be fairly assumed.

Sullivan had recovered sufficiently to travel up to Liverpool on 7 November to be present at a performance of *The Golden Legend* conducted by Charles Hallé; and on the same day he wrote to Otto Goldschmidt to send his condolences on hearing of the death of his wife, Jenny Lind. Sullivan recalled the time when, as a Chapel Royal chorister, he had first heard her sing. "She it was," he told Goldschmidt, "who made me think that Music was divine."[31]

The revival of *HMS Pinafore* opened at the Savoy on Saturday 12 November 1887. Sullivan dined at Carte's with Helen Lenoir, Fanny Ronalds, her daughter, and Michael Gunn before going along to the Savoy. He was particularly impressed by the new set. "Curtain rose at 8.30 on the most splendid 'set' ever seen on the stage. The stage was a real ship—great enthusiasm."[32] The opera was greeted, in the words of *The Times*, like "an old friend after a long separation." As for Carte's anxiety about the song "Fair Moon," Barrington's conviction that he could succeed with it was fully justified by the same paper: "a more comic captain of the Navy than Mr. Rutland Barrington singing to a small guitar by the light of the moon, it would be impossible to imagine."[33] Gilbert and Sullivan took their bows together and afterward, with Kitty and Fanny Ronalds, they all went off to Carte's for an oyster supper.

A few days later, Sullivan's physical condition deteriorated. This time he began a course of permanganate injections but as the side-effect to the injection was irritation of the bladder, he soon stopped them. While still in a low state, both physically and mentally, he received an invitation from Villiers Stanford, recently appointed professor of music at Cambridge, to conduct *The Golden Legend* in Cambridge the following June for the University Musical Society. In his reply, he told Stanford that he found it impossible to be definite about such a long time in the future. "I get ill and nervous, and consequently have refused to pledge myself to any public engagements a long way ahead."[34]

THE IDEA FOR THE NEW opera that Gilbert had told Sullivan about in October had been developing in his mind and in his plot book. He said that he had got the idea when he saw an advertisement for the Tower Furnishing Company, while waiting for his train one day at Uxbridge Station. His first title for the piece was "The Tower Warder," and by 12 December he was ready to go over the plot with Sullivan, inviting him to dinner for 14 December. Sullivan was too ill to go; he had a "cold in the bladder & swollen testicle" and was forced to stay in bed.[35] The next day his temperature was up to 105° F and he was injecting himself with morphia. Ten days later, on Christmas Day, Sullivan was still in bed, but well enough to receive Gilbert and Carte and to listen to Gilbert reading the plot: "immensely pleased with it," Sullivan wrote in his diary. "Pretty story, no topsy turvydom, very human, & funny also." In the evening Sullivan was able to get up for dinner with his guests, Fanny Ronalds and her parents, but by 10:45 he was back in bed.[36]

The year came to an end with Sullivan feeling "depressed & low."[37] Since Christmas, he had been unable to stand without being in pain. Fanny Ronalds and her parents came to dinner on New Year's Eve and together they saw in the New Year, a new year that brought no relief for Sullivan from the continual pain. Gilbert called with the first four lyrics for "The Tower Warder" on 2 January, and six days later he brought him three more, but Sullivan was in no fit state to start work.

Neither was he prepared to give a direct answer to the Leeds Festival Committee, which had asked him in November if he would write a symphony for the 1889 festival. The committee had still not reached a decision about their conductor for the next festival, and, through his secretary, Sullivan declined to give an answer until the appointment had been made. By 18 January, Sullivan felt strong enough to write himself to Fred Spark and to expand on his previous letter, but he had not moved from his original opinion that the appointment of a conductor should be made before the music was arranged. The committee were not convinced; they had their appropriate procedures for the appointment of a conductor, and General and Executive Committees were set up for each festival, Spark told him. Sullivan's voice was lost in the wilderness of procedures.

A new acting talent was introduced to Gilbert in January 1888: Julia Neilson, a twenty-year-old student at the Royal Academy of Music who was eager to acquire stage experience before embarking on a career in opera. She asked Joseph Barnby, who was then professor of conducting at the Royal Academy, to write her a letter of introduction to Gilbert. Barnby was only too pleased; he thought that, as a singer, Julia Neilson would only ever be a charming drawing-room mezzo.[38] Gilbert agreed to listen to her. He was impressed, and advised her to give up any idea of going into opera and to concentrate on the stage.

The day after the audition, Gilbert wrote to Mary Anderson, who was thinking of playing *Pygmalion and Galatea* at the end of her season of *Comedy and Tragedy*, telling her that he had found "a magnificent Cynisca . . . the most remarkable novice I have ever seen."[39] A fortnight later he wrote to Carte, suggesting a matinee of *Broken Hearts* at the Savoy in May, with Julia Neilson playing the part of the Lady Hilda. "I am astonished at her Cynisca —," he wrote. "It is simply superb."[40]

Excited though Gilbert was to find new talent and to nurture it, the old stagers at the Savoy remained important to him. Jessie Bond was ill again at about this time and unable, or merely reluctant, to play in *Pinafore*. Gilbert wrote to encourage her, saying "I shall be very glad indeed to see you back again. The Savoy is not itself without you."[41]

Gilbert's mindfulness of old friends was matched by his long memory of old insults. W. H. Kendal wrote to him on 6 February asking for permission to play *Sweethearts* with his wife in their autumn tour, and requesting Gilbert to state his terms. In reply, Gilbert took Kendal back to 1875 and the difference that had occurred then over *Broken Hearts*. In case Kendal had forgotten, Gilbert reminded him that he had said he "would never again allow Mrs. Kendal or yourself to speak a line of mine upon the stage."[42]

Now in his early fifties, Gilbert was as vigorous as ever: hard-working, engaged on a new piece, ready to keep an eye on new talent, ready to take on an old opponent with all his old energy. Sullivan, by contrast, had been sapped of energy. After his months of illness, he was more than ever in need of going in search of sunshine. In early February he left for Monte Carlo, but not before signing a new five-year contract with Gilbert and Carte, renewing the one they had made in 1883. For Gilbert to have signed that contract is not surprising; what is surprising is that Sullivan was prepared to do so after his recent illness and the resulting depression. The answer lies in his increasing friendship with Carte and his increasing dependence on Carte who was promising him a brighter future.

On 9 February, Gilbert and Carte attended a supper and ball given to celebrate the five hundredth performance of *Dorothy*. Carte was uneasy at the success of this rival opera, and wrote to Sullivan on 13 February. The two men had already discussed Carte's plans for the future, and it had been agreed that Sullivan would write to Gilbert giving his own views on Carte's idea of building a new theater, of putting the new opera on there, disbanding the old Savoy company and "making a fresh start."

From Carte's point of view the matter was urgent. He had to let the Savoy or sell it, otherwise his scheme for a new theater would fail. Carte knew he would not be able to convince Gilbert but hoped that Sullivan would succeed. "Now, if you wish the scheme to go through," he wrote to Sullivan, "you will not delay writing to him at once and putting your views with that incisive clearness which is always at your command. . . . But *there is not a day to lose*." Carte urged Sullivan on: he had a good tenant, Charles Wyndham, who was interested in taking on the Savoy. As for *Dorothy* at the Gaiety, he insisted: "we should not let *other people get **ahead**.*"[43]

Sullivan wrote his letter to Gilbert. It has not survived, but it was no doubt written with that "incisive clearness" that Carte envied. There is no doubting the clarity of Gilbert's reply. "I can't for the life of me, understand the reasons that urge you to abandon a theatre and a company that have worked so well for us, and for whom we have worked so well. Carte has his own interests." Gilbert's instincts were correct: he knew that Sullivan still had ambitions for grand opera, but he saw that this particular scheme was in accordance with Carte's own agenda. At this point it was Gilbert who held the Savoy Company together; had he not, *Ruddigore* would have been the end of the series at the Savoy.

Gilbert was dismayed at the timing of the suggestion coming from Sullivan, when he had been working on the next opera for some time: "now that the piece is half finished, you propose to scatter the company, abandon the theatre—& start anew with a new company in (I suppose) a new theatre!" Gilbert's reasons for continuing at the Savoy were straightforward:

> We have the best theatre, the best company, the best composer, & (though I say
> it [)], the best librettist in England working together—we are as world-known,
> & as much an institution as Westminster Abbey—& to scatter this splendid
> organization because Dorothy has run 500 nights is, to my thinking, to give up
> a gold mine.[44]

Gilbert's letter was written without acrimony; he quite simply did not understand why they should contemplate changing. He ended his letter to Sullivan with a cheerful, "I hope you've been lucky at the tables," and then outlined his own system, at which no doubt Sullivan, far more experienced (at losing) at the tables than Gilbert, would have simply smiled. At least the Savoy was safe—for the moment.

CHAPTER TWENTY-TWO

"A New Departure"—
The Yeomen of the Guard

IT WAS BACK TO BUSINESS as usual at the Savoy. Plans were already in hand to revive *The Pirates of Penzance* after *Pinafore*, and Jessie Bond was expressing concern about her part as Edith, another small part following that of Hebe. She asked Gilbert to improve it for her. Gilbert was no more enthusiastic about changing *The Pirates* than he had been about changing *Pinafore*, but he was sympathetic to her problem. Any addition to the dialogue, he told her, would be mere padding, and obvious as such. "My difficulty is increased by Sullivan being abroad, for he might have consented to a song to precede Frederic's entrance from the cave — and I would gladly have written such a song — but he is at Monaco and quite unlikely to work." Instead, Gilbert held out to her the prospect of "a particularly good part" in the next opera.[1] Jessie Bond played Edith, as written, and patiently waited for that better part.

The weather had not been kind to Sullivan in Monte Carlo and he decided to cross over to Algiers. Before leaving, he paid a visit to the German crown prince Frederick, who was staying at San Remo. While Sullivan was there, the prince received news that his father, the old kaiser William I, had died, and he had to return immediately to Berlin as the new emperor, Frederick III. It was to be a short reign: he was already suffering from throat cancer and had only a few months to live. Sullivan sailed from Marseille on 6 March and stayed in Algiers for a fortnight. During that period, *HMS Pinafore* came to the end of its run of 120 performances on Saturday, 10 March, leaving a few clear days for rehearsals before the opening of *The Pirates of Penzance*.

At rehearsal on the Tuesday, Gilbert objected to the girl who had been chosen to rehearse the part of Kate "on approval," and criticized Carte's choice in front of Barker and Cellier. Carte was deeply offended; he considered that Gilbert was undermining his position in the theater in front of the others. Later in the week, Gilbert objected to the appearance of another girl in the chorus. Exasperated, Carte wrote a lengthy letter to relieve himself of his frustration at Gilbert's criticisms: "if you and Sullivan say that you want none but handsome girls in the chorus, the matter can easily be discussed. I do not think however that it could be done without dismissing the vocal power of the chorus." That was not the real cause of his frustration. He objected to Gilbert's "tone"; it was as though Gilbert thought him incompetent. If the "carping and criticism" and the general lack of confidence continued, he said, "I would really rather terminate the business management between us at some period that will not cause anyone inconvenience."[2]

As the week wore on, Gilbert's behavior became more unpredictable. The opening of *The Pirates of Penzance* had been rescheduled from Thursday, 15 March, to Saturday, 17 March, and the dress rehearsal moved to Friday. Gilbert had been informed of the change but, as the days went by, he became confused over the time. As it happened, the time clashed with a dinner engagement he had made, and frantic phone calls from Kitty, Helen Lenoir, Carte, and Gilbert only managed to increase the confusion. When Gilbert turned up at Beaufort House on Friday, he insisted to Carte that everybody would have to wait until 6:00 to start the rehearsal, because he had now rearranged his dinner engagement. Carte thought "that it was most undesirable to keep them waiting for an hour." According to Carte, at that point Gilbert "got very much excited and annoyed about it," but finally arranged to be there at 5:30.[3]

When Gilbert arrived in the evening he was even more "excited" and accused Carte of being dictatorial. He claimed that, as they paid everybody's salary, they had a right to keep them waiting as long as they liked. The rehearsal went ahead, but Carte was deeply upset by Gilbert's behavior toward him and by Gilbert's accusations.

Gilbert's increasing anxiety as an opening night approached and his differences of opinion with Carte or Sullivan were not new, but even allowing for Gilbert's volatile temperament, his behavior at the Savoy had been out of the usual. Is it simply a coincidence that, during that week, Gilbert's mother lay dying? There is no evidence that he was ever in contact with his mother again after 1876, when his parents had separated, an event for which he laid the blame at her door. He was a stubborn man, capable of keeping to his resolution of cutting off all relations in order to demonstrate his grave displeasure. But he also was a sensitive man. Through his sisters he would certainly have heard about the state of his mother's health, and the fact that she was near to death. There is no hard evidence, only the evidence of Gilbert's behavior, which, in the words of D'Oyly Carte, was a departure from "the courteous consideration" with which he had always until then treated the staff at the Savoy.[4] Gilbert's mother died on Sunday, 20 March, aged seventy-six.

After putting forward his own scheme for "a fresh start," Carte now found himself faced with the possibility of breaking off business relations with Gilbert. On

22 March, he sent a telegram to Sullivan, who was due back in Marseille: "Serious row on with author dont really see how things are to go on you must stick to me."[5] Two days later, after Gilbert had returned to a calmer state of mind, Carte sent another telegram to Sullivan, at the Hotel de Paris, Monte Carlo: "Row made up all is peace for the moment."[6]

The Pirates of Penzance had opened successfully on 17 March. *The Times* thought "the occasion was shorn of much of its interest by the absence of Sir Arthur Sullivan from the conductor's seat," but the audience were enthusiastic at the return of the opera.[7]

Four days later, Julia Neilson made her debut as Cynisca in *Pygmalion and Galatea* at the Lyceum, with Mary Anderson playing Galatea. Despite her inevitable nervousness, the "high anticipations" of her talent "were to a large extent confirmed," thought *The Times*,[8] though in Gilbert's opinion not all the press did "justice to the performance." He told Mrs. Barnby that the part was played "more perfectly than it has ever been played before" and was "little short of phenomenal." His plan was to put on *Broken Hearts* for her, and then to write a play especially for her, which he hoped would be produced in October.[9]

Sullivan arrived back from France on 1 April, and over the next few days resumed the sittings for his portrait begun with Millais before the trip to Monte Carlo. On 11 April, Carte called on him: "Carte came to tell me of his marriage next day," he observed in his diary.[10] Sullivan was to be best man. D'Oyly Carte and Helen Lenoir were married at the Savoy Chapel and in his diary, Sullivan noted mischievously, "saw the young couple off at Charing Cross."[11]

Home from their honeymoon, D'Oyly and Helen Carte settled into 4 Adelphi Terrace. Only a few minutes' walk from Beaufort House and the Savoy, Adelphi Terrace, built by Robert and James Adam, stood high above the embankment, giving a commanding view of the Thames. With the aid of Whistler, Carte transformed the sober tone of the house by the use of bright colors, "guilding and colouring the carvings and ceiling mouldings in the principal rooms."[12] In the front room on the first floor, where three French windows gave onto the balcony, an ornately molded ceiling had as its centerpiece a painting of the three Graces by Antonio Zucchi, or by his wife, Angela Kaufmann, both of whom carried out decorative paintings for the Adam brothers.

Millais's portrait of Sullivan was given a private viewing at the Grosvenor Gallery on 28 April. It was not quite finished; the final sitting was to take place the following day and Sullivan avoided the gallery. "Hadn't the courage to go & see it," he noted.[13] He had his first sight of the finished portrait with Millais the following day. He was too moved to say anything at the time but wrote to the painter afterward to show his appreciation of such a "splendid and princely gift."[14]

Just as moving an experience occurred shortly after. By royal command, a performance of *The Golden Legend* took place at the Albert Hall on 8 May. In his diary, Sullivan recorded the queen's words to him after the performance: "At last I have

W. S. Gilbert—the mature librettist, taken about 1883 (Peter Joslin Collection)

heard the Gold: Legend, Sir Arthur!" and later, "you ought to write a grand opera—
you would do it so well!"[15]—words that the queen would later forget she ever said,
but that remained engraved on Sullivan's mind as if they were a royal command.

The Pirates of Penzance closed after eighty performances on Wednesday 6 June
and the third and last of the revivals, *The Mikado*, opened the next day: "there was

no lack of applause," said *The Times*, "and of that continued ripple of subdued laughter which is even more flattering to an author than noisy demonstrations." The only changes to the original cast were in the parts of Nanki-Poo, played by J. G. Robertson, and Yum-Yum, played by Geraldine Ulmar, whose voice, "if a little shrill" was "fully equal to the demands here made on it, and, although not a little, she was at least a pretty, maid from school."[16]

The next day, Gilbert called on Sullivan at 11 a.m. and read him act 2 of "The Tower Warder." After a discussion lasting three hours, Gilbert left Sullivan the rest of the lyrics. At this stage, the dialogue had, as usual, still to be completed, but it had been sketched out "in the rough," as Sullivan noted in his diary.[17] Because the new opera was now scheduled for the middle of September, Gilbert considered he had enough time to complete the dialogue and also to write his play for Julia Neilson, which would appear at the St. James's Theatre some time in the autumn, under the management of Rutland Barrington, who was leaving the Savoy at the end of *The Mikado*.

Sullivan, too, considered that three months was ample time to write the music for the new opera. He had two engagements to fulfill before making a start: one was to conduct *The Golden Legend* on 12 June for the Cambridge Musical Society, the engagement he had been reluctant to agree to during his illness the previous year; the other engagement was to join a house party as the guest of Russie Walker with his friends Ernest Dresden and Edward Dicey for a few days at the Ascot races. While he was at the racecourse, Sullivan learned by telegram of the death of the German emperor, Frederick III. He was to be succeeded by his twenty-nine-year-old son, William II, whom Sullivan had met at Kiel and who was to be the last kaiser of Germany.

It was now time for Sullivan to start work on the new opera. On 18 June, he leased a house called Booth Lodge at Fleet, four or five miles away from York Town, and therefore in familiar country. Only a short distance away lived the empress Eugénie in her house Farnborough Hill, to the north of Farnborough. A few days after moving into Booth Lodge, Sullivan was invited to tea. "Had a long walk with the Empress," he wrote in his diary.[18] Because he had more time than usual to complete the music, he led a more balanced existence during July. His nephew, Herbert, arrived for a stay, and halfway through July, Fanny Ronalds arrived with her mother and stayed until the end of the month. Sullivan found time for more exercise than usual, one day rowing with Herbert and his friend Russie Walker from Fleet up the river as far as Odiham, a distance of some seven or eight miles, and then back again. He had a day out at the races at Sandown on 27 July and the next day traveled up to Chester to conduct another performance of *The Golden Legend*.

Music rehearsals for act 1 of the new opera began under the direction of François Cellier on Friday, 10 August, and on the Monday Sullivan left Fleet to return to Queen's Mansions and work on act 2. A few difficulties in act 1 remained to be ironed out: Gilbert sent an altered lyric for the second verse of "To Thy Fraternal

Care" in the finale of act 1, and Sullivan wanted an alteration to a duet between Phoebe and Wilfred in the first scene. That problem was solved by cutting the duet completely.

But when Sullivan started on act 2 he saw serious difficulties in the musical situations. He raised the matter with Gilbert. From Sullivan's point of view, he was simply proceeding as usual: drawing Gilbert's attention to any difficulties, which they would then solve together. From Gilbert's point of view, Sullivan was arriving at this stage of his work at a very late hour; in his opinion, Sullivan should have been much further advanced in the work. There was an inevitable clash. "You might have told me of these requirements six months ago," complained Gilbert.[19] "Haughty letter from Gilbert," Sullivan wrote in his diary for 16 August, the day he attended his first rehearsal at the Savoy. "Wrote him back a snorter," he added.[20] Sullivan pointed out that he had not seen act 2 until 8 June. He had been working on it for the last three weeks, trying to overcome the difficulties in the musical situations, but could make no further progress without modifications from Gilbert. Sullivan asked if the rehearsals were to continue, because he was not prepared to "set the piece as it was."[21]

To that "snorter," Gilbert responded by pointing out that they had been through the musical construction of act 2, and on 8 June Sullivan had seemed delighted with it; only now had he discovered difficulties after writing five numbers of the second act. It was not that he objected to Sullivan's requiring alterations, it was the scale of them—practically a reconstruction, he complained—and the lateness, to which he objected.

Gilbert had relieved his feelings, but he had no realistic alternative; he had to make the changes Sullivan required. At the next rehearsal, Sullivan described Gilbert as being "mild & conciliatory" and everything was arranged satisfactorily between them.[22] Not that Sullivan had been able to set the first act without encountering difficulties. The most famous are the difficulties Sullivan grappled with when trying to set "I Have a Song to Sing, O!" Once Gilbert had enlightened him that it was suggested by an old sea shanty, which is well known in various forms, such as, "I'll sing you one, O! / What is your one, O?" then Sullivan had no further trouble and it turned out to be one of his most popular and best appreciated songs.

Among Gilbert's papers in the British Library is a "Summary of Incidents. Act 1.," followed by "*Opening of Act 2—Amended Version.*" That it is entitled "amended" suggests it does not predate the correspondence between Gilbert and Sullivan of mid-August. Comparison with the published libretto shows interesting differences. At that stage, the lyrics for "Free from His Fetters Grim" had not been written, and a song for Elsie (later cut), "There's Many a Maid in Her Best Arrayed," was included. The act 1 "Summary of Incidents" includes a song written for Wilfred Shadbolt, which is headed "*Barrington* (sung to J. Bond)" and begins "When jealous torments rack my soul." The mention of Barrington dates the first part of the paper (the act 1 summary) to a time before Barrington's decision to leave the Savoy to go into management. There is also a recitative for Elsie, "'Tis Done! I Am a Bride! Oh Little

Ring," which was missing from the license copy, giving rise to speculation that it had been added late. Following that piece of recitative is the familiar song by Elsie, in Gilbert's handwriting, but with changes by Sullivan, which give an insight into his method of working. Gilbert had written the song out as it appears in the published libretto, and called it a "Ballad," which Sullivan crossed out, substituting the word "Song." Sullivan wrote out the lyric again, but in a form better suited to his needs, marking the first half of the first line with his own rhythmic notation, as he settled on the rhythm for the music.

> Though tear and long drawn sigh ill fit a bride
> No sadder wife than I the whole world wide
> > Ah me! Ah me!
> Yet maids there be who would consent to lose
> The merry rose of youth, the flower of life
> To be in honest truth a dowered wife. ["dowered" is crossed out by Sullivan
> > and replaced with "wedded"]
> > No matter whose!
> Ah me, what profit ye, O maids that sigh
> Though gold should live if wedded love must die.[23]

Now that good relations had been restored, and while Gilbert was making his adjustments to act 2, Sullivan went over to Belfast with Fanny Ronalds and her son, Regie, to visit her daughter who, from comments in Sullivan's diary, was probably expecting a baby. It was only a short stay for Sullivan. A few days later, he returned to London and his scoring, leaving Fanny and Regie in Belfast. Gilbert held his first stage rehearsal for act 1 on Thursday, 6 September, after which Sullivan carried on with the music for act 2, calling the principals to a Sunday rehearsal followed by dinner at Queen's Mansions. At the end of the week, he was in Hereford, conducting *The Golden Legend*; then it was back to Queen's Mansions, and back to his scoring.

According to their custom, Gilbert and Sullivan had made no final decision about the title of their new work, always referring in correspondence to "the new piece" or "the new opera." The working title that Gilbert had first used was "The Tower Warder" (or "The Tower Warders"), but now he wrote to Sullivan with an alternative: "The more I think of it, the more convinced I am that The Beefeater is the name for the new piece."[24] Whose idea it was to change the title to *The Yeomen of the Guard* is not known, nor is it known when the change was made. Gilbert often wrote the title later as "The Yeoman of the Guard"; a frequent slip, perhaps, or another intermediate title. While Gilbert was pondering the use of "The Beefeater," Sullivan was still anxious about what was happening in Belfast. He wrote to Fanny Ronalds on 14 September, and the next day wrote in his diary. "Wrote to Belfast. . . . no news yet."[25] He appears to have adopted the whole family as his own, and was behaving like an expectant grandfather.

The song that caused Sullivan most difficulty in *The Yeomen of the Guard* was the tenor solo "Is Life a Boon?" in which Gilbert was at his most poetic. Sullivan is reported to have written three versions until Gilbert was satisfied that justice had been done to the rhythm of his lyric. The final version had still not been written when Sullivan composed the tenor song in the second act, "Free from his fetters grim." When it came to the rehearsal of this number, Sullivan handed the voice part to Courtice Pounds, and after running through it with him at the piano, told Pounds to stand on the stage and to sing it as well as he could "to impress Gilbert."[26]

The troublesome "Is Life a Boon?" was to be the last number to be written. Sullivan finished scoring the rest of the opera at 5 a.m. on 21 September and then gave his mind to the overture, which for this, the most serious of his operas with Gilbert, he wanted to write himself. He had by now received news from Belfast, in a telegram that said simply "All right!" "Thank God," Sullivan added in his diary.[27] He began sketching the overture on Sunday 23 September and then scored it over the next two days, at the same time beginning orchestral rehearsals at St. Andrew's Hall. At the end of the week, on Friday, 28 September, he held a full music rehearsal at the Savoy. With less than a week to the opening, Gilbert was becoming increasingly agitated. "Had a regular flare up with Gilbert between the parts," Sullivan wrote in his diary. "He worried everyone & irritated me beyond bearing—in one of his worst moods— I can't stand it any longer, & get as angry & irritable as he is. Eventually we made it up. Rehearsed the Overture."[28]

After 116 performances, the revival of *The Mikado* ended its run on Saturday, 29 September. "Great excitement, and tremendous enthusiasm for Barrington," noted Sullivan, as they said good-bye after his eleven years with them. Barrington had started as a young Dr. Daly in *The Sorcerer*, and was now finishing as a mature Pooh-Bah, although still only thirty-five, in *The Mikado*. Farewell speeches were made, first to the audience and then later to the company, as he embarked on his new career in management. That day, Sullivan had written the final version of "Is Life a Boon?" He rehearsed it with Pounds at Queen's Mansions the next day, and on Monday, Pounds sang it at a full rehearsal at the Savoy, "to everyone's amazement and delight!" recorded Sullivan.[29]

The final dress rehearsal started at 4:00 p.m. on Tuesday and lasted for six hours. Gilbert was irritable and Sullivan was bloody-minded. Gilbert was anxious about Temple's song in the first act, "A Laughing Boy but Yesterday," and wanted to cut it; "am anxious myself to cut it," noted Sullivan, "but object to be [*sic*] 'hectored' in the matter."[30] Gilbert's nerves were stretched taut, and on the morning of the opening, Wednesday, 3 October 1888, he wrote to Sullivan to record his disquiet about certain disputed points. The "success of the first Act will be most seriously imperilled," he maintained, unless Meryll's "wholly irrelevant song" were withdrawn. There were already too many numbers of a serious, grim, or sentimental character for "a professedly comic opera." The finale, too, was a cause of concern. He wanted the couplets reduced by half. "This, you will observe, is not 'cutting out your music,' but cutting out a *repeat* of your music. And I may remind you that I am proposing to cut, not only your music, but my words."[31]

The two men arranged to meet at the Savoy at 8:00 p.m. in order to go over the points raised by Gilbert. It was agreed to cut down the couplets in the finale, but to leave Meryll's song in for the first night. That way at least, Temple would be able to sing the number he had rehearsed and Sullivan would have an opportunity of letting his music be heard once, before it passed into oblivion. Gilbert then went and fussed around making sure everything was ready for the performance, and as Jessie Bond recalled, "was almost beside himself with nervousness and excitement."[32] Bond felt the strain of an anxious and fussing Gilbert as she sat on the stage at her spinning wheel, ready for the first number, while on the other side of the curtain Sullivan was already conducting his overture. At last Gilbert left the stage, and the theater, and went to while the time away at the Alhambra, leaving Kitty to act as his eyes and ears for the performance. Next to her in her box, on this occasion, sat William Gilbert senior.[33]

Sullivan, too, was nervous—"awfully nervous," he commented, "—& continued so until the duet 'Heighdy' which settled the fate of the Opera. Its success was tremendous—*3 times* encored! After that everything went on wheels and I think its success is even greater than the *Mikado*—9 encores—."[34]

From the rise of the curtain on the single figure of Phoebe at her spinning wheel, an image that Gilbert had used in *Ages Ago*, Gilbert signaled that this opera was different. According to *The Times*, author and composer had "turned over a new leaf."[35] The *Era* wondered if admirers of Gilbert and Sullivan's "topsy-turvy" operas would be so enthusiastic about "the new departure" they had made.[36] Both audience and critics were delighted and most enthusiastic about the new opera. The *Daily Telegraph* thought that "the music follows the book to a higher plane, and we have a genuine English opera, forerunner of many others, let us hope, and possibly significant of an advance towards a national lyric stage." The same reviewer thought that "I Have a Song to Sing" was perhaps "Mr. Gilbert's most successful lyric" and with "Sir Arthur Sullivan's quaintly beautiful music" the song may "rank in popular esteem as the gem of the work."[37] The same number elicited further praise from the *Morning Advertiser*, "Sir Arthur Sullivan has never written anything more delicately melodious and elegant than this, in fact of its kind he has never equalled it and probably never will, for it is not given to any composer to match such an exquisite thing."[38]

Punch took pleasure in pointing out that Gilbert's plot bore a strong resemblance to elements of Wallace's *Maritana*, which in turn had been based on a French play, *Don César de Bazan*, but generally the press was full of praise. Courtice Pounds was praised by *The Times* as "a better actor and a better tenor than any of his predecessors" and the same paper gave qualified praise to W. H. Denny, who had the difficult task of replacing such a popular comedian as Rutland Barrington. "Upon the whole," continued *The Times*, "we can agree with the popular verdict. Mr. Gilbert is in a way a man of genius, and even at his worst is a head and shoulders above the ordinary librettist . . . . his lyrics are suave and good to sing, and, wedded to Sir Arthur Sullivan's melodies, they will no doubt find their way to many a home where English song is appreciated."[39]

If Gilbert and Sullivan opera is a unique genre, then *The Yeomen of the Guard* is unique within the genre. Both men thought that it was the best of their operas, and for Gilbert it was just about as serious as he would want to go. He had created the character of Jack Point, the jester, who "may wear a merry laugh upon his lip" but whose "laughter has an echo that is grim." And he had created the lugubrious jailer, Wilfred Shadbolt, who with his "pretty wit" saw himself as a possible jester. Together, they make a comical couple and in their duet, "Hereupon We're Both Agreed," they never fail to captivate the audience.

Sullivan was justly proud of his overture, which Courtice Pounds said Sullivan thought "could be played at any Symphony concert, and be a credit to it."[40] Having given it his loving attention, he was sadly disappointed when the audience talked all through it. "I shall never take the trouble to write another," he said to the young Henry Wood, who had been engaged as accompanist for the rehearsals. "Next time I shall get you or Ernest Ford to score a medley of tunes."[41] Among all the overtures, it stands out, with its imposing "Tower of London" theme, lightened by the theme of "Were I Thy Bride" and the poignant "When a Wooer Goes A-Wooing." A snatch of Jack Point's "Oh a Private Buffoon," is rendered sad by being taken at a slower tempo and by the plaintive notes of the clarinet. Sullivan had captured the moods of the opera and summed up the whole work brilliantly: all to no avail, he thought, as the audience chatted and fumbled about. He felt as though he was casting pearls before the unappreciative.

CHAPTER TWENTY-THREE

1888-1889

"I Have Lost the Liking for
Writing Comic Opera"

D'OYLY CARTE HAD NOT given up on his idea to move his theatrical interest away from the Savoy Theatre. It was not his intention to sell the theater, merely to rent it. Following the building of the Savoy Theatre, it had taken him much longer than he had anticipated to raise the capital for his next two major ventures: the hotel and the opera house. Among his shareholders in the "Savoy Mansions Hotel" scheme were relatives, friends, and business associates, including his brother and sister, Carl Rosa, George Grossmith, François Cellier, George Edwardes, and Augustus Harris. Fanny Ronalds worked on a commission basis, receiving one share for every ten shares she sold.[1] Sullivan and Michael Gunn were major shareholders and directors of the board.

By the end of 1888, while the Savoy Hotel was beginning to rise on the Embankment, Carte's new theater also was beginning to take shape on its site in the recently developed Shaftesbury Avenue. As slum houses were cleared in the area and the roads widened, sites became available for development, and Gilbert, also intending to build a theater, acquired a site in the new Charing Cross Road, opposite the Beefsteak Club.

As soon as *The Yeomen of the Guard* had opened, Carte contacted Charles Wyndham, his prospective tenant for the Savoy Theatre to assure him that they would be moving. Certainly Gilbert's position had shifted a little; he was at least considering, reluctantly, the possibility of a move to Shaftesbury Avenue. Carte ended his letter to Wyndham by pointing out that he had had the Savoy cleaned and a new curtain put in. No complaint from Gilbert over the expense has come to light; presumably there was none. Gilbert had his own problems at the time over the building of his new theater, the Garrick. During construction, an underground stream had been discovered, giving rise to a joke from Gilbert that he was thinking of leasing the fishing rights rather than a theater. Progress had been slow and unsatisfactory, and in October Gilbert was forced to dismiss the architect and employ C. J. Phipps to complete the job.[2]

Gilbert had "plunged all [his] available capital & a good deal more" into building the Garrick, he explained to John Hare, who would be its manager for the next seven years. It had cost £43,000 to build, and £15,000 of that sum Gilbert had obtained on a loan. Repayment on the loan plus other expenses, such as ground rent, rates, and insurance, came to about £2,500 a year, resulting in a rent for Hare of about £4,000. At first, Hare queried the high rent, but acquiesced after Gilbert detailed the costs of this "most risky & utterly inconvertible form of security."[3] The theater was to open on 24 April 1889 with Pinero's *The Profligate*, in the absence of Gilbert, but in the presence of Sullivan who wrote a song, "E Tu nol Sai," especially for the play.

The Yeomen of the Guard opened in New York at the Casino Theatre on 17 October 1888. J. H. Ryley, who was popular with American audiences, played Jack Point, but on the whole it was a weak cast, and the opera ran for only 100 performances. By contrast, the first provincial performance of *The Yeomen*, at the Prince's Theatre Manchester on 1 November, had a strong company that included many of those who had appeared in New York in *The Mikado* and *Ruddigore*: George Thorne as Jack Point, David Fisher as Shadbolt, and Fred Billington as Sergeant Meryll. It was at Manchester that George Thorne interpreted the final scene as ending with the death of Jack Point. A month later in Bath, Henry Lytton, with the "E" Company, also played the tragic ending for Jack Point. The stage direction states simply, "Fairfax *embraces* Elsie *as* Point *falls insensible at their feet*." It does not require an imaginative leap of genius for an actor to see the possibility of playing that scene tragically; most actors playing Jack Point have interpreted it in this way, and it is not surprising that both Thorne and Lytton did so. Years later, a dispute arose over who thought of it first, with both men claiming Gilbert's sanction for the interpretation.[4] The fact that "the tragic death" was allowed to continue shows that Gilbert was satisfied to leave the interpretation open.

During the course of October, Sullivan solved two problems that had bothered him so much when he had been ill earlier in the year. First, as president of the Birmingham and Midland Institute, he agreed to distribute prizes and deliver an address in Birmingham Town Hall on 19 October. The prospect of this ordeal had terrified him. He delivered his carefully written address, which George Grove had helped him prepare, slowly and clearly, and felt afterward that it had been well received. His speech was in praise of English music. He recalled past achievements, stressed the increased role of music in education, and singled out for praise George Grove and his staff at the Royal College of Music. "We must be educated to appreciate," he said, "and appreciation must come before production. Give us intelligent and educated listeners and we shall provide composers and performers of corresponding worth."[5]

The second problem was the question of a new composition for the Leeds Festival of 1889. This he resolved at the end of October, by writing to the committee to decline their invitation. More to his liking was a commission that he accepted from Henry Irving: to write the incidental music for *Macbeth* at the Lyceum. The performance was scheduled for 29 December, and with his usual last-minute rush Sullivan completed his score on Boxing Day.

Gilbert had been faced with a frantic rush of his own in the preceding month. Rutland Barrington's first play at St. James's was a failure, and Gilbert's play was needed as soon as possible. He rushed on an old play, *Brantinghame Hall,* which had not previously been produced.[6] The play was considered sentimental, and a few good comedy scenes for Barrington and his brother, Duncan Fleet, could not redeem it. Some of the more recently written dialogue in *Brantinghame Hall,* however, gave a foretaste of Gilbert's next work with Sullivan: "And all property ought to belong to everybody or nearly everybody—equally. And there oughtn't to be any Bishops, or rich men—or scarcely any—."[7]

The Cartes were sufficiently impressed by the manuscript to offer to place the play in New York, and Gilbert willingly accepted their terms, but when the play opened at the St. James's on 27 November, it was a failure. Gilbert was bitterly disappointed, not only for himself but also for Julia Neilson, particularly when his old friend Clement Scott attacked the play. He assured Scott he had written his last play, and trusted that Scott was gratified to think that he had effectively stifled the career of a promising actress suffering from stage fright.

Both Gilbert and Julia Neilson recovered from the failure: Gilbert wrote a few more plays, and Julia Neilson went on to a highly successful career in the theater, both in acting and later in management with her husband, Fred Terry. Meanwhile, Gilbert had broken off all friendly relations with Clement Scott, and threatened to sue Scott for libel when a rumor was circulated that Gilbert had suggested to the editor of the *Daily Telegraph* that he sack Scott. The ensuing publicity was detrimental to Gilbert and did nothing to save *Brantinghame Hall* nor Rutland Barrington, who had two failures behind him in his new role as manager. More seriously for Barrington, he was now bankrupt.

Three days after the opening of *Brantinghame Hall,* Gilbert released Carte "unconditionally" from his agreement to place the play in New York.[8] While thanking Gilbert for his "generous offer," Carte's first reaction was to ignore the press and wait to see what the reaction of the public would be to the play.[9] He did not have to wait long for the answer.

The last weeks of 1888 had not brought Gilbert the success he had hoped for. Neither did Sullivan achieve with his music to *Macbeth* the kind of congratulations he would have expected. "Self restraint, subordination, and assimilation to a higher purpose," commented *The Times,* "become in such circumstances almost as important as creative genius; and these virtues Sir Arthur Sullivan has had every opportunity of practising during his long association with Mr. Gilbert."[10] To judge from Sullivan's reaction shortly after *Macbeth*, these words may well have affected his attitude to further work with Gilbert.

On Christmas Eve, Kitty went to the Savoy to see *The Yeomen* and reported back to her husband. Judging from Gilbert's letter to Carte, written on Christmas Day, it was not her first report on the piece.

> My wife was at the Savoy yesterday. She saw nothing to object to in the "business" of the duet—"Were I thy bride." Perhaps they have toned it down on a hint from you. But she *did* see a good deal to object to in the business of the trio "a man who would woo a fair maid" in Act 2. She says that Ulmar & Bond go a great deal too far in pinching & tickling Grossmith—tweaking his nose & punching him about. Now whatever they do should be done *neatly* & *delicately*—& not *over*done. I wish you would look at this, some night & judge for yourself.
>
> Have you thought over my proposition re the new Theatre?[11]

Gilbert was referring to a suggestion that Carte use his new theater for revivals of Offenbach as well as revivals of their own work. Carte did not receive Gilbert's letter until 27 December—a delay of only two days, and that over Christmas—but Carte concluded that the post must be out of order: an interesting comment on the efficiency the Victorians expected from the postal service. He immediately looked into the matter raised by Gilbert and wrote to him on 28 December, reporting that he had spoken to the actors concerned "and it will be I have no doubt right tonight. I shall see that it is." He had given careful thought to Gilbert's idea for the new theater. "I think it is a good idea and I have no doubt that those operas done anew by you, with the great advantage of your personal supervision and stage arrangements, and done as we would do them, would draw. The only question is to what extent, and how long would they run."[12]

By temperament, Carte was against the idea of revivals. He was an innovator. He had opened the first theatrical agency in the country; he had built a theater for English comic opera; he was the first to light a theater by electricity—he wanted new works in a new theater. He deferred any decision until they met Sullivan and heard his views about a new opera.

Carte's original idea of "a fresh start" with a new company had run up against Gilbert's more pragmatic idea of continuing with the old Savoy company but playing a mixture of revivals. Carte was opposed to Gilbert's suggestion on business grounds. As events turned out, Gilbert's suggestion was a better business proposition than the one Carte eventually opted for.

As the year drew to its close, Carte saw the possibility of losing his tenant for the Savoy as Charles Wyndham, tempted by an available site near Gilbert's theater in Charing Cross Road, was beginning to talk of building his own theater.

Carte and Gilbert called on Sullivan in Queen's Mansions on 9 January to discuss the issue. In his diary for the day, Sullivan has left a clear and concise account of the views he put to Gilbert.

Explained to [Gilbert] my view as to the future—viz: that I wanted to do some dramatic work on a larger musical scale, & that of course I should like to do it with him if he would—but that the music must occupy a more important position than in our other pieces—that I wished to get rid of the *strongly marked rhythms*, and rhymed *couplets*—& have words which would give a chance of developing *musical* effects. Also that I wanted a voice in the *musical construction* of the libretto. He seemed quite to assent to all this.[13]

The diary account makes no mention of the other issues, concerning the future of the Savoy company and the Savoy Theatre. This is not surprising. Three people at a meeting will have three different perceptions of what took place, and Sullivan's mind was concentrated on the single issue of his grand opera. Carte had not got the clear-cut decision he wanted concerning his new theater.

"Very weak & depressed," Sullivan wrote in his diary for 17 January.[14] It was time for Sullivan to take a long break away from London. Before leaving, he was invited as one of the prince of Wales' house guests to Sandringham on 18 January, where he met the widow of the Kaiser Frederick with her three daughters. "I was quite touched by her affectionate greeting of me. I really couldn't speak."[15]

Sullivan left for the south of France on Tuesday, 12 February, crossing over from Calais on a "special" boat with the prince of Wales and Reuben Sassoon. After supper with the prince in Calais, Sullivan and Sassoon continued their journey to Paris and then Sullivan went on to Monte Carlo. By now, Sullivan's reputation as a gambler was being talked about in the press, and he hastened to assure his secretary, Smythe, that what was written about him was "untrue rubbish. I did one day have 5 louis on Zero & it came up—that has been my most distinguished feat!"[16] His diary reveals a different picture. Tuesday, 19 February, shows him losing 3,000 francs, then, having drawn more money out of the bank, winning 11,000 francs before going on to play bezique, where he won another 1,600 francs. Visits to the casino did not improve his mental state. He was still in low spirits, with the pressure of having to do another comic opera weighing on him, whereas he much preferred the idea of writing a grand opera—with Gilbert, if that were possible.

From Monte Carlo, Sullivan wrote to Gilbert, expanding on what he had said in their meeting on 9 January. Gilbert's reply on 20 February takes up the points of Sullivan's letter. Gilbert was sympathetic to Sullivan's wish to write a grand opera, but pointed out that such an opera would require "a much more powerful singing & acting company" than they had at the Savoy. A grand opera would not, he thought, give him a chance of doing what he did best—"the librettist of a grand Opera is always swamped in the composer." As for the subject of a proposed opera, Gilbert thought that *The Yeomen* was about as serious as they should go in a work together. "We have a name, jointly, for humorous work, tempered with occasional glimpses of earnest drama—I think we should do unwisely if we left, altogether, the path which we have trodden together so long & so successfully."

He understood Sullivan's desire to write a bigger work, but suggested that Sullivan should do both:

Are the two things irreconcilable? As to leaving the Savoy—I can only say that I should do so with the profoundest reluctance & regret. I dont believe in Cartes new Theatre—the site is not popular—and cannot become popular for some years to come. Our names are known all over the world in connection with the Savoy, & I feel convinced that it would be madness to sever the connections with that theatre.[17]

If Sullivan wanted to write a grand opera, Gilbert suggested Julian Sturgis as the "best serious librettist of the day."[18] Gilbert's own attempts at such work, he was convinced "would be, deservedly or otherwise, generally pooh-poohed."[19]

This was not the reply Sullivan expected or wanted; it did nothing to lift him out of his despondency. He replied to Gilbert on 12 March, saying that he had hoped *The Yeomen of the Guard* was the beginning of "works of a more serious & romantic character." He could not go back, he said. "I have lost the liking for writing comic opera." It had even become "distasteful" to him, writing for the usual stock-characters such as "the middle-aged woman with fading charms."[20]

By this point in his letter, he would have managed, though not out of malice, to upset Gilbert deeply. But he went even further. He took up Gilbert's point about his having to sacrifice himself as a librettist if he were to attempt a grand opera. "I say that this is just what I have been doing in all our joint pieces, and, what is more, must continue to do in Comic Opera to make it successful." He wanted to do a work where the music was "the first consideration—where words are to suggest music not govern it." To Gilbert's concern that it would be foolish to leave the Savoy, Sullivan reminded him that, by September, few of the old Savoy company would be left. "Grossmith goes; Barrington has gone. Temple wants to go, & Miss Ulmar *must* go. We can't keep her on. Consequently there will remain on [*sic*] Jessie, Brandram, Pounds & Denny, two of them admirable for comic opera—the other two stronger vocally than histrionically."

Sullivan claimed to be looking for some "modus vivendi," and having categorically stated that he did not want to write any more comic operas, he then hinted at the possibility of their working together again, leaving Gilbert to make the next move—"we seem to be in an 'impasse,' & unless you can solve the difficulty I don't see my way out of it."[21]

Gilbert's reply on 19 March was sent to Venice where Sullivan arrived, via Genoa and Verona, on 20 March. "Your letter has filled me with amazement & regret," he began. He was more wounded by the first part of Sullivan's letter than he was encouraged by Sullivan's slight hint that he might change his mind. Sullivan had wanted to be wooed; and Gilbert was not in the mood for wooing. If Sullivan thought that he had been "effacing" himself for the last twelve years and wanted to write an opera in which "the music shall be the first consideration (by which I understand an opera in which the libretto, & consequently the librettist, must occupy a subordinate place)," said Gilbert, then there could be no satisfactory "modus vivendi." As in Sullivan's letter, so in Gilbert's: the first part seemed final and unmoving, and then came a glimmer of hope. "You are an adept in your profession & I am an adept in mine. If we meet, it must be as master & master—not as master & servant."[22]

Now it was Sullivan's turn to feel annoyed and hurt; but instead of replying directly to Gilbert, he decided to write to Carte on 26 March and to express his feelings about his own position in the theater in comparison with Gilbert's, feelings that must have been festering over a long period. The letter was addressed "My dear Carte," and not his usual "My dear D'Oyly"—a clear indication to Carte that the whole letter was intended for Gilbert's eyes. Sullivan complained that Gilbert's reply to his letter was "only a few lines of huffy resentment at one or two of my sentences." If Gilbert was not prepared to argue the points he raised, then Sullivan regretted that there was nothing further he could do to settle the issue. "There is one point in Gilbert's letter on which I cordially agree with him—If we meet it must be as master & master, not as master & servant."

If only that were the case, Sullivan argued, "unnecessary friction" would be avoided, "for *excepting during the voice rehearsals, and the two Orchestral rehearsals I am a cipher in the theatre* once the stage rehearsals begin *and Gilbert is supreme* until the fall of the curtain on the last rehearsal . . . *the music has always had to give way to words & business. In nothing else is my opinion allowed to have weight*, in dresses, scenery, make up, or lights. *They are Gilbert's pieces, with music added by me.*" Twelve years of working in this way had made him tired of the process and unless changes were made to their method of working, he would rather "give it up altogether."

On the rehearsal system Sullivan felt particularly strongly. Everyone was called to each rehearsal and there was too much waiting around; as a result, everyone was tired and "my music gets cruelly murdered." The solution was for Gilbert to hold "all his preliminary rehearsals in sections—Dialogue, Chorus, & Principals all separate, and bringing them all together the last week or ten days."

If Gilbert was prepared to agree to his views, then Sullivan would collaborate in a new piece. Otherwise, that would be the end of the matter. And then, knowing full well that Gilbert would read his letter, Sullivan concluded: "I write to *you* because I hate quarrelling with old friends, & I should certainly say something unfortunate if I wrote to Gilbert."[23]

Carte immediately took the letter around to Gilbert and left it with him; and on the same day, Friday, 29 March, Gilbert responded. "I return Sullivan's letter. I needn't tell *you* that it is most monstrous & unfair & unjust & false in every detail. Will you & Mrs. Carte dine with us tomorrow at 8. We can then discuss the future of the Theatre at our leisure. It is of course impossible that I can ever write with Sullivan again."[24]

That very day Carte cabled Sullivan. "Have you received my three letters are you coming straight from Venice to Adelphi Terrace now is the crisis if nothing settled before Gilbert leaves Saturday week whole thing must break up cannot leave matters in suspense."[25]

By that time, Sullivan's second letter had already been written and was on its way to England. It arrived on 30 March, dated 27 March; this time it was addressed directly to Gilbert. In a sense, it is the second part of one letter to Gilbert, the first part purportedly to Carte. Splitting the letter in this way enabled him to be more forthright in his views while claiming that he did not want to upset Gilbert in expressing them. In the second half, he expressed himself in a way that he hoped Gilbert would find unobjectionable.

Sullivan asked for three things: first, that his judgment and opinion should have some weight in the musical situation; second, that he should have "a more important share in arranging the attitudes and business in all the musical portions"; and third, that "the rehearsals should be arranged in such a way as not to weary the voices, & cause everyone to sing carelessly and without any regard for tune, time, or accent. . . . If you accept all this in the same spirit in which I write, we can go on smoothly as if nothing had happened, & I hope successfully. If not, I shall regret it deeply, but, in any case, you will hear no more recriminations on my part."[26]

What had led to this volte-face on Sullivan's part—from a categorical refusal to write another comic opera, to the point where he suggests, reasonably, an alteration in their method of working together, leaving it to Gilbert to decide if they are to continue?

The answer probably lies in the three letters that Carte had sent Sullivan, and to which he had received no reply. The reality of the situation, which Carte would have impressed on Sullivan, was that *The Yeomen of the Guard*, whose returns were down during Lent (mentioned in Sullivan's letter of 26 March) could not survive until the new theater was ready. Important income for Carte would be lacking, he would not be able to keep the Savoy Theatre open, he would not have the necessary finance to produce a large work at the new theater; and Sullivan's own income would be drastically reduced. The picture was clear in Carte's mind: he needed another Gilbert and Sullivan opera for the Savoy, and then he could offer Sullivan the opportunity of opening the new theater with his own grand opera.

Gilbert replied to Sullivan's second letter on 31 March. "The requirements contained in your letter of the 27th are just & reasonable in every way," Gilbert began. So far so good. Gilbert agreed to Sullivan's first point about his judgment and opinion being important in "the laying out of the musical situations, even to making important alterations after the work has been framed." However, Gilbert challenged Sullivan to name an instance when it was not already the case in their work together. As to the third point in Sullivan's letter, concerning rehearsals, Gilbert replied, "how am I to know that you object . . . unless you tell me so?" and went on to suggest that acting and singing rehearsals might be taken separately until the last week. On Sullivan's second point, concerning Sullivan's share "in arranging the attitudes & business in all the musical portions," Gilbert tartly commented that Sullivan was *"probably . . . not present at more than one* [rehearsal] *in six during the first fortnight when the business has to be arranged."* But as far as Gilbert was concerned, those matters were not now the only consideration.

> If that letter stood alone there would be nothing to prevent our embarking at once, in a cheerful & friendly spirit, upon the work which (subject to your approval) I have been constructing during the last 10 days. But unhappily the letter does not stand alone. It was preceded by a letter to Carte (avowedly written that its contents might be communicated to me) which teems with unreasonable demands & utterly groundless accusations—.

Gilbert rejects Sullivan's claim that he was "a cipher in the theatre" and that his opinion carried no weight in the arrangement of "business."

> You say that our operas are "Gilbert's pieces with music added by you," & that Carte can hardly wonder that 12 years of this has a little tired you. I say that when you deliberately assert that for 12 years you, incomparably the greatest English musician of the age—a man whose genius is a proverb wherever the English tongue is spoken—. . . deliberately state that you have submitted silently & uncomplainingly for 12 years to be extinguished, ignored, set aside, rebuffed & generally effaced by your librettist, you grievously reflect, not upon him, but upon yourself & the noble art of which you are so eminent a professor.[27]

Gilbert did not say in this letter, as he had in his note to Carte, that he would not work with Sullivan again. Sullivan's second letter had made a difference, even if Gilbert had seen through his ploy.

Gilbert's letter did not reach Sullivan until 6 April, the day Gilbert and Kitty left on a Mediterranean cruise heading for Gibraltar, their first port of call. The same day Sullivan decided to leave Venice, travel to Budapest and then on to Vienna. Both Gilbert and Sullivan were on the move, but heading in different directions.

After several days in Vienna, including a night at the opera to see *Lohengrin*, Sullivan traveled on to Paris. On 17 April, he met up with Carte, who was there with his two sons and Sullivan's nephew. Serious discussions began about the future, and the possibility of another opera with Gilbert. They traveled back to London together, where they continued their discussion until they came to an agreement. They both decided to write to Gilbert on 24 April, the very day that Gilbert's new theater, the Garrick, opened.

Meanwhile, the Gilberts had continued with their cruise: sailing to Algiers, then on to Malta and Palermo, and back through the Straits of Gibraltar, to call at Trafalgar and Cadiz. On 1 May they set sail from Cadiz and docked at Plymouth on Sunday, 5 May. Gilbert had left his itinerary with Carte and it was to Trafalgar that Carte and Sullivan addressed their letters of 24 April; to be on the safe side, Sullivan had sent another letter to Cadiz. Gilbert received none of them. As Carte had heard nothing, on 4 May he sent a copy of his original letter together with a covering note to Plymouth. Only on his arrival at Plymouth did Gilbert receive Carte's news:

> Sullivan is prepared to write you at once another Comic Opera for the Savoy on the old lines, if you are willing also. . . . As an inducement to him I have agreed with him that his "Grand Opera" shall be produced at my New Theatre later on. I think this is not a bad arrangement. . . . I think too that he really likes to keep up the collaboration which has existed for so many years, as I need not say I do.[29]

Sullivan, too, had written to Gilbert and sent copies of his earlier letters to Plymouth, saying much the same as Carte: "I am quite prepared to set to work at once upon a light or comic opera with you, (provided of course that we are thoroughly agreed about the subject) and to think no more of our rather sharp discussion." Now that he had been given the opportunity of producing an opera "on a large scale," and had been promised that the new theatre would be kept for this purpose, Sullivan felt that he could "realize the great desire of [his] life," while at the same time continue a collaboration which he regarded "with a stronger sentiment than that of pecuniary advantage." He was prepared to set to work immediately on the new Savoy piece. "How will this fit in with your arrangements?"[30]

Gilbert must have found his homecoming more welcome than he had anticipated.

CHAPTER TWENTY-FOUR

The Gondoliers

WHEN GILBERT ARRIVED BACK in London on Tuesday 7 May, he contacted Carte. He was still feeling hurt by Sullivan's comments, but was willing to move forward and collaborate again. Sullivan assured him that, if his previous comments had caused him pain, he regretted having made them. Carte had passed on to Sullivan Gilbert's idea of using the subject of a theatrical company for the new opera, and Sullivan was not slow in reminding Gilbert that it was a subject that had once before nearly brought their collaboration to an end. He preferred an alternative idea, a subject connected with Venice and Venetian life, which held out the possibility of writing bright music. The next day Gilbert and Sullivan met for a frank discussion, airing their differences and their grievances. At the end of the day, Sullivan recorded in his diary, "Shook hands & buried the hatchet."[1]

Back on friendly terms, Sullivan invited Gilbert and Kitty to dinner to celebrate his birthday on 13 May. That year it was a dinner for close friends and family. As well as the Gilberts, Sullivan invited George Lewis and his wife, Tom Chappell and his wife, Fanny Ronalds and her son Reg, and Bertie. There was to have been one other guest, "William Lacy asked but didn't turn up," says Sullivan's diary for the day.[2]

The happiness of that friendly reunion was shortly followed by sadness when, in the early hours of 22 May, Fanny Ronalds's father died. Along with Fanny and her two children, Sullivan had been at his bedside. Three days later, "in the sunshine & under a large plane tree, we consigned the poor old gdpa to his last rest," he wrote.[3] Sullivan was like one of the family, calling Fanny's parents "grandpa and grandma," while Bertie used to call Fanny "auntie." Sullivan, too, began to refer to her in his diary as auntie from that year onward, showing the change that had taken place in their relationship. No longer did the checks and numbers occur beside the initials L.W.; instead Sullivan was showing interest in another woman who appears in his diary around this time. For 7 June, he wrote, "Drove down to Richmond to dine with ABC.✓"[4]

A month after starting work on the new opera, Gilbert had his sketch plot ready for Sullivan and called at Queen's Mansions on Saturday afternoon, 8 June, to read it to him. Sullivan was pleased, noting that he thought it "Bright, interesting, funny & very pretty."[5] In the evening, they both went to see Frank Wyatt in *Paul Jones*, in search of a replacement for George Grossmith, who was leaving the Savoy company in August. Barrington, by contrast, after his disastrous venture into management, wanted to return to the Savoy. "He now asks £27.0.0 a week," said Carte to Gilbert in a letter of 18 June. Carte offered him £25, an increase of £3 on his last engagement. "I dont suppose that anything he has done since has rendered him more valuable to us than he was then."[6] Barrington was signed on, and so was his brother, Duncan Fleet, to be one of Barrington's understudies.

When Jessie Bond was asked to renew her contract she declined, unless she were paid £30 a week. Such a salary was too much for Gilbert. He wrote to tell her so, pointing out that much of her success was due to the parts written for her. Nevertheless, Gilbert was outvoted by Sullivan and Carte, and to his annoyance Jessie Bond was given her £30.

Having received Sullivan's approval of the sketch plot, Gilbert went off to his country house, Breakspears, to work on the lyrics. Following Sullivan's request that the music play a more important part, Gilbert decided on a long musical introduction to the opera. He worked intensively on it over the next fortnight, and on Friday, 21 June, offered to read Sullivan act 1 the following Wednesday, telling him that "The first nine pages of MS are *all Music*, & no dialogue."[7]

Before making a start on the music, Sullivan decided to rent a house for the summer outside London, and in early July took Fanny Ronalds down to Weybridge to view Grove House, which proved suitable. His priority was the Leeds Festival, for which he had works to prepare and rehearsals to conduct. He traveled up to Leeds on 1 July, and again toward the end of the month, returning in time for 27 July and a "house-warming" supper for 210 guests at the Savoy Hotel.

On the last day of July, Sullivan was visited in Weybridge by Julian Sturgis who brought him a scenario of "Ivanhoe" to look over, and that they settled, in Sullivan's opinion, "very satisfactorily."[8] Sturgis would work at the libretto for Sullivan's grand opera while Sullivan got down to the music for the next opera with Gilbert. By this time he had already made a start on the first lyrics from Gilbert, writing the opening chorus "List and Learn" and Antonio's song, "For the Merriest Fellows Are We," on 15 July. A week later, he wrote the "entrance of the Duke of Vallodolid" who was to be renamed the Duke of Plaza-Toro.

While Sullivan continued with the music, composing "the Duke's song and the Grand Inquisitor's song" on 24 July, Gilbert was producing more lyrics for act 1, as well as making additions, improvements, and changes according to Sullivan's requirements and suggestions. On 8 August, Gilbert sent another verse to "Thank

You, Gallant *Gondolieri*" (Tessa's "Gay and gallant *gondolieri*") and also what he called an "expostulatory song for either of the girls, when the Grand Inquisitor informs them that they must be separated from their husbands." This number, "Kind Sir, You Cannot Have the Heart," Sullivan assigned to Gianetta. In the same batch, Gilbert included a "farewell duet, addressed by Tessa & Gianetta to their husbands—before the final chorus," namely the two verses, "Now, Marco Dear" for Gianetta, and "You'll Lay Your Head" for Tessa. In the note enclosing this group of famous songs, Gilbert added a modest, "I hope you will like the numbers."[9] After Sullivan's severe criticisms, Gilbert was making every effort to be as accommodating as possible.

A scenario for *The Gondoliers*, which dates almost exactly from this point in the construction of the opera, was sent to Sullivan, possibly with the letter of 8 August.[10] It still includes what has been called the "growling chorus," which Sullivan wanted cut and that was replaced by "For Everyone Who Feels Inclined." In a letter to Sullivan on 10 August, Gilbert objected to the idea of cutting this number, explaining that the "Venetians of the 15th Cent were red hot Republicans" who objected to the idea of one of them being made king. The story would be unintelligible, he claimed, without the chorus.[11]

Gilbert was deliberately exaggerating and was unable to convince Sullivan. A second chorus was cut; the political satire was weakened, but it was not lost; and the substitute song from Gilbert ("Rising Early in the Morning") was more in keeping with the joyful mood of the opera. The piece was to lose its fifteenth-century dating and to finish up somewhere in the eighteenth; Sullivan understood perfectly well that Gilbert's pieces only looked realistic, but all took place in some timeless "fairyland"—part of their enduring charm.

That same scenario contains a song for Gianetta, which was later cut. It was sung to the Grand Inquisitor and began: "Good sir, I wish to speak politely— / Forgive me if my words are crude —."[12] Gilbert must have forgotten that he sent Sullivan this particular song. Much later, on 9 November, he sent it to him again because Sullivan had wondered whether Gianetta's song, "Kind, Sir, You Cannot Have the Heart," was too long for the situation. "I have come across a song," Gilbert said, "which I wrote for the same situation. . . . If you don't like it as well as the other, tear it up."[13] Sullivan did not like it as well, and "Kind, sir," remained.

Also in the scenario of August, was the Grand Inquisitor's recitative, "Do Not Give Way to This Uncalled-for Grief," to which Gilbert had added a note: "*This can be expressed in dialogue if thought advisable*," and to which Sullivan appended "I have set this to music." The scenario continues with: "Then One of Us Will Be a Queen [Tessa or Gianetta or Quartette]," under which Sullivan wrote "Quartett [*sic*] much better (with chorus perhaps)." The final number in the scenario is "With Ducal Pomp & Ducal Pride," after which, Sullivan has written: "this I think might come out—it seems to me in the way & too much like the entrance in 1st. Act."[14] This time Gilbert insisted, and the number remained.

Eaton Square—number 90 was Gilbert's winter home for the last five years of his life

George Grossmith played Jack Point for the last time on Saturday, 17 August. Gilbert wanted to mark the occasion with a testimonial, and suggested that they present him with "a piece of plate worth (say) £50—which wont hurt us three much."[15] Grossmith's understudy, John Wilkinson, took over as Jack Point and played the part until the end of the run. Gilbert was opposed to the selection of Wilkinson, "but as I am in the minority I must give in," he had said resignedly to Sullivan.[16]

Sullivan broke off from composing *The Gondoliers* to attend the Three Choirs Festival, obliging him to travel down to Gloucester twice: first, for a day's rehearsal on 2 September, and then for the performance itself on 5 September. After conducting *The Prodigal Son, In Memoriam,* and *The Golden Legend* he preferred to return home the same evening, arriving in London at 2:25 a.m.

On the same day that Sullivan was rehearsing in Gloucester, one of Gilbert's old pieces opened in Plymouth. It was his adaptation of Offenbach's *Les Brigands* (with words by Meilhac and Halévy), which he had written twenty years before. The production in Plymouth was to be a prelude to later performances at the Avenue Theatre in London. Gilbert objected to the fact that arrangements had already being made without consulting him, and maintained that his adaptation had been made for Boosey's only for copyright purposes and not for performance. Gilbert's memory was at fault, as he later admitted, and the production went ahead despite his objection.[17] Gilbert applied for and was granted a temporary injunction to restrain Boosey's from publishing the libretto, but when the case came up the following

1889

week, Gilbert lost and was ordered to pay costs. Gilbert's objection to the publication of the libretto was occasioned by the addition of two songs of inferior quality. He published one of the songs in a letter to *The Times*, commenting ironically, "I think I am entitled to ask that I shall not be made to shine with the lustre of another man's intellect."[18]

A different class of lyric altogether from the interpolated songs in *Les Brigands* was that of "In a Contemplative Fashion," which Gilbert was working on at exactly the same time as the dispute with Boosey's. After conducting at Gloucester, Sullivan had studied Gilbert's lyric and asked him for some alterations. In view of the subsequent success of the song, it is surprising now to think that Gilbert had not made a copy of the lyric and had to ask Sullivan on 11 September to return the original to him. This particular number caused a sensation when it was first heard, and the weaving together of two melodies was found intriguing. It is also intriguing to consider the stages through which the song passed before reaching its finished form.

Gilbert's original lyric consisted of the quartet of Marco, Giuseppe, Gianetta, and Tessa singing in unison:

> In a contemplative fashion,
> And a tranquil frame of mind,
> Free from every kind of passion,
> Some solution let us find. [etc.][19]

The first half of the number then consisted of a verse of four lines sung by each of the four singers:

> I, no doubt, Giuseppe wedded —
> That's, of course, a slice of luck. [etc.]

Gilbert's suggestion to Sullivan was that the chorus "In a Contemplative Fashion" be sung at the same time as the verses. Sullivan set it as requested, but when it came to setting the second half of the number, he did not wish to repeat himself, so he asked Gilbert for lines that would be a contrast to the first half.

On 12 September, Gilbert sent him the new lines, saying: "Will this do? Its dactylic but it is difficult to get the contrast you want without dactyls."[20] The lines he sent in dactylic meter (one stressed syllable followed by two short) produced the following:

Mar	Now it seems that when we were two beautiful babies,
	A lady was married to one of us here.
Gia	And if I can catch her
	I'll pinch her and scratch her
	And send her away with a flea in her ear.
Giu.	It certainly seems that whichever she wedded
	Must yield to her title, & cannot refuse

Tess.	If I overtake her
	I'll warrant I'll make her
	To shake in her aristocratical shoes!
Gia.	If she should turn out to have married Giuseppe
(to Tess.)	Then you from Giuseppe would have to depart
Tess	If I have to do it
(to Gia)	I'll warrant she'll rue it—
	I'll teach her to marry the man of my heart!
Tess	If Marco she married, your lot will be bitter—
(to Gia)	Her mother's the mightiest Duchess of Spain
Gia	No matter—no matter
(to Tess)	If I can get at her
	I doubt if her mother will know her again![21]

Gilbert's letter to Sullivan continued:

> Probably it will be impracticable to set the accompanying lines "In a contemplative fashion," so as to be a running accompaniment to the verses as they now stand. If so, I suppose they could be omitted during the verses and introduced at the end to finish with. If the verses won't do, send them back and I'll try again.[22]

If Sullivan were to achieve the same effect as in the first half, he would need changes to Gilbert's lines for the second half. The first half had been in iambic meter (a stressed syllable followed by an unstressed) and had served his needs very well, and he needed the monotony of the dactylic meter to be broken up. On 22 September, Gilbert wrote to Sullivan:

> I have altered the "In a contemplative fashion" as you suggested. The only question is whether the last two verses, which the girls sing at each other—& with which the two men have nothing to do—wouldn't be better in the original flowing metre, as lending itself better to the volubility of two angry girls. I dont care a pin, myself, which it is, but I thought you might find the original dactylic metre better for that particular purpose. Just as you like—here it is, in both forms.[23]

The paper in the D'Oyly Carte Collection that contains Gilbert's original dactylic meter as just quoted has the new alternative lines written alongside, squeezed in on the original sheet:

Alongside	Now it seems that when we were two beautiful babies.
	A lady was married to one of us here.
is written	Now when we were pretty babies
	Someone married us—that's clear.
and beside	It certainly seems that whichever she wedded
	Must yield to her title, & cannot refuse

is written	He whom that young lady married,
	To receive her can't refuse.[24]

And the lyrics continue in exactly the form that they finally appeared in the libretto.

Gilbert concludes his letter of 22 September with a postscript. "It has just occurred to me that a good effect might be produced by continuing the 'Let us grasp the situation (pp) through the second half of the number . . . Is it practicable—& if so, will it be an improvement?"[25]

If this theoretical reconstruction is correct, one cannot help but think that Sullivan had already foreseen Gilbert's request and had been working toward such an effect, but went further by having all the singers repeating some of their lines together in total confusion before the final calm chorus. Gilbert's initial idea had been paid back with interest, and matured into one of Gilbert and Sullivan's most successful numbers.

Sullivan left his house in Weybridge on 19 September, and a period of intense activity followed. He was in Leeds on Saturday, 21 September, for a choral rehearsal and then was back in London on the Sunday, rehearsing Geraldine Ulmar, Courtice Pounds, Jessie Bond, and Rutland Barrington, the four singers in the complicated number he had written, "In a Contemplative Fashion." The following day he took orchestral rehearsals for the Leeds Festival; this did not require his traveling to Leeds, as the orchestral players were engaged in London. All the time he was in communication with Gilbert about requirements for *The Gondoliers*; Gilbert was tackling "The Nurse's Ballad" at the end of act 2, and told Sullivan he had decided to turn it into a dramatic recitative, to avoid reminding the audience of Buttercup's song at the end of *Pinafore*. But the stage had now been reached when any response from Sullivan would have to wait; *The Gondoliers* had to take second place for a while as Sullivan devoted all his time to Leeds.

On 4 October, with Louis and Clotilde and two other servants, Sullivan traveled to Leeds, where the Judge's Lodgings were again to become his temporary home during the festival. Rehearsals filled the first three days and then the festival itself ran from Wednesday to Saturday. Two performances a day were given, and apart from two new works conducted by the composers themselves, Sullivan conducted them all. On the Saturday evening, the festival concluded with Sullivan conducting *The Golden Legend*: "Last Concert superb performance of 'Golden Legend,'" he recorded. "The finest I have ever heard—afterwards the enthusiasm was indescribable—cheering & waving their handkerchiefs at me for minutes."[26] To have conducted what he considered his finest work at the Leeds Festival and to find it greeted with such acclaim was a high moment in his musical career. To the orchestra he showed his gratitude by seeing them off at the station on their "special" train to London. Only then did he go off for supper and enjoy a period of quiet satisfaction.

While Sullivan had been busy in Leeds, Gilbert attempted to finish the libretto. He had written "a nice little ballad for Pounds . . . and a good rattling song for Barrington," he told Sullivan. He also had transferred "Now I'm About to Kiss Your Hand" from the Grand Inquisitor to the Duke, as Denny already had a song in act 2. "I couldn't consult you about this, as you were busy in Leeds, so I have done it on the chance of your agreeing to it—if you don't, it can be restored to Denny." Sullivan agreed to that particular change. Gilbert had also decided to cut the Duchess's song, "On the Day When I Was Wedded," saying that it "stopped the action of the piece" and he did not think "it was the kind of song that would show her [Rosina Brandram] off effectively. However it can easily be restored, if you like."[27] Sullivan disagreed, and the song was restored. Gilbert's customary reading of the libretto took place at the Savoy Hotel on Thursday, 17 October, in front of only six of the principals, and was followed by a music rehearsal with Sullivan.

The opera was still not finished: Sullivan had several numbers to write, as well as the alterations suggested by Gilbert. On 25 October, Gilbert told Sullivan that he wanted to rewrite "Now I'm About to Kiss Your Hand," "making it more musically rhythmical & ending with a minuet for Wyatt & Barrington . . . Wyatt & Barrington are both such excellent dancers that it seems a pity to miss so good a chance of utilizing them. What do you think? (Pounds could accompany them on a mandolin—play the dance music, I mean)."[28] Sullivan preferred a gavotte, and Pounds joined in the dancing.

And so it went on: Gilbert suggesting alterations, Sullivan producing countersuggestions, Sullivan asking for modifications, Gilbert supplying alternative lyrics. If Gilbert and Sullivan were not exactly working "as one individual," they were working together more closely than ever before. In the early days of November, Sullivan was feeling exceptionally tired. After a prolonged period of composition for *The Gondoliers*, he had gone straight into the Leeds Festival, with its hours of preparation and rehearsals before the additional drain on his energy of the performances themselves; he had then gone back immediately to working on the opera with Gilbert, all the time trying to come up with something bright and cheerful. Unusually for Sullivan, he was too tired to visit his mother's grave on her birthday, which was his normal practice, and he sent his servant Clotilde to lay a cross of flowers on the grave for him. The following day, he felt too tired to go to a music rehearsal that had been called, and in its place Gilbert held a makeshift stage rehearsal of part of act 1. Instead of reacting ill temperedly to this sudden change of plan, Gilbert showed his concern for Sullivan by calling around to see him after the rehearsal, and the next day called on Sullivan to accompany him to the Savoy.

Despite his tiredness, on 2 November Sullivan wrote "Here Is a Fix," a name that was later changed to "Here Is a Case Unprecedented," one of the brightest and merriest numbers of all the Gilbert and Sullivan operas. Starting work at 11:00 p.m. on 4 November, the day he was too tired to attend rehearsals, he composed three numbers, and rewrote "Rising Early in the Morning." On his last day of composition, Friday, 8 November, Sullivan rewrote two numbers and then composed "There Lived a King" followed by "Take a Pair of Sparkling Eyes," finishing at 5:00 a.m. on the Saturday morning.

Gilbert — self-portrait drawn in Homburg, 1893 (V&A Picture Library)

The next day he began scoring the opera and proceeded at a remarkable rate. It took him only four days to score the first lengthy number, eighteen minutes or so of music, unbroken by dialogue, and for which he completed ninety pages of scoring. He kept up the pace until he finished on 25 November. He had made an exception to attend a dinner at the Savoy to mark the resignation of his friend Edward Dicey as editor of the *Observer*, but otherwise stuck to his task every day. The day before he finished scoring, 24 November, Sullivan noted in his diary, "Poor old Freddy [Clay] died at Marlow."[29] The next day, Sullivan scored the finale.

On 26 November, with his work virtually finished, Sullivan wrote in his diary: "I am out of prison at last," and went to the theater for the evening. The next evening he was on the train to Manchester, on his way to attend a performance of *The Golden Legend* given by Charles Hallé's orchestra at the Free Trade Hall on 28 November: another excellent performance, with tumultuous applause for Sullivan at the end. Instead of remaining in Manchester to savor the acclaim, he caught the night train for London, in order to be in time to attend Fred Clay's funeral the next day at the Brompton Cemetery.

After the weekend, Sullivan began orchestral rehearsals for *The Gondoliers* at the Prince's Hall and that evening, after dinner, he settled down to write the overture. Having finished his own stage rehearsal at the Savoy, Gilbert called in at Queen's Mansions at 11:15. Together they settled the title of the opera: "The Gondoliers" or "the King of Barataria" Sullivan wrote in his diary, "good title I think." After his business meeting with Gilbert, Sullivan went back to the overture: "arranged & scored the Overture, finishing at 3 a.m."[30]

At the end of a full music rehearsal at St. Andrew's Hall on 3 December, Sullivan was pleased to note: "everyone delighted, especially G!"[31] On 5 December, the day before the dress rehearsal, a last-minute change was made to act 2. Instead of "Till Time Shall Choose," the quintet, "Here Is a Case Unprecedented," which had been previously cut, was reinstated, "much to everyone's delight," Sullivan commented.[32] There was the now customary lengthy and semipublic dress rehearsal that lasted nearly seven hours, from 4 until nearly 11, before Gilbert and Sullivan were satisfied that *The Gondoliers* was ready for performance.

The cast had been completed with the engagement of a young soprano, Decima Moore, as Casilda, making her stage debut four days before her eighteenth birthday; and Wallace Brownlow (who had played the Lieutenant in *The Yeomen*) had been chosen to play Luiz.

The Savoy was "crammed" for the first night.[33] Friends and former colleagues filled the boxes and the stalls: Lord Dunraven (from the old Opera Comique days), Augustus Harris, John Hollingshead, John Hare, and the former Savoyards Julia Gwynne, Sybil Grey, J. G. Robertson, and Richard Temple.

"From the time the curtain rose," said the *Sunday Times*, "there reigned in the Savoy Theatre but one steady, undisturbed atmosphere of contentment—contentment with the music, the dances, the piece, the scenery, the dresses, and not the least of all, with the talented and loyal members of Mr. D'Oyly Carte's company."[34] The reviewer for *The Times* found it difficult to single out particular musical items for praise, but gave special mention to "In a Contemplative Fashion" as "the cleverest thing that the composer has accomplished."[35] The *Sunday Times* described the same number as "the musical gem of the opera . . . a marvel of contrapuntal ingenuity, as mirth-provoking as it is clever, and notwithstanding its great difficulty, rendered with ease and humour that fairly astounded the musical listener."[36]

In the first act "A Right Down Reg'lar Royal Queen" produced cries of "All of it" when Sullivan attempted to encore only the last part, "a request laughingly granted by Sir A. Sullivan," reported the *Daily News*.[37] As for the Cachucha, the *Sunday Times* called it "a treat to witness. . . . Nothing in its way to equal this has ever been done at the Savoy. We predict that all London will want to see the Cachucha danced by Geraldine Ulmar, Jessie Bond, Courtice Pounds, Rutland Barrington, and the incomparable Savoy chorus."[38]

The Gondoliers succeeded as a complete piece of joyous theatrical entertainment; Gilbert and Sullivan had worked hard together to produce this total effect, with Gilbert being more conscious than usual of Sullivan's desire to be closely involved in the development of the musical situations. It was the music that received most attention from the critics, who were overwhelmed by the display of musical fireworks that Sullivan had produced. *The Illustrated London News*, however, gave full weight to Gilbert's contribution. "Mr W. S. Gilbert has returned to the Gilbert of the past, and everyone is delighted. He is himself again. The Gilbert of *The Bab Ballads* . . . this is the Gilbert the public want to see, and this is the Gilbert who on Saturday night was cheered, till the audience was weary of cheering any more."[39] "Gilbert and I got a tremendous ovation —," wrote Sullivan, "we never had such an enthusiastic house and such a brilliant first night."[40]

Never again were Gilbert and Sullivan to experience such success.

CHAPTER TWENTY-FIVE

1889-1890

Carpets, Etc.

"I MUST AGAIN THANK YOU," wrote Gilbert to Sullivan, the day after the opening of *The Gondoliers*, "for the magnificent work you have put into the piece. It gives one a chance of shining right through the twentieth century with a reflected light."[1] "Don't talk of reflected light," replied Sullivan. "In such a perfect book as 'The Gondoliers' you shine with an individual brilliancy which no other writer can hope to attain."[2]

Their working relationship had reached its apogee: "master & master" were appreciative of each other's genius. This latest opera, in many ways their most brilliant, had been born not only out of their combined talent and hard work but also out of an unusual degree of willingness on Gilbert's part to give full weight to Sullivan's requests. As for Sullivan, he had fought hard with a man who was not used to giving way in order to exert greater influence over the construction of the musical settings. For the present, they could both bathe in the glory their success had brought them; and Gilbert was right — that glory would last right through the twentieth century.

As *The Gondoliers* settled into its run, Rutland Barrington was, as usual, on the lookout for ways to "work up" his part. He wrote to Gilbert on 10 December, making two requests:

> I beg of you to give me a different dress for the *second act*—the present one hampers my movements most horribly and is most hot and uncomfortable. . . . Also—would you object to the Chorus remaining on the stage after my solo in commencement of second act ("Rising early") until I dismiss them?[3]

Passing the letter to Carte, Gilbert commented:

Here's an amazing letter! I wish you'd see Barrington & find out what he means.

As to the Chorus remaining on the stage until he dismisses them—there never was a more preposterous suggestion. Why, the song he has just been singing explains that he is the humble servant of the courtiers who order him about as they please as if he were a menial—& then he proposes to "dismiss them"! I never heard a more inartistic "suggestion." The man's personal vanity is at the bottom of it all. He wants an encore for his song & doesn't think his legs look handsome in white tights! So that he is all right, he doesn't care what becomes of the piece. I hope youll give him a good drubbing down.[4]

Carte was left not only with that problem but also with the question of casting and rehearsing a company to take *The Gondoliers* to America. Gilbert was off to India with Kitty, and would be away for the next three months. On 20 December, they set out from Fenchurch Street, seen off at the station by a crowd of well-wishers from the Savoy, and accompanied to the ship, the *SS Orizaba*, by a few close friends.

Sullivan spent part of Christmas Day at a final rehearsal for the New York Company before dining at home with Fanny Ronalds, her family, and a few friends. Gilbert and Kitty were at sea for Christmas, and unaware that, on the evening of 25 December, in The Close in Salisbury, William Gilbert senior suffered a stroke. Over the next few days he rallied a little and by Sunday, 29 December, was able to sign his will with a cross; but by the following Thursday, it was clear that he was close to death. Gilbert had left Naples on 30 December, heading for Egypt and the Suez Canal, and perhaps it was there that he received new of his father's death. On 4 January, the *Daily News* carried an obituary written by Sutherland Edwards, who described his uncle as "an author of marked originality. . . . Apart from its realistic side, there was a fantastical element in Mr. Gilbert's talent, which his son, Mr. W. S. Gilbert, may be said to have inherited with new developments."[5]

William Gilbert had left instructions that his funeral was to be as simple as possible, costing no more than £20. He bequeathed the furniture and contents of 14 Pembridge Gardens to his daughters Mary Florence and Ann Maude, and his library and three paintings to his son. He left £100 to his daughter-in-law, Lucy Gilbert, to be spent on a piece of jewelry as a memorial of his affection. The rest of his estate, which amounted to about £8,000, was to be shared equally among his four children.[6]

D'Oyly Carte's New York company for *The Gondoliers* opened on 7 January at the Park Theatre. The whole operation had been meticulously planned by Helen Carte. She had assured Gilbert as early as November that she would leave "no stone unturned" to send a good company: "With the 'Yeomen' it turned out wrong _because_ we didn't send out our own company."[7] Despite her best efforts, the company was severely criticized in America.

When D'Oyly and Helen Carte arrived in America on 26 January, having unsuccessfully urged Sullivan to join them, Carte had to defend himself to the American press.[8] Angered by the suggestion that he had sent a cheap company to New York he resolved to make whatever changes in cast were necessary. When *The Gondoliers* moved to Palmer's Theatre on 18 February, several major changes were made. Fred Billington took over as Don Alhambra, and Richard Temple replaced Duncan Fleet as Giuseppe. But a major problem remained over the part of the Duke of Plaza-Toro, which was eventually solved—but too late—by bringing over Henry Lytton.

Instead of joining the Cartes, Sullivan went to Paris and then on to Monte Carlo, staying at the Hôtel Metropole. It was only a short stay. He went north to Brussels in March to see a performance of a new opera by Ernest Rayer, based on Flaubert's novel *Salambô*, giving him an opportunity to see how the composer had treated an historical novel before he embarked on *Ivanhoe*. He returned to Monte Carlo, this time accompanied by Fanny Ronalds and her mother. Although the relationship with Fanny Ronalds's family was a permanent feature in Sullivan's life, there were other initials, "R." and "E.W.," appearing in his diary around this time. On the return home via Milan and Basle they stopped in Paris, where Sullivan stayed in a separate hotel from Fanny and her mother, leaving them there to return home on 19 April by himself.

In India, meanwhile, Gilbert kept in touch with Carte, who was back at the Savoy. Gilbert had heard that *The Gondoliers* was not doing well in New York, and from Agra wrote to Carte, "I am sorry for that, but it is a very difficult piece to cast properly & I confess I was not very sanguine. . . . I found the Mikado & Trial by Jury, playing at Calcutta—it seems that our pieces are continually played there & it seems monstrous that we have no agent to protect our interest."[9] The Gilberts left Bombay on 7 March and ten days later, from Port Said, Gilbert wrote to Carte to inform him of their itinerary on the homeward journey, expecting to arrive in London on 27 March.

Once home, Gilbert was soon into Savoy business in response to Helen Carte's anxiety over "gagging" in *The Gondoliers*. When Barrington "worked up" his part, he usually made small changes and additions to the text as laid down by Gilbert. Gilbert suggested that Barrington should provide him "with a book marked with the alterations & additions he wants to make, & I will sanction them if possible."[10] Gilbert was not always intransigent over small changes to the text, if he thought they were merited; but neither was he so liberal that he would allow such a notorious ad-libber as Barrington to have a free rein. In the end, Gilbert came to a compromise with Barrington over suggested alterations.[11]

Heavy financial dealings were occupying Carte in April 1890. On 8 April, he applied to the Charing Cross Branch of the Union Bank for a loan of £45,000.[12] Not that Carte was personally in financial difficulties. He continued to invest and speculate to increase his personal wealth. On 18 April, he wrote to Sullivan strongly recommending that they both invest in a wine syndicate and went on to advise Sullivan about making money. "I have made a great deal of money during some years on the margins scheme—i.e. by borrowing at 5 per Ce[nt] or less and getting a difference in increased interest and you seem to have neglected this very easy form of making money for other various and uncertain . . . speculations."[13]

It is unlikely that Gilbert knew anything about the state of Carte's personal finances. If he had known, it might have saved some of his anxiety and suspicion over the following months. He was aware that Carte was involved in large speculations concerning his new theater, and what worried Gilbert was that Carte was actually speculating with his money. What grieved him particularly was the thought that Carte was only in a position to speculate at all because he and Sullivan had been responsible for the accumulation of Carte's fortune.

In mid-April, Gilbert learned that the preliminary expenses of *The Gondoliers* had amounted to £4,500. He asked Helen Carte for details. She replied on 15 April: she had found that the preliminary costs had included "some things in front (new carpets etc)" but she had not gone through the details of the account.[14]

When Gilbert received details of the preliminary expenses on Monday 21 April, he immediately went to see Carte in his office in Beaufort House. Also present at the meeting was Helen Carte. What actually took place, and what actually was said, can only be surmised from the accounts of those present. One thing is certain: there was a blazing row between Gilbert and Carte. For Gilbert to express his anger was not unusual; for Carte to respond in anger was a new departure. And in that situation, Gilbert lost his temper. "You seemed so very different from your usual self," Helen Carte told Gilbert later, "and it all came so suddenly and was really so entirely unprovoked."[15]

"When you first burst out," Helen Carte recalled in her account of what took place, "it was when you said we were robbed right & left and you said Mr Carte did not even check his carpenters accounts and that you made him what he was or words with that meaning." She described his manner as "violent & insulting" and completely unprovoked.[16] During this tirade, she said, Carte managed to keep control of himself and remain calm.

Gilbert moved on to the matter of the carpet. According to their agreement, Gilbert claimed, they were "liable only for 'repairs incidental to the performances'—that carpets in the lobbies & on the staircases in front" could not be considered as "incidental to the performances."[17] Carte disagreed: Gilbert and Sullivan shared responsibility as tenants for the upholstery in front. Why then, Gilbert responded, if they were jointly responsible, were not he and Sullivan consulted over major expenditure? With conflict over the existing agreement, Gilbert called for a fresh agreement. By this stage, Carte's anger had been roused: "Very well, in that case we would make the rent £5000 instead of £4000."[18] Helen Carte claimed that Gilbert countered with, "Then you will have to find a new author for the Savoy" (a statement that Gilbert refuted), and that Carte replied, "That might be practicable."[19]

Gilbert was furious and threw at Carte the same question he had put to him in New York in 1880: what had Carte done for his share of their successful enterprise? At that point Carte declined any further discussion, and suggested that if Gilbert were "dissatisfied with the existing state of things" he should go and talk to Sullivan;

whereupon Gilbert stormed out with the comment that Carte was kicking down the ladder by which he had risen.[20]

In that overheated atmosphere, little light had been shed on their difference of opinion. Their perceptions of what had taken place at the meeting had more to do with the emotional atmosphere than with the content of the disagreement. Gilbert considered that he had been treated "very unceremoniously, arrogantly and insolently."[21] Carte was of the opinion that Gilbert's observations "were so insulting, so absolutely unprovoked and uncalled for" that he could not meet Gilbert as if nothing had happened.[22] As far as Helen Carte was concerned, although her husband had become very excited in the course of the interview, "he was never excited in the way" Gilbert was. "Anything in the conversation that might be considered insulting," she recalled to Gilbert, "was certainly in some of the things you said to Mr Carte — not in anything he said to you."[23] Their individual perceptions of the meeting, however, were the reality in which they would develop their own positions over the coming months.

Gilbert's version of events was given the following day in a letter to Sullivan, which started with the understatement "I've had a difficulty with Carte." He went on to relate the substance of their disagreement. Gilbert had been "appalled" to learn that the preliminary expenses of *The Gondoliers* had amounted "to the stupendous sum of £4500!!!" He listed some of the items of expenditure for Sullivan, items amounting to £1,962. He mentioned costumes, especially Rosina Brandram's second dress, which cost £100 ("this costly garment has now," said Gilbert, "for some occult reason, gone on tour"); he mentioned carpentry and other items and saved his most interesting item for last: "But the most surprising item was £500 *for new carpets for the front of house.*" Gilbert stressed to Sullivan the words of their agreement, which did not say anything about *replacing* items but only mentioned *repairs* described as "repairs incidental to the performances." He hoped Sullivan would agree that "a distinct understanding should be arrived at" if they were to work for Carte again.[24]

Sullivan reacted calmly. In his reply to Gilbert on 23 April, he said how much he regretted "that any heated personalities should have entered into the discussion about the accounts." He was not prepared to give an opinion on the question of renewals and repairs, but would go into the matter. He reminded Gilbert that it was Gilbert himself who controlled the preliminary expenses, and that he left everything in Gilbert's expert hands. "Let us talk the matter over," he suggested.[25]

They met for a long talk on Saturday, 26 April. "Gilbert . . . gave his version of the row between him and Carte," noted Sullivan, "— very different to Mr [and] Mrs. Carte's version"—a version he had heard at Adelphi Terrace on the day the "row" took place.[26] Sullivan could not agree with Gilbert about the renewal of carpets and the responsibility of preliminary expenses, but he undertook to arrange a meeting with Carte at Queen's Mansions for "calm deliberation," without any mention of what had taken place in their "heated conversation." Sullivan wanted to let the matter "stand over" for a week; he was going "out of town and the delay would tend to smooth matters."[27] Sullivan's solution appears reasonable. He was able to shelve problems in this way, and anyway he wanted to go up to Newmarket for the races where he had been invited to stay with his friend Russie Walker. Gilbert's temperament was completely the opposite. He would constantly worry at a problem, working himself more firmly into a feeling of self-righteousness until the problem was resolved, if necessary, in a court of law.

On the same day that Gilbert and Sullivan met, Carte wrote a long letter to Gilbert, disputing the accuracy of Gilbert's statements in two letters to Sullivan that had been shown to him. Carte agreed that the preliminary expenses were high, "enormously and unnecessarily so," but then Gilbert was responsible for those expenses. Carte had found it impossible to get estimates for costumes and sets and was told that Gilbert "had not definitely settled this or that consequently no estimate could be given." To avoid controversy, Carte had simply accepted the situation as it was. He noted that, in his second letter to Sullivan, Gilbert had mentioned the cost of £330 for carpets, "the actual amount being £140 odd," said Carte, adding that it was a "fair sample of the general inaccuracy" of Gilbert's letters.

As for Gilbert's remark about Rosina Brandram's costumes, which "for some occult reason, have been sent on tour," Carte reminded him that he was "perfectly aware . . . that these costumes had been sent on tour because Miss Brandram had resigned her engagement" in London on medical grounds but was able to tour in the country.

Carte rejected Gilbert's claim, in his first letter to Sullivan, that he had said, "You write no more for the Savoy," and insisted that it was Gilbert who had said, "Then you will have to find another author for the Savoy." After calm reflection, Carte was now ready to answer Gilbert's question about what he did for his share of the profits, a question that at the time Carte had declined to answer. "I have devoted the greater portion of my time and energies during the best years of my life to the management of the Theatre in London and the tours in the country and abroad."[28] And so far, he claimed, everyone had been satisfied with his management.

The following day, Carte sent another letter to Gilbert making good a paragraph omitted in copying up his first letter, and concluding: "If you do not know—or have forgotten what I have done the first passer by in the street could probably tell you."[29]

With his mind fixed on the idea of a fresh agreement, Gilbert had already drawn up a list of points that he took around to Sullivan on Sunday morning, 27 April, leaving the paper with Sullivan for his consideration. Sullivan again proposed leaving the matter for a week, saying he had noticed that Carte had been irritable of late, and after a few days they would be able to meet in a more "tranquil frame of mind." "Gilbert agreed with me," recorded Sullivan, "in this quoting from *The Gondoliers*." Sullivan's impression was that Gilbert wanted relations to be back on their "former amicable footing."[30]

Nevertheless, Gilbert's attitude to Barrington's "gagging" grew harsher. He had received several reports, including one from Kitty, who had been to the Savoy on 29 April, and the next day he wrote to Carte. "The piece is, I think, quite good enough without the extraneous embellishments suggested by Mr. Barrington's fancy. Anyway it must be played *exactly as I wrote it.* . . . If once a licence in this direction is accorded it opens the door to any amount of tomfoolery."[31]

The next few days were crucial in determining the course of events. On Saturday, 3 May, Gilbert wrote two letters to Helen Carte seeking greater clarification over the preliminary expenses. He begged Sullivan to make an appointment with Carte to discuss the fresh agreement and a way to restore good relations with Carte, provided that there was no possibility of Carte repeating his insult.[32] Sullivan thought it better to let the new agreement stand over until a new piece was needed for the Savoy, which would not be for some months because of the success of *The Gondoliers.* He was too busy, he added, at the moment to give his mind to a new agreement.

But on Monday, 5 May, after Gilbert's two letters to Helen Carte had arrived, Carte responded to Sullivan. He addressed his letter "Dear Sullivan": an indication perhaps that, if he had not already sought advice from his solicitor, Frank Stanley, he had it in mind to do so; or perhaps that the letter was intended for Gilbert. He had considered Sullivan's suggestion of a meeting of all three of them. He had waited for a week, he said, to see if some opening would occur, but Gilbert's two letters to Helen Carte showed that he was "still much in the same state of mind."[33] Reflecting on Gilbert's insulting remarks to him at their meeting at Beaufort House, Carte could not see how he could meet Gilbert as though nothing had happened between them.

On the same day, probably hearing of Carte's refusal to meet him, Gilbert wrote a formal letter to Carte, giving notice that "from and after Xmas 1890" he revoked Carte's licence to produce his libretti. "I further give you notice," he added, "that from and after the withdrawal of the Gondoliers I revoke your licence to produce and perform such libretti in London."[34]

He sent a copy to Sullivan, informing him that the time had arrived to end their collaboration, and that after the withdrawal of *The Gondoliers* "our united work will be heard in public no more."[35] This dramatic flourish from Gilbert was answered by Carte's prosaically reminding him that their agreement for the provinces expired at Christmas 1891 (offering the suggestion that Gilbert had made a clerical error in stating Christmas 1890); that the agreement was binding on all parties; and that the London agreement already ended with the run of *The Gondoliers.* "Your letter of notice therefore hardly seems to have been necessary."[36]

Sullivan's reaction to the break was less sanguine than Carte's appeared to be. "Felt ill all day," he wrote in his diary; "received letter from Gilbert, . . . breaking off finally our collaboration—*nothing* would induce me to write again with him. How have I stood him so long!! I can't understand."[37] On the same day, Gilbert had written Sullivan another letter accusing him of "marked discourtesy," "consistent hostility, veiled or otherwise," "contemptuous indifference," and "placidity in tolerating insults inflicted on [him]."[38] Sullivan refuted these charges as baseless. Twice Gilbert had asked to meet him to discuss a new agreement, twice Sullivan had declined "whilst the present one was still under dispute." He referred to the matter as a "lamentable affair" and said that he was trying to heal the breach, a task that he believed that Gilbert had entrusted to him, when Gilbert had interfered. Because Gilbert's "imperious will" had received a check, Gilbert had now taken a step that caused him "the deepest pain."[39] This does not tally with his diary, in which he expressed relief at the end of the collaboration. It is possible that Sullivan was peeved that it was actually Gilbert who had broken off the collaboration—in the past it had been Sullivan who controlled whether the partnership was to continue or not.

In another letter to "Dear Sullivan," on 7 May, Carte enclosed copies of Gilbert's official letter of "resignation" and his own reply, adding "I think you will see that a meeting would have been of no use."[40] As a further sign that Carte was already preparing for legal action, he asked Sullivan to let him have any letters he may have received from Gilbert "bearing on the recent affair, with his letter to you of April 23rd (or copies of any such letters) that I may *see* whether there is anything in them affecting me."[41] Gilbert, too, was preparing for further developments and wrote to Carte asking for a copy of their agreement.

It was Helen Carte who replied, in a lengthy letter started on 7 May and completed the following day. She agreed with Sullivan and Carte that the preliminary expenses were Gilbert's responsibility. As to "the front of house matter," she reminded Gilbert that Carte had paid for the carpets and furniture of the Savoy when it opened, and since then, the theater had been kept "spick and span" by redecoration and repairs, expenses that they had all three shared. She concluded with her account of the "interview" between Gilbert and Carte at Beaufort House.[42] By the time she had finished her exhaustive account, Gilbert had already put the interpretation of the agreement into the hands of his solicitor.

On the same day, Gilbert wrote to Sullivan, explaining his accusation of Sullivan's marked discourtesy toward him, saying that Sullivan had declined to comment on Gilbert's relations with Carte; had declined to meet him because many months would have to elapse before a new piece would be needed; that Sullivan could not give any time to future Savoy matters, as he wanted to give himself entirely to his opera; that Sullivan had implied that it was he who was to decide when Gilbert was to commence a libretto. All this amounted, in Gilbert's opinion, to "marked discourtesy." As to Sullivan's reference to his "imperial will" (corrected next day to "imperious will," the term Sullivan had actually used), Gilbert said that it was he who was insulted by Carte and therefore for him to say on what terms he would continue their association. In a second letter on the same day, he denied that he had ever asked Sullivan to heal the breach between him and Carte. Sullivan had, he claimed, volunteered to see Carte and "to point out to him the enormity" of Carte's letter.[43]

This was all too much for Sullivan, and in his reply he informed Gilbert that he had no intention of continuing "a correspondence which can result in no practical good."[44]

Gilbert had already moved on, however, and by 9 May was negotiating terms for a comic opera with the theater manager Horace Sedger. Gilbert set out his terms to Sedger, stipulating 15 percent on gross receipts, and insisting that he was to be responsible for "the entire stage-management in the most comprehensive interpretation of the term."[45] An agreement was subsequently signed by Gilbert and Alfred Cellier to write a comic opera to be produced at either the Lyric or the Prince of Wales's, to be ready by September 1891.[46]

No longer having to consider Gilbert's opinions, Carte went ahead with his plans for his new theater. He approached Frederic Cowen on 13 May, asking if he would be interested in writing "a grand opera or a comic opera."[47] Without Gilbert and Sullivan operas to fall back on, he would have to build his own repertoire; and at this stage he was not restricting himself to grand opera.

On that same day, 13 May, the two solicitors became involved in the unfolding drama. Frank Stanley offered the check and accounts for the period up to 4 April 1890 to Bolton, Gilbert's solicitor. In his acknowledgment, Bolton added that they proposed asking for the accounts and books since 25 November 1882, the day of the opening of *Iolanthe*, the first of the operas to be produced exclusively at the Savoy. Reopening the old accounts would introduce further complications, prolonging the dispute.

In the meantime, word had reached the press that the partnership of Gilbert and Sullivan had come to an end. Carte gave an interview to the press on 15 May, and the following day the *New York Times* published an article quoting Carte. It attributed statements to him that Carte could not possibly have made, saying that Gilbert and Sullivan met in the theatre "to balance accounts," that Gilbert had shouted, "You are both blackguards," before rushing out of the office; and Sullivan was reported to have written to Gilbert saying that he was "thoroughly disgusted" at his "ungentlemanly conduct."[48]

When he learned of the report, Carte felt obliged to correct the distorted picture that had been presented, saying that there was "scarcely anything correct" in the article. He could not in justice allow it to be supposed that Gilbert had spoken or acted in the way reported.[49]

Gilbert was preparing his own statement for the *Sunday Times,* intending to say that the collaboration had come to an end because Sullivan was writing "an opera of a different character." He sent his draft to Sullivan, who had moved down to Grove House, Weybridge, hoping for some peace and quiet to work on *Ivanhoe.* Writing on 16 May, Sullivan declined "to be a party to letting this statement go forth," saying that he himself had refused to give interviews and considered that Gilbert's proposed note implied that it was he who had broken up their collaboration. He was quite ready to continue with Gilbert if he were always to be as pleasant as he had been during the production of *The Gondoliers.* He was amazed and indignant to find he had been "unceremoniously chucked aside."[50]

On 20 May, the *Pall Mall Gazette* announced to its readers that the "rumoured rupture at the Savoy is now an admitted fact." It gave as the reason "the development of Mr. Carte's grand opera schemes," and regretted the breakup "for it is hardly likely that Gilbert will find another Sullivan or Sullivan another Gilbert."[51] Gilbert responded immediately, denying that his "secession" had any connection with Sullivan's new opera. He had withdrawn from further collaboration, he said, for his own reasons and without "putting an end to the friendly relations which have existed between Sir A. Sullivan and myself for many years."[52]

Carte was not so diplomatic in his explanation of the turn of events. He gave an interview to *The Star,* published on 23 May, in which he was quoted as saying, "I don't think I am saying anything that is not perfectly well known when I say that Mr. Gilbert is a very difficult man to get on with."[53]

Sullivan had in the meantime made a start on *Ivanhoe,* and by 11 June had almost completed his sketch of the first act. Then he put it away for revision, and made a start on act 2. He gave himself a fortnight's break from composing, during part of the time going to Ascot for the races, and then resumed work on 29 June. He had already made an early decision about the next Leeds Festival, turning down the invitation to produce a composition for them. He wanted to concentrate his mind on *Ivanhoe,* after which, he told Fred Spark, he was not sure he would have the strength to undertake a work for the festival. To commit himself, two and one-half years in advance, to produce a creative work was too much for a man of his age. At the age of forty-seven, Sullivan was beginning to look on himself as an old man.

Sullivan was already involved in the delicate matter of discussing terms with Carte for *Ivanhoe.* He had been hoping for a similar arrangement to the one he had with Gilbert at the Savoy, but was to be disappointed. Carte sent him a formal letter on 7 June, telling him that ideally he and Mrs. Carte would have shared equally in the profits, and then explained that because of expenses and the need of a run, the matter was complicated, and so he had worked out a sliding scale, depending on receipts.[54] *Ivanhoe* was already overdue, and the financial position would become increasingly more delicate with the passing months.

WHEN THE TIME CAME to complete the accounts for the quarter ending 4 July 1890, Stanley thought it advisable to see the remarks from Gilbert's solicitor on the former accounts before any further action was taken. These remarks were sent to Stanley on 14 July and the following day Stanley also received a report from Gilbert's accountant. Gilbert had tried to interest Sullivan in his proposal that the Savoy accounts should be kept differently, but Sullivan was not interested and told Gilbert so; he considered the involvement of a lawyer and accountant "a deplorable step. . . . My object now is to do nothing that will add fuel to the fire, and consequently I hold entirely aloof from taking part in this unhappy dispute."[55] Unfortunately for Sullivan, being so tied up over *Ivanhoe* in the fortunes of Carte, he would not be allowed to remain aloof. Carte wanted him on his side.

Having studied the remarks from Gilbert's solicitor, Stanley advised the Cartes to do nothing until he had had a full discussion with them. No plans were made for this discussion and D'Oyly and Helen Carte went down to Hastings for a few days' rest, as Carte was unwell and suffering from abscesses on his hands. By 26 July, Gilbert's solicitors were becoming impatient to see the quarterly accounts and sent a reminder to Stanley. He put them off by saying that Carte was away ill, and that there had been no discussion yet of the accounts. The Cartes returned to London on 28 July, but Gilbert's solicitors clearly thought they had waited long enough and that they were being unnecessarily delayed. On 30 July they issued a writ. The following day, Bolton wrote to Stanley asking for a payment of £2,000.

There was no reply. Gilbert's solicitors delivered a second letter, by hand, on Saturday, 2 August, stipulating that unless £2,000 was paid on the morning of Tuesday, 5 August, they would apply for a receiver. To no avail. It was bank holiday weekend. Stanley had left London and the Cartes had gone to Lynton, in Devon.

Gilbert had meanwhile contacted Sullivan concerning the late arrival of the quarterly accounts and payment. Sullivan replied on 5 August: "I am very sorry affairs are taking this turn. With regard to last quarter's divisions, I have asked Carte to send me an account in the usual way, and if I am satisfied with its detail, shall of course, demand my share of the profits."[56]

The Cartes moved on from Lynton to Westward Ho, and it was Thursday, 7 August, before Stanley managed to contact them. Immediately Carte sent a check for £2,000 to Stanley, telling him that he was ready to offer more if the accounts justified it. That check, via Stanley, did not reach Bolton until Monday, 11 August. Nearly a month had passed since Bolton had sent his report on the previous accounts. Gilbert had already filed an affidavit on 8 August and Bolton filed his on 11 August, the day on which notice was served for an application for a receiver.[57]

Penalized along with Gilbert, and now concerned at the delay in receiving his quarterly payment, Sullivan wrote to Carte. Carte was aggrieved that Sullivan should be so concerned and took issue with him for what he had written in his letter of 5 August to Gilbert. Because Gilbert had put matters into his solicitor's hands, Carte said, he had been obliged to do the same and "naturally having done so I must either abide by my solicitors advice or withdraw my business from his hands." He suggested a meeting with Stanley, to hear what he had to say. What upset Carte was that Sullivan had written to Gilbert, saying "that by a little conciliation and concessions *all round* affairs need never have reached their present stage. I don't know if this means that *I* ought to have made concessions or been conciliatory." It was Gilbert who had initiated the legal proceedings, he insisted, Gilbert who had sent in an accountant, and Gilbert who had issued a writ and commenced an action. He repeated his suggestion that Sullivan should see Stanley about the affair. Carte could cheerfully bear all the trouble that "the Gilbert bothers" were causing him. "But," he pleaded to Sullivan, "if *you* — my friend of so long standing with whom I have been working so long, who has advised me through this worry, for whose great work I have actually built my new theatre, if you — I say are not going to back me up thoroughly in the trouble — then it *is* hard and I feel disheartened for the first time and in a way that nothing else could make me."[58]

After Carte's emotional appeal, and mindful of his dependence on Carte for the success of his grand opera, Sullivan saw Stanley and swore an affidavit the very next day, and Stanley filed his own affidavit on 19 August, the day before *Gilbert v. Carte* came to court.[59] As far as Gilbert's solicitors were concerned, these two affidavits altered matters and in court the next day a request was granted for the case to stand over for a week in order to give Gilbert an opportunity to answer them and to amend the writ by adding Sullivan as a defendant.[60]

Another week of intense activity followed on the part of the solicitors of both Gilbert and Carte as they maneuvered to outwit their opponents. Stanley told Carte that it would be useful if they could show "a vindictive spirit or malice" on Gilbert's part, and Carte was anxious to see a letter he had heard about, which Gilbert had written to Sullivan, and which he was convinced was libelous. Sullivan would not part with the letter nor show it to Carte, who hoped that Stanley would succeed in getting hold of that letter and any other written by Gilbert.[61]

When the case came up on Wednesday, 27 August, Gilbert's counsel informed the court that Gilbert had gone to Carlsbad because of ill health and had no opportunity of swearing an affidavit. Application was made for the case to stand over for another week.

The day before the case came up again, Gilbert filed two affidavits. In response, on 3 September, three further affidavits were filed, one from Carte and two from Sullivan. In all, the court was presented with fourteen affidavits: three by Gilbert, three by Sullivan, one by Carte, and the rest by the solicitors.[62] Gilbert had argued that from the nightly returns supplied to him by Carte, the takings amounted to £20,000; with average expenses of no more than £11,000, his share of the profits should amount to £3,000. Stanley's argument, put forward by Carte's counsel, was that because of outstanding liabilities, the accounts had frequently not been rendered until several weeks had elapsed and, he claimed, there were certain outstanding liabilities not yet brought into account. An affidavit from Sullivan supported the claim.

Details of the amounts that had been paid over the years to Gilbert and Sullivan were then revealed: in eleven years Gilbert had received £70,000 for performances in London and £20,000 for provincial and American performances. After this, an affidavit from Sullivan was read in which he stated "that in his judgement it would be most injurious to the interests of all the parties if the conduct of the business were interfered with by the appointment of a receiver." In reply, Gilbert's affidavit was read in which he quoted Sullivan's letter of 5 August, when Sullivan had said that, if he were satisfied with the accounts, then he would demand his share of the profits. But it was a further sworn statement by Gilbert that was to be the severest blow to Carte and that lies at the center of this unhappy dispute. Gilbert had pledged his oath that "he believed his property was being misapplied." £9,000 had not been divided, and he "believed the money had not been paid because Mr. Carte, being engaged in other speculations, had used it for purposes of his own." Furthermore, Gilbert had sworn that "apart from the Savoy Hotel, which was, of course, an enormous undertaking, Mr. Carte was engaged in large speculations."[63]

Carte's defence argued that the action for a receiver was unreasonable, as £2,000 had already been paid; Sullivan's counsel contended that Sullivan had taken no part in "this unfortunate quarrel, and did not desire to be mixed up in it." Carte's counsel then offered to pay Gilbert £1,000 on account on the day after the hearing, and to deliver the accounts in three weeks. This offer was accepted by the court, and no order was made to appoint a receiver.[64]

What had been achieved? Considerable bitterness, certainly. Gilbert received no more than he would have done if he had not gone to court, and he had to pay the costs into the bargain. Carte had succeeded to the extent that no receiver had been appointed by the court, and he had been obliged to do what he had already decided to do in sending Gilbert a further payment of £1,000 on account, followed by the accounts three weeks later. And Sullivan had found himself drawn into the dispute in order to support Carte, on whom he was dependent, and, in the process, had been influenced by Stanley to swear an affidavit that there were outstanding legal liabilities that had not been brought into account. The money referred to concerned the Lillian Russell affair in 1884, at the time of *Princess Ida*, an affair that had been settled apart from a small amount of which Gilbert knew nothing.

Was the cause of the breakup really a carpet, an argument over a piece of property at the Savoy? The particular piece of property at the Savoy that Gilbert was passionately concerned with was his own property, or his shared property with Sullivan: the operas that had become known as the Savoy operas. He had resisted Carte's plans to ditch the Savoy and start afresh in a new theater with a different agenda, and had become convinced that his property (even in the sense of the profit derived from his property) was being misapplied, as he saw it, in building up Carte's empire. A sense of the ownership of property lay at the center of Gilbert's thinking. At the rational level he appeared to be behaving irresponsibly; at an instinctual level he was fiercely protecting his property.

CHAPTER TWENTY-SIX

1890-1891

Disentangling the Knot

THE ONE THING THAT Gilbert, Sullivan, and Carte would not have bargained for was that their private differences, made public in a court of law, would make them all ill. Sullivan's kidney ailment and Gilbert's gout were worsened by the stress that both were under; and Carte's abscesses were no doubt a direct result of the anxiety caused by his battle with Gilbert. "I have been miserable since this wretched affair began," said Gilbert to Sullivan on 6 September, "& would gladly end it. The notion of your being a defendant in a suit in which I am a plaintiff has thoroughly upset me."[1] "Don't think me exaggerating," replied Sullivan, "when I tell you that I am physically & mentally ill over this wretched business."[2] And a little later, Carte confessed to his wife, "I shall be very glad when the day comes, if it *does* come, when Gilbert and I can shake hands and forget that all this ever occurred."[3]

The first move in a reconciliation came from Gilbert. But it was a tentative move only; they still had a long and painful road to travel, along which injured pride could only gradually be repaired, before they reached anything like a full reconciliation.

Three days after the court case, Gilbert approached Helen Carte, addressing her, "Madam." "You will, no doubt, be surprised at receiving a letter from me, and still more surprised when you find that it is an overture of reconciliation." His motive for writing, he told her, was his distress that "associations of so uniformly pleasant a character & of so many years' standing should be exchanged for feelings of lasting antipathy & resentment."[4]

He proposed to meet Helen and D'Oyly Carte and Sullivan, at Beaufort House, without lawyers, to try to settle their differences, suggesting that they all withdrew any "angry expressions" that had been used and "generally look upon byegones [*sic*] as having gone by."[5] "He is extraordinary," was Sullivan's comment in his diary after reading a copy of Gilbert's letter.[6]

Helen Carte replied formally to Gilbert on the same day, agreeing that it was regrettable that their friendly relations had been terminated, but pointing out that "certain injurious statements" had caused resentment in Carte's mind.[7]

Sullivan expressed his own feelings about the difficult time they had all been through in his reply to Gilbert on 8 September: "My old personal regard for you as a friend pleads very strongly to let the past five months be blotted out of our years of friendship as if they had never been lived through—." But he, too, was "still smarting under a sense of the unjust and ungenerous treatment" he felt he had received.[8] If there was to be a reconciliation, he wanted it to be a thorough one; but that could not happen while Gilbert still held the view that legal action had been his only option. He would much rather believe that Gilbert had acted out of anger aggravated by bad health. He did not feel able to sit down and discuss the original dispute calmly, and suggested that Gilbert drop his action against Carte and that the matter be settled by friendly arbitration.

His letter did nothing to placate Gilbert. He insisted that his solicitors had informed him that the form of action made application for a receivership essential. He rejected outright Sullivan's suggestion that his behavior was the result of ill temper or ill health. He had acted the way he had because he would not bow to Carte's refusal to let him examine the books and because he would not, he told Sullivan, "allow him to retain money long since due & constantly accruing which you know that he had no more right to than my watch & chain. I deeply regret that I should have exposed myself to the magisterial reproof contained in your letter."[9]

Having considered Gilbert's proposal for a meeting, and after a few days' rest in Folkestone, Helen Carte wrote to him on Wednesday, 10 September. She wanted his mind to be "disabused on certain points." For that reason she suggested that the two of them should meet so that she could "clear the ground" by showing him that his sense of injustice was founded on a misapprehension of what had occurred. One of the consequences of Gilbert's affidavit, she told him, had been the postponement of a mortgage on the new theater that Carte was negotiating, "and I need not say that some steps will have to be taken in this matter to set things right."[10]

The meeting was eventually scheduled for Monday afternoon, 15 September, and as Gilbert preferred not to meet at Beaufort House, it was arranged for 4 Adelphi Terrace. Helen Carte wanted to present Gilbert with documentary evidence to show that D'Oyly Carte had never refused to pay him the money due to him. She took him carefully through the stages detailed earlier about payment of the £2,000 on account that Carte had made as soon as he received a request from Gilbert's solicitors. She did not, of course, refer to the delaying tactics used by Stanley. The point she wanted to press home was that Gilbert had not been justified in his affidavit when he stated that he believed the money had not been paid because it was being used by Carte for his own purposes.[11] Gilbert was ready to admit at the meeting that he would not have sworn his affidavit if he had been aware of the facts put to him; the statement in his affidavit had been made in anger.[12]

The next day, Sullivan received a report of the meeting when Helen Carte called on him at Queen's Mansions. "She seems to have put everything straight before him," he recorded in his diary, "& not minced matters. He ought to feel thoroughly ashamed of himself but I don't suppose he does."[13] Gilbert was sufficiently contrite, if not "ashamed," to ask Helen Carte that any friendly settlement should not be made public.

Gilbert wanted a reconciliation, but believed there was still a case to be answered. Carte, too, was willing to settle the dispute, but believed that he had been wronged by Gilbert's insinuations. Nevertheless, he was ready to go over the situation and state his position clearly. This he did in a long letter written to Helen Carte on 19 September, hoping to arrive at an equitable solution. Of course the letter was really for Gilbert, with whom he was not communicating directly, and it was copied out by Helen Carte and forwarded to Gilbert.

Carte's primary concern was that Gilbert's affidavit read out in court had "actually had a most injurious effect." Now that Gilbert was prepared to admit that the affidavit was sworn in anger, and would not have been made at all if he had been informed of the details of the correspondence between the solicitors, then it should be withdrawn publicly.

Moving on to the question of the accounts, he argued that, if there were items charged to the account that should not have been charged, then he was entitled to claim that items had been credited that need not have been credited.

Carte was referring to revenue derived from program advertisements and bar profits. He had credited them because he had thought it "a fair and right thing to do," not because he was bound by an agreement. In the same way that he thought it was "right to charge against them repairs and renewals rendered necessary by wear and tear in the front of the theatre. One thing goes with another," he claimed. The profits on the programs alone, since Helen Carte had taken them in hand, he estimated, were far in excess of any charges for repairs and renewals. "Of course I have made a splendid thing out of Gilbert & Sullivan's operas, but so have Gilbert & Sullivan; and I strongly object to Gilbert's taking the line that he and Sullivan have made my fortune. They have made their own as well, and it has been a benefit all round."[14]

Helen Carte wrote her own letter to Gilbert. She wanted to know how he was going to undo "the injurious effect of the statements" in his affidavit, which he had acknowledged privately should not have been made. But they had been made "and repeated in newspapers all over the country." The public should now be told that his affidavit was made with a lack of information and, now that he knew the facts, that he withdrew it.[15]

No retraction was forthcoming, but he wrote to Sullivan a few days later, saying that he did retract an epithet he had applied to Carte and which, "on reflection," he now considered unjustifiable. No doubt this unrevealed "epithet" was in the letter Carte had been anxious to see. "I am sorry that I used it and I unreservedly withdraw it," wrote Gilbert.[16] Meanwhile, Helen Carte tackled Gilbert again, taking him in minute detail through all the correspondence, the events concerning the check for £2,000 and the harmful effect of his affidavit.[17]

The long and detailed letter from Helen Carte, begun on 27 September and not finished until the 29th, coincided with Gilbert's move to a new address: Graeme's Dyke, Harrow Weald. The house took its name from the original Grimes Dike that ran from Harrow Weald Common to the northern edges of Pinner, and by the end of 1891 Gilbert's address was to revert to the more accurate "Grim's Dyke." Gilbert bought the estate of 110 acres of woodland and farmland from a banker named Henriot, but the Tudor-style house in the grounds originally had been designed by Norman Shaw in about 1870 for the painter Frederick Goodall, who sold it to Henriot in 1882. The painter's studio on the first floor was converted into a huge drawing room, having as its central feature a tall, pink alabaster fireplace. Gilbert was to make many alterations over the years to the house and to the gardens. He employed seven servants in the house itself, including a butler, housekeeper, and ladies' maid; and in the grounds stood five cottages for his outside staff (including a gamekeeper) and their families. Counting the children of these employees, all living on the estate, there was upward of thirty people who depended on Gilbert for their livelihood. His butler, John Warrilow, then a young man in his early thirties, was to remain in service at Grim's Dyke until Gilbert's death, and afterward to continue as butler to Kitty.

One of his first letters after the move to Grim's Dyke was Gilbert's reply on 30 September to the exhaustive letter from Helen Carte. He put off a detailed reply, telling her that his memory was "too treacherous" to allow him to reply without reference to the correspondence between the solicitors.[18]

And then, in a letter from Helen Carte on 10 October, Gilbert learned a piece of information that was a revelation to him. The costs in the Lillian Russell case of £400 had been paid at the time of that particular dispute. There remained a balance of a little over £40 to be charged on the Savoy account. This new information now became the focus of Gilbert's attention. Far from there being "outstanding financial liabilities" as sworn by Stanley, and verified by Sullivan in his affidavit, the financial liabilities had been largely settled. He wrote to Sullivan on 12 October—a letter in which he expressed himself, according to Sullivan, "in friendly terms."[19] "What were the legal expenses not yet brought up to account to which you referred in your affidavit— . . . I have been cudgelling my brains to discover what legal proceedings had been taken with my authority, & I can honestly think of nothing but the Lilian [*sic*] Russell business."[20]

Two days later, he tackled Sullivan more openly about his affidavit. He stressed that the only outstanding expense was the "insignificant sum of £46," dealing with matters for which he had no personal liability. "I am willing to believe that your affidavit, (which, in effect, charges me with perjury) was made under an entire misconception, owing, no doubt, to deceptive representations which were made to you by persons interested in procuring your evidence."[21] What Gilbert wanted was a retraction of Sullivan's affidavit — in writing.

No reply has survived, but it is probably the letter that Gilbert later referred to as "an evasive reply."[22] Sullivan had noted in his diary: "[Gilbert's] letter of Sunday was a 'trap' — went up to consult George Lewis — Mrs. Carte also there — Lewis gave me sketch of letter to write in answer."[23] Hence, the "evasive reply" mentioned by Gilbert. For her part Helen Carte wrote to Gilbert again, going into painstaking detail over the events and ending with sharp criticism of Gilbert's own affidavit. It could easily be withdrawn, she insisted, "without casting aspersions on the Solicitors on either side."[24]

Gilbert's response was that he could say nothing without seeking counsel's opinion. With the prospect of further legal proceedings a possibility, Helen Carte contacted Frank Stanley. Her letter reveals a different aspect of her character from the calm, rational quality she displayed in all her dealings with Gilbert. In this hastily written letter, her thoughts — and feelings — tumble out in her excitement at the thought of beating Gilbert, even if it meant sacrificing Sullivan. She was not sure what arguments would be used to support their case.

> Would it stand therefore entirely on the question as to whether the a/cs should be finally made up on the whole run? If so might we not be upset on this as, Mr. Carte having the right to run the piece indefinitely he might find it answer his purpose to run it on losing business (failing getting a suitable tenant) and just make the rent received cover *his* loss while Gilbert & Sullivan might be compelled to share the loss whether they liked or not — having no power to stop the run? I don't want to go in & be beaten — and I don't quite understand what arguments we shall lean on.[25]

The situation changed the very next day when, after taking counsel, Gilbert wrote to her. He was prepared to withdraw his questioning of the past accounts and to take the Cartes's view as to "the repairs etc being properly charged —."[26]

Replying to Gilbert on 30 October, Helen Carte returned to her usual careful and rational style. Referring to Gilbert's original objection, which had apparently started off the whole dispute, she assured Gilbert that "anything fresh" that was bought for the Savoy would be the property of the joint account, eventually to be sold off for their joint benefit. The original cost of everything in the theater had been borne by Carte but repairs and renovations were always necessary—"The celebrated carpets of last autumn do not look very fresh now."[27]

She suggested that Gilbert now withdraw any legal action against Carte and that an arbitrator be appointed to decide whether redecorations, repairs, and renewals should be charged to the joint account, and whether the profits on advertisements and bar receipts should have been credited. The last point was not to Gilbert's liking, but at last it looked as though between Gilbert and Carte, after months of dispute, a settlement was near.

WHILE PEACE WITH GILBERT was approaching on one front, from another direction came Sullivan to assail the Cartes with further cause for anxiety. Not only was he well behind schedule in finishing *Ivanhoe*, but he also was unhappy about the terms they had agreed. On 5 November, writing in a much more forthright style than she used with Gilbert, Helen Carte launched into him: "I may say at once that I am sorry to have to have any sort of discussion about the main terms of that agreement I hoped that was [all agreed] and I feel that after all that has taken place it would have been better had you not *wanted to go back* on the arrangement you had yourself proposed & settled." She outlined the three arrangements that had been proposed at different times: a profit share (thought unworkable, "with the best of friends it must be apt to lead to friction"); the sliding scale; and finally a percentage.

"—On the doorstep at Weybridge, however, it was settled it *should* be the per cent and at the same time the question was raised as to what should be done as to the out of pocket cost of keeping back the opening of the Theatre all this autumn." Sullivan had shown himself willing to pay a half share of the expense, paid back weekly out of his percentage. If the opera failed to run long enough for Sullivan to pay his half share, then Carte would bear the loss.

> There isn't any doubt the theater could have been ready for April, [said Helen Carte] and would have been had there seemed any chance of the opera being. You naturally didn't like the idea of any other musical attraction opening it — and although we tried to get Bernhardt or something else of first class *dramatic* we did not succeed, being too late in the field. Now from what you tell us it looks like its being *nine* months in all later than originally proposed.

She hammered away at Sullivan, telling him that there was now £90,000 invested in the new theater on which interest had to be paid. There was ground rent, insurance, staff salaries, "and the question of the artists themselves which must shortly arise." Sullivan had told her that he did not like the idea of being "fined" for being late. "It is not a question of any body being *fined*," she told him. "It is only a question of what is to be done with a bad job. . . . The production is turning out infinitely more expensive than contemplated—*all* the expenses are rising." Any profit for D'Oyly Carte looked increasingly unlikely.

> But now you seem to want to throw over the ***whole*** thing—and at the last moment—just as you are breaking to us that even a further postponement is probable—you speak as if you wanted to throw everything on to d'Oyly. . . . I thought you felt satisfied you had been well treated in all ways about this opera—no work & no expense spared—nothing grudged—*enormous risks* run by D'Oyly over it—in fact with this postponement, I tell you honestly I fear to *think* how we are to manage—I am at my wits' end. It is pay, pay, pay every minute of every day—and it will be a tough struggle to hold on till this later date.

I don't *mind* all the worry even if only *you* didn't seem to be disatisfied [*sic*] after it all—that is the last straw.

After that outburst, longer than she intended, she calmed down. "Shall I come down to see you as soon as I can get free here?"[28]

The closer relationship with Sullivan than with Gilbert, and the anxiety over the risks they were taking, explains Helen Carte's frank talking. Her anxiety was increased by the worry she shared with her husband over the illness of D'Oyly's elder son, Lucas, now a student at Oxford, who had contracted typhoid. Gilbert had already expressed his sympathy, which Carte gratefully acknowledged when he wrote to Gilbert agreeing to meet him.[29]

The meeting took place at Adelphi Terrace on Tuesday, 11 November, and Sullivan noted in his diary, "Gilbert met Mr. and Mrs. Carte by appointment . . . discussed the disputes—admitted he had been wrong & 'badly advised.'"[30] A week later Carte agreed to Gilbert's request that their settlement was "of a friendly and private nature," and that he would give no statement to the newspapers. He added, "I am glad to say my boy is better and I believe is on the high road to recovery."[31]

SULLIVAN HAD BEEN DRIVING himself on with the score of *Ivanhoe*. Fighting tiredness and illness, he finished act 1 on 13 October, and two days later saw his nephew Bertie off at Liverpool Street station as he departed for his new job, laying a cable between Haiti and Brazil. His intensive and punishing schedule continued. He had no sleep at all on 6 December, and after a discussion with Julian Sturgis that day, rewrote the ending of the opera in order to finish on a brighter tone. At last on 13 December, Sullivan was able to record, "Put the last note to score at 6. p.m.—*absolutely finished*! Thank God. Seven months' hard labour. 715 pages of score."[32]

Working under Sullivan at the new theater were François Cellier and Ernest Ford, and also Henry Wood as répétiteur, whom Sullivan had engaged personally, paying his fees himself. Cellier had begun rehearsals of the chorus in November, and rehearsals with Sullivan began at the end of December.

While Sullivan was involved with *Ivanhoe*, Gilbert was planning for the production at the Lyric of *The Mountebanks*, which was scheduled for October 1891. He wrote to Jessie Bond in December, offering her "an excellent part," and asked Percy Anderson to design the costumes.[33]

But it was not long into 1891 before Gilbert ran into trouble with his new collaborator. Cellier had gone to Australia and, as far as Gilbert was concerned, seemed unwilling to engage in any detailed correspondence about their work. Cellier was looking for a drier climate for the sake of his health, as he began to suffer from the early stages of tuberculosis. He wrote a short letter to Gilbert from Suez. He had heard that Gilbert had chosen a Spanish setting for their opera, but as his last work had been set in Spain, he preferred an alternative. Gilbert had already completed act

1. Angry and frustrated, he decided it was time to end "a collaboration upon which (having regard to our respective temperaments[)] perhaps we never should have embarked."34

A few weeks before the opening of *Ivanhoe*, Gilbert's *Songs of a Savoyard* was published by Routledge. Gilbert had dedicated the book to Sullivan, who, after receiving a copy from the publishers, wrote to thank Gilbert for "such a graceful & flattering compliment" and, at the same time, to say how much he hoped Gilbert would attend the first night of *Ivanhoe*. "I should take it much to heart if you were not present, so pray come."35 Gilbert replied to Sullivan's few words of invitation with a lengthy letter recapitulating the old quarrel and justifying the action he had taken. He reminded Sullivan of the affidavit he had sworn, and claimed that when he had given Sullivan the opportunity of withdrawing it, he had made an evasive reply, forbidding any further reference to the legal proceedings or Gilbert would forfeit his personal friendship. He would gladly accept Sullivan's invitation, if Sullivan would only admit that his statements had been made "under mis-information."36

Both Gilbert and Sullivan had sworn affidavits that later had been shown to be false. When informed of the relevant facts by Helen Carte, Gilbert had admitted he was wrong, although he declined to make a public retraction of the statement, on the grounds that it would have damaged his solicitors' reputation. Gilbert now expected Sullivan to act likewise. To Gilbert it was a straightforward matter of justice. Sullivan did not agree.

"My dear Gilbert," he wrote. "I thought that byegones were to be byegones [*sic*], and that no further reference was to be made to any of the matters lately in dispute." Sullivan would neither apologize for his affidavit nor retract it. He had wanted to remain neutral in the dispute between Gilbert and Carte; it was Gilbert who had made him a defendant in the case. The difference between the two men was stark: Gilbert wanted to confront the issue; Sullivan preferred to set the issue aside. "Surely, my dear Gilbert, you can afford to let things rest as they are now, and let us forget the past. Let your presence at the theater tonight[,] be an intimation that you are as ready & willing as I am to think no more of what has happened, & to allow nothing to disturb our old friendship."37

With his letter, Sullivan enclosed two orchestra seats for *Ivanhoe*. Gilbert replied on the same day. He had moved his ground. He was not asking for an apology or a retraction, but simply an admission that Sullivan would not have sworn his affidavit if he had known the facts. "If you will give me this," said Gilbert, "I will use the stalls with the utmost pleasure."38

Sullivan still refused to admit he was wrong and referred Gilbert to Stanley. "I have no faith in Stanley," replied Gilbert (in a letter which Sullivan described in his diary as "a rough & insolent refusal),39 "& I want nothing from him. You deliberately swore that the costs in Russell v Carte were still unsettled and by so swearing you defeated me & put me to an expense of £400 in costs[.] I have it in Stanleys own hand that all the costs in that action were settled 5 years ago, & so have you. I decline your stalls."[40]

This hectic exchange of letters on 31 January did not spoil the grand occasion for Sullivan. He arrived at Carte's new theater, now named the Royal English Opera House, at twenty to eight. "Tremendous crowd outside," he noted, ". . . tremendous reception by a brilliant & packed house. The night was really superb, . . . Great enthusiasm at the end—everyone called—I went on with Sturgis. Gave all the stage hands 5/- each afterwards. Supped at the Orleans—large party given by E. Dresden and G. Foâ. Then to Portland—home at 4."[41]

"I would say that I look upon this Opera—'Ivanhoe,'" Sullivan had written to selected music critics before the production, "—as the most important work I have yet written—not only from its magnitude, but also from the strength of the musical work I have put into it. I have endeavoured to be before all things Dramatic."[42] Carte set out his own aim in a program note, claiming that a run was the only way the expenditure could be recouped. To support such a run, a double cast was required for seven of the principal roles. Sullivan was to conduct again on 2 and 4 February in order to launch all the principals in their roles, and afterward the conducting was shared between François Cellier and Ernest Ford.

The opening night had been well attended by royalty: the prince and princess of Wales, the duke and duchess of Edinburgh, and the princesses Victoria and Maude. At Osborne in the Isle of Wight, Queen Victoria asked her daughter, Princess Louise, to write to Sullivan and congratulate him on his success, saying that it was a particular satisfaction to her as she believed that it was "partly owing to her own instigation" that Sullivan had written the work.[43] In his reply Sullivan asked Princess Louise to assure the queen "that it was indeed in deference to Her Majesty's expressed desire and gracious encouragement" that he had written his opera. He took the opportunity to ask to be allowed to dedicate the opera to the queen, and if "Her Majesty would graciously accept this tribute of my devotion and respect, I should look upon it as the crowning point of my career."[44]

Correspondence resumed between Gilbert and Sullivan immediately after the opening of *Ivanhoe*. On 1 February, anxious to clarify what he had written "in extreme haste" in the letter Sullivan had described as "rough & insolent," Gilbert wanted confirmation that Sullivan had made his affidavit "under a misapprehension . . . & I ask for no more than your simple word to that effect. . . . I am sorry to be the only discordant note in the chorus of praise with which your work was received last night. I would gladly have been present to render my tribute to a great work if you had rendered it possible for me to do so. As it is I will meet you when & where you please, if you think that such a meeting would promote a better understanding."[45]

Gilbert wanted matters neatly settled, if not entirely settled. Sullivan wanted matters forgotten: "We look at things from such different points of view," he replied, "that I fear neither will ever be able to convince the other. You assume I am in possession of facts, of which in reality I am absolutely ignorant. . . . I am afraid the matter must rest where it stands."[46] He was in no hurry to meet Gilbert, and did not take up his invitation.

Gilbert tried again the next day, 5 February. It was another appeal to Sullivan to "rectify his error . . . I am heartily sorry," he concluded, "that the attitude you have assumed appears to preclude all possibility of a complete reconciliation."[47] Sullivan did not budge.

Having left a decent interval of time, Gilbert made a visit to the Royal English Opera House to see *Ivanhoe* on 11 February, telling Helen Carte the next day that the opera "was more tuneful" than he expected.[48] Meanwhile, after a weekend at Sandringham as one of the guests of the prince of Wales at a "males only" house party, Sullivan left London accompanied by Bertie, bound for Monte Carlo. He did not feel obliged to wait for the command performance ordered by the queen for Windsor Castle—a performance not of *Ivanhoe* but of *The Gondoliers*. On Friday 6 March, the Savoy was closed for the night while the full company, having traveled down to Windsor by special train from Paddington at midday, gave their performance in the Waterloo Chamber at Windsor Castle.

With his hoped-for reconciliation with Sullivan blocked, as he saw it, and with his attempted collaboration with Alfred Cellier run aground, Gilbert was turning his mind in a different direction. On 1 May, he was notified that he had been appointed as justice of the peace and was invited to swear "Statutable Oaths" at the Guildhall, Westminster, at the end of the month.[49] Then on 6 May, Gilbert received a letter from Alfred Cellier's wife, Harriet. Cellier was too ill to write himself, she told Gilbert, but she was at pains to point out that her husband had not intended treating Gilbert "with the slightest discourtesy" and thought it an honor to collaborate with "so distinguished and successful a librettist."[50] If Gilbert had a book ready, then Cellier was willing to set it to music. Not only did Gilbert overlook their earlier differences, he also overlooked the ominous sign that Cellier was too ill to write a letter although willing to write an opera.

The month of May 1891 was to run in Gilbert's favor. He had been appointed justice of the peace, *The Mountebanks* was to be restarted, the publishers Routledge agreed to pay him £80 for his illustrations in *The Songs of a Savoyard*, Sullivan sent him a check for £147.15.6 for performances of their work in Germany, and Helen Carte, having told him in April that the electric lighting charges were to be reduced, confirmed that he was due a refund of £330. Writing to thank Sullivan for the German check, Gilbert mentioned the overcharge on the electric lighting accounts, and while claiming that this was the result of his action against Carte, with tongue in cheek commented, "As you will, I suppose, benefit considerably by this re-adjustment of accounts I thought it possible that you might wish to share with me the cost of the action by which it was brought about."[51]

Sullivan returned from Monte Carlo in time to conduct the one hundredth performance of *Ivanhoe* on 25 May. "Crowded & enthusiastic house," he recorded.[52] Meanwhile, Carte was faced with difficult management and financial questions. At the Savoy, *The Gondoliers* came to the end of its run of 554 performances on 20 June; the end also of nearly nine years of exclusively Gilbert and Sullivan operas at the theater. Ten days later, the Savoy reopened with *The Nautch Girl*, with music by Edward Solomon to a book by George Dance and Frank Desprez. Frank Thornton had returned to the Savoy, and another noted return was that of the stage director, Charles Harris, who had quarreled with Gilbert in 1878 at the Opera Comique. But as far as Jessie Bond was concerned, the Savoy was not the same place without Gilbert, whom she described as her "kind and constant friend."[53]

At the Royal English Opera House, Carte's problems were more severe. Negotiations with Frederick Cowen had proved fruitless, and Carte had nothing else ready to follow *Ivanhoe*. On 17 June he approached Bret Harte, asking to use one of his stories and have it arranged in "scenic form"; with Harte perhaps writing the lyrics and Sullivan the music.[54] Another fruitless attempt. By July Carte was in financial difficulties, and on 19 July the Opera House was mortgaged for £85,000 to Hubert de Burgh Canning, marquess of Clanricarde.[55] Less than a fortnight later, on 31 July, *Ivanhoe* finished its run of 155 performances. It had been a costly experiment on Carte's part, and a managerial failure. For Sullivan it had been a failure financially, and not successful enough musically to encourage him to repeat the experience. From then on, he stuck to what he did best.

In early July, Sullivan learned that he was suffering from a buildup of uric acid and knew that further kidney trouble lay in store for him. His doctor ordered him to Contrexéville, a spa in the east of France, about seventy miles northeast of Dijon. Sullivan left on 19 July and two days later, having stopped off for the races at Vincennes, arrived at Contrexéville, beginning the "cure" the next day. For the next month, until 20 August, he subjected himself for the sake of his health to the rigors of the regime: rising at 6 a.m., drinking six pints of mineral water before breakfast at 10, then nothing until dinner at 6 p.m. and bed at 10. In a letter to his composer friend Ethel Smyth, he described the experience as "a constant delirious whirl of dullness" and closed with, "May an old man's blessing rest on you"—he was forty-nine.[56]

Sullivan left Contrexéville on 22 August and traveled south, via Dijon and Macon, to Aix-les-Bains, where he met up with Fanny Ronalds and her mother, after their "cure" at the spa there. All three went off to Switzerland for a fortnight, followed by a few days' stay in Paris before finally traveling back to England.

Gilbert was still in the process of casting *The Mountebanks*. At the beginning of August he had approached Helen Carte to try to have Decima Moore released by D'Oyly Carte so that she could join the cast. "I don't ask this in my own interest," Gilbert said, "but entirely in the girl's. . . . I promised the girl's father that I would help her on if I had the chance of doing so & I should like to be of service to her."[57]

Before the end of the month, Gilbert was in a position to read *The Mountebanks* to the company, under the impression that Cellier was well advanced with the music. Three weeks later, only four choruses had arrived from Cellier, and a music rehearsal had to be postponed. Cellier had found it impossible to have the music ready for all the principals, and told Gilbert he hoped to send the music to the singers individually. He added, "I will let you know the next music call."[58] Gilbert was exasperated. He decided to "abstain" from the music rehearsals; "conduct them as you please," he told Cellier, "without reference to me." When all the music was known, Gilbert would attempt to "pick up the measures" from Ivan Caryll, the music director.[59] Only then would Gilbert begin stage rehearsals.

Perhaps fearing that the music for *The Mountebanks* would never be completed, Gilbert was already at work on his next opera. This time he had asked George Grossmith to collaborate with him. But neither Cellier nor Grossmith was a substitute for Sullivan. It was an appropriate moment for Gilbert to try to settle his differences with his former collaborator, and he had several conversations with Tom Chappell about a reconciliation. On 4 October, Sullivan wrote to Gilbert, prepared "to let byegones be byegones" and to meet him, "provided that the disagreeable events of the past eighteen months are never alluded to, or at least never discussed."[60]

Gilbert's temperament would not allow him simply to forget the past; he had to find a way of justifying to himself that a reconciliation was in keeping with his own code of honor. He took Sullivan through the two meetings he had had with Tom Chappell, looking for a way ahead; the sticking point was always Sullivan's affidavit. He had been over events again and again in his mind, but could not see how he had acted in any way inconsistent with "the character of a gentleman & a man of honour." He assured Sullivan that all bitterness had passed from his mind but he still felt unfairly treated: "if you can suggest any reasonable means whereby this cloud can be removed, it will give me infinite pleasure to adopt it."[61]

"Let us meet and shake hands," replied Sullivan, casting Gilbert's scruples aside. "We can dispel the cloud hanging over us by setting up a counter-irritant in the form of a cloud of smoke."[62] Gilbert, however, still fretted over the affidavit, and in a letter to Sullivan, on 11 October, the day before they had arranged to meet, he spelled out his problem again, quoting from Sullivan's affidavit and Helen Carte's letter to him of 10 October 1890. "I quote these matters," he said, "because while it is impossible to ignore these altogether I wish to dispense with written documents when I come to you tomorrow. . . . So, in the interests of peace I shall bring none with me." In that way, Gilbert could satisfy his own conscience and trust in a successful conclusion to their meeting. "If, on the face of the facts I have set forth," he said to Sullivan, "you see your way to saying anything that can place us upon a thoroughly cordial footing, I am sure you will say it—if not, we must do as well as we can without it."[63]

On Monday, 12 October 1891, Gilbert arrived at Queen's Mansions at midday. The two men sat and talked for two hours. "Full reconciliation & shook hands," noted Sullivan.[64] The last thread of that particularly troublesome knot had finally been disentangled.

Part V

1891-1911

Utopia and Beyond

CHAPTER TWENTY-SEVEN

1891-1893

Picking up the Thread

PART OF THE CONVERSATION between Gilbert and Sullivan during their reconciliation meeting at Queen's Mansions revolved around the prospect of a future collaboration. Eighteen months before, Sullivan had been adamant that *nothing* would induce him to work again with Gilbert; and now something had changed his mind.

Most of Sullivan's income came from the Savoy, from his work with Gilbert; and that source had now dried up. Whatever artistic satisfaction he had derived from *Ivanhoe*, the material benefits were nil. Working again with Gilbert was a practical solution. He had already entered, however, into negotiations with Carte to write an opera with Sydney Grundy; and Gilbert himself was engaged on two pieces of his own. The timing of their new work therefore was, as Sullivan said in a letter written from Newmarket, "a matter for consideration and discussion." He was most anxious "that nothing should ever arise which would lead to another misunderstanding between us."[1]

Gilbert was ready to start on a new plot. He fully understood Sullivan's position, and taking Sullivan's opera with Grundy into consideration together with his work for the next Leeds Festival, he estimated that it would be twelve or eighteen months before they could collaborate. "Now I need not say," he replied to Sullivan on 15 October 1891, "that I can't afford to remain idle during this long period—I *must* write & produce at least one libretto during this time."[2] He preferred that libretto to be for Sullivan, but in early November Sullivan told him that negotiations with Grundy had reached a stage where he felt obliged to agree to start work on the piece at once. "I look upon our renewed joint collaboration as merely postponed for a little time, & hope that we shall soon have another success together."[3]

Carte reopened the opera house on 3 November with Messager's *La Basoche*, planning to intersperse six more performances of *Ivanhoe* during the first month. Although no lover of grand opera, Gilbert showed his support for Carte by attending the first night with Kitty and a group of relations. Reporting on the experience to Helen Carte, he thought that the music was "very pretty" but "much too long." "The staging is perfect," he added, "— too good for high class opera."[4]

He had already agreed to scenery and properties from past Savoy productions being sold off, and asked Helen Carte if he could buy the executioner's block and ax from *The Yeomen of the Guard* "as a relic," he said, "of the best of our joint work at the Savoy," later making an additional request for the "gong & bell."[5]

Frequent letters to Helen Carte at the time show a friendly, cooperative spirit on Gilbert's part, with even a mild dig at previous problems made with a touch of humor. The recalculation of the electricity account had come about because there had been a change in the supply system. Instead of the Savoy Theatre having its own supply, the electricity for the theater was now supplied from the Savoy Hotel. Where the supply came from was immaterial, said Gilbert, "as I regarded the Savoy Hotel & your husband as practically one & the same, for the purpose of the Electric Lighting, I did not think it necessary to discriminate."[6]

But the good will Gilbert showed toward the Cartes in their current endeavors was tinged with nostalgia for the old days at the Savoy. Replying to birthday wishes from the old Savoyard Marion Johnson, now Mrs. Long, he told her: "We are busy rehearsing at the Lyric but its very different to the Savoy. Instead of the old familiar faces of the Chorus (too old sometimes) I see a gang of uninterested young ladies whom I don't know from Adam, or at all events from Eve. It was always a pleasure to me to work with the Savoyards."[7] Before long, Gilbert established as warm a relationship with the choristers at the Lyric as with those at the Savoy. While rehearsals continued in the run up to Christmas, the Gilberts had moved up to London, as they had done the previous winter and were to do for the rest of Gilbert's life. In those first two years after the move to Grim's Dyke, they stayed at the home of their friends the Mertons, at 18 Chesham Place, off Belgrave Square.

As the opening night of *The Mountebanks* approached (it was now scheduled for Thursday, 31 December 1891), Gilbert became increasingly nervous and anxious. He allowed his tetchiness with Alfred Cellier to appear in the *Pall Mall Gazette* on 26 December. He blamed the lateness of the opera's appearance on Cellier's "many engagements, coupled with ill health," adding that he had not seen as much of Cellier as he would have liked.[8] Gilbert had not forgiven Cellier for being late with the music and had fastened his mind on Cellier's reputation for being reluctant to get down to work, instead of taking seriously the state of Cellier's health.

Two days after the publication of this newspaper report, Alfred Cellier died. "I can hardly see the paper for the tears which are in my eyes," Sullivan wrote from Paris to François Cellier; and, referring to the article in the *Pall Mall Gazette*, commented, "Anything more selfishly egotistical or in worst taste, I cannot conceive & even *he* ought I think to feel a bit sorry now."[9] Accompanied by his nephew and his two faithful servants, Louis and Clotilde, Sullivan was on his way to Roquebrune, near Monte Carlo, where he had rented a villa with the intention of working on the music for *Haddon Hall*, his opera with Sydney Grundy.

Alfred Cellier's death delayed the opening of *The Mountebanks* by only a few days. It opened at the Lyric on Monday, 4 January 1892, with a cast that included Frank Wyatt, Geraldine Ulmar, and J. G. Robertson. Instead of remaining to take a curtain call on his own, Gilbert had chosen to return to Grim's Dyke after the last rehearsal.

> I feel quite lost now the rehearsals are over, [wrote Esme le Neve, one of the choristers] as I *really* enjoyed them, & on Saturday when you said you should not come on Monday, I felt I was saying good-bye to one of my best friends. You have been *so kind* to us all, but you would feel repaid for it, if you knew the esteem & *admiration* with which we all regard you. I am not commissioned by anyone to say this, . . . I *know it*.[10]

At the end of the rehearsals, Gilbert had sent all the chorus a week's salary because of the enforced delay following Cellier's death. A letter of thanks came from Lina Hicks and was signed by another twenty-eight choristers. "We shall ever remember, with pleasure," she wrote, "the kindness & consideration you bestowed on us, during the rehearsals; and could wish no better, than always to be in your productions, to be ever under your kind surveillance. . . . We are, with best wishes, your 'Mountebank' girls."[11]

Gilbert's opera with George Grossmith was now running into difficulty with Horace Sedger, who managed not only the Lyric but also the Prince of Wales's, where he had agreed to produce *Haste to the Wedding*. He was arguing over terms that Gilbert had understood were settled. Sedger felt that the terms agreed for *The Mountebanks* had been excessively high and that he had been "unfairly cornered in the matter."[12] Gilbert's response on 29 January 1892 was predictable: "You have charged me, practically, with having swindled you," he thundered, and threatened to refer the matter to his solicitors. "It is as well that you should learn that charges of this class are not to be made against gentlemen with impunity."[13] Gilbert and Kitty then left for Egypt. If Sedger wanted to reply, Gilbert told him, he would have to post his letter to Brindisi.

At the Royal English Opera House, *La Basoche* had come to the end of its run on 16 January. Carte closed the theater for a time and then let it for a season of drama to Sarah Bernhardt. Carte's dream for English opera had been shattered. Dispirited, he made plans to cut his losses and dispose of the theater. The Savoy, too, closed on 16 January, at the end of two hundred performances of *The Nautch Girl*, only to reopen on 28 January with a revival of *The Vicar of Bray*, a comic opera by Sydney Grundy with music by Edward Solomon.

In Roquebrune, Sullivan had made a start on *Haddon Hall*, but was suffering again from his old kidney ailment. He grew progressively worse until, in early April, he was seized by a severe attack—so severe that Sullivan feared for his life, and Herbert and the servants, in desperation, seeing that the morphia that he usually took to control the pain was insufficient, could think of no means of relief other than to lower him into a hot bath. Whether or not that was a lifesaver, as his nephew thought, the crisis passed and in two days he began to recover. News of the seriousness of his condition reached England, Carte rushed out to Monte Carlo and plans were made to bring Sullivan home. Edward Dicey, alerted of the danger, telegraphed Carte, asking to be told as soon as they started back, as he wanted to meet them in Paris on their return journey. When the party reached Calais, Sullivan was so weak that he had to be carried on board ship. By the time he arrived home, his debilitated condition demanded a long period of recuperation.

On his own arrival home, from Egypt, Gilbert ran straight into a controversy at the Lyric. Sedger had decided to reduce the number of choristers in *The Mountebanks* "from motives of economy," and Gilbert immediately applied for an injunction. In his affidavit Gilbert argued that the reduced number of choristers "would seriously affect not only the musical value of the performance, but also the stage management," the piece would be less attractive and his income would be affected.[14] Against Gilbert it was argued that a reduced number of choristers, from fifty-three to forty-five, was quite sufficient "to render the music effectively," and the judge was not convinced that Gilbert would suffer "any serious injury."[15] He ruled that the case should stand over to the next term.

Gilbert had been defeated; and, as usual in such cases, he had his final word in a letter to *The Times*. His reason for applying for an injunction, he said, was to protect "the unfortunate choristers, who, having devoted from two to three months to unpaid and very arduous rehearsals, now find themselves unexpectedly dismissed."[16] As the case had been ordered to stand over, the choristers were, in effect, dismissed and Gilbert instructed his solicitor to discontinue further proceedings.

The Mountebanks continued for another seven weeks, reaching 229 performances before closing. Because of Gilbert's battle with Sedger, *Haste to the Wedding* was now without a venue until Gilbert negotiated terms with Charles Wyndham, who agreed to produce the opera at the Criterion. At the same time, despite Sullivan's weak condition, Gilbert was eager to come to an arrangement about terms, so that he could start on the plot for their new work. He wrote to Sullivan on 27 April. "I had a long & (I think) satisfactory interview with Mr. & Mrs. Carte yesterday—that is to say, I propounded my views & they seemed to think them fair & reasonable—& all that remains (I suppose) is that you shall think them fair & reasonable too."[17]

In optimistic mood, Gilbert expected financial terms to be similar to their previous practice, but "open to modifications of detail if necessary."[18] He was reluctant to involve Sullivan in details until *Haddon Hall* and the coming Leeds Festival were out of the way, but if Sullivan agreed, he would put all other proposals aside and start work on a plot to be ready for Sullivan to consider when he was free.

Still in a weak condition, Sullivan was in no fit state to respond immediately to Gilbert's suggested terms. Because of his illness, when *The Vicar of Bray* ended its run on 18 June, there was no opera ready to replace it and the Savoy Theatre was closed. Both Carte's theaters now stood empty and were losing money. Gilbert suggested to Helen Carte that the opera house could be used "for the production of new & good versions of the Offenbach Operas. Of course they would have to be done to perfection," he advised, implying his own involvement.[19] Carte did not take up his offer; he was in the final stages of his arrangements for the disposal of the Royal English Opera House that was sold to a company headed by Augustus Harris, turned into a music hall, and renamed the Palace Theatre of Varieties.

By 20 July, Sullivan was well enough to travel to Leeds to hold his first choral rehearsal, and shortly after he resumed work on *Haddon Hall*. By August, he was able to write to Gilbert, "I am getting better & stronger every day & hope to be in harness again soon—also to come down to see you at Grim's Dyke."[20] The visit had to be postponed. On 9 August, he told Gilbert, "I am so hard at work I have not been able to get away for a day, otherwise I should certainly have claimed your hospitality. It is very stuffy in London." He was "quite willing & ready" to do a new piece with him, and could make a start in about November. "I think a new opera by you & me would be a great hit, after the long cessation."[21]

Toward the end of August, claiming pressure of work and probably anxious to avoid any protracted dispute, Sullivan pulled out of a meeting with Gilbert and Carte, leaving Gilbert to discuss terms alone with Carte. Sullivan could not escape: Gilbert involved him by correspondence. Gilbert had been content to be paid on a percentage basis, assuming the same terms for both of them. Sullivan was happy with a percentage for Gilbert, but not for himself. Gilbert interpreted Sullivan's position as one of apathy. All he wanted was a broad agreement to work "on sharing terms."[22]

The problem was left unresolved until Sullivan had time to attend a meeting. As terms had not been settled, Gilbert made no start on a plot, but he grew increasingly more impatient to make a start when *Haste to the Wedding*, which had opened at the Criterion in July, hastened to its ending after only twenty-two performances.

Haddon Hall opened at the Savoy on Saturday, 24 September. The old Savoyards Rutland Barrington, Courtice Pounds, W. H. Denny, and Rosina Brandram were in the cast and were joined by Charles Kenningham and Lucille Hill, who had sung in *Ivanhoe*. Jessie Bond, who had turned down a part in *Haddon Hall*, had hoped to attend the first night, but to her surprise Sullivan wrote asking her not to attend because of his disappointment at not having her in his work, and also because he thought her presence might make the girl who had taken over her part nervous. In compensation, he offered her the opportunity of going to one of his orchestral rehearsals for the Leeds Festival.[23] Needless to say, Jessie Bond never forgot the slight. Gilbert was a welcome member of the first-night audience, however, and went around to congratulate Sullivan at the end of the performance.

Orchestral rehearsals for the Leeds Festival took place the following week, from Monday to Wednesday. It had been arranged for Joseph Barnby to share the conducting with Sullivan on the Monday, but as he had just taken up his appointment as principal of the Guildhall School of Music, that arrangement proved impossible. On Friday, Sullivan traveled up to Leeds and started rehearsals that very evening. The festival opened on Wednesday, 5 October, with a performance of *Elijah*, and for the next four days Sullivan conducted most of the heavy program himself, apart from the Saturday morning concert, when individual composers conducted their own works. Included among them was the young Edward German, who conducted his *Richard III Overture*. German felt honored at the end of the performance when Sullivan went up to congratulate him and shook his hand "in full view of the audience."[24]

After leaving what he thought a decent interval, Gilbert contacted Sullivan on Thursday, 20 October. "I have been waiting in daily expectation of hearing from you appointing a meeting to discuss arrangements for the projected new Opera."[25] Sullivan replied on the same day from Brighton. "Since Leeds, I have been roaming about, to get clear of London, & to avoid all business, for I was very tired.... On Saturday week (29th.) I shall be back in town for a day or two. Will you let me know then, if & when you are coming up to town, & want a chat!"[26] " 'If I want a chat with you'?" replied Gilbert. "Certainly, if *you* want one with *me*. That is to say if we both want one with each other. I can be at Queens Mansions at any hour on Monday the 31st. you like to appoint. Shall we say 3 p.m.?"[27] "Monday at 3," said Sullivan, "& a cup of tea, by all means. We can discuss the future, & I think we can arrive at a satisfactory arrangement."[28]

An immediate start on a new work with Gilbert was out of the question. "My doctor won't let me," Sullivan told him, "& I am not fit for it. I feel that I must let my brain lie fallow for a bit."[29]

They met at Queen's Mansions as arranged on Monday, 31 October, and both men left the meeting satisfied that an agreement had been found. But by Thursday the situation had changed. Carte had shown Sullivan a copy of a letter he had received from Gilbert that, according to Sullivan, "put fresh difficulties in the way."[30] Their understanding of their meeting on 31 October differed. Sullivan had no intention of reverting to the old tripartite management. "What had happened may happen again & I am too old now to be worried with ructions & disputes."[31] The Savoy had changed since Gilbert had left; control must be in the hands of Sullivan and Carte. Sullivan agreed to equal financial terms. "But for expenditure, accounts &c you must trust to my judgment, accuracy & honour."[32]

Disgruntled, Gilbert replied briefly on 4 November. "Having regard to the tone & purport of your last letter I must assume that it was written with the definite object of putting an end to the possibility of a collaboration."[33] "I am unfortunate in my letters to you," replied Sullivan on 8 November, "and it distresses me greatly that you should have misconstrued the 'tone and purport' of my last one." He was sorry that Gilbert could not agree to the arrangement he had suggested, and added "it is of little use discussing by correspondence a matter upon which we seem so hopelessly at variance; and I don't want to quarrel with a man for whom I entertain a sincere regard."[34]

At great length in a letter on 9 November, Gilbert summed up their old quarrel and did so, he said, because Sullivan had used the quarrel as a reason for having a different agreement with Carte. He claimed that he had attempted to address his grievances "by the only means that your indifference and supineness left open to me."[35]

"Your recollection of many past incidents," replied Sullivan, "differs so entirely from mine that a discussion upon them is useless, and I will confine myself to stating what my feeling is about the present condition of affairs."[36] He was quite willing to share the profits in three ways, but would not return to tripartite management, leaving himself open to disputes and litigation.

> You cannot for a moment imagine that I will ever again put myself into the position of being liable to suffer so much worry and anxiety as I did in the year following the production of the "Gondoliers." I would rather give up writing for the stage altogether.[37]

That letter from Sullivan prompted two more from Gilbert on 12 November, the second letter of which he ended by saying, "I think the least you can do is to withdraw the horrible imputation upon my honour & good faith contained in your last two letters."[38] Sullivan was shocked. "God forbid," he said, "that any such idea should be in my mind for a second . . . it really makes me ill going on in this somewhat acrimonious style with an old and valued friend — No good can come of it." He suggested that they cease their correspondence for a while, until matters had calmed down.[39]

Sullivan had come to the end of his tether; and so had Gilbert. Unaware of it, Sullivan had in his honest and heartfelt letter hit on the right tone, and on 15 November Gilbert wrote to him, "Your frank disclaimer of any intention to reflect upon my honour & good faith takes an immense load from my mind . . . by dwelling on the subject day & night I have magnified it to the proportions of a nightmare." He suggested they meet Carte to arrange terms and then he could start work on the piece, hoping to have the first act ready for Sullivan by February or March. "I hope your journey will set you up again."[40]

The journey Gilbert referred to was Sullivan's return to Roquebrune, again renting a villa for the winter months. By the end of November, Gilbert had agreed with the Cartes to take a percentage of the receipts in the new opera, estimating 11 percent to approximate to one-third of the net profits. Helen Carte, on past evidence, agreed and the situation was finally settled. Gilbert would now, at last, be able to begin his plot for the new opera. Sullivan had left final negotiations in the hands of Carte. "I thought it hardly fair to interfere," he wrote to Gilbert from Roquebrune on 12 December, "unless I were referred to. . . . I am sending you some sweets for Christmas time. Don't make yourself ill."[41]

Because of his changed position in questions of management of the Savoy, Gilbert now began to worry about casting and whether his voice would carry the sway it once did. Sullivan reassured him in a letter on 22 December. "Our pieces have been distinguished by the extraordinary *one ness* in idea and construction they display." Surely they could still work together "without special clauses to meet difficulties which cannot arise if we are all acting in good faith. . . . I hope Mrs. Gilbert will get her Christmas Box (of sweets) and that you will not eat them all yourself."[42] Sullivan had decided on a different sort of Christmas box for his old friend, George Grove: an invitation to spend Christmas with him, and a first-class return ticket to Roquebrune.

On Christmas Day, Gilbert wrote to Sullivan. He was now worried about changes in cast *after* production, but was prepared to waive that difficulty until a later date in order to push on with the plot. "When I have *quite* combed out the plot," he told Sullivan, "(it is rather tangled at present) I propose to run over to Monte Carlo with it that you may know exactly what it is (say in a fortnight) & make any suggestions or objections that may occur to you."[43] A further letter from Gilbert, while "laid up with a nasty attack of gout,"[44] again seeking reassurance on casting, crossed with one from Sullivan insisting that Gilbert should stay at his villa in Roquebrune. Gilbert had intended to set out on 25 January, but was now seeking clarification on performing rights.

Again Sullivan had to write a letter of reassurance, proposing that all fees and payments should be shared equally between them. He urged Gilbert to pack his portmanteau and start out at once, giving him instructions on trains to catch in order to arrive at Mentone. "Bring also (concealed in greatcoat pockets &c) your own cigars, as it is impossible to get a decent one here."[45]

On Friday, 27 January 1893, Gilbert and Sullivan were at last sitting together in the Villa Diodato at Roquebrune discussing their work. "Think things can be arranged on a satisfactory basis," noted Sullivan.[46] Gilbert had read his plot to both Sullivan and George Grove, and reported back to Kitty. "The reading went off *most successfully*—both Sullivan & Grove enthusiastic—declaring its the best plot I've done."[47] Although he found Sullivan "extremely pleasant & hospitable," Gilbert's stay was short. He left Roquebrune on the Sunday to return home via Paris, meeting up with his friends the Mertons for a few days, and arrived home on Thursday, 2 February, ready to start on the next stage of his libretto.

CHAPTER TWENTY-EIGHT

1893

Utopia, Limited

THE PLOT GILBERT HAD READ in Roquebrune had started out in his plot book as a scene on a "romantic sea shore" populated by sea nymphs. It was once again the image of an idealized female society before the arrival of man, bringing human love. As the plot develops in draft after draft, it is monarchical government that is brought to the island before settling finally as a model of English society imported into "the happy valley." The ensuing chaos is only resolved by the notion of "government by party." Satire had for the first time become central to the plot.

A month after his return from Roquebrune, Gilbert had written "seven or eight numbers (but some of them are alternatives)," he told Sullivan on 4 March, "& a considerable amount of detached dialogue."[1] He presumed Sullivan would rather wait until act 1 was complete before he sent him any lyrics. Sullivan was in no hurry—at that time he was busy with two concerts to be given at Roquebrune: the first on Sunday, 5 March 1893, a concert of his own music including his symphony, which on the program he called "In Ireland"; the second, a concert including music from other "English composers" including Hubert Parry, Mackenzie, Stanford, Sterndale Bennett, and Cowen.

As Gilbert worked on the lyrics of their new work, his thoughts turned to casting the characters, even the minor characters. Writing to Carte on 12 March, he asked: "Would Miss Jenoure be of any use to you in the piece that is to follow Haddon Hall? . . . I think there is a part for her in *our* piece—if Sullivan & God Almighty approve—at all events—I would take care there was one, if she was already at the Savoy."[2] Aida Jenoure had played Zorah in the New York *Ruddigore* company, but she was not taken on for the next Savoy piece. Whatever the reason for her nonappearance, it is evident from Gilbert's letter that he was not at all confident that in casting his voice would carry as much weight as Sullivan's. But it was impossible to ignore Gilbert, and in practice his voice would be heard more frequently as work on the opera proceeded.

Sullivan and Grundy's *Haddon Hall* had been a success for the Savoy. It ended its run of 204 performances on 15 April 1893, but it was a month before the next production—*Jane Annie* by J. M. Barrie and Conan Doyle, for which Ernest Ford had written the music. Gilbert preferred to let the piece run a fortnight or so before going to see it, until "the people have settled down to their work," he told Carte. "I have been laid up with a most violent attack of gout in both feet & in the right hand so I have not been able to do anything but swear for the last 18 days."[3] *Jane Annie* managed only fifty performances, after which the Savoy was closed until the new opera was ready.

Following his return to England in April, Sullivan's first musical engagement was the opening of the Imperial Institute by the queen, on 10 May, when he conducted an orchestra of ninety-eight as they played his *Imperial March* specially written for the occasion. Three days later, on his fifty-first birthday, he was inundated with telegrams, one of which was from his old friend Nina Lehmann. The telegram conjured up in his mind the memory of a glamorous past, and in a wistful reply he said, "to me the romance of my life is in the past—the present is all hard—prosaic facts, although twenty years hence today probably will be in the realms of romance also."[4]

On Saturday, 27 May, accompanied by Bertie, Sullivan caught the train to Harrow. "Gilbert met me at station with wagonette," he noted, "— looked far from well, gout very bad—drove to his house 'Grim's Dyke[']—lovely place—noone but ourselves there—very quiet & pleasant."[5] Gilbert's attack of gout had come on toward the end of April, keeping him housebound most of the time and unable to work. "Fortunately," he told Helen Carte, "I had finished Act 1 & about 7 numbers (no dialogue) of Act 2 before the attack came on."[6] At least he was able to give Sullivan the completed act 1 as he had promised.

Waiting until he had moved out of London, down to Dorney House in Weybridge Sullivan started work on Monday, 19 June, noting at the end of the first day, "slow work."[7] The following day, Gilbert wrote to say that he had discovered a promising American soprano, Nancy McIntosh. "She is rather tall, extremely fair—very nice looking, without being beautiful—good expressive face—no appreciable American twang."[8] Gilbert had met Miss McIntosh at a party given by her singing tutor, George Henschel. Originally from Cleveland, Ohio, she had recently begun her career as a concert singer, making her professional debut in the Popular Concerts at St. James's Hall on Saturday, 5 November 1892. *The Times* described her voice as "a soprano of great beauty and considerable power," and the *Musical News* thought that she was "doubtless destined to rank among the best of our sopranos."[9]

Gilbert found her charming and told her that he was looking for a soprano for his new piece with Sullivan. She had never acted before, but Gilbert was not deterred. Decima Moore had never acted before she was given the part of Casilda in *The Gondoliers*; and Julia Neilson was a complete beginner when Gilbert began coaching her for the stage. He was confident he could turn Nancy McIntosh into an actress.

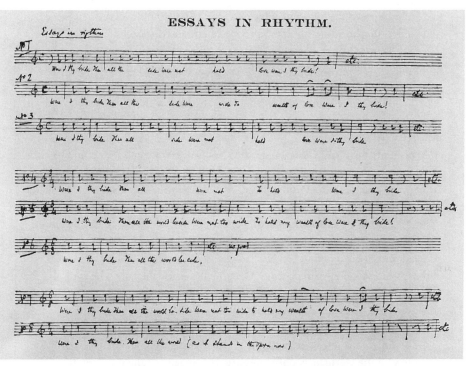

Essays in Rhythm — Sullivan demonstrates his method of trying various
rhythmic possibilities before settling on one and then composing the melody
(Reproduced from *Sir Arthur Sullivan* by Arthur Lawrence, Da Capo Press edition)

In his next letter to Sullivan, on 22 June, sending him an amended finale to act 1
following their discussions at Grim's Dyke, Gilbert mentioned that Nancy McIntosh
would be glad to sing for him at any time he found suitable. Sullivan was in no hurry
and did not hear her until 30 June, when he was due to attend a session at the Savoy.
He found her voice disappointing but liked her pleasant personality: "I don't think
she was at her best — however she will do as she is nice, sympathetic & intelligent."[10]
Gilbert, Sullivan, and Carte heard other singers that day; they decided to engage
Walter Passmore, who had appeared in the cast of *Jane Annie*, to play Tarara, the
Public Exploder; R. Scott Fishe (also from *Jane Annie*) to play Goldbury, a Company Promoter; Florence Perry as Princess Kalyba; and Emmie Owen (described by
Sullivan as "a little treasure") to play Princess Nekaya.[11] It also had been decided,
with Gilbert's agreement, that Charles Harris would retain his position as stage director, working under Gilbert, but not before Harris had formally apologized for his
behavior toward Gilbert in 1878. Gilbert's reply was a formal acknowledgment,
adding, "I am quite willing to overlook & forget the occurrence to which it relates."[12]
It was only after the meeting at the Savoy, when he had returned to Weybridge,

that Sullivan raised the question of the character of Lady Sophy in the new piece. He told Gilbert that he found the part "unsympathetic and distasteful." He had thought that Katisha was to be the last such character; "the elderly spinster, unattractive and grotesque — either bemoaning her faded charms, or calling attention to what is still left of them, and unable to conceal her passionate longing for love, is a character which appeals to me vainly, and I cannot do anything with it."[13] Possibly Sullivan was being sensitive to the feelings of Fanny Ronalds, a contralto whose charms Sullivan recently found faded.

In his reply on 3 July, Gilbert reminded Sullivan that he had raised no objection to the plot in Roquebrune: "you expressed full & unqualified approbation," said Gilbert, "of every incident in the piece." He had left Sullivan a copy of the sketch plot and, apart from the ten weeks of his illness, Gilbert had worked steadily at the opera "& at least 5/6 of it are finished." He went into detail on the characterization of Lady Sophy, saying that she was not "very old, ugly raddled or grotesque" as Sullivan had said in his letter, in fact she "*should be. . . . a dignified lady of 45 or there-abouts, & no more ugly [than] God Almighty has made the lady who is to play the part.*" He suggested they should meet to discuss the question, "I have no doubt we shall come to a pleasant understanding on this very important point."[14] Sullivan had made his objection; and the character of Lady Sophy remained unchanged.

Gilbert had finished act 2 by 17 July and, following doctor's orders, was making plans to visit the German spa of Homburg. Before leaving, he was keen to read act 2 to Sullivan and to make final arrangements about costumes and scenery with Carte. He had agreed with Helen Carte to visit the theatrical costumiers and, in the interests of economy, to look for appropriate uniforms for the opera. What uniforms he saw he described as "very seedy, not suitable . . . & so unsavoury in smell — that I confess I did not go very minutely into the matter — There was a 1st. Class Ministers dress which possibly might do for the Ld. Chamberlain — it was no doubt an old one of Grossmiths & would, I am afraid be too small for anybody else."[15]

The revised finale to act 1 was ready by 21 July, when Sullivan played it to Gilbert, noting in his diary that Gilbert "thought it the best Finale I had done."[16] Gilbert then left for Homburg, where he kept up his correspondence with Sullivan and with Carte, making changes here and there. He changed the name of the King, which had already changed from Rasselas to Philarion (and which he now thought too like Hilarion), and settled for Paramount. Princess Sabina, the King's eldest daughter, had already been changed to "Princess Zara," the working title of the opera.

Added to the pain from his gout, Gilbert now suffered from the fear that by his own miscalculations he had put himself in an inferior position financially. He wrote to Sullivan to share his misgivings, but added "whether you hold me to my ill-considered bargain or not, I shall join cheerfully & loyally with you both in all the hard work before us."[17] Sullivan reassured Gilbert that both he and Carte would "make things absolutely satisfactory to all three" and hoped he would come back from Homburg "healed by the water."[18] Gilbert, however, thought that the waters of

Homburg had done him very little good. Walking had become too difficult and he had to make the trip to and from the waters in a bath chair. Both his feet were painful: "My right foot (which I call Labouchere) is very troublesome—& I take a vicious pleasure (not unalloyed with pain) in cramming him into a boot which is much too small for him. My left foot (known in Homburg as "Clement Scott") is a milder nuisance but still tiresome—& would hurt me a good deal if he could."[19]

The old tripartite management system may have changed on paper, but from the correspondence exchanged while Gilbert was away, the image emerges of Gilbert, four hundred miles away in Homburg, controlling things from his bath chair. In correspondence with Helen Carte over the costumes, he kept a close eye on detail.

I think Princess Zara's dress should be somewhat distinctive but at the same time, such a dress as would be worn by the Princess of Wales's eldest daughter, at a drawing room. Miss Brandrams should be sober & *sad* coloured such a dress as a depressed old dowager might wear—at the same time, quite handsome. . . . We shall want any quantity of *diamonds*—tiaras—rivieres &c. for *all* the ladies—or very nearly all. Of course the two young girls of 15 would not wear diamonds—but all married ladies should have them conspicuously.[20]

The same day, 4 August, he wrote to Helen Carte again, insisting that all the materials for dresses should be set out for inspection on the stage "by electric light *by night.*" Of the twenty-eight girls in the chorus, sixteen were to wear dresses with trains (at £25 each) and eighteen without trains (at £18 each). "The '*train girls,*'" suggested Gilbert, "ought to be the very best looking & showiest of the chorus—the short stumpy ones wont look well in trains. They can be chosen irrespective of their voices, as they dont sing in that scene."[21]

Correspondence with D'Oyly Carte concerned casting and the roles that remained unfilled. Before leaving London, Gilbert had suggested engaging Frank Thornton or Cairns James, who had played the leading comedy roles in touring companies. Now on 8 August, he was doubtful about James. "If C. James is decided upon, I should need a special clause about gagging &c.—The first offence to be followed by instant dismissal."[22] That was probably enough to decide Carte against engaging Cairns James.

Sullivan, too, needed to be in communication over difficulties that he had encountered since starting work on act 2 on 6 August. The tenor song for Fitzbattleaxe, he noted, was "impossible to set."[23] He wrote to Gilbert outlining his difficulties with act 2, saying that it was only when he tackled the numbers that he saw what was really needed. Gilbert accepted his suggestions, relieved that the difficulties raised by Sullivan were not more serious. But it made him all the more anxious to get home, so that they could settle act 2 together. Frustrated, he told Carte, "My gout is as bad as ever & this place has done me no good whatever. I shall return on Sunday reaching home on Monday."[24] Gilbert arrived back on Monday, 14 August, and the next day contacted Sullivan. "I will come on Thursday as you suggest, by the train arriving

MISS ROSINA BRANDRAM IN "UTOPIA. LIMITED."
ALFRED ELLIS.
20, UPPER BAKER STREET,
LONDON, N.W.
COPYRIGHT

Rosina Brandram as Lady Sophy in *Utopia, Limited*
(By permission of the British Library)

12.23—returning from Weybridge by the 5.47. I assume that you are not averse to standing a bit of bread & cheese & a drop of beer to a pore working man wots been out of work for some years."[25]

Gilbert had returned to England in the middle of a heatwave. "Terribly hot," noted Sullivan in his diary on 14 August.[26] The next day, "Heat awful—couldn't do much."[27] On 16 August, "Terrible heat continued," said Sullivan as he composed the duet between Lady Sophy and King Paramount.[28] The next day, he noted, "Terrible heat, 90°—Impossible to work owing to regatta & fair being held."[29] In the evening, however, he managed to go over the music with Frank Cellier in preparation for rehearsals. Gilbert actually arrived at Sullivan's on Friday, 18 August, not Thursday as first arranged, and after lunch they worked at the opera together, with Gilbert making alterations in response to Sullivan's suggestions. "Real good day's work," Sullivan noted. "Heat awful—93° in the shade."[30] Gilbert did not leave early. Instead, at seven o'clock, as the intense heat of the day abated, Sullivan took Gilbert down to the Thames. There, at the end of a glorious day, Sullivan rowed his old colleague the few miles down the river to Halliford and then back into the setting sun. An image of serene harmony.

By the end of August, chorus rehearsals had begun under François Cellier, and Sullivan gave himself a little break on 1 September with a visit to the races at Sandown. The day before he had attended auditions for the part of Phantis, when they heard nine different singers. Gilbert was due to read the piece to the company on Thursday, 7 September, but on 5 September he wrote to Helen Carte, "I am sorry to say I have had a bad relapse & am now completely crippled. I am sending up to town for a pair of crutches—so that I may be enabled to turn up at the reading on Thursday."[31] Sullivan was at the same time keen on the principals going down to Weybridge for a rehearsal before the reading;[32] while Gilbert in his letter to Helen Carte, said that he was "*particularly* anxious to read the piece *before* the principals learn their music" and was determined to read the piece on 7 September.[33] How that particular problem was solved to the satisfaction of both Gilbert and Sullivan is not known, but about that time Sullivan wrote to Helen Carte to say, "*For your sake*, poor child I am very glad you have a satisfactory letter from the Dyke (*Devil's* Dyke it ought to be called.)"[34] The harmony had once more been broken.

Still composing act 2, Sullivan found great difficulty with "Oh Admirable Plan": "impossible to get it into shape," he noted.[35] Two days later, with revised words from Gilbert, he succeeded with that number as well as the revised song "A Tenor, All Singers Above." On 16 September, he composed the delightful music for the drawing room scene before going off to Kempton races for the afternoon. The finale of act 2 proved to be another stumbling block, so Gilbert asked Sullivan to compose the music first (the only example of this ever occurring), and then attempted to fit words to it, describing the result as doggerel.

With his customary all-out effort, Sullivan finished the score in the early hours of Saturday morning, 30 September. The following Friday was given to a full-dress rehearsal, starting at 11:30 in the morning and finishing at 5:30. It was to be the most lavishly produced of all the operas. Sullivan had earlier expressed concern over the cost and had suggested some curtailment of the expenses. Gilbert agreed to cut down on "the ladies' bouquets & diamonds. . . . The merest paste (mixed with glass emeralds and rubies) will do for the jewellery."[36] Gilbert made a few other suggestions for economy, but on the whole both Sullivan and Carte let Gilbert have his way as usual over the costs of production. The estimates had come to £6,750; the actual cost was £7,200, and included two sumptuous sets designed by Hawes Craven.

Closed since 2 July, the Savoy Theatre reopened its doors on Saturday, 7 October 1893, for the first performance of *Utopia (Limited); or, The Flowers of Progress*. (The parentheses around "Limited" were to be removed later.) The line had formed at 10 a.m. for the first new Gilbert and Sullivan opera to appear for nearly four years; there had been no Gilbert and Sullivan in London since *The Gondoliers* had closed more than two years before, after an unbroken run of operas over a period of fourteen and a half years. Since *The Gondoliers*, musical comedy had appeared on the scene when George Edwardes produced *In Town* at the Gaiety in December 1892. Would the old Gilbert and Sullivan formula be able to compete successfully in the new musical world? Were the old collaborators still able to produce their magic? Gilbert was now fifty-six, and Sullivan fifty-one.

In the orchestra seats, two old Savoyards, George Grossmith and Jessie Bond, no doubt joined with the rest of the audience in wanting to see the new Savoyards secure another success for the old partnership of Gilbert and Sullivan. Sullivan was "shockingly nervous as usual — more than usual" when he went into the orchestra at 8:15. But he was cheered for over a minute before raising his baton.[37] "Everybody was glad to see Mr. Gilbert, Sir Arthur Sullivan, and Mr. Carte working together again," said the *Globe*; "everybody was prejudiced in favour of the production; and everybody joined in making it a success."[38]

In *Utopia (Limited)*, Gilbert had departed from the successful formula of the other operas. Without his stock company to write for, the nearest recognizable character-type he produced was that of Lady Sophy. Two comic characters, Scaphio and Phantis, are really unscrupulous rogues and are led away into custody; and King Paramount's role as a pawn, first in the hands of the two Wise Men and later in the limited monarchy, which supersedes the old order, moves satire center stage.

But what mattered most for the success of any Gilbert and Sullivan opera was the happy combination of words and music. In *Utopia (Limited)*, Gilbert produced his share of clever lyrics and Sullivan wrote his share of bright melodies; but the two did not always come together. Perhaps the best of Sullivan's music occurs where there are no words at all: the drawing room scene, the dances (for example the dance following the duet between Paramount and Sophy in act 2), and in incidental music.

The lyrics posed immense problems for Sullivan, and he seems to have been uninspired by the words of "Bold-Raced Ranger" and "First You're Born," where being able to follow the narrative line or argument is essential and where Sullivan had to give even greater prominence to the words than usual. It is little wonder that Sullivan had difficulty in setting the wordy argument of the finale. He did manage to soften some of the heaviness of the satire in the introduction of the "Flowers of Progress," with some beautiful orchestral work in the finale of act 1, and words and music arguably came together best in the duet "Words of Love Too Loudly Spoken," sung by Zara and Fitzbattleaxe, and in the amusing trio of Scaphio, Phantis, and Tarara, "With Wily Brain." The throwback to *Pinafore* provided by "I'm Captain Corcoran, K.C.B.," proved to be a show-stopper, but was a reminder of former glory.

For all its success — and *Utopia (Limited)* was successful with a run of 245 performances (one short of *Princess Ida*) — and for all its good points, this opera does not stand comparison with those of the golden days of Gilbert and Sullivan. The collaborators had lost that "oneness" that had characterized their work until *The Gondoliers*. It can, however, be considered as a success in its own right, namely as a light opera of the 1890s, when musical comedy was taking over from comic opera.

At the end of the first-night performance of *Utopia (Limited)*, "Sir Arthur Sullivan and Mr. Gilbert came forward, and shaking each other by the hand, the old comrades bowed their thanks."[39] Afterward, recorded Sullivan, they had supper at the Savoy Hotel, Gilbert, Carte, and himself, "asking about 8 friends each — Miss Macintosh [*sic*] in the chair!"[40] Sullivan's exclamation mark indicates perhaps his surprise at one so young being given the place of honor, or even perhaps his astonishment at her being feted after her performance.

The inevitable alterations followed the first night. The first casualty was Zara's solo, "Youth Is a Boon Avowed." The decision to cut the song had, in fact, been made earlier; the song was omitted from the dress rehearsal and given its only performance on the first night. As a result of press criticism, Gilbert agreed to make alterations to the dialogue at the end of the opera. Zara's speech had been adversely criticized in the papers, but Gilbert was unwilling to cut it completely and change the ending of the opera. Instead he cut out the lines, "Inexperienced civilians will govern your Army and Navy; no social reforms will be attempted, because out of vice, squalor, and drunkenness no political capital is to be made." Sullivan's finale had also been the subject of criticism, and Sullivan agreed to set Gilbert's original lines, provided that Gilbert removed the line spoken by Tarara that he found offensive: "You know you can't help believing an affidavit."[41] The line was removed and Sullivan reset the finale, which was first heard on 13 October. A small change was made to the title when, on 17 October, Gilbert told Helen Carte that he thought "the brackets in Utopia (Limited) should be omitted."[42]

Then, after *Utopia* had been running a month, it was brought to Gilbert's attention that the prince of Wales was not pleased that Rutland Barrington, as King Paramount, appeared in act 2 wearing the Order of the Garter, as well as wearing the uniform of a field-marshal. It was thought that the only man who had that privilege was the prince of Wales, and therefore the use of the two insignia together was considered a little too pointed. Gilbert wrote to Sullivan on 5 November suggesting that it would be "a graceful thing" to remove the cause of the prince of Wales' complaint.[43]

All in all, it was not a long list of changes — no more than in *The Yeomen of the Guard* and certainly fewer than in *Ruddigore*. *Utopia, Limited* was promising a good run and Gilbert was keen to collaborate again; Sullivan was less enthusiastic.

CHAPTER TWENTY-NINE

1893-1896

The Grand Duke

"PERHAPS HE'S NOT VERY KEEN about doing another piece. If so, & if he will say so, I will make my arrangements accordingly."[1] Gilbert had approached Sullivan within two weeks of the opening of *Utopia, Limited*, ready to make an immediate start on the next opera; and now, writing to Carte on 12 December 1893, he was wondering what had happened to Sullivan.

Carte and Gilbert were agreed that they should start thinking of a new piece. Gilbert had written to Sullivan twice, and Sullivan had promised it would be his priority when he returned from Germany; "but," said Gilbert, "I have heard nothing from him since. Is he in London? And if so, will you jog his memory?"[2]

Sullivan had gone to Berlin on 18 November, staying in the Hotel Bristol, Unter den Linden. Although *Ivanhoe* was not to make an appearance in Berlin for another two years, Sullivan had hoped to arrange a performance of the opera as soon as possible. The opportunity of having his serious work performed in Germany was more pressing to him at the moment than the prospect of another piece with Gilbert.

In the course of the next few months, four companies were rehearsed to take *Utopia, Limited* on tour, while plans were also under way for a production at the Broadway Theatre in New York the following Easter. At the Savoy *Utopia, Limited* had settled into its run, but Nancy McIntosh had not settled into her part. Gilbert's unerring instinct for spotting a promising actress had erred, and the effort that he had put into his personal coaching of her had not been productive. Moreover, through involving himself closely in the personal life of Miss McIntosh, inviting her to stay at his home, as years before he used to invite Marion Terry, both he and Kitty had found themselves emotionally bound up with the young singer.

There was no question of Kitty looking on Nancy as a young rival, as may have been the case with Marion Terry; this time both Gilbert and Kitty were becoming closely attached to a young woman who, at twenty, was the age a daughter of their own might have been. Nancy, now living in London with her father and sister, had been brought up in a wealthy environment, but her father's failure in business had made their financial future insecure. Gilbert felt doubly bound to further Nancy's career, in the way that he had helped other actors and actresses in the past, by using his influence where he could. Gilbert had introduced her into the world of the theater; he now felt morally responsible to help her.

D'Oyly and Helen Carte, and Sullivan, too, saw things differently. They had a principal soprano who was a good singer but no actress. She may have had a nice, pleasant and sympathetic personality, but she was not good for business. There would be no question of engaging her again; in fact, they would have preferred her present engagement to be terminated.

On 16 December, Gilbert and Sullivan met to discuss a future collaboration, and immediately afterward Gilbert went off to construct a plot. He worked away in his usual systematic fashion over the Christmas period at Grim's Dyke. Nancy McIntosh joined Gilbert and Kitty for the weekend before New Year, and on 1 January she had a long talk with both of them, during which she told them about her precarious financial circumstances, and together they discussed her future.[3]

As a result of that talk, when he saw Sullivan a few days later, Gilbert begged him to let him write a small part for Nancy in their next work and so "save her from starvation." "What could I reply," Sullivan wrote in his diary. "I said 'give me till Monday to think over it'—to which he replied 'Come, why not say so at once', & nothing more was said. He went away delighted. I was upset."[4] Sullivan promptly saw her the next day, Saturday 6 January, and then heard her sing for two hours on the Monday. He was encouraging, told her he thought her voice was "much finer than he had any idea of" and then, hoping she would take the hint, told her that she had "an enviable career" ahead of her if she returned to the concert stage.[5]

When they met the next day, 10 January, Gilbert had "the rough outline of the plot" ready for Sullivan.[6] Reporting back to Carte, Gilbert's impression from the meeting was: "we quite understand one another."[7] Already he was thinking about casting. "I had a letter from Grossmith," he told Carte, "as to the possibility of an engagement for the new piece—He wants £70 a week—which is absurd & not to be thought of—but my belief is that if he could be got for £50 (which might be saved by getting rid of our two present big salaries) it would be quite worth while to secure him."[8]

If they were to make much profit the preliminary expenses of the new piece had to be considerably less than those of *Utopia*, and Carte stressed the point. After a good start with *Utopia*, business at the Savoy was beginning to fall off, and he was worried by competition from musical comedy at the Gaiety. He had suggested £2,000 for the preliminary expenses, and a reduction in the salary bill. Gilbert now proposed going further: keeping the expenses down to £1,500, hiring a cheaper scenic designer than Hawes Craven and restricting the principals' costumes to £20 apiece. Then came a setback to Gilbert's plans, as he explained to Carte. "Since I last wrote to you I have received a letter from Sullivan recanting all that he fully agreed to last night, & declining to write with me again unless the piece is to consist of broad & unrelieved low comedy from first to last. The situation is getting serious & I think I ought to have a talk with you about it as soon as possible."[9]

This was clearly an exaggeration of Sullivan's views, but it is equally clear that on reflection Sullivan was not pleased with Gilbert's idea for the next opera. After seeing Carte on Saturday, 13 January, Gilbert offered to let Sullivan see the scenario of the new piece before he had to commit himself to setting the music. "I have received a very satisfactory reply from Sullivan," Gilbert told Carte on 18 January, "who tells me that my last letter to him is 'most reassuring.'"[10]

Gilbert's concern over Nancy McIntosh and her financial situation extended to trying to make sure she lived within her means. He lectured her on the virtues of economy and, taking his advice to heart, she started traveling to and from the theater by train instead of catching a cab. Then she caught a cold, developed a sore throat and blamed it on traveling by train. It was to be the beginning of a series of colds and sore throats, made worse by anxiety, during January and February. She missed three performances in January, after breaking down in tears before going on stage, and having to be physically supported at times during the opera by Barrington and Kenningham. On her return, Sullivan sent her a brace of pheasants. "Everybody very kind to me at the theater," she wrote in her diary.[11] Her friends and colleagues were sympathetic and supportive. Both Gilbert and Sullivan sent her gifts on Valentine's Day; Rosina Brandram welcomed her back with flowers when she missed a performance in February; Rutland Barrington sent her lilies; Kitty Gilbert brought her violets and eggs; and Fanny Ronalds came to the theater one evening to offer encouragement by singing with her before one of the performances.

Nancy's anxiety was increased when Gilbert used his influence to get her the part of Dorothy in a benefit matinee performance of *Dan'l Druce* at the Strand. When she came to play the part on 20 February, she had little voice and no confidence; but a week later she repeated the role in a performance at the Crystal Palace. This time she felt that she had redeemed herself, and Gilbert congratulated her with a present of four cases of champagne.

Her closeness to the Gilberts was growing throughout this period. On 10 January, Gilbert and Kitty had moved into Prince's Gardens, an elegant square near the Albert Hall, which they made their London home until 22 March. Nancy lunched with them on several occasions over the months and dined there on a couple of occasions, once when she met the Hares and the Crutchleys (Sybil Coke and her husband), and once with her father and sister. She visited Grim's Dyke, "played with the monkeys" and stayed there over Easter, being shown over the grounds, watching Gilbert and Kitty "ride through the fields" and looking round Gilbert's library. She had experienced one "uncomfortable visit," as she called it, at Prince's Gardens, when Gilbert talked business with her. Her diary, which she kept for the first months of 1894, does not mention what kind of business they discussed, but a few weeks later she noted that Gilbert spent an hour at the Tax Office, "arranging about my summons for income tax."[12]

By 2 March, Gilbert was becoming agitated again over the whereabouts of Sullivan. He dropped a brief note to Carte. "Have you any news of Sullivan? I am at a standstill & must remain so until he comes."[13] Gilbert heard from Sullivan a few days later. On 8 March Nancy McIntosh, who had been invited to tea at Prince's Gardens, was taken down by Gilbert to the library, where he read her Sullivan's letter in which, she recorded, he said that "he will not write another piece if there is a part for me or a part suited to me in it. . . . This letter is the beginning of the end."[14] The next day Gilbert went to see Carte, who was anxious to "smooth things over," Nancy noted. "This uncertainty is most wearing—it & my throat together make me almost useless."[15] Carte was unsuccessful in his attempt to "smooth things over," and on 13 March Gilbert received a letter from Sullivan breaking off their collaboration.[16]

A lack of documentation surrounding these events means it is impossible to be clear about all the details. The one thing certain is that Sullivan would not write again with Gilbert if Nancy McIntosh were in the cast. Gilbert approached George Henschel with his libretto (the one intended for Sullivan, to be called *His Excellency*) and on 22 March everything appeared settled. Then Carte refused to produce the opera at the Savoy and, on 7 April, Nancy McIntosh noted sadly in her diary, "Mr. G. told me of H's lying letter about me & that Carte won't produce this opera & that it may fall through. Made me wretched & gave me a sleepless night."[17] Now that Gilbert's opera with Nancy McIntosh in the cast would be produced elsewhere, leaving the Savoy clear, Sullivan wrote to Gilbert on the same day, saying that he was still open to the possibility of their writing an opera together. From Gilbert's reply, it was now a question of timing. It would be impossible to have a new piece ready for June, and July would be too late in the season.

The proposed opera with Henschel was still a live issue, even if Carte had refused to produce it at the Savoy, and Gilbert now turned to the unlikely Horace Sedger on 10 April, asking for 20 percent (10 percent each) of the gross receipts. The proposal foundered; either Sedger declined or Henschel pulled out, and no more was heard of the collaboration. Neither was Gilbert's meeting with Sullivan productive. There was no time to produce an opera to replace *Utopia*; Sullivan did not want to write an opera that included Nancy McIntosh; and Gilbert wanted to pursue the piece he already had in mind, which included a part for Nancy. It was stalemate.

That summer Sullivan rented a house at Walton-on-Thames and, no longer encumbered by a libretto to set to music, he embarked on a season of racing: Sandown, Kempton, Newmarket, and Doncaster. It was the season in which Sullivan became a racehorse owner, buying "Blue Mark" for £500 after he had seen it win, and then selling it for £400 when it failed to repeat its success.

After 245 performances, *Utopia, Limited* closed on 9 June 1894. The final accounts revealed that Gilbert had made £4,600 for his 11 percent of gross receipts, whereas Carte and Sullivan, sharing the net profits between them, had each received only £1,800. Compared with previous operas, *Utopia* had not been a financial success, but at least the Savoy opera had held its own in competition with musical comedy at the Gaiety. Carte turned once more to Messager and on 3 July put on *Mirette* in an English adaptation by Harry Greenbank and Fred E. Weatherby. It would not be long before both *Mirette* and the Savoy were in trouble.

In June, Gilbert had teamed up with the young composer Osmond Carr who undertook to write the music for *His Excellency*, and it was agreed to produce the opera at the Lyric Theatre under the management of George Edwardes. The cast that Gilbert and Edwardes engaged had the look of an old Savoy company about it, with George Grossmith, Rutland Barrington, Jessie Bond, Alice Barnett, George Temple (who had played Samuel in the first London performance of *The Pirates* and toured as Captain Corcoran and Pooh-Bah), and the newer performers Charles Kenningham and Nancy McIntosh. They also engaged two promising young actors: Arthur Playfair, who had appeared in *The Mountebanks*, and Ellaline Terriss. At the Savoy, *Mirette* collapsed on 11 August, after only forty-one performances, and the theater was closed until the Cartes could arrange for a new adaptation of the opera. When some of the Savoy chorus, now unemployed, began to go over to the Lyric, it must have looked to the Cartes as though Gilbert was stealing the Savoy company away from them.

There began a long correspondence between Helen Carte and Gilbert, in which she accused him of enticing members of the Savoy chorus to go over to the Lyric. "You have been entirely misinformed," replied Gilbert on 6 September, and proceeded to discuss the individual instances quoted to him.[18] Helen Carte was not satisfied with his answer and wrote again, insisting that the choristers were already engaged at the Savoy. "The choristers were, no doubt 'already engaged' at the Savoy," Gilbert replied, "but you omit to add that they were under a fortnight's notice of dismissal. . . . It seems to me that if you wish to retain your choristers, your clear course is to give them engagements for a term."[19] Helen Carte took exception to the tone of that particular letter and Gilbert was obliged to write again, with further explanation, maintaining his original position, but attempting to be less strident, even apologizing if he had expressed himself "with unnecessary acrimony."[20]

Helen Carte would not let go. In an argument she was as persistent as Gilbert. She returned to the charge and Gilbert was forced to respond: "You persist in either misunderstanding or disbelieving me."[21] He denied emphatically that he had induced any chorister to leave the Savoy. Eventually, Helen Carte had to admit that she had been misinformed.

The sensitivity Helen Carte exhibited over the whole issue was symptomatic of the anxiety both she and D'Oyly Carte experienced at the downturn in their fortunes. The Savoy stood empty after the failure of *Mirette* and, because Gilbert refused to allow any of his operas to be performed without Nancy McIntosh, the only piece the Cartes had to offer was another version of *Mirette*. Public interest meanwhile had switched from the Strand to Shaftesbury Avenue and to the Lyric Theatre in particular, where great excitement had been generated at the prospect of Gilbert's new work with Dr. Osmond Carr, with a cast that had a familiar ring about it, led by Grossmith, Barrington, and Bond. It was all the more poignant for the Cartes to see that Gilbert's expected success was due to take place such a short distance away from Carte's spectacular failure in Shaftesbury Avenue.

A few days after Gilbert's last letter to Helen Carte, on 13 September, rehearsals began for *His Excellency*, with a refreshed Nancy McIntosh recently returned after a vacation in the United States.[22] At that point, Sullivan stepped in to help out his old friends at the Savoy, not with a new idea but with an old idea reworked. With F. C. Burnand he had agreed to revive their *Contrabandista*, which had first been performed in 1867. Burnand would rewrite the dialogue and Sullivan would write the music for a revised second act, the whole to be ready to replace the revised *Mirette* when it ended its run.

Shortly before the opening of *His Excellency* at the Lyric, a journalist named the comtesse de Brémont wrote to Gilbert asking for an interview for her paper, *St. Paul's*. Fully occupied in the last days of rehearsal, Gilbert wanted to put her off and told her that his fee for interviews was 20 guineas. The comtesse de Brémont replied that "she anticipated the pleasure of writing his obituary for nothing." Outraged, Gilbert wrote to *The Times* and the *Daily Telegraph*, sending a copy of her reply to him and referring to her as "a lady who styles herself the Comtesse de Brémont" who was already known to him "by repute."[23] Now it was the turn of the comtesse to be outraged, and she sued Gilbert for libel.

The action was to come to court on 19 December 1895. Gilbert had made his own enquiries through his solicitors, building up a picture of the comtesse de Brémont, ready to defend his comments published in *The Times* and elsewhere. She was originally Anna Elizabeth Dunphy from Cincinnati, Ohio, who at the age of twenty-five, in 1878, had married the compte de Brémont, then aged forty-four, who generally called himself Dr. de Brémont. In a letter to Helen Carte, Gilbert told her that he had previously received press notices of the comtesse's poems, "which are awfully improper"; and his solicitors had found out that she had a "bad reputation" in Johannesburg.[24] Little of all this was needed in court. Some of her poems were read out and described by counsel as "rather warm." Without even leaving their box, the jury returned a verdict in favor of Gilbert.[25]

Having won his point, Gilbert wrote to Anna de Brémont to tell her that he had instructed his solicitor not to insist on her paying her costs of the action. She thanked him for his courtesy and apologized for any pain she may have caused him. "This I have accepted unreservedly," said Gilbert, relating the incident to a friend, "— so, now, she is my sister."[26]

Public interest had grown as the first night of *His Excellency* approached, and speculation had increased about the plot of the opera. The *Star* published an account of the plot, and Gilbert applied for an interim injunction to prevent the paper reissuing that number. But by the time the injunction was granted, the opening of *His Excellency* was only one day away. Gilbert had gone to court to obtain justice;

that was his way, but in the process he had obtained excellent publicity for *His Excellency*, which duly opened on Saturday, 27 October. Writing to Helen Carte a week later, on 4 November, Gilbert said of it: "The piece is doing admirably & seems in for a long run. If it had had the advantage of your expensive friend Sullivan's music, it would have been a second Mikado."[27]

While Gilbert was gloating over his success at the Lyric, at the Savoy the revised version of *Mirette* closed after sixty-one performances on Thursday, 6 December. The following Wednesday, Sullivan and Burnand's revised *Contrabandista*, now called *The Chieftain*, opened with a strong cast including Rosina Brandram, Courtice Pounds, and Walter Passmore. *The Chieftain* was not, however, going to save the Savoy; at best, it would tide them over for a while. To reverse their fortunes, they were in need of a Gilbert and Sullivan opera. To make matters worse, just along the Strand, at the Gaiety, a new musical comedy had opened on 24 November. It was called *The Shop Girl*, with music by Ivan Caryll. Enormously popular, it would run for two years. Carte was out of ideas; he was tired, dispirited and, by the middle of December, he was seriously ill.

At the end of December, as Carte slowly recovered, Sullivan tried to assure him about business at the Savoy. "The Chieftain goes _well_. Splendid house last night, the alterations I have made are great improvements and much appreciated."[28] Sullivan was trying to be optimistic; further improvements were needed, and by then he was already working on his *King Arthur* music for Comyns Carr's play, which was to be produced by Henry Irving at the Lyceum. In the meantime, *Cox and Box*, with Richard Temple as Bouncer, was brought on from 31 December alongside *The Chieftain* to bolster the program.

Sullivan finished the music to *King Arthur* in the early hours of Tuesday, 8 January 1895, and at the Lyceum on Saturday, 12 January, he conducted the first night of the characteristically flamboyant Irving production, with Ellen Terry as Guinevere and with scenery and costumes designed by Burne-Jones. Shortly after the opening Sullivan left for Monte Carlo, staying at the Hôtel de Paris, where he then set about writing new numbers for *The Chieftain*. He was still struggling with them at the end of January, unable to set a new song for Rosina Brandram because of Burnand's meter, which prevented him giving it a Spanish dance rhythm as they had arranged. It was all very late: *The Chieftain* had little life left in it.

On 16 January 1895, Gilbert, Kitty, and two young friends—one of them the daughter of their Harrow Weald neighbours, the Blackwells—set sail for a two-month cruise to the West Indies, calling first at Tenerife and then sailing across the Atlantic to a comprehensive tour of the islands. Two days before leaving England, Gilbert had replied to a letter sent to him at the end of November by Bertram Ellis, editor of the *Keene Evening Sentinel* in New Hampshire. Ellis had sent a copy of an editorial he had written on "Electrical Execution," dealing with the "resuscitation of an executed criminal," and he suggested that it might make a theme for the plot of a comic opera.[29]

In his reply, Gilbert said that he had been working for some months on a piece that dealt with "an imaginary law by which under certain circumstances, a man who is physically alive is regarded as civilly & socially dead. Through the agency of a *deus ex machina*, the operation of this law (made to last 100 years) comes suddenly & unexpectedly to life again." Gilbert admitted that his plot had similarities with the article, but if he did use Ellis's suggestions "it would involve an entire reconstruction of the second act."[30] However, he promised to pay Ellis £50 if he made use of any of his ideas.

From what he told Ellis, Gilbert had started to think about his next opera soon after the opening of *His Excellency*, which would date his earliest draft to November 1894. He pasted the cutting from Ellis into the front of his plot book, possibly as a reminder of his obligation to Ellis rather than as a source. An alternative possibility that has been suggested is that, despite what he had told Ellis, Gilbert's idea for his plot was derived from Ellis's article.[31] But Gilbert's usual practice was to start work on a new plot very shortly after his previous piece had opened (in this case shortly after 27 October 1894), and Ellis's letter, dated 28 November, would not have reached Gilbert much before the middle of December 1894.

The plot was written originally bearing in mind the Lyric, where Gilbert and George Edwardes had thought of producing another opera in the spring of 1896. In an early draft, Gilbert jotted down a suggested casting, using actors from the cast of *His Excellency*: Alice Barnett, George Grossmith (as Wilhelm, the Grand Duke of Hesse Halbfennig), Rutland Barrington, Gertrude Aylward, Jessie Bond, Ellaline Terriss, Nancy McIntosh (as Casilda, daughter of the Prince and Princess of Monaco), and Richard Temple, who was no longer at the Savoy.

But the picture changed dramatically soon after Gilbert's return from his cruise to the West Indies. Due to an influenza epidemic, returns at the Lyric box office had taken a dive and Edwardes had decided to close. Despite attempts by the cast to stave off the end by expressing their willingness to take a cut in salary, after 162 performances *His Excellency* finally closed on 6 April. Plans were set in motion to take *His Excellency* to America with as many of the original cast as possible, including Nancy McIntosh. And then Nancy made an important decision: after *His Excellency* she wanted to return to the concert platform. She wrote to Sullivan to inform him. It is unlikely that this decision was reached without long discussion with Gilbert, and her writing to Sullivan told him that the obstacle standing in the way of a future collaboration with Gilbert at the Savoy had been removed.

Sullivan was in Paris when Nancy's letter arrived at Queen's Mansions. He returned to London on 24 April, and replied to Nancy's letter a week later. "I am so glad," he told her, "you mean to take up Concert and Oratorio work again, for I am convinced that that, and not the stage is your proper sphere. I am sure with a little help to start you, you will do well there."[32]

The way was now clear, in theory at least, for the Cartes and Gilbert to come to an agreement about the future. Gilbert and Edwardes had already agreed to put off a new opera to a later date. At the Savoy, matters were at a standstill. When *The Chief-tain* had come to the end of its meager run of ninety-eight performances on 16 March, Carte let the Savoy to the Carl Rosa Company, who played Humperdinck's *Hansel and Gretel* for a season until 15 June. The Savoy Theatre was then closed once more. Tentative negotiations began between Gilbert and the Cartes. According to a letter from Helen Carte to Sullivan in August 1895, she had been in correspondence with Gilbert for more than six months, from the time of his cruise to the West Indies, and before Nancy McIntosh's decision to quit the stage.

In June, Sullivan moved out of Queen's Mansions for the summer, while his apartment was redecorated. He left Herbert to supervise and provided him with a detailed list of tasks to keep him occupied. Sullivan went off to Ascot for the races, staying with his friend Russie Walker, and then rented River House at Walton-on-Thames. Meanwhile, the Cartes kept him informed on progress in their negotiations with Gilbert. In early July Gilbert fell ill with gastric flu, but he had recovered in a few weeks and was well enough to travel down to Walton on Thursday, 8 August, to read his sketch plot to Sullivan, leaving him the manuscript to go over in his own time. The following Sunday, Sullivan responded. After studying the sketch plot he liked it even more than on first reading. "It comes out as clear and bright as possible. I shall be very pleased to set it, and am prepared to begin (as soon as you have anything ready for me) and have written to Carte to tell him so."[33]

What Sullivan then suggested carried important implications for casting the new opera. He proposed making one of the soprano parts a contralto, arguing that this would make life easier for him when setting concerted pieces, because he would have a soprano and contralto instead of two sopranos. What he was doing was turning the character of Countess Krakenfeldt (which Gilbert had intended for Rosina Brandram) into that of a soprano and at the same time was ridding himself of his problem of the aged contralto with faded charms. Gilbert was sympathetic to the musical difficulties Sullivan experienced, but pointed out that the changes Sullivan proposed were far-reaching. In a countersuggestion, he left Brandram as the Countess Krakenfeldt.

On Monday, 12 August, Sullivan saw the Cartes and matters appeared settled. But when Sullivan returned to Weybridge, he had another idea, this time to have the Countess Krakenfeldt played by Florence Perry, and Rosina Brandram given another part—another possible attempt to avoid the middle-aged, plain lady character. He wired Gilbert and understood from the reply that Gilbert agreed. Overjoyed, Sullivan broke the news to the Cartes.

Helen Carte was furious and, on Wednesday, 14 August, sent Sullivan a long telegram reprimanding him severely for contacting Gilbert without clearing with them first as he had promised. What Sullivan was proposing played havoc with the casting. She followed up the telegram with a letter reminding Sullivan that she had begged him "never again; *until all questions were settled*—to send off important letters or telegrams to Mr. Gilbert without giving us a chance of consulting with you *first."* They had spent months in careful negotiations, and Sullivan was in danger of wrecking everything. Simply because Gilbert had agreed to Brandram playing Lisa, she told Sullivan, "you thought no more of what was to be done with the rest of the cast."[34]

A meeting was held at Adelphi Terrace on Friday, 16 August, when Gilbert, Sullivan, and the Cartes agreed terms for the production of *The Grand Duke*. Gilbert sold Carte complete rights to the opera for a total of £5,000, and at the same time agreed that Carte had the rights to produce revivals of his operas in London. One of the reasons for keeping to the casting that already had been agreed was that the Cartes had engaged a new leading soprano, Ilka Palmay, a Hungarian who had played Yum-Yum in *The Mikado* in Germany. She had come to England with the Saxe-Coburg Company and had made a favorable impression on London audiences. *The Sketch* described her as having "a face which alters with every shadow and shade of feeling" and "a personality as charming as the tilt of her well-shaped head."[35]

It was soon evident to Sullivan that production of the new opera before the end of the year was impossible, and with Gilbert and Carte decided in the interim to bring on a revival of *The Mikado*. Out of Gilbert's *His Excellency* cast, Charles Kenningham was still on contract to the Savoy, and Barrington and Jessie Bond had turned down an engagement with George Edwardes to go to America; therefore, all three were available for *The Mikado*. Gilbert was happy to have Jessie Bond in the cast, "for you were the life and soul of the piece," he told her. "Barrington without you is flint without steel (in that piece), as I told Carte three weeks since."[36] Having complimented her so handsomely, he was able to let her down lightly over her request for a new song. There was little hope, he told her, of Sullivan being able to find time to write a new song for *The Mikado*. "He is like me in one respect (only in one) — when he is in full swing of his work, as he is now, he won't stand interruption."[37]

Barrington, Brandram, and Bond played their original roles and were joined by the newcomers to the opera: Walter Passmore (Ko-Ko), Charles Kenningham (Nanki-Poo), Robert Scott Fishe (the Mikado), Florence Perry (Yum-Yum), and Emmie Owen (Peep-Bo). Gilbert supervised the rehearsals, and Sullivan conducted the first night on Wednesday 6 November 1895. The Savoy Theatre was alive again. The performance was, in the words of *The Times*:

> a triumph from first to last. All the old favourite numbers in the score were encored — "The flowers that bloom in the spring" had to be twice repeated — and both artists and composer were loudly cheered by an exceptionally large audience.

The newcomers to the cast were considered to be as good as the original cast, although according to the reviewer for *The Times*, Walter Passmore "does not succeed in effacing recollections of the humour of his predecessor."[38]

The day after the opening, Gilbert and Sullivan spent nearly three hours together at Queen's Mansions "going through the new piece," Sullivan told Helen Carte. "I played him all I have done, & he is delighted!"[39] Gilbert was far from delighted, however, with Florence Perry and Emmie Owen in *The Mikado*. Miss Owen had retaliated when Gilbert pointed out the error of her ways in a piece of business with their fans, which Gilbert had not sanctioned in rehearsal. Sullivan reported to Helen Carte:

> Gilbert is angry with both of them, but especially with Owen—talked of reducing her part in the new piece to "cues" &c. as he couldn't possibly work with a girl who attacked him like a tigress &c &c. you know the sort of thing.

He suggested that Emmie Owen should write a short note of apology to Gilbert.

> He wont of course alter her part as I have settled that all right, but he might make it unpleasant for her at rehearsals, & she had better get the right side of him. So will you suggest it to her? They are a couple of little fools, harried into such conduct by Jessie.
>
> The taps with the fans were *never done*, (only the motion of tapping) [neither] by Braham nor Ulmar, & both Gilbert & myself dislike it. I don't know who told you it was done formerly, but it certainly never was.[40]

Shortly after the opening of the revival of *The Mikado*, Sullivan left for Berlin to prepare for the performance at the Berlin Court Opera of *Ivanhoe*. He was told that £3,500 had been spent on the production, but from what he could observe he was not convinced. Neither was he impressed by the soloists, and he thought the chorus was awful. By contrast, he told his new secretary, Wilfred Bendall, he was satisfied with the orchestra, and also with "the excellent little conductor Dr Muck."[41] Although supervising rehearsals, Sullivan managed to find time to begin work on act 2 of *The Grand Duke*.

After the disappointment of having his work postponed for two years since his preparatory visit to Berlin, and after seeing the quality of the cast and chorus engaged for the opera, Sullivan was not confident of its success when it was performed on 26 November 1895. His worst fears were confirmed. The opera was greeted with respect but without enthusiasm. *The Times* correspondent in Berlin commented, "in the future, as in the past, Sir Arthur Sullivan's great popularity here will continue to be associated with those works which, like *The Mikado*, bear the full impress of his original genius."[42]

Sullivan returned to his work with Gilbert. The libretto for *The Grand Duke* had been subject to numerous changes since Gilbert had started work on it a year before. At the beginning he was writing for a small cast, as in the old days, but when he later introduced modifications for the Savoy, he increased the cast and complicated the plot by embedding into the original a secondary plot involving a theatrical company. In his original plot, Nancy McIntosh was to have been Casilda, the daughter of the Prince and Princess of Monaco; for the finished version, Gilbert had to produce a plot that made good use of the engagement of Ilka Palmay. He had created for her the part of an English actress among a company of Germans, whose foreign accent was commented on by the other players as being English, while everybody else was presumed to be speaking in German. Grossmith was no longer to be the Grand Duke, and Barrington's part as the leading comedian in the theatrical company became the major comedy role. The complications brought about by the new and involved plot were never solved to Gilbert's entire satisfaction. Overall he thought he had produced an "ugly misshapen little brat."[43]

As in all the operas, more depended on the quality of the lyrics than on the plot. In his sixtieth year, Gilbert had passed his best as a writer of comic verse, especially the kind of comic verse that had so effectively inspired Sullivan in the past to produce his stream of melodies. There is a wealth of patter, but Sullivan found it difficult to be inspired by much of it. In the old days, he would take a difficult number back to Gilbert and ask him to put it into a different meter or make a suggestion for improvement, in order to produce the effect he was seeking. Perhaps one of Gilbert's more successful numbers was the Grand Duke's "When You Find You're a Broken-Down Critter," describing the horrors of being ill. Gilbert had evidently been pleased with it as he had written a slightly different version for *The Mountebanks*, but Cellier had been too ill to set it. Sullivan set it to a slower tempo than usual for what was originally intended as a patter song, and turned it into a pleasantly tuneful number.

The best of the combined work of Gilbert and Sullivan was now in the past. Nevertheless, there are several numbers from *The Grand Duke* with bright and cheerful melodies, including the opening chorus, "Won't It Be a Pretty Wedding?" And Sullivan showed he had not lost his gift for the clever interweaving of melodies when, in the "catty" duet between Julia and Lisa ("Oh, listen to me, dear—/ I love him only, darling!"), a deliciously slinky, feline melody on the clarinet roams around behind the girls' mock politeness. Sullivan took the trouble to write the overture himself: a sample of the best melodies in the opera, woven together rather than stitched together as in earlier medleys.

Last-minute changes to the libretto before the first night included changing the Grand Duke's name from Wilhelm to Rudolph and his duchy from Hesse Halbpfennig to Pfennig Halbpfennig. Reference to the Grand Duke as "of German royalty a sprig" was neutralized to "in his own opinion, very very big," and instead of being termed "a miserable pig," he was called "a miserable prig." All these changes were made to avoid giving offence not to Germans in general but to Kaiser Wilhelm in particular, and they were possibly Gilbert's response to a request from Sullivan, who highly valued his friendship with the German emperor. Gilbert kept Sullivan waiting, though—the changes were made just in time for the first night.

Among the cast on that first night, 7 March 1896, playing minor roles in *The Grand Duke; or, The Statutory Duel* were three singers destined for a bright future at the Savoy: Ruth Vincent (Gretchen), Jessie Rose (Bertha), and C. H. Workman

(Ben Hashbaz), who had appeared as Calynx on tour with *Utopia, Limited*. It was a splendid first night, the audience glittering with the rich and famous, among them a sprinkling of the aristocracy, and old friends such as Lord Marcus Beresford and Sir Eyre Massey Shaw, George Edwardes and Julia Gwynne, Jessie Bond, and Arthur Pinero. The evening produced a goodly crop of encores: including two for Barrington ("By the Mystic Regulation" and "At the Outset I May Mention"); an encore for the quintet, "Strange the Views Some People Hold," and one for one of Sullivan's loveliest melodies, "Take Care of Him," sung by Florence Perry. From the critics there was praise for the cast, for Gilbert's stage management, for Ilka Palmay's singing and acting, and for Walter Passmore—who "comes nearer to Mr. Grossmith's level than he has done yet," said *The Times*—but of the opera as a whole, the same reviewer also commented, "This time the libretto is very conspicuously inferior to the music."[44] At the end of the night, both Gilbert and Sullivan received their traditional call to come onto the stage to acknowledge the applause of the audience, but neither man was really satisfied. That night Sullivan wrote in his diary, "Thank God opera is finished & out."[45]

CHAPTER THIRTY

1896-1898

They Went On . . . "But Did Not Speak to Each Other"

ONCE THE GRAND DUKE had opened, Sullivan wasted no time, but packed his bags and set off for Monte Carlo. "Why reproach me?" he wrote back to Frank Burnand on 12 March, "*I* didn't write the book!! . . . Another week's rehearsal with W.S.G. & I should have gone raving mad."[1] Did Sullivan ever, during his stay, recall Gilbert's words from *The Grand Duke*, words sung by the Prince of Monte Carlo and to which Sullivan had given a real French flavor in his music?

> Take my advice—when deep in debt,
> Set up a bank and play Roulette!

Sullivan was not in Monte Carlo to set up a bank, but to indulge his passion for gambling. If Sullivan did recall the song, he took no heed of the lines,

> For every time the board you spin,
> The bank is bound to win![2]

Certainly *The Grand Duke* was no banker. After playing to about £1,600 a week for the first two months, it had dropped to £900 by the end of the third. From 25 April, it was faring badly against the newest of the musical comedies, *The Geisha* by Sydney Jones, which had opened at Daly's Theatre.

Gilbert was keeping an eye on the libretto and was still ready to wield the pruning knife nearly two months into the run. On 3 May he wrote to Helen Carte: "I return your book with the suggestions for cuts. I have agreed to all that appear to me to be possible—I have given my reasons for objecting to those to which I *have* objected." As a matter of principle he was against allowing any "gags" that had not been submitted to him before production, but he was sensitive to Barrington who liked to "work up" his part. "I have no desire to injure the prospects of the piece," he said, "— &, consequently, your interests — by doing anything that would give <Barrington> [name crossed out] any actor an excuse for walking sulkily through his part — so I will leave it to you to do exactly as you think best."[3]

With *The Grand Duke* fading, six matinee performances of *The Mikado* were put on. The cast was the same as in the revival at the beginning of the year, and included Jessie Bond who returned to play Pitti-Sing. On Friday, 11 July, after 123 performances, *The Grand Duke* was taken off and the very next evening *The Mikado* took its place. Rutland Barrington stayed for the first week and then left the Savoy to join the cast of *The Geisha* at Daly's while Fred Billington was called in from the "C Company" to take over as Pooh-Bah.

Back from Monte Carlo, Sullivan was soon in poor health. After suffering from his old kidney ailment in May, he caught influenza in June and was eager to seek the mountain air in Switzerland. He left for St. Moritz on 22 July, hoping "to pick up strength & return D.V. well & robust" he explained to Helen Carte.[4] His trip to Monte Carlo, it appears, had left him temporarily embarrassed, and he was obliged to ask Helen Carte to redirect his next two checks to pay off his debts. "I don't want to worry you, but I am overdrawn at Goslings, *& must* pay some things from their bank — So will you like a dear, pay my Grand Duke money to my account *there*, as soon as you can."[5]

In the company of his friend Adolf Hirsch, Sullivan traveled to St. Moritz, and for the next five weeks he spent his time in the "delirious dullness" shared by other wealthy English visitors. The duchess of York was there, with her mother the duchess of Teck, and other hotel guests included Leo Rothschild and his wife, Henry Labouchère and his wife, Henrietta Hodson, and Charles Wyndham, who was there with Mary Moore, Decima Moore's sister. Together with royal guests he was invited to dinner by the Rothschilds, and later returned the favor by giving a dinner for more or less the same party, entertaining them afterward with "a little music" in his sitting room.[6] On one occasion, he was invited to lunch with the royal party in their rooms, for which event he took gifts for the duchess of Teck and Princess May, and in return the princess gave him a "beautiful photo of herself & children."[7]

In a letter to his nephew, Sullivan described a typical day at the hotel: "I get up in the morning (before I go out even), breakfast, read The Times and Telegraph, & then I stroll about till lunchtime, if it doesn't pour. Out again from lunch to dinner time, if it doesn't pour — then the regular Swiss Hotel evening, sitting in the large Hall, smoking, talking, and passing the time until we come up into my sitting room, for an hours chat before going to bed."[8]

> In open idleness we live,
> With lyre and lute
> And silver flute,

The life of Lazyland!
In lazy languor—motionless,
We lie and dream of nothingness.[9]

Gilbert's words from *Utopia*—so well interpreted by Sullivan. And in his "dream of nothingness" Sullivan was able to forget—so effectively it seems, that he even forgot Fanny Ronalds's birthday.

The weather was mixed: "When it rains," he told his nephew, "it does so conscientiously—never ceasing even for meals"; but after the rain, the sun rejuvenated him, "there was a crystal sort of coldness in the air which made one feel 21 again."[10] Sullivan moved on to Lucerne, and, no doubt still feeling twenty-one, he fell in love with a girl of twenty—Violet Beddington. Sullivan had known her since she was a child, when Rubinstein had introduced him to the family. Over the next few weeks, he spent much of his time in the company of "Miss Violet," as he very properly addressed her. And then the old romantic in him imagined the possibility of life being renewed by this beautiful young woman, blooming with the vital energy of youth. Sullivan proposed marriage; he told her he did not have many years left to live, and afterward he would leave everything to her as Lady Sullivan. She thought it over, and declined the proposal. Sullivan found the refusal so painful, and no doubt so embarrassing, that he left Lucerne the very next morning.

He traveled up to Munich, then across to Vienna before moving back into Germany to answer an invitation from the dowager empress of Germany, Queen Victoria's eldest daughter, to stay at Friedrichshof, where he arrived on Wednesday, 23 September. He was given a warm welcome and after dinner sat at the piano and played for the pleasure of the empress. The next day he was on his way again, this time homeward bound via Frankfurt and Paris.

While Sullivan had been away, *The Mikado* had passed its thousandth performance, but celebrations to mark the occasion were delayed until Saturday, 31 October, for the 1037th performance. Festoons of chrysanthemums were hung across the front of the boxes, the proscenium, and the back of the stalls; Japanese lanterns concealed the electric lights and special programs were printed in the shape of Japanese fans. Everyone in the audience received a *Gilbert & Sullivan Birthday Book* as a souvenir, containing extracts from the operas for every day of the year. Of the original cast only Jessie Bond and Rosina Brandram remained, but, said *The Times*, "the newer generation of performers can show some remarkably good representatives, such as Miss Florence Perry . . . and Mr. Walter Passmore, who is steadily improving as an exponent of the class of parts associated with the name of Mr. Grossmith."[11] At the close of the evening, Gilbert and Sullivan appeared in answer to the usual call, and an apology was read for D'Oyly Carte, who, it was announced, "was kept at home by illness."[12]

Carte's illness continued throughout November. "I hope the relapse is only temporary," said Gilbert to Helen Carte on 9 November,[13] and then again on 24 November, "I am extremely sorry to hear that Carte has been so ill. It must be a serious anxiety to you & I assure you of my fullest sympathy."[14] Carte was only fifty-two, but like Sullivan was suffering from constant ill-health and was aging prematurely. Sullivan was temporarily restored to better health after his stay in Switzerland, and a few weeks after conducting the gala night at the Savoy, he conducted *The Golden Legend*, on 19 November, at the Albert Hall. It was to be the last time that he conducted the work.

At the end of November, Helen Carte sent a repertory company out to South Africa on a tour that lasted until July 1897. For the sale of the libretto in South Africa, Gilbert left everything in the hands of Helen Carte. "Make any arrangements you think right about S. African books," he told her. "I know it will be fair & just."[15]

Over the years, Gilbert had often involved Helen Carte in his charitable causes, and at the end of November approached her with an unusual request. He had been appointed as the honorary secretary of the Bushey Cottage Hospital, a few miles from Grim's Dyke; it was a post that he filled in his customary conscientious way for the rest of his life. He wanted to have a circular for the hospital typed. "Now I dont know any one who has a type writer except yourself—& I am not sure that *you* have. But *if* you have, will you kindly allow one copy to be made & sent to me?"[16]

Any thought of doing another opera was far from Gilbert's mind. "Personally I am not keen about doing any more—at least that is my feeling now," he said to Helen Carte, offering to let her make use of any "likely material" he came across for a possible libretto.[17] He was off to Burma, with Kitty, leaving on 4 December, for a three-month trip.

By the end of the year, Sullivan also had left England, to spend the winter months in the south of France, where he rented the Villa Mathilde at Beaulieu, a short distance from Nice. He had taken Clotilde and Louis with him, but left Herbert in London. He also had left behind Fanny Ronalds, who had been deeply upset when she learned of Sullivan's proposal to Violet Beddington. Although still "really fond of her," Sullivan could not admit to loving her as he once did. In a letter to Herbert from Beauvais, he attempted to explain and to divorce himself from any role of responsibility in her depression. He told Herbert that when he had first known her she had men, in Paris and in London, throwing themselves at her. "Now, the years will tell," he said, recommending that they should be "gentle and considerate" to her at this difficult period of her life. Complications in their relationship were causing pain on both sides. "I think," he confessed to Herbert, "we all touched the bottom of misfortune and unhappiness this past year . . . be a friend & guide to her."[18] For the present, Sullivan preferred to cope with these complications by being far away.

Apart from putting himself at a distance from any unpleasantness, Sullivan was engaged in writing ballet music to a scenario by Carlo Coppi commissioned to celebrate Queen Victoria's diamond jubilee. Because of his usual delay in making a start, he was short of time and at the end of January sent a frantic message to Wilfred

Bendall to search out his *Ile enchantée* music for him in the libraries at Crystal Palace and Covent Garden.

It fell to Bendall again to help out when Sullivan was appointed chairman of the music section for a Victorian Era exhibition planned for Earl's Court in May. In Sullivan's absence, many of the duties must have fallen on Bendall as vice chairman. Sullivan's personal contribution would be *Victoria and Merrie England*. He had finished his score by the end of March and shortly after started for Paris, where he intended to spend some time on vacation with Fanny Ronalds.

Having fulfilled one commission, Sullivan found himself presented with another. On 6 April, he traveled south to Cimiez, near Nice, where Queen Victoria was staying. He was to see Sir Arthur Bigge, the queen's private secretary, "about a 'command' hymn for the Jubilee."[19] The queen wanted the hymn played on 20 June in every church throughout the British Empire and wanted Sullivan to compose the tune. For the words of the hymn, Sullivan suggested the bishop of Wakefield, William Walsham How, author of the well-known hymn "For all the saints." While in Cimiez, Sullivan met his old friend the duke of Edinburgh, now the duke of Saxe-Coburg, and through him earned for himself an official invitation from the queen to play the harmonium in the chapel at the Regina Hotel, for the royal party. As for the hymn, How and Sullivan were each deeply appreciative of the other's contribution. Sullivan expressed his admiration of the poetry and religious feeling of the words, but feared his music did not come up to their level. How, by contrast, was convinced that his words could only be enhanced when set by a composer of Sullivan's genius.

By the time Gilbert had returned to England, after his Far Eastern voyage, he had recovered from his despair following *The Grand Duke*, and was ready to embark on another libretto for the Savoy. What he had in mind was a plot based on *The Wicked World*. He suggested an all-female chorus, but Carte objected. "I am no musician," said Gilbert to Helen Carte, in a letter on 11 April, "& cannot express a useful opinion on such a point—but I should suggest that when the composer is decided upon, *he* should be consulted upon the point."[20] Over the next few days, Gilbert suggested that his new piece could be set in the period of Richard III, or perhaps given a contemporary setting, but in either case he wanted to make it more humorous than *The Wicked World*. Carte remained unenthusiastic.

While Gilbert and Sullivan were both abroad, the revival of *The Mikado* had come to an end on 17 February 1897 after 226 performances. It made way for a new comic opera, *His Majesty*, with words by F. C. Burnand, R. C. Lehmann, and Adrian Ross, and music by Alexander Mackenzie. It had only a short run. A revised version had to be produced after a month, and on 24 April, after sixty-one performances, *His Majesty* finally closed. The Cartes were forced once more to fall back on Gilbert and Sullivan, and a decision had been made to revive *The Yeomen of the Guard*.

With Hawes Craven Gilbert spent a morning at the Tower of London selecting a scene that would be suitable for a new set for act 2, from which Craven could build

Arthur Sullivan—the mature composer (V&A Picture Library)

a model for Gilbert's consideration. Gilbert had already agreed to the cast drawn up by the Cartes: Richard Temple had returned to play Sergeant Meryll, and Rosina Brandram, the only other member of the original cast, played Dame Carruthers. The newcomers were Walter Passmore (Jack Point), Henry Lytton (Wilfred Shadbolt), Ilka Palmay (Elsie), Florence Perry (Phoebe), and the promising Ruth Vincent in the small part of Kate. The opera opened on Wednesday, 5 May, and was conducted on the first night by Sullivan. "Great reception," he noted in his diary. "Opera went splendidly—Palmay very unfitted for Elsie. Passmore & Lytton excellent—also Perry as Phoebe. Gilbert & I took calls at the end—Supper at Savoy afterwards."[21]

At the Alhambra Theatre, on 25 May, after a private dress rehearsal in the afternoon, Sullivan and Coppi's ballet *Victoria and Merrie England* was danced for the first time. Sullivan was pleased with its reception: "Magnificent house—all the élite of London present, including Princess Louise, Duke of Cambridge & the Adolphus Tecks. Great enthusiasm. Conducted the performance myself—Genuine success."[22] The ballet was indeed popular, and continued to be performed at the Alhambra over the next six months.

Sullivan's contribution to the diamond jubilee earned him the gratitude of the queen and an invitation to Windsor Castle. On 5 July, after dinner with the household, he was "received by the Queen in the Long Corridor. Had twenty minutes conversation with Her Majesty who was most kind & gracious," he recorded. "After I retired she sent me the Jubilee Medal by Miss Phipps—played billiards and smoked with the Household till bedtime."[23] Queen Victoria's intense dislike of smoking confined it to the billiard room.

Having fulfilled his royal duties, Sullivan left for Germany and the Bayreuth Festival, accompanied by his secretary Wilfred Bendall. *Parsifal*, on 11 August, impressed him immensely; but three days later he was very disappointed in the performers of *Rheingold*, saying that the orchestra under Siegfried Wagner was "rough & ragged."[24] On Sunday, 15 August, at a house party at which the prince and princess of Wales and Arthur Balfour were guests, he had a "good lunch," fell asleep and missed the first act of *Walküre*. From what he saw, he thought there was "much that is beautiful in the opera—less dreary padding than in the others."[25] The next day he found *Siegfried* "intolerably dull & heavy . . . I am weary of Leitmotiven," he noted. "What a curious mixture of sublimity & absolutely puerile drivel are all these Wagner Operas."[26] On Tuesday he heard *Götterdämmerung*, and although he thought the first act "Dull & dreary" and the second act "Just as dull & dreary," he judged the third act "Very fine and impressive. The Leitmotiven seemed all natural and not dragged in, and the whole Act is much more dramatic & musically finer than any of the others."[27] On the final day he heard *Parsifal* again—a less impressive performance, he thought. And so finished a week of Wagner; what for others had been a musical feast, Sullivan had found most indigestible at times. From Bayreuth he took off for the Alps, visiting Innsbruck, Thusis, Splügen, and Disentis with Fanny Ronalds.

A fortnight later he was back in England, writing in his diary on Sunday, 5 September: "Glad to be at home. Sat up till 12.15 recounting my experiences to Clotilde."[28] More than just a housekeeper, Clotilde was now confidante and at times a partner at cards.

Nothing had come of Gilbert's suggestion of a new libretto based on *The Wicked World* and its all-female chorus. Carte had not been impressed with the idea, and possibly he was not happy to put on a new piece by Gilbert without Sullivan. A piece by Sullivan was another matter, and he commissioned him to write an opera with the book supplied by Comyns Carr and Arthur Pinero.

Blocked in one direction, Gilbert moved to his next work, *The Fortune Hunter*, a play originally commissioned by Edward Willard; but as the work progressed, Willard had misgivings. Similarly, George Alexander, manager of the St. James's, who also had asked Gilbert for a play, found it unsuitable. Gilbert decided to offer it to May Fortescue, whose company worked in the provinces. *The Fortune Hunter* opened at the Theatre Royal, Birmingham, on 27 September, and it so happened that on that same day Gilbert wrote a letter to *The Times*, complaining about the deterioration in punctuality of local trains on the London and North-Western Railway. The letter has become famous; part of it appears in books of quotations to this day, long after *The Fortune Hunter* has been forgotten. The quotations vary, but Gilbert's original letter read:

> In the face of Saturday the officials and the company stand helpless and appalled. This day, which recurs at stated and well-ascertained intervals, is treated as a phenomenon entirely outside the ordinary operations of nature, and, as a consequence, no attempt whatever is made to grapple with its inherent difficulties. To the question, "What has caused the train to be so late?" the officials reply, "It is Saturday"—as who should say, "It is an earthquake."[29]

Shortly after that letter, Gilbert had cause to use the railways, to travel up to Edinburgh where *The Fortune Hunter* was opening after its short run in Birmingham. Immediately on arrival he wired and then wrote to "Dearest Kits," "I arrived all right (but half an hour late)."[30] His problem with trains was not confined to punctuality. He had found his sleeping berth already occupied, but the mixup was eventually sorted out and he ended the journey with a first-class compartment to himself. In Edinburgh, he was welcomed with the news that *The Fortune Hunter* had done good business in Birmingham. It may have done, but the play was panned in *The Times*: "In dialogue *The Fortune Hunter* does not bear signs of the hand to which we owe the witty and ingenious librettos of Savoy opera."[31]

The press was to prove even more troublesome to Gilbert over the next few weeks. After the performance on 4 October, Gilbert gave an interview to Isaac Donald of the Edinburgh *Evening Despatch*, and in the newspaper the next day he was reported as saying, "I hear Sydney Grundy put on the same level with Arthur Pinero, while the fact is that Mr. Grundy is only a translator." Asked about blank-verse plays, Gilbert was quoted to have said, "we have no actor on the stage that can make a thirty-line speech interesting." Asked if that criticism applied to Henry Irving, George Alexander, and Beerbohm Tree, Gilbert agreed.[32]

An article based on the interview appeared in the *Evening Despatch* the following day, by which time Gilbert had already left Edinburgh. It was not until 13 October, when reference to the article appeared in the *World*, that Gilbert was made aware of the comments attributed to him. He wrote to the *Era* and to the *Evening Despatch* denying that he had spoken of Sydney Grundy in the way quoted. The *Evening Despatch* made no reply; but the *Era*, in its issue of 16 October, commented: "Mr. Gilbert's abnormal self-esteem has with advancing years developed into a malady. In his own estimation he is a kind of Grand Llama or Sacred Elephant of dramatic literature." He was not "a cruel or spiteful man," the article continued, but "his real kindliness and good-nature have simply been obscured by the abnormal protuberance of his bump of self-esteem."[33]

Gilbert responded by suing the editor of the *Era* for libel, but would have to wait until the following year before the case came to court. In the meantime, in reply to a "very generous letter" from Sydney Grundy, Gilbert claimed that the words he used in the interview were "Of course I speak of Mr. Grundy only as an adapter." Gilbert was distressed by the suggestion that he had spoken "slightingly" of Grundy; although he had to admit his choice of words was no doubt unwise.[34]

The revival of *The Yeomen of the Guard* came to an end on 20 November 1897, after 186 performances. Ilka Palmay had left the cast in July, and various sopranos were tried as Elsie before Ruth Vincent was settled on for the rest of the run. In December, Carte turned to Offenbach with a new adaptation of *The Grand Duchess of Gerolstein*. It would be another six months before Sullivan would have his new opera ready; he planned to spend Christmas in London before going to the south of France, where he hoped to compose the music.

After rehearsals for *The Grand Duchess of Gerolstein*, which opened on 4 December, Carte had to take to his sickbed again at Weybridge. "I hope," said Sullivan in a letter to Carte on 14 December, "this means nothing more serious than a little fatigue after the rehearsals, or a little cold. They tell me at rehearsals you exhibited superhuman energy—that you gave directions in stentorian tones, and that generally, you displayed the combined qualities of a C. Harris, an R. Barker, a W.S.G. an Arthur Sullivan *and* a Louis Quatorze!"[35] He tried to raise Carte's spirits. "I have spent most of my time lately at Windsor, and have had *three* long & pleasant chats with the Queen (bless her, she is so kind and gracious)[.] We are beginning to be talked about!"[36]

Even before settling terms with his new collaborators, Sullivan had a long discussion about the opera with Carr and Pinero one evening after dinner at Carr's house. "First signs of difficulties likely to arise," Sullivan noted in his diary. "Both Pinero and Carr gifted & brilliant men, with *no* experience in writing for music, & yet obstinately declining to accept any suggestions from me, as to form and construction."[37] Sullivan found it heartbreaking to try to make a musical piece out of their involved sentences.

Although unsettled business was now compounded by misgivings about the libretto, Sullivan still undertook to write the music. Terms were not agreed until February 1898, and even then the terms were not what Sullivan would have preferred. "As I wired you yesterday," he wrote to Helen Carte on 3 February, "I have written to Pinero a second letter to say that I will consent to share profits instead of taking a percentage." Sullivan explained that he had told Pinero that his decision was motivated by his hearing that they felt "discouraged" by having a different agreement from his. But his real motive, he told Helen Carte, was to avoid adding to her worries. "I thought of you and all the trouble you have had already—of the work you have had to do with the hotels as well as the theater—of your anxiety about D'Oyly, & of your standing quite alone."[38]

Helen Carte had questioned his reasons for not settling terms when he received the scenario, but Sullivan deflected the question by throwing the onus onto Pinero and Carr. They were wrong, he said, to have made an agreement with her without reference to him, while knowing that he did not like the terms.

Sullivan made himself sound like an innocent among wolves; but the truth is he had not settled business arrangements carefully before going any further in the collaboration. Gilbert had always fought for them both in the past; Sullivan, without Gilbert, was vulnerable. "My love to D'Oyly," Sullivan concluded. "I wish you could bring him to Beaulieu—the air is lovely, & it would do him a world of good. He might come by sea all the way."[39] Carte did not travel out to Beaulieu, but Comyns Carr did, staying several weeks.

Sullivan would get up very late, Carr related, perhaps even in the afternoon; after dinner he liked to play a few games of bezique before settling down to work while everyone else slept, working through the night until four or five in the morning. Visits to the casino were restricted to twice a week. When he played, he played alone. For this most sociable of men, the thrill and excitement of the gaming table was a solitary experience; after three hours at the tables, he would go back to Beauvais exhausted.[40]

When *The Gondoliers* was revived, on 22 March 1898, Sullivan was still on the Riviera. "I am sorry," Gilbert wrote to Helen Carte, from 27 Prince's Gardens where he was spending the winter months, "that Sullivan wont come over—the more so as it is impossible for me to take the call (if there should be one) alone. It is a piece of egotism to which I am really not equal." The time was approaching for Gilbert's libel action against the editor of the *Era*, and he asked Helen Carte to stand as a witness for him, if necessary, just to say that she had seen nothing in him to suggest that he was "a man in whom vanity & egotism have degenerated into a disease—that I do not desire (as far as you know)," he suggested to her, "to dominate the universe ; & that I am not in the habit of abusing and insulting the actors who play in the pieces."[41]

In spite of his fear of being considered egotistic at such a sensitive time, Gilbert did step forward in answer to a call at the end of *The Gondoliers* on 22 March. He apologized for Sir Arthur Sullivan's absence, said *The Times*, "by making the welcome announcement that the composer [was] at work upon a new opera."[42] The only link with the original *Gondoliers* among the cast that evening had been Rosina Brandram as the Duchess, who according to *The Times* gave "as refined and quiet a performance as ever."[43]

The following Monday, Gilbert was in court to prove that he was not the vain egotist that the *Era* had made him out to be. Edward Carson, counsel for Ledger, the editor of the *Era*, put Gilbert into the witness box and in a long cross-examination was allowed to range widely over Gilbert's past quarrels: his quarrel with Clement Scott, over his criticism of *Brantinghame Hall*, and his legal action against the *Pall Mall Gazette*. Carson asked him if he had quarreled with Sullivan, or with D'Oyly Carte, or with Horace Sedger, or with John Hare, as he built up his picture of a quarrelsome Gilbert. At one point, Carson put it to Gilbert that the *Era* had made many favorable comments about him. "Very possibly," Gilbert replied. "I never read them, for I know how good I am, but I do not know how bad I am." The trial continued into Tuesday and the special jury then retired to consider their verdict. After two and one-half hours they returned, unable to agree, and the foreman insisted that there was no chance of an agreement. The trial closed without a verdict.[44]

"As you will have seen," Gilbert reported to Helen Carte, "the jury disagreed—10 were for me & 2 against. The judge summed up like a drunken monkey—he is in the last stage of senile decay & knew absolutely nothing about the case. It was impossible to convince him that I was not bringing the case against the *interviewer*!"[45] On Friday, 1 April, Gilbert and Kitty set sail for Naples for a three-week vacation in Italy. "I want to blow the 'froust' of the Law Courts out of my brain," he explained to Helen Carte.[46]

Sullivan, too, left for the continent in April, going to Paris at the end of the month for a short vacation with Fanny Ronalds, who was grieving following the death of her mother. The Leeds committee was hoping that he would write a cantata for the next festival, but Sullivan was almost certain in his own mind that he would decline. He fully realized that this might cost him the conductorship, and knew he could be easily replaced. "There will be no difficulty about a conductor," he confided to Wilfred Bendall, with a hint of bitterness, "as Stanford is ready—aye, and willing! What else did he accept the Leeds Phil. Soc. for?"[47] Fanny Ronalds was better for the vacation, she "now & then has a bit of colour in her cheek," he told Bendall.[48]

When they returned home, it was Sullivan's turn to be ill, with a bout of influenza in early May. As he recovered, he intended to go to Brighton "to get a change of air" but instead felt well enough to go to Newmarket for the races.[49] Once again, he was short of ready money and wrote to Helen Carte.

I have been staggered by receiving two accounts which for the moment I am unable to pay.

A short time ago I was to the good, & in the last few days the slump has been so rapid and unexpected, that I am much to the bad. Can you (I know you *will* if you can) lend me the money (£1700) for three weeks? . . . If you can't do all, perhaps you can manage a thousand of it, & I will do the rest. . . . The insult is, as you understand, a cash transaction, as Pooh Bah would say, payable in three weeks — may be less.[50]

To judge from Sullivan's next note to Helen Carte, the touch of humor had not amused her sufficiently to make her do exactly as Sullivan had requested. "When I came in just now (8.40) & saw your note, I was in hopes it was to say you were at the Island & would supper [*sic*] or billiards — and after all it is only a question of a miserable thousand pounds. Did you get my letter yesterday, sent by train? and has sufficient been paid to Herries to save me from ruin & disgrace?"[51]

After the relaxed atmosphere of the south of France, where he was able to work steadily when he chose to, Sullivan had come back to a series of anxieties, the kind of situation he found difficult to handle. With his new opera, *The Beauty Stone*, only a few weeks away, the question of a cantata for the Leeds Festival remained unresolved, and he had received an offer from Rudyard Kipling to set his poem "Recessional." Sullivan's solution was to cancel the cantata and to put off "Recessional." He recognized that the poem as it stood presented difficulties to a composer, and wrote to Kipling to tell him so. Kipling understood, but would prefer that the poem was left unset rather than be badly done by another composer. "Please accept the thing as yours," Kipling wrote, "if you care to use it, and when you care to use it. There will be no other setting authorized by me."[52] The poem remained unset.

Described as a "Romantic Musical Drama," *The Beauty Stone* opened at the Savoy on 28 May 1898, a week after *The Gondoliers* had been taken off, to allow a full week for rehearsals. The cast was full of the established Savoy stars of the new generation: Henry Lytton, Walter Passmore, Emmie Owen, and Ruth Vincent, alongside the veteran Rosina Brandram. Assuming that he would receive an invitation to the first night, Gilbert had invited a few friends to dinner with the intention of taking them on to the Savoy afterward. But no invitation arrived and Helen Carte told him that Sullivan had objected to his being invited.[53] Sullivan later denied that Gilbert's exclusion had been his own decision, but the damage had been done. Gilbert considered his exclusion as a slight, one for which he would later exact payment.

The Beauty Stone flopped, and was taken off on Saturday, 16 July, after fifty performances. On the Monday, *The Gondoliers* was brought back, with one important change of cast: Robert Evett, who had been in the touring companies since 1892, appeared as Marco. Helen Carte offered Gilbert a box for the performance, but he declined: "I never sit in front when a piece with which I am concerned is being played, & my ladies are going to Daly's."[54]

Sullivan did not allow the failure of *The Beauty Stone* to deter him. In July, he entered into negotiations with James Davis, the librettist of *The Geisha*, in the hope of producing a piece together. Sullivan had none of the qualms that he had experienced over producing a serious piece for the Leeds Festival. He had thought at the time of *Ivanhoe* that comedy-opera writing was behind him, but his financial situation had changed his mind, and he told Davis quite openly, "I want to devote the next three or four years to making money and nothing else, and as there are very few other ways open to a composer, I might as well go on."[55] However, nothing came of these particular negotiations.

In search of better health, Sullivan left for the Alps in late July, going first to a spa in Austria, Badgastein, where he stayed three weeks, and then, after a visit to Innsbruck, traveling to Thusis in Switzerland. Against his expectations, the Leeds committee renewed his conductorship for the next festival, and in September he made another trip, this time to Spa in Belgium, trying to build up his strength to face the taxing demands of the Leeds Festival in October.

While Sullivan was away in Belgium, Gilbert was rehearsing the next revival at the Savoy to follow *The Gondoliers*. The double bill of *Trial by Jury* and *The Sorcerer* opened on 22 September, with Walter Passmore as John Wellington Wells and Henry Lytton as Dr. Daly. "I think the Company gave a capital performance last night," Gilbert wrote to Helen Carte. "Personally I was very much pleased with it. You have a valuable man in Evett. I should secure him for a good term."[56]

Gilbert was still pushing to further Nancy McIntosh's career on the stage. "She has so enormously improved," he told Helen Carte, "that I'm sure it will be worth your while to hear her."[57] In spite of Nancy's earlier decision to return to the concert platform, so clearing the way for Sullivan to collaborate again with Gilbert, she had not done so. Indeed, at the end of 1897, she had been appearing in *The Circus Girl* and in *The Geisha* in America. In the event, there was no time to arrange an audition before Gilbert, Kitty, and Nancy left on 29 September for a long trip to the Crimea, planning to return on 8 November.

Orchestral rehearsals for the Leeds Festival began toward the end of September at St. James's Hall. A young and nervous Edward Elgar traveled to London to rehearse his *Caractacus*, which was to be given its first performance at Leeds. Elgar wrote to Sullivan at the end of the rehearsals to thank him for making his opportunity possible: "this is of course only what one knows *you* would do but it contrasts very much with what some people do to a person unconnected with the schools."[58] Years later, in a letter to Herbert Sullivan, Elgar recalled how he had urged Sullivan to rest while he went through *Caractacus*, but Sullivan had remained and "made notes of anything which struck him, in that most charming self-sacrificing way which was always his."[59]

It was to be Sullivan's last Leeds Festival; he knew that the committee would be looking for a new conductor for the next. They had already employed Frederick Cowen and Charles Stanford for this festival, in case Sullivan's strength should prove inadequate to the task. The final day of the festival was Saturday, 8 October. "After last performance," Sullivan recorded in his diary, "the chorus cheered me so tremendously, that I suddenly broke down, & ran off the orchestra crying like a child[.] When I came out of my room again, *all* the chorus were waiting for me, & I shook hands with all!"[60] He accompanied the orchestra to the station to see them all off on their special train to London and only then went for supper. "When at supper at home," he wrote in his diary, "was surprised by a serenade (by about 30 of the male chorus[)]. I invited them in, gave them champagne & cigars, & they sang half a dozen pieces, retiring at 1. a.m. Went to bed tired—rather a trying day!"[61]

His association with the Leeds Festival had come to an end. He was ready to embrace the theater once more, and his next opportunity presented itself when he was introduced by Wilfred Bendall to the young dramatist Basil Hood. On 11 November, Hood called on Sullivan and they discussed the possibility of doing a piece together. "I know noone so good now," Sullivan recorded, "(putting Gilbert out of the question, of course)."[62]

Was Gilbert out of the question professionally, or for personal reasons? Sullivan had been made well aware of Gilbert's feelings after the first night of *The Beauty Stone*, and was going to be made even more aware of them on 17 November at the twenty-first anniversary of *The Sorcerer*. "Tremendous house," Sullivan noted, "—ditto reception. Opera went very well. Passmore inimitable. Call for Gilbert & self—we went on together, but did not speak to each other! He is mortally offended about the 'Beauty Stone', insisting that *I* kept him out of the theatre on the 1st. night! As he will not allow me to explain that I had nothing whatever to do with it, of course there is nothing to be done."[63]

Having been snubbed by Gilbert on stage at the Savoy, now Sullivan, as well as Gilbert, was hurt. The tragedy of that night was that this was the last occasion when Gilbert and Sullivan were to meet.

CHAPTER THIRTY-ONE

1899-1900

"I Am Sorry to Leave"

WITH THE PASSING of the old year *The Sorcerer* was taken off at the Savoy, and on 7 January 1899 a new opera opened, *The Lucky Star* by Ivan Caryll. Its eastern setting presented a problem to Basil Hood, whose libretto for Sullivan had the working title "Hassan." To produce another opera with an eastern setting straight after *The Lucky Star* would be impossible. Hood needed a fresh idea.

Gilbert and Kitty were planning another cruise to the Crimea in April, and stayed at Grim's Dyke for most of the winter. In February, they had a short stay at the Royal Palace Hotel, Kensington, but Gilbert was attacked by gout in both feet and they had to return to Grim's Dyke. Although his condition had improved by April, he was not completely over the attack and the cruise was postponed.

Sullivan, however, did go away. Having drawn up his will on 4 March at his solicitors, Lewis and Lewis in Ely Place, he left for France; but instead of his usual destination on the Riviera, this time he chose Biarritz, on the Atlantic coast.

From Biarritz Sullivan wrote to Wilfred Bendall, asking him to prepare a statement for the press about the invention he had worked on in the previous autumn. Following a fatal accident suffered by a friend, Lady Alice Lathom, wife of the lord chamberlain, when the horse drawing the carriage in which she was traveling had bolted, Sullivan had been applying his mind to a safety device. He worked on the idea of a "safety shaft," to be known as the "Sullivan safety shaft," which could be pulled to release the animal. It could be operated either by the driver or, if he had been thrown, by a passenger reaching through the front window of the carriage. A model was made to Sullivan's design, and a patent was granted. But Sullivan's world of horse-drawn carriages was coming to an end. It would not be long before the invention made a decade earlier by Daimler and Benz would change the focus of road safety to motorcars.

The next question to which Sullivan was obliged to give considerable thought was a contract made with the Cartes, and that he had signed without reading. It committed him to write one piece a year for the Savoy, and once he had woken up to that requirement he set about freeing himself from the contract. Since 1890, and the end of the run of *The Gondoliers*, the Savoy had been losing money. When *The Grand Duke* closed in July 1896, ownership of the Savoy was transferred by Carte to a limited company, the Savoy Theatre and Operas Limited, with D'Oyly and Helen Carte on the board of directors. In order to reverse their ill fortune, the Cartes were eager to harness Sullivan's talents to the Savoy. Sullivan was unwilling to be tied. He sent a letter, addressed to Helen Carte, for Bendall to copy, telling him that he had had "to weigh and choose *every word* with the greatest care, because they are both so sensitive—especially do they dislike any reference at all to myself or Gilbert having contributed to their rise and fortune."[1]

Sullivan was back in England by 29 April, when he conducted his symphony at the Crystal Palace. It appeared on the program as his "Irish symphony," and Sullivan felt obliged to write to *The Times* to explain that he no longer used its original title in deference to Stanford's more recent *Irish* Symphony. "When my symphony was performed in France," he wrote, "I entitled it 'En Irlande' in order to avoid any confusion with Professor Stanford's work."[2]

Sullivan's ballet music for *Victoria and Merrie England* was still being heard at the Alhambra (where Sullivan and Fanny Ronalds attended a performance on 4 May), and now his music was returning to the Savoy: *The Lucky Star* was to be replaced by the double bill of *Trial by Jury* and *HMS Pinafore*. Rehearsals at the Savoy had begun at the beginning of May, under the supervision of Gilbert. "The rehearsals are going on capitally," Gilbert wrote to Helen Carte. The only drawback, he told her, was the interfering presence of Barker, "who is simply intolerable."[3]

HMS Pinafore would now be a buffer between *The Lucky Star* and Sullivan and Hood's new piece. Therefore, "Hassan"—or *The Rose of Persia*, as it was eventually called—was back in the picture, provided Sullivan was able to come to an agreement with the Cartes. A meeting was arranged for 25 May, and beforehand Sullivan wrote to Helen Carte, setting out his position. He was not, as they supposed, eager to write for the Savoy, but he was happy to write for Carte. He suggested that it was time the Cartes gave up the Savoy and even gave up management altogether; not only were they losing money but their health was suffering. As for the agreement, Sullivan was scathing in his criticism of it. He was bound to supply an opera a year and the Cartes were not even obliged to produce it. Sullivan wanted an agreement that referred to the new piece and nothing else. If the opera were a success, he would not need an agreement to induce him to write another. If it were a failure, the Cartes would not want another.

"Frankly," replied Helen Carte, "I am not excited about doing any more comic operas; I am anxious simply to do what is RIGHT by everybody." She thought they should go ahead with the new opera, because Hood would be disappointed if they did not, "and he is such a very good fellow."[4]

HMS Pinafore opened on Tuesday, 6 June, and was to hold the stage until *The Rose of Persia* was ready. Walter Passmore, now firmly established as George Grossmith's heir, played Sir Joseph, Rosina Brandram was Little Buttercup, and to the delight of those who had seen the original cast, Richard Temple had returned to play Dick Deadeye.

Gilbert had managed to supervise the rehearsals, but his condition had not improved by July when his doctor ordered him off to take the mineral waters of Buxton, hoping they would clear the gout from his system. Meanwhile, Sullivan ordered himself off to Switzerland, partly for health reasons and partly to compose the music for *The Rose of Persia*. By the end of July, in Disentis, he had made a start, and with a visit from Basil Hood was able to iron out any difficulties. But progress was slow, and in the middle of August he returned to England, renting a house in Ashridgewood, Berkshire, not far from York Town, before moving down to Dorney House in Weybridge after six weeks.

In September 1899, Gilbert and Kitty were planning another trip to India for December, rather than returning to the Crimea as originally planned. For the first time Gilbert was not working on a libretto or a play, and if an idea came to him, he would be likely to suggest it for someone else. "I have a wonderfully good & fresh idea for a libretto," he told Helen Carte on 22 September, "—would you like to hear it? Of course I dont intend to do it myself, but the idea is quite at your service if you care for it."[5] He was referring to a short story called "The Fairy's Dilemma," which he was writing for the Christmas number of the *Graphic*. Helen Carte did not take up the offer, and it was Gilbert himself who later turned the story into a play.

IN OCTOBER 1899 —when in South Africa the Boers laid siege to Mafeking at the start of the Boer War—jingoistic fever was sweeping the country. Sullivan was asked to set the music to Kipling's words of "The Absent-Minded Beggar," as part of an appeal to raise funds for the families left behind in poverty, when the soldiers went off to fight for their country. Sullivan set aside *The Rose of Persia* to compose the music for Kipling's song and on 13 November at the Alhambra theater, after a rehearsal in the morning, he conducted the song for its first performance. "Packed house," he wrote in his diary, "—wild enthusiasm—all sang chorus! I stood on the stage & conducted the *encore*—funny sight!"[6] Fanny Ronalds, too, was called on to play her part in the war effort. At a meeting at Lady Randolph Churchill's house, she was elected treasurer on a committee set up to finance an American hospital ship to be sent out to South Africa.[7]

Gilbert's fundraising at the time was closer to home. He was involved in helping to organize a bazaar to raise funds for the Bushey Heath Cottage Hospital. Kitty was running a stall, and they asked Helen Carte for a box and stalls at the Savoy to offer as prizes in a raffle. Helen Carte's cooperation was immediate and more generous than asked for; but when she offered Gilbert a box for the first night of *The Rose of*

Persia for his personal use, he rejected the offer, still smarting from Sullivan's objection to his presence at the first night of *The Beauty Stone*. He preferred to go to the second or third night.

In the early hours of Sunday, 19 November, Sullivan finished the score of *The Rose of Persia*, and with a sense of release could now concentrate on the final rehearsals. Monday's rehearsal he described as "*dull* as ditchwater."[8] Tuesday's dress rehearsal was brighter, he thought, "but I don't anticipate very great success."[9] On Wednesday, 29 November, *The Rose of Persia* opened at the Savoy. "I conducted as usual," Sullivan noted. "Hideously nervous as usual — great reception as usual — great house as usual — excellent performance as usual — everything as usual — except that the piece is really a great success I think, which is *un*usual lately."[10]

"Sullivan's music was enough to delight the expert and to please the less sophisticated listener," reported the *Daily Telegraph*.[11] Walter Passmore played the part of Hassan, Henry Lytton was the Sultan, and the cast included other Savoy favorites: Rosina Brandram, Emmie Owen, Jessie Rose, and Robert Evett, all contributing to the first real success at the Savoy, apart from the Gilbert and Sullivan revivals, since *Utopia, Limited*. The American soprano, Ellen Beach Yaw, engaged by the Cartes at the insistence of Sullivan, who in turn had been influenced by Fanny Ronalds, proved less successful than hoped for, and was replaced after a few weeks by Isabel Jay.

Before the first night, Sullivan had made a point of telling Helen Carte that he hoped Gilbert would be there. Helen Carte tried again to have Gilbert present, reserving a box for the occasion without his asking for it. Gilbert again declined: "How . . . could I possibly accept an invitation from you to be present at his next première, on the strength of a conveyed message from him that he hoped I would come?"[12]

Gilbert and Kitty did not go to India in December as they had planned. For the last four years, Kitty's sister Grace had been suffering from heart problems, and in September had gone down to Bournemouth to benefit from the sea air. Kitty was with her when suddenly, on 28 September, she had a heart attack and died. For Kitty to leave her distressed mother at such a time was out of the question. India and a visit to her brother Compton, now Major-General Turner, would have to wait. Instead, Gilbert and Kitty saw out the old year and ushered in the new century at Grim's Dyke. Gilbert revealed their plans for New Year's Eve to Kitty's great-niece, Dorothy de Michele, whose mother, Beatrice Lake, had been a frequent visitor to the Gilberts, even going on vacation with them in the days before she was married. He jokingly told her that in her honor he had built a lake "because her mother was once one," that it measured 170 yards by 50 yards, and that they were going to turn on the water at midnight on 31 December.[13]

Sullivan's year ended on a somber note, with the announcement in the *Musical Times* in December that he had resigned from the conductorship of the Leeds Festival. The decision had been taken much earlier, and the Leeds committee wanted

Sullivan to give ill health as the reason. He refused, claiming that there was no possibility of a recurrence of his old ailment; he would have been happy to continue until 1901 and so complete a public career of forty years, counting from his return from Leipzig. The committee finally agreed to his announcing his resignation without stating a reason.

ON THE FIRST DAY of the new century, Gilbert sent Helen Carte "every good wish for centuries to come." Sullivan had begun the year vigorously enough, playing his part in bolstering the national spirit in a time of war. He conducted massed bands at the Albert Hall on 20 January in a program that included a march based on "The Absent-Minded Beggar," and again conducted massed military bands in a display of patriotic sentiment at Her Majesty's Theatre on 18 February. Then kidney stones began to bother him again, and the London winter was always something he wanted to escape from; before the end of the month he was once more in Monte Carlo.

"I passed portions of a 'quarry' before I left London, and suffered a good deal," he told Helen Carte, "—So, I came down here to hang about in the sunshine, and the result was that the rest of the quarry came away or a good portion of it if not all."[14] His health picked up, but he was disappointed in the lack of sunshine; even so, he went for a long walk every afternoon with his friend Arthur Wagg. On 20 March, he agreed to write another opera with Basil Hood, and was prepared to sign an undertaking for Helen Carte to that effect. This time he would be writing for the Savoy, and not necessarily for D'Oyly Carte—D'Oyly and Helen were considering giving up management of the theater.

Sullivan had himself urged Helen Carte to give up management and to look after her own health, which was suffering. "I heard you were far from well and that the doctors urged your going away for rest without delay. I fear, my dear Helen, there is too much truth in this. You are overworked, and if you don't stop in time, you will break down suddenly."[15] And if she did follow Sullivan's advice and take off somewhere with D'Oyly, then Sullivan had another suggestion, "would you care to let the 'Island' to me — say for three months? . . . I must go into the country when I return of course, as composing is impossible in London."[16] The Cartes did not go away; Sullivan was unable to rent the "Island," and he had to look elsewhere.

The Cartes were among his guests to celebrate his birthday that year, a month after his return to London, when he gave a dinner party at the Savoy Hotel for what he called "waifs and strays."[17] The party of thirteen guests included Lionel Monckton, whom he had met in Thusis in 1898, and described as a "very nice fellow" with "a real gift for music."[18]

Monckton was part of a glittering cast, two days later, assembled for a matinee performance of *Trial by Jury* at Drury Lane. He appeared as one of the extras in court along with Joseph Comyns Carr and Sydney Grundy. Henry Lytton was one of the jurymen and Decima Moore a bridesmaid, while the Learned Judge was played by Rutland Barrington. And seated in the center of the stage below the Learned Judge, in the nonspeaking part of the Associate, was W. S. Gilbert, assisted by a new character created for the occasion, the Associate's Wife, played by Lady Bancroft. Perhaps on such occasions Gilbert turned a blind eye to "gagging."

Sullivan's search for a house for the summer had led him to Shepperton, on the Thames, and to "River Bank," less than half a mile from Carte's island. He was ready to start work on *The Emerald Isle*, but on 26 May he received a visit from Sir George Martin, the organist at St. Paul's Cathedral, and Colonel Arthur Collins, one of the royal equerries. In the Boer War, Mafeking had been relieved after a six-month siege, and the London streets had been alive with celebrations day and night. The end of the war was in sight, it was thought. Sullivan was asked to write a *Te Deum* to thank God for the coming victory. It was to be Sullivan's last completed work, but would never be performed in his lifetime.

The following day Kipling wrote to Sullivan, hoping to write another song with him and enclosing a copy of his "Recessional." "I do hope," he said, "the spirit will move you to set it."[19] The work was piling up for Sullivan—not a situation he relished. Kipling was set aside, and so was *The Emerald Isle*; his priority was the *Te Deum*.

News had reached Sullivan that George Grove had died, aged seventy-nine, but Sullivan felt unequal to the ordeal of attending the funeral. Thoughts of their particular friendship in the early days, when Sullivan was starting out on his career in music, must have weighed heavily. Grove's death also coincided with the time when Sullivan commemorated his own mother's death, and on 29 May he visited Brompton Cemetery to lay flowers on her grave. As he thought of what he owed to those who had passed away before him, he noted in his diary under 7 June, "Father's birthday—born 1805!"[20] Sad days for Sullivan; and he responded in the way that was probably best for him. As part of the prince of Wales's party, he went down to Epsom and watched the Derby.

Plans were already under way at the Savoy to take off *The Rose of Persia*, to put on a revival of *The Pirates of Penzance* and to ask Gilbert to supervise the rehearsals. The state of Gilbert's health was a consideration, and he was at that time in the last days of rehearsal for a revival of *Pygmalion and Galatea* and *Comedy and Tragedy*, due to open on 7 June at the Comedy Theatre. He replied to Helen Carte on 5 June, assuring her he was considerably better and able to work, but was reeling after what he described as

> a series of "wild cat" rehearsals with the most awful & insolent woman I have ever had to encounter. . . . A few days rest will, no doubt, set me right again.[21]

In an attempt to avoid similar problems in rehearsing *The Pirates* he appealed to Helen Carte, "By the way, I trust I am not to have Mr Barker inflicted upon me at rehearsal." He reminded her of rehearsals for *HMS Pinafore*. "He actually used to occupy the armchair placed for my use—leaving me stand although I was lame with gout, & continually interfered with his corrections until I gave him a hint to be quiet."22

The problems Gilbert encountered with Barker were as nothing compared to the "wild cat" rehearsals with Janette Steer. Gilbert had given her a three months' licence to produce *Pygmalion and Galatea* as well as *Comedy and Tragedy*, subject to his control of the stage management. As Galatea she refused to follow his stage directions, and Gilbert warned her that unless she did so, he would take out an injunction to prevent her playing the piece. On the day of the opening, 7 June, Gilbert made his views public in the *Pall Mall Gazette*: "Although I have by contract expressly reserved to myself the right of stage management in every detail, circumstances have arisen which have caused me to cease to concern myself with the parts of Galatea and Clarice. These parts will, presumably, be played by Miss Steer in accordance with her own view."23

Those words were turned against him when his application for an injunction came before the High Court on 29 June. "The defendant," said the judge, "had in fact played the part in accordance with her own view, as the plaintiff had publicly announced. After that letter she was entitled to do so."24 Gilbert had ineptly played into Janette Steer's hands.

At the same time as Gilbert was being inept, Sullivan was being indiscreet. He had gone to Berlin at the invitation of the kaiser, to conduct a "command performance" of *The Mikado* on 10 June at the Berlin Opera House. Later, in an interview with an English reporter, he revealed that he had assured the kaiser of an even warmer welcome in England than before the Boer War. He was assuming too much. In December 1895, following the disastrous Jameson Raid on the Transvaal, the kaiser had sent a telegram congratulating Paul Kruger, president of the Transvaal, for defending his country against the British invasion. On 17 June, Sullivan noted in his diary that he had been brooding "all day long over unfortunate interview. Curse the press and its correspondents." After years of discretion about anything to do with the royal family, he noted ruefully, "I should have let my enthusiasm run away with my discretion & related before professional reporters what had passed between H. Majesty & myself."25 In his political naiveté, Sullivan was more concerned at the possibility of having upset a royal personage than at having offended many of his compatriots.

The Rose of Persia ended its run of 213 performances on Thursday, 28 June, to be replaced by the revival of *The Pirates of Penzance* on Saturday, 30 June. Sullivan resisted Helen Carte's pressure on him to appear at the first night of the revival, even though Gilbert had told her that he wanted Sullivan to take a curtain call with him. Sullivan feared a repeat of Gilbert's snub at *The Sorcerer* in September 1898, and since then Gilbert had added to his humiliation. "He committed the outrage as I told you, of cutting me dead in the street. I survived it, but I am not going to, wittingly, indulge him in a similar pleasure if I can help it."26 Informed of Sullivan's decision, Gilbert gave an unsympathetic reply: "I am sorry Sullivan won't come, but I don't think he cares to face me.—He need not have minded—I wouldn't have hurt him!"27

On the Sunday after the opening of *Pirates*, Gilbert went off to Buxton in yet another attempt to rid himself of the gout that had now become an almost permanent companion. Sullivan continued working on his *Te Deum* and was enjoying reasonably good health; he was certainly fit enough on 12 July to take out his tricycle and, accompanied by Bertie, cycle the two miles to Laleham, where his servants had gone for a picnic on the Thames.

Toward the end of July, on a blazing hot Saturday, Sullivan traveled up to London. He had lunch with Fanny Ronalds and in the afternoon, with Bertie and Bendall, he went down to the Crystal Palace to distribute prizes at the first National Brass Band Festival. The idea for the festival had been suggested by Sullivan to J. Henry Iles, who had organized the brass band concert Sullivan had conducted at the Albert Hall in 1898. And now the son of a military bandmaster was in the place of honor at a competition of the military band's close cousin, the brass band. First prize, with a selection from *Tannhäuser*, went to "the Black Dykes — really splendid," Sullivan noted, "with brilliant fire and go."[28] After the presentation Sullivan himself conducted the bands. His first experience of music performed in public was that of the military band. His life had come full circle. At the Crystal Palace, the scene of his first musical triumph, his last performance in public was to conduct massed brass bands, not in a performance of his finest music, but in his march "The Absent-Minded Beggar." He ended the day dining at the Crystal Palace with Bertie and Bendall as they watched a firework display before he returned to Shepperton.

News reached Sullivan on 30 July of the death of the duke of Saxe-Coburg; "upset me dreadfully," he wrote, "— another of my oldest and best friends gone."[29] It was shortly followed by news of another death on 10 August: that of Charles Russell, the lord chief justice. "Another friend gone!" Sullivan wrote. "They go with cruel rapidity."[30] At that stage there was nothing to suggest that Sullivan himself would soon fall seriously ill. He had finished his *Te Deum*, and had already started on *The Emerald Isle* when he set off for Switzerland accompanied by Louis.

He had arranged to visit Albert Visetti in Pontresina, and after reaching Thusis by train he undertook a hazardous journey by carriage across the Albula Pass. It was "pitch dark, pouring, and a thick fog [had] arisen," he wrote in his diary. He had been warned not to attempt the pass, but the warning had been given in Romansch and only afterward did Sullivan find out what had been said. "The coachman couldn't see the horses' heads. Louis sat outside to support and help the driver." It was a terrifying journey across the narrow pass on a road made treacherous in the pouring rain. "If a horse had stumbled and fallen, I think nothing could have saved us. But thank God we got down safely. . . . I felt as if I had just passed thro' the most critical hour of my life."[31] By 25 August he was back in Thusis, staying at the Hotel Viamala, and ready to carry on with *The Emerald Isle*.

In his first full week of work, Sullivan finished composing act 1 and on Monday 3 September, began the next stage of "framing." But he was soon struggling. He was stricken with neuralgia, so severely that it put a stop to his work. "I seem very short of ideas," he noted on 5 September.[32] The next day, looking at his work, he commented, "I think it is paltry stuff, but it worried me all the same."[33] Reporting on progress to Helen Carte on 8 September, he described his violent neuralgia. "It takes the form of a violent headache with deadening pain all down the side of my face, and renders me incapable of even writing a letter when it comes on, which happens five or six times a day. It has almost stopped my work for five days, for it invariably comes on when I begin to write."[34]

He pointed out that he had only received act 2 from Hood on 5 September and, because Hood was unable to go out to Thusis and go over any difficulties, as Sullivan had hoped, progress had been slowed down. The only solution was to go back home as quickly as possible. He tried to be optimistic: "I should think you might fairly count upon beginning the vocal rehearsals about the 23rd."[35] Helen Carte's experience and instincts told her that the opera would not be ready in time to replace *The Pirates* when takings began to fall. In that case, she was considering a revival of *Patience*. Sullivan assured her that the first act of *The Emerald Isle* was done, and that only his neuralgia had prevented him from completing the framing. He was against the idea of putting on revivals of the old operas, and would prefer to see her bring back *The Rose of Persia*: ". . . it would be much better to do that than to go to the expense of reviving one of the pieces not in stock. Oh dear—you must forgive me for stopping now, my dear Helen, I can hardly see the paper I am writing on, my head is so bad. I am taking quinine—that's all I can do. Is there any other remedy?"[36]

The following day, with some relief from the deadening pains in the side of his face, Sullivan was back at work, trying to finish the framing of act 1. But within a week, feverish symptoms appeared and he developed bronchitis, making work impossible. He left for home, arriving in London on 19 September. He could not shake off his illness; he had lost his voice, was too weak to work and was frightened by his condition. At the end of September, he went down to the old spa of Tunbridge Wells and stayed at the Wellington Hotel, hoping to be able to work away from London. He was in low spirits and wrote in his diary on 30 September, "awfully nervous & in terror about myself." To make matters worse, his kidney trouble flared up. "After dinner, while having my coffee, felt old pain coming on—in half an hour I was *writhing* & bathed in sweat." He sent for a doctor, who got him into bed and injected something, "I don't know what, but certainly not morphine, which relieved me directly & gave me a good night's rest."[37] The next day he was still weak, but able to go out for a walk and could even turn his mind to work.

Unaware of the seriousness of Sullivan's illness, Helen Carte complained of the delay in finishing the opera, suggesting it was a mistake that he had undertaken to write his *Te Deum*. "The 'mistake' of writing the Te Deum," he replied, "had no more to do with the backward state of the Opera, than conducting the Leeds Festival in 1898, or writing 'The Golden Legend' in 1886 had. The Te Deum was finished & out of hand," he told her, before he left Shepperton. He had finished everything that Hood had sent him in Switzerland, and he had done all he could without consulting Hood. Then his health broke down. "Physical pain, and nervous terror combined are not conducive to good mental work," he told her. He had produced nothing in four days, but now felt better. "However, it is a comfort to know that the 1st. Act is absolutely finished and I feel strong enough now to get on quickly with the 2nd. Act: at which Hood (who is here) and I are working now. This place has done me much good, & I hope to return home on Monday next."[38]

Over the weekend, Hood's place at Tunbridge Wells was taken by François Cellier, and together they worked at an accompaniment for the vocal score. After a fortnight in Tunbridge Wells, in the privacy of his diary and not having to put the best picture possible on the situation for Helen Carte, Sullivan asked himself, "what have I done? Little more than nothing, first from illness and physical incapability. Secondly from *brooding*, and nervous terror about myself."[39] On Sunday, 14 October, he was examined by a doctor and found to be "sound enough," but his throat was still "in a bad state." He had to admit that he had practically "done nothing *for a month*." At least he could write in his diary, "Have now finished & framed 1st. Act, & they are rehearsing it."[40]

On Monday, 15 October, Sullivan left Tunbridge Wells, but left reluctantly. It was a lovely day, he recorded in his diary; and after Frank Cellier had left the hotel, Sullivan made what was to be his last entry: "I am sorry to leave—such a lovely day."[41]

Back at Queen's Mansions, he had to answer a further request from Helen Carte about progress on the opera. He replied on Tuesday, 16 October. "Forgive me," he began, "for dictating this letter, as I want to save my hand for music writing." He tried to put on a brave face, claiming that he was "into the swing of work again." He estimated that, provided his health held up, she could rely on being able to produce the opera by 1 December.[42]

From that letter, Helen Carte had to make a decision as a business woman, not as a friend of Arthur Sullivan. It was clear to her that the opera would not be ready for 1 December. She decided to work toward 8 December for the new opera and to bring on the revival of *Patience* for a short run. If the new opera were ready for 8 December, all well and good; if not, she had *Patience* to fill in the gap. Sullivan found it difficult to accept the inevitable decision, and wrote to her on 17 October to express his disappointment and to point out that, in his opinion, it was impossible to bring on *Patience* in three weeks' time. In addition, she would be taking away rehearsal time from the new opera. He was arguing as though he were confident he would finish on time; Helen Carte was not prepared to take the risk.

To his dictated letter, he added a postscript in his own hand, "Who is to do the delicate stage management of 'Patience,' Gilbert being ill?"[43]

Gilbert had indeed been ill. He had lost sixty pounds at Buxton and was barely able to walk. In spite of his disabling condition, he still managed to provide someone with the opportunity of spreading the "scandal" about him that he had been seen out with a young lady, and noise of it reached the ears of Helen Carte. "No scandal," Gilbert assured her,—the "young lady["] was my wife—aged 53."[44]

Gilbert agreed to supervise the rehearsals for *Patience* and to start on Monday, 29 October.

> I will drive straight to the side door in Beaufort Buildings [he told her]—my man will be with me & will help me down to the stage. I am sending a wheel chair (the same that I used in rehearsing Utopia) & I shall be glad if you will allow this to be on the stage for my use. I am also sending a carrying chair to take me up the steps from the stage to the side door in Beaufort Buildings. I can manage to walk down stairs, but when I am tired, I cant walk up stairs.[45]

He also asked to have a rehearsal for principals at Grim's Dyke on Friday, 26 October. Walter Passmore and Henry Lytton were to be in the major roles of Bunthorne and Grosvenor; Rosina Brandram was Lady Jane; and Patience was to be played by Isabel Jay. "Kindly let me know how many will come on Friday," Gilbert suggested to Helen Carte, "that I may provide carriage accommodation for them."[46]

Helen Carte would not hear of his arriving at the side entrance. Capitalizing on her thoughtfulness, Gilbert asked if it was possible to heat the stage. "My great fear is the risk of catching a chill from sitting all day on a cold stage. . . . I feel that I am giving you a great deal of trouble, but you are too kind to mind that."[47]

Meanwhile, Sullivan was still struggling to work: "I work hard," he told Helen Carte on 27 October, "and waste no time knowingly and wilfully, but I am *very slow* at it. . . . I cannot get my strength back. . . . But I plod on, and have no doubt but that I shall be up to tune."[48]

Gilbert's rehearsal on Monday, 29 October "went as smooth as butter," he reported afterwards to Helen Carte. "I was not at all tired after it & indeed could have gone through it all again."[49] Helen Carte was no doubt pleased with the smoothness of the rehearsal, but what she also wanted was a smoothness in relations between Gilbert and Sullivan. Gilbert was only too pleased when she suggested Sullivan taking a call with him on the first night. She tried Sullivan again. He replied on Friday, 2 November:

> I think that if three such noble wrecks as Gilbert, D'Oyly & myself were to appear on the stage at the same time, it would create something more than a sensation. . . . It wasn't my intention to come to the first night of "Patience," but if it would really please Gilbert to have me there & go on with him, I will come—not to conduct of course, but to take the call with him (and D'Oyly too,) if there should be one. Let us bury the hatchet, & smoke the pipe of peace. I have no doubt we can get both from the property room, and if the result is to relieve G. of some of that awful gout, I shall be well pleased.[50]

As she moved from one invalid to the other—from D'Oyly at home, to Gilbert and Sullivan in correspondence—Helen Carte hit on an idea for the first-night call. Writing to Sullivan to tell him how pleased she was that he was going to come to the first night ("I know it will *truly* please Mr. Gilbert much—I could see how *very much* he wished it"), she added: "I suggested to D'Oyly last night that he should have an original effect of *three bath chairs* discovered — or a procession of bath chairs! Or you standing and they two in a bath chair each at the sides."[51]

It was not to be. On Wednesday, 7 November, Helen Carte received a note from Sullivan. It is his last letter, written in blue pencil and in a very shaky hand.

In bed

Dear Helen,

It's not a question of taking a chill if I come out, but of ever getting out at at [*sic*] all again. I am regularly bowled over — kidneys and throat. Pray tell Gilbert how very much I feel the disappointment.

Good luck to you all. Three invalid chairs would have looked *very well* from the front.

Ever yours,

A.S.[52]

Helen Carte sent the note to Gilbert. He had already heard the news; his reply reached her before the performance. "I return Sullivan's note. I had written him a conciliatory letter to-day expressing my regret that he could not come tonight & saying that I had looked forward to that opportunity to shake hands over past differences & I am extremely sorry he is so ill."[53]

Even then Gilbert did not fully realize the gravity of Sullivan's illness. He had planned to go off to Egypt with Kitty and Nancy, and wrote to Sullivan on Friday, 9 November. He would have liked to see him but in his "present enfeebled condition," he told Sullivan, the journey up to London would be exhausting. "I sincerely hope to find you all right again on my return & the new opera running merrily." He added, "The old piece woke up splendidly."[54]

Sullivan was sinking, too weak now to attend to any correspondence. By Wednesday, 21 November, his condition appeared grave and the royal physician, Sir Thomas Barlow, was contacted. He was due to call the next day. But suddenly, on the morning of Thursday, 22 November, Sullivan's heart gave out, and he died.

CHAPTER THIRTY-TWO

1900-1905

A Gilbert without a Sullivan

THE EXACT CIRCUMSTANCES of Sullivan's dying moments are uncertain. Later accounts by relations, Sullivan's cousin B. W. Findon in 1908 and his nephew Herbert in 1927, both preferred an account in which Sullivan died in the arms of his nephew, but there are discrepancies in the details of both accounts. Contemporary accounts in newspapers are probably nearer the truth. The end came suddenly, with only Clotilde and Louis (or perhaps Clotilde alone) present when he died. Sullivan's own doctor, Buckston Browne, was sent for and certified the cause of death as bronchitis and cardiac failure.[1]

Out of respect to Sullivan, the Savoy Theatre was closed on the evening of his death. Both D'Oyly and Helen Carte were deeply saddened at the news, and sympathized with Fanny Ronalds. Helen Carte wrote to her on Friday, 23 November. "It is all so inexpressibly sad—and, although I realize the enormous loss the world generally has suffered—I can think of nothing at present but the **_personal_** loss—the loss of so very dear and true a friend—. . . a friend from whom I have never had one unkind word and who has never varied in all these long years."[2]

On Saturday afternoon, 24 November, writing in pencil, D'Oyly Carte sent his own note to Fanny Ronalds:

My dear friend
I cannot write or speak yet of what has taken place. I am broken down with illness myself have been in bed since Sunday last with an attack of bronchitis and my temperature from 100 to 101, and am still in bed . . . I am very weak. As I say I cannot talk about this yet to anyone or write, but _you_ will not require this to believe in my sympathy and common grief with you in the loss of him whom we all loved.[3]

Fanny Ronalds replied to them both on Sunday, 25 November.

I can find no words to express the sympathy I feel for you in your great sorrow, and you know how deep & terrible my grief is at the loss of my oldest, dearest, and most valued friend left to me on earth. Our loss is irreparable. No one can ever take the place of the dear one who has passed away—I dare not think how many years it is since first we met, but from that that [sic] day we have been firm, true friends, through all the joys & sorrows of life.

She prayed that they might all be united in "The Better Land," "in perfect harmony, and find there 'The Lost Chord' of our happiness."[4]

Sullivan had left directions for his funeral, written eighteen years earlier. He directed that his body should be embalmed and that he should be buried in the family grave at Brompton Cemetery. For his funeral he requested "Yea, though I Walk" from *The Light of the World*, or the Funeral Hymn from the *Martyr of Antioch*. The embalming was carried out as directed, and on 24 November it was announced that the queen had commanded a service to be held at the Chapel Royal, St. James's Palace, before the burial. Then, because a considerable number of Sullivan's fellow musicians, led by Sir George Martin, suggested that Sullivan should have a public funeral in St. Paul's Cathedral, the dean and chapter agreed. The Brompton Cemetery funeral arrangements were canceled, but the service ordered by the queen for the Chapel Royal would be conducted as arranged.[5]

At noon on Tuesday, 27 November, the first part of the funeral service began. The Chapel Royal had been decorated with white lilies and chrysanthemums and with a lyre of mauve orchids, and a wreath of laurels was presented by the queen's representative, Sir Walter Parratt, master of the queen's music. The United States ambassador was present and among the mourners were Lady Katherine Coke, Gilbert's sisters Florence and Maude, Mr. and Mrs. Francis Burnand, Rutland Barrington, George Grossmith, Charles Wyndham, Otto Goldschmidt, and Basil Hood.

The procession leading the coffin into the chapel was headed by the boys of the choir of the Chapel Royal, in the traditional scarlet and gold coat that Sullivan had been so proud to wear; and among the pall bearers were Sir Squire Bancroft, François Cellier, Sir Alexander Mackenzie, and Sir John Stainer. Behind the coffin followed the chief mourners: his nephew Herbert, John Sullivan (his uncle), Mrs. Holmes (Amy Coghlan, a cousin), Jane Sullivan (daughter of Uncle John), B. W. Findon, Edward Dicey, Helen Carte, Rupert D'Oyly Carte, and Sullivan's servants.

Included in the music was "Yea, though I Walk thro' the Valley of the Shadow of Death," as Sullivan had requested. After the service at St. James's, the cortege moved along Pall Mall to Trafalgar Square and then down Northumberland Avenue to the Embankment. As it made its way along the Embankment, D'Oyly Carte would have been able to see everything clearly from his high vantage point in Adelphi Terrace. From the Embankment, the procession turned left toward Ludgate Circus and then, for the final part of the journey, up Ludgate Hill to St. Paul's.

In the cathedral, a border of white chrysanthemums crowned by sprays of lilies of the valley had been placed around the opening in the nave through which the coffin would be lowered into the crypt, and the sides of the shaft were hung with creepers and tendrils; the whole floral decoration was provided by Tom Chappell and his wife. On the coffin were placed the wreaths of the queen, of the prince and princess of Wales, and of Princess Louise. Fanny Ronalds had requested that her floral cross might be lowered into the grave with the coffin, but she was informed that only the queen's wreath was allowed. After the coffin had been lowered into the grave, the whole Savoy company, conducted by François Cellier, sang "Brother, thou art gone before us," and the service closed with the "Dead March" from *Saul* on the organ.[6]

The crypt was filled with the heavy perfume from the floral tributes; there were so many that three carriages had been needed to carry them in the procession from the Chapel Royal. The numerous wreaths had been sent not only by individuals but also by the various musical societies with which Sullivan had been connected. Everyone who had known him wanted to be part of this final tribute.

"I wish I had been in England," Gilbert wrote to Herbert Sullivan, "that I might have had an opportunity of joining the mourners at his funeral." He expressed his "personal sorrow" and sympathy at Sullivan's "terribly sudden death," but found satisfaction, he told Herbert, "that I was impelled, shortly before his death, to write to him to propose to shake hands over [our] recent differences & even a greater satisfaction to learn, through you that my offer of reconciliation was cordially accepted."[7]

A musical tribute was paid to Sullivan on Saturday afternoon, 8 December, in a concert at the Crystal Palace. August Manns conducted a program of Sullivan's sacred and secular music, opening with *In Memoriam* and including selections from *The Martyr of Antioch, The Golden Legend,* and his music to the *Tempest*. Songs in the program included "The Lost Chord" and "O Hush Thee, My Babie," and the concert concluded with a selection from *The Merchant of Venice*.[8] It was a musical selection that left aside the essential humor and charm of Sullivan's personality.

Probate of Sullivan's will was granted on 12 January 1901 to his executors, Charles Mathews, Edward Dicey, and D'Oyly Carte. Sullivan had remembered all his relatives and his close friends. To each of the surviving children of his brother he left £1,000, and smaller amounts to his Uncle John and his cousins, including a cousin of his mother, Helen Phillips, to whom he left the house he had bought her in Bridgetown, Barbados. There were gifts for the prince of Wales (a tortoiseshell and silver card box and clip to match), for the duke of York (a silver mounted cocoanut), for D'Oyly Carte (a silver inkstand and the couch in his study), and pictures, ornaments, embroidery, and china were variously given to Helen Carte, Fanny Ritchie (Fanny Ronalds's daughter), Sybil Crutchley, and Mrs. Beach Grant. "To my old and dear friend Mary Frances Ronalds" he left a dinner service (either "the old Vienna" or "the old Worcester china"), his Sèvres dessert service, four silver candlesticks, twelve silver ornaments, his Louis XV writing table, and the original manuscript of "The Lost Chord." Mementos were left to his close friends Russell Walker,

Arthur Wagg, Ernest Dresden, George Lewis, and Edward Dicey. Sullivan thoughtfully distributed his original scores: to the Royal Academy of Music he left *The Martyr of Antioch* and *The Mikado*; to the Royal College of Music, *The Golden Legend* and *The Yeomen of the Guard*; to the duke of Saxe-Coburg (who predeceased Sullivan), *The Light of the World* ("in remembrance of the many happy hours I spent with His Royal Highness when I was writing it"); to Wilfred Bendall, *King Arthur* and *Macbeth*; to François Cellier, *Patience* and *The Pirates of Penzance*; to D'Oyly Carte, *Iolanthe*; and to Gilbert, *Ruddigore*.

To his "faithful servant and good friend" Louis Jaeger, and to his "devoted servant and good friend" Clotilde Raquet who had nursed him "through so many illnesses" he left £1,000 each. They also received a number of other gifts: books, clothing, and cigars for Louis, and for Clotilde furniture, cutlery, and ornaments. The rest of his estate and effects, which included manuscripts, letters, and diaries, Sullivan left to his nephew Herbert. His gross estate was valued at £54,527 10s 8d.; in December 1902 it was resworn at £56,536 13s 10d.[9]

GILBERT STARTED 1901 in Egypt, still suffering from gout and arthritis. "I am just as great a cripple as when I left England," he told an American friend, Mary Talbot, who suffered from a disabling illness herself but was always cheerful. In regular correspondence with her Gilbert had begun by addressing her as "Dear Mrs. Talbot," but over the years, as he became more familiar with his "American cousin," he used to address her "My dear Cousin Mary" and sign off as "Cousin Bill." He had only left the hotel, he told her, to be wheeled to the sulfur baths, which he described as "rotten eggy" and of no help. He had been told by the doctor that he might never walk again. "However, I'm not going to howl about it," he wrote. "But I should like to be able to wash the back of my neck. It is not a lofty aspiration, but at present it is the goal of my ambitions."[10]

Gilbert's first outing from the hotel, on 14 February, turned out to be very nearly his last. With Kitty and Nancy he was traveling by train to Cairo, when suddenly the engine left the rails and tumbled down an embankment, dragging one carriage with it and leaving Gilbert's carriage perched perilously on the edge of the slope. They had all been "tossed about the carriage like parched peas in a drum," said Gilbert to Mary Talbot. He was unable to move, but Nancy managed to get him onto his feet and out of the carriage, while Kitty, although bruised, was able to get down on her own. Nancy climbed back into the carriage to collect their luggage, and then clambered down the embankment to rescue Gilbert's hat for him. She "then set off in the boiling sun to walk two and a half miles to old Cairo to get a carriage." Seven people had been killed and about twenty injured in the disaster. "I shall never forget the shrieks of the wounded and dying," he wrote.[11]

The Victorian era, which had embraced the whole of Sullivan's life, had come to an end on 22 January, with the death of Queen Victoria. Out of respect, the Savoy

Theatre was closed from 23 January until 3 February. In January, Carte had invited Edward German to complete the music of *The Emerald Isle*, but Carte was never to see its performance. On Wednesday morning, 3 April, at Adelphi Terrace, D'Oyly Carte died. He was fifty-six. His funeral, a private family affair, took place three days later at Hastings, while at the same time a memorial service was held at the Savoy Chapel, attended by the Savoy cast and other theatrical friends and colleagues, including George Edwardes, Jessie Bond, Fanny Ronalds, Courtice Pounds, Richard Barker, and Stanley Boulter. On the day of the funeral, Saturday, 6 April, the Savoy Theatre was closed.[12]

On the day Carte died, Gilbert was on his way home from Egypt. He heard the news when he reached Marseille on 5 April, and wrote immediately to Helen Carte.

> The sad news of your husband's death—which only reached me on landing here half an hour ago—has touched me profoundly.
>
> Believe me, I sympathize with you in your bereavement & I sincerely wish I could have been in England to pay the last token of respect to his memory— ... I am deeply sorry for you—deeply sorry for the grief that has overtaken a lady for whom, in all the vicissitudes of our business relations, I have always felt a sincere admiration &, I hope I may add, affection.[13]

It was a time of profound sadness for Gilbert and Kitty. In January, they had received news that Kitty's brother Compton had died in India on 31 December, and Kitty's anxiety over her sick husband can only have been increased by the quick succession of deaths coming little more than a year after her sister's. More than ever would her mother depend on her for emotional support; more than ever would Kitty need Nancy beside her. From Marseille the Gilberts moved along the Riviera to Bordighera, where they spent ten days before returning on 17 April. They had been away from England for five months, in search of better health for the only one of the famous triumvirate left alive.

On 25 April probate was granted for D'Oyly Carte's will to the sole executrix, Helen Carte. Carte's estate was valued at £240,817, and his will reflected his life: one of total dedication to work and family. His individual legacies remembered his employees, right down to bar attendants and messengers at the Savoy, loyal servants to the company such as John Beckwith, his acting manager and treasurer, and the long-term stage manager, William Seymour. To Rosina Brandram, the sole member of cast remaining from the earliest days, who had never left his company for other theaters, he left £1,000. All his household and personal effects were left to Helen Carte, as well as one-third of his residuary estate. The rest was divided into two parts, providing a fund for his sons and a fund for his brother and sisters. No friends were mentioned.[14]

Helen Carte continued with preparations for the last opera that her husband had commissioned. When the music was completed, German gave her details of what he and Sullivan had each contributed. Sullivan had composed twelve out of the fourteen numbers in act 1, and five out of the fourteen numbers in act 2, with the finale being completed by German. "Sir Arthur left Nos. 1 & 2 complete ... With this exception," said German, "my task has been to orchestrate & harmonize the entire Opera."[15]

Gilbert and Kitty were in the Savoy audience on the first night of *The Emerald Isle* on Saturday, 27 April. The Gilbert household was well represented. Four of their servants had taken an upper box, paid for by Gilbert. "I heartily wish you all good fortune on Saturday," he had written to Helen Carte. "I am afraid however that the melancholy events of the past 5 months will tend to deprive me of much of the enjoyment I should otherwise have experienced."[16] Afterward he congratulated Helen Carte on the success of the opera: "German had a most delicate & difficult task to discharge," he said, "& I think he acquitted himself admirably."[17] *The Emerald Isle*, under the direction of François Cellier and with a cast including Walter Passmore, Henry Lytton, Robert Evett, Rosina Brandram, and Isabel Jay, went on to complete 205 performances, not far short of the success of *The Rose of Persia*.

While *The Emerald Isle* was enjoying success in London, the "Savoy Touring Company" took the opera around the provinces, visiting the major cities, traveling up to Scotland and across the sea to the Emerald Isle itself. Sullivan's other music was not forgotten that autumn. In early September, during a season of promenade concerts conducted by Henry Wood, an evening of Sullivan was included in the program: *In Memoriam*, the incidental music to the *Tempest* and *Henry VIII*, the masque music from the *Merchant of Venice*, the *Di Ballo* overture, solos from *Ivanhoe*, and quartets from *The Mikado* and *The Yeomen of the Guard*. Henry Wood was to conduct Sullivan's music again at the Queen's Hall, in a memorial concert on the anniversary of his death, performing *In Memoriam*, *The Golden Legend* with the Wolverhampton Choral Society, and a selection from the second act of *Ivanhoe*.

After seeing *The Emerald Isle* into production, Helen Carte gave up the management of the Savoy, and the theater was leased to William Greet, who put on a double bill of musical plays by Basil Hood: *Ib and Little Christina*, with music by Franco Leoni, and *The Willow Pattern*, with music by Cecil Cook. The bill ran for sixteen performances from 14–29 November. If it had been intended as a stopgap before the next major piece by Hood and German was ready, it fell far short of expectations. A Gilbert and Sullivan revival was again needed to rescue the Savoy from disaster. Helen Carte, who had retained the London rights of the operas, having resisted a suggestion from Herbert Sullivan that he and Gilbert buy them back from her, had contacted Gilbert within the first week of *Ib and Little Christina* asking him to supervise rehearsals for *Iolanthe*.

Gilbert's attention to detail was no less in the revival of *Iolanthe* than in the original production. It had been wrong, he pointed out to Helen Carte, to put the two earls in act 2 into plain court dress, and he suggested a real clock for act 2, showing the actual time during the performance, which would make a good advertisement and a talking point for the opera. A nucleus of established performers — Rosina

Brandram (Queen of the Fairies), Henry Lytton (Strephon), Walter Passmore (Lord Chancellor), Robert Evett (Tolloller), and Isabel Jay (Phyllis) — continued the tradition for which the company was famous. At the end, Gilbert was as usual called before the audience, but for the first time Helen Carte also was required to take a bow.[18] W. H. Seymour, who had been with the company since he first understudied Ralph Rackstraw in the original *Pinafore*, was no longer stage manager. He was in poor health and died during the run of the revival.

Gilbert's own health had improved since his return from Egypt and Italy. He was on his feet again, and the wheelchair had not been needed at rehearsals. At Christmas, however, he had a relapse. In a letter to Mary Talbot, written on Christmas Day, he apologized for complaining of his own "twaddling grievances" when she had so much to suffer, but in the cold weather he felt he was "a growing cripple."[19]

WHILE THE BOER WAR drew on during 1902, the *Iolanthe* revival was replaced in March by a new opera by Hood and German recalling a former period of English history, *Merrie England*. News of the end of the fighting in South Africa reached London on 1 June, and the next day cheering, flag-waving crowds filled the streets of the West End. An official and more sober response followed a week later on Saturday, 8 June, when a service of public thanksgiving was held at St. Paul's Cathedral and Sullivan's *Te Deum* was played, two years after its composition.

Far away from the public celebrations of 8 June, Gilbert spent the weekend quietly at Grim's Dyke, entertaining his old neighbors from Harrington Gardens, Henry Coke and Lady Katherine, together with their daughter, Sybil, and her husband, Colonel Charles Crutchley. The Crutchleys were to be among his closest friends over the remaining years of his life. Now sixty-five, and having recovered from his severe gout and the worst of his arthritis, Gilbert was entering on a happy and contented phase of his life. Horse riding and tennis belonged to the past, and had been replaced by croquet and swimming. Facilities for both sports were close at hand. His library, with its wide French windows, looked out onto the croquet lawn, and beyond was the lake he had recently had built and in which he bathed during the summer months. The work of lining the bottom of the lake with clay, in which Gilbert had joined, had been blamed by family and friends for his severe rheumatic illness in 1900, and Kitty vainly attempted to dissuade him from swimming in the cold water. He agreed, on medical advice, not to swim if the water was too cold; but if the temperature in the lake was 58° F or more, Gilbert would plunge in before breakfast.

He had written nothing for the theater since *The Fortune Hunter* in 1897 and the last of the revivals had ended at the Savoy. It looked as though Gilbert had this time truly retired.

He was retired, but not inactive. His duties as a local magistrate took him to court in Edgware most weeks, and in 1902 he was given the ceremonial title of deputy lieutenant of the county of Middlesex. He had also discovered a new hobby, as he explained on 6 October in a letter to his friend Mary Talbot. "I daresay you have read in the papers that I've taken to motoring & that I made my début [*sic*] by spoiling a parson, who came round from under a dead wall on a bicycle." The car ended up in a ditch, Gilbert was thrown across the dashboard and hit his head, and Kitty "was pitched, very compactly, into a hedge, where she looked like a large & quite unaccountable bird's nest." The parson admitted it was not Gilbert's fault and asked them to lunch. "So that was all right. The car is a steam one—a Locomobile—an AMERICAN one in honour of yourself—& it travels quite noiselessly."[20]

The allusion to the "papers" was a reference to a letter he had written to *The Times* on 27 September, writing in support of the twelve miles an hour speed limit. He related the story of his accident, although in a more serious tone, and concluded, "had I been going at the rate of 25 or 30 miles an hour, as advocated by so many of your correspondents, the bicyclist would almost certainly have been killed and the occupants of the car most seriously injured."[21]

At that time, Gilbert placed more value on his motorcar than he did on an original manuscript of one of his early works that Helen Carte had come across. Helen Carte, who had remarried and was now Mrs. Stanley Boulter, told him about the discovery of the manuscript of *Ruy Blas*. "The MS has no interest for me," Gilbert replied, "I should only tear it up if I had it." He added a postscript. "After writing the above my wife came in & I read her your note—She said 'Oh do buy it'—So, if you will kindly arrange for it, I will."[22] It cost Gilbert £5.5.0 to buy back his manuscript of *Ruy Blas*, which now resides with his papers in the British Library.

Gilbert's work for the Bushey Heath Cottage Hospital continued, and to help raise money he put on four performances of his *Rosencrantz and Guildenstern*. Gilbert himself played King Claudius, Nancy McIntosh was Queen Gertrude, and Sybil Crutchley played Ophelia. Also in the cast were Captain Robert Marshall, the dramatist, Henry Rowland Brown, a barrister friend, and Kitty's niece, Mabel Turner. That was not Gilbert's only dramatic performance in 1902: on 5 December at the Lyric, he appeared in a part that he was beginning to claim as his own, that of the Associate in a testimonial benefit performance of *Trial By Jury*, put on as an afterpiece to Sheridan's *The Critic*.

IT WAS NOW MORE than two years since Sullivan's death, and a committee was set up to provide a memorial to him in London. The sculptor William Goscombe John was commissioned to model a bust, and Herbert Sullivan suggested that Gilbert provide a fitting quotation from one of the operas as an inscription. Sending his lines to Herbert, Gilbert commented, "It is difficult to find anything quite suited to so sad an occasion, but I think this might do."[23] He had chosen:

> Is life a boon?
> If so, it must befall
> That Death, when e'er he call
> Must call too soon.[24]

The monument, standing in the Embankment Gardens, not far from the Savoy, was unveiled by Princess Louise on 10 July. The plaintive notes of "The Lost Chord" rang out across the gardens, played by a solo cornet. Speeches were made; Gilbert proposed a vote of thanks to the committee and to Princess Louise; and the mood changed as the deep tones of a euphonium boomed out, "Ho, Jolly Jenkin."

As for the Savoy, so closely associated with the words and music of Gilbert and Sullivan over the years, a new reality, brought about by the passage of time, had to be faced. After a new Hood and German opera, *A Princess of Kensington*, which ran until May 1903, the old Savoy company was disbanded. (The faithful Rosina Brandram had remained until the end, a period of almost twenty-five years since the days of *The Sorcerer*.) The Savoy Theatre and Operas Limited considered that the value of its assets had reduced considerably since its formation in 1897, and on 27 August, the company made an application in court to reduce its capital from £75,000 to £41,250.[25] Helen Boulter, who in business continued to call herself Helen D'Oyly Carte, was to keep the Gilbert and Sullivan operas alive with her main "Repertory Company" touring the country.

Gilbert was suspicious that the devaluation of his "property" while it was in the possession of another, would result in a poor sale value when he came to renew with the company. It was not that he distrusted Helen Carte; many times he had commended her for her fairness and sense of justice. But he suspected that, since her remarriage, she was no longer a free agent, and this suspicion was to rankle and be the cause of some acrimonious letters from Gilbert in the years to come.

Negotiations for a new contract began shortly afterward and on 29 September 1903 Gilbert entered into an agreement with Helen Carte in which he assigned to her for five years, from 30 May 1905, rights of performance of all his operas with Sullivan plus *The Mountebanks* and *His Excellency*. For this, he would receive £5,000, payable in twenty installments of £250.

At the same time that Gilbert was negotiating this agreement, he learned of the serious illness of his old colleague and former friend, Clement Scott. They had not been on speaking terms for years, but now that Scott was near death, Gilbert tried to make amends by doing what he could to help Scott's wife. He called regularly at their house or wrote or telephoned, anxious for news. Margaret Scott, recalling years later how Gilbert helped her, wrote, "He helped me with my work, he wrote articles for me, and to his last hour I am sure he never breathed a word of what he had done for me."[26] At Scott's funeral, at St. Etheldreda's, Ely Place, Gilbert was noticeably moved to tears.

Many of his former colleagues had already died. Gilbert was conscious of the loss, especially the loss of his closest collaborator. For his birthday in 1903, he received the usual crop of congratulations from well-wishers. To Frank Cellier, he replied: "Many thanks for your good wishes. Personally Im rather sick of birthdays—I've had so many of them. A Gilbert is of no use without a Sullivan—& I can't find one!"[27]

But Gilbert did find himself a new publisher in 1903. He had met Frederick Macmillan, liked him and trusted him. "For good & sufficient reasons," Gilbert wrote to Macmillan, "I have withdrawn 'The Bab Ballads' from Routledge Ld. who have published them, with excellent results for themselves during 38 years. Do you feel inclined to take them up?"[28] On Macmillan's acceptance, Gilbert trustingly replied, "Any arrangement that you may think fair will satisfy me."[29]

Publication of an old work was not enough. Gilbert was itching to be creative again. Before the end of the year, he had started on a new play.

GILBERT AND KITTY MOVED UP to London for the first three months of 1904, staying at 52 Pont Street, a short distance from Sloane Square. Gilbert worked at his new play, *The Fairy's Dilemma*, adapting his short story that he had earlier offered to Helen Carte. The play was intended for Arthur Bourchier at the Garrick; and as well as working on the new, he was preparing for publication of the old, settling terms for "The Bab Ballads" with Frederick Macmillan. Gilbert was offered less than he asked for, but he settled amicably: "I'm not disposed to haggle over a trifle & if you think 25% too much I"ll take 20%."[30]

Helen Carte kept him informed on Savoy matters. After the run of *A Princess of Kensington* had ended on 16 May 1903, the theater had been closed for nearly a year and was now due to reopen on 10 February 1904 under new management, with a musical comedy called *The Love Birds*. "It's sad to think of the old show being handed over to the Philistines," Gilbert wrote to Helen Carte. "I'm sure that you & I could have worked the theater together to the advantage of both. But its too late now?"[31] Nothing came of Gilbert's hint of a suggestion.

Musical comedy had taken over the position once held by the operas of Gilbert and Sullivan, and the dramatic critic of *The Times* was of the opinion that the one had 'snuffed out" the other. Such a suggestion was too much for Gilbert to let pass without comment, and he protested to the editor: "Savoy opera was snuffed out by the deplorable death of my distinguished collaborator, Sir Arthur Sullivan. When that event occurred, I saw no one with whom I felt that I could work with satisfaction and success, and so I discontinued to write *libretti*."[32]

It was not the whole truth as to the end of their partnership; and neither had he given his honest opinion of what had replaced the Savoy opera. That he gave in a letter to Helen Carte: "I am deeply sorry for the fate that has overtaken the Savoy. I hear, on all sides, that the 'Love Birds' is an insult to one's understanding."[33] As for writing any more libretti himself, he told her, "The difference between working for

NANCY MCINTOSH.

Prince,

31 Union Square, New York.

Penn. Ave & 11th St. Wash. D.C.

Nancy McIntosh in America, about 1897 (By permission of the British Library)

the Savoy where I had a free hand & working under a Manager of any other Theatre would (apart from other considerations)[,] place my doing so out of the question."[34] Gilbert wanted to remember the best of times, and to forget the worst of times.

The Fairy's Dilemma, "a domestic pantomime," opened at the Garrick on 3 May, with Arthur Bourchier and his wife, Violet Vanbrugh, in the cast. Max Beerbohm, writing in *The Saturday Review*, spoke of Gilbert being "enshrined among [his] minor gods." "And the 'Bab Ballads'—," said Beerbohm, "how shall I ever express my love for them?"[35] Having offered his admiration of the old Gilbert, he then proceeded to severely criticize his latest piece as something out of the 1870s. The play managed ninety performances and was taken off on 22 July.

Gilbert and Kitty took a late holiday that year, going to Biarritz, then on to Paris for a week before returning home in mid-October. Writing from Biarritz to the critic William Archer, Gilbert expressed his opinion that "English is (next to Italian) the very best of all European languages for singing purposes," provided that the songwriter avoided "a harsh collocation of consonants & a succession of close vowels. I wrote two of the songs in 'The Yeomen of the Guard' ('Were I thy bride' & 'Is life a boon') for the express purpose of proving this."[36] Consideration of the comparative qualities of languages may have contributed to a decision Gilbert made shortly after this letter. The holiday at Biarritz and Paris had been their first French holiday for many years, and Gilbert's first opportunity for a long time of using his French. He had been a fluent speaker of the language since his schooldays in Boulogne, and he may have noticed he was a little rusty. He decided to go back to keeping a diary, but this time he would keep it in French, forcing himself to write French every day.

The diaries have a simplicity, even a naiveté, about them as Gilbert records how he spent each day. They were not written for posterity: had they been, Gilbert would have taken greater care over his French. He was practicing his French, not trying to improve it. Characteristically, Gilbert had a cavalier approach to the correct use of French accents but, more than that, he made no use of a dictionary. If the word he was searching for did not come to him readily, because he had forgotten it or had never known it, he was content to leave it in English, giving his sentences at times a certain "franglais" flavor.

THE WINTER MONTHS OF 1905 were again spent at 52 Pont Street. Gilbert had begun to suffer from arthritis in his leg and was recommended to a new doctor, called Hokansson. A month's course of treatment brought him some relief—but it was only temporary.

One advantage of spending the winter months in London was the opportunity of more frequent visits to the theater, allowing Gilbert to go several times a week, mostly with Kitty and Nancy and friends. Kitty held an "at home" every Wednesday afternoon; and they would give one or two formal dinner parties during their three-month stay. More frequently and less formally, they entertained friends and relations to lunch or dinner: the Crutchleys, Luke Fildes's daughters, Mabel Turner (now Mabel Dugdale), and Gilbert's nephew (and stockbroker) Stanley Weigall. Kitty rode occasionally on Rotten Row, and they would both attend "Church Parade" on a Sunday morning in Hyde Park.

In March, Gilbert returned to his idea of writing a libretto based on *The Wicked World*. He worked on a 'scenario" over four days, from 9 March, had the manuscript printed and then sent it off to Messager. On 28 March, the "scenario" was returned. Messager was not interested. The "scenario" would be put away again but not forgotten.

Two days later, Gilbert was back at Grim's Dyke: back to his croquet and his photography, to watching for the first strawberries in the greenhouse, to feeding the fish and going for walks in the grounds. His usual partner at croquet was Nancy, sometimes playing several games a day. Kitty preferred not to play croquet. She went riding most mornings, was an avid bridge player, and in the evening enjoyed a game of billiards with Gilbert or the male guests, usually Rowland Brown or Arthur Helsham Jones, a magistrate colleague of Gilbert who often stayed over.

Visits to London were frequent, once or twice a week: to the theater or to friends, and Kitty regularly visited her mother, who lived in Scarsdale Villas, a short distance from their old home in Victoria Road. Gilbert went up to London on 29 April for the Academy dinner; his diary entry suggests he went more out of a sense of duty than from pleasure. His immediate companions at table included "le sacré Kipling" ["bloody Kipling"], he noted, adding, "Speeches dull & commonplace."[37]

Most Wednesday mornings Gilbert was driven by his chauffeur, Hardy McHardy, in their Cadillac (one of the two cars that replaced the steam car) to the Magistrates Court at Edgware. Afterward, McHardy, evidently a cut above the rest of the employees, would often have lunch with Gilbert and Kitty. On 10 May, instead of going to court, Gilbert and McHardy tried out a new car, a 20.30 Napier, driving through Stanmore and putting the car through its paces up Brockley Hill and Barnet Hill. "Le motor très bien sur le top speed—beaucoup de bruit au middle speed. Je préfère mon 16.24."[38]

The best of Gilbert's plays were still in demand and *The Palace of Truth* was revived in May at the Great Queen Street Theatre. From *The Palace of Truth* he went straight into a week's rehearsals at the Criterion for *Comedy and Tragedy*. He was in full swing, reinvigorated by being back in the theater and feeling much better than he had for years. He was prepared to undertake more. He wrote to Helen Carte. "If I can make arrangements for the production of the Operas in London, will you sell me back the London rights—&, if so on what terms? I expect [Herbert] Sullivan will agree to anything I agree to, but I've not consulted him. I can quite understand that you dont care to be bothered with the responsibility of running a London Theatre, but it would amuse me to do so."[39]

Gilbert and Sullivan were to appear in London again; but not exactly in the way Gilbert planned.

CHAPTER THIRTY-THREE

1905-1906

The Trouble with Casting

GILBERT'S HOPES OF TAKING over the management of a London theater to stage revivals of the operas were soon dashed by Helen Carte. As long as she ran her touring company, she told him, she was unwilling to separate the London rights from the touring rights. Her own suggestion was to revive the operas by bringing her touring company to London, which would reduce preliminary expenses. Each opera could be played for two weeks initially and then all of them played as a repertoire. "With classic works such as these," she said, "which are not novelties, the public undoubtedly like a Repertoire."[1]

Gilbert did not appear to be too disappointed. On the same day that he recorded in his diary "Premier 'Gooseberry Tart' pour lunch,"[2] he told her that he quite understood her point of view and was ready to support her endeavors, "with all the energy I can command."[3]

He was feeling mellow. These were mellow times. It was beautiful weather; he had had the lake cleaned and could take his customary morning swim; there was croquet on the lawn; photography; and in the evening after dinner, billiards, or the gramophone or perhaps the mechanical organ, the "orchestrelle."

In early June, he went into London one day with Nancy, bought two lemurs, and then all four of them caught the 5:20 from Euston back to Grim's Dyke. After a brief spell in captivity, the lemurs broke their chains and escaped, only to be recaptured two days later in the grounds. Later Gilbert would occasionally let them free to roam at leisure, even so far as to roam into the dining room and eat the nectarines and the bananas.

July produced a glorious spell of weather: Gilbert was able to swim daily, enjoy several games of croquet a day, or take a boat out on the lake. He spent a day at Lord's watching the annual Oxford versus Cambridge cricket match, while Kitty and Nancy went to Lord's the following week to see the Eton and Harrow game.

Kitty's mother was staying nearby, at Caldecote Hill, for the summer and as usual Kitty kept up her regular visits, cycling along the country lanes the mile or two from Grim's Dyke.

When the time came for their annual garden party, the good weather had departed and it was even too fresh and blustery for Gilbert to swim. But it stayed dry and the party went ahead as planned, with music provided by a Hungarian Band on the sunken lawn. The next day Gilbert's arthritis attacked him again, and for several weeks he was forced to lie on the sofa or go to bed for part of the day. "Ma jambe me fait mal en cou," he wrote in his diary on 10 September; which presumably meant, "My leg is a pain in the neck."[4]

His leg showed no sign of improvement until he was on vacation in Italy with Kitty and Nancy, going for a three-week stay to Lake Como. They had originally planned to go to Cadenabbia, but to Gilbert's disgust they discovered on arrival that rooms had not been reserved for them. Instead, they were rowed across to Bellagio and given excellent accommodation in a hotel called the "Great Britain." Toward the end of the vacation, they moved on to Milan, where they heard High Mass at the cathedral and climbed to the roof to admire the view. The next day they went to see da Vinci's "Last Supper." Gilbert thought that the painting had deteriorated so badly that it was impossible to judge anything but its composition, which he described as "faible."[5]

While they were away, a baby lemur had been born at Grim's Dyke. Almost the first thing Gibert did on their return home on 10 October was to visit the lemurs, but it was too dark to see anything and he had to wait until morning to catch sight of the new arrival. This was the first lemur to have been born in captivity in England, and Gilbert recorded the increasing length of its survival in his diary as he watched over its progress.

At the end of October, Kitty started to look for a suitable house in London for the first three months of the next year. After several trips and after viewing various houses in Belgravia, her efforts were rewarded when they were finally offered, for a rent of £351 for three months, an address that they would use each year for the rest of Gilbert's life: number 90 in the prestigious Eaton Square.

The improvement in Gilbert's arthritis had been maintained. The season for swimming and croquet was over, and in their place Gilbert was taking long walks, one November day setting off for London on foot and walking ten miles before rain forced him to catch a bus. He sold his old Cadillac in November for £85, and bought a new one. In his anglo-français he commented: "Le car ne va pas trop bien puisque le 'clutch slips.'"[6]

Christmas was spent by Gilbert and Kitty at Grim's Dyke. Kitty went to church on Christmas morning, and both Gilbert and Kitty gave up their afternoon on Boxing Day to entertaining the patients at the cottage hospital, with the assistance of a conjuror, who in Gilbert's judgment was rather poor.

The year ended quietly—the quietest year of Gilbert's life—his only year of true retirement.

THE MOVE UP TO LONDON in 1906, for the first time to 90 Eaton Square, was supervised by Nancy. She usually took charge of the organization on these occasions and Gilbert liked to keep out of the way, going to the Junior Carlton Club for lunch and only returning in the evening when domestic order had been established. The rhythm of London life was resumed, with Kitty's "At Homes" on Wednesdays, her outings on Rotten Row, and frequent visits of both of them to the theater. Gilbert was nearer to his clubs and regularly called in at the Beefsteak or the Junior Carlton, but the club whose membership he dearly prized was the Garrick. Thirty-seven years before, Gilbert had been blackballed, through an inexplicable case of mistaken identity, and his injured pride would not allow the matter to be rectified.

But it was the Garrick Club that made the first move. The committee told Gilbert he would be elected if he were willing to be proposed. Robert Marshall proposed his name and on 22 February Gilbert was officially elected to membership.

Around the same time, Gilbert negotiated the sale of his two Napiers in part exchange for a new 20.32 hp Darracq. He was again finding it difficult to walk. He had undergone another course of treatment from Dr. Hokansson, but immediately afterward his leg had begun to trouble him again.

His leg was still causing him pain when they returned to Grim's Dyke in April. As new life appeared around Grim's Dyke, Gilbert recorded each event in his diary: *Premieres Fraises* (6 April), "Premier concombre" (11 April), "Première feuille de beech" (19 April). Almost daily, he mentions the pain in his leg and is often unable to play croquet, preferring to drift in his boat or sometimes simply to rest.

His arthritic pains forced him to take to his bed for a few days. When his decision to stay in bed was turned into an order by the doctor, Gilbert felt like a condemned man, but cheered up later when he heard his "premier cou-cou" and when Nancy came to sing to him with her guitar.[7] Four days in bed were enough. On the fifth day he got up for lunch, and with Nancy drove to London in the Darracq. Gilbert attended a rehearsal at the Garrick for *Rosencrantz and Guildenstern*; Nancy went for a singing lesson; and the Darracq went to have its throttle examined.

Over the days and weeks his leg gradually improved, and by the middle of May he had begun work again, trying to improve *The Fortune Hunter*, now calling it "Cynthia's Husband." On 23 May, he was in London to produce *Rosencrantz and Guildenstern* at Lincoln's Inn Fields in aid of King's College Hospital, and the next day he was back in London, at Drury Lane, for the first rehearsal for a benefit performance of *Trial by Jury*. The "Ellen Terry Benefit" production of *Trial by Jury* took place at Drury Lane on 12 June. As usual on such occasions, it was a cast packed with celebrities, with Rutland Barrington as the Judge and Courtice Pounds as the Defendant. The jury included Francis Burnand, Arthur Conan Doyle, Anthony Hope, and Brandon Thomas; Decima Moore was one of the bridesmaids; and among the crowd in court was Rosina Brandram, as well as Sydney Grundy and John Martin-Harvey. The Associate was played by W. S. Gilbert, assisted by his Wife, played on this occasion by Fanny Brough.

On the same day, Gilbert started another month's course of treatment for his arthritic leg, this time with a Dr. Horne. The pain in his leg had made croquet impossible and it was not until the end of June that he was able to finish a game. Apart from the days when his leg was most painful, he managed to swim, taking his twenty-ninth swim of the year, he carefully noted in his diary, with Bertie Sullivan, who was staying at Grim's Dyke for the weekend.

On 26 July, Gilbert received news of the death of his sister Jane in Salisbury. Gilbert had not been to Salisbury in recent years, and no family correspondence between Gilbert and his sisters has survived. But Jane's children were frequent visitors to Grim's Dyke. Jane Weigall had had ten children—seven boys, three of whom became clergymen, and three girls. A commemorative plaque was erected in Salisbury Cathedral "by her grateful children": "In loving memory of Jane Morris Weigall— For nearly forty years a daily worshipper in this Cathedral." Jane was sixty-seven when she died.

In mid-August, after five days without pain, Gilbert recorded hopefully in his diary, "Ma jambe parait guéri [My leg appears to be cured]." He could enjoy the rest of that glorious summer, sometimes swimming twice a day, enjoying frequent visits from friends and developing his skills with a telephoto lens. Kitty was spending more time on her bicycle than her horse, visiting the hospital at Bushey and her mother who had again gone to Caldecote Hill for the summer after a brief stay at Grim's Dyke. One of Kitty's regular calls at the hospital was to their butler Warrilow, who had fractured his femur getting awkwardly out of the car at Grim's Dyke, trapping his leg behind the running board.

At fifty-eight, Kitty was in good health, fit and active, but had been suffering from an eye complaint that resulted in her doctor recommending a trip to Wiesbaden. On 7 September, Gilbert, Kitty, and Nancy set off for the health resort on the Rhine. It was in Wiesbaden that Gilbert received a letter from Helen Carte telling him that she intended to bring on a revival of *The Yeomen of the Guard*. Gilbert was pleased, but he had reservations.

> If the cast is a good one it will, I think, inflict a severe blow on "musical comedy"—but if it is inferior, on the whole, to the original cast, it will place further revivals out of the question. So, at least, it seems to me. I wont conceal from you that I am very anxious on this point.[8]

His warning was moderate, but it was clear. It came as a surprise to Helen Carte. Her intention had been to use her existing touring company. That was not good enough for Gilbert. He wanted her to engage the principals expressly for the London revival. Writing to Helen Carte on 5 October, the day before he left Wiesbaden, he suggested Nancy McIntosh as the soprano, assuring Helen Carte that her voice had improved and that she had benefited from her experience at Daly's. He made a further suggestion: "Could you get Lytton for Jack Point & Denny for the gaoler? With this cast I should feel certain of success. As many old Savoyards as possible!"[9]

Helen Carte's reply concerning Nancy McIntosh was firm, saying that "existing arrangements" would not allow her to offer an engagement. Neither was she receptive to Gilbert's request for "old Savoyards." "Were the original cast of the 'Yeomen' 20 years ago to appear now—such of them as are still alive—I think we must agree that the result would be deplorable and the piece could not run a week. Mr. Denny and Mr. Temple are probably the only ones who could get through their old parts— and neither is available."[10]

To make her point, she was exaggerating the problem. She also pointed out the financial difficulties of staging revivals, saying that it would take three months of "big business" to recoup the preliminary expenses. She was only considering a revival because Gilbert had expressed the wish for one and because interest had also been shown "by some of the public and press." "If I should proceed into the matter (which is uncertain) I will in due course send you my cast." She had originally written, "my proposed cast," but had changed her mind.[11]

Gilbert's response was immediate. "I must disabuse your mind of the idea that in putting the piece on the Savoy Stage, with what I presume is simply your country company, you are fulfilling any expressed desire of mine." Gilbert wanted a bolder approach "with a flourish of trumpets, an admirable cast, approved by me," he said, and would like to see the operas interspersed with other light operas, such as *La Sonnambula* or *L'Elisir d'Amore*. His particular grievance was that he was to have no voice in casting and thought it would be "a useless form," he said, "to send me a list of the people who are to play in it." Surely some of the famous names of the past were available—Lytton, Temple, Denny, and Barrington—names that would add value to the production. "However, I have no right to prejudge a cast of which I know nothing. I will attend rehearsals & if I find the people practicable I will carry them through to the best of my ability."[12]

He did not hear again from Helen Carte until 20 October, when a firm decision had been made to bring on a revival of *The Yeomen of the Guard* for 8 December, running for about two months, and having a second opera ready by then to take its place. In total, she hoped to produce three or four operas, but it depended on her state of health. Despite her earlier show of reluctance to engage new artists for the revival, she had made enquiries about Denny and Temple. Denny was in America and Temple had signed with David Bispham for the run of *The Vicar of Wakefield*. "Miss Brandram," she told Gilbert, "the only other member of the original cast who could have been all right had she been *well*, is, as you know a confirmed invalid. I wrote to her, but of course I knew it was hopeless."[13] After the old Savoy Company had been disbanded, Rosina Brandram had first appeared at the Adelphi and then opened in

May 1904 in Messager's *Veronique* at the Apollo. But in September that year she was involved in a carriage accident and her injuries put an end to her career.

Gilbert admitted to Helen Carte that he had no right to complain that he had not been consulted, as he had not stipulated this as a condition in the agreement he had made with her. "My grievance, such as it is," he told her, "is a purely sentimental one. You have always treated me with so much courtesy & consideration . . . that I confess I am surprised, & not a little hurt, that I have not been consulted on this occasion."[14] But he promised to do his best to make the production effective.

Two days later, on 22 October, Helen Carte sent Gilbert a telegram asking him to see the bass she proposed for the part of Sergeant Meryll. Gilbert's pride had been hurt in not being consulted initially, and he would have nothing to do with her proposal. Hurriedly he replied, "Seeing him here would be useless. As I have been totally ignored in casting the piece I prefer to leave the entire responsibility with you."[15] So ready was his response, he had not read the telegram carefully, and noted in his diary that day that Helen Carte had suggested sending him the tenor who was to play Leonard Meryll.

The revival of *The Yeomen of the Guard* was at the same time reviving public interest in Gilbert himself. He was interviewed at Grim's Dyke by the *Pall Mall Gazette* on 20 October, by the *Daily Mail* on 25 October, and on 6 November a reporter and a photographer arrived from the *Graphic*, taking photos of him in his library, in the drawing room and in the garden. The *Daily Mail* interview appeared in the paper on 30 October, and Gilbert was quoted as saying of the revival that it was "the very first occasion on which the entire cast has not been selected by me, so that whatever merit is due to the selection will belong to Mrs. D'Oyly Carte. So far, I don't know the name of a single individual in the cast."[16] The difference of opinion with Helen Carte was now public.

While waiting for the next development in the production of *The Yeomen of the Guard*, Gilbert had returned to rewriting *The Fortune Hunter*, which he was now calling "Diana's Husband." Kitty's eye problem had not been cured at Wiesbaden, and in the autumn evenings Gilbert would often read to her, from the newspaper or a novel, on one occasion reading from *Pickwick Papers*. He bought her, in advance of her birthday and in part exchange for a diamond necklace, a pearl necklace costing £800. On his own birthday, his seventieth, he treated his guests to a reading after lunch of his now completed "Diana's Husband." He made no record in his diary of their reactions, but it would seem that "Diana's Husband," alias "Cynthia's Husband," aka *The Fortune Hunter,* was due to be laid to rest. He made other attempts later to revive interest in the play, but was never successful.

It was also on his birthday that Gilbert received confirmation from Helen Carte of the time of the first rehearsal for *The Yeomen of the Guard*. She tried to reassure him that the cast had been carefully chosen and, "with the great advantage of [his] personal rehearsal," she hoped it would prove "worthy of the Savoy traditions."[17] By now Gilbert was even more indignant. "If Sullivan had been alive," he wrote to her, "you would no more have thought of casting one of the operas without obtaining his approval of every minute detail of the cast than you would have thought of setting the Savoy on fire."[18]

The volcano was rumbling and gathering force. Helen Carte must have wondered if or when it would eventually erupt. Her reply attempted to cool him down. "I hope I am not really as bad as you think I am. In any case, I shall always preserve the greatest regard and most friendly feelings for yourself."[19]

Between tea and dinner on Sunday 25 November, Gilbert locked himself away in his library to work on *The Yeomen of the Guard* in preparation for the first rehearsal the next day. In the morning, the cast assembled before him at the Savoy contained only one member who had been rehearsed by him before: Herbert Workman, who had played the First Citizen in the 1897 revival. Gilbert's impression that day is recorded in his diary: "Assez bonne troupe [Fairly good company] excepte Serg. Meryll qui est terrible."[20] The second day was similar: "Assez bien—mais Meryll impossible."[21] The singer in question was Overton Moyle, engaged by Helen Carte on François Cellier's advice.

At the end of rehearsals on the second day, Gilbert mentioned his unease about Moyle to Helen Carte. She wrote to Gilbert that evening. "Mr. Moyle is a Concert singer, with an exceptionally fine voice; who should, in the course of time, be a very suitable artist." She admitted that as an actor he was only a novice, and that is why she had asked Gilbert to see him.[22]

Gilbert had only himself to blame. He had acted hastily, had misread her telegram, and now placed Helen Carte in an awkward situation. Moyle had given up concert engagements and his name had been announced to the press; "I think," said Helen Carte, "he would have a great and legitimate grievance, and I hesitate very much to be a party to it." She asked Gilbert to give him a further rehearsal. If he still felt the same, they should both see Moyle and Gilbert could give his opinion. "Having myself engaged him, I should not be justified in taking the part from him excepting for the strong view which you as the author of the piece, hold on the subject."[23] The next day Gilbert noted in his diary simply: "Bonne repetition [Good rehearsal]";[24] and there is no further mention of Moyle.

On the day of the dress rehearsal, Helen Carte wrote Gilbert a long letter in which she went into meticulous detail over their dispute about casting. She reminded him of the agreement made in 1895, where it was stated that if Gilbert did not like the cast and did not care to supervise rehearsals, he could take £1,000 instead. She went over their correspondence concerning the revival, stressing that there were no old Savoyards available except Henry Lytton, and her "understanding with Mr. Workman made it impossible for [her] with any decency" to offer the part of Jack Point to Lytton. "I also saw," she said, "no artist likely to be better—if as good—as Miss Jessie Rose." Rather than give up the idea of the revivals, which she felt inclined to do, she knew that she had to construct her own cast or, she added, "an alternative which I refused to contemplate, I must enter into a controversial correspondence with yourself."

It was only after much thought, she told him, "and also after pressure brought on me from various quarters," that she decided to proceed. "I am not expecting by anything I say, to alter your views—I should like to, but I fear I should wish in vain."[25] Then she added, but decided to omit from the fair copy sent to Gilbert: "It has been very painful to me that you should have taken the line you have. I do not feel that I have deserved it." [26]

Gilbert would not be moved by Helen Carte's reasonable arguments. He replied to her on the day of the opening. He accepted that she had kept to their contract. "I have never suggested that you have violated it in the smallest particular," he admitted. But he held to his view that he should have been consulted, as Sullivan would have been, he repeated. As for the members of cast mentioned by Helen Carte, he expressed his satisfaction with Workman and Jessie Rose, "who are both admirable." But he added, "the other parts are but indifferently filled."[27]

The public enthusiasm generated because the operas were to return—because "the ancient glories of the Savoy were to be renewed," as *The Times* expressed it,[28]—found early expression on the day of the opening. The line formed at 10 a.m. at the gallery doors and by 11 a.m. at the pit entrance. In the afternoon, the management made a decision to open the doors early and tea was served to the weary devotees. In that day's *Evening Standard*, Rutland Barrington was quoted as saying, "I should think that the revival would have had better chances of success if [Mrs. D'Oyly Carte] could have got some of the Old Savoyards."[29] Gilbert was clearly not alone in his point of view.

That evening Gilbert and Kitty dined at the Savoy Hotel with Kitty's niece, Mabel Dugdale, and her husband. Afterward, in accordance with his tradition, Gilbert left his guests while they went to their box in the theater. As though to justify Gilbert in his battle with Helen Carte over the casting, *The Times* commented, "It was obviously desirable, above all things, to secure the services of as many as possible of the old 'Savoyards' . . . surely some might have been induced to take up their old parts again . . ." and highlighted the applause that had greeted the arrival at the theater of Jessie Bond and Henry Lytton.[30] As for the present company, the same paper praised Jessie Rose "as a genuine successor of Miss Jessie Bond" and considered that C. H. Workman was "at least as good as either of his predecessors in the part of Jack Point. . . . His was the chief triumph of Saturday night."[31]

With the exception of John Clulow as Wilfred Shadbolt, other members of the cast were not considered up to the old standard. Included among the performers that night was a young actor making his first appearance in a Gilbert and Sullivan opera: Leo Sheffield, who played the Second Yeoman and was to have a swift rise to prominence.

Gilbert's instincts about the cast chosen for him seemed to have been justified, but his treatment of Helen Carte had been brutal. To the cast and to the public, whatever they knew or guessed of the differences behind the scenes, Gilbert was a hero. He was applauded "with great enthusiasm" at the end of the opera by both audience and performers, said *The Times*, and Helen Carte "also appeared and was warmly applauded."[32]

After the first night, the war of letters between Gilbert and Helen Carte resumed. Gilbert returned to his suggestion of engaging Henry Lytton. If he could not have played Jack Point, because that part had been given to Workman, he could have been engaged as Wilfred Shadbolt. "However Mr. Lyttons reception by Mr. Boulter," said Gilbert, "when he applied for an engagement, placed it out of the question." Gilbert was convinced that Stanley Boulter was influencing Helen Carte's selection of artists, and he wanted his displeasure felt. "With the exception of Mr. Workman & Miss Rose (who were both admirable) the performance was a performance of understudies. The tenor, as an actor, was an impossibility."[33]

The following day, 11 December, Gilbert returned to the fray, all the time becoming more aggressive in his attitude toward Helen Carte, although making it clear that it was the man behind her, Stanley Boulter, who was the real target of his abuse.

> The production, as a whole, is discreditable to the memory of Sullivan, to me, & to the magnificent reputation which he & I built up for the Savoy Theatre. The piece has received a blow from which it will never recover—& I presume that a similar blow is to be struck at the other pieces you propose to produce. I can only hope that your astounding change of attitude towards me is due to the influence of Mr. Boulter[.] It is horrible to me to think that it is the outcome of your own volition.[34]

To win his point, Gilbert became increasingly more outspoken. On 12 December Helen Carte wrote to him again, mainly to discuss a problem that had arisen over the storage of scenery; but also to say: "I have, I think, replied with unfailing courtesy to your letters; but this seems only to result in their assuming a more and more discourteous—I might say abusive—tone[.]"[35]

At the same time as he was firing volley after volley at Helen Carte, Gilbert's diary shows him over this same period leading a perfectly contented existence at Grim's Dyke, tending his lake and trying to deal with the scum that built up on the surface. The same persistence with which he pursued practical problems until they were resolved, and that showed itself in his constancy in taking up the battle on behalf of friends (as Henry Lytton was now finding), was that same persistence that an opponent must have found extremely wearing, once Gilbert had set his hand to the task. To Helen Carte's letter of 12 December, Gilbert wrote a long letter on 13 December. "I cannot allow your statement that I have been discourteous, not to say abusive, in my very painful correspondence with you to pass unchallenged."[36] Again he went over the history of the dispute, and then chose to add insult to his previous injurious statements: "I must remind you that when an unoffending man has been so treated by a lady whose large fortune he has been so directly instrumental in helping to make, the offence lies with her in so treating him rather than with him for protesting in plain terms against such treatment."[37]

"Longue lettre à Mrs. Carte," Gilbert recorded in his diary for 17 December.[38] This was in reply to a letter he had received from her that day, going over old ground and reminding him yet again of their agreement of 1895. "It is difficult, therefore," she told him, "for me to see that you have any kind of grievance."[39]

In his reply, Gilbert, too, went through the whole issue again, step by step, and challenged her to quote an expression he had used that could be classed as "discourteous, unchivalrous, unwarranted & abusive."[40]

Helen Carte refused to rise to the challenge, preferring to pass over it in silence. Gilbert returned to consideration of the weeds in his lake; to entertaining his friends; and to Christmas shopping for some of his lady friends (a Kelly's Directory for the writer Elizabeth de la Pasture, the "World's Classics" for Mary Talbot, and chocolates for his younger friends—Dorothy Fildes, Edmée and Yolande de la Pasture, Margery and Pamela Maude). That Christmas the Crutchleys stayed over at Grim's Dyke. On Boxing Day, they woke to six inches of snow that had fallen overnight. The snow did not deter them from their annual visit to the Bushey Cottage Hospital where, after tea, the entertainment consisted of listening to the gramophone, followed by Sybil Crutchley reciting "The Yarn of the Nancy Bell."

The Gilberts started their winter stay in London a little early, moving up to 90 Eaton Square on 29 December. The following evening, Gilbert was guest of honor at a dinner given by the O. P. Club at the Hotel Cecil, to which 450 guests had been invited. Gilbert, seated between the president of the club, Sidney Dark, and Mrs. Dark, replied to the toast, "The Savoy Operas." About forty old Savoyards were present; Gilbert praised all his "dear old comrades" from past Savoy companies and recalled the names of those who had already died: Alfred Cellier, Harriette Everard, George Bentham, Alice Barnett, Emmie Owen, D'Oyly Carte, Richard Barker, Charles Harris, William Seymour, and especially Arthur Sullivan. He was not at his "merriest," he said, when remembering all Sullivan had done for him "in allowing his genius to shed some of its lustre upon my humble name."[41]

But even here, on this public occasion, Gilbert could not resist a reference to the quarrel that divided him from Helen Carte, albeit a reference that wrapped itself around a roll call of honor. "And when the operas revert, as they will, to their original proprietors, they (or their executors) will hold out their hands to George Grossmith, to Rutland Barrington [then followed a long list of old Savoyards including Nancy McIntosh] . . . and implore them to return to the arena in which they achieved so many triumphs."[42]

From what they had heard of the battle between Gilbert and Helen Carte, old Savoyards such as Lytton, Barrington, and others would have seen it as Gilbert fighting for them against an intransigent management. For that, he would have their undying support; in after years, Lytton went so far as to say that Gilbert had "a genius for friendship."[43] Gilbert also was fighting to get his own way; but he had been right in supposing that, when playing the operas at the Savoy, a cast that included the old Savoyards would increase the popularity of the revivals.

As far as Helen Carte was concerned, she was acting according to the letter of the agreement with Gilbert drawn up in 1895, when D'Oyly Carte was still alive. It is not clear why she did not attempt to enter into a new agreement with Gilbert, now that they were the only two left. Was it because of outside pressure, as Gilbert had suspected? Or was it a miscalculation on her part, hoping to save herself from long discussions by correspondence with Gilbert if she drew up the cast herself? Gilbert had proved her mistaken on the last point.

Bruised but unflinching, Helen Carte wrote to Gilbert on the last day of 1906. She proposed producing *The Gondoliers* on Tuesday, 22 January 1907, and "in accordance with [their] agreement of Sept 30th. 1903" asked if he were willing to undertake the stage management. She ended her letter with the bald statement: "I enclose the cast."[44]

CHAPTER THIRTY-FOUR

1907-1908

Interpolations

IGNORING ANY REFERENCE to the cast that Helen Carte had sent him for the revival of *The Gondoliers*, Gilbert contented himself with a brief acknowledgment that rehearsals were due to start on 7 January 1907. Only when rehearsals had actually begun did Gilbert refer to the company that had been engaged.

They were substantially the same performers as in *The Yeomen of the Guard* with the addition of Richard Green, who had sung in *Ivanhoe* and who was to play the part of Giuseppe. Writing to Helen Carte, Gilbert told her that the cast was, "with few exceptions, so very unsatisfactory" to him that he wanted to disclaim all responsibility for it. He declared his intention to write to critics of the main newspapers to point out that the selection was Helen Carte's and not his. "It will leave the press," he claimed, "the liberty to form an independent opinion as to whether the selection is judicious or otherwise."[1]

Helen Carte was not slow to point out the flaw in his argument. "I fail to see," she replied, "how you consider you will assist the critics to form an independent opinion of my artists by the letter you propose writing to them. Their independent opinion cannot be affected by the question of who selected the artists. If it were it would not be independent." She then moved from logic to supposition, and in a sentence that she later regretted, she summed up Gilbert's intentions: "I can only, therefore, assume that your letter is intended to give me notice that you wish to prejudice the minds of the critics beforehand, to the damage of my artists and possibly my business, by a letter which cannot be taken to have any other object than to express your disapproval of the cast."[2]

While accepting the logic of her first statement, Gilbert took issue with her interpretation of his intention. He wanted to place himself beyond praise or blame, he said, "in the matter of the cast of 'The Gondoliers,' in which I have had no voice whatever." This was so obviously "the only interpretation" that could be attached to his proposed letter, he claimed, that her suggestion amounted to "a gross and gratuitous insult."[3]

It would not be in his best interests, he told her, to damage the operas, especially as the copyright of the libretti would soon revert to him. At his most indignant, Gilbert concluded: "I must ask you to withdraw, explicitly and unreservedly, the grossly disgraceful & altogether unwarrantable charges you have made against me."[4]

In addition, Gilbert did not think that enough rehearsal time had been allowed and after initially suggesting a postponement of the opening night, which would have proved impossible at that late stage, suggested two rehearsals on 21 January, the day before the opening. As that would entail additional expense in employing the orchestra for an evening rehearsal, he wrote to Helen Carte on Friday, 11 January, offering to cover the expense himself. To that suggestion, she replied on Monday, 13 January: "Is it really necessary for you to continue to adopt such a gratuitously offensive attitude towards me?" Would it not have been kinder, she asked, if he had enquired about any difficulty, before suggesting financial assistance, "which can only be done for the purpose of giving pain?"[5]

For the second time Helen Carte, under intense pressure and unwell, had given way uncharacteristically to assuming Gilbert's intentions. She assured Gilbert that there was no difficulty in his holding two rehearsals on 21 January and that "the extra expense of the orchestra would be most willingly met" by her.[6] But it was her opening remarks on which Gilbert seized. Replying on Tuesday, 14 January, he repeated his previous challenge to her, asking her to quote examples of his abusive treatment of her, and "now" he continued, "you think proper to describe me as offensive for no better reason than that I have offered to defray an expense that I had no right to expect you to incur. . . . May I suggest that we are more likely to arrive at a satisfactory understanding on points that may arise if you can contrive to restrict your epithets to those usually employed by ladies in their correspondence with gentlemen?"[7]

She ignored Gilbert's implied insult, and chose to defend her former statements. "I did not describe you as offensive, I asked you if you really thought it necessary to adopt such a gratuitously offensive attitude towards me — which I take to be an attitude calculated to wound." His suggestion that she would let the payment of the orchestra stand in the way of a rehearsal seemed to her "very much calculated to wound my feelings, and most certainly did so. I have no desire to continue a painful correspondence."[8]

The pain and the hurt that Helen Carte experienced in this bitter exchange had no effect on Gilbert. He wanted her to feel the consequences of flouting his wish to be consulted over the casting and was remorseless in pressing home his point. He replied on 15 January, asking her to withdraw "the abominable charge . . . of deliberately plotting" to injure her company and business. Unless he received an apology, "all friendly relations — even of the most formal kind" were at an end.[9] Whenever she took it on herself, he threatened, to cast one of the operas without consulting him, he would publicly disclaim responsibility in order to protect himself.

Helen Carte was not going to win this battle of words with Gilbert. He had the capacity to go on and on, wearing his opponent down without pity. Helen Carte found it too painful and backed away. Giving further consideration to the letter she had written on 10 January, she said, "I think I can trace your indignation, expressed in such strong language, to a misconception, owing to my not having expressed my meaning in clear language. I did **_not_** mean to charge you with a wish to injure my Company or my business." She was referring to the result of his action, not its purpose. She had no hesitation therefore in withdrawing the words that unintentionally offended Gilbert. "It has always been my desire to treat you with courtesy, and will continue to be so. It ought not to be impossible to conduct such business communications as may be necessary between us in a friendly manner; and, so far as I am concerned, I shall endeavour to do so."[10]

The argument proved to be futile. It would appear from Gilbert's diary that only one rehearsal was held on 21 January after all, and the following morning readers of *The Times* were able to see Gilbert's letter disclaiming any responsibility for the production of *The Gondoliers* except the stage management.[11] In the evening, he drove a young friend, Dora Critchett, to the Savoy, and then spent the evening at the Beefsteak Club until it was time for him to return and take a call at the end of the opera.

He was received with rapturous applause; *The Gondoliers* had charmed the audience once more. The cast had acquitted themselves well, on the whole: "Mr. Workman surpasses both his predecessors," said *The Times*; "Miss Jessie Rose [Tessa] . . . must seem delightful to those who never saw the original"; and "Mr. Clulow is more than satisfactory as the Grand Inquisitor." The reviewer drew attention to Gilbert's letter, which had appeared that morning, and thinking back to the breakup in the Gilbert and Sullivan partnership after the original *Gondoliers*, expressed the hope that the letter did not signify "the beginning of another breach between [Gilbert] and the management. As the surviving member of the famous triumvirate, he has an authority to which no one else can possibly pretend; and everything should of course be done to obey his wishes in every detail."[12]

The opening of *The Gondoliers* coincided with Gilbert's going down with a heavy cold that worsened over the following week and led to the curtailing of his social life as he called off dinner engagements and theater visits. He developed a hacking cough, which kept him awake all one night, and he spent the next night in an armchair in front of the fire. Dr. Hokansson used to call most days. He was fussed over by Elizabeth de la Pasture, who frequently visited him, reading him her latest play and keeping him company if Kitty and Nancy were both out. Sybil Crutchley called, and Dora Critchett sent a basket of flowers; he was not neglected. By 6 February, he had recovered sufficiently to give his third interview to Edith Browne, who was writing his biography, and on Sunday, 10 February, he was out in Hyde Park for "Church Parade"—on his own, as Nancy had taken to attending Mass on Sundays at Brompton Oratory and was usually accompanied by Kitty.

On 27 February, Gilbert put on the uniform of a deputy lieutenant and was driven in an old-fashioned brougham to the Central Criminal Court in the Strand for the official opening by Edward VII and Queen Alexandra. The whole area had been developed in recent years: Clement's Inn, where Gilbert had once had rooms, had gone and the broad Kingsway road had been constructed to run from Holborn down to the Aldwych, the new wide crescent of roadway north of the Strand. The development represented a new, more open era under Edward VII and had necessitated sweeping away the old, narrow streets and alleys, like Wych Street where the Opera Comique once stood. And one of the old stars, who had begun her career with Gilbert and Sullivan at the Opera Comique and was so much a part of the old era, Rosina Brandram, died the following day at Southend, in Argyllshire.

"Jai reçu les proofs de la biographie," Gilbert noted in his diary for 8 March. "Mdlle est très sévère sur mes comedies."[13] Two days later, he returned the proofs to Edith Browne, making "some very candid & outspoken comments." Her judgment of the literary quality of his plays "especially those in verse," he found particularly hard to bear.[14] Miss Browne's reply calmed him down; he had to admit that his position as leading dramatist belonged to a former time "& it hurt me not a little," he told her, "to find that work which was so well esteemed when it was produced, appealed so feebly to so keen an intelligence as your own."[15]

Edith Browne had been most complimentary in her book about Gilbert's work in the theater as a stage director.

> He is naturally endowed with the qualities of a ruler, [she wrote] who can impose discipline; and even now at the age of seventy, this finely-built, erstwhile officer of the Gordon Highlanders . . . walks into a room or on the stage with the alert step and dignified carriage of a commander who charges his whole environment with power. Merely to see him is to be instinctively impelled mentally to stand to attention, but to know him is to realise that he is just and generous as he is strong.[16]

No wonder Gilbert overlooked her less complimentary comments on his early plays.

It had been Helen Carte's intention to bring on a revival of *The Mikado* as the third of her planned repertoire of four operas. Her planning was already well advanced when she learned that the lord chamberlain had banned *The Mikado* from being performed in order to avoid offending the Japanese during the proposed visit of Prince Fushimi. She appealed against the ban and in a personal interview presented her case, without success. After spending two hours in tears in the lord chamberlain's office, a distressed Helen Carte wrote to Gilbert sending a copy of her correspondence with the lord chamberlain and telling him about her interview. If she had hoped for Gilbert's sympathy, she received none. "I can only say," he replied on 2 April, "that if the Mikado was to be produced with the same ignorant ineptitude that has characterized the other productions at the Savoy, I am heartily glad that its performance has been prohibited."[17]

Despite the ban, on 29 March the D'Oyly Carte touring company put on a performance of *The Mikado* in Sheffield, the management of the theater claiming that they had received no official notification of the ban. Every seat in the theater was taken and many people had to be turned away.[18]

In place of *The Mikado*, Helen Carte decided to revive *Patience*, and Gilbert began rehearsals on 18 March. On the opening night, Thursday, 4 April, he went to the Palace Theatre to watch the "performing sea lions," but he was at the Savoy by 10:30, in time for his call. *The Times* praised John Clulow (Grosvenor), Louie René (Lady Jane), and Clara Dow (Patience), because they kept up "something of the old tradition. They have realized something of the great truth that it is better to let Mr. Gilbert make them funny than to try and make Mr. Gilbert funny. He is quite funny enough without embroidery."[19]

For Gilbert, it was back to Grim's Dyke and the care of his lake and gardens: sowing grass seed along the banks of the lake, bringing the water-level up to the full (a depth of five feet ten and one-half inches), getting rid of the worms and the weeds on the croquet lawn; and back to affairs at the cottage hospital, as part of a subcommittee set up to oversee the building of two wings to increase the number of beds available at the hospital. There were the occasional visits and shopping trips to London: to buy new boots and shoes from the American Boot Company and a cigar case from Harrod's; to purchase a wardrobe for the hospital, a piano for Nancy; and to order a new truss for his hernia. "We are very quiet here," he wrote to Mary Talbot, "— the weather has been too cold & raw for us to invite visitors here &, except Mrs. de la Pasture, the novelist, we have had no visitors." He told her about the coming revival of *Iolanthe*. "I fancy it will be better played than the others — Mrs. Carte is beginning to discover that her policy has been folly. They have engaged Lytton for the principal part — they scorned him & insulted him grossly when he applied for an engagement 4 months ago."[20]

Rehearsals for *Iolanthe* began on Tuesday, 28 May: six stage rehearsals over two weeks, then a dress rehearsal on 7 June and the final dress rehearsal on the 10th. For the first night, Gilbert had bought a box at £3.3.0; twenty stalls at 10s. 6d.; seven seats in the balcony at 7s. 6d.; eight seats at 5 shillings; and ten seats at 4 shillings: a total bill of £20.5.6. Apart from his guests in the box with Kitty and Nancy, he had invited forty-five other guests, probably including his servants. As for Gilbert himself, he dined at the Beefsteak Club and then, as usual, arrived at the Savoy in time for his call. According to *The Times*, Henry Lytton had enriched the cast by returning to play Strephon, while Workman's Lord Chancellor was rated as a masterpiece, with the "Nightmare Song" being "sung with marvellous glibness." Overton Moyle was praised for his singing in the part of Private Willis — "even Mr. Charles Manners did not sing the sentry's song better."[21]

The next morning, Gilbert was on the magistrates' bench at Edgware, carrying out his civic duties and embodying the law for the local community. Ten days later, he received a letter from the prime minister, Sir Henry Campbell-Bannerman, offering him a knighthood. "It is an offer which I gratefully accept," Gilbert replied.[22]

Grim's Dyke, with the French windows of Gilbert's library open
(By permission of the British Library, Add MS 49,353 C)

The announcement was made public in the *Gazette* on 27 June, and Gilbert was inundated with congratulations: telegrams from Savoyards old and new, such as Ruth Vincent as well as Rutland Barrington and Henry Lytton; and telegrams from the Kendals, who sent one each. "Congratulations on an honour which ought to have been conferred on you twenty years ago," said George Grossmith, and Bertie Sullivan went even further, "Sincerest congratulations only it ought to have been a Dukedom."[23] Rutland Barrington followed up his telegram with a letter: "I should have told you that you impressed me as still being hale and harty [*sic*] enough to hold your position as being the only "producer" of plays, to perfection, it has ever been my lot to work with."[24] Gilbert belittled the award, but all the same, he was proud of the recognition given to him as a dramatic author.[25]

By 3 July Gilbert had received over three hundred letters of congratulations, and Kitty had received nearly a hundred. A constant stream of visitors called at Grim's Dyke, and between visits Gilbert was kept busy writing replies. A late letter of congratulations arrived from the Sisters of Nazareth at their convent, Nazareth House in Hammersmith, the district where Gilbert had spent the first years of his life: "We rejoice exceedingly that you the great friend of the poor, should be thus honoured and we pray God to spare you many many years."[26]

Gilbert was knighted by Edward VII at Buckingham Palace on 15 July, driven there in his Darracq. He had lunch afterward at the Savoy Grill and was home in time for tea followed by a swim in the lake: his second of the day and his forty-third of the year. And life returned to normal. Lady Gilbert was often to be seen on her bicycle along the country lanes on her visits to the hospital or to see her mother, and Sir William could be found swimming daily and playing croquet, increasing his menagerie at Grim's Dyke by buying Siberian cranes and making arrangements for a loft conversion, a scheme which was later abandoned.

The season of revivals at the Savoy came to an end on Saturday, 24 August, in a performance that started at 4 p.m. and consisted of act 1 of *The Yeomen* and act 2 of *The Gondoliers*; then after an interval, act 2 of *Patience* and act 1 of *Iolanthe*. Despite the ban still being in force, the scene between Ko-Ko and Katisha from act 2 of *The Mikado* was played as a finale. Gilbert stayed at Grim's Dyke. After his ninety-ninth swim of the year in the morning and a game of croquet with Nancy in the afternoon, he was having a quiet evening at home.

The season's tally of swims reached 118 on 10 September, and the next day Gilbert, with Kitty and Nancy, set off for a vacation at Territet, near Montreux on Lake Geneva, where they were joined later by Kitty's niece, Nonie, and her husband, Harold Messel. They visited Lausanne, Vevey, and St. Gingolph; they had boat rides and trips on the funicular; they met their old friends Marcus Stone and his wife, and generally had a restful three weeks' vacation. They returned to England at the end of the month, and the next morning Gilbert was back to his duties on the bench at Edgware.

That autumn Gilbert decided to buy a new 50 hp Darracq for £1,000 and was offered £475 for his old one. It was months before he was satisfied, finally taking possession of the car on Christmas Eve. On Boxing Day, he was traveling between Stanmore and the Edgware Road at 40 mph and doing 16.5 mph up Brockley Hill in third gear. Service from the garage had not improved since his first car, but his speed certainly had.

Christmas 1907 at Grim's Dyke was without Nancy. Her aunt had died in October and on 30 November she left for America to visit her uncle. Gilbert and Kitty went to Euston to see her off, but whereas Kitty and Nancy had lunch at the Euston Hotel, Gilbert was too nervous and fidgety to eat and went for a walk until it was time to say good-bye at the station, where Nonie and Harold Messel also were waiting to see Nancy off.

Writing to Mary Talbot at the end of the year, Gilbert mentioned Nancy's absence. "We go to Eaton Square on the 7th. Jan—we shall Miss Nancy McIntosh when we move as she took all the trouble off our hands. I only hope she wont be tempted to remain with her uncle."[27] Gilbert's fear was that the "rich old man" would ask Nancy to stay as a companion to his daughter. Writing to "Dearest Nancy" a few days later, on 3 January 1908, and signing himself "Your affectionate Judge," the nickname Nancy used for him, Gilbert showed how much he and Kitty wanted her to continue to be a close part of their lives. "My wife sends her best love & all wishes for a happy new year *which we hope & trust you will spend with us*, but we seem to see difficulties ahead. I only hope you are not going to chuck us after so many years."[28]

Their guests at Christmas were Sybil and Charles Crutchley and their teenage son, a pupil at Harrow, who managed to aggravate Gilbert by behaving like a normal teenager. "The Crutchleys are here with their son Gerald," Gilbert wrote to Mary Talbot, "— a young gentleman of 17 — quite spoilt — does what he pleases without consulting any one — breaks into the middle of one's conversation — & generally gets on my nerves — I am obliged to retire to the morning room to write this, as it has occurred to him to play the Orchestrelle."[29]

In the same letter, Gilbert told her, "I am still hammering away at my fraudulent parson." Gilbert was referring to a case he had taken up after discovering that the £5 he had donated for the relief of four sisters had not gone straight to the ladies concerned but had gone to the National Blind Relief Society, whose honorary secretary was the Rev. J. Pullein Thompson. Gilbert demanded his money back and then sent it personally to the four ladies, the Misses Griffin, in Wells, Norfolk. Thompson subsequently asked the ladies to return the money that Gilbert had sent, so that it could be added to the fund that was earmarked for them. When he learned what had happened, Gilbert doggedly set about righting what he saw clearly to be an injustice, appealing to the Charity Organization Society through whom Thompson was working, and writing to the bishop of London to acquaint him with the misdirected behavior of one of his clergymen; but Gilbert was frustrated in all his attempts. The bishop thought that Gilbert was exhibiting "suspicion run mad," but did agree to an interview with Gilbert and Thompson, at which he stated that the contents of the meeting should remain secret, and that there should be no consideration of legal action. Gilbert refused absolutely to abide by those conditions.[30]

Gilbert spent nearly a year "hammering away" and in the end, following legal advice, settled for producing a printed brochure that he presented to the Committee of the Charity Organization Society, detailing his case against Thompson. Gilbert's own summing-up of Thompson after meeting him was that, although he was probably honest enough, he thought he was weak and foolish. He had not been dealing with a real fraud but with a man whose accounting methods fell some way short of satisfactory.

NANCY RETURNED FROM AMERICA on 31 January, and was met at Euston by Gilbert and Kitty with the new Darracq; their fear of losing her was past and they returned to being a family of three. In the eyes of their friends, Nancy had assumed the role of an adopted daughter. All three were soon back into the social round, being entertained to dinner by friends, giving dinners at Eaton Square, and of course making frequent visits to the theater.

In celebration of Gilbert's knighthood, Bertie Sullivan, Robert Marshall, and Willie Mathews (director of public prosecutions, and now Sir Charles Mathews) had arranged a dinner for 2 February, with more than one hundred guests at the Savoy. "It is the most gratifying compliment that I have ever received," said Gilbert to Bertie Sullivan, "and I thank you heartily for it."[31]

In his after-dinner speech, Gilbert recalled his early days as a journalist and the happy meetings of "The Serious Family" (whose members had all since died); his days as a naive dramatist, when he was cheated out of a fair rate for his work, an occurrence that he had never forgotten; and he recalled especially his old collaborator. "That my share of the operas profited inestimably by Sullivan's magnificent work is a common-place of stage criticism, and if my simple muse has succeeded in overtopping the clouds, it has been carried thither on the wings of his mighty Pegasus." Time and again he had been astounded when he heard the music Sullivan had written for his lyrics. Surprisingly, Sullivan had maintained that there was no such thing as humor in music, "but," said Gilbert,

> in my humble judgment he was, himself, a musical humorist of the very highest order. In justification of this belief I may indicate the clergymans song in the "Sorcerer" the trio "Ring the Merry bells on board ship" in the "Pinafore," The three little Maids from School from the Mikado, the wonderful accompaniment to the Dream song in "Iolanthe" & the exquisite duet between Elsie & Jack Point in the first act of the "Yeomen of the Guard."[32]

When Gilbert received notification in March of Helen Carte's intention to stage a revival of *The Mikado* and an invitation to undertake the stage management, he accepted without argument. Apart from Workman as Ko-Ko, Henry Lytton had been engaged to play the part of the Mikado and Rutland Barrington that of Pooh-Bah. He had a preliminary discussion with Workman at Eaton Square about allowable interpolations, and rehearsals proper began on Monday, 1 April.

In place of criticism of the cast, Gilbert took issue with Helen Carte over the "interpolations and excrescences" that had crept into the libretti in the touring companies. "I believe," Gilbert wrote to her on 21 April, "that, inter alia, an encore verse has been sung in connection with KoKo's entrance in the Mikado & Mr Workman has had the coolness to send me the text of it & ask my consent to his singing it."[33] Helen Carte denied that any interpolations were allowed except those that Gilbert himself authorized from time to time, "and no encore verse is ever sung by Mr Workman in 'The Mikado,'" she insisted. "On the last production of 'The Mikado' in London you authorised an encore verse, suggested I believe by Mr. Passmore, and referring to the Chinese; but this is never sung on tour."[34] If Gilbert had any authentic information about interpolations and would let her know, she assured him that she would deal with the matter. The next day, Gilbert noted in his diary that he had written an encore verse for Workman.

Gilbert was pleased to have two old Savoyards in the cast: he invited Rutland Barrington to lunch with Kitty and himself at Simpson's during a break in rehearsal on 23 April, and the next day Barrington and Henry Lytton invited Gilbert and Jessie

Rose to lunch, again at Simpson's, after the rehearsal for the day had finished. Gilbert had the confidence of the cast, and it would appear that he also had their confidences. Writing to Helen Carte on 25 April, he acknowledged the receipt of his £200, his fee for rehearsing each of the revivals, and then launched into her yet again.

> You are quite mistaken in supposing that the libretti are not freely "gagged." I was informed this morning by a member of the Savoy Company that it is the practice for KoKo, addressing the Mikado in Act 2, to exclaim "High tiddley hi ti! And when I say 'High tiddley high ti, I refer to your Majesty." I am informed that similar interpolations occur throughout that & other pieces, but that the gagging is more frequent & more insolent in "The Gondoliers" than in any other.[35]

Surely, he suggested, if she had any respect for their agreement, it was possible for her "to send a short hand clerk to the performances, who would take note of all the embroideries with which your buffoons are in the habit of decorating my work."[36] Unless she took some such action, he threatened, he would proceed for breach of contract.

Even after the opening of the revival on Tuesday, 28 April, the question of interpolations had still not been resolved. Helen Carte was confident that there were no unauthorized interpolations in *The Mikado* or any other opera. "Several months ago," she told Gilbert, "I had the exit words spoken by Pooh Bah 'No money, no grovel' taken out, because although I remembered Mr. Barrington used to mumble some words to take him off, I could not trace these exact words in any of the old prompt books as having been authorized by you. I understand you have now reinstated them with two additional lines."[37]

She urged Gilbert to write into a copy of the libretto of *The Mikado* all the authorized alterations which she could then have printed by Chappells. She admitted that "there had been a considerable number of alterations, chiefly interpolations made by Mr. Barrington"; if she had a correct printed version, it would help her to put an end to gagging. Gilbert's earlier reference about the agreement prompted her to send him a copy, but she assured Gilbert that she did not need an agreement to prevent any additions being made to the libretti. "I have too much respect for them to do otherwise."[38]

Gilbert replied that it was Workman who had given him the example of gagging in *The Mikado* that he had quoted. He also had been told by members of the company, he insisted, that nearly all the pieces were liberally "gagged" but none so much as *The Gondoliers*. "Your sending me a copy of any agreement to prove your right to sanction alterations of my pieces at your pleasure evinces, clearly enough, your contemptuous attitude towards the works that have been the foundation of your fortunes. But, as I said before, I do not hold *you* morally responsible."[39]

Helen Carte was adamant that her respect for the operas would not let her treat the matter of interpolations lightly. If any actor "continued an interpolation after he had been told it was not authorized by you," she told Gilbert, "[he] would have his engagement terminated." She had seen all the principals at the Savoy who were from the touring company and they denied "absolutely that the pieces were 'gagged' on Tour." She enclosed a signed statement from the actors involved.[40] Gilbert rejected the statement. "The people who signed the document you have forwarded to me are all dependent on your goodwill for their engagement & they were not likely to give themselves away by declining to put their names to it."[41]

The very idea that her company should be accused of dishonesty brought an indignant reply from Helen Carte. "They spoke freely, and under no constraint of any kind" she insisted.[42] On the same day, 5 May, with the letters crossing, Gilbert wrote referring to specific examples.

> Some of Barrington's "gags" are justified by long use or are otherwise unobjectionable, or too trivial for notice — others are redundant & weak. Among the latter I should include "Chop it off" "I think we might manage to wait till then" and "You haven't got one" (a big right arm)[.] This latter was introduced in Grossmith's time — he used to bare his arm which was extremely thin — it does not apply to Workman's arm which is of ordinary dimensions. I will write to Barrington & ask him to suppress these last three.

"This lengthy correspondence," Gilbert told her, had arisen because he had mentioned the "High tiddley hi ti" gag and because Workman had asked permission to retain other interpolations. Because Gilbert had objected to them, Workman had omitted them. "All this is strictly true or is a deliberate invention of mine. You can judge for yourself which is more likely to be the case."[43]

Helen Carte was still convinced it was Lytton and not Workman who had told Gilbert about the "High tiddley hi ti" gag, but the hair-splitting correspondence finished on that point.[44]

Gilbert's health was now better than it had been for years. He still had occasional trouble with his arthritic leg, but his diabetes, which had been checked regularly over the last few months, had been brought under control. He was keeping fit with his regular swims, sometimes as many as three a day, depending on guests, as he rarely left a young lady to swim unaccompanied.

Rehearsals for the next revival at the Savoy, *HMS Pinafore*, began on 30 June. There was no dispute over the cast, which, along with Workman, Barrington, and Lytton (as Dick Deadeye) included a new soprano, Elsie Spain, and a new tenor, Henry Herbert; neither was there a dispute over interpolations; but after the dress rehearsal Gilbert found another reason to complain to Helen Carte. "If you are content to degrade the Savoy stage by the hideous & contemptible dresses which you have provided for the ladies' chorus, I am not disposed to take any responsibility for them. I shall let it be known that they are the outcome of your own choice & your own ideas of taste."[45]

The revival of *Pinafore* opened on 14 July, and three nights later Gilbert was back in London with Kitty and Nancy to see *Il Barbiere di Seviglia* at Covent Garden. As he left the opera house and was getting into a cab, a young man rushed at him, punched him in the mouth and made a grab at his watch and chain. "Fortunately," Gilbert related in a letter to *The Times*, "the bow of the watch broke, and the swivel of the chain gave out, and so he got nothing." What the young man did get from the quick-thinking old gentleman he had attacked, was a punch in the face, which sent him running down the road to make his escape.[46]

While enjoying the fine days of summer at Grim's Dyke, swimming daily and entertaining a stream of guests, Gilbert turned his attention to a children's version of *The Mikado*. On 27 August, after three weeks at the task, he completed his tale: "So this exciting story, which is crammed full of thrilling incidents, and hair-breadth escapes, ended quite happily and without any bloodshed after all!"[47] Not so happily for Gilbert, while he was writing the story, his pet lemur Paul, who had been born at Grim's Dyke, died and was buried in the grounds. He had lived for nearly three years.

Gilbert's swimming season in 1908 finished early because of cold weather at the end of August and rheumatism in his arm. He took his 161st and last swim of the year on 29 August and on 9 September, with Kitty, Nancy, and a friend, Mary Gillham, he left Tilbury for a Mediterranean cruise, calling at Gibraltar, Valetta, Corfu, and Fiume before taking a four-day stop in Venice. As the ship sailed from Venice to Messina, on the return journey, the ship's sports were held. At the end of the competition, Lady Gilbert was called on to distribute the prizes. Unfortunately, there was no prize for her sporting seventy-one-year-old husband. "J'assiste au Veterans' race," Gilbert wrote in his diary, "mais je nai pas gagné."[I take part in the Veterans' race, but I didn't win.][48] The cruise ended at Marseille, and by train they traveled to Paris, where Gilbert bought Kitty a tiara for £450 "chez Lacloche" in the rue de la Paix. The Darracq was waiting for them at Charing Cross Station when they arrived back on Sunday evening, 11 October.

At the Savoy, Helen Carte put on two more revivals: *Iolanthe*, which opened on 19 October; and *The Pirates of Penzance*, on 30 November. Gilbert had not been invited to supervise rehearsals for *Iolanthe* and had not thought it necessary, as there were few changes in cast from the previous revival. Neither did he dispute the cast for *The Pirates of Penzance*, which included Henry Lytton as the Pirate King. He was now sure of his cast and confident of success.

That autumn Gilbert bought another lemur to replace Paul—this time a female. He called her Babs and was so delighted with her that he ordered another. The new lemur was enjoyed and spoiled by Gilbert: sitting on his knees while he had tea, sitting on his shoulders while he walked around the garden, and even balancing on his head while he had a photo taken.

Shortly before Christmas 1908, Gilbert made one more attempt to find a composer for his new version of *The Wicked World*. He had unsuccessfully tried Edward Elgar and then, on 21 December, he wrote to Edward German. Gilbert told German of the piece's peculiarity: "that the chorus *must all be ladies*." "As I see the piece in my mind's eye," said Gilbert, "it might be productive of exquisitely beautiful effects — but your mind's *ear* may be altogether opposed to the notion."[49] German was interested. Gilbert's *Fallen Fairies* would at last take the stage.

1909-1910

Enter Fairies—Their Flight and Fall

REHEARSALS FOR THE NEXT Savoy revival, *The Gondoliers*, began on 7 January 1909. Gilbert considered his supervision of rehearsals essential, as there had been several changes in the cast since its last revival. Even the experienced Rutland Barrington was new to the part of the Grand Inquisitor, and Gilbert had two newcomers in Henry Herbert as Marco and Dorothy Court as Casilda.

It was Gilbert's intention, after his new opera with Edward German and when the rights to perform the old operas reverted to him in May 1910, to stage a series of revivals himself. Replying to a letter from Richard Temple, Gilbert mentioned his hope "that a wealthy Syndicate may be formed for their proper production." He regretted Temple's absence from the recent revivals, saying he had been "shamefully treated" in not being consulted over the casting. "I believe this to be entirely due to Mr. Boulter's interference—as I am sure that Mrs. Carte, if left to herself, would have treated me with the courtesy that I have always received at her hands."

Temple had expressed a wish to make a farewell performance as the Pirate King or as Sir Roderick Murgatroyd. *Ruddigore* would be out of the question for the present, Gilbert told him, because of expense and "difficulties attending its production." But he held out hope, adding, "I propose to commence my season in 1910 with that piece—& if, you are still available, we might arrange for you to play your old part."[1]

Edward German called at Eaton Square on Sunday 10 January to discuss *The Wicked World*, which Gilbert had started working on a week before. German liked the plot and was willing to continue, while recognizing that the lack of a male chorus was a potential problem. Gilbert took the opportunity, while German was there, of getting Nancy to sing to him. According to Gilbert's diary comment, German was delighted with her singing, although he may have been simply showing polite appreciation. Nancy was now thirty-five and had little recent experience, but Gilbert was still convinced of her ability and was determined that she should play the leading soprano role of Selene. With German's approval of the plot, Gilbert could begin work on the lyrics, once he had finished rehearsals for *The Gondoliers*.

After *The Gondoliers*, which opened on 18 January 1909, Helen Carte had no intention to bring on any more "fresh revivals," but she had it in mind to finish the season with a few performances of *The Yeomen of the Guard*. If Gilbert wanted to attend any rehearsals, she hoped the £200 she was sending him for *The Gondoliers* would cover them. "The *second* revival of any opera," she said, "within a short period, cannot pay expenses."[2] After such a straightforward letter, Helen Carte must have been unprepared for the onslaught that assailed her the next day.

Gilbert pointed out that *The Yeomen* would in reality be a new revival, and therefore come under the terms of their agreement. Only three of the earlier cast would be in the revival and most of the chorus was new. "You take upon yourself, aided by wholly incompetent advisers, to cast the pieces without consulting me in any way & I am compelled, in my own defence, to do my best to counteract the deficiencies of the cast by stage managing the piece & instructing the actors to the best of my abilities." He admitted that recent casts were considerably better, "but still certain members — important members — of your company require careful handling, or catastrophe is likely to result." As to the question of the financial success of a second revival, his thinking was clear. She was not obliged to produce it at all, "but if it is produced I must claim to stage manage it under our agreement."[3]

Helen Carte did not respond immediately. When she did reply, ten days later, it was with one of her lengthy and detailed letters, referring to their agreement and showing that she had not contravened it. Their agreement, she said, did not entitle her to ask him to rehearse second revivals. However she did not want to argue. She was too ill "to enter into a controversy on a matter not of serious importance," and she agreed to pay £200 for rehearsing *The Yeomen*.[4]

Mention of her being ill brought a slightly more gentle response from Gilbert, but he was still incapable of refraining from going over old ground.

I am sorry that you are ill & I certainly have no desire to worry you with an unnecessarily unpleasant correspondence. . . . To do you justice I firmly believe that you have not been a free agent in these matters, & that if you had been free to do so you would have treated me with the perfect courtesy & consideration which you extended to me for twenty years. As you said to me in one of your letters "If you knew all you would not blame me," and I do not.[5]

In her reply on 31 January, Helen Carte said she could not recall the sentence quoted by Gilbert without going through all their correspondence, and added, "I cannot tell to what I was referring. But it could just have been to me not being a free agent." Nevertheless, she accepted full responsibility for her decisions, while at the same time defending her casting. Lytton, she said, was now willing to play parts he did not wish to play two years before, and generally the difficulty was getting "especially at short notice, artists who can sing, act, speak and look these parts as well as those whom we could select gradually—and then train for years."[6]

Her gentle admission and frank speaking were not reciprocated by Gilbert. He preferred to blast at her once more.

> I prefer to believe [he told her on 2 February] what *I know to be the case*. You are not a free agent, or you would never have treated me with the gross insolence & black ingratitude which have characterized the Savoy methods during the last 2¼ years. With regard to Mr Lytton. I happen to have heard, from his own mouth, an account of what took place when he came to the Savoy about an engagement two years ago. Your casts have been in very many instances deplorable—the operas have been insulted degraded, & dragged through the mire—& I have been exposed to humiliating ridicule in the face of the entire company.[7]

Gilbert continued in this bombastic fashion until he blew himself out in the postscript: "Probably you do not hear candid opinions about the character of your productions. *I do*."[8]

The next letter from Gilbert to Helen Carte, only five days later, on 7 February, was in startling contrast to what had gone before. He had completed the first act of his new opera, which he was still calling *The Wicked World*, and had read it to Edward German, and then to Nancy, on 6 February. He approached Helen Carte, in a letter marked "*Secret*." He told her about his libretto, his collaboration with Edward German, and his hope that the opera would be ready by the autumn. Because of their long association, he wanted to offer the piece to her before any other manager. It was as though his earlier intemperate remarks had not been aimed at her personally. "Difficulties have arisen during the past 2¼ years to which I refer merely to express my assurance that nothing connected with those difficulties has occurred to affect my regard & respect for you personally both in your public & private capacities. Whether this condition of things is reciprocal I do not know, but it at least justifies me in making a suggestion which you may (or may not) care to entertain."[9]

Helen Carte was unable to split herself in two: as the person to be assailed by Gilbert's criticism, and then as the person worthy of his regard and respect. She responded briefly, thanking him, but turning down the offer. "I feel that the many anxieties and responsibilities of London management are more than my health and strength allow me to continue."[10] Gilbert went back to working on act 2, reducing the original three acts of *The Wicked World* to two, and in the meantime sent off the first act to German.

From the middle of February, work on the libretto for *The Wicked World*, which was to be given the provisional title "Selene," continued alongside Gilbert's rehearsals for *The Yeomen of the Guard*. Gilbert completed the libretto and sent it off for typing on 28 February, and the next day, Monday, 1 March, the last of the revivals opened at the Savoy.

What was particularly significant about this revival of *The Yeomen of the Guard*, the last of the operas that Gilbert would supervise, was the return of Richard Temple, at the age of sixty-two, to play the part of Sergeant Meryll. He and Rutland Barrington, now fifty-six and playing Wilfred Shadbolt for the first time at the Savoy, were the only members of cast from *The Sorcerer*, almost thirty-two years earlier. It was Richard Temple's farewell, and after a few performances his place was taken by Leo Sheffield. Missing from the cast of *The Yeomen* was Henry Lytton, who had taken a short engagement as the leading comedian in the touring company. That short engagement became something more permanent. He was to remain as leading comedian until his retirement in June 1934.

With Kitty and Nancy present, Gilbert read act 2 of "Selene" to German on 4 March, and afterward German played them a selection of the numbers he had composed for act 1. They were making good progress together, but so far had found no one to produce the opera. Gilbert tried Frederick Harrison, manager of the Haymarket, but he turned it down. Next, Gilbert saw Seymour Hicks at the Garrick Club on 20 March when they had a preliminary discussion, and after consulting with German he suggested reading the libretto to Hicks. Hicks must have had second thoughts. The reading never took place. Then came a letter from Helen Carte.

For nearly the whole of March Helen Carte had been ill in bed, first with influenza and then with pneumonia. She had decided to give up management of the Savoy Theatre but to retain her touring company. She was against the idea of separating ownership of the London rights and country rights of the operas, and although she had no intention of running another series of revivals in London, she wished to retain the London performing rights. She suggested that, if the operas were assigned to her for five years from 30 May 1910, she would give Gilbert a written guarantee that she would not authorize any revivals in West End theaters, but that the right to do so would be reserved to Gilbert. She suggested a payment to her of £250 a year for each opera Gilbert revived. Gilbert agreed to her proposal, but with some modification. Gilbert's idea was to produce the new opera and then follow it with another opera, which he had already "at the back of [his] mind," and then to follow that with revivals of *Ruddigore, Princess Ida, The Mountebanks*, and *His Excellency*. That would carry him through a year, after which he would let the operas "lie fallow" for the remaining four years of the agreement, before reviving them again with the rest of the operas. As the total fee for reviving the operas for a year would be "absolutely prohibitive," he suggested a payment of £100 each from Bertie Sullivan and himself and £100 for *The Mountebanks* and *His Excellency*, in which Sullivan had no interest.[11]

Other details had to be worked out. For example, Helen Carte was anxious that none of the members of her touring company, including understudies, should be lured away for Gilbert's revivals. But with a guarantee from Gilbert on that score, they soon came to an agreement, which was signed on 15 April. There remained for discussion the matter of alterations to the librettos of the revived operas: if there were material alterations and Helen Carte wanted to use them, then Gilbert would not have to pay the £100 agreed; if there were only small verbal alterations, then Helen Carte would be at liberty to use them without payment.

The business arrangements between the two of them had proceeded swiftly, efficiently, with give and take and without any acrimony whatsoever. On 9 April, Gilbert informed Workman of his agreement with Helen Carte and also told him about his plans for revivals after the new opera. With that clear information Workman was able to approach the members of the Syndicate that he was forming to finance the whole enterprise.

The future looked promising for Gilbert; and in a mood of optimism he decided to upgrade his cars. First, he wanted to exchange his 16.20 hp Cadillac for a 20.30 hp and, second, he wanted to sell his Darracq for £500 in part exchange for a Rolls Royce. After a test drive in a Rolls on 20 April, and with the part-exchange agreed, Gilbert ordered his new car, optimistically insisting on delivery for the middle of June. Kitty chose the color: it would be blue, with light blue lines along the coachwork, blue morocco upholstery, and the monogram "WSG" on the side doors and the back of the car. To offset the additional expense, Gilbert put up 63 Prince's Gate for sale. He had owned the house for twenty-five years, without raising the rent in all that time. The agent valued it at £5,500; Gilbert thought that was too high, put the house up for sale at £5,000, and finally sold it for £4,725.

As work progressed on "Selene"—or, as it was eventually called, *Fallen Fairies*— Gilbert and German collaborated happily. Although German had misgivings about the piece, he was complimentary about Gilbert at this stage. "Gilbert is delightful to work with, and he seems to have great faith in me; he treats what I say with respect and often acts on it. The fact is he is such a giant that he can afford to be doubly polite and nice."[12]

The relationship with Workman, however, was of a different order. Workman had set up his syndicate by 17 May, but through lack of management experience had not worked out in detail his operating powers. Having agreed terms with Gilbert, subject to his approval of the libretto and music, and having agreed that Nancy McIntosh would play the leading soprano role, Workman went to Grim's Dyke on 26 May, when Gilbert read him the libretto and German played him the music. A week later, after consultation with his financial masters in the syndicate, Workman wrote to Gilbert offering lower terms and informing him that he was committed to engage Elsie Spain as the leading soprano for the first three productions under his management at the Savoy (*Fallen Fairies* being planned as the second of the three productions). Gilbert was adamant. "With regard to the terms, I never haggle. They are immutable and must be accepted or rejected *en bloc*."

Gilbert rejected Elsie Spain as unsuitable for the part of Selene and regretted the time lost in what he termed "idle negotiations," having been misled into confiding details of the music and the libretto. "I decline to have dealings with a man who is capable of such conduct. . . . Please return my libretto *at once*."[13]

Workman did not return the libretto, but came straight back to Gilbert to renegotiate. Gilbert insisted, however, on 15 percent on the gross receipts, 10 percent for himself, and 5 percent for German. On the engagement of Nancy, Gilbert said, "I do not press Miss McIntosh on you. I only say that German & I are completely satisfied with her. . . . If you can find a better at her salary (£25 per week) we will accept her."[14]

It was another month before Workman returned to Gilbert ready to settle. Gilbert drew up a draft agreement on 6 July. Workman would have the right to produce at the Savoy: *Ruddigore, Princess Ida, Utopia Limited, The Grand Duke, The Mountebanks,* and *His Excellency*. For each of the pieces, Workman was to pay Helen Carte £100, and Gilbert's share of the gross receipts would be 10 percent. On 14 July, everything appeared "finally settled," with an agreement giving German total control of the music. "Workman tells me," said Gilbert in a letter to German, "that they have contrived to get rid of Cellier."[15]

While German busied himself with the music of *Fallen Fairies*, Gilbert concerned himself with his new Rolls Royce. Although he had insisted on delivery of the car by the middle of June, it was not until 5 July that he finally took possession of it. "The Rolls-Royce is a huge success," he wrote to Margery Maude, a few days later.[16] He had spoken too soon. The day he wrote that letter, they had been invited to dinner by the Crutchleys at Chelsea Hospital, where Charles Crutchley had recently been appointed the lieutenant-governor with the rank of major-general. The car reached the hospital, but then broke down: "quelque trouble dans le gear-box," Gilbert noted.[17] The Rolls had to be left overnight in the courtyard while they returned home by train. On this occasion, repair of the car was prompt: McHardy collected the car from Rolls Royce the following evening and drove it back to Grim's Dyke.

After almost two months of trouble-free motoring, the Rolls Royce broke down again on 2 September. It was more than a week before his car was ready and Gilbert's verdict, after taking the car for a drive, was that it was running "abominablement."[18] That was the third time the car needed repairs in two months, he complained, sending the car back to Rolls Royce and asking for his money back: £1,349.11.0, which represented the purchase price plus accessories. Rolls Royce insisted that he was under an obligation to keep the car. Gilbert disagreed. Rolls Royce sent a representative to placate him, and the following day his Rolls was delivered, running perfectly. It was not to be the end of his troubles. Even in November he was complaining about its performance on hills, but after that the complaints ceased.

On the whole, Gilbert was proud of his Rolls Royce. Margery Maude's sister Pamela recalled years later the fun the children had when Gilbert took them to see his car. The children all clambered into the car and Gilbert sat behind the wheel and pretended to drive. "Where to?" he asked. "Home, please," replied Margery in the same tone of voice her mother used to their chauffeur. And Gilbert, remembering one of his "Bab Ballad" characters, added, "Then we must go round by Rum-ti-Foo, so that you can call on the dear Bishop." As far as the children were concerned, that "seemed a perfectly sensible suggestion."[19]

German had referred to Gilbert as "a giant" in theatrical circles, and it is true that his seniority was recognized by many in the profession. As a member of the council of the Academy of Dramatic Art, he played a major role in the appointment of Kenneth Barnes, brother of Violet and Irene Vanbrugh, to be the new administrator. Barnes was appointed after a weekend at Grim's Dyke, where he was under close scrutiny from Gilbert and Cyril Maude. In time, Barnes was to become the first principal of the Royal Academy of Dramatic Art, a post that he was to hold until 1955.

In 1908, Gilbert had been chosen by his fellow dramatists to act as spokesman, along with Arthur Pinero and J. M. Barrie, in a deputation to the home secretary, Herbert Gladstone, on the question of dramatic censorship. And now, in the summer of 1909, Gilbert was called on to give evidence to a parliamentary committee, set up to investigate censorship. Gilbert was in favor of censorship, but against leaving it in the hands of one man, the lord chamberlain. He preferred the idea of an appeal panel of three arbiters: one appointed by the author, one by the lord chamberlain, and the third agreed by both of them.[20]

At the end of the summer and before Gilbert had to concern himself with the production details for *Fallen Fairies*, he set off on 17 September with Kitty and Nancy for another visit to Wiesbaden. They stayed at the spa for three weeks, following the various treatments prescribed for each of them, and enjoying a monotonously restful time. Jigsaw puzzles—a new interest already begun at Grim's Dyke—occupied part of their time at Wiesbaden. But the most exciting event of their stay was recorded by Gilbert in his franglais: "J'ascends dans le ballon."[21] No comment or explanation follows of what appears to be Gilbert's only experience of air travel.

Once back in England, he was into Savoy business, and on 12 October he met with German and Workman, and later with German and the syndicate. The syndicate had produced their first piece, called *The Mountaineers*, on 29 September, and were now ready to turn their minds to their second production. What had seemed to Gilbert before he had gone away as a settled matter was beginning to look less sure. The syndicate did not agree with the terms arranged by Gilbert and Workman on 6 July.

To Gilbert's astonishment, Workman claimed he had not kept a copy of the original contract; and Gilbert's astonishment turned to anger when he was told that the syndicate wanted him to read them his libretto and wanted German to play them his music before they accepted the piece. That, Gilbert emphatically told Workman, was entirely out of the question.

After further correspondence between Gilbert and Workman, the syndicate stepped in, asking for a meeting with Gilbert. He refused, saying his agreement was with Workman and he had now handed the matter over to his solicitors.[22] The syndicate gave way and accepted the terms agreed earlier by Gilbert and Workman.

Work resumed on the opera, with Gilbert working on alterations with German; and both of them auditioning and selecting the cast. The only three male characters in the cast were to be played by C. H. Workman, Leo Sheffield, and Claude Fleming.

Among the ladies, Nancy McIntosh would be joined by Jessie Rose, Ethel Morrison, and a few protégées of Gilbert, including Marjorie Dawes, a chorister from the last revivals, who had been coached by Gilbert and had received singing lessons from Nancy. At last Nancy was to be given the chance that Gilbert believed had been denied her for so long; but if Gilbert had really been as confident of Nancy as he had claimed when insisting she play the part of Selene, then she would not have needed the intensive coaching he gave her from the time the libretto was read to the company on 8 November until the first stage rehearsal on 29 November. She had also received preferential treatment by being provided with the music to practice as soon as each act had been completed by German.

On the first night of *Fallen Fairies* at the Savoy, on Wednesday, 16 December, Gilbert dined at the Beefsteak Club and at 9:30 went to the theater, where he waited out the second act in Nancy's dressing room. At the end, he recorded in his diary, he received a "Belle reception."[23] The next morning, however, he found that the critics were not enthusiastic about the opera. And then, a week after the opening, on Wednesday, 22 December, Gilbert received a letter from Herbert Workman telling him that they wanted to take Nancy out of the cast.

Gilbert's first reaction was to ask German for his frank opinion. If it were German's opinion that Nancy should give up the part, then both she and Gilbert would accept his decision "without the smallest feeling of resentment."[24]

Then Gilbert tackled Workman. First he wrote to him; but, unable to sit around waiting for a reply, in the afternoon he caught the train into Euston and went straight to the Savoy to confront him and protest about the decision. German meanwhile replied to Gilbert: "I am not going to pretend her singing, latterly, has been quite what I expected—her voice seems of less volume than when she sang at Grim's Dyke, but I put it down to over-work & nervousness."[25]

Instead of registering German's admission that Nancy's voice was not as good as he thought, Gilbert fastened onto the suggested reason. His belief, he told German, was that there were "wheels within wheels" and that someone in the syndicate was trying to replace Nancy with their own preference, "a Miss Evans, I believe."[26]

On Christmas Eve, a Friday, Gilbert told Nancy of the decision to take her out of the role of Selene. At eleven o'clock in the morning, Workman rang to tell Gilbert that Nancy was not to play the part on the Monday after Christmas, as they had a replacement ready. Nancy was devastated—unable to play the part any more. To attend the theater that evening was impossible.

After discussion with German at Grim's Dyke on Christmas Day, Gilbert sent a long letter to Workman setting out his objections to Nancy's sudden removal from the cast. Workman had told Gilbert that Nancy sang out of tune. Gilbert launched a countercharge: "If, as you told me on the telephone, nine people rose from their stalls during her final scene & left the theatre in disgust (which I do not for a moment believe) it was because you sent them there to do so."[27] Gilbert was convinced that Workman's "utterly unfounded charge" had an ulterior motive. "It is on that assumption that I shall rest such proceedings as I may be advised to take."[28]

On Monday, 27 December, Gilbert drove over to see Birkett, his solicitor, in order to apply for an injunction against Workman to stop him playing *Fallen Fairies* except with Nancy McIntosh or her "accredited understudy" in the part of Selene; but it was a bank holiday and impossible to obtain a writ that day.[29] Gilbert now began to prepare for legal proceedings against Workman for breach of contract. He wanted German to swear an affidavit, calling on him on 29 December to take him by taxi from St. John's Wood to the City of London. German was willing to sign an affidavit that he and Gilbert were satisfied that Nancy should play the part; but he was reluctant to become involved in a court case. The next day, Gilbert notified Workman that the rights of revival of the operas, which were to have been assigned to him, were now withdrawn.

In the space of a week, the situation at the Savoy had been totally transformed. Gilbert's hopes for a successful run for *Fallen Fairies*, followed by another new opera and then a series of Gilbert and Sullivan revivals, had been frustrated; Workman's dream of managing the operas had evaporated, and with it the prospect for the syndicate of getting a substantial return on their capital investment. At the center of the fiasco was Nancy McIntosh. Gilbert's blindness to the possibility that Nancy was not good enough, either as singer or actor, to hold the lead in a production was met by the conviction of Workman and the syndicate that it was she who stood in the way of their success. *Fallen Fairies* proved to be the downfall of the whole enterprise.

Gilbert did not remain idle. Immediately he set about trying to revive *Ruddigore* elsewhere, first offering it to Malone at the Adelphi. "We propose to cut out a good deal of the heavy music in Act 2," Gilbert told him, on 30 December. "There have been numerous enquiries about the piece & there is every prospect of its revival being entirely successful."[30] Within a week, Gilbert had received his first refusal for *Ruddigore*. Malone was not interested in it for the Adelphi. His next attempt, on 6 January 1910, was to send the libretto to Seymour Hicks;[31] but Hicks was no more enthusiastic over *Ruddigore* than he had been over *Fallen Fairies*.

In one more attempt to interest a manager in *Ruddigore*, Gilbert went to see Arthur Bourchier at the Garrick Theatre. It was to be another fruitless attempt.

In the meantime, Workman had decided to change Gilbert's libretto for *Fallen Fairies* by reinstating one of Nancy McIntosh's solos, "Oh Love that rulest our land," which had been cut at an early stage and replaced by a duet. Gilbert sent Workman a telegram on 13 January forbidding him to introduce a song that had not been authorized, and followed it up with a letter to say he was applying for an injunction. The injunction was granted on 14 January, and on 17 January Workman's solicitors agreed to Gilbert's demand. Gilbert now wanted an apology and continued to pursue his case against Workman for breach of contract.

On 29 January, Gilbert heard from Edward German that *Fallen Fairies* was to finish that evening, after a run of six and one-half weeks. Although the piece was now history, Gilbert's sense of justice had still not been satisfied. He continued to prosecute his case against Workman throughout February and March, with Nancy swearing an affidavit on 18 March; but at the end of the month he instructed his solicitor to drop the case, provided that Workman and the Syndicate were prepared to pay costs.

What led to his change of mind? Gilbert usually pursued matters into court to await the judicial decision. Over Easter, his guests at Grim's Dyke were Kitty's niece and her husband, close friends of Nancy. It would appear that Nancy found the prospect of a court case too hard to bear.

At a time of frustration and failure for Gilbert, his friend Frederick Macmillan stepped in to ask him to write his memoirs, offering a royalty of 25 percent. Gilbert promised to give it a "trial trip." He made a start on 31 March, made one other attempt and then tried no more.[32] He was never to return to it.

Shortly after their return to Grim's Dyke that year, great excitement swept the house when they caught a burglar who had stolen a purse from the bedroom of Kitty's lady's maid. The household was first alerted that something was wrong by Huti, a pekinese, who was found barking insistently outside a door on the top floor. When one of the maids went into the room, a burglar, who was hiding behind the door, made a run for it, but Warrilow, the butler, and Arthur Dowling, a footman, caught him by the back door. The burglar had almost succeeded in getting away from them when a heftily built gardener appeared at the back door, bringing a rose for Gilbert's buttonhole. The burglar was quickly overpowered.

"After he had been caught," explained Nancy in her account of the incident, "Sir William had him lashed up like a seaman's hammock, seven turns & a clove-hitch & then had some conversation with him about the art of burgling in general & this case in particular." They phoned the police, and the man was driven to the police station in Gilbert's Cadillac, said Nancy, as Sir William thought "he must be very much exhausted after the dreadful struggle in which he had been engaged."[33]

Gilbert extended his range of interests in 1910. He had discovered the cinema, going frequently to a cinema in Bear Street, near Leicester Square; and he had also become a keen observer of the skies at night, having an observatory built in the grounds and its telescope installed by the middle of May.

Full use of the observatory would have to wait, as he was leaving with Kitty on a cruise to the Azores on 21 May, this time without Nancy, who had already gone off on her own to Vienna.

CHAPTER THIRTY-SIX

1910-1911

"A Very Honorable End"

BY WAY OF LISBON, TANGIERS, and Gibraltar, Gilbert and Kitty, accompanied by Harold and Nonie Messel, sailed to the Canaries, calling at Santa Cruz, La Palma, and Madeira before sailing on to the Azores. From Gilbert's diary, it does not appear to have been one of their more successful cruises. His most frequent entry is: "Rien de remarkable" [*sic*]. Gilbert had been elected president of the sports committee but was not active himself, spending the best part of two or three days ill in bed as they sailed back toward Spain. By the time he recovered, they had reached Vigo, where he went ashore. "Promenade dans la ville, qui est puante," he commented.

On the journey home from Spain, he found little of note to comment on except a magnificent sunset, as they crossed the Bay of Biscay, and a hysterical outburst from one of the passengers. On their penultimate evening on board, Lady Gilbert distributed the prizes on behalf of the sports committee, and on the final evening Gilbert proposed the health of the captain on behalf of everyone. They docked at Tilbury on the morning of 13 June, and were home at Grim's Dyke at 1:20, when Gilbert immediately went for a swim in the lake before lunch.[1]

It was to be another week before Gilbert could take his next swim. At tea on the afternoon of their arrival home, he knocked over a pot of boiling water and scalded his foot. He spent the next few days with his foot up or lying on a chaise longue in the garden, but he was well enough on 18 June to carry out the official opening of the Grim's Dyke Golf Club as its first president. Ten days later Kitty, still fit and sprightly at the age of sixty-two, took her first golf lesson at the club.

Bertie Sullivan made a quick visit to Grim's Dyke on 22 June to consult about a proposition he had received from Herbert Workman. If Gilbert had no intention to revive the operas as he had originally planned, then Workman was interested in buying the rights. Gilbert's memory was long, and his patience with Workman was short. "I do not intend to waste any epithets upon you —," he told Workman, "you can easily supply them for yourself. It is enough to say that no consideration of any kind would induce me to have dealings with a man of your stamp."[2]

Gilbert's foot took a long time to heal. It was 6 July before Kitty stopped bandaging it for him, and that day they both went into London by train. Kitty was in search of a servant to replace Arthur Dowling, the footman who had helped to catch the burglar in April. Without waiting to collect his wages, Dowling had walked out the evening before, after Kitty had reprimanded him for being slightly drunk.

On 1 August Gilbert made a note in his diary of the arrest of Dr. Hawley Harvey Crippen. Accused of murdering his wife, Crippen had been arrested, along with his lover Emily Le Neve, on the *SS Montrose* sailing to Quebec. He was the first suspected criminal to be arrested as a result of a radio message, and the case caught the public imagination. Traveling up to London by train at the beginning of September, Gilbert happened to bump into his friend Sir Charles Mathews, the director of public prosecutions, who promised him an admissions ticket for the Bow Street hearing. Gilbert attended all five sessions, which finished on 21 September, when Crippen and Le Neve were committed for trial at the Old Bailey.

By the time the trial came up at the Old Bailey, Gilbert was miles away, en route for Constantinople, with his traveling companion, Philip Hogg. Kitty and Nancy meanwhile had gone down to Bath, intending to stay until 5 November, the day before Gilbert was due to return from his cruise.[3]

Gilbert and Hogg set off on 12 October on what was to prove an eventful journey. Their first hurdle was to get across France, which had been hit by a partial train strike. They had to travel by car from Dieppe to Paris, arriving with only twenty minutes to spare to catch the train for Marseille. There was no dining car on board, and their only nourishment throughout the sixteen-hour journey was a sandwich. At Marseille, they learned that their ship, instead of sailing to Naples as planned, had been diverted because of an outbreak of cholera; but at least the detour gave them the opportunity to visit Monte Carlo, where Gilbert won 15 francs at the casino. It was only on 17 October, when they reached their next port of call, Palermo, that Gilbert realized he had left his passport at home, and Hogg had done the same, omissions that they would have to put right before Constantinople. From Palermo they went to Messina, still in ruins following the earthquake at the end of 1908, when 75,000 people had lost their lives. "The city is a pitiable spectacle," said Gilbert, writing to Kitty on 19 October, "—miles & miles of ruined houses, with many dead bodies buried in the debris—the smell of the bodies quite perceptible."[4]

From the British Consul in Piraeus, Gilbert and Hogg finally obtained their passports, and from the Turkish Embassy their visas for Constantinople. They went sight-seeing in Athens, in a temperature of "80° in the shade," Gilbert told Kitty, with a day devoted "to the Acropolis, Temple of Jupiter, &c & I took about three dozen photographs, all of which were quite successful." He had been away a fortnight and had still not received any mail or newspapers since he had left England. "It is very annoying to be so long without hearing from you, but it isn't your fault or mine."[5]

After forty-three years of marriage, Gilbert still found it difficult to be away from Kitty for long. In his first letter on the trip, he had told her, "I need not say that I miss you greatly & heartily wish you were here."[6]

At Smyrna, where they arrived on 25 October, Gilbert was able to get copies of the *Daily Telegraph*, the earliest dated 19 October, which gave details of the first day of Crippen's trial at the Old Bailey, but by that time Gilbert had already heard that Crippen had been found guilty. They sailed on, through the Dardanelles and on to Constantinople. He visited St. Sophia and the tombs of the sultans, and spent part of his time on board reading the papers and writing to Kitty. "Le Neve acquittée," he noted in his diary on 29 October.[7]

The return journey took them to Corsica, where Gilbert visited Napoleon's house at Ajaccio, before setting sail for Marseille. He finally arrived back in London on Sunday evening, 6 November, to find Kitty and Nancy waiting for him at Charing Cross station.

Gilbert returned to a quiet life at Grim's Dyke that autumn. He had his regular duties to attend to as a justice of the peace, now at court in Wealdstone as well as Edgware, he spent a great deal of time on his photography, went for walks with Kitty or Nancy, and entertained friends and relations. He made the occasional visit to London, to the Junior Carlton or the Garrick, but it was generally life at a slower pace than Gilbert usually led.

His mind that year had frequently turned to the thought of mortality, his own mortality in particular; and, at Bow Street Magistrates' Court in September, he had spent long hours looking at the face of a man who was eventually to be condemned to death. On 20 December, in a letter to Mary Talbot, he wrote, "I received yesterday my diary for 1911, and as I looked through its blank pages it set me thinking. At my time of life (turned 74) the future becomes a serious consideration & one can't help wondering what miseries[,] sorrows, calamities, deaths & other horrors will have to be set down before it is finished — if ever it *is* finished, which seems unlikely."[8]

The day after his letter to Mary Talbot he had lunch at the Junior Carlton Club with James Welch, resident actor at the Coliseum, who was always on the lookout for short plays to perform. Gilbert suggested a one-act play, dealing with the last hours of a man in the condemned cell. Welch was enthusiastic, and Gilbert agreed to develop the idea into a play — but not until after Christmas. Christmas was a time for entertaining guests. The day before Christmas Eve at Grim's Dyke was party time for the children of Gilbert's employees: the children came for tea and games, and each child went back home with a present. The Crutchleys came for Christmas, and at the traditional party at the cottage hospital a few days after Christmas, Nancy sang to her own accompaniment on the guitar.

THE ANNUAL MOVE TO Eaton Square took place on 5 January 1911, and while the house was being put in order Gilbert lunched at the Garrick, and went to the cinema before arriving home in time for tea. They all went out to dinner that evening—which made life easier for the servants on the first evening in London—to the Crutchleys at Chelsea Hospital. The next day, despite an attack of diarrhea, Gilbert was at the Academy of Dramatic Art to do his duty as an examiner. The rest of the day he spent at home, lying on the sofa and feeling weak. He managed some soup for lunch, a cigar in the evening, and for dinner he settled for fish. After a good night's sleep, he was back to normal.

Gilbert now turned his mind to his one-act play, which he called *The Hooligan*. Having obtained permission from the Home Office, he set off for Pentonville Prison on 13 January. His appointment was with the warden, and Gilbert questioned him about the details of the last hour on earth of the condemned man before he was hanged. Gilbert worked at *The Hooligan* intermittently from 16 January and had it finished by 2 February.

He made a further visit to Pentonville Prison on Monday, 13 February, this time taking the set designer to have a look at the condemned cell and to interview the chief guard. Gilbert's reading of the play and the first rehearsal followed the next day, but it was almost a week before the second rehearsal, partly because Gilbert was suffering from a heavy cold and had virtually lost his voice. At the third rehearsal, on 21 February, Gilbert walked out almost immediately, infuriated by Welch's "gagging." Afterward, Welch wrote an amusing letter of apology to Gilbert, which achieved its objective, and rehearsals were resumed.[9]

The first showing of *The Hooligan* took place at the Coliseum on Monday, 27 February 1911. While Kitty went to the theater with a friend, Gilbert was at the Beefsteak Club, only going around to the Coliseum to collect Kitty at the end. Kitty had been to the "first night" of all her husband's London productions, including the revivals of the operas, since the very first, *Dulcamara*, way back in 1866. And now, nearly forty-five years later, in contrast to the early burlesques, he had written a one-act serious play, his last for public performance, ending with the death of the protagonist from heart failure.

Gilbert was not quite ready to go himself. "The old crumbling ruin has been propped up and under-pinned," he wrote to Mary Talbot, "and will, I think, stand a few months yet."[10]

The Hooligan had been a success for Welch as well as for Gilbert, and at the end of its four-week run, Welch agreed a price of £200 for the acting rights in the United Kingdom for two years. Gilbert went back to writing once more—this time a play called *Trying a Dramatist*, intended for the students of the Academy of Dramatic Art, and that he completed in a few days. Shortly after, Gilbert was busy revising his plays for publication by Chatto and Windus.

He was still planning for the future. Another opportunity to revive *Ruddigore* presented itself when the agent Henry Mapleson expressed an interest in producing one of the operas. Gilbert suggested *Ruddigore*, but Mapleson was really interested in producing *The Mikado*. "I told him," Gilbert said to Helen Carte, "that if he wished to produce that piece he must arrange terms with you, in the first place & with me afterwards . . . if you & Mapleson can agree on terms for its production, I should only ask a small fee beyond the £300 for rehearsing it."[11]

The Gilberts had returned to Grim's Dyke in early April and a new addition to the Grim's Dyke menagerie arrived the same day—a gazelle. After a week, Gilbert had introduced the new arrival to his library and had begun taking her for walks around the croquet lawn. A month later he bought a young stag for his gazelle, and called him Florian. Before long both gazelles were visiting his library.

There were conventional visitors, too—weekend guests, such as Mary Talbot, now confined to a wheelchair, and a constant stream of friends, to tea or to lunch or to swim.

On Wednesday, 24 May, Kitty left for Newbury to spend a few days with Mr. and Mrs. Helsham Jones and their daughters. Gilbert went up to London and called in at the Dramatists' Club. It is possibly there that he met Sydney Grundy, who later referred to a conversation they had about old age. "What does age matter," said Grundy, "with such health as yours?" "Nothing," answered Gilbert: "my experience is that old age is the happiest time of a man's life. The worst of it is, there's so little of it."[12]

After his customary appearance on the bench at Edgware on 25 May, Gilbert spent the rest of the day on photography and croquet with Nancy. The following evening he was driven in the Rolls to the Middle Temple, where he attended a dinner marking the centenary of Thackeray's birth, and afterward went on to a reception where, he noted in his diary, he met Anna Pavlova. Kitty returned from Newbury by lunchtime on Saturday, 27 May, and after lunch Gilbert went into Wealdstone to contribute his views to an enquiry concerning the proposed amalgamation into one borough of Harrow Weald and Wealdstone. It was magnificent weather. He returned home for his twenty-first swim of the year, and in the course of the afternoon welcomed more visitors to Grim's Dyke, including Sir Frederick and Lady Macmillan.

On Sunday, 28 May, Gilbert took his early morning swim and swam again in the afternoon with his lunch guests. After all the guests had gone, Gilbert, Kitty, and Nancy had a quiet evening at home, with just the three of them for dinner. He had written a letter to Isabel Emery, a local drama teacher and niece of Cyril Maude's wife, Winifred, who had often come to Grim's Dyke to swim, and Gilbert made arrangements for the next day. He told her that he was going into London, but would arrive back at Harrow-on-the-Hill station at 3:38 and would drive her to Grim's Dyke with her young pupil.

On the morning of 29 May, another warm, sunny day, Gilbert said good-bye to Kitty and drove to London to be present at the annual parade and inspection, known as Oak-Apple Day, at the Chelsea Hospital. He turned down an invitation from Sybil Crutchley to stay to lunch, saying that he wanted to visit May Fortescue who was ill, and that he had to be back at Grim's Dyke for an appointment with two girls who wanted to swim in the lake. May Fortescue was recovering from a riding accident, and had been advised to lie in a darkened room. When Gilbert arrived at the house, May Fortescue's mother said to him, "I won't ask what you think of her appearance, for you can scarcely see her." "Her appearance matters nothing," he replied. "It is her disappearance we could not stand."[13]

From there, Gilbert went to the Junior Carlton Club for lunch. Seeing W. H. Kendal, Gilbert went up to him and asked if he could sit at his table. Relating the incident later to his wife, Kendal said that

> [Gilbert] talked of everything,—of you and your brother Tom [Robertson] who introduced him to John Hare! He was witty; he was full of spirits; he ate an enormous lunch, he flattered you and he flattered me—which astonished me so much that I could not eat mine.
>
> After lunch, he sat and talked for a time, then he looked at his watch and said, "I must be off, as I have an appointment to teach a young lady to swim." He went away, but came back and shook hands with me twice, in the most cordial manner.[14]

Isabel Emery and her pupil, Ruby Preece, met Gilbert as arranged at Harrow-on-the-Hill station. They arrived at Grim's Dyke a little after four o'clock and went straight to the lake. The two girls were first into the water, and swam out into the middle. Ruby Preece tried to put her feet down, failed to touch the bottom, and cried for help. Gilbert was still on the steps, but immediately struck out in the cold water and quickly swam out to her. When he reached Ruby, he said, "Put your hands on my shoulders and don't struggle." As she did so, Gilbert sank beneath the water. The girls scrambled to the bank and screamed for help. Two gardeners arrived, took the boat out, managed to find Gilbert, pulled him into the boat and rowed to the side of the lake; but he was already dead.

The doctor was called. Dr. Wilson said that when he arrived on the scene everything possible had been done to provide artificial respiration. "Sir William was lying on his back on a rug, and there were pillows under his shoulders. Lady Gilbert and others were applying hot-water bottles." The doctor himself attempted further artificial respiration, but there was no sign of life.[15]

An inquest was held in the billiard room at Grim's Dyke on Wednesday, 31 May. Gilbert's usual doctor, Dr. Shackleton, said that Gilbert had suffered from "high tension & an intermittent pulse & slight aneurism" and he had warned him not to bathe if the water was too cold. In his opinion, Gilbert had died from "syncope, the result of excessive exertion." The coroner, Dr. Gordon Hogg, summing up for the jury, said that "the evidence made it quite clear that Sir William died in endeavouring to save a young lady in distress. It was a very honourable end to a great and distinguished career."[16]

HUNDREDS OF TELEGRAMS, cards, and letters of condolence had been pouring in to Kitty. Among the telegrams were those from Jessie Bond, Dion Boucicault (from

New York), Sir Francis and Lady Burnand, George Grossmith, Henry Lytton (with the touring company in Dublin), Bertie Sullivan, Richard Temple, and Marion Terry. A letter of sympathy came from 14 Pembridge Gardens, where Gilbert's sister Mary Florence lay dying, unaware of her brother's death. One of his neighbors, S. J. Blackwell, who was chairman of the Bushey Cottage Hospital Committee, said of Gilbert, "I was struck by his fairness & the more I knew him, the more I appreciated his kindness, large heartedness & cleverness." One of his former protégées, Amy Brandon Thomas, said, "He was so good & kind, the kindest friend I shall ever have, I can never be grateful enough for all he taught me." Helen Carte, who had battled hard with Gilbert over the years, wrote, "It seems to me as if the last great link with the past had gone—it is a very sad thought. Very few have done as great work as he in their lives and it will live after him."[17]

Kitty's relatives shared in her sorrow. Her niece, Beatrice (Lake) de Michele, now a grandmother and widow, told Kitty, "Never was there a man who was so good and kind to his friends and my recollection of his many kindnesses to me is overwhelming." Her widowed sister-in-law, Ellen Turner, living at 6 Essex Villas, recalled "that thro" all your long life together you have been such a loyal, true, & good wife to him. And a real right hand. . . . [f]or myself, I can only feel great gratitude to him for his unfailing kindness & generosity to my dear ones." Her cousin Harold bemoaned the fact that Gilbert had lost his life bathing, "To think that the cause of his death should have been due to the reason that you were always most anxious about—I so well remember how constantly you & Nancy used to try & persuade him not to go & bathe—but he always wd. have his own way—wouldn't he?" Letters came from Gilbert's nephews Gilbert, Howard, Spenser and Stanley Weigall, and from his niece Mary. "You always seemed so happy together & I know how terribly you will miss him," said Mary, the wife of Stanley Weigall.[18]

Gilbert's close friends for many years were deeply moved. "I cannot realize," wrote John Hare, "that the best friend of so many years is gone, & to think I shall see him no more." Bruce Seton, a friend of Gilbert's own age, whose friendship went back to the time they were young men, could not write straight away—"he broke down completely on hearing the news," wrote his wife. When he did write, Seton told Kitty, "I cannot tell you how much I valued the friendship of your husband. Outside the small range of my own relations, I think he was the dearest friend I possessed!"[19]

Many moving tributes to Gilbert were among these letters of condolence, giving an insight into the relationship between Gilbert and Kitty and the role of Nancy in their lives. One of Kitty's closest friends, Sybil Carlisle, poured out her own grief to "My dearest dearest Kitty. . . . How painful and dreadful for you to feel that in spite of your many warnings, the cold plunge and exertion were too much for him. I know you have always feared the lake, the cause of his bad illness. . . . How happy you have made him and what a wonderful wife you were, no one can realize except you and his life long friends."[20]

"That wonderful vitality of his," wrote another friend, Constance Hope, "that made him the centre wherever he might be, must have been even more marked at home, where he was always so bright & gay & energetic. . . . I am so thankful to think you have yr. dear adopted daughter to share yr. grief, as I feel sure she does to the full." And Kitty's niece—and close friend in recent years—Nonie Messel said of Gilbert, "He was & always will be a sort of hero for us not only because of his work but for his great, warm genial personality. No one who knew him & loved him could ever forget him."21

Fanny Ronalds shared in Kitty's grief; "Words are no consolation when our nearest and dearest are taken. . . . I earnestly hope you are as well as possible in your great grief." The Sisters of Nazareth House in Hammersmith added their message to the ever-growing pile of letters: "Sir William was a good Benefactor to our poor—He never forgot them. . . . We shall never forget him."22

Among all the letters was one from a recent friend and visitor to Grim's Dyke, Madame Thérèse Wittmann. Gilbert had met her in March, when she came to see him about doing a translation into French of *The Hooligan*.23 She had first visited Grim's Dyke in April and then again as recently as 17 May; Gilbert was expecting her on 26 May, but she had not arrived, so he had written to her inviting her to come on 30 May. In her imperfect English, she wrote to Kitty:

> When I was at Grim's Dyke the other day do you remember that I did not want to have a swim!—he asked me times and times and at the end I told him that I had not a heart strong enough to be in safety in the cold water and that I did not want to give him an emotion and obliged [*sic*] him to save me! . . . And then he laughed and told me, "You see me, I go three times a day—" and I answered "Well I really think you might be more careful."24

Gilbert had expressed the wish to be buried at Stanmore, in the churchyard of St. John the Evangelist, which he used to pass in the car on his way to and from Edgware. But the burial was refused by the rector, the Rev. S. F. L. Bernays. His parishioners objected to the idea of outsiders taking up space in their churchyard. The rector suggested that Kitty have Gilbert cremated and then have "a quiet service in the churchyard. Of course this at once overcomes all objections raised by Parishioners, as it does not fill up the Churchyard."25

Shortly after eight o'clock in the morning on Friday, 2 June, accompanied by Arthur Helsham Jones and Henry Rowland Brown, Gilbert's body left Grim's Dyke to be driven to the crematorium at Golders Green. The ashes, in a plain oak casket, were then taken to St. John the Evangelist's, Stanmore, where the funeral took place at 3:00 p.m. Along with Kitty and Nancy in the front pew were Sybil and Charles Crutchley and Kitty's cousin, the Rev. Henry Turner. The servants from Grim's Dyke occupied two separate pews. Friends and associates from the theater were among the many friends who attended the funeral: John Hare, Arthur Pinero, Mr.

and Mrs. Walter Passmore, Rutland Barrington, George Alexander, Cyril Maude, Rupert D'Oyly Carte, and Arthur Bourchier.[26]

At the end of the church service, Bertie Sullivan and Henry Rowland Brown carried the casket to the graveside, just outside the door of the church, while the choir sang, "O God our help in ages past." There were about 130 wreaths, among them those from Mr. and Mrs. François Cellier, Ellen Terry, Sir Squire and Lady Bancroft, and Kenneth Barnes, and one from the students of the Academy of Dramatic Art ("an anchor because his opinion in matters to do with the Academy was always so sound and well-placed," said Kenneth Barnes). The same motif was used by the sisters from Wells, in Norfolk, whom Gilbert had continued to help since their impoverished condition became known to him. One of the sisters, Thirza Griffin, wrote, "we are sending an anchor of Flowers symbolical of what he has been to myself & Sisters."[27]

After the funeral, Mary Talbot, the close friend of both Gilbert and Kitty, who had received so many letters from Gilbert but who was too ill to attend the funeral, wrote: "I wanted to come to-day, but I have hunched up & can't.—& perhaps it is as well as I like to keep the remembrance of my dear dear Cousin Bill as I saw him last, leaving him a goodbye with a smile on his dear face."[28]

KITTY WAS ANXIOUS TO publish the last two plays her husband had written, *The Hooligan* and *Trying a Dramatist*. Rowland Brown had made an initial contact with the *Century* magazine in America, but had then gone traveling for six weeks. Kitty contacted Frederick Macmillan at the end of June, and working through him she received £100 for their eventual publication in the magazine.

Probate of Gilbert's will was granted on 9 August to the executors: Kitty, Nancy, and Percival Birkett, his solicitor, who also were named as the trustees of the will. Gilbert's estate was valued at £111,971. He left his portraits by Frank Holl and Herman Herkomer and the bronze statuette of him by Andrea Lucchesi to his trustees, but Kitty was to have possession of them during her life. After her death, the portrait by Holl was to be offered to the National Portrait Gallery and, if they did not want it, to the Garrick Club; if they in turn refused it, then it was to go to Nancy. After Kitty's death, the portrait by Herkomer was to go to Nancy and the statuette to Cara Pillans, matron of the Bushey Heath Cottage Hospital. To Kitty, he bequeathed Grim's Dyke and everything it contained, all his money at the bank, all his stocks and shares and other securities, all his copyrights, and the Garrick Theatre. The Garrick was then to pass to Nancy and afterward to the trustees of the Actors Benevolent Fund.

Gilbert left his cameras and photographic equipment to Arthur Helsham Jones and his microscope to Henry Rowland Brown. His cigars were to be shared between Carlo Perugini and Rowland Brown. To a few friends such as Helsham Jones, Sybil Crutchley, Mabel Dugdale, and Mary Talbot, he left £100 each to buy some memento of him. Two hundred pounds was bequeathed to the Bushey Heath Cottage Hospital. He left money to all his servants according to their years of service with him.

After Kitty's death, his property was to be converted into money and divided into two halves. The first half was to be divided among Stanley Weigall, Mary Weigall (Stanley's wife), Mary Weigall (daughter of Alfred and Jane), Harold Turner, and Herbert Guy Turner (sons of Lucy's late brother), but the shares were not to exceed £4,000 each. The second half, up to a maximum of £1,000 each, was to be shared among his sister Jane's children, as well as Dorothy and Audrey, the daughters of Stanley Weigall. Any remainder after the allocation of these amounts was to be given to the Royal General Theatrical Fund. Kitty was asked to keep up his annual payment of £20 to the Kitty Cot in the Victoria Hospital for Children, and his annual payment of £10.10 to the Cottage Hospital.[29]

Of their nature, wills are legalistic and prosaic documents, spelling out the details of what is to happen to material possessions as they are handed on to named individuals. But the abiding legacy of both Gilbert and Sullivan was bequeathed to a much wider audience. The series of thirteen operas written between 1875 and 1896 was their legacy to succeeding generations, who have been enchanted by their unique combination of words and music.

CURTAIN CALL

A Selection of the Characters in the Story and What Happened to Them Subsequently

RUTLAND BARRINGTON HAD A STROKE in January 1919 and was forced to retire from the stage. He died in poverty on 31 May 1922, aged sixty-nine.

Fred Billington continued to work with the touring company until, after a good meal and a good cigar (the way he wanted to go), he collapsed and died on 2 November 1917.

Jessie Bond, who was so often sick and having to miss performances, lived until she was eighty-nine. She died on 17 June 1942.

Leonora Braham was the only English soprano to create the leading soprano role in any of the operas from *The Sorcerer* to *The Grand Duke* — she created five of them, from Patience in 1881 to Rose Maybud in 1887. After the Savoy, her career took her to Australia, South America, South Africa, and the United States. She died on 23 November 1931, aged seventy-eight.

Helen D'Oyly Carte, after all her battles with Gilbert, wrote to Lady Gilbert on 9 June 1911, a week after Gilbert's funeral: "I want to thank you very sincerely for writing to me so kindly in the midst of all your trouble. Even though I had seen little of him for so long I always felt he was *there* & the blank is very great."[1] Helen Carte had worked unceasingly for the Gilbert and Sullivan operas from almost the beginning of the partnership, before *The Sorcerer* was produced. She continued to manage the touring company as long as she was able. She died on 5 May 1913, at the age of sixty-one. Her estate was valued at £117,670. All her debentures and shares in the Savoy Theatre and Operas Ltd. and all her preference shares in the Savoy Hotel she left to Rupert D'Oyly Carte, who took over the touring company on her death. He managed the D'Oyly Carte Opera Company until his own death, at the age of seventy-two in 1948, when his daughter, Bridget D'Oyly Carte, took over the company until it closed in 1982.

François Cellier died at his home in Kingston, Surrey, on 5 January 1914, aged sixty-four. His son, Frank Cellier, married Florence Glossop-Harris, the daughter of Augustus Harris.

Robert Evett became codirector of Daly's Theatre in 1915 on the death of George Edwardes and subsequently became managing director of the theatre until he retired in 1925. He died on 15 January 1949, aged seventy-four.

May Fortescue, the thought of whose "disappearance" Gilbert "could not stand," lived until 2 September 1950. She was eighty-eight.

Lucy Gilbert had a memorial tablet to her husband put up in the church of All Saints, Harrow Weald. (A memorial in London was unveiled in 1915: it is on the wall of the embankment near Hungerford Bridge and opposite the entrance to the Embankment underground station. The inscription on the memorial reads, "His Foe was Folly and His Weapon Wit.") After the death of her husband, Lady Gilbert was unanimously elected by the hospital committee in July 1911 as honorary secretary of the Bushey Cottage Hospital. At the beginning of World War I, she compiled *Kitty's Cookery Book*, which included recipes for Curzon Street Gingerbread, Sally Lunns, and two varieties of milk punch, the punch being provided by rum and brandy. She kept up her enthusiasm for her husband's work. Writing to Frederick Macmillan on Christmas Day 1926, she referred to the last night of the season at the Prince's Theatre, which ended on 18 December with act 1 of *Iolanthe* and act 2 of *The Yeomen*: ". . . it was a grand night, I never heard such enthusiasm, I had a splendid reception & was photographed on the stage afterwards."[2] She lived at Grim's Dyke for the rest of her life; some of her servants who remained with her all that time had been at Grim's Dyke since before her husband's death, including her chauffeur, Hardy Mc-Donald McHardy, who was still with her when she made her will in December 1934. She died on 12 December 1936, aged eighty-nine. Apart from individual legacies, she left everything else to Nancy McIntosh, who along with Gerald Crutchley was executor and trustee of her will. To Herbert Sullivan's widow, Elena (by then Mrs. Percy Bashford), she left "all [her] interest in the Gramophone Records of the Gilbert and Sullivan Operas and Songs in any Countries." Her legacies show that she kept up a lifelong friendship with Sybil Crutchley, Sybil Carlisle, and Molly Hare, the daughter of John and Mary Hare, as well as her surviving relatives, especially Mabel Dugdale. Her mother, Herbertina Turner, died at the end of 1913, aged ninety-eight.

Mary Florence Gilbert survived her brother by just over three months. She died on 12 September 1911, aged sixty-eight. Her sister, Anne Maude Gilbert, the youngest of the Gilbert family, was the most long-lived, reaching eighty-seven when she died in 1932.

George Grossmith lived less than a year after Gilbert. He died at Folkestone on 2 March 1912, aged sixty-four.

Durward Lely sang in opera and oratorio after leaving the Savoy company. He toured in America in 1893–1894 and later toured with the Carl Rosa Opera Company. He died in Glasgow on 29 February 1944, aged ninety-one.

Henry Lytton was knighted in 1930 for his services to Gilbert and Sullivan. He played more than twenty different parts over the years, an achievement that was probably only surpassed by Sydney Granville, who began his career as Bill Bobstay at the Savoy in July 1908, and by Leo Sheffield. Lytton appeared for the last time with the D'Oyly Carte Opera Company at the Gaiety Theatre, Dublin, on 30 June 1934, as Jack Point. The following Christmas he appeared in *Aladdin* at the Prince of Wales's, Birmingham. He died 15 August 1936, aged sixty-nine.

Nancy McIntosh, as executor of Lady Gilbert's will, ensured that the statue of Charles II, which had stood near the dyke when Gilbert bought Grim's Dyke, was restored and reerected in the Soho Square Garden, where it had been originally situated; also that Frank Holl's portrait went to the National Portrait Gallery, and that the large rigged model of *HMS Queen*, which had stood in the hall at Grim's Dyke, went to the Science Museum. The ax and block from *The Yeomen of the Guard* were given to the London Museum. On the whole, she had resisted attempts by collectors, and the bulk of Gilbert's papers, including Gilbert's original sketches for the *Bab Ballads,* went to the British Museum. After the sale of Grim's Dyke, she spent the rest of her life in Kensington and Knightsbridge. She died on 20 February 1954, aged eighty. Her estate was valued at £25,581.

Decima Moore married Brigadier-General F. Gordon Guggisberg, who was governor of British Guiana from 1928 to 1929. Decima was awarded the C.B.E. in 1918 for her social and charitable work during World War I. She died 2 February 1964, aged ninety-three.

Courtice Pounds appeared in August 1916 at His Majesty's as Ali Baba in *Chu-Chin-Chow*, and remained in the cast for almost the whole of its five-year run. In December 1922, he played Franz Schubert in *Lilac Time*. He died 21 December 1927, aged sixty-five.

Fanny Ronalds died at 7 Cadogan Place on 28 July 1916, aged seventy-six. The manuscript copy of "The Lost Chord," which Sullivan had left her, was buried with her in Brompton Cemetery.

Leo Sheffield returned to the D'Oyly Carte Opera Company in 1915, taking over all the "Barrington" roles from Fred Billington in 1917. After the 1929–1930 season at the Savoy, he appeared in musical comedy. During World War II, he worked with the Entertainments National Service Associations and later with the BBC Repertory Company. After the war, he toured in *Naughty Marietta, The Gypsy Baron,* and *The Melody of Love.* He died on 3 September 1951, aged seventy-seven.

Herbert Sullivan died 26 December 1928, aged fifty-nine. He left Arthur Sullivan's papers to trustees for his wife, Elena Margaret. She married again, and when she died, as Mrs. P. F. R. Bashford, the papers were left to trustees for the daughter of her second marriage, Ruth Bashford. In 1966, the papers, including Sullivan's diaries, were sold by the trustees for Ruth Bashford to collectors. (The diaries, apart from 1879 – 1880, are part of the Beinecke Rare Book and Manuscript Library at Yale University. The papers that formed Reginald Allen's collection, including the 1879 – 1880 diary, are in the Pierpont Morgan Library in New York.)

Richard Temple spent the latter years of his life teaching and died, 19 October 1912, aged sixty-five.

Ellaline Terriss was not a Savoyard. She appeared in Gilbert's *His Excellency* at the Lyric in 1894 and was married to Seymour Hicks. She was the last surviving link with the Gilbert and Sullivan era. She died on 16 June 1971, at the age of one hundred.

Geraldine Ulmar, who created two of the leading soprano roles, Elsie and Gianetta, toured later in *The Geisha.* She died on 13 August 1932, aged seventy.

C. H. Workman appeared in September 1910 at the Lyric in *The Chocolate Soldier*. In January 1914 he left for Australia with J. C. Williamson Ltd. He died suddenly on 1 May 1923, aged forty-nine.

NOTES

Abbreviations

AS	Arthur Sullivan
BRB	Beinecke Rare Book and Manuscript Library, Yale University
DC/TM	D'Oyly Carte Papers, Theatre Museum, London
LMA	London Metropolitan Archives
PML	Gilbert and Sullivan Collection, Pierpont Morgan Library, New York
PRO	Public Record Office, Kew
PRO/FRC	Family Record Centre, Islington
Soc Gen	Society of Genealogists, London
WCA	Westminster City Archives
WSG/BL	Gilbert Papers, British Library

Curtain-raiser: The London Grocer and the Irish Soldier

1. Parish Register of Over Wallop, Hants, Soc Gen.

2. Memorandum on Pedigree by Thomas Webb Gilbert, son of William Gilbert and Alice (Whitmarsh), WSG/BL Add MS 49,345. C. R. Everett, in *The Genealogist's Magazine,* vol. 7, no. 9, March 1937, pp. 463–469, convincingly traces W. S. Gilbert's family back a further eight generations from Thomas Gilbert to a Richard Gilbert, who was tenant of the Parsonage Manor, Shipton Bellinger, Hampshire, in the fifteenth century.

3. Apprenticeship Records, PRO IR 1/54 f 76. The only William Gilbert recorded as an apprentice at this period served under a gingerbread baker named Peter Hellyer of Fareham near Portsmouth. The apprenticeship was served for the usual seven years starting on 4 July 1761. It was quite possible to change guilds once the apprenticeship period had been served; it also is possible that William was released from his indentures a month or so before 4 July 1768, by which time he had already opened his business in London and then married. It would have been a happy connection to make, given W. S. Gilbert's known weakness for gingerbread, but the absence of the father's name on the apprenticeship records means that this connection cannot be proved.

4. Memo WSG/BL Add MS 49,345.

5. Kent's Directory, 1770 ff, LMA.

6. Parish Register of Bramshaw, Hampshire Count Record Office. Bramshaw is about ten miles southeast of Salisbury and about fifteen miles from Fareham. Near Bramshaw is the village of Sherfield English where William Gilbert's grandfather, Henry Gilbert, still lived. He had been born in 1695 and died in March 1785, aged ninety, and was blind for the last fifteen years of his life. He was W. S. Gilbert's great-great-great-grandfather.

7. Ibid.

8. Parish Register of St. George, Hanover Square, WCA.

9. Parish Register of St. Margaret's, Westminster, WCA.

10. Kent's Directory 1779 ff, LMA.

11. Will of William Gilbert of Tooting, PRO/FRC. Mortgage from Mr. F— of Falmouth, Cornwall. The exact dating of the mortgage is unsure.

12. Lowndes Directory 1789 ff, LMA.

13. *Survey of London*, vol. 22, ed. Sir Howard Roberts and Walter H. Godfrey. Includes photograph of no.7 Blackfriars Road taken in 1947. The houses have since been demolished.

14. Parish Register of Christ Church, Blackfriars Road, LMA.

15. International Genealogical Index, Guildhall Library.

16. Will of William Gilbert of Tooting, PRO/FRC.

17. St. Margaret's Westminster Parish Register, WCA.

18. Parish Register of Christ Church, Blackfriars Road, LMA. The son of great-grandfather William's third marriage, Thomas Webb Gilbert, eventually retired to Salisbury where he bought a house in The Close. After the death of his widow, the house was left to William Gilbert, the father of W. S. Gilbert.

19. Second Battalion Fifty-seventh Regiment of Foot Muster Rolls and Pay Lists PRO WO 12/6706.

20. Ibid.

21. First Battalion Fifty-seventh Regiment of Foot Muster Rolls and Pay Lists PRO WO 12/6644.

22. Glover, *Peninsular War*, p. 219.

23. Longford, *Wellington*, p. 299.

24. PRO WO 12/6644.

25. Out Pensions Royal Hospital PRO WO 116/32. Includes physical description of the soldiers.

26. Hibbert, *Wellington*, p. 140.

27. PRO WO 12/6645.

28. Ibid.

29. Admissions of male children to Royal Military Asylum PRO WO 143/17.

30. PRO WO 12/6645.

31. PRO WO 12/7475. Private Thomas Sullivan was paid from 25 July 1815 by the Second Battalion Sixty-sixth Foot. There is some discrepancy in the army records; elsewhere he is shown as enlisting in the Sixty-sixth at Portsmouth 31 July 1815. His discharge document gives 25 July 1815, having served in the Fifty-seventh until 24 July, therefore showing continuity of service that would be important for his pension.

32. Ibid.

33. PRO WO 116/32.

1: Gilbert: A Dramatic Childhood; Sullivan: A Musical Background

1. *Strand Magazine*, autobiographical sketch in How, *Illustrated Interviews*, p. 10.

2. Kent's Directory 1809, LMA.

3. *Gentleman's Magazine*, May 1812, p. 492.

4. Will of William Gilbert of Commercial Row, PRO/FRC.

5. Parish Register of St. James's Piccadilly, WCA.

6. Obituary of William Gilbert by Sutherland Edwards, *The Daily News*, 4 January 1890 p. 3.

7. Parish Register, St. Paul's Covent Garden, PRO/FRC.

8. Kent's Directory, 1800 ff, LMA.

9. *The Medical Directory*, 1845, Soc Gen.

10. *Survey of London*, vol. 36, St. Paul's Covent Garden 1970, p. 207.

11. Parish Register, St. Paul's Covent Garden, WCA.

12. Census 1841, PRO/FRC; *Survey of London*, vol. 6, Hammersmith, 1915. Fairlawn, no. 159 Hammersmith Road (with plate). The *Red Cow* stood on the south side of Hammersmith Road at the corner of Cow Lane (now Colet Gardens).

13. Wilson, *Murray*, pp. 271–272.

14. Murray, *Autobiography*, p. 79.

15. *Gilbert and Sullivan News*, vol. 2, no. 17, Spring 2000, p. 5 "The Kidnapping of Gilbert," by Michael Walters.

16. Browne, *W. S. Gilbert*, p. 10.

17. 1841 Census PRO/FRC. The census was taken on 6 June 1841, at which date there were three children of Joseph and Catherine Gilbert staying with the Schwencks at Merton. The eldest child was William, aged four, who disappears by the end of the year. There is no mention of him in surviving correspondence.

18. Will of Jane Gilbert of Merton, PRO/FRC.

19. WSG/BL Add MS 49,345 ff 3–4 Catherine Gilbert (4 Portland Place) to Mrs. Henry West [undated].

20. Will of Joseph Mathers Gilbert of Nightingale Lane, Clapham, PRO/FRC.

21. *The Times*, 21 Jan. 1845, p. 6 e.

22. Will of Catherine Gilbert, PRO/Somerset House, written 8 April 1849, in which she divided her trust property in four equal shares to her brother John Skinner Francis, her sister Julia Lavinia Laing, her mother Sarah (Mrs. Thomas Fredericks), and her friend Lieutenant Norman Baillie Hopper.

23. WSG/BL Add MS 49,345 Mary Schwenck (Weybridge Common) to Mrs. West, (Pangbourne) 20 June 1845.

24. *The Times*, 10 July 1845, p. 8 a; R. Meeson and W. N. Welsby, *Reports of Cases Argued and Determined in the Courts of Exchequer and Exchequer Chamber*, vol. 14, 1846.

25. Death Certificate of Christiana Morris, 3 April 1845, who died at 17 Southampton Street in the presence of her grandson Frederick Edwards. PRO/FRC.

26. Will of Thomas Morris of Southampton Street, Covent Garden. PRO/Somerset House.

27. *The Times*, 13 February 1833, p. 7.

28. *Survey of London*, vol. 16 Southern Kensington: Brompton, p. 67.

29. How, *Illustrated Interviews*, p. 10.

30. Joseph Foster. *Alumni Oxonienses*, vol. 3. 1968. Dr Francis Nicholas graduated BA from Oxford 1815; MA (Oxford) 1818 and DCL (Oxford) 1839.

31. 1851 Census PRO/FRC. Dr Francis Nicholas was aged fifty-five in 1851 and his twelve-year-old son, Francis, was a pupil at the school.

32. "Haunted" first appeared in *Fun* 24 Mar. 1866, Ellis, *Bab Ballads*, p. 81.

33. Dark and Grey, *W. S. Gilbert*, p. 5. The friend referred to is Rowland Brown.

34. Ridley, *Napoleon III and Eugénie*, pp. 334–335.

35. Stedman, *W. S. Gilbert*, p. 4.

36. PRO WO 143/17.

37. Ibid.

38. Jacobs, *Arthur Sullivan*, pp. 5–6.

39. Findon, *Sir Arthur Sullivan*, p. 10. Findon actually cites Hampstead as the place of

Clementina Sullivan's education; this may have been a familiar way of referring to East-hampstead near Camberley.

40. Saxe Wyndham, *Arthur Seymour Sullivan*, p. 2.

41. Birth Certificate, Frederick Sullivan, PRO/FRC.

42. Jacobs, *Arthur Sullivan*, p. 6.

43. Sullivan and Flower, *Sir Arthur Sullivan*, p. 2.

44. Census 1841 PRO/FRC. Thomas Sullivan describes himself as professor of music, de-noting that he considered teaching as his main occupation.

45. Parish Register, St. Mary at Lambeth, LMA.

46. Jacobs, *Arthur Sullivan*, p. 7.

47. Census 1851 PRO/FRC.

48. Sullivan and Flower, *Sir Arthur Sullivan*, p. 4.

49. The whole area around Bolwell Terrace was redeveloped and the site of Sullivan's birthplace is now in the playground of the Lilian Baylis School.

50. Lawrence, *Sir Arthur Sullivan*, pp. 4–5.

51. 1851 Census (30/31 March) shows Arthur and Frederick Sullivan, both "scholars," still living with their parents at Sandhurst. Plees's school had not yet opened at 20 Albert Terrace, Bayswater. By 1861, the school had either closed or moved.

2: The Chapel Royal and King's College

1. Lawrence, *Sir Arthur Sullivan*, pp. 237–239.

2. Helmore, *Thomas Helmore*, p. 76.

3. AS to his parents [undated], in Baily, *Gilbert and Sullivan and their World*, pp. 11–12.

4. F. C. Burnand, *Records and Reminiscences*, p. 442.

5. Cellier and Bridgeman, *Gilbert, Sullivan and D'Oyly Carte*, p. 11.

6. Mrs. Sullivan (Yorktown) to AS, 23 December 1855, in Allen, p. 5.

7. Birkett Foster, *Philharmonic Society*, p. 249.

8. Smart Papers/BL Add MS 41,771 ff 177–178. Cipriani Potter (39 Inverness Terrace, Bayswater) to George Smart, 17 July 1857.

9. Jacobs, *Arthur Sullivan*, p. 18.

10. Census 1861, PRO/FRC.

11. Ibid.

12. Smart Papers/BL Add MS 41,771.

13. George T. Smart to Harry Fowler Broadwood, 26 June 1858, in Wainwright, *Broadwood*, p. 181. An approximate equivalent of monetary values can be obtained by multiplying by fifty.

14. Hearnshaw, *King's College*, p. 238.

15. How, *Illustrated Interviews*, p. 338.

16. Skeat, *King's College London Engineering Society*, p. 16.

17. *The Times*, 5 October 1855, Report on examination in August 1855 for commissions in the Royal Artillery and Engineers; 12 October 1855, Report on revised examinations for Jan-uary 1856; 3 January 1856, letter from W. C. Lake, classical examiner for Artillery and Engi-neer Appointments; 12 March 1856, list of successful candidates; 15 August 1856, list of suc-cessful candidates in examinations of 30 June held at King's College.

18. Gilbert to Mrs. German Reed, 30 December 1875, requesting a copy be made of his play *Ages Ago* for his mother and sisters to put on in an amateur performance in Algiers.

19. W. S. Gilbert, "To My Bride," 9 June 1866, Ellis, *Bab Ballads*, p. 86.

20. Education Department papers: PRO/T1/6082A/15282; 6133A/13673; 6250A/9059.

21. 1861 Census, PRO/FRC.

3: Sullivan at Leipzig; Gilbert at Law

1. Walter Bache to his parents, 8 October 1858, in Bache, *Brother Musicians*, p. 132.

2. Barnett, *Musical Reminiscences*, pp. 38–39.

3. Baily, *Gilbert and Sullivan Book*, pp. 23–26.

4. Rogers, *Memories*, pp. 155–160.

5. AS to Clara Rogers, in Baily, *Gilbert and Sullivan Book*, p. 27.

6. Moscheles, *Life of Moscheles*, p. 282.

7. AS (3 Ponsonby Street) to Smart, 22 April 1861, Smart Papers BL/Add MS 41,771 f 135. Copy, read to the Mendelssohn Committee 13 May 1861; original sent to Carl Klingemann.

8. Miss Hamilton (Mrs. Walter Carr) to *Musical Times*, 1 February 1901, in Saxe Wyndham, *Arthur Seymour Sullivan*, p. 59.

9. Young, *Sir Arthur Sullivan*, p. 29.

10. Sullivan and Flower, *Sir Arthur Sullivan*, p. 39.

11. Charlotte Brontë to William Smith, [1849], in Juliet Barker, *The Brontës*, London: Phoenix, 1994, pp. 621–622.

12. There is an alternative but less likely account of Grove's first meeting with Sullivan taking place at St. James's Hall, which appears in Graves, *Sir George Grove*, p. 92.

13. Grove to AS in Young, *George Grove*, p. 84.

14. *The Times*, 7 April 1862, P.12 e.

15. *The Times*, 9 April 1862, p. 9 f.

16. Jacobs, *Arthur Sullivan*, p. 31.

17. Sullivan and Flower, *Sir Arthur Sullivan*, p. 37.

18. Marriage Certificate of Frederic Sullivan and Charlotte Lacy, PRO/FRC.

19. AS (3 Ponsonby Street) to Nina Lehmann, 23 November 1862, in Sullivan and Flower, *Sir Arthur Sullivan*, pp. 40–41.

20. Photograph in Sullivan and Flower, facing p. 42.

21. Lawrence, *Sir Arthur Sullivan*, p. 52.

22. Baily, *Gilbert and Sullivan Book*, p. 33.

23. PRO/Education Department papers/1857 T1/6082A/15282; 1858 T1/6133A/13673; 1860 T1 6250A/9059; 1860 T1/6283A/20075.

24. *The Theatre*, vol. 1, pp. 217–224.

25. *London Gazette*, 1859, Indexes, p. 49, Guildhall Library.

26. Merrick, *Civil Service Rifle Volunteers*, p. 18.

27. Ibid., p. 82.

28. *The Times*, 3 October 1860, p. 11.

29. Merrick, *Civil Service Rifle Volunteers*, p. 25.

30. Gilbert to W. H. Swanborough, 17 October 1860, in Stedman, *W. S. Gilbert*, p. 9

31. *The Theatre*, vol. 1, pp. 217–224.

32. 1861 Census, PRO/FRC.

33. *The Theatre*, vol. 1, pp. 217–224.

34. Clement Scott, *Wheel of Life*, p. 104.

35. *The Theatre*, vol. 1, pp. 217–224.

4: Gilbert and Sullivan: The Ballad Writers

1. Clement Scott, *Wheel of Life*, p. 104.

2. Terence Rees, "A Melodrama Written by W. S. Gilbert at 22" in *The Times*, 27 October 1966, p. 6.

3. Pearse, *Inns of Court and Chancery*, pp. 384–395; notes to the author by Adrian Blunt, Deputy Librarian, The Honorable Society of the Inner Temple.

4. How, *Illustrated Interviews*, p. 11.

5. Archer, *Real Conversations*, p. 114.

6. Army Lists PRO.

7. Will of Mary Schwenck of 14 Canterbury Villas, Brixton, PRO/Somerset House.

8. Speech by Gilbert at complimentary banquet on his knighthood, given at the Savoy Hotel, 2 February 1908. WSG/BL Add MS 49,306 ff 118–123.

9. WSG/BL Add MS 49,303. Attendance book of the "Serious Family." Last entry: 19 May 1866, present: George Rose, C. J. Stone, W. S. Gilbert, Clement Scott, Alfred Thompson, Paul Gray, Tom Hood.

10. WSG/BL Add MS 49,306 ff 118–123.

11. WSG/BL Add MS 49,345.

12. Hood, *Bunch of Keys*, Preface.

13. Stedman, *W. S. Gilbert*, pp. 43–45.

14. Ellis, *Bab Ballads*, p. 81.

15. Ibid., p. 86.

16. Army Lists of East India Company, BL / India Office.

17. 1861 Census, PRO/FRC.

18. Birth Certificate of Lucy Agnes Blois Turner, PRO/FRC.

19. 1861 Census, PRO/FRC.

20. Goodman, *Gilbert and Sullivan at Law*, p. 27.

21. How, *Illustrated Interviews*, p. 12.

22. Tom Hood, ed., *Warnes's Christmas Annual, Five Alls.*

23. *The Theatre*, vol. 1, pp. 217–224. Elsewhere, Gilbert refers to a different period of time; whatever the case, it was written and rehearsed very quickly.

24. Ibid.

25. Ibid.

26. Nicoll, *Late Nineteenth Century Drama*. Vol I. p. 69.

27. *The Theatre*, Vol 1 pp. 217–224.

28. AS (Greenheys, Manchester) to Nina Lehmann, 23 January 1863, PML.

29. Post Office Directory, 1872, indicates vacant possession after Sullivan had moved with his mother to Albert Mansions, therefore suggesting that the Sullivans had occupied the whole house.

30. Emmerson, *Arthur Darling*, pp. 5–6.

31. Wolfson, *Sullivan and the Scott Russells*, p. 6.

32. Saxe Wyndham, *Arthur Seymour Sullivan*, p. 239.

33. Sullivan and Flower, *Sir Arthur Sullivan*, pp. 46–47.

34. AS to his father, 11 September 1864, in Allen, *Sir Arthur Sullivan*, p. 18.

35. AS (Richmond Lodge, Holywood, Belfast) to his mother, 30 August [1865], in Allen, *Sir Arthur Sullivan*, p. 19.

36. Sullivan and Flower, *Sir Arthur Sullivan*, p. 41.

37. F. C. Burnand to the *Spectator*, in Wells, *Souvenir of Sir Arthur Sullivan*, pp. 21–22.

38. Jacobs, *Arthur Sullivan*, p. 42.

39. Saxe Wyndham, *Arthur Seymour Sullivan*, pp. 88–89.

40. Thomas Sullivan to AS, Allen, *Sir Arthur Sullivan*. p. 22.

41. AS to Nina Lehmann, 18 October 1866, PML.

42. Grove to Olga von Glehn, 28 October 1866, in Graves, *Sir George Grove*, p. 133.

5: Gilbert and Sullivan in the Theater

1. AS to his mother, 10 February 1867, in Lawrence, *Sir Arthur Sullivan*, p. 72.
2. *The Times*, 11 May 1867, p. 9 f.
3. Baily, *Gilbert and Sullivan and their World*, p. 29.
4. Rachel Scott Russell to AS, 9 July 1868, PML.
5. Rachel to AS, 24 May 1867, PML.
6. Rachel to AS, 24 May 1867, PML.
7. Rachel to AS, 12 June 1867, PML.
8. Rachel to AS, n.d., PML.
9. Rachel to AS, 30 August 1867, PML.
10. Rachel to AS, 28 August 1867, PML.
11. Marriage certificate of WSG and Lucy Turner, PRO/FRC.
12. WSG/BL Add MS 39,345 f 12.
13. Mary Craushay to Lucy Gilbert, WSG/BL Add MS 49,343.
14. *The Times*, 24 January 1868, p. 10 e. There has been confusion over the first name of Miss Everard. In programs, her name was given as Miss H. Everard; in Stedman and Jacobs, it appears as Harriet; Rollins and Witts give her name as Helen Everard in their lists of early casts. The birth registers of PRO/FRC give her name as Harriett, but she appears to have added an "e" later. On a contract for 1878 in the D'Oyly Carte papers, she is Harriette Everard, and she gave Harrriette as the spelling of her name in the 1871 census, when she was living in the Old Kent Road with her husband, the actor Arthur Parry.
15. Ibid.
16. Note by Grove in the Crystal Palace program, 14 December 1867, in Young, *George Grove*, p. 95; Jacobs, *Arthur Sullivan*, p. 58 & p. 435 note 7.3.
17. Grove's account, in Graves, *Sir George Grove*, pp. 147–148.
18. *The Times*, 31 July 1867, p. 9 f and letter, 3 August 1867, p. 12 d.
19. Louise to AS, 14 April 1868, PML.
20. Louise to AS, 25 April 1868, PML.
21. Rachel to AS, 27 April 1868, PML.
22. Jacobs, *Arthur Sullivan*, p. 35 and note 4.10 p. 432. Jacobs suggests the possibility that *The False Heiress* was the retitled opera with Chorley, *The Sapphire Necklace*.
23. Notes by Canon T. P. Mannington, husband of D'Oyly Carte's sister Blanche, DC/TM.
24. Unsigned notes DC/TM.
25. AS to Richard D'Oyly Carte, 10 August 1868, DC/TM.
26. Louise to AS, 28 November 1868, PML.
27. Louise to AS, 3 December 1868, PML.
28. Louise to AS, 7 December 1868, PML.
29. Louise to AS, [December 1868], PML.
30. WSG to Kitty, February 1868, WSG/BL Add MS 49,345.
31. Ellis, *Bab Ballads*, pp. 157–159.
32. Army List, 1868, PRO.
22. Judd (The Phoenix Printing Works) to WSG, 14 December 1868, WSG/BL Add MS 49,330.
34. *The Times*, 11 December 1868, p. 4 f.
35. *The Times*, 24 December 1868, p. 3 f.
36. Hollingshead, *Gaiety Chronicles*, p. 57.

6: The Meeting of Gilbert and Sullivan—*Thespis*

1. Stedman, *W. S. Gilbert*, p. 69.

2. Hollingshead, *Gaiety Chronicles*, p. 94.

3. Hollingshead, *Good Old Gaiety*, p. 16.

4. Jacobs, *Arthur Sullivan*, p. 66.

5. Stedman, *W. S. Gilbert*, p. 76.

6. *The Times*, 28 June 1869, p. 6 d.

7. *The Theatre*, vol. 1, pp. 217–224.

8. Arthur Jacobs, *Gilbert and Sullivan*, p. 17.

9. In the libretto of *Our Island Home* the Pirate King is named Captain Bang (see Stedman, *Gilbert before Sullivan*). However, the libretto includes a song from Goldberg, pp. 111–114, which contains the lines, "I'm Captain Byng, / The Pirate King."

10. WSG to Lucy Gilbert, [undated], WSG/BL Add MS 49,345.

11. Rachel to AS, 3 February 1869, PML.

12. Rachel to AS, [3 April 1869], PML.

13. Young, *Sir Arthur Sullivan*, p. 89.

14. Rachel to AS, 4 June 1869, PML.

15. Rachel to AS, [undated], PML.

16. Rachel to AS, 11 September 1869, PML.

17. Rachel to AS, 26 October 1869, PML.

18. AS to Charles Gruneisen, 13 December 1869, in Jacobs, *Arthur Sullivan*, p. 61.

19. Goss to AS, 22 December 1869, PML.

20. Rachel to AS, 9 May 1870, PML.

21. Louise to AS, 24 May 1870, PML.

22. Findon, *Sir Arthur Sullivan*, p. 170.

23. *Palace of Truth*, Gilbert, *Original Plays*, First Series, p. 171.

24. How, *Illustrated Interviews*, p. 14.

25. "A Scrap of Autobiography," WSG/BL Add MS 49,348.

26. Burnand, *Reminiscences*, p. 53.

27. Speech at the Savoy Hotel, 2 February 1908, WSG/BL Add MS 49,306 ff 118–123.

28. *The Theatre*, vol. 1, pp. 217–224.

29. *New York Times*, 9 May 1871, 4.7.

30. Millais to AS, 19 August 1870, PML.

31. 1871 Census, PRO/FRC.

32. *Graphic*, 6 May 1871, p. 411.

33. As to his mother, 5 June 1871, PML.

34. Rees, *Thespis*, p. 10.

35. AS (Langholm) to his mother, PML.

36. *New York Times*, 16 November 1871, 5.2.

37. Edward English to R. M. Field, 30 October 1871, in Allen, *First Night Gilbert and Sullivan*, p. 2.

38. WSG/BL Add MS 49,306.

39. Rees, *Thespis*, p. 90.

40. *New York Times*, 31 December 1871, 5.2.

41. Ibid., 4 October 1872, 5.1.

42. Hollingshead, *Gaiety Chronicles*, p. 202.

43. Lawrence, *Sir Arthur Sullivan*, pp. 85–87.

44. Notes for *Ballet Music, L'Ile Enchantée—Thespis*, recorded by Radio Telefis Eirann, Marco Polo (1992).

45. English to Field, 28 December 1871, in Allen, *First Night Gilbert and Sullivan*, p. 2.

46. AS to his mother, 28 December 1871, ibid., p. 6.

47. *Morning Advertiser*, 27 December 1871, p. 3.

48. Hollingshead, *Good Old Gaiety*, pp. 14–15.

49. *Daily Telegraph*, 27 December 1871, p. 2.5.

50. Ibid.

51. *Daily News*, 27 December 1871, p. 2.3.

7: Different Worlds

1. Buckstone to WSG, 14 January 1872, WSG/BL Add MS 49,330.

2. *New York Times*, 31 December 1871, 5.2.

3. *Era*, 28 January 1872, p. 11.

4. Ibid., 5 May 1872, p. 11.3.

5. Stedman, *W. S. Gilbert*, p. 97.

6. Innes, *Aberdeenshire Militia*, p. 31.

7. *The Times*, 6 January 1873, p. 8 a.

8. *Pall Mall Gazette*, 6 January 1873, p. 10.

9. Ibid., 23 January 1873, p. 3.

10. Buckstone to WSG, 12 January 1873, WSG/BL Add MS 49,330.

11. *The Times*, 10 March 1873, p. 8 b.

12. WSG (Guestley Lodge, Hastings) to Mrs. Robertson [Marie Litton], 27 June 1873; WSG to Marie Litton, 22 October 1873, WSG/BL Add MS 49,330.

13. Archer, *Real Conversations*, p. 112.

14. Stedman, *W. S. Gilbert*, pp. 109–110.

15. *The Times*, 28 November 1873, p. 11 a.

16. Ibid., 2 December 1873, p. 12 f.

17. Buckstone to WSG, 17 November 1873, WSG/BL Add MS 49,330.

18. *The Times*, 2 May 1872, P.5 e.

19. Frederick Lehmann to AS, January 1872, in Jacobs, *Arthur Sullivan*, p. 85.

20. AS to Frederick Lehmann, January 1872, PML.

21. Young, *Sir Arthur Sullivan*, p. 66, note 26.

22. *The Times*, 18 September 1872, p. 8 d.

23. AS to his mother, 16 September 1872, PML.

24. AS to Davison, 16 May 1873, in Allen, *Sir Arthur Sullivan*, p. 71. Sullivan and Flower, *Sir Arthur Sullivan*, p. 72, mention a lover in Ireland who was his inspiration at this time, but detail is lacking.

25. AS to Ernest von Glehn, 14 December 1872, and subsequent note by E. de Glehn [*sic*] in Saxe Wyndham, *Arthur Seymour Sullivan*, p. 115.

26. *The Times*, 28 August 1873, p. 10 c.

8: *Trial by Jury*

1. Goodman, *Gilbert and Sullivan at Law*, pp. 151–152.

2. Stedman, *W. S. Gilbert*, p. 121.

3. *Athenaeum*, in Stedman, *W. S. Gilbert*, p. 123.

4. *Rosencrantz and Guildenstern*, Gilbert, *Original Plays*, Third Series, p. 75.

5. AS (Balcarres) to his mother, 21 September 1874, PML.

6. AS (Franzensbad) to his mother, 8 August 1874, PML.

7. AS to his mother, 6 September 1874, PML.

8. Bennett, *Forty Years of Music*, pp. 68–70.

9. *The Times*, 23 January 1875, p. 8 f.

10. *The Times*, 22 February 1875. "There was a fall of snow on Saturday morning in London and at intervals during the day. The snow remained in the parks yesterday and had not disappeared in the streets last night when a sharp frost set in." These weather conditions in London during the period best match the account given by Sullivan.

11. Lawrence, *Sir Arthur Sullivan*, p. 105.

12. Program, DC/TM.

13. *The Times*, 29 March 1875.

14. *Daily News*, 27 March 1875, p. 3.5.

15. *Daily Telegraph*, 26 March 1875, p. 3.2.

9: In Search of a Manager

1. *Era*, 6 June 1875, p. 12.

2. In his diary entry for 12 April 1888, Sullivan spells Helen Lenoir's real name as Cowper-Black. This has possibly led to that spelling being repeated in biographies. The marriage registers at PRO/FRC give Couper-Black. According to Paul D. Sealey ("Who was Helen Lenoir" in *The Savoyard*, February 1983), her original name was Susan Couper Black, and she registered at the University of London (1871–1874) as Helen Susan Black. See also Jacobs, p. 444.

3. Innes, *Aberdeenshire Militia*, p. 33.

4. AS to his mother, August 1875, PML.

5. WSG to AS, 28 October 1875, WSG/BL Add MS 49,338 f 87.

6. WSG to AS, 9 November 1875, ibid., f 106.

7. WSG to AS, 11 November 1875, ibid., f 111.

8. WSG to AS, 23 November 1875, ibid., f 136.

9. Browne, *W. S. Gilbert*, p. 51.

10. Townley Searle, *Bibliography*, pp. 36–37.

11. Dark and Grey, *W. S. Gilbert*, p. 54.

12. WSG to AS, 8 December 1875, WSG/BL Add MS 449,338 f 155.

13. WSG to Clement Scott, in Mrs. Clement Scott, *Old Days in Bohemian London*.

14. AS to his mother, 27 December 1875, PML.

15. WSG to Wybrow Robertson, 2 December 1875, WSG/BL Add MS 49,338 f 146.

16. WSG to Robertson, 15 December 1875, WSG/BL Add MS 49,338 f 174.

17. "Mr. W. S. Gilbert and the Organ Grinder," *Era*, 28 November 1875, p. 6, and "Topics of the Week," p. 11.

18. WSG to J. Pender, 11 December 1875, WSG/BL Add MS 49,304 ff 44–46.

19. WSG to James Saunders, 10 December 1875, ibid., f 47.

20. Sothern to WSG, 22 April [1875], WSG/BL Add MS 49,331 ff 90–91.

21. WSG to Sothern, 13 December 1875, WSG/BL Add 49,338 f 165.

22. WSG to AS, 3 December 1875, WSG/BL Add MS 49,338 f 147.

23. WSG to Carte, 17 December 1875, ibid., f 180.

24. WSG to AS, 4 January 1876, ibid., f 208.

25. AS to the duke of Edinburgh, PML.

26. WSG to Morton, 26 January 1876, WSG/BL Add MS 49,338 f 230.

27. WSG and AS to Morton, 7 February 1876, ibid., f 242.

28. WSG to AS, 15 February 1876, ibid., f 248.

29. WSG to Carte, 11 March 1876, [copy in Typed Capitals] ibid., ff 263–264.

30. Sothern to WSG, 10 February 1876, WSG/BL 49,331 ff 80–82.

31. WSG to Sothern, 23 February 1876, WSG/BL Add MS 49,338 ff 254–255.

32. Sothern to WSG, 12 March 1876, WSG/BL Add MS 49,331 ff 83–84.

33. WSG to Morton, 25 March 1876, [copy in Typed Capitals] ibid., f 272.

34. WSG to Fred Sullivan, 14 May 1876, [copy in Typed Capitals] ibid., f 296.

10: Sullivan Is Honored; Gilbert Is Ridiculed

1. AS to his mother, June 1876, PML.

2. Baily, *Gilbert and Sullivan Book*, p. 11.

3. Anne Gilbert to WSG, 1 June 1876, WSG/BL Add MS 49,331 f 100.

4. WSG to his mother, 29 May 1876, WSG/BL Add MS 49,304 ff 31–34.

5. Ibid.

6. WSG to his mother, 6 June 1876, ibid., ff 41–43.

7. WSG to his mother, 4 June 1876, ibid., ff 35–37.

8. WSG to Captain Algernon Hawkins Thomas (Lord Inverurie), president of the mess committee, 25 July 1876, WSG/BL Add MS 49,338 f 310.

9. WSG to Colonel Innes, 16 November 1876, ibid., ff 367–368.

10. *Dan'l Druce Blacksmith*, WSG, *Collected Plays*, Second Series, p. 109.

11. Stedman, *W. S. Gilbert*, p. 139.

12. WSG to Sothern, 9 November 1876, WSG/BL Add MS 49,338 ff 360–361.

13. WSG to Sothern, 30 November 1876, ibid., f 380.

14. Sothern to WSG, 12 January 1877, WSG/BL Add MS 49,331 ff 124–127.

15. WSG to Sothern, 30 January 1877, WSG/BL Add MS 49,338 ff 420–423.

16. Sothern to WSG, 30 January 1877, WSG/BL Add MS 49,331 ff 130–131.

17. WSG to Knight, 28 November 1876, WSG/BL Add MS 49,338 f 373.

18. WSG to Henrietta Hodson, 29 November 1876, ibid., ff 378–379.

19. WSG to Buckstone, 3 December 1876, ibid., f 383.

20. WSG to Henry Howe, 7 December 1876, ibid., ff 385–386.

21. WSG to Buckstone, 9 February 1877, ibid., f 434.

22. Buckstone to WSG, 18 February 1877, ibid., f 462.

23. WSG to Henrietta Hodson, 25 February 1877, ibid., ff 459–460.

24. WSG to Mrs. Kendal, 25 April 1877, ibid., f 495.

11: The Comedy Opera Company and *The Sorcerer*

1. Findon, *Sir Arthur Sullivan*, p. 171.

2. AS to Herbert Sullivan, 30 December 1896, PML.

3. Martin, *Lady Randolph Churchill*, p. 111.

4. WSG/BL Add MS 49,338 f 448.

5. Lewis Carroll to AS, 31 March 1877, PML.

6. John Hare to WSG, 16 February 1877, WSG/BL Add MS 49,331 f 132.

7. WSG to Hare, 17 February 1877, WSG/BL Add MS 49,338 ff 451–452.

8. WSG to Hare, 26 June 1877, ibid., ff 517–518.

9. WSG to Hare, 30 January 1878, ibid., ff 586–589.

10. AS to his mother, 5 July 1877, PML.

11. Carte to G. Metzler, 4 July 1877, extracts in DC/TM.

12. WSG to AS, 11 November 1875, WSG/BL Add MS 49,338 f 111.

13. Helen Carte to Rutland Barrington, [undated], DC/TM.

14. Barrington, *Rutland Barrington, By Himself*, pp. 15–30.

15. Baily, *Gilbert and Sullivan Book*, (Spring Books ed.) pp. 134–135.

16. WSG to Sothern, 2 August 1877, WSG/BL Add MS 49,338 ff 519–520.

17. Will, Mary Turner of Dorset Square, PRO.

18. WSG to W. H. Kendal, 19 September 1877, WSG/BL Add MS 49,338 f 527.

19. AS to his mother, 18 August 1877, PML.

20. AS to his mother, 8 September 1877, PML.

21. Program, DC/TM.

22. WSG/BL Add MS 49,338 ff 542–543.

23. AS to Isabella Paul, 23 October 1877, PML.

24. Grossmith, *Society Clown*, pp. 92–95.

25. Ibid.

26. Ibid., p. 91.

27. Ibid., pp. 92–95.

28. Ibid.

29. Ibid.

30. Ibid., p. 97.

31. AS to his mother, 1 November 1877, PML.

32. Archer, *Real Conversations*, pp. 129–130.

33. Barrington, *Rutland Barrington, By Himself*, p. 27.

34. Grossmith, *Society Clown*, p. 102.

35. Barrington, *Rutland Barrington, By Himself*, p. 29.

36. *The Times*, 19 November 1877, p. 6 b.

37. Ibid.

38. AS to his mother, 25 December 1877, PML.

12: *HMS Pinafore*

1. Program, DC/TM.

2. WSG to AS, 27 December 1877, facsimile in Allen, *Sir Arthur Sullivan*, p. 99.

3. WSG/BL Add MS 49,306.

4. "The Bumboat Woman's Story," Ellis, *Bab Ballads*, p. 284.

5. WSG/BL Add MS 49,306.

6. "Captain Reece," Ellis, *Bab Ballads*, p. 143.

7. WSG/BL Add MS 49,306.

8. *HMS Pinafore*, Gilbert, *Original Plays*, Second Series, p. 271.

9. Ibid.

10. WSG Diary, 1 January 1878, WSG/BL Add MS 49,332.

11. Ibid.

12. Ibid., 6 January 1878.

13. Ibid., 12 January 1878.

14. Will of Lucretia Ann Turner, PRO.

15. Will of Mary Turner, PRO.

16. WSG Diary, 5 January WSG/BL Add MS 49,332.

17. WSG to General Turner, 8 January 1878, WSG/BL Add 49,338 f 581, but noted in 1878 Diary as written 6 January 1878.

18. WSG Diary, 7 January 1878, WSG/BL Add MS 49,332.

19. Ibid., 22 June 1878.

20. WSG to Carte, 8 January 1878, DC/TM.

21. WSG Diary, 9 January 1878, WSG/BL Add MS 49,332.

22. Ibid., 8 January 1878.

23. AS to Carte, 5 February 1878, DC/TM.

24. Ibid.

25. AS to his mother, 5 January 1878, PML.

26. Hollingshead, *My Lifetime*, vol. 2, p. 124.

27. *The Times*, 23 January 1875, p. 1.

28. WSG Diary, 18 February 1878, WSG/BL Add MS 49,332.

29. Ibid., 25–27 February 1878.

30. Ibid., 27–28 February 1878.

31. Ibid., 6 March 1878.

32. Ibid., 11 March 1878.

33. Ibid., 12 March 1878.

34. Ibid., 13 March 1878.

35. AS to his mother, 16 January 1878, PML.

36. AS to his mother, 25 February 1878, PML. This would be a Requiem Mass, not the burial service, for Pius IX who died 7 February 1878. In previous biographies, the word "Pope" has been misread as "Doge," for example, Jacobs, p. 121.

37. AS to Frederick Spark, 12 March 1878, in Spark and Bennett, *Leeds Music Festivals*, p. 146.

38. WSG Diary, 25 March 1878, WSG/BL Add MS 49,322.

39. Ibid., 15 April 1878.

40. Ibid., 25 April 1878.

41. Ibid., 28 April 1878.

42. AS to his mother, 20 April 1868, PML.

43. AS to Carte, 23 April 1878, in Young, *Sir Arthur Sullivan*, p. 116.

44. AS to Carte, 23 April 1878, DC/TM.

45. Contract, DC/TM.

46. WSG Diary, 13 May 1878, WSG/BL Add MS 49,322.

47. Bond, *Life and Reminiscences*, p. 53.

48. Notes on overtures, DC/TM.

49. WSG Diary, 24 May 1878, WSG/BL Add MS 49,322.

50. Ibid., 25 May 1878.

51. *Era*, 2 June 1878, p. 5.1.

52. *The Times*, 27 May 1878, p. 6 d.

53. *Ibid.*, 3 June 1878, p. 12.

54. AS to his mother, 2 June 1878, PML.

55. AS to Miss Anna, PML.

13: Troubled Waters

1. E. H. Bayley to Carte, 6 July 1878, DC/TM.

2. Weather reports in *The Times* between 27 May and 18 August 1878. In that period the temperature was over 80°F on only four days. On almost half the days, the temperature varied between 56 and 69°F.

3. AS to his mother, 16 August 1878, PML.

4. WSG Diary, 28 June–9 July 1878, WSG/BL Add MS 49,322.

5. WSG to Charles Harris, 27 June 1878, WSG/BL Add MS 49,338 f 606.

6. WSG Diary, 4 and 5 July 1878, WSG/BL Add MS 49,322.

7. Ibid., 11 July 1878.

8. Ibid., 11–16 July 1878.

9. Ibid., 17–26 July 1878.

10. Ibid., 27 July–5 August 1878.

11. *The Times*, 5 August 1878, p. 8 e.

12. *The Times*, 12 August 1878, p. 8 a; 19 August 1878, p. 8 a; 26 August 1878, p. 4 d; 2 September 1878, p. 5 f.

13. WSG Diary, 31 August–16 September 1878, WSG/BL Add MS 49,322.

14. Ibid., 20 September 1878.

15. AS to Carte, 12 September 1878, DC/TM.

16. WSG Diary, 6 October 1878, WSG/BL Add MS 49,322.

17. Ibid., 9 April 1878.

18. AS to Directors, Comedy Opera Company Limited, 13 November 1878, Copy, DC/TM.

19. WSG Diary, 23–30 December 1878, WSG/BL Add MS 48,322.

20. AS to A. J. Hipkins, [27 December 1878]. PML.

21. WSG to Neville, 3 February 1879, WSG/BL Add MS 49,338 f 634.

22. Sothern to WSG, copy by Gilbert in WSG to Kendal, 19 February 1879, ibid., ff 642–643.

23. WSG to Hare, 18 February 1879, ibid., ff 639–640.

24. Lucy Gilbert to Mary Fairs, 3 March 1879, ibid., ff 649–651.

25. Carte to WSG and AS, 8 April 1880, DC/TM.

26. WSG to Carte, 15 September 1879, DC/TM.

27. Carte's Diary Notes, DC/TM.

28. Richard Barker to WSG, 22 July 1879, DC/TM.

29. AS to Gunn, 30 July 1879, DC/TM.

30. AS to Hollingshead, 30 July 1879, in Hollingshead, *Gaiety Chronicles*, pp. 275–276.

31. WSG to AS, 2 August 1879, WSG/BL Add MS 49,338 f 658.

32. Ibid.

33. WSG to AS, [6 August 1879], in Allen, *Sir Arthur Sullivan*, facsimile p. 100.

34. Carte to AS, 26 August 1879, DC/TM.

35. Carte to AS, 26 August 1879, DC/TM.

36. Ibid.

14: America and *The Pirates of Penzance*

1. Collard Aug. Drake to *The Times*, 8 October 1879, p. 6 f.

2. WSG to Carte, 15 September 1879, DC/TM.

3. AS to Carte, 4 October 1879, DC/TM.

4. *The Times*, 16 October 1879, p. 11 c.

5. *Era*, 16 November 1879, p. 6.

6. AS to his mother, November 1879, PML.

7. AS to his mother, 21 November 1879, PML.

8. AS to his mother, 10 November 1879, PML.

9. AS to his mother, 21 November 1879, PML.

10. AS to his mother, 10 December 1879, PML.

11. Ibid.

12. AS to his mother, 12 December 1879, PML.

13. WSG to Percy de Strzelecki, 14 August 1902, in Allen, *First Night Gilbert and Sullivan*, pp. 99–100.

14. AS Diary, 16 December 1879, PML.

15. AS to his mother, 20 December 1879, PML.

16. Ibid.

17. Program, DC/TM.

18. AS Diary, 31 December 1879, PML.

19. AS to his mother, 2 January 1880, PML.

20. AS to his mother, 2 January 1880, PML.

21. *New York Herald*, 1 January 1880, p. 10.1.

22. WSG/BL Add MS 49,340.

23. Bradley, *The Complete Annotated Gilbert and Sullivan*, p. 194.

24. WSG to Marion Johnson, 12 February 1880, DC/TM.

25. AS Diary, 1 January 1880, PML.

26. 'Cynisca' to WSG, [undated], WSG/BL Add MS 49,331 ff 217–220.

27. Spark to AS, 14 February 1880, Spark and Bennett, *Leeds Music Festivals*, p. 171.

28. AS Diary, 24 February 1880, PML.

29. WSG/BL Add MS 49,340.

30. Carte to WSG and AS, 8 April 1880, DC/TM.

31. George R. Sims, in *The Referee*, 4 June 1911, "Gilbertian Memories: Some Personal Reminiscences."

32. Carte to WSG and AS, 8 April 1880, DC/TM.

33. *Daily News*, 5 April 1880, p. 2.3.

34. *The Times*, 5 April 1880, p. 4 e.

35. Barrington, *Rutland Barrington, By Himself*, p. 39.

36. *The Times*, 5 April 1880, p. 4 e.

15: *Patience*

1. WSG to Alfred Watson, [April 1880], in Watson, *A Sporting and Dramatic Life*, p. 86.

2. Carte to WSG and AS, 8 April 1880, DC/TM.

3. Ibid.

4. Ibid.

5. Ibid.

6. Ibid.

7. Memo 11 May 1880, DC/TM.

8. WSG to AS, 1 November 1880, WSG/BL Add MS 49,338 ff 700–701.

9. WSG to Miss Everard, 9 July 1880, WSG/BL Add MS 49,338 ff 693–694.

10. Carte to AS, 15 September 1880, DC/TM, Letter book 1880–1891, ff 223–226.

11. Grove to Mrs. Sullivan, 21 July 1880, in Young, *George Grove*, p. 166.

12. *Daily Telegraph*, 16 October 1880, p. 3.3.

13. *The Times*, 14 December 1880, p. 8 c.

14. Joseph and Edith Barnby to AS, 7 October 1880, PML.

15. Baily, *Gilbert and Sullivan Book*, p. 173.

16. WSG to AS, 3 December 1880, in Allen, *Sir Arthur Sullivan*, facsimile of copy made by Nancy McIntosh, p. 141.

17. WSG to AS, 1 November 1880, WSG/BL Add MS 49,338 ff 700–701.

18. *Patience*, Gilbert, *Original Plays*, Third Series, p. 91.

19. Ibid.

20. AS Diary, 1 January 1881, BRB.

21. Carte to WSG, 21 December 1880, DC/TM, 1880–1891, ff 252–253.

22. Carte to Fladgate, 9 December 1886, ibid., f 458.

23. Mary Cowan to WSG, 12 December 1881, WSG/BL Add MS 49,331.

24. *The Times*, 2 March 1881, p. 4 c; 3 March 1881, p. 4 e.

25. Ibid., 1 August 1881, p. 4 d.

26. AS Diary, 21 April 1881, BRB.

27. Oscar Wilde to George Grossmith, in Allen, *Sir Arthur Sullivan*, facsimile, p. 147.

28. *Patience*, Gilbert, *Original Plays*, Third Series, p. 91

29. *Daily News*, 25 April 1881, p. 2.3.

30. Ibid.

31. Ibid.

32. *The Times*, 25 April 1881, p. 10 b.

16: The Savoy Theatre

1. Martin-Harvey, *Autobiography*, p. 47.

2. AS Diary, 17 and 18 May 1881, BRB.

3. Carte to AS, 24 May 1881, DC/TM, 1880–1891, ff 267–272.

4. AS Diary, 1881, BRB.

5. AS to his mother, 27 June 1881, PML.

6. Lawrence, *Sir Arthur Sullivan*, pp. 245–247.

7. Carte to WSG, 1 September 1881, DC/TM, 1880–1891, ff 281–282.

8. WSG to Clay, 19 September 1881, WSG/BL Add MS 49,338 f 756.

9. *The Times*, 3 October 1881, p. 7 f.

10. Ibid.

11. Ibid.

12. *The Daily Chronicle*, 11 October 1881, p. 5.7.

17: *Iolanthe*

1. AS Diary, 19 October 1881, BRB.

2. AS Second Diary 1881, BRB.

3. Carte to booking agents in America, 8 November 1881, in Ellmann, *Oscar Wilde*, p. 146.

4. *The Times*, 29 December 1881, p. 4 e.

5. Booking notes, DC/TM.

6. WSG to Clayton, 23 November 1881, WSG/BL Add MS 49,338 f 761.

7. WSG to Michael Gunn, 10 January 1882, DC/TM.

8. WSG to Carte, 14 January 1882, DC/TM.

9. Carte to AS, [February 1882], DC/TM.

10. Ibid.

11. Ibid.

12. AS to his mother, 29 January 1882, PML.

13. AS to his mother, 12 February 1882, PML.

14. AS Diary, 14 January 1882, BRB.

15. Ibid.

16. AS Diary, 6 March 1882, BRB.

17. AS to his mother, 26 February 1882, PML.

18. AS to his mother, 19 March 1882, PML.

19. *The Times*, 25 April 1882, p. 8 e.
20. AS Diary, 25 May 1882, BRB.
21. Ibid.
22. Ibid., 26/27 May 1882.
23. Ibid., 1 June 1882.
24. Ibid., 2 June 1882.
25. Ibid., 5 June 1882.
26. Ibid., 7 June 1882.
27. Ibid., 9 June 1882.
28. Ibid., 13 June 1882.
29. AS Second Diary 1881, BRB.
30. WSG to Carte, 10 August 1882, DC/TM.
31. Ibid.
32. WSG to Carte, 13 October 1882, DC/TM.
33. Ibid.
34. Carte to Helen Lenoir, 11 October 1882, DC/TM, 1880–1891 ff 316–317.
35. Carte to Helen Lenoir, 26 October 1882, ibid., ff 332–333.
36. AS to Alfred Cellier, 29 October 1882, DC/TM.
37. Ibid.
38. Jacobs, *Arthur Sullivan*, p. 184.
39. AS to Alfred Cellier, 29 October 1882, DC/TM.
40. DC/TM.
41. *Era*, 2 December 1882, p. 6.2.
42. "The Fairy Curate," Ellis, *Bab Ballads*, p. 287.
43. *Iolanthe*, Gilbert, *Original Plays*, First Series, p. 243.
44. Bond, *Life and Reminiscences*, p. 110.
45. AS Diary, 25 November 1882, BRB.
46. *The Times*, 27 November 1882, p. 10 c.
47. *Era*, 2 December 1882, p. 6.2.

18: *Princess Ida*

1. Carte to Helen Lenoir, 31 December 1882, DC/TM, 1880–1891, f 340.
2. Ibid.
3. *The Era*, 2 December 1882, p. 4.4.
4. Memorandum Agreement, facsimile in Allen, *Sir Arthur Sullivan*, p. 150.
5. AS Diary, 8 February 1883, BRB.
6. Program, DC/TM.
7. *The Times*, 17 February 1883, p. 4 b.
8. Ibid., 3 January 1883, p. 10 e.
9. Program, DC/TM.
10. AS Diary, 29 April 1883, BRB.
11. Gladstone to AS, 3 May 1883, PML.
12. AS Diary, 7 May 1883, BRB.
13. *Musical Review*, in Goldberg, *Story of Gilbert and Sullivan*, p. 291.
14. AS Diary, 22 May 1883, BRB.
15. Ibid., 4 June 1883, BRB.
16. WSG to Carte, 7 July 1883, DC/TM.
17. AS Diary, 31 July 1883, BRB.

18. Ibid., 13 October 1883, BRB.

19. *The Times*, 12 November 1883, p. 9 f.

20. WSG to Carte, 7 December 1883, DC/TM.

21. AS Diary, 15 December 1883, BRB.

22. Ibid., 31 December 1883, BRB.

23. Ibid., 4 January 1884, BRB.

24. Ibid., 5 January 1884, BRB.

25. *Sunday Times*, 6 January 1884, p. 5.4.

26. *The Times*, 7 January 1884, p. 7 c.

27. Ibid., 9 January 1884, p. 9 f.

28. Ibid., 14 January 1884, p. 9 f.

29. AS to Nina Lehmann, 22 January 1884, PML.

30. AS Diary, 29 January 1884, BRB.

19: *The Mikado*

1. AS to Bret Harte, 2 February 1884, in Goldberg, *Story of Gilbert and Sullivan*, pp. 304–306.

2. Hare to WSG, 3 February 1884, WSG/BL Add MS 49,332 ff 26–27.

3. WSG to Hare, 3 February 1884, ibid., ff 28–29.

4. Carte to AS, 22 March 1884, PML.

5. AS to Carte, 28 March 1884, PML.

6. WSG to AS, 30 March 1884, PML.

7. AS to WSG, 2 April 1884, PML.

8. WSG to AS, 4 April 1884, PML.

9. AS to WSG, 7 April 1884, PML.

10. Ibid.

11. AS Diary, 10 April 1884, BRB.

12. WSG to AS, ?10 April 1884, PML.

13. WSG to AS, 3 May 1884, PML.

14. AS to WSG, 4 May 1884, PML.

15. WSG to AS, 5 May 1884, PML.

16. AS to WSG, 6 May 1884, PML.

17. WSG to AS, 8 May 1884, PML.

18. AS to WSG, 8 May 1884, PML.

19. AS Diary, 9 May 1884, BRB.

20. Browne, *W. S. Gilbert*, p. 68.

21. AS Diary, 21 May 1884, BRB.

22. WSG to Burnand, 27 May 1884, PML.

23. AS Diary, 30 April 1884, BRB.

24. Ibid., 28 April 1884, BRB.

25. Emmerson, *Arthur Darling*, p. 119.

26. Carte to WSG, 5 August 1884, DC/TM, 1880–1891, ff 358–364.

27. Carte to WSG, 18 August 1884, ibid., ff 366–369.

28. Carte to AS, 29 August 1884, ibid., ff 370–371.

29. Ibid.

30. AS Diary, 11 October 1884, BRB.

31. *The Times*, 13 October 1884, p. 4 c.

32. AS to Spark, October 1884, Spark and Bennett, *Leeds Music Festivals*, p. 283.

33. AS Diary, 20 November 1884, BRB.

34. Ibid., 8 December 1884, BRB.

35. Ibid., 11—21 December 1884, BRB.

36. MS lyrics, DC/TM.

37. *The Times*, 10 January 1885, p. 6 d.

38. MS lyrics, DC/TM.

39. Ibid.

40. *The Mikado*, Gilbert, *Original Plays*, Third Series, p. 175.

41. *New York Daily Tribune*, 9 August 1885, p. 9.1.

42. Carte to AS, 30 October 1884, DC/TM 1880–1891, ff 377–378; Carte to Leonora Braham, 18 July 1885, ibid., ff 429–430.

43. *The Era*, 17 January 1885, p. 10.1.

44. William Lacy to AS, 2 February 1885, PML.

45. Jacobs, *Arthur Sullivan*, p. 212.

46. Sullivan's will, PRO/Somerset House.

47. *The Era*, 21 February 1885, p. 14.2.

48. AS Diary, 2 March 1885, BRB.

49. Ibid., 3 March 1885, BRB.

50. Ibid., 11 March 1885, BRB.

51. Ibid., 14 March 1885, BRB.

52. Barrington, *Rutland Barrington, By Himself*, p. 55.

53. WSG to Algernon Mitford, 17 March 1885, in Stedman, *W. S. Gilbert*, p. 225.

54. *The Daily News*, 16 March 1885, p. 2.4.

55. Allen, *First Night Gilbert and Sullivan*, p. 239.

20: *Ruddigore*

1. Shirley Nicholson, *A Victorian Household*, p. 64.

2. Carte to Stetson, 13 June 1885, DC/TM, 1880–1891, f 407.

3. Ibid., ff 409–410.

4. Ibid., f 405.

5. Carte to WSG, 31 May 1885, ibid., typed copy, ff 271–281.

6. WSG to Carte, 1 June 1885, DC/TM.

7. Carte to WSG, 2 June 1885, DC/TM 1880–1891 , ff 397–398.

8. Carte to WSG, 5 June 1885, ibid., ff 399–401.

9. WSG to AS, 21 June 1885, PML.

10. Carte to Stetson, 13 June 1885, DC/TM, ff 412–413.

11. Carte to AS, 23 June 1885, DC/TM, 1880–1891, ff 415–416.

12. AS Diary, 11 July 1885, BRB.

13. Ibid., 18 July 1885, BRB.

14. Ibid., 4/5 August 1885, BRB.

15. Ibid., 7 August 1885, BRB.

16. Ibid.

17. Thorne, *Jots*, p. 78; Passenger List, Cunard Line—*R.M.S. Aurania*, DC/TM.

18. Program, DC/TM.

19. *New York Times*, 30 September 1885, p. 4.7.

20. AS Diary, 24 September 1885, BRB.

21. *New York Times*, 25 September 1885, p. 5.2.

22. Thorne, *Jots*, p. 81.

23. Carte to Leonora Braham, 18 July 1885, DC/TM, 1880–1891, ff 429–430.

24. Carte to WSG, 18 November 1885, ibid., ff 438–441.

25. WSG to Carte, 19 November 1885, DC/TM.

26. Carte to WSG, 21 November 1885, typed transcript, DC/TM.

27. Carte to AS, 21 November 1885, DC/TM, 1880–1891, f 437 B/C.

28. Carte paid Desprez £20 for *The Carp*, 13 February 1886, DC/TM.

29. AS Diary, 12 March 1886, BRB.

30. AS to Spark, 3 February 1886, in Spark and Bennett, *Leeds Music Festivals*, p. 283.

31. Carte to AS, 23 March 1886, DC/TM, 1880–1891, ff 442–443.

32. AS Diary, 23 March 1886, BRB.

33. Ibid., 1 April 1886, BRB.

34. *The Times*, 3 June 1886, p. 6 b.

35. William, prince of Prussia, to AS, 3 July 1886, PML.

36. AS to Spark, 30 July 1886, in Spark and Bennett, *Leeds Music Festivals*, p. 286.

37. Ibid., 16 and 24 August 1886.

38. AS Diary, 26 August 1886, BRB.

39. *Liverpool Mercury*, 18 October 1886, p. 7.1.

40. *The Times*, 18 October 1886, p. 8 b.

41. WSG to AS, 21 October 1886, PML.

42. Carte to Helen Lenoir, 27 November 1886, DC/TM, 1880–1891, ff 446–447.

43. *The Times*, 24 January 1887, p. 4 c.

44. Barrington, *Rutland Barrington, By Himself*, p. 59.

45. *The Times*, 24 January 1887, p. 4 c.

46. Ibid.

47. *Daily News*, 24 January 1887, p. 3.5.

48. *The Times*, 24 January 1887, p. 4 c.

49. *Graphic*, 29 January 1887, p. 107.1.

50. WSG to AS, 23 January 1887, PML.

51. WSG to Alfred E. T. Watson, 24 January 1887, in Watson, *A Sporting and Dramatic Life*, p. 85.

21: "A Fresh Start"

1. Lytton, *Secrets of a Savoyard*, pp. 36–39.

2. *The Times*, 16 February 1887, p. 9 f.

3. AS Diary, 22/23 February 1887, BRB.

4. Carte to AS, 5 March 1887, DC/TM, 1880–1891, ff 472–479.

5. Carte to AS, 8 March 1887, DC/TM, 1880–1891, ff 482–484.

6. Carte to Carl Rosa, 11 March 1887, ibid., f 485.

7. Carte to AS, 5 March 1887, DC/TM, 1880–1891, ff 472–479.

8. *The Times*, 11 May 1887, p. 6 f.

9. AS Diary, 25 March 1887, BRB.

10. Ibid., 26 March 1887, BRB.

11. Ibid.

12. Ibid., 2 April 1887, BRB.

13. Ibid., 8 April, BRB.

14. *The Times*, 8 May 1887, p. 6 f.

15. AS to John Stainer, 4 May 1887, PML.

16. WSG to Carte, 28 [August 1887], DC/TM.

17. WSG to Marion Johnson, 25 July 1885, DC/TM.

18. AS to Marion Johnson, 30 April 1885, typed copy, DC/TM.

19. Watson, *A Sporting and Dramatic Life*, p. 89.

20. AS Diary, 4 September 1887, BRB.

21. AS Diary, 10 October 1887, BRB.

22. Ibid., 13 October 1887, BRB.

23. AS to Grove, 12 October 1887, PML.

24. AS Diary, 31 October 1887, BRB.

25. Ibid., 3 November 1887, BRB.

26. Carte to WSG, 8 October 1887, DC/TM, 1880–1891, f 499.

27. Ibid.

28. WSG to AS, 26 October 1887, PML.

29. Carte to AS, 5 November 1887, DC/TM, 1880–1891, f 502.

30. Ibid.

31. AS to Otto Goldschmidt, 7 November 1887, PML.

32. AS Diary, 12 November 1887, BRB.

33. *The Times*, 14 November 1887, p. 7 d.

34. AS to Stanford, 15 November 1887, in Young, *Sir Arthur Sullivan*, p. 148.

35. AS Diary, 14 December 1887, BRB.

36. Ibid., 25 December 1887, BRB.

37. Ibid., 31 December 1887, BRB.

38. WSG to AS, 26 February 1888, PML

39. WSG to Mary Anderson, 22 January 1888, in Dark and Grey, *W. S. Gilbert*, pp. 155–156.

40. WSG to Carte, 6 February 1888, DC/TM.

41. WSG to Jessie Bond, 16 January 1888, PML.

42. WSG to W. H. Kendal, 7 February 1888, WSG/BL Add MS 49,332 ff 38–39.

43. Carte to AS, 13 February 1888, DC/TM 1880–1891 ff 513–515.

44. WSG to AS, 19 February 1888, PML.

22: "A New Departure"—*The Yeomen of the Guard*

1. WSG to Jessie Bond, 11 February 1888, in Bond, *Life and Reminiscences*, pp. 84–85.

2. Carte to WSG, 19 March 1888, DC/TM 1880–1891 ff 517–523.

3. Carte to WSG, 20 March 1888, ibid., ff 529–531.

4. Carte to WSG, 19 March 1888, ibid., ff 517–523.

5. Carte to AS, 22 March 1888, ibid., f 532.

6. Carte to AS, 24 March 1888, ibid., f 534.

7. *The Times*, 19 March 1888, p. 4 e.

8. Ibid., 22 March 1888, p. 5 f.

9. WSG to Mrs. Barnby, in Neilson, *This for Remembrance*, pp. 37–38.

10. AS Diary, 11 April 1888, BRB.

11. Ibid., 12 April 1888, BRB.

12. *Survey of London*, vol. 18, The Strand (1937), ed. Sir George Galter and Walter H. Godfrey.

13. AS Diary, 28 April 1888, BRB.

14. AS to Millais, 30 April 1888, in Allen, *Sir Arthur Sullivan*, p. 135.

15. AS Diary, 8 May 1888, BRB.

16. *The Times*, 9 June 1888, p. 17 b.

17. AS Diary, 8 June 1888, BRB.
18. Ibid., 23 June 1888, BRB.
19. WSG to AS, 15 August 1888, PML.
20. AS Diary, 16 August 1888, BRB.
21. Ibid.
22. Ibid., 21 August 1888, BRB.
23. WSG/BL Add MS 49,298.
24. WSG to AS, 13 September 1888, PML.
25. AS Diary, 15 September 1888, BRB.
26. Note by Courtice Pounds in DC/TM.
27. AS Diary, 22 September 1888, BRB.
28. Ibid., 28 September 1888, BRB.
29. Ibid., 1 October 1888, BRB.
30. Ibid., 2 October 1888, BRB.
31. WSG to AS, 3 October 1888, PML.
32. Bond, *Life and Reminiscences*, p. 148.
33. Stedman, *W. S. Gilbert*, p. 251.
34. AS Diary, 3 October 1888, BRB.
35. *The Times*, 4 October 1888, p. 11 a.
36. *The Era*, 6 October 1888, p. 9.1.
37. The *Daily Telegraph*, 4 October 1888, p. 7.7.
38. *Morning Advertiser*, 4 October 1888, p. 3.5.
39. *The Times*, 4 October 1888, p. 11 a.
40. Goldberg, *Story of Gilbert and Sullivan*, p. 52.
41. Wood, *My Life of Music*, p. 54.

23: "I Have Lost the Liking for Writing Comic Opera"

1. DC/TM, 1880–1891, ff 540–542.
2. WSG to W. Emden, 22 October 1888, WSG/BM Add MS 49,335 f 57.
3. WSG to Hare, 22 November 1889, WSG/BL Add MS 49,335 f 86.
4. *Graphic*, 25 February 1922, p. 214; Lytton, *Secrets of a Savoyard*, pp. 46–48.
5. *The Times*, 20 October 1888, p. 9 f.
6. Stedman, *W. S. Gilbert*, p. 253.
7. *Brantinghame Hall*, Gilbert, *Original Plays*, Fourth Series, p. 267.
9. WSG to Carte, 30 November 1888, DC/TM.
9. Carte to WSG, 2 December 1888, DC/TM, 1880–1891, f 580.
10. *The Times*, 31 October 1888, p. 10 f.
11. WSG to Carte, 25 December 1888, DC/TM.
12. Carte to WSG, 28 December 1888, DC/TM, 1880–1891, ff 575–576.
13. AS Diary, 9 January 1889, BRB.
14. Ibid., 17 January 1889, BRB.
15. Ibid., 18 January 1889, BRB.
16. AS to Smythe, 1 March 1889, PML.
17. WSG to AS, 20 February 1889, PML.
18. Ibid.
19. Ibid.
20. AS to WSG, 12 March 1889, PML.

21. Ibid.
22. WSG to AS, 19 March 1889, PML.
23. AS to Carte, 26 March 1889, DC/TM.
24. WSG to Carte, 29 March 1889, DC/TM.
25. Carte to AS, telegram, DC/TM 1880–1891, f 590.
26. AS to WSG, 27 March 1889, PML.
27. WSG to AS, 31 March 1889, PML.
29. Carte to WSG, 24 April 1889, DC/TM 1880–1891, ff 595–596.
30. AS to WSG, 24 April 1889, PML.

24: *The Gondoliers*

1. AS Diary, 9 May 1889, BRB.
2. Ibid., 13 May 1889, BRB.
3. Ibid., 25 May 1889, BRB.
4. Ibid., 7 June 1889, BRB.
5. Ibid., 8 June 1889, BRB.
6. Carte to WSG, 18 June 1889, DC/TM, 1880–1891, ff 603–604.
7. WSG to AS, 21 June 1889, PML.
8. AS Diary, 31 July 1889, BRB.
9. WSG to AS, 8 August 1889, PML.
10. WSG/BL Add MS 49,298.
11. WSG to AS, 10 August 1889, PML.
12. WSG/BL Add MS 49,298.
13. WSG to AS, 9 November 1889, PML.
14. WSG/BL Add MS 49,298.
15. WSG to Carte, 14 August 1889, DC/TM.
16. WSG to Sullivan, 8 August 1889, PML.
17. *The Times*, 16 September 1889, p. 6 c.
18. *The Times*, 8 November 1889, p. 10 f.
19. *The Gondoliers*, Gilbert, *Original Plays*, Third Series, p. 307.
20. WSG to AS, 12 September 1889, PML.
21. MS lyrics, DC/TM.
22. WSG to AS, 12 September 1889, PML.
23. WSG to AS, 22 September 1889, PML.
24. MS lyrics, DC/TM.
25. WSG to AS, 22 September 1889, PML.
27. WSG to AS, 11 October 1889, PML.
28. WSG to AS, 25 October 1889, PML.
29. AS Diary, 24 November 1889, BRB.
30. Ibid., 2 December 1889, BRB.
31. Ibid., 3 December, BRB.
32. Ibid., 5 December 1889, BRB.
33. Ibid., 7 December 1889, BRB.
34. *Sunday Times*, 8 December 1889, p. 5.6.
35. *The Times*, 9 December 1889, p. 12 a.
36. *Sunday Times*, 8 December 1889, p. 5.6.
37. *Daily News*, 9 December 1889, p. 3.1.

38. *Sunday Times*, 8 December 1889, p. 5.6.

39. *Illustrated London News*, 14 December 1889, p. 770.1.

40. AS Diary, 7 December 1889, BRB.

25: Carpets, Etc.

1. WSG to AS, 8 December 1889, PML.

2. AS to WSG, quoted in WSG to AS, 8 May 1890, PML.

3. Barrington to WSG, DC/TM.

4. WSG to Carte, 11 December 1889, ibid.

5. *The Daily News*, 4 January 1890, p. 3.

6. Will of William Gilbert, of The Close, Salisbury, PRO/Somerset House.

7. Helen Carte to WSG, 13 November 1889, DC/TM, 1880–1891 ff 610–611.

8. *New York Times*, 27 January 1890, p. 8.2.

9. WSG to Carte, 11 February 1890, DC/TM.

10. WSG to Helen Carte, 8 April 1890, ibid.

11. WSG to Helen Carte, 12 April 1890, ibid.

12. DC/TM 1880–1891, 8 April 1890, f 625.

13. Carte to AS, 18 April 1890, ibid., ff 641–642.

14. Helen Carte to WSG, 7/8 May 1890, ibid., ff 661–671.

15. Ibid.

16. Ibid.

17. WSG to AS, 22 April 1890, WSG/BL Add MS 49,333 ff 64–68.

18. Helen Carte to WSG, 7/8 May 1890, DC/TM, 1880–1891 ff 661–671.

19. Ibid.

20. Ibid.

21. WSG to AS, 22 April 1890, PML.

22. Carte to AS, 5 May 1890, DC/TM 1880–1891 ff 648–649.

23. Helen Carte to WSG, 7/8 May 1890, DC/TM 1880–1891 ff 661–671.

24. WSG to AS, 22 April 1890, PML.

25. AS to WSG, 23 April 1890, PML.

26. AS Diary, 23 April 1890, BRB.

27. Ibid., 26 April 1890, BRB.

28. Carte to WSG, 26 April 1890, DC/TM 1880–1891 ff 628–637.

29. Carte to WSG, 28 April 1890, ibid., f 638.

30. AS Memo, 27 April 1890, in Jacobs, *Arthur Sullivan*, p. 317.

31. WSG to Carte, 30 April 1890, DC/TM.

32. Referred to in WSG to AS, 8 May 1890, PML.

33. Carte to AS, 5 May, DC/TM 1880–1891 ff 648–649.

34. WSG to Carte, 5 May 1890, ibid., f 654.

35. WSG to AS, 5 May 1890, PML.

36. Carte to WSG, 6 May 1890, DC/TM 1880–1891 ff 650–651.

37. AS Diary, 6 May 1890, BRB. Jacobs, p. 318, edited this diary entry to read, "How I have stood him so long I can't understand."

38. AS to WSG, 6 May 1890, PML.

39. Ibid.

40. Carte to AS, 7 May 1890, DC/TM 1880–1891 ff 652–653.

41. Ibid.

42. Helen Carte to WSG, 7/8 May 1890, ibid., ff 661–671.

43. WSG to AS, 8 May 1890, PML.

44. AS to WSG, 9 May 1890, PML.

45. WSG to Horace Sedger, 9 May 1890, WSG/BL Add MS 49,332 ff 44–45.

46. WSG/BL Add MS 49,332 ff 48–49.

47. Carte to Frederick Cowen, 13 May 1890, DC/TM 1880–1891 f 674.

48. *New York Times*, 16 May 1890, p. 1.6.

49. Ibid., 10 June 1890, p. 4.7.

50. AS to WSG, 16 May 1890, PML.

51. *Pall Mall Gazette*, 20 May 1890, p. 1.2.

52. Ibid., 21 May 1890, p. 2.1.

53. *The Star*, 23 May 1890, p. 2.7.

54. Carte to AS, 7 June 1890, DC/TM

55. AS to WSG, 16 July 1890, WSG/BL Add MS 49,333 ff 75–76.

56. AS to WSG, 5 August 1890, letter used as exhibit by Gilbert in court, *Daily News*, 4 September 1890, p. 7.1.

57. Cause Book 1890, J 15, 1948, PRO.

58. Carte to AS, 13 August 1890, DC/TM 1880–1891 ff 695–702.

59. Cause Book 1890, J 15, 1948, PRO.

60. *The Times*, 21 August 1890.

61. Carte to Frank Stanley, 22 August 1890, DC/TM 1880–1891 ff 703–704.

62. Cause Book 1890, J 15, 1948, PRO.

63. *The Times*, 4 September 1890 p. 3 d; *The Daily News*, 4 September 1890, p. 7.1.

64. Ibid.

26: Disentangling the Knot

1. WSG to AS, 6 September 1890, PML.

2. AS to WSG, 8 September 1890, WSG/BL Add MS 49,333 ff 77–80.

3. Carte to Helen Carte, 19 September, DC/TM 1880–1891 ff 712–721.

4. WSG to Helen Carte, 6 September 1890, DC/TM.

5. Ibid.

6. AS Diary, 6 September 1890, BRB.

7. Helen Carte to WSG, 6 September 1890, DC/TM 1880–1891 f 705.

8. AS to WSG, 8 September 1890, WSG/BL Add MS 49,333 ff 77–80.

9. WSG to AS, 9 September 1890, ibid., ff 81–82.

10. Helen Carte to WSG, 10 September 1890, DC/TM 1880–1891 ff 708–709.

11. Details of their meeting: Helen Carte to WSG, 27 September 1890, DC/TM ff 165–181.

12. Carte to Helen Carte, 19 September 1890, ibid., 1880–1891 ff 712–721.

13. AS Diary, 16 September 1890, BRB.

14. Carte to Helen Carte, 19 September 1890, DC/TM 1880–91 ff 712–721.

15. Helen Carte to WSG, 19 September 1890, DC/TM.

16. WSG to AS, 24 September 1890, PML.

17. Helen Carte to WSG, 27 September 1890, DC/TM ff 165–181.

18. WSG to Helen Carte, 30 September 1890, DC/TM.

19. AS Diary, 12 October 1890, BRB.

20. WSG to AS, 12 October 1890, PML.

21. WSG to AS, 14 October 1890, WSG/BL Add MS 49,333, ff 83–84.

22. WSG to AS, 31 January 1891, ibid., ff 87–90.

23. AS Diary, 14 October 1890, BRB.

24. Helen Carte to WSG, 15 October 1890, DC/TM.

25. Helen Carte to Stanley, 24 October 1890, DC/TM, 1882–1891 f 206.

26. Helen Carte to Stanley, 27 October 1890, ibid., ff 208–211.

27. Helen Carte to WSG, 30 October 1890, ibid., ff 214–217.

28. Helen Carte to AS, 5 November 1890, ibid., ff 221–228.

29. Carte to WSG, 6 November 1890, ibid., f 229.

30. AS Diary, 11 November 1890, BRB.

31. Carte to WSG, 18 November 1890, DC/TM 1882–1891 ff 235–238.

32. AS Diary, 13 December 1890, BRB.

33. WSG to Jessie Bond, 7 December 1890, in Bond, *Life and Reminiscences*, pp. 167–168.

34. WSG to Alfred Cellier, 13 January 1891, WSG/BL Add MS 49,332 ff 60–61.

35. AS to WSG, 28 January 1891, WSG/BL Add MS 49,333 ff 85–86.

36. WSG to AS, 31 January 1891, ibid., ff 87–90.

37. AS to WSG, 31 January 1891, ibid., ff 91–93.

38. WSG to AS, 31 January 1891, ibid., ff 95–96.

39. AS Diary, 31 January 1891, BRB.

40. WSG to AS, 31 January 1891, WSG/BL Add MS 49,333 f 94.

41. AS Diary, 31 January 1891, BRB.

42. AS to [music critics], 22 January 1891, DC/TM.

43. Princess Louise to AS, 2 February 1891, PML.

44. AS to Princess Louise, 4 February 1891, PML.

45. WSG to AS, 1 February 1891, WSG/BL Add MS 49,333 ff 97–98.

46. AS to WSG, 4 February 1891, ibid., f 99.

47. WSG to AS, 5 February 1891, ibid., ff 100–101.

48. WSG to Helen Carte, 12 February 1891, DC/TM.

49. Clerk of the Peace to WSG, 1 May 1891, WSG/BL Add MS 49,332 f 81.

50. Harriet Cellier to WSG, 6 May 1891, ibid., ff 77–78.

51. WSG to AS, 28 May 1891, ibid., ff 103–104.

52. AS Diary, 25 May 1891, BRB.

53. Bond, *Life and Reminiscences*, p. 169.

54. Carte to Bret Harte, 17 June 1891, DC/TM 1882–1891 f 246.

55. Memo, DC/TM.

56. AS to Ethel Smyth, 10 August 1891, in Smyth, *Impressions that Remained*, p. 284.

57. WSG to Helen Carte, 4 August 1891, DC/TM.

58. Alfred Cellier to WSG, 24 September 1891, WSG/BL Add MS 49,332 ff 92–93.

59. WSG to Alfred Cellier, 25 September 1891, ibid., ff 94–95.

60. AS to WSG, 4 October 1891, WSG/BL Add MS 49,333 ff 105–106.

61. WSG to AS, 5 October 1891, ibid., ff 107–108.

62. AS to WSG, 6 October 1891, ibid., f 109.

63. WSG to AS, 11 October 1891, ibid., ff 112–113.

64. AS Diary, 12 October 1891, BRB.

27: Picking up the Thread

1. AS to WSG, 14 October 1891, WSG/BL Add MS 49,333 f 114.

2. WSG to AS, 15 October 1891, ibid., ff 115–116.

3. AS to WSG, 2 November 1891, ibid., f 117.

4. WSG to Helen Carte, 4 November 1891, DC/TM.

5. WSG to Helen Carte, 3 November 1891, DC/TM.

6. WSG to Helen Carte, 12 October 1891, typed copy, ibid.

7. WSG to Marion Johnson, [19 November 1891], ibid.

8. *Pall Mall Gazette*, 26 December 1891, p. 1.

9. AS to François Cellier, 29 December 1891, in Hyman, *Sullivan and his Satellites*, p. 104.

10. E. Le Neve to WSG, 5 January 1892, WSG/BL Add MS 49,332 ff 104–105.

11. Lina Hicks to WSG, 9 January 1892, ibid., ff 106–107.

12. Horace Sedger to WSG, 28 January 1892, ibid., ff 109–110.

13. WSG to Sedger, 29 January 1892, ibid., ff 111–112.

14. *The Times*, 14 April 1892, p. 8 a.

15. Ibid.

16. Ibid., 15 April 1892, p. 4 e.

17. WSG to AS, 27 April 1892, ibid., Add MS 49,333 ff 118–119.

18. Ibid.

19. WSG to Helen Carte, 17 June 1892, DC/TM.

20. AS to WSG, August 1892, WSG/BL Add MS 49,333 f 120.

21. AS to WSG, 9 August 1892, ibid., ff 121–122.

22. WSG to AS, 31 August 1892, WSG/BL Add MS 49,330 ff 126–127.

23. AS to Jessie Bond, 16 September 1892, in Bond, *Life and Reminiscences*, pp. 171–172.

24. Scott, *Edward German*, p. 59.

25. WSG to AS, 20 October 1892, WSG/BL Add MS 49,333 ff 128–129.

26. AS to WSG, 20 October 1892, ibid., f 130.

27. WSG to AS, 21 October 1892, ibid., ff 131–132.

28. AS to WSG, 25 October 1892, ibid., ff 133–134.

29. Ibid.

30. AS to WSG, 3 November 1892, ibid., ff 135–137.

31. Ibid.

32. Ibid.

33. WSG to AS, 4 November 1892, ibid., f 138.

34. AS to WSG, 8 November 1892, ibid., f 139.

35. WSG to AS, 9 November 1892, ibid., ff 140–142.

36. AS to WSG, 11 November 1892, ibid., f 143.

37. Ibid.

38. WSG to AS, 12 November 1892, ibid., ff 146–148.

39. AS to WSG, 14 November 1892, ibid., ff 149–150.

40. WSG to AS, 15 November 1892, ibid., f 151.

41. AS to WSG, 12 December 1892, ibid., ff 154–155.

42. AS to WSG, 22 December 1892, ibid., ff 158–159.

43. WSG to AS, 25 December 1892, ibid., ff 160–161.

44. WSG to AS, 7 January 1893, ibid., ff 162–163.

45. AS to WSG, 19 January 1893, ibid., f 168.

46. AS Diary, 27 January 1893, BRB.

47. WSG to "Dearest Kits," [28 January 1893], WSG/BL Add MS 49,345.

28: *Utopia, Limited*

1. WSG to AS, 4 March 1893, PML.

2. WSG to Carte, 12 March 1893, DC/TM.

3. WSG to Carte, 9 May 1893, DC/TM.

4. AS to Nina Lehmann, 13 May 1893, PML.

5. AS Diary, 27 May 1893, BRB.

6. WSG to Helen Carte, 3 June 1893, DC/TM.

7. AS Diary, 19 June 1893, BRB.

8. WSG to AS, 20 June 1893, PML.

9. Press cuttings, WSG/BL Add MS 49,345.

10. AS Diary, 30 June 1893, BRB.

11. Ibid.

12. WSG to Charles Harris, 29 June 1893, WSG/BL Add MS 49,332 f 140.

13. AS to WSG, 1 July 1893, ibid., Add MS 49,333 ff 169–171.

14. WSG to AS, 3 July 1893, ibid., ff 173–174.

15. WSG to Helen Carte, 20 July 1893, DC/TM.

16. AS Diary, 21 July 1893, BRB.

17. WSG to AS, [25 July 1893], WSG/BL Add MS 49,333 f 177.

18. AS to WSG, 26 July 1893, ibid., ff 175–176.

19. WSG to AS, 27 July 1893, PML.

20. WSG to Helen Carte, 4 August 1893, DC/TM.

21. WSG to Helen Carte, 4 August 1893, ibid.

22. WSG to Carte, 8 August 1893, ibid.

23. AS Diary, 6 August 1893, BRB.

24. WSG to Carte, 8 August 1893, DC/TM.

25. WSG to AS, 15 August 1893, PML.

26. AS Diary, 14 August 1893, BRB.

27. Ibid., 15 August 1893.

28. Ibid., 16 August 1893.

29. Ibid., 17 August 1893.

30. Ibid., 18 August 1893.

31. WSG to Helen Carte, 5 September 1893, DC/TM.

32. AS to Frank Cellier, 1 September 1893, ibid.

33. WSG to Helen Carte, 5 September 1893, DC/TM.

34. AS to Helen Carte, [September 1893], ibid.

35. AS Diary, 12 September 1893, BRB.

36. WSG to AS, 30 August 1893, PML.

37. AS Diary, 7 October 1893, BRB.

38. *Globe*, 9 October 1893, p. 3.4.

39. *Sunday Times*, 8 October 1893, p. 4.6.

40. AS Diary, 7 October 1893, BRB.

41. WSG to AS, 9 October 1893, in Wolfson, *Final Curtain*, p. 57.

42. WSG to Helen Carte, 17 October 1893, DC/TM.

43. WSG to AS, 5 November 1893, PML.

29: *The Grand Duke*

1. WSG to Carte, 12 December 1893, DC/TM.

2. Ibid.

3. Nancy McIntosh Diary, 1 January 1894, WSG/BL Add MS 49,345.

4. AS Diary, 5 January 1894, BRB.

5. Nancy McIntosh Diary, 8 January 1894, WSG/BL Add MS 49,335.

6. WSG to Carte, 11 January 1894, DC/TM.

7. Ibid.

8. Ibid.

9. WSG to Carte, 11 January 1894, DC/TM.

10. WSG to Carte, 18 January 1894, DC/TM.

11. Nancy McIntosh Diary, WSG/BL Add MS 49,335.

12. Ibid.

13. WSG to Carte, 2 March 1894, DC/TM.

14. Nancy McIntosh Diary, 8 March 1894, WSG/BL Add MS 49,335.

15. Ibid., 10 March 1894.

16. Ibid., 13 March 1894.

17. Ibid., 7 April 1894.

18. WSG to Helen Carte, 6 September 1894, DC/TM.

19. WSG to Helen Carte, 8 September 1894, ibid.

20. WSG to Helen Carte, 10 September 1894, ibid.

21. WSG to Helen Carte, 13 September 1894, ibid.

22. *Era*, 28 July 1894, p. 10.

23. *The Times*, 23 October 1894, p. 6 e.

24. WSG to Helen Carte, 4 December 1895, ibid., 21/97; WSG/BL Add MS 49,335 f 183.

25. *The Times*, 20 December 1895, p. 13 f.

26. WSG to Lord Shand, 24 December 1895, WSG/BL Add MS 49,335 f 198.

27. WSG to Helen Carte, 4 November 1894, DC/TM.

28. AS to Carte, 27 December 1894, ibid.

29. Bertram Ellis to WSG, 28 November 1894, WSG/BL Add MS 49,332 f 166.

30. WSG to Ellis, 14 January 1895, ibid., ff 175–176.

31. For a fuller discussion of this theory, see Wolfson, *The Final Curtain*, pp. 68–69; and for an earlier suggestion that the plot was partly borrowed from Tom Taylor's short story "The Duke's Difficulties," see Stedman, p. 307.

32. AS to Nancy McIntosh, 30 April 1895, WSG/BL Add MS 49,345.

33. AS to WSG, 11 August 1896, WSG/BL Add MS 49,333.

34. Helen Carte to AS, 14 August 1895, PML.

35. *The Sketch*, 15 April 1896, p. 522. Ilka Palmay has often been referred to incorrectly as von Palmay.

36. WSG to Jessie Bond, 25 October 1895, in Bond, *Life and Reminiscences*, pp. 172–173.

37. Ibid.

38. *The Times*, 7 December 1895, p. 8 a.

39. AS to Helen Carte, [7 November 1895], DC/TM.

40. Ibid. Geraldine Ulmar played Yum-Yum in the 1888 revival.

41. AS to Wilfred Bendall, 16 November 1895, PML.

42. *The Times*, 28 November 1895, p. 5 f.

43. WSG to Mrs. Bram Stoker, 9 March 1896, PML.

44. *The Times*, 9 March 1896.

45. AS Diary, 7 March 1896, BRB.

30: They Went On . . . "But Did Not Speak to Each Other"

1. AS to Burnand, 12 March 1896, PML.

2. *The Grand Duke*, Bradley, *The Complete Annotated Gilbert and Sullivan*, p. 1187.

3. WSG to Helen Carte, 3 May 1896, DC/TM.

4. AS to Helen Carte, 22 July 1896, DC/TM.

5. Ibid.

6. AS Diary, 23 August 1896, BRB.

7. Ibid., 7 August 1896.

8. AS to Herbert Sullivan, 22 August 1896, PML.

9. *Utopia Limited*, Gilbert, *Original Plays*, Third Series, p. 405.

10. AS to Herbert Sullivan, 22 August 1896, PML.

11. *The Times*, 2 November 1896, p. 6 f.

12. Ibid.

13. WSG to Helen Carte, 9 November 1896, DC/TM.

14. WSG to Helen Carte, 24 November 1896, DC/TM.

15. WSG to Helen Carte, 24 November 1896, DC/TM.

16. WSG to Helen Carte, 25 November 1896, DC/TM.

17. WSG to Helen Carte, 28 November 1896, DC/TM.

18. AS to Herbert Sullivan, 30 December 1896, PML.

19. AS Diary, 6 April 1897, BRB.

20. WSG to Helen Carte, 11 April 1897, DC/TM.

21. AS Diary, 5 May 1897, BRB.

22. Ibid., 25 May 1897.

23. Ibid., 5 July 1897.

24. Ibid., 14 August 1897.

25. Ibid., 15 August 1897.

26. Ibid., 16 August 1897.

27. Ibid., 17 August 1897.

28. Ibid., 5 September 1897.

29. *The Times*, 28 September 1897, p. 10 c.

30. WSG to Kitty, 4 October 1897, WSG/BL Add MS 49,345.

31. *The Times*, 28 September 1897, p. 4 f.

32. Ibid., 29 March 1898, p. 12 a.

33. *Era*, 16 October 1897.

34. WSG to Sydney Grundy, 21 October 1897, WSG/BL Add MS 49,332 ff 227–228.

35. AS to Carte, 14 December 1897, DC/TM.

36. Ibid.

37. AS Diary, 15 December 1897, BRB.

38. AS to Helen Carte, 3 February 1898, DC/TM.

39. Ibid.

40. Comyns Carr, *Some Eminent Victorians*, pp. 265–286.

41. WSG to Helen Carte, 18 March 1898, DC/TM.

42. *The Times*, 23 March 1898, p. 7 f.

43. Ibid.

44. Ibid., 29 March 1898, p. 12 a; 30 March 1898.

45. WSG to Helen Carte, 28 March 1898, DC/TM.

46. WSG to Helen Carte, 31 March 1898, DC/TM.

47. AS to Bendall, 21 April 1898, PML.

48. Ibid.

49. AS to Helen Carte, [May 1898], DC/TM.

50. Ibid.

51. AS to Helen Carte, DC/TM.

52. Rudyard Kipling to AS, 14 May 1898, PML.

53. WSG to Helen Carte, 22 November 1899, DC/TM.

54. WSG to Helen Carte, 16 July 1898, DC/TM.

55. AS to James Davis, 1 July 1898, in Jacobs, *Arthur Sullivan*, p. 387.

56. WSG to Helen Carte, 23 September 1898, DC/TM.

57. Ibid.

58. Edward Elgar to AS, [29 September 1898], in Allen, *Sir Arthur Sullivan*, p. 179.

59. Elgar to Herbert Sullivan, 29 December 1926, in Young, *Sir Arthur Sullivan*, p. 216.

60. AS Diary, 8 October 1898, BRB.

61. Ibid.

62. AS Diary, 11 November 1898, BRB.

63. Ibid., 17 November 1898.

31: "I am Sorry to Leave"

1. AS to Bendall, in Jacobs, *Arthur Sullivan*, p. 392.

2. *The Times*, 2 May 1899, p. 9 f.

3. WSG to Helen Carte, 3 May 1899, DC/TM.

4. Helen Carte to AS, in Jacobs, *Arthur Sullivan*, pp. 393–394.

5. WSG to Helen Carte, 22 September 1899, DC/TM.

6. AS Diary, 13 November 1899, BRB.

7. Lady Randolph Churchill, *Reminiscences*, p. 309.

8. AS Diary, 27 November 1899, BRB.

9. Ibid., 28 November 1899.

10. Ibid., 29 November 1899.

11. *Daily Telegraph*, 30 November 1899, p. 10.7.

12. WSG to Helen Carte, 22 November 1899, DC/TM.

13. WSG to Dorothy de Michele, 24 December 1899, in Dark and Grey, *W. S. Gilbert*, pp. 186–187.

14. AS to Helen Carte, 20 March 1900, DC/TM.

15. Ibid.

16. Ibid.

17. AS Diary, 13 May 1900, BRB.

18. Ibid., 11 August 1898.

19. Kipling to AS, 27 May 1900, PML.

20. AS Diary, 7 June 1900, BRB.

21. WSG to Helen Carte, 5 June 1900, DC/TM.

22. WSG to Helen Carte, 6 June 1900, ibid.

23. *The Times*, 30 June 1900, p. 17 e.

24. Ibid.

25. AS Diary, 17 June 1900, BRB.

26. AS to Helen Carte, 28 June 1900, DC/TM.

27. WSG to Helen Carte, 29 June 1900, ibid.

28. AS Diary, 21 July 1900, BRB.

29. Ibid., 31 July 1900.

30. Ibid., 10 August 1900.

31. Ibid., 19 August 1900.

32. Ibid., 5 September 1900.

33. Ibid., 6 September 1900.

34. AS to Helen Carte, 8 September 1900, DC/TM.

35. Ibid.

36. Ibid.

37. AS Diary, 1 October 1900, BRB.

38. AS to Helen Carte, 12 October 1900, DC/TM.

39. AS Diary, 14 October 1900, BRB.

40. Ibid.

41. Ibid., 15 October 1900. Close examination of the diary shows a short dash after the words "I am sorry to leave"; the following "s" of "such a lovely day" is slightly larger than usual for a "small letter," but sometimes Sullivan wrote the letter in this way and it is not a "capital letter." The interpretation, "I am sorry to leave — such a lovely day," makes good sense. Sullivan was not saying good-bye to the world yet. He walked out of the hotel in Tunbridge Wells, still hoping to recover, although terrified at the thought that his illness might be fatal.

42. AS to Helen Carte, 16 October 1900, DC/TM.

43. AS to Helen Carte, 17 October 1900, DC/TM.

44. WSG to Helen Carte, 21 October 1900, DC/TM.

45. WSG to Helen Carte, 24 October 1900, DC/TM.

46. Ibid.

47. WSG to Helen Carte, 26 October 1900, typed copy, DC/TM.

48. AS to Helen Carte, 27 October 1900, DC/TM.

49. WSG to Helen Carte, 29 October 1900, DC/TM.

50. AS to Helen Carte, 2 November 1900, DC/TM.

51. Helen Carte to AS, in Baily, *Gilbert and Sullivan Book*, p. 376.

52. AS to Helen Carte, DC/TM.

53. WSG to Helen Carte, 7 November 1900, DC/TM.

54. WSG to AS, 9 November 1900, PML.

32: A Gilbert without a Sullivan

1. *The Times*, 23 November 1900, p. 9 a; *Daily Telegraph*, 23 November 1900, p. 7.1.

2. Helen Carte to Fanny Ronalds, 23 November 1900, DC/TM.

3. D'Oyly Carte to Fanny Ronalds, [24 November 1900], ibid.

4. Fanny Ronalds to Mr. and Mrs. Carte, 25 November 1900, ibid.

5. *The Times*, 27 November 1900, P.11 a.

6. Ibid., 28 November 1900, p. 12 a.

7. WSG to Herbert Sullivan, PML.

8. Musical Tribute, program, DC/TM.

9. Sullivan's Will, PRO/Somerset House.

10. WSG to Mary Talbot, 30 December 1900, in Dark and Grey, *W. S. Gilbert*, p. 172.

11. WSG to Mary Talbot, 18 February 1901, ibid., pp. 172–173.

12. *The Times*, 8 April 1901, p. 7 f.

13. WSG to Helen Carte, 5 April 1901, DC/TM.

14. Richard D'Oyly Carte's Will, PRO/Somerset House.

15. German to Helen Carte, DC/TM.

16. WSG to Helen Carte, 24 April 1901, DC/TM.

17. WSG to Helen Carte, 30 April 1901, ibid.

18. *The Times*, 9 December 1901, p. 7 c.

19. WSG to Mary Talbot, 25 December 1901, in Dark and Grey, *W. S. Gilbert*, pp. 173–174.

20. WSG to Mary Talbot, 6 October 1902, DC/TM.

21. *The Times*, 29 September 1902, p. 4 f.

22. WSG to Helen Carte, 4 October 1902, DC/TM.

23. WSG to Herbert Sullivan, [19 March 1903], PML.

24. *The Yeomen of the Guard*, Gilbert, *Original Plays*, Third Series, p. 261.

25. *The Times*, 28 August 1903, p. 5 c.

26. Mrs. Clement Scott, *Old Bohemian Days*, p. 71.

27. WSG to François Cellier, 19 November 1903, DC/TM.

28. WSG to F. Macmillan, 8 December 1903, Macmillan Papers/BL Add MS 54,999 ff 1–2.

29. WSG to F. Macmillan, 11 December 1903, ibid., ff 3–4.

30. WSG to F. Macmillan, 9 January 1904, ibid., ff 5–6.

31. WSG to Helen Carte, 12 January 1904, DC/TM.

32. *The Times*, 12 March 1904, p. 9 c.

33. WSG to Helen Carte, 12 March 1904, DC/TM.

34. WSG to Helen Carte, 19 March 1904, ibid.

35. *The Saturday Review*, 14 May 1904, p. 621.

36. WSG to William Archer, 5 October 1904, Archer Correspondence/BL Add MS 45,291 ff 192–193.

37. WSG Diary, 29 April 1905, WSG/BL Add MS 49,323.

38. Ibid., 10 May 1905.

39. WSG to Helen Carte, 23 May 1905, DC/TM.

33: The Trouble with Casting

1. Helen Carte to WSG, 25 May 1905, DC/TM.

2. WSG Diary, 26 May 1905, WSG/BL Add MS 49,323.

3. WSG to Helen Carte, 26 May 1905, DC/TM.

4. Ibid., 10 August 1905, WSG/BL Add MS 49,323.

5. Ibid., 9 October 1905.

6. Ibid., 28 November 1905.

7. Ibid., 6 May 1906 WSG/BL Add MS 49,324.

8. WSG to Helen Carte, 4 October 1906, DC/TM.

9. WSG to Helen Carte, 5 October 1906, ibid.

10. Helen Carte to WSG, 8 October 1906, WSG.BL Add MS 49,333 f 186.

11. Ibid.

12. WSG to Helen Carte, 9 October 1906, DC/TM.

13. Helen Carte to WSG, 19 October 1906, WSG/BL Add MS 49,333 f 189.

14. WSG to Helen Carte, 20 October 1906, DC/TM.

15. WSG to Helen Carte (telegram), 22 October 1906, DC/TM.

16. *Daily Mail*, 30 October 1906, p. 5.

17. Helen Carte to WSG, 17 November 1906, WSG/BL Add MS 49,333 f 198.

18. WSG to Helen Carte, 18 November 1906, ibid., f 199.

19. Helen Carte to WSG, 20 November 1906, ibid., f 200.

20. WSG Diary, 26 November 1906, WSG/BL Add MS 49,324.

21. Ibid., 27 November 1906.

22. Helen Carte to WSG, 27 November 1906, WSG/BL Add MS 49,333 ff 200–201.

23. Ibid.

24. WSG Diary, 28 November 1906, WSG/BL Add MS 49,324.

25. Helen Carte to WSG, 7 December 1906, WSG/BL Add MS 49,330 f 203 (first page only, copy of complete letter in DC/TM).

26. Ibid. From copy in DC/TM.

27. WSG to Helen Carte, 8 December 1906, DC/TM.

28. *The Times*, 10 December 1906, p. 8 a.

29. *Evening Standard*, 8 December 1906, p. 9.3.

30. *The Times*, 10 December 1906, p. 8 a.

31. Ibid.

32. Ibid.

33. WSG to Helen Carte, 10 December 1906, DC/TM.

34. WSG to Helen Carte, 11 December 1906, DC/TM.

35. Helen Carte to WSG, 12 December 1906, DC/TM.

36. WSG to Helen Carte, 13 December 1906, DC/TM.

37. Ibid.

38. WSG Diary, 17 December 1906, WSG/BL Add MS 49,324.

39. Helen Carte to WSG, 16 December 1906, WSG/BL Add MS 49,333 ff 203–204.

40. WSG to Helen Carte, 17 December 1906, DC/TM.

41. Dark and Grey, *W. S. Gilbert*, pp. 193–195.

42. Ibid.

43. Lytton, *Secrets of a Savoyard*, p. 53.

44. Helen Carte to WSG, 31 December 1906, WSG/BL Add MS 49,333 f 210.

34: Interpolations

1. WSG to Helen Carte, 8 January 1907, DC/TM.

2. Helen Carte to WSG, 10 January 1907, DC/TM.

3. WSG to Helen Carte, 12 January 1907, DC/TM.

4. Ibid.

5. Helen Carte to WSG, 13 January 1907, DC/TM.

6. Ibid.

7. WSG to Helen Carte, 14 January 1907, DC/TM.

8. Helen Carte to WSG, 14 January 1907, DC/TM.

9. WSG to Helen Carte, 15 January 1907, DC/TM.

10. Helen Carte to WSG, 16 January 1907, WSG/BL Add MS 49,333 f 217.

11. *The Times*, 22 January 1907, p. 11 a.

12. Ibid., 23 January 1907, p. 4 e.

13. WSG Diary, 8 March 1907, WSG/BL Add MS 49,325.

14. WSG to Edith Browne, 10 March 1907, BL C132.g.72.

15. WSG to Edith Browne, 21 March 1907, ibid.

16. Browne, *W. S. Gilbert*, pp. 65–66.

17. WSG to Helen Carte, 2 April 1907, DC/TM.

18. *The Times*, 3 March 1907, p. 5 f.

19. Ibid., 5 April 1907, p. 3 f.

20. WSG to Mary Talbot, 25 May 1907, photocopy, DC/TM.

21. *The Times*, 12 June 1907, p. 9 f.

22. WSG to Campbell-Bannerman, 21 June 1907, WSG/BL Add MS 49,336 f 3.

23. WSG/BL Add MS 49,337.

24. Barrington to WSG, 30 [June 1907], WSG/BL Add MS 49,336 f 24.

25. Dark and Grey, p. 197.

26. Sisters of Nazareth to WSG, 7 July 1907, WSG/BL Add MS 49,337.

27. WSG to Mary Talbot, 29 December 1907, DC/TM.

28. WSG to Nancy McIntosh, 3 January 1908, WSG/BL Add MS 49,345.

29. WSG to Mary Talbot, 29 December 1907, DC/TM.

30. "My case against the Rev. J. Pullein Thompson," WSG/BL Add MS 49,348; WSG Diary, 26 November 1907, Add MS 49,325.

31. WSG to Herbert Sullivan, 24 December 1907, PML.

32. WSG/BL Add MS 49,306 ff 118–123.

33. WSG to Helen Carte, 21 April 1908, DC/TM.

34. Helen Carte to WSG, 21 April, typed copy, DC/TM.

35. WSG to Helen Carte, 25 April 1908, DC/TM.

36. Ibid.

37. Helen Carte to WSG, 28 April 1908, DC/TM.

38. Ibid.

39. WSG to Helen Carte, 30 April 1908, DC/TM.

40. Helen Carte to WSG, 1 May 1908, DC/TM.

41. WSG to Helen Carte, 4 May 1908, DC/TM.

42. Helen Carte to WSG, 5 May 1908, DC/TM.

43. WSG to Helen Carte, 5 May 1908, DC/TM.

44. Helen Carte to WSG, 6 May 1908, DC/TM.

45. WSG to Helen Carte, 13 July 1908, DC/TM.

46. *The Times*, 20 July 1908, p. 13 e.

47. WSG/BL Add MS 49,299.

48. WSG Diary, 5 October 1908, WSG/BL Add MS 49,326.

49. WSG to Edward German, 21 December 1908, ibid., Add MS 49,339 f 48.

35: Enter Fairies—Their Flight and Fall

1. WSG to Richard Temple, 10 January 1909, WSG/BL Add MS 49,339 ff 65–66.

2. Helen Carte to WSG, 15 January 1908, DC/TM 1907–11 f 58.

3. WSG to Helen Carte, 16 January 1909, DC/TM.

4. Helen Carte to WSG, 26 January 1909, DC/TM, 1907–11 ff 65–66.

5. WSG to Helen Carte, 26 January 1909, DC/TM.

6. Helen Carte to WSG, 31 January 1909, DC/TM.

7. WSG to Helen Carte, 2 February 1909, DC/TM.

8. Ibid.

9. WSG to Helen Carte, 7 February 1909, DC/TM.

10. Helen Carte to WSG, 9 February 1909, DC/TM.

11. WSG to Helen Carte, 5 April 1909, DC/TM.

12. German to his sister Rachel, May 1909, in Scott, *Edward German*, p. 136.

13. WSG to Workman, 3 June 1909, ibid., WSG/BL Add MS 49,339 ff 166–167.

14. WSG to Workman, 7 June 1909, ibid., ff 169–170.

15. WSG to German, 14 July 1909, ibid., f 204.

16. WSG to Margery Maude, 8 July 1909, in Dark and Grey, *W. S. Gilbert*, p. 188.

17. WSG Diary, 8 July 1909, WSG/BL Add MS 49,327.

18. Ibid., 10 September 1909.

19. Maude, *Worlds Away*, p. 135.

20. *The Times*, 20 August 1909, p. 16 b.

21. WSG Diary, 2 October 1909, WSG/BL Add MS 49,327.

22. WSG to W. M. Kerr, 25 October 1909, WSG/BL Add MS 49,339 f 272.

23. WSG Diary, 16 December 1909, WSG/BL Add MS 49,327.

24. WSG to German, 22 December 1909, WSG/BL Add MS 49,339 ff 298–299.

25. Quoted in WSG to German, 11 January 1910, ibid., ff 316–317.

26. WSG to German, 23 December 1909, ibid., f 301.

27. WSG to Workman, 26 December 1909, ibid., Add MS 49,339 ff 304–307.

28. Ibid.

29. WSG Diary, 27 December 1909, WSG/BL Add MS 49,327.

30. WSG to Malone, 30 December 1909, WSG/BL Add MS 49,339 f 311.

31. Diary note of Nancy McIntosh, 6 January 1910, WSG/BL Add MS 49,328.

32. WSG to Macmillan, 22 March 1910, Macmillan Papers/BL Add MS 54,999 ff 21–22; 1 April 1910, ibid., f 23.

33. *The Times*, 13 April 1910, p. 9 a; Nancy McIntosh, MS article, WSG/BL Add MS 49,345.

36: "A Very Honorable End"

1. WSG Diary, May–June 1910, WSG/BL Add MS 49,328.

2. WSG to Workman, 22 June 1910, ibid., Add MS 49,339 f 349.

3. *The Times*, 12 October 1910, p. 11 a.

4. WSG to Kitty, 19 October 1910, WSG/BL Add MS 49,345.

5. WSG to Kitty, 25 October 1910, ibid.

6. WSG to Kitty, October 1910, ibid.

7. WSG diary, October 1910, WSG/BL Add MS 49,328.

8. WSG to Mary Talbot, 20 December 1910, in Dark and Grey, *W. S. Gilbert*, pp. 180–181.

9. Blow, *Through Stage Doors*, pp. 204–207.

10. WSG to Mary Talbot, 10 March 1911, in Dark and Grey, *W. S. Gilbert*, p. 181.

11. WSG to Helen Carte, 10 May 1911, DC/TM.

12. *Daily Chronicle*, 1 June 1911, p. 4.

13. Dark and Grey, *W. S. Gilbert*, p. 222.

14. Madge Kendal, *Dame Madge Kendal by Herself*, pp. 179–180.

15. *The Times*, 1 June 1911, p. 6 b.

16. Ibid.

17. WSG/BL Add MS 49,341–49,343.

18. Ibid.

19. Ibid.

20. Ibid.

21. Ibid.

22. Ibid.

23. WSG Diary, 11 March 1911, WSG/BL Add MS 49,329. Gilbert's entry reads: "A 6.20 Visite de Mrs. Whitburn qui desire traduire le Hooligan en Francais [*sic*] pour le Guignol." Later references in the diary are to "Mrs. Wittmann" and "Mdme Wittmann." In signing her letter to Lady Gilbert, Thérèse Wittmann finishes her signature with a flourish, which makes her name look like Wittmanny.

24. WSG/BL Add MS 49,343.

25. Ibid.

26. *Harrow Observer*, 9 June 1911; *The Times*, 3 June 1911, p. 11 c.

27. WSG/BL Add MS 49,343.

28. Ibid.

29. Gilbert's Will, PRO/Somerset House.

Curtain Call

1. Helen Carte to Lady Gilbert, 9 June 1911, WSG/BL Add MS 49,345.

2. Lady Gilbert to Sir F. Macmillan, 25 December 1926, Macmillan Papers/BL Add MS 54,999 f 91.

SELECT BIBLIOGRAPHY

Allen, Reginald, ed. *The First Night Gilbert and Sullivan*. New York: Heritage Press, 1958.

Allen, Reginald (in collaboration with Gale R. D'Luhy). *Sir Arthur Sullivan, Composer and Personage*. New York: Pierpont Morgan Library, London: Chappell, 1975.

Archer, William. *English Dramatists of To-day*. London: Sampson Low, Marston, Searle, & Rivington, 1882.

—— *Real Conversations*. London: William Heinemann, 1904.

Ayre, Leslie. *The Gilbert and Sullivan Companion*. London: W. H. Allen, 1972.

Bache, Constance. *Brother Musicians, Reminiscences of Edward and Walter Bache*. London: Methuen, 1901.

Baily, Leslie. *The Gilbert and Sullivan Book*. London: Cassell, 1952; Spring Books, 1956.

—— *Gilbert and Sullivan and Their World*. London: Thames and Hudson, 1973.

Bancroft, Marie, and Squire Bancroft. *The Bancrofts, Recollections of Sixty Years*. London: John Murray, 1909.

Barnett, John Francis. *Musical Reminiscences and Impressions*. London: Hodder and Stoughton, 1906.

Barrington, Rutland. *Rutland Barrington, by Himself*. London: Grant Richards, 1908.

Bennett, Joseph. *Forty Years of Music, 1865–1905*. London: Methuen, 1908.

Bibby, Cyril. *T. H. Huxley: Scientist and Educator*. London: Watts, 1959.

Blow, Sydney. *Through Stage Doors*. Edinburgh: W. & R. Chambers, 1958.

Bond, Jessie. *The Life and Reminiscences of Jessie Bond*. London: John Lane, Bodley Head, 1930.

Boosey, William. *Forty Years of Music*. London: Ernest Benn, 1931.

Borer, Mary Cathcart. *Illustrated Guide to London 1800*. London: Holt, 1988.

Bradley, Ian. *The Complete Annotated Gilbert and Sullivan*. Oxford: Oxford University Press, 1996.

Browne, Edith. A. *W. S. Gilbert*. London: John Lane, Bodley Head, 1907.

Burnand, Sir Francis C. *Records and Reminiscences, Personal and General*. London: Methuen, 1904.

Carr, J. Comyns. *Some Eminent Victorians*. London: Duckworth, 1908.

Cellier, François, and Cunningham Bridgeman. *Gilbert, Sullivan and D'Oyly Carte*. London: Pitman, Second Edition, 1927.

Churchill, Lady Randolph. *The Reminiscences of Lady Randolph Churchill*. London: Edward Arnold, 1908.

Copenian, W. S. C. *The Apothecaries of London, A History 1617–1967*. London: Pergamon Press, 1967.

Cox-Ife, William. *W. S. Gilbert: Stage Director*. London: Dennis Dobson, 1977.

Dark, Sidney, and Rowland Grey. *W. S. Gilbert, His Life and Letters*. London: Methuen, 1923.

Eden, David. *Gilbert and Sullivan, the Creative Conflict*. Cranbury, N.J.: Associated Universities Presses, 1986.

Ellmann, Richard. *Oscar Wilde*. London: Hamish Hamilton, 1987.

Emmerson, George S. *Arthur Darling: The Romance of Arthur Sullivan and Rachel Scott Russell*. London, Ont.: Galt House, 1980.

Findon, B. W. *Sir Arthur Sullivan and His Operas*. London: Sisley's, [1908].

Fitzgerald, Percy. *The Savoy Operas and the Savoyards*. London: Chatto & Windus, 1899.

Fitz-gerald, S. J. Adair. *The Story of the Savoy Operas*. London: Stanley Paul, 1924

Foster, Miles Birkett. *The History of the Philharmonic Society of London, 1813–1912*. London: Bodley Head, 1912.

Gielgud, Kate Terry. *An Autobiography*. London: Max Reinhardt, 1953.

Gilbert, W. S. *Original Plays*. 4 vols. London: Chatto and Windus, 1920–1923.

—— *Topsyturvydom*, with Letters [including letters from Lady Gilbert] and Portraits. London: Criterion Theatre, 1874; republished by Oxford University Press, 1931.

—— *The Bab Ballads*. James Ellis, ed. Cambridge, Mass.: The Belknap Press, 1980

—— *The Lost Stories of W. S. Gilbert*. Peter Haining, ed. London: Robson Books, 1982.

Glover, Michael. *The Peninsular War 1807–1814, A Concise Military History*. London: David & Charles, 1974.

Goldberg, Isaac. *The Story of Gilbert and Sullivan*. London: John Murray, 1929.

Goodman, Andrew. *Gilbert and Sullivan at Law*. London: Associated Universities Presses, 1983.

—— *Gilbert and Sullivan's London*, Robert Hardcastle, ed. Tunbridge Wells: Spellmount, 1988; second edition, London: Faber, 2000.

Granville-Barker, Harley. *Exit Planché—Enter Gilbert*. London: London Mercury, vol 25, nos. 149/150, March 1952.

Graves, Charles L. *The Life and Letters of Sir George Grove*. London: Macmillan, 1903.

Grossmith, George. *A Society Clown*. Bristol: J. W. Arrowsmith, 1888.

Hearnshaw, F. J. C. *The Centenary History of King's College London*. London: Harrap, 1929.

Helmore, Frederick. *Memoir of Rev. Thomas Helmore, M.A*. London: J. Masters, 1891.

Hibbert, Christopher. *The English, A Social History, 1066–1945*. London: Guild, 1987.

—— *Wellington, A Personal History*. London: HarperCollins, 1997.

Hicks, Seymour. *Between Ourselves*. London: Cassell, 1930.

Hollingshead, John. *My Lifetime*. 2 vols. London: Sampson Low, Marston, 1895.

—— *Gaiety Chronicles*. London: Archibald Constable, 1898.

—— *Good Old Gaiety*. London: Gaiety Theatre, 1903.

Hood, Tom, ed. *A Bunch of Keys*. London: Greenbridge and Sons, 1865.

How, Harry. *Illustrated Interviews*. London: George Newman, 1893.

Howard, Diana. *London Theatres and Music Halls, 1850–1950*. London: Library Association, 1970.

Hudson, Roger. *London, Portrait of a City*. London: Folio Society, 1998.

Hughes, Gervase. *The Music of Arthur Sullivan*. London: Macmillan, 1960.

Hyman, Alan. *Sullivan and His Satellites*. London: Chappell, 1978.

Innes, Thomas. *The Aberdeenshire Militia and the Royal Aberdeenshire Highlanders, now Third Battalion The Gordon Highlanders, 1798–1882*. Aberdeen: Aberdeen Journal Office, 1884.

Jacobs, Arthur. *Gilbert and Sullivan*. London: Max Parrish, 1951.

—— *Arthur Sullivan, A Victorian Musician*. Oxford: Oxford University Press, 1984; second edition Aldershot, Hants.: Scolar Press, 1992.

James, Alan. *Gilbert and Sullivan*. London: Omnibus Press, 1989.

Jones, John Bush, ed. *W. S. Gilbert: A Century of Scholarship and Commentary*. New York: New York University Press, 1970.

Kendal, Madge. *Dame Madge Kendal by Herself*. London: John Murray, 1933.

Klein, Hermann. *Thirty Years of Musical Life in London, 1870–1900*. London: Heinemann, 1903.

Lawrence, Arthur. *Sir Arthur Sullivan, Life Story, Letters and Reminiscences*. New York: H. S. Stone, 1900; reprinted, New York: Dacapo Press, 1980.

Lehmann, R. C. *Memories of Half a Century*. London: Smith, Elder, 1908.

Leslie, Anita. *Jennie, The Life of Lady Randolph Churchill*. London: Arrow, 1974.

Longford, Elizabeth. *Wellington, The Years of the Sword*. London: Weidenfeld and Nicolson, 1969.

Lytton, Henry A. *The Secrets of a Savoyard*. London: Jarrolds, 1933.

Mander, Raymond, and Joe Mitchenson. *A Picture History of Gilbert and Sullivan*. London: Vista Books, 1962.

––––– *The Lost Theatres of London*. London: Rupert Hart-Davis, 1968.

Martin, Ralph G. *Lady Randolph Churchill*. London: Literary Guild, 1969.

Martin-Harvey, Sir John. *Autobiography*. London: Sampson Low, Marston, 1933.

Maude, Pamela. *Worlds Away*. London: John Baker, 1904.

McIntyre, Ian. *Garrick*. London: Penguin Press, 1999

Meeson, R., and W. N. Welsby. *Reports of Cases Argued and Determined in the Courts of Exchequer & Exchequer Chamber*. vol 14. London: 1846.

Merrick, Edward. *A History of the Civil Service Rifle Volunteers*. London: Sheppard and St. John, 1891.

Moscheles, Charlotte. *Life of Moscheles*, adapted from the original German by A. D. Coleridge. 2 vols. London: Hurst and Blackett, 1873.

Murray, George Gilbert Aimé. *An Unfinished Autobiography*. London: George Allen and Unwin, 1960.

Neilson, Julia. *This for Remembrance*. London: Hurst and Blackett, 1941.

Newsome, David. *The Victorian World Picture*. London: Fontana, 1998.

Nicholson, Shirley. *A Victorian Household, Based on the Diaries of Marion Sambourne*. Stroud, Glos.: Alan Sutton Publishing, 1994.

Nicoll, Allardyce. *A History of Late Nineteenth Century Drama 1850–1900*. Cambridge: Cambridge University Press, 1946.

Orel, Harold, ed. *Gilbert and Sullivan, Interviews and Recollections*. Basingstoke: Macmillan, 1994.

Pearse, Robert R. *A Guide to the Inns of Court and Chancery*. London: 1853.

Pearson, Hesketh. *Gilbert and Sullivan*. Harmondsworth: Penguin, 1950.

––––– *Gilbert, His Life and Strife*. London: Methuen, 1957.

Rees, Terence. *Thespis, A Gilbert and Sullivan Enigma*. London: Dillon's, 1964.

Ridley, Jasper. *Napoleon III and Eugénie*. London: Constable, 1979.

Rogers, Clara Kathleen. *Memories of a Musical Career*. Boston: Privately printed at the Plimpton Press, 1932.

Rollins, C., and R. J. Witts. *The D'Oyly Carte Opera Company in Gilbert and Sullivan Operas*. London: Michael Joseph, 1962.

Scott, Clement. *The Wheel of Life*. London: 1897.

Scott, Mrs. Clement Scott [Margaret]. *Old Bohemian Days in London*. London: Hutchinson, [1919].

Scott, William Herbert. *Edward German, An Intimate Biography*. London: Cecil Palmer, 1932.

Searle, Townley. *A Bibliography of Sir William Schwenck Gilbert*. London, 1931.

Sherson, Errol. *London's Lost Theatres of the Nineteenth Century*. London: John Lane, Bodley Head, 1925.

Sims, George R. *My Life, Sixty Years' Recollections of Bohemian London*. London: Eveleigh Nash, 1917.

Skeat, W. O. *King's College London Engineering Society 1847–1957*. London: King's College, 1957.

Smyth, Ethel. *Impressions That Remained*. 2 vols. Second edition. London: Longmans, Green, 1923.

Spark, Fred R., and Joseph Bennett. *History of the Leeds Music Festivals, 1858–1889*. London: Novello, Ewar, 1892.

Stedman, Jane W. *Gilbert Before Sullivan*. London: Routledge and Kegan Paul, 1969.

——— *W. S. Gilbert, a Classic Victorian and His Theatre*. Oxford: Oxford University Press, 1996.

Stern, Robert A. M., Thomas Mellins, and David Fichman. *New York 1880: Architecture and Urbanism in the Gilded Age*. New York: Monacelli Press, 1999.

Sullivan, Herbert, and Newman Flower. *Sir Arthur Sullivan, His Life, Letters and Diaries*. Second edition. London: Cassell, 1950.

Terriss, Ellaline. *Just a Little Bit of String*. London: Hutchinson, 1955.

Thorne, George. *Jots*. London, J. W. Arrowsmith, [1884].

Treuherz, Julian. *Victorian Painting*. London: Thames and Hudson, 1993.

Wainwright, Davod. *Broadwood by Appointment, A History*. London: Quiller Press, 1982.

Warre, H. J. *Historical Records of the Fifty-Seventh, or West Middlesex Regiment of Foot*. London: W. Mitchell, 1878.

Watson, Alfred E. T. *A Sporting and Dramatic Life*. London: Macmillan, 1918.

Wearing, J. P. *The London Stage*. Metuchen, N.J.: Scarecrow Press, 1976–1993.

Wells, Walter J. *Souvenir of Sir Arthur Sullivan*. London: George Newnes, 1901.

Williamson, Audrey. *Gilbert and Sullivan Opera*. Rev. edition, London: Marion Boyars, 1982.

Wilson, Gwendoline. *Murray of Yarralumba*. Oxford: Oxford University Press, 1968.

Wolfson, John. *Final Curtain, The Last Gilbert and Sullivan Operas*. London: Chappell, 1976.

——— *Sullivan and the Scott Russells*. Chichester: Packard Publishing, 1984.

——— *The Savoyards on Record*. Chichester: Packard Publishing, 1985.

Wood, Christopher. *The Pre-Raphaelites*. London: Phoenix Illustrated, Orion, 1997.

Wood, Henry. *My Life of Music*. London: Victor Gollancz, 1938.

Wyndham, Henry Saxe. *Arthur Seymour Sullivan*. London: Kegan Paul, J. Curwen, 1926.

Young, Percy M. *Sir Arthur Sullivan*. London: J. M. Dent, 1971.

——— *George Grove*. London: Macmillan, 1980.

INDEX

Turner, Lucretia Anne, 53, 148–149
Turner, Lucy. *See* Gilbert, Lady Lucy
Turner, Mabel, 395, 400, 408, 443, 446
Turner, Mary, 53, 135, 148
Turner, Major-General Samuel Compton, 52, 148, 379, 392
Turner, Dr. Thomas, 53
Turner, Captain Thomas Metcalfe Blois, 52
Twiss, Quintin, 65

Ulmar, Geraldine, 248, 253, 263, 268, 277, 286, 288, 299, 303, 333, 359, 448
Uncle Baby (W. Gilbert), 48
Utopia, Limited or, The Flowers of Progress, 161, 346–350, 352–353, 361, 364, 379, 386, 430

Van Biene, Auguste, 170
Vanbrugh, Violet, 399, 431
Vezin, Hermann, 123
Viardot-Garcia, Pauline, 43, 71
Vicar of Bray, The (Solomon), 333–334
Victoria, Princess (later Empress to Frederick III), 121, 200, 287, 364
Victoria, Queen, 27, 100, 121, 221, 256, 265, 275–276, 325–326, 365–366, 368, 370, 390–391
Victoria Hospital for Children, 444
Vincent, Ruth, 360, 368, 370, 373, 417
Visetti, Alberto, 383

Wagg, Arthur, 380, 391
Wagner, Richard, 30, 72, 225, 368
Walker, Russell, 277, 309, 357, 390
Walküre (Wagner), 368
Wallack's Theatre, New York, 90, 93, 96–97, 135
War of 1812, 8
Warrilow, John, 320, 404, 434
Warwick, Giulia, 134, 140, 152
Watson, Alfred, 186, 261, 267

Weigall, Alfred, 35, 44, 69, 122, 148
Weigall, Jane, 17, 35, 44, 69, 122, 148, 404, 444
Weigall, Mary, 441, 444
Weigall, Stanley, 400, 441, 444
Welch, James, 437–438
Wellington, duke of, 7–8, 28
Western Grammar School, 20
Whistler, James McNeil, 191–192, 242, 244, 259, 265
Whitmarsh, Alice, 5–6
Wilde, Oscar, 188, 191, 195–196, 205
Wilkinson, John, 296
Willard, Edward, 369
William, prince of Prussia (later Kaiser William II), 200, 257, 277, 360, 382
William I, emperor of Prussia, 263, 273
Williamson, J. C., 204
Wilton, Marie. *See* Bancroft, Lady
Wittmann, Thérèse, 442, 484 n.23
Wolseley, Field Marshal Garnet, 182, 208
Wood, Sir Henry, 282, 323, 393
Workman, C. Herbert, 360, 407–409, 414, 416, 420–422, 429–435, 448
World, 370
Wortley, Charles, 135
Wyatt, Frank, 294, 300, 333
Wylam, Edward, 49, 78
Wyndham, Sir Charles, 104, 129, 194, 198, 271, 283, 286, 334, 363, 389

Yates, Edmund, 45
Yaw, Ellen Beach, 379
Yeomen of the Guard, The, or The Merryman and His Maid, 279, 283–284, 287–288, 290, 305, 332, 348, 366, 370, 391, 393, 399, 400, 405–407, 412, 418, 420, 426, 428, 446–447
Young, Duncan, 263

Zucchi, Antonio, 275